RAC

GOLF GUIDE

RAC

GOLF GUIDE

EDITED BY MITCHELL PLATTS
GOLF CORRESPONDENT OF 'THE TIMES'

RAC Publishing

Published by RAC Enterprises, Ltd, RAC House, Bartlett Street, South Croydon, CR2 6XW

British Library Cataloguing-in-Publication Data
1. Great Britain. Golf
I. Royal Automobile Club
796.3520941

ISBN 0-86211-091-2
ISBN 0-86211-092-0 pbk

CONTENTS

INTRODUCTION

In 1969 Tony Jacklin became the first "home" player to win the Open Championship for 18 years. This victory had a dramatic effect on the game of golf in Great Britain and Ireland. For so long the Americans had dominated the game, but Jacklin's victory boosted the morale of all "home" golf fans – players and spectators alike.

The number of golfers affiliated to the English Golf Union alone has risen to more than 500,000 as we enter the 1990s. It is predicted that by the turn of the century that figure will be 1¼ million.

In broader terms, in 1990, the number of golfers throughout the British Isles stands at more than 2 million, compared with 400,000 in 1968.

The game has hooked so many people because it sets natural targets. To break 100 is an achievement which once accomplished makes 90 the figure in mind then 80 and 70. It might not be too long, with the appliance of science and more hi-tec equipment, before breaking 60 on today's present courses will be commonplace for professionals.

Yet perhaps the greatest aspect of golf is that amateurs can compete in a professional world. Not too many sporting enthusiasts get the chance to grace Wembley's turf or walk to the crease at Lords.

In golf you can pay a green fee and tee-up anywhere from St. Andrews, the mecca of the game, to St. Mellion, where Jack Nicklaus designed his first course in Britain; from Royal Birkdale, on the Lancashire coast, to Wentworth in Surrey.

The RAC Golf Guide provides not only an in-depth guide to how to play those great Championship courses, but places the spotlight on a multitude of gems scattered around the countryside.

"Golfers who know but from their pro" was the old adage. Golfers who know will also do well to use this book to telephone ahead to confirm when and on which course they can play. I hope it will prove as valuable as a "hot" putter.

Mitchell Platts
Golf Correspondent, ***The Times***

GOLF IN THE 'NINETIES

Martin Hardy, Golf Correspondent, *The Daily Express*

Golf worldwide is swinging towards the 21st century on a course full of optimism and strength.

The sport in Britain has never been more popular, the quality never greater and the feeling for the future never more confident. Among professionals and amateurs, men and women alike, there is not only a massive sense of achievement, but also a sense of pride and excitement.

Before we look too far forward, it is necessary to journey into history to study the foundations upon which this future of promise was built.

The sportsman's sportsman

About the only thing that has not changed over the last 100 years and more is golf's sense of values. Today it holds a unique place in sport. There is no 'cleaner' game and none which has embedded itself as firmly in true sportsmanship than golf.

Nobody takes defeat harder than Seve Ballesteros. Yet any player who has been paired with the Spaniard in the last round of a major championship, when they have been in contention and Ballesteros has not, will tell of the sincere encouragement they have received from the world's best player.

Visit any practice area on the Volvo Tour and you will see players analysing one another's swings, pointing out problem areas and generally passing on tips. It doesn't seem to matter that one player may use his new knowledge to beat the player who gave it to him when the two next meet on the course.

Home heroes

Generally, golf has evolved slowly, although there were phases when it quickened its step. The late Sir Henry Cotton gave our game a much needed fillip before and after the Second World War with his grace and style.

The interest in the game spread through the achievements of Arnold Palmer and Jack Nicklaus, while Tony Jacklin gave our youngsters at home a hero to follow when he won Opens on both sides of the Atlantic within a year.

Jacklin may have faded as a player, but his influence on golf has not diminished. Indeed, there are those who believe that despite his many successes on the course, he will be remembered more for what he achieved after hanging up his spikes.

Significant factors in the golf explosion and continuing boom, centre on Europe's Ryder Cup achievements. It was Jack Nicklaus who suggested during the 'seventies that unless Great Britain and Ireland wanted a 'Stand-'em-up, knock-'em-down' type of match, then Europe would have to be included.

European victory

Even with the introduction of the likes of Ballesteros, the Americans continued to dominate, until, just a few months before the 1983 encounter, Jacklin accepted the position of captain.

He transformed everything, on and off the course. Our heroes were made to feel like first class citizens at last and in his baptism at PGA National, West Palm Beach, Florida, Europe lost by only one point.

In 1985, the Belfry was the scene for our first win in 28 years and Jacklin followed it by leading the first ever triumph on American soil two years later – ironically against an American side captained by Nicklaus and on the magnificent course he designed at Muirfield Village, Ohio.

Those magic moments of Ryder Cup history, along with the personal achievements of players such as Nick Faldo, Sandy Lyle, Ian Woosnam and Seve Ballesteros, have encouraged an interest in the game unsurpassed in its history.

The ladies' successes

It is not just the male professionals who are enjoying this marvellous period. The likes of Laura Davies, from Surrey, a player with an awesome talent and the first Briton to win the US Open, are ensuring that the women are establishing a strong European circuit of their own.

Our amateur women made history in the 'eighties – indeed before the Ryder Cup men – by winning the Curtis Cup in America for the first time. And Great Britain and Ireland's top amateurs completed the hat-trick when, in the Walker Cup in 1989, they too, beat the United States on American soil.

It had been a decade when the balance of power switched from one side of the Atlantic to the other, providing all Europe with optimism and confidence for the run up to the turn of the century.

And the future?

What can we expect along the way? Our teams, who entered the 'nineties holding the Curtis, Ryder and Walker Cups all at once for the first time, seem assured of parity at least for several battles to come, despite America's greater strength in depth.

But can the golden age of British and European golf be expected to continue on an individual front in the same way that it so dominated the world in the 'eighties, a period during which the Americans searched in vain for a new superstar as Tom Watson faded?

Again it is necessary to look over our shoulders and consider those who have done most to make us rejoice and America cry.

Ballesteros, Lyle, Faldo, Langer and Woosnam, golf's Royal Flush, all came to the sport through different routes: Ballesteros through the caddie shack; Lyle through birth; Faldo through watching it on television; Langer through perseverance and Woosnam by accident.

They had very little in common, if anything, off the course, but are united in their attitude and greatness on it – the common denominator being sheer dedication.

None of them needs to swing a club again to ensure they live a life of luxury and that includes Woosnam, who at the start of the 'nineties had still to win a major championship, the normal basis for riches.

But when such players enter a tournament, the sponsors are guaranteed value for money, as all of them will be trying their hardest to win. They do not play just for fat cheques, their prize is the pride of winning of a major tournament.

As long as the top players retain the desire to win – and the signs are that it is increasing rather than diminishing – then the future of our game is in safe keeping.

You only have to see the extra people attracted to playing

tennis during Wimbledon fortnight; the increased numbers in swimming pools during the Olympics or know how popular middle distance running has become since Coe and Ovett, to realise the effects success has on sport.

A growing game

Golf in the 'eighties for Britain and Europe was one glorious success story. So much so that today golfing facilities in Britain and Ireland came nowhere near close to satisfying demand while on the Continent the boom has triggered an astounding growth in the building of golf courses.

An astonishing 700 more courses need to be built in the British Isles before the turn of the century (and that may yet prove to be a conservative number) to keep pace with the enormous interest in the game.

People with no sporting tradition find themselves hooked just as soon as they hit their first shot into the air: club waiting lists grow longer and longer and queues to get on local municipal courses start before first light in some parts of Britain.

All the signs are that golf addiction is still advancing at a phenomenal rate. And nowhere more so than on the Continent and particularly France. The French connection is a formidable one and several clubs have already made our top greenkeeping brains offers they have not been able to resist. This has prompted a loud if unpopular call by the English Golf Union for club subscriptions to be increased to help stop the drain before it becomes a serious problem.

Etiquette

There are other small areas for concern as golf's popularity graph continues its sharp rise, the need to replace divots and repair pitchmarks is continually emphasised yet repeatedly overlooked by too many, to the immense frustration of the diligent few. It should occur to golfers that courses would be generally in better condition if greenkeepers could concentrate on the difficult task of the upkeep of greens instead of having to spend too much precious time carrying out jobs which should not be their responsibility. But this aside, what do we have to look forward to?

The future will undoubtedly see the continued increase in the number of youngsters wanting to turn professional. While this, of course, is to be desired there should be warning signs pinned to every Junior Section noticeboard. For every Faldo there are a hundred golfers struggling to make putts drop and ends meet. It is a long and arduous climb to the top and few do it without the background of a distinguished past in the amateur ranks. Too many turn professional too quickly and although the return to the amateur ranks is not barred, it is neither a quick nor easy journey.

What many youngsters fail to realise is that the difference between being a top amateur and even a middle-of-the-road professional is still quite a big one, and one that is all too frequently overlooked.

'Look before you leap' is an old adage, but it is the best advice to youngsters whose expectations outstrip their abilities. For if they cannot beat the best amateurs then they have no chance against the professionals.

But while Britain and Europe continue to dominate the world scene, the clamour will continue at every level of the game. The future of golf has never looked better. It has had a distinguished past and those rich traditions look like being extended for many years to come.

THE CHAMPIONSHIP COURSES

THE BELFRY

Gordon Richardson, Golf Correspondent of
The News of the World

Built on what were once potato fields, The Belfry, near Sutton Coldfield in the Midlands, was the stage on which Tony Jacklin's Europeans played their way to the first victory over the Americans for 28 years in the 1985 Ryder Cup. The trophy was retained two years later in 1987, with the first ever defeat of the Americans on United States soil. The Belfry was once again home to the Ryder Cup in 1989 when the matches produced a nail-biting draw.

More than £8 million has been spent on developing the famed Brabazon course and neighbouring Derby courses, hotel and leisure complex, which houses the headquarters of the Professional Golfers' Association (PGA).

THE COURSE

Hole 1 (408 yards) Par 4 Bunkers left and right must be bisected with the tee-shot and the ideal landing place is just to the left of the smaller right-hand trap. This opens up the green. Drive too far left and the big bunker guarding the green on that side comes very much into play.

Hole 2 (340 yards) Par 4 With a stream 10 yards or so short of the green, players have no option but to lay up from the tee, generally with a one or two iron, avoiding bunkers left and right. The pitch to the green must be exact, as it is guarded to left, right and front by sand.

Hole 3 (455 yards) Par 4 As at the 1st, the best line from the tee is down the right but avoiding the huge bunker sited around 210 yards out. With a depression on the left awaiting long hitters the premium is on accuracy, and bunkers left and right of the green demand precision with the long second shot.

Hole 4 (569 yards) Par 5 Most players will have to hit two solid woods in order to lay-up short of the stream that fronts a narrow, sideways-on green at this genuine par five.

Hole 5 (389 yards) Par 4 A 200-yard carry from the tee to clear a stream crossing the fairway is not too daunting, unless the wind is blowing head on. The drive should favour the right side in order to set up the ideal approach to a narrow, two-level green beyond three sand traps.

Hole 6 (386 yards) Par 4 A lake to the left threatens all the way from the pitching area to the green as you drive over a stream. Beware of driving too far right into a cunningly sited bunker before tackling a second shot that must be fired between water and sand to a sizeable green.

Hole 7 (173 yards) Par 3 Not much room for mistakes in club selection and positive strike at The Brabazon's first short hole. The elevated green is protected by a new re-vetted, horseshoe-shaped front bunker and another to the rear. Beyond the water, to the right, there are trees awaiting cut or sliced shots.

Hole 8 (476 yards) Par 4 A dauntingly difficult hole with three right-hand side bunkers waiting to catch tee-shots played too safely away from the lake on the left. A long iron or even a wood is required to reach the well-bunkered green, which lies beyond a stream.

Hole 9 (390 yards) Par 4 In favourable conditions this hole back to the hotel plays only a drive and short iron. But going too far right to avoid sand and trees on the left, leaves a testing second to a steeply upward sloping green across the edge of the lake.

Hole 10 (301 yards) Par 4 The trick here is not to be misled by the yardage of The Belfry's most celebrated par four. They call it the 'Ballesteros Hole' because Seve drove it when it measured 300 yards. Would-be emulators must fly their tee-shots in over the lake and trees. Lesser mortals should hit mid-irons short of the water and sand, leaving a short pitch onto the green.

Hole 11 (365 yards) Par 4 The 11th's secret is to avoid driving too far left on this gentle right-hand dog-leg or else the tee-shot will probably finish in one of two big bunkers. The approach shot must be aimed accurately between two more big sand traps which are placed front left and right of the green.

Hole 12 (225 yards) Par 3 The Brabazon's second short hole is even more testing than the first and a three wood or even a driver is needed to reach the back of the two-tier, upsloping green which lies beyond the stream.

Hole 13 (364 yards) Par 4 From the back tees, two big bunkers on the right come very much into play along with another on the left. Landing just left of centre sets up the second shot to the green. The green is protected by a huge trap runnming from 2 o'clock to 5 o'clock around its perimeter.

Hole 14 (184 yards) Par 3 This is the last of the one-shotters and the most inviting. The only danger here is straying into the bunkers placed left and right of a two-tiered, angled green with mounds behind.

Hole 15 (540 yards) Par 5 Most players will drive to the right of the left-hand fairway bunker, pitching short of a larger one on the right. The second shot should be played to pitch over a stream that runs across the fairway to the right and beyond a mid-fairway sand trap in order to set up the pitch to a heavily guarded three-tiered green.

Hole 16 (400 yards) Par 4 The drive on the 16th should cut the corner and land left of centre, positioning the ball ideally for a short second to the green. The green itself slopes right to left, and a big left-hand bunker puts the pressure on.

Hole 17 (555 yards) Par 5 This is the last of the long holes. It is a difficult left to right dog-leg. Trees on the right-hand edge of the tee and the corner of the dog-leg act as a deterrent against trying to cut too much off the corner. However, those who dare, face a less daunting second shot across the stream towards an open green.

Hole 18 (455 yards) Par 4 Galleries and television viewers who watched player after player find a watery grave at this fearsome final hole in the 1989 Ryder Cup will need no reminding that you must clear the lake twice to reach an uphill, three-tiered, 60-yard long green.

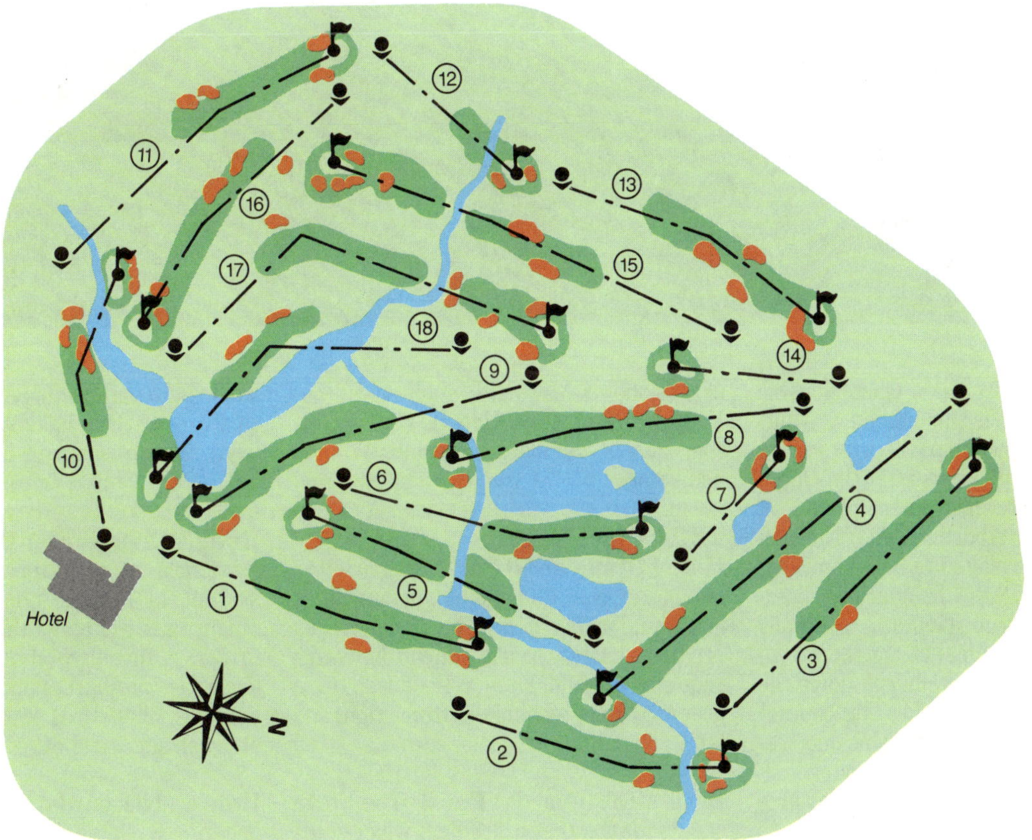

MUIRFIELD

Mitchell Platts, Golf Correspondent of
The Times

Nick Faldo won the Open Championship in 1987 when last it was staged at Muirfield. The Championship will return there in 1992 exactly 100 years after the Open, which previously had been played at Prestwick, St. Andrews and Musselburgh, was first played over 72 holes. It was in 1891 that the Honourable Company of Edinburgh Golfers, generally recognised as the oldest club in the world, moved east from Musselburgh down the Firth of Forth to Muirfield. The course, surrounded by a stone wall, was once referred to as an old water meadow, although one drama after another has produced a succession of wonderful Open champions at Muirfield, such as Hilton, Vardon, Braid, Ray, Hagen, Perry, Cotton, Player, Nicklaus, Trevino, Watson and Faldo.

THE COURSE

Hole 1 (449 yards) Par 4 Regarded as one of the most demanding opening holes in championship golf. The landing area can be as narrow as a dozen yards, with a required second shot a long iron to a green guarded by bunkers front, right and left.

Hole 2 (349 yards) Par 4 The brave can go for the green although wiser souls will lean towards a three wood and a pitch to a green which has five bunkers to the right. There is out of bounds down the left.

Hole 3 (379 yards) Par 4 Most professionals regard this hole, like the second, as a birdie opportunity and the smart ones will resist the urge to use the driver. A three wood or one iron should leave the ball short of encroaching fairway bunkers, 280 yards from the tee, and a shortish second shot.

Hole 4 (181 yards) Par 3 An elevated green, excellently bunkered, represents a difficult target especially as the land falls right away at the back. The green is also 40 yards deep, which poses problems with club selection.

Hole 5 (558 yards) Par 5 If the hole is played downwind then this monster hole can be reached in two. But five bunkers to the right, scattered from between 200 to 290 yards, present a problem, as do the 10 which surround the green.

Hole 6 (471 yards) Par 4 This hole is so good that opinion is split on whether or not it is the drive or the second shot which causes the biggest headache. The hole dog-legs to the left, with four bunkers guarding the corner, and the second shot is made difficult by a bunker on the right and out of bounds, which edges its way to the green from the left.

Hole 7 (185 yards) Par 3 This hole is more often than not played into the prevailing wind. The green is quite narrow with cavernous bunkers guarding the left-hand side. If the pin is at the back it might require a three iron from the tee.

Hole 8 (444 yards) Par 4 The hole dog-legs to the right where there lies a cluster of eight bunkers. They must be avoided at all cost although the second shot is deceptive with bunkers 30 yards short of the green, which appreciably shorten the distance to the eye.

Hole 9 (510 yards) Par 5 The drive should be aimed down the right so as not to flirt with the out-of-bounds wall all the way up the left-hand side to Greywalls Hotel. It has been lengthened in recent years although it can still be reached in two.

Hole 10 (475 yards) Par 4 This is widely regarded as a wicked hole where it is not too difficult to drop a shot. The obvious dangers, apart from the length and the notorious Muirfield rough, are the bunkers on the right, 250 yards and 280 yards from the tee, and the two bunkers to the right of the green.

Hole 11 (386 yards) Par 4 If played into the wind this hole, with a blind tee-shot over a mound, can prove troublesome. The green, surrounded by bunkers, is a mass of subtle dips and hollows.

Hole 12 (381) yards) Par 4 The elevated tee from which this hole is played exposes it to the capricious nature of the wind. Into a westerly wind, the drive must be a very exacting shot, with a bunker some 250 yards down the left. The pin, if at the back of the green, can be beyond the seven bunkers which guard it.

Hole 13 (153 yards) Par 3 The green is almost 50 yards long, so club selection is important, but this is one of the most gorgeous short holes in the game. It is teasing to the eye and it requires a precise, knocked-down shot as so often it is played into an easterly wind.

Hole 14 (447 yards) Par 4 Driving is a problem with three bunkers, the first at about 220 yards, on the left and one on the right narrowing the landing area. The second shot, too, is difficult and it requires an authoritative strike.

Hole 15 (396 yards) Par 4 This hole was lengthened for the 1987 Championship so increasing the importance of hitting the fairway from the tee, since as good a lie as possible is required to play a typical links run-up shot onto the green.

Hole 16 (188 yards) Par 3 The longest of Muirfield's short holes and it can play to more than 200 yards with the wind against. That will mean using a long iron and although the green is generous in size, it is still encircled by seven bunkers.

Hole 17 (542 yards) Par 5 Jack Nicklaus played a three iron from the tee and a five iron for his second when, in 1966, he won the Open. The key most certainly is to miss the bunkers down the left since they are so severe that to extract a ball from them usually requires a sand-iron shot hit sideways.

Hole 18 (447 yards) Par 4 Nicklaus has said that he cannot think of a better hole anywhere in golf and Faldo must have felt the same in 1987 when he hit the green with a five iron then two-putted to complete a round of 18 successive pars. The hole plays every inch of its yardage.

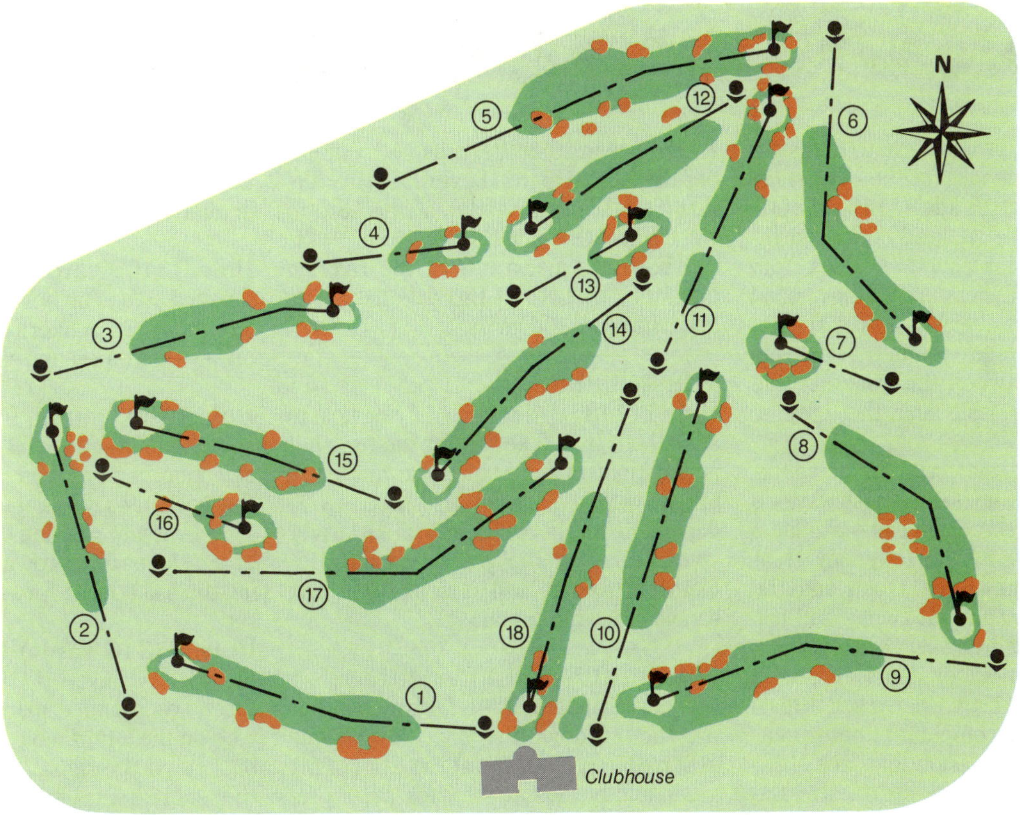

ROYAL BIRKDALE

Frank Clough, Golf Correspondent of
The Sun

From the finest professional to humblest hacker, everyone falls for the bewitching charms of Royal Birkdale. Birkdale is a jewel of a course situated on the north-west coast, just a couple of miles from Southport in Lancashire. Huge sand dunes on almost every hole give spectators ideal vantage points at the big events, and between the dunes lie the fairways, often fast, and the greens, always tricky.

It's a course that calls for power as well as accuracy; if you miss a fairway or a green, clinging scrubland can make life a misery. Birkdale has hosted many great golfing occasions – the Open and the Ryder Cup to name but two – and has seen its share of drama and history.

You may remember Arnold Palmer's Open triumph in 1961 when gales threatened to blow the competitors out to sea, or the classic concession that Jack Nicklaus gave to Tony Jacklin to halve the Ryder Cup in 1989. Perhaps you remember the 'best two iron I ever hit in my life' that Tom Watson rifled in at the 18th to win his first Open on English soil in 1983?

Those are just a few of the riveting memories that Royal Birkdale has given golf fans down the years.

THE COURSE

Hole 1 (448 yards) Par 4 A fine hole to start the round. The line for the tee-shot is just right of the bunker on the left – taken with a driver or three wood depending on the wind. A well-hit driver gives a view of the green and the problems around it and a solid four iron should reach the green.

Hole 2 (417 yards) Par 4 There's a rise in the middle of the fairway and hitting the ball down that line provides the best route. Six bunkers at the front of the green and bushes at the back put a premium on accuracy with the second shot. If the drive's good, a six iron should be enough to gain the target.

Hole 3 (409 yards) Par 4 A straightforward hole. The best drive finishes just left of the two bunkers on the right, leaving a nine-iron second shot to the green.

Hole 4 (203 yards) Par 3 Again wind speed and direction will play a part in club selection. A three iron should reach from the back tees. Four bunkers guard the green but just clearing them is fine as the green slopes down towards the hole making the ball bounce forward.

Hole 5 (346 yards) Par 4 This hole provides a choice of tee-shot, either a three wood aimed just right of the last tree on the left or a big driver flying over bushes on the right. The second way is the short route but does risk getting tangled up in rough. Seven bunkers guard a smallish green, but a good wedge should be sufficient.

Hole 6 (490 yards) Par 5 A great golfing hole. The best drive is a well-hit driver, aiming just left of the bunker on the right. A corker leaves a one or two iron onto a long elevated green, but it has to pitch all the way.

Hole 7 (154 yards) Par 3 The tee-off is from an elevated tee, but it's a straightforward hole and a seven iron should be enough. The green is well-bunkered, but the gap between the trap on the left and the first one on the right is quite wide.

Hole 8 (458 yards) Par 4 This usually plays into the wind. The favoured line for the drive is just left of the bunkers down the right side of the fairway. It's quite a tight fairway, so accuracy is important. A five or six iron should do the rest but the four bunkers at the front of the green can cause problems in erratic, windy conditions.

Hole 9 (414 yards) Par 4 This is a blind tee-shot where the ball must be fired just left of the marker post. Go right and the ball will run down a slope, leaving a tricky shot. If the correct line is taken, the ball will finish near the top of a ridge, leaving an eight iron onto the green.

Hole 10 (395 yards) Par 4 The safe line is down the right but the brave will take the left side (where there is trouble) hoping for a good drive that will get round the corner of the dog-leg, leaving a seven or eight iron to the green.

Hole 11 (409 yards) Par 4 Driving from the back tees ensures a fairly formidable carry over some bushes in front. The green is long and elevated with only one bunker to worry about, but the second shot can vary between a seven and nine iron, depending on the wind.

Hole 12 (184 yards) Par 3 One of the finest par threes in the world. Although the drive is hit downhill the club selection will range from a one iron to a seven iron! That's how tricky the wind makes it. The green is well-guarded and the ball doesn't usually bounce down from the hills that surround the green.

Hole 13 (506 yards) Par 5 There's a stream running down the left but it shouldn't come into play. The best line for the drive is left of the bunkers on the right. For the second, a three wood could reach the green, but a nice four iron leaves only an 80-yard pitch. The dangers are a tight fairway and bunkers left and right that can come into play.

Hole 14 (199 yards) Par 3 Another downhill par three although the green is elevated. Five bunkers and sloping ground around the green demand accuracy off the tee – a three iron is usually the club.

Hole 15 (543 yards) Par 5 A good long drive is required here, just to the right of the three sand traps down the left. To reach the green in two a wood is needed, but the shot must clear five more sand traps. Going left of them with a five or six iron leaves a nice wedge in.

Hole 16 (414 yards) Par 4 Palmer's hole. He was in deep trouble in the 1961 Open, took a divot 'bigger than a donkey's dinner' as one observer put it, and hit the green. A plaque down the right commemorates his glorious shot. It is safer going down the left because the fairway is quite wide. Five bunkers protect the elevated green but a five iron is usually enough.

Hole 17 (525 yards) Par 5 Two huge sand dunes that stand like guardians at the mouth of the fairway must be bisected with the drive. Lee Trevino tried to, but failed, took seven and still won the 1971 Open. If you get through the gap, there are no real problems with the second shot because the fairway is generous. The green, however, is heavily protected by bunkers and trees.

Hole 18 (472 yards) Par 4 Out of bounds runs down the right so the smart tee-shot is just to the left of the second bunker on the right. If you hit it as far as Tom Watson, a two iron will get you on – that's what he hit to win the 1983 Open. Three bunkers guard the green and with out of bounds through the back.

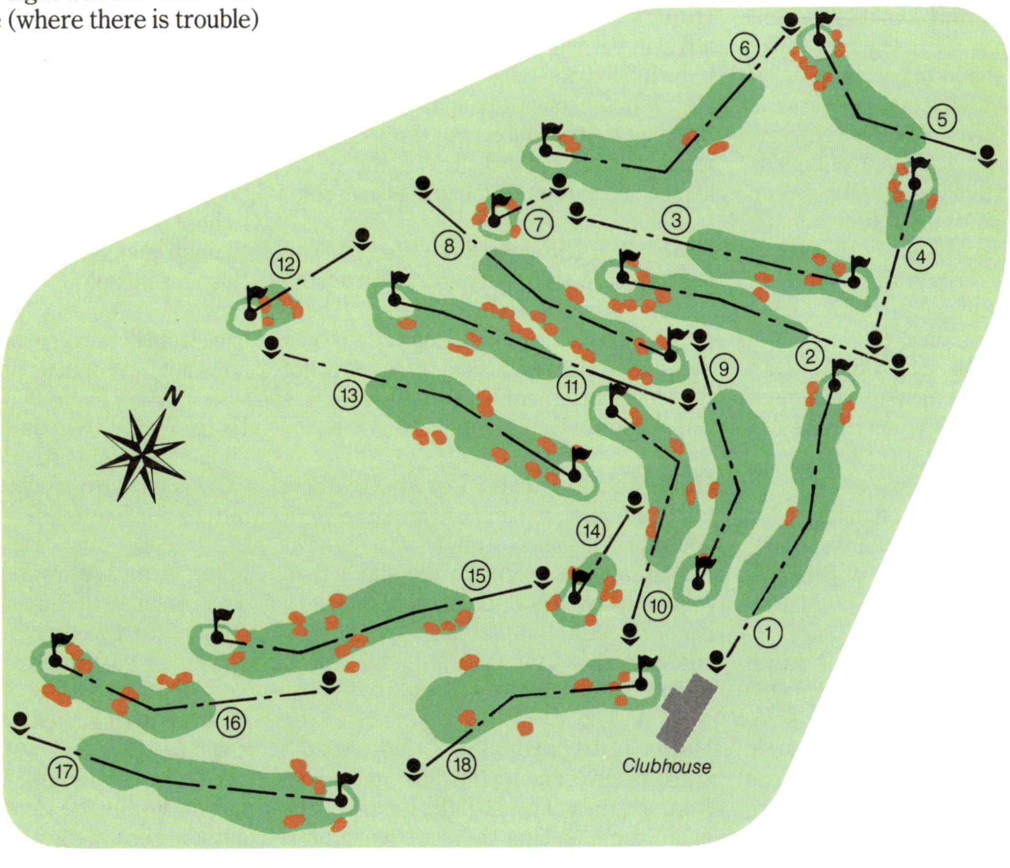

ROYAL LYTHAM AND ST. ANNES

Ron Moseley, Golf Correspondent of The Press Association

The texture of the turf leaves no doubt that Royal Lytham and St. Annes is a links course, but there is little to suggest that the sea is nearby. In fact the course is almost entirely surrounded by red-brick houses, with a menacing out-of-bounds railway line threatening several holes on the outward half. Bobby Jones made Royal Lytham famous with his shot out of the bunker at the 17th in the first Open here in 1926, but the course has not been so kind to Americans since then.

Europe has fared well though with Tony Jacklin breaking the overseas monopoly in 1969, while Severiano Ballesteros won twice in 1979 and 1988.

Lytham is famed for some of the most difficult finishing holes in golf and also for the only left-handed winner of the Open, Bob Charles of New Zealand, in 1963.

THE COURSE

Hole 1 (206 yards) Par 3 Royal Lytham is the only Open championship course which begins with a short hole, and a testing one at that. The tee-shot is played from a cluster of trees to a green surrounded by seven bunkers with two others short of the target.

Hole 2 (420 yards) Par 4 The bold, attacking drive down the right over a large mound and bunkers, while also flirting with the out-of-bounds railway line that flanks the entire length of the hole, reaps a rich reward. From there the angled green is much more approachable.

Hole 3 (458 yards) Par 4 The cowardly tee-shot, left and away from the railway fence, is right this time. There are also trees and undulating rough to be avoided on the other side, but that is not the ideal place to attack the pin when it is classically set back right of the green.

Hole 4 (393 yards) Par 4 This hole takes the players back towards the clubhouse and, usually, straight into the prevailing wind. An accurate tee-shot has to avoid the bunkers at the corner of the left-hand dog-leg but, in any event, the approach shot from the right offers much the preferable option.

Hole 5 (188 yards) Par 3 Not all of the bunkers surrounding this hole are visible from the tee. The slightly raised green takes some holding and club selection is vital, depending on the strength and direction of the wind.

Hole 6 (486 yards) Par 5 For the experts a good birdie hole, especially if it is being played downwind. The receiving area for the drive narrows away and the right of the fairway is safer because of the spinney and bunker on the other side. Bunkers in front of the green have to be carried but tentatively, as a pitch or chip back from barish ground behind the green does not have much appeal.

Hole 7 (551 yards) Par 5 A newish bunker, at 250 yards down the left-hand side, is likely to trouble only the biggest hitters but that is the best line to take at the second successive par five. The green is tucked away and masked by a small mound to the right. Unless conditions are favourable it will take most players at least three shots to get home.

Hole 8 (394 yards) Par 4 An iron could be the best bet for the tee-shot here, largely because the out-of-bounds railway line on the right comes very much into the reckoning again. There is plenty of trouble on the left too, but the approach shot is played to a plateau green, high in the sky-line. Huge bunkers are there to catch anything short.

Hole 9 (162 yards) Par 3 Not much of a look of links about this hole with its backdrop of red-brick buildings. It is target golf at its best though, with the fear that the overclubbed ball might land in the street. In fact the 10 bunkers around the putting surface are the real obstacles to the hole.

Hole 10 (334 yards) Par 4 A short par four which starts off with a blind tee-shot over mounds to a narrow fairway with little room, even on the ideal line. The next shot may only be a pitch, but lack of definition makes judgement of distance somewhat difficult. The green tends to slope away on all sides.

Hole 11 (485 yards) Par 5 The gamble here is presented by the large bunkers at 256 yards range, which rise some 15 feet into the air on the corner of this left-hand dog-leg. Carry them and the chances are that the green is reachable, but the more cautious line to the right will almost certainly require three shots to get home.

Hole 12 (189 yards) Par 3 Trees surround the tee and it is all too easy on this hole to make a mistake with club selection. The green, which has a considerable slope from the right, is protected by seven bunkers, along with a road and out of bounds at the back.

Hole 13 (339 yards) Par 4 Anyone could easily be misled into thinking that this hole represents the calm before the storm that lies ahead. This right-hand dog-leg hole is relatively short, but the tee-shot should be hit left to leave the best approach to a narrow, heavily guarded green that has more slopes than any other on the course.

Hole 14 (445 yards) Par 4 Although one of the easier holes on the course, the drive still must be carefully placed to avoid the humps and bunkers on the right-hand side of the fairway. The green slopes towards the back where there is an out of bounds problem for the overhit approach shot.

Hole 15 (468 yards) Par 4 Big hitters will drive over the right-hand bunkers placed about 230 yards down the fairway, because a recently added sand trap guards the route on the other side. Usually the 15th plays straight into the wind, making it one of the hardest holes on the course. Many more bunkers lie around the green awaiting any shot that is less than perfect.

Hole 16 (356 yards) Par 4 Lytham used to boast 356 bunkers, but now there are only about half that number; however, 16 of them are on this one hole alone. The tee-shot is blind and must be aimed further left than seems apparent, in order to set up a short-iron approach shot to a green that slopes from right to left.

Hole 17 (413 yards) Par 4 The 17th has 11 more bunkers, each one threatening the shorter route across the angle of the dog-leg. Any shot aimed right 'stretches' the hole, making the approach much more testing, especially into the prevailing wind.

Hole 18 (386 yards) Par 4 From a recently added back tee, the bunkers at around the 240-yard mark are now in play and so too is the shrubbery around the club's flag-pole on the right. There is a narrow entrance to the green, itself enormous and producing more three-putts than any other on the course.

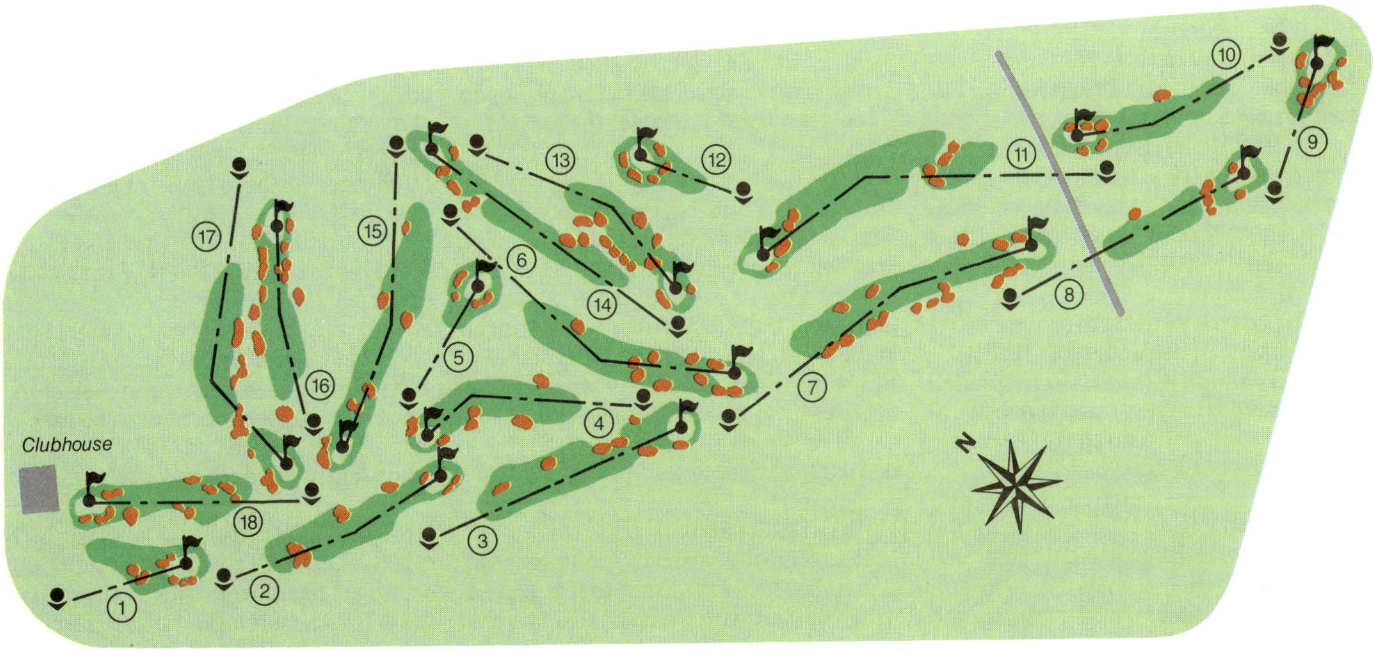

ROYAL ST. GEORGE'S GOLF CLUB, SANDWICH

Ron Moseley, Golf Correspondent of The Press Association

Royal St. George's may not be popular with some American golfers, but it carries a lot of affection in British hearts. For two very good reasons.

In 1934 Henry Cotton ended a long period of American domination of the Open with the first of his three victories, including a second round of 65 (after which the famous Dunlop 65 ball was named). Then, in 1985, Sandy Lyle became Open Champion to score the first success by a British golfer for 16 years.

The course was the first in England to stage an Open in 1894 and has held 10 others since, more than any other course south of the border.

It went off the Open rota for 32 years, but came back in 1981 after many of the blind shots had been eradicated and changes made to five holes. St. George's has strong amateur links, and was the venue for the Walker Cup in 1967.

THE COURSE

Hole 1 (448 yards) Par 4 The 'kitchen', which has been the mysterious name for the hollow across the first fairway for nearly 100 years, is the ideal landing area for the drive. But then the problems start. The second shot has to be played with exactly the right club, over three deep bunkers, to get the ball close to the flag.

Hole 2 (377 yards) Par 4 Any player who has got away with a four on the 1st hole will be thinking of a birdie here. But there is a big risk, namely a carry of over 230 yards, if the ball is to be fired straight at the green across the left-hand dog-leg. From the right side of the fairway the approach will be with a longer club and anything short will probably slip back down a sharp slope.

Hole 3 (215 yards) Par 3 One of the best, and most demanding, short holes in golf. The tee-shot used to be played blind, but now with a raised tee and a plateau green, everything is in view, including the total absence of any bunkers. However, the rough on the surrounding hillocks is lethal.

Hole 4 (471 yards) Par 4 Possibly the hardest hole on the course. The tee-shot must carry a massive sand dune, in which is set an enormous bunker. The alternative route, left, is narrow and approach shots that finish short of the green leave fiendishly difficult putts up a slope. Overhit shots do not have far to travel to be out of bounds.

Hole 5 (422 yards) Par 4 The fairway, in a valley enclosed by dunes, appears an inviting target. However, it is only the perfectly placed drive that presents a sight of the green between two hillocks. Even then the second shot can be hard to judge, as wind speed and direction on the other side of the dunes is often erratic.

Hole 6 (157 yards) Par 3 This hole is called The Maiden, after the enormous sand dune that towers above the green on the left. The prevailing wind is usually against, making club selection difficult. Four bunkers guard the edges of the green.

Hole 7 (532 yards) Par 5 The first of the par fives presents a frightening drive with the carry from the new back tee, over the cross-bunkers, measuring about 200 yards. There are nine other sand traps dotted around the hole, while the green lies beyond another ridge, and anything off-line will be severely punished.

Hole 8 (420 yards) Par 4 This hole was formerly a par three but was changed to give the course a better balance. The fairway is divided by a stretch of rough, sandy scrub. Two straight and long shots are needed to find the target – a long and undulating green.

Hole 9 (391 yards) Par 4 Ideally the drive should be placed on the right-hand side of the fairway to give the best approach shot. This will have to carry two bunkers, named Corsets because they pinch into the fairway. The green is heavily bunkered and runs away sharply to the right.

Hole 10 (401 yards) Par 4 It is not so much the drive that presents the problem on this hole but the approach shot. And, for once, it might even pay to be short of the exposed and elevated green rather than take the risk of going over the back, where severe penalties may be incurred.

Hole 11 (218 yards) Par 3 This was a par four which has been shortened. The high tee presents the best view of Pegwell Bay from which a straight tee-shot is essential to avoid five bunkers guarding a green that has many subtle contours.

Hole 12 (367 yards) Par 4 A dog-leg and an obvious birdie chance. There is not a great deal to be gained by trying to 'shorten' the hole and drive across the angle where lots of bunkers are ready and waiting. A good tee-shot aimed left will still leave only a short-iron second shot.

Hole 13 (455 yards) Par 4 The tee-shot has to carry a line of dunes and it is wiser to aim right of centre rather than to attempt the shorter, but more dangerous route left. Bunkers abound and a long second shot has to find a green divided by a ridge, with out of bounds at the back.

Hole 14 (509 yards) Par 5 The second and last of Sandwich's two par fives, bisected by the famous 'Suez Canal' lying about 310 yards from the back tee. The out-of-bounds fence runs all the way down the right and there is plenty of trouble, such as bunkers and rough on the port side too. Experts, in favourable conditions, might get home in two; for lesser mortals, crossing the water in that many strokes may be accomplishment enough.

Hole 15 (468 yards) Par 4 A classic golf hole with innumerable problems along the whole route. Bunkers await the drive on either side of the fairway, but the approach is even more intimidating; the choice is either playing short or carrying the cross-bunkers, to try to find the green. The green itself is perilous with a bank on the left and a severe drop on the right.

Hole 16 (165 yards) Par 3 The last short hole is probably the easiest, producing three holes-in-one during the 1981 Open and a Tony Jacklin televised 'ace' during the 1967 Dunlop Masters. The green is entirely surrounded by sand and, if the wind is against, a big club may be necessary to get there.

Hole 17 (427 yards) Par 4 The drive has to avoid two well-positioned bunkers on either side but, yet again, it is the approach which will have some players worried. The green, wider than it is long, is on a plateau and anything short of the target will roll back to leave an extremely difficult chip.

Hole 18 (470 yards) Par 4 A tough finishing hole with the better drive going left, as the other side poses more problems in having to cross a bunker with cuts into the green. Left of the putting surface is 'Duncan's Hollow' named after George Duncan who failed to get down in two and lost the 1922 Open.

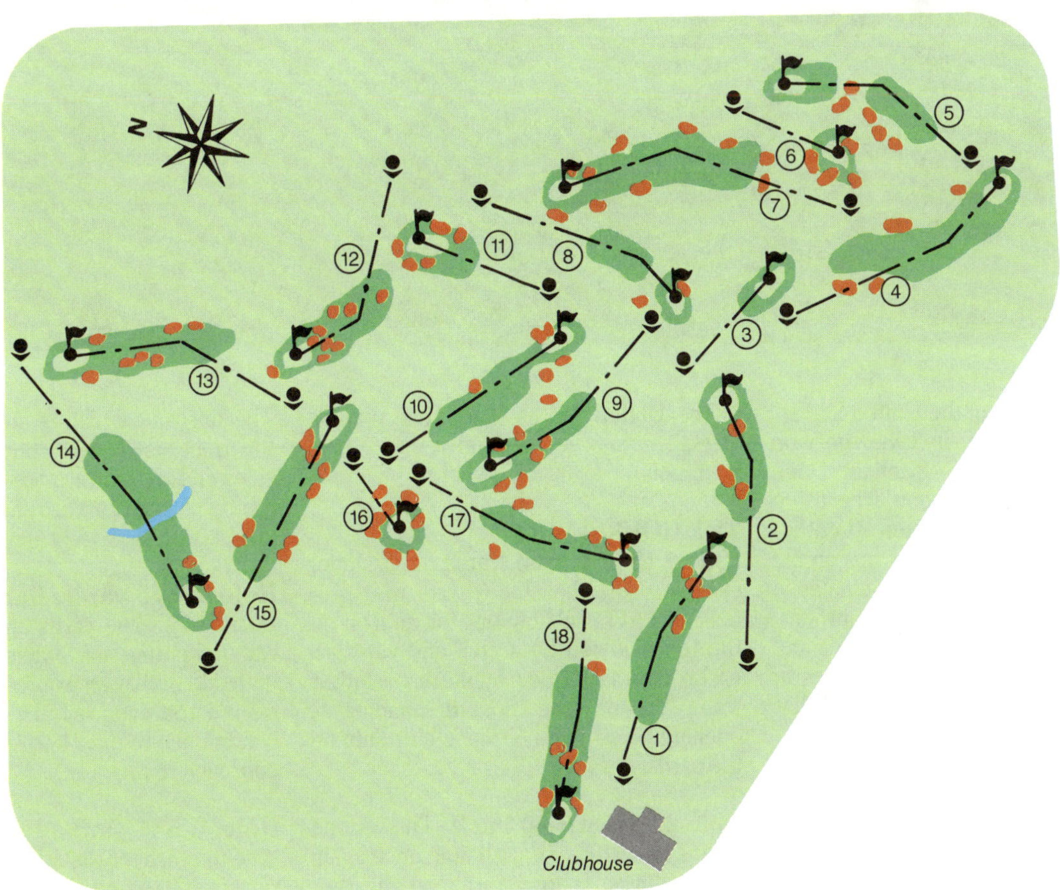

ROYAL TROON

Mitchell Platts, Golf Correspondent of
The Times

Mark Calcavecchia, of the United States, created history when, in 1989, he won the first four holes play-off for the Open Championship at Royal Troon, where golf was first played in 1878. Then 23 enthusiasts, whose first clubhouse was an old railway carriage, began with five holes in wild country festooned with broom, heather and whins, and full of dunes and hillocks. It was extended to 18 holes in 1886, although it was not until 1923 that the Open was taken there when the previously arranged venue, Muirfield, was being rebuilt. Arthur Havers won that year, since when Bobby Locke (1950) of South Africa, Arnold Palmer (1962) of the United States, Tom Weiskopf (1973) also of the United States, and Tom Watson (1982), another American, have triumphed.

THE COURSE

Hole 1 (364 yards) Par 4 A flat hole, close to the beach, where the professional will probably opt for an iron off the tee followed by a chip and run to a green which has two bunkers on either side. It is not the most demanding of opening holes and a birdie is certainly on the cards.

Hole 2 (391 yards) Par 4 The second hole is more difficult, although once again it probably calls for an iron off the tee. The fairway, which is angled slightly to the right, is cleverly bunkered on both sides and an accurate tee-shot will set-up a fairly straightforward shot to a generous green.

Hole 3 (379 yards) Par 4 The Gyaws Burn, some 300 yards ahead of the tee, can be in range for longer hitters, so it is quite likely that an iron will again be used off the tee especially in fast, downwind conditions. It then leaves for a positive approach to the green.

Hole 4 (557 yards) Par 5 Now is the time to reach for the driver although accuracy is still the premium as the fairway is often narrowed by the rough being grown-in. A fairway bunker some 240 yards out on the right, in which direction the hole dog-legs, must be avoided so that the green, well-protected by bunkers, can be reached in two.

Hole 5 (210 yards) Par 3 In general the wind comes from the right which does not exactly help since the green slopes from right to left towards deep bunkers. It is rated by the professionals as an exceptionally good short hole with the length making it all the more difficult to keep the ball on the green.

Hole 6 (577 yards) Par 5 This is the longest hole in Open Championship golf and it is made all the more testing by the narrow fairway with two bunkers to the left and one to the right. The green, also long and narrow, represents a difficult target considering the length of the hole and pitching left of it will leave a tricky chip.

Hole 7 (402 yards) Par 4 Time to return to an iron from the tee, although some may prefer a three wood. The drive must navigate tricky mounds, leaving a medium iron into a green which has a ramp at the front.

Hole 8 (126 yards) Par 3 In 1950 Herman Tissies, an amateur from Germany, took 15 at this hole, known as The Postage Stamp, whereas Gene Sarazen, one of only four men to win all four major championships, holed-in-one in 1973! It is far from easy, despite the length, and it can play to as much as a five iron if the prevailing wind is blowing against.

Hole 9 (423 yards) Par 4 The place not to finish here is over the back of the green, which is on a slight plateau, because there trees and bushes will interfere with a recovery shot. From the tee it is a case of playing for position again, probably with an iron, leaving a bump and run to the green.

Hole 10 (438 yards) Par 4 There is not a bunker in sight but that does little to ease the strain as the hole can play extremely long into the wind. The drive over dunes is forbidding, with danger lurking on both sides. The second shot is a long iron into the hogsback green.

Hole 11 (481 yards) Par 5 It is entirely possible to extract a birdie from this hole although it commands two good shots to be on the green. The drive must miss the gorse, to leave a second shot which is made all the more difficult by the knowledge that the gorse extends down the left, while the out-of-bounds railway line runs down the right.

Hole 12 (431 yards) Par 4 Following a solid drive the key here is to run a positive approach into a two-tiered green making sure to avoid the cavernous bunker to the right. The green slopes from back to front.

Hole 13 (465 yards) Par 4 Once again there are no bunkers on this hole although there are many humps and hollows. In fact the fairway has been described as looking like the back of the moon. Into the wind it is a hole which is extremely difficult to hit in two and par is considered a virtue at all times.

Hole 14 (179 yards) Par 3 The key, which so often is the case in golf, is to take one club more than it looks especially as the green, fully visible from the tee, has two bunkers front right and one similarly placed on the left.

Hole 15 (457 yards) Par 4 Out of bounds is to the right, where the tented village is built during the Open, and the drive to a plateau-style fairway must be long and accurate to avoid bunkers on both sides. The green, set in a tiny valley with a little swale in front of it, is also well guarded by bunkers.

Hole 16 (542 yards) Par 5 The decision to be made here is whether or not to drive the stream. If that option is successfully accomplished then it is possible to hit the green, which is narrow and well-bunkered, in two. Otherwise it becomes a three-shotter with an eight iron probably required for the third.

Hole 17 (223 yards) Par 3 What a demanding hole to face at this stage. The green represents a teasing target because it is difficult in dry conditions to stop the ball on the putting surface. There is a little flat area in front of the green on which is it possible to land the ball so that it gently rolls forward up towards the flag.

Hole 18 (452 yards) Par 4 The 18th was stretched by 25 yards for the Open in 1989 although Greg Norman still managed to drive into the fairway bunker which proved his undoing. The need to be positive with the second shot is there for all to see with out of bounds at the back of the green. It is a wonderful, if rather severe, finishing hole.

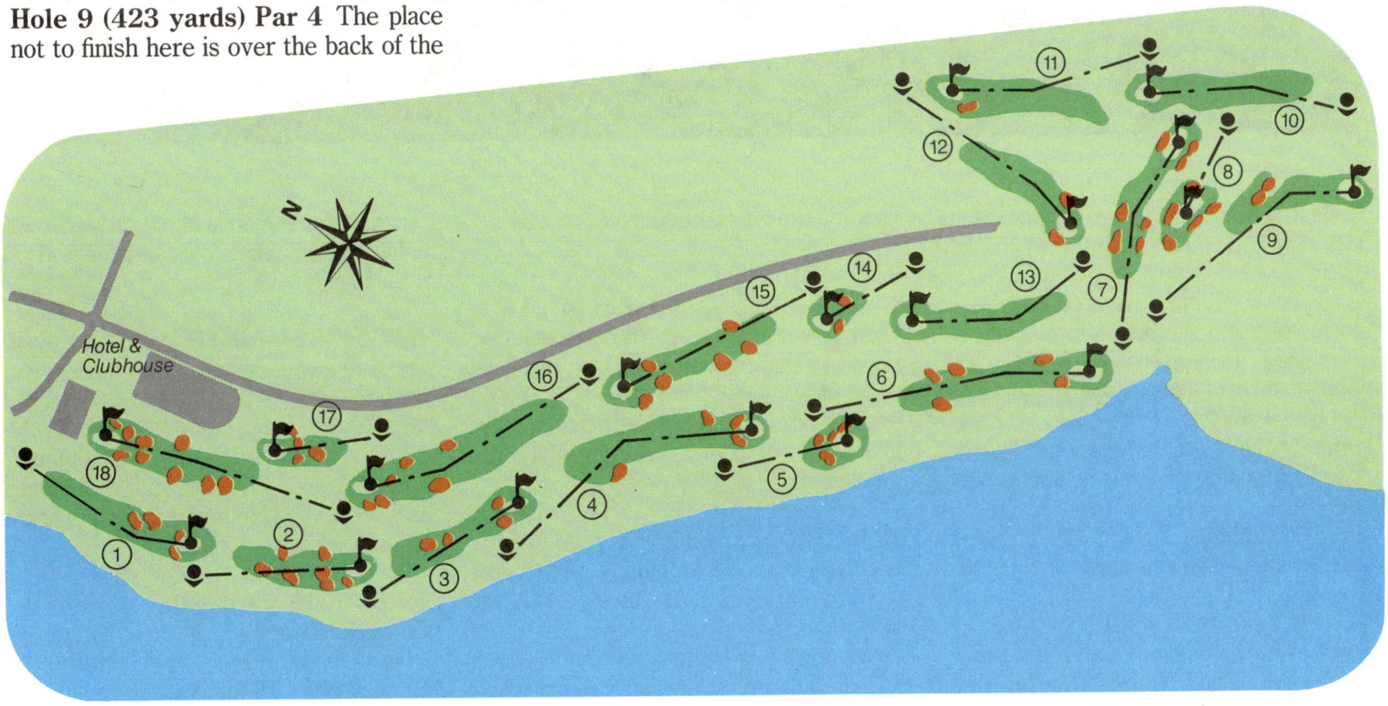

ST. ANDREWS

Tim Glover, Golf Correspondent of
The Independent

The Royal and Ancient Golf Club of St. Andrews stands as a shrine to the auld game and a beacon to the new. This historic links course was created, not by man, but by mother nature and has remained unspoilt since time immemorial. A form of golf has been played at St. Andrews since the 16th century. Appropriately the Royal and Ancient Golf Club has its imposing clubhouse standing sentinel over the 1st tee and the 18th green of the Old Course. 'Truly, if I had to select one course on which to play the match of my life, I should have chosen the Old Course', said the great Bobby Jones. St. Andrews, the birthplace and the home of the game of golf, represents the way it was and the way it should be.

THE COURSE

Hole 1 (370 yards) Par 4 Granny Clark's Wynd crosses the 1st fairway, which is shared with the 18th, at a distance of 150 yards from the tee. No bunkers to contend with but the Swilken Burn guards the front of the green, which has subtle borrows.

Hole 2 (411 yards) Par 4 A good drive is critical at the Dyke Hole with the perfect line to the right of Cheape's bunker. Down the right-hand side there is heavy rough and a few hidden bunkers to watch out for. The green lies concealed in a hollow and the shot has to be played over higher ground which conceals the bottom of the flag.

Hole 3 (352 yards) Par 4 A relatively straightforward par four with the best line being to the right of the bunker facing the tee. The green opens up better from the right but it is guarded by the small bunkers and rough. The green itself slopes away from the player requiring a delicate approach shot.

Hole 4 (419 yards) Par 4 Here the approach is the difficult shot. There are no hazards on a direct line from the tee but thereafter 15 bunkers lie in wait for anything off-line. Again the right side is favoured but a pushed shot will take the ball the wrong side of the track. A little hump protects the front edge of the green.

Hole 5 (514 yards) Par 5 The drive is the critical shot at the first of the par five holes on the Old Course. There is heavy rough on the right-hand side and at around 250 yards from the tee there is a group of seven bunkers which cannot be seen from the tee. Beyond a hill, short of the green, is a deep gully. The 5th shares the green with the 13th and is the biggest of the double greens.

Hole 6 (374 yards) Par 4 The drive must carry the deep gullies in front of the tee and then there is big trouble both to the left and right of the fairway. On the left lie the Coffins bunkers and on the right, deep gorse. The ideal line is straight on the airfield hangars that can be seen across the Eden Estuary on the RAF base at Leuchars.

Hole 7 (359 yards) Par 4 There is a choice from the tee; well to the left opens up the green and makes access to the pin easier but requires a longer, although less dangerous shot. The more favoured line is tight on the right side, over the edge of the whins. The huge Cockle bunker dominates the approach to the green.

Hole 8 (166 yards) Par 3 The first hole of the Loop where a good player would hope to pick up one or two strokes to par. The prevailing wind is from the right and it can be difficult to get close to the pin. The green has several subtle borrows.

Hole 9 (307 yards) Par 4 One of the easiest holes on the course. There are a few bunkers down the middle but the fairway is generous. There are no reference points around the green which is flat and accommodating.

Hole 10 (318 yards) Par 4 The Bobby Jones hole is another that offers a birdie opportunity. A lone bunker down the right threatens the drive but the approach requires a delicate touch to get the ball close to the flag. A pitch and run would pay better dividends.

Hole 11 (172 yards) Par 3 The wind is the critical factor when it comes to tackling this famous hole. The pin is usually cut behind the Strath bunker which eats into the front part of the green. Hill bunker to the left, a cavern more than 10 feet deep, is also in play. The green has a steep slope from back to front and left to right.

Hole 12 (316 yards) Par 4 Not a very long hole, but a tricky one. Hidden bunkers lie in the middle of the fairway and the green has a plateau that is only 10 steps wide. Anything short or long will mean a very difficult putt.

Hole 13 (398 yards) Par 4 The Coffins bunkers must be passed on the left or the right but a long, high ridge can create a problem for the drive down the right. It is not difficult to hit the huge green but it is easy to have a long approach putt.

Hole 14 (523 yards) Par 5 The drive at the Long Hole is one of the key shots in the round. There is out of bounds over the wall on the right and the Beardies bunkers guard the left side of a very narrow landing area. After that comes another line of defence and it is not called the Hell bunker for nothing.

Hole 15 (401 yards) Par 4 The drive should follow the line of the church spire to the right of the town. There are bunkers on the left and out of bounds on the right. An approach shot to the left, even if it is on the green, could still leave the player with a greenside bunker between him and the hole.

Hole 16 (351 yards) Par 4 The Principal's Nose, a group of bunkers down the middle, is the dominating feature of this hole. A drive down the left leaves an approach back towards the disused railway line, which runs the length of the hole down the right. The more adventurous drive to the right leaves an easier approach, but the landing area is tight.

Hole 17 (461 yards) Par 4 After a drive over the railway sheds, the Road Hole requires one of the most courageous shots in world golf. A narrow green, which is set at an angle, demands a perfectly struck iron. Too short and the Road Hole bunker, which has destroyed many a good score-card, will trap the ball. Too long and the horrors of the road beyond lie in wait.

Hole 18 (354 yards) Par 4 The final hole has no bunkers and acres of space although too far left is out of bounds. The line to aim for is the clock on the R and A Clubhouse. The Valley of Sin is a deep depression on the front left corner of the green.

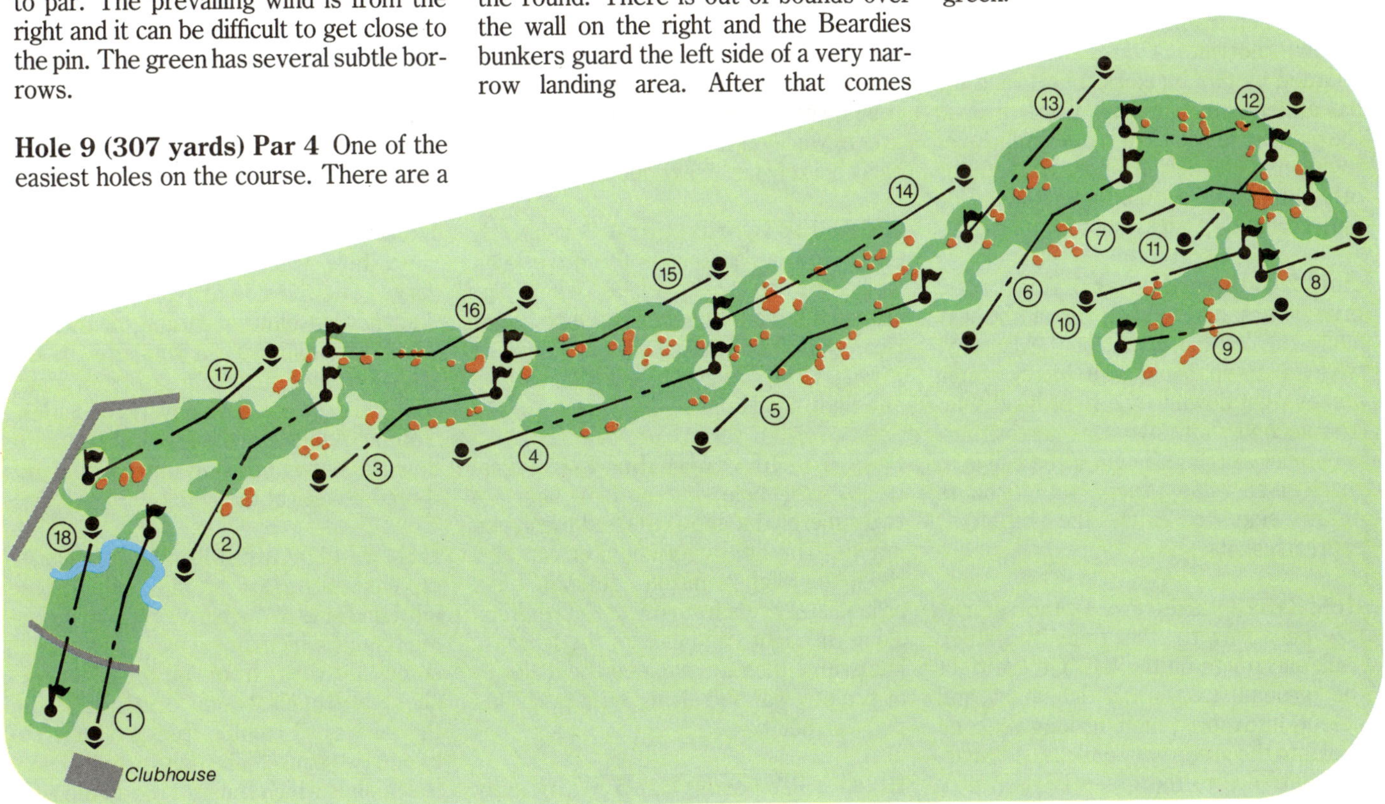

ST. MELLION

Ron Wills, Golf Correspondent of
The Daily Mirror

St. Mellion, some ten miles from Plymouth, is the site of the only course that Jack Nicklaus has designed in Great Britain. It is a superb golf course, and one that must rank alongside some of Nicklaus' other great course design achievements.

The owners of the St. Mellion Country Club, Martin and Hermon Bond, purchased an extra 200 acres of land to accommodate Nicklaus' ambitious plans to construct a quality course which would win international recognition. The Bond brothers no doubt winced from time to time as they signed the cheques, but it was money well spent.

Streams have been re-directed, others have been opened up to form lakes, and entire hillsides have been bulldozed aside to create memorable holes on a course that largely runs around the perimeter of the old course.

Nicklaus has utilised every square yard of the extra 200 acres (and it's a shame more land still was not available) to produce a majestic course that is a test for all, whether you are a scratch golfer or a humble 18-handicapper.

THE COURSE

Hole 1 (420 yards) Par 4 A comparatively gentle start. An opening shot from an elevated tee into a wide fairway runs away downhill and dog-legs gently to the right. Then comes the difficult bit, a second shot into a tiny, raised green, guarded by two bunkers. Short, and the ball either lands in a bunker or in a dip in the ground, leaving a delicate wedge over the bunker. A sliced shot will find the other bunker, or worse, deep rough. Too far left and it's a tricky shot from a bank.

Hole 2 (543 yards) Par 5 An accurate drive is essential. Trees run all the way along the left-hand side of the fairway, while a steep bank with heavy rough comes right down to the right-hand side. The second shot down this narrow fairway must also be straight if the ball is to reach a slim-line green, with bunkers either side to catch the off-target approach shots.

Hole 3 (373 yards) Par 4 Another narrow fairway with, this time, the steep bank and rough on the left. On the right the ground falls away suddenly and steeply into more rough, making a second shot into the green very difficult. The narrow entrance to the green is again protected by bunkers – three of them. One on either side, with a third, 35 yards short of the green, to catch underclubbed shots or over ambitious shots from the rough.

Hole 4 (185 yards) Par 3 Built into the side of a hill, the 4th hole once again demands accuracy from the tee. On the left another steep bank, complete with rough, comes down onto the fringe of the green, while on the right, the ground falls away sharply into trees and more rough.

Hole 5 (354 yards) Par 4 A relatively easy par four, as long as the drive is hit well. The carry over a lake, which laps around the tee, is 180 yards. Once that is cleared, it's plain sailing from a wide open fairway to a large green, guarded only by one right-hand bunker.

Hole 6 (430 yards) Par 4 A largely trouble-free hole, but nothing short of two superbly hit shots will find the green in two. The hole's sole bunker can also catch the slightly mishit tee-shot – it's around 200 yards from the tee. Trees run along the right-hand side of the fairway, but even if they are avoided the majority of players will be relying on a pitch and putt for their pars.

Hole 7 (502 yards) Par 5 With a fairly wide fairway, the ideal tee-shot here should finish into the right half which opens up the green on this dog-leg left hole. Too far left and the ball could finish in trees, some of which almost encroach onto the fairway. A sprayed second shot could also land in trouble – either trees on the left or a large bunker on the right, which guards the front of the green. Missing the green on the left can cause problems, as the ground falls away dramatically.

Hole 8 (140 yards) Par 3 Another short hole where the green has been carved into the side of a hill, and one that demands absolute accuracy off the tee. The green is large but it is guarded by two trees on the left, the branches of which will punish a tee-shot straying too far left. Too far right, and the ball will run away down a slope, probably into one of the three bunkers at the bottom.

Hole 9 (410 yards) Par 4 An accurate drive is vital here, preferably aimed at the left-hand side of the fairway to avoid sloping ground which runs down into a bunker some 250 yards from the tee. The tee-shot is also uphill, but once on the plateau, the fairway is trouble-free and runs between two banks. The only hazard of note is a bunker which runs alongside the right of the green, ready to trap a second shot that has been overfaded.

Hole 10 (448 yards) Par 4 A delightful start to the second half. The 10th is played from a raised tee and the drive has to carry a stream into an ample fairway which dog-legs to the right. But even the best of drives leaves a demanding second shot of anything up to 190 yards, with wayward shots being severely punished. A slice will carry the ball into trees or, worse, into a stream which runs the entire length of the fairway and past the green. More trees await a pulled shot, and the green itself is small. Wisdom might dictate playing up short and hoping for a pitch and putt to salvage par.

Hole 11 (202 yards) Par 3 This, the most picturesque par-three hole on the course, is anything but a doddle. To reach the green demands a carry of at least 190 yards over water. There is a short cut over water, but the chances are the ball will finish in a largish bunker guarding the green's right-hand edge. Any par three will have been earned.

Hole 12 (546 yards) Par 5 Another hole where water can play a vital role. A stream runs down the entire right-hand side of the fairway and then turns sharp left to run across the entrance to the green. It's a brave, confident and very big hitter who would try to reach the green in two here. A 280-yard drive still leaves close to 260 yards to the centre of the green. But two sensible woods and a pitch over the stream yield a par to most.

Hole 13 (404 yards) Par 4 No major problems here, other than the fact that the hole is uphill all the way to a heavily bunkered green. A large bunker awaits the pulled tee-shot some 200 yards or more from the tee. Avoid that and the biggest problem is choosing the right club for the second shot to cover the ever-rising ground.

Hole 14 (174 yards) Par 3 The final short hole, and probably the simplest of the four. The carry to the front of the green is a mere 160 yards, and only a cut tee-shot will land in real trouble – either a bunker right and just short of the green or trees. Perhaps the hole that gives the last chance for a breather before the testing finish.

Hole 15 (442 yards) Par 4 A generous fairway, but a tee-shot of at least 200 yards is required to carry the rising ground and on to the flatter surface. Once up there, the dangers are still apparent. A pulled second shot and the ball runs away down a slope; a pushed second could finish in trees or heavy rough. The narrow entrance to the green is protected on either side by bunkers. A par here is always well earned.

Hole 16 (554 yards) Par 5 The longest hole on the course, it dog-legs left and then the fairway rises steeply to an elevated green. But it should provide plenty of pars, assuming the rash of bunkers is avoided. A trio of them, beginning 200 yards from the tee, await the sliced tee-shot, and another three, one either side and one in the centre of the fairway, are hungry for mishit second shots. Three more surround the raised green, but traps apart, it's a hole that shouldn't scare most golfers.

Hole 17 (456 yards) Par 4 A testing par four, with trees and out of bounds on the right-hand side of this dog-leg right hole. But it's also a hole that demands two majestic shots to reach the green which dog-legs even further right. Most players will hit two shots and then pitch over the road at this slightly uphill hole and rely on a single putt for a par.

Hole 18 (472 yards) Par 4 There are not many longer par fours than this one, and it begins with a daunting tee-shot down a narrow avenue between trees. Hit an accurate tee-shot into a generous fairway, and there are still 200 yards or more to go to the green which curls around a small lake. It's an intimidating shot, too intimidating for most who will, one suspects, pitch onto the green and, as with the 17th, hope for a single-putt par.

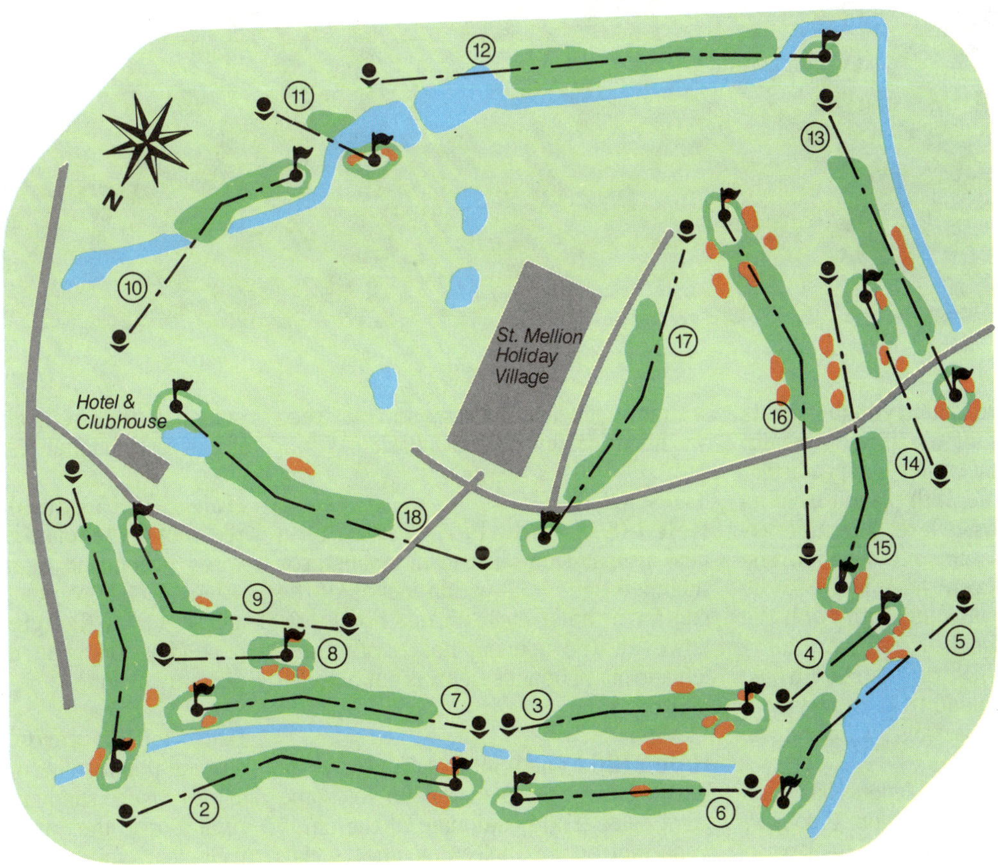

ST. PIERRE

Gordon Richardson, Golf Correspondent of
The News of the World

St. Pierre Golf and Country Club, with its panoramic views of the distant Severn Bridge, is best-known for its spectacular 237-yard par-three 18th played from an elevated tee across a lake. When Severiano Ballesteros won the Epson Grand Prix Matchplay event here in 1989, the hole was turned into the 16th (with the 10th becoming the 17th and the 9th the 18th) to ensure further matches would be played here to add to the enjoyment of millions of golf fans watching on television.

The original course layout has subsequently been resumed on this near 7,000-yard layout in a former deer park, with its abundance of majestic old trees and historic mansion and church.

THE COURSE

Hole 1 (576 yards) Par 5 In the Epson final against Denis Durnian, Ballesteros thumped two shots within inches of the cup for a tap-in eagle three. For most, however, the opening hole, with trees left and out of bounds right, is out of reach in two.

Hole 2 (364 yards) Par 4 The drive on the 2nd must keep to the left of some giant oaks. The positioning of the pin is important on this hole as it affects club selection for the approach to a raised green, with bunkers left and right.

Hole 3 (135 yards) Par 3 The third tee-shot of the round is hit to another elevated green and demands precise club selection. There are bunkers front, left and right of the green and the hole, depending on wind direction, can play deceptively long.

Hole 4 (379 yards) Par 4 The tee-shot on this hole is tricky as it is necessary to bisect sand traps placed left and right down the fairway while steering well-clear of some big trees to the right.

Two more bunkers guard the entrance to a slightly crowned green.

Hole 5 (420 yards) Par 4 The 5th heads back down towards the valley bottom. Thick woods on the right of the fairway are the greatest danger here. The second shot is often played from a sloping lie, which must carry a big dip to a green with a very narrow entrance.

Hole 6 (165 yards) Par 3 Wind speed and direction must be taken into account before hitting down from an elevated tee to a green that looks nearer than it is. A range of sand traps guards the front of the green, with bushes behind.

Hole 7 (442 yards) Par 4 The 'sky-high' tee at this hole gives an exhilarating view of the fairway below. The drive must be accurate, avoiding big trees on the left-hand side. However, the ball must not stray too far right otherwise the long and virtually blind second to a small, well-bunkered green is not possible.

Hole 8 (309 yards) Par 4 The temptation here is to have a direct drive at the green, which is eminently reachable. But the prudent select a long iron and aim to keep left of a big tree jutting into the fairway on the right, leaving an easy pitch over a bunker to the target.

Hole 9 (444 yards) Par 4 A bunker on the right and trees on the left make this a hugely demanding tee-shot. Two more bunkers short of the green can trick players into believing the approach is shorter than it is. The second shot must be bold to be up onto the green.

Hole 10 (362 yards) Par 4 If the longer hitters avoid the bunker on the right at this left-hand dog-leg the ball will reach the green from the tee. Any ball hit with draw, however, will tend to kick away down the left-hand slope. An iron off the tee followed by a short pitch, therefore, is often the preferred way to play the hole.

Hole 11 (369 yards) Par 4 At all costs the tee-shot must avoid the bunker on the right of the fairway to make the approach to the green at the crest of the slope possible. Coming up short from an uphill lie is a common failing.

Hole 12 (545 yards) Par 5 This is the second of St. Pierre's par fives and demands two huge blows to reach the green for a birdie or eagle opportunity. To create this chance, the ball must draw round the trees at the corner of the dog-leg.

Hole 13 (219 yards) Par 3 The elevated tee at this long par three gives a birdseye-view of the five big bunkers that are placed short, left, right and behind the green.

Hole 14 (521 yards) Par 5 Steering to the right of the trees from the tee provides a clear view of the distant tree-ringed green, situated beyond more fairway-narrowing oaks. Only the purest golf shots will get to the green in two.

Hole 15 (375 yards) Par 4 The landing area for the tee-shot on this hole is ideally a narrow stretch of turf between the big trees on the left and an angled row of bunkers cutting in from the right. The proximity of the lake beyond the green inhibits bold approaches.

Hole 16 (426 yards) Par 4 As long as the drive avoids tangling with the giant chestnut tree growing 150 yards from the tee on the right-hand side of the fairway, this left-to-right dog-leg gives most players the chance of a birdie down the home straight.

Hole 17 (412 yards) Par 4 A slight dog-leg to the right calls for an accurate drive from an elevated tee in the trees. If the ball lands too far right, the approach shot is either played out of the trees, or at least over them. The green has bunkers front left and right.

Hole 18 (237 yards) Par 3 With out of bounds over the wall on the left and a steep slope all the way up to the green from the lake, the premium at one of golf's most spectacular finishing holes is to fly the ball all the way to the putting surface beyond three bunkers – no easy feat with a long iron or wood.

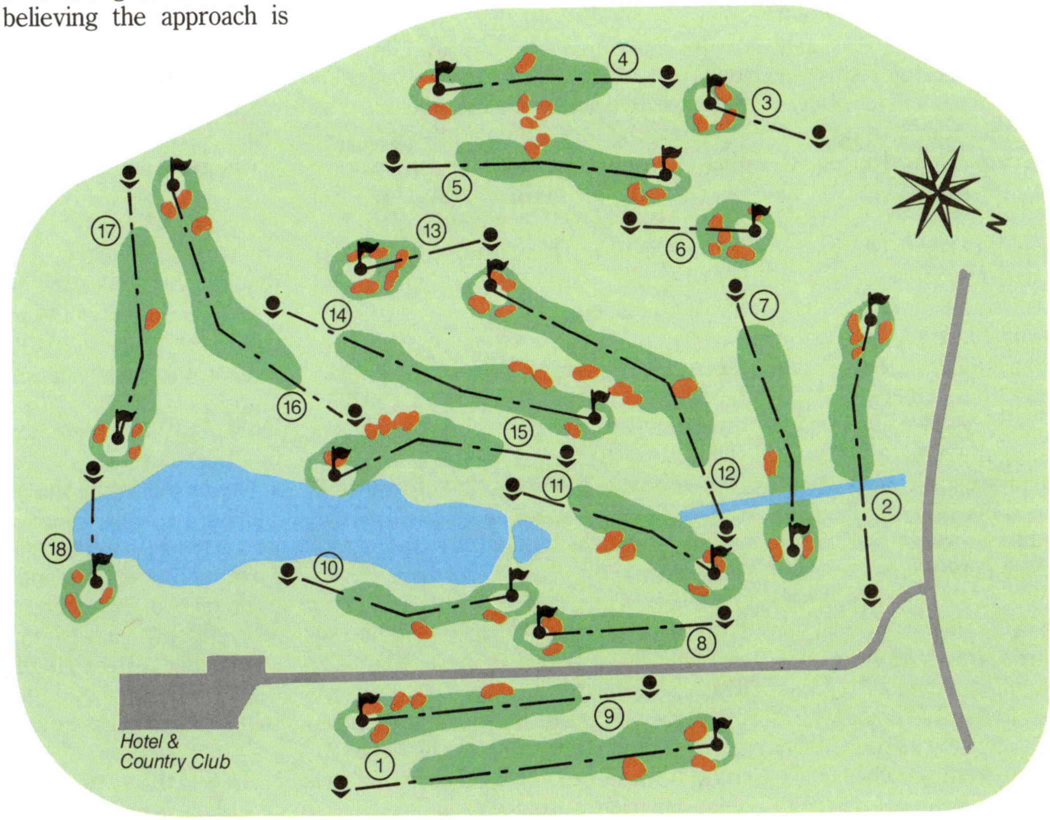

SUNNINGDALE

Renton Laidlaw, Golf Correspondent of
The London Evening Standard

Sunningdale Golf Club, which boasts two excellent courses, the Old and the New, can arguably provide two of the best inland championship tests in the country. The members of the Royal and Ancient Golf Club of St. Andrews certainly thought so when they created history by taking the biennial Walker Cup match, played between the top amateurs of America, Great Britain and Ireland, to this course in 1987. Previously all matches on this side of the Atlantic had been played, like the Open Championship, on links courses by the sea.

Built on pleasantly undulating Surrey heath, on sandy soil that drains easily, the courses provide an interesting test of golf without requiring the player to be a power-driver. The character of Sunningdale's two golfing gems puts a premium on the ability to hit accurate shots avoiding the well-placed bunkers and keeping out of the heather, pines and silver birches that line the fairways.

THE COURSE

Hole 1 (494 yards) Par 5 Henry Longhurst, doyen of golf commentators, was of the opinion that the 1st hole, which stretches gently away downhill on ground sloping right to left from the clubhouse, was one of the best opening holes in golf. The ideal line is down the right-hand side, skirting the trees in order to set up the chance of hitting the green in two with a long iron or three wood.

Hole 2 (484 yards) Par 5 Played at right angles to the 1st, the 2nd also demands two good hits. The line this time is across the heather down the left, cutting off as much as possible to ensure a spot on the fairway from which to hit a second shot over the brow of a slight hill. The green slopes from front to back and is guarded by a deep bunker, which cuts into it on the left.

Hole 3 (296 yards) Par 4 The big hitter may well drive this hole as long as they are careful to avoid the bunker on the right, close to the putting surface. The danger on this green is rolling into one of the left-hand bunkers at the back of the green, owing to the natural slope of the surface.

Hole 4 (161 yards) Par 3 The first of Sunningdale's par threes is played uphill. The base of the pin is obscured from most of the tees. The club is a six or seven iron but the margin for error is small, but even if the ball reaches the green, its natural slope can make putting a problem.

Hole 5 (410 yards) Par 4 This hole provides a panoramic and much-painted view from the tee. That pleasure, however, is offset by a carry of heather some 200 yards long. It is possible to reduce the carry by going right, but then the ball might run into two well-placed bunkers. The small green is over the pond creating just that little extra pressure.

Hole 6 (415 yards) Par 4 This is a hole where a thick band of rough that crosses the fairway catches the mishit drive. The second shot is uphill to a green that falls away sharply to the right and is guarded to the front and left by sand traps.

Hole 7 (402 yards) Par 4 The drive at the roller-coaster 7th is blind. The line is down the left into a valley to avoid a sand trap on the right. The second shot is up the hill to a two-tiered green protected by a bunker on the front and a series of sand traps on the left where the ground falls away sharply. Like so many of the holes at Sunningdale, the 7th, if played sensibly should provide a par, but one wayward shot can prove dramatically costly.

Hole 8 (192 yards) Par 3 The second short hole is played across the valley to a green surrounded by sand traps. Tee-shots hit short and right can kick off down the hill and any pulled left can end on a heather bank from which a delicate recovery is difficult. Few putts on this green are straight.

Hole 9 (267 yards) Par 4 The 9th green, again a double-tiered test, is reachable with a driver, but the entrance to the green, set at an angle, is tight and guarded by no fewer than four bunkers stretched diagonally across the fairway.

Hole 10 (478 yards) Par 5 Standing on the tee is always a great delight. Like the 5th, the view is spectacular. The fairway stretches way down the hill then up far enough to make the second shot a demanding one with a long iron. Once again the green is full of subtle borrows. The delight at hitting the green in two can be marred by failing to two-putt.

Hole 11 (325 yards) Par 4 This hole is blind off the tee, with trouble on either side, and trees blocking the short cut down the right. The green is placed beyond heather and a ditch. It is best to play for position on this hole, leaving a full wedge to a putting surface that slopes from back to front and which falls away sharply at the back.

Hole 12 (451 yards) Par 4 A dog-leg gently to the left and uphill at the end. The drive should go down the right, missing an astutely placed fairway bunker, to set up a medium- or long-iron second shot to a green lying diagonally halfway up the hill. Shortening the second shot by going down the left often leaves the ball in another sand trap. A necklace of bunkers stretches across the fairway, 80 yards short of the green which is narrower at the back than at the front. No-one is disappointed to make par here.

Hole 13 (185 yards) Par 3 Played from a high tee down to a green protected by a gully on three sides. The wind swirls more cunningly beside the green than on the sheltered tee, making it more difficult to hit that side of the ridged green on which the pin has been set.

Hole 14 (509 yards) Par 5 The longest hole but still reachable in two shots. The second shot is played over a string of bunkers positioned diagonally across the fairway. As long as the ball stays out of the heather and sand a par should not be too difficult.

Hole 15 (226 yards) Par 3 Made more difficult by the fact that it is usually played in a right-to-left crosswind, more often than not the tee-shot requires a three wood. The trick is to miss the bunkers on the left-hand side, but even if the green is reached, a tantalising ridge can cause problems when lining up for a birdie putt.

Hole 16 (438 yards) Par 4 The fairway is wide providing no real problem on the drive, but the second shot is made more difficult by having to hit off a downhill lie to an elevated green. Club selection for the second shot is important here. Anything hit short can run into a bunker, shrewdly positioned front and to the left of the putting surface.

Hole 17 (421 yards) Par 4 The brave line off the tee is down the right, taking care to avoid the two bunkers, one of which is almost invisible from the tee. Playing an iron off the tee down the centre for safety means the ball will run left, leaving a further demanding 200-yard shot over a bunker positioned near the green, this time sloping from left to right.

Hole 18 (432 yards) Par 4 The 18th is just eight yards longer than the 17th, but very different in character. Having played downhill at the 17th, the 18th is played back up the hill to the clubhouse. Any drive hit left can end up in ghastly trouble either in gorse or a difficult bunker. The line is up the left, leaving only a medium iron to the green. The green itself is set at an angle and positioned in front of the huge oak tree, the Club's symbol. The green is again well-bunkered both left and right and the hole is demanding enough to ensure that the making of a closing par gives considerable satisfaction.

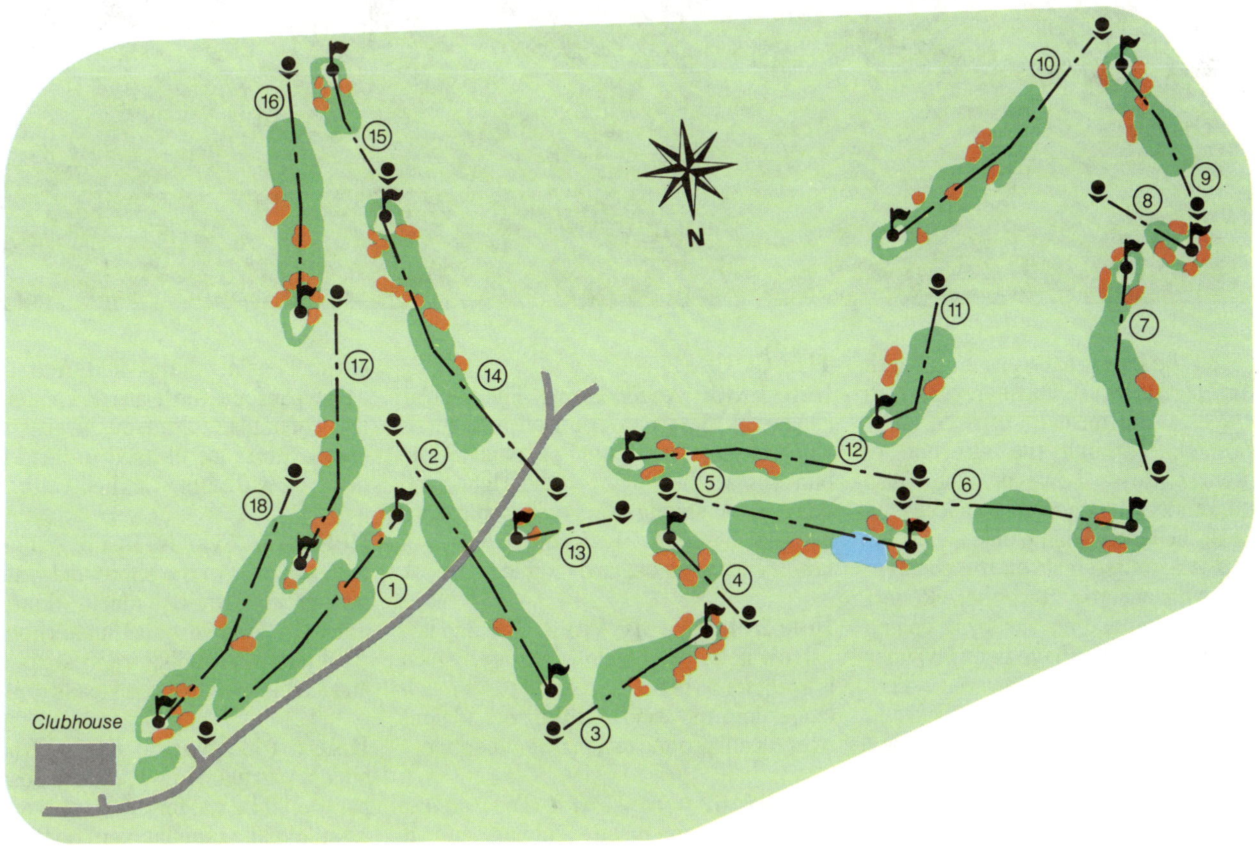

TURNBERRY HOTEL

Mitchell Platts, Golf Correspondent of
The Times

Not even the two great wars of the 20th century could thwart Turnberry, though Mae Wests and tarmac strips certainly intervened. Through the direction of Mackenzie Ross, however, the Ailsa course emerged to become a successful venue of the Open Championship.

This is a course built on the countryside scarred by battle. It was here Robert the Bruce defended his castle. In golfing terms, though, there have been few finer confrontations than that between Tom Watson, the victor, and Jack Nicklaus, the vanquished, in 1977. Greg Norman, in 1986, went on to win the Open with a score of 63 in the second round which tied the record low for a major Championship.

THE COURSE

Hole 1 (350 yards) Par 4 The popular choice off the tee is one iron or a three wood to play for position so avoiding the bunkers at the angle of the right-hand dog-leg. A strong wind will complicate matters especially with the pitch to a green which can be hard to hold.

Hole 2 (428 yards) Par 4 The 2nd is a narrow hole, played along a ridge, which is a test for all players. It often plays much longer into the wind and the second shot over 'dead' ground can prove deceptive.

Hole 3 (462 yards) Par 4 The rough at Turnberry can be demanding and it certainly protects this hole. Although it is a long par four, there are no bunkers to be wary of until the three by the green. Most competitors are pleased to head for the next tee with a four on their card.

Hole 4 (167 yards) Par 3 A tantalising hole adjacent to the shore and with a pulpit green where much drama has unfolded. A cavernous bunker, set front right below a sandhill, represents danger and a hit left of the green leads to trouble.

Hole 5 (441 yards) Par 4 What was once a par five is now a much respected par four. The line for the drive is down the right, avoiding the bunkers on the left, so leaving a clear shot into a cleverly protected, angled green.

Hole 6 (222 yards) Par 3 This hole, especially into a head wind, is a nightmare for many players. Although a par three, there are times when it is necessary to reach for the driver; mostly, however, it requires a long iron or a three wood, played across a shallow valley to a tilting green.

Hole 7 (528 yards) Par 5 It requires precision and more than a touch of courage to extract an eagle from this hole. The green can be reached in two if, from the elevated tee, a long drive is struck so that the ball nestles on the fairway which dog-legs left. The rough, so often calf-deep, lies in wait and most approach shots will kick in right from the green.

Hole 8 (427 yards) Par 4 The saucer-like fairway is dominated by a single bunker. What poses a bigger problem, however, is the two-tiered green, which, being elevated, makes it particularly difficult to get the ball close with the second shot particularly when the pin is placed at the back.

Hole 9 (455 yards) Par 4 There are few more invigorating tees on which to stand than this one which is lashed by the waves below. The cairn stone marks the centre of the fairway but the optimum place to drive is down the left, towards the wall of the lighthouse, from where it is best to view the green.

Hole 10 (452 yards) Par 4 Considered by most professionals to be a better hole than the much-photographed 9th. A difficult fairway to find into the wind especially as the ball should be shaped to follow the left-hand dog-leg. But the ball must not be hooked or it will finish on the beach. The putting surface is protected by a cross-bunker short of the green.

Hole 11 (177 yards) Par 3 There is out of bounds to the left and it is on that side of the green that the pin is often set so that it sits close to a bunker. The hole is played from a pulpit tee and it is the least testing of the par threes.

Hole 12 (441 yards) Par 4 Humps and hollows abound down the middle of the fairway, which is better protected by bunkers on the left since it was decided to lengthen the hole by 50 yards. The green sits to the left of the war memorial which itself is to be found on top of a large dune.

Hole 13 (411 yards) Par 4 The tiger line cutting the corner of the hole, which dog-legs to the right, leaves a straightforward, although at times deceptive shot, to an unguarded, raised green.

Hole 14 (440 yards) Par 4 Not the longest of the par fours, but most definitely a gruelling one when played with the wind blowing off the sea towards which the hole points. There is one bunker to the left which often swallows the drive. A drive down the right will also erase the prospect of having to hit the second shot over a huge bunker fronting the left side of the green.

Hole 15 (209 yards) Par 3 It was on this hole in 1977 that Tom Watson holed from off the green for a birdie two. That enabled him to catch Jack Nicklaus and from there he went on to win. He was fortunate, of course, to miss the bunkers which protect a green that has a steep drop to the right.

Hole 16 (409 yards) Par 4 The tee-shot makes few professionals tremble in their spikes, although the same cannot be said of the second shot, especially when the pin is placed to the front of the green. Then it is all too easy to underclub and watch in agony as the ball tumbles back into the stream known as Wilson's burn.

Hole 17 (500 yards) Par 5 The second of the two par fives meanders through a shallow valley and the fairway, though narrow, is more often than not hit with a driver. A closely contested Open could be decided here as it is possible to extract an eagle from the hole.

Hole 18 (431 yards) Par 4 By using the 18th tee on the neighbouring Arran course the Royal and Ancient, organisers of the Open, have not only lengthened the hole but also turned it into a sharp dog-leg left. Two bunkers to the left come into play, although a drive hit straight and true will leave a comfortable approach to the green.

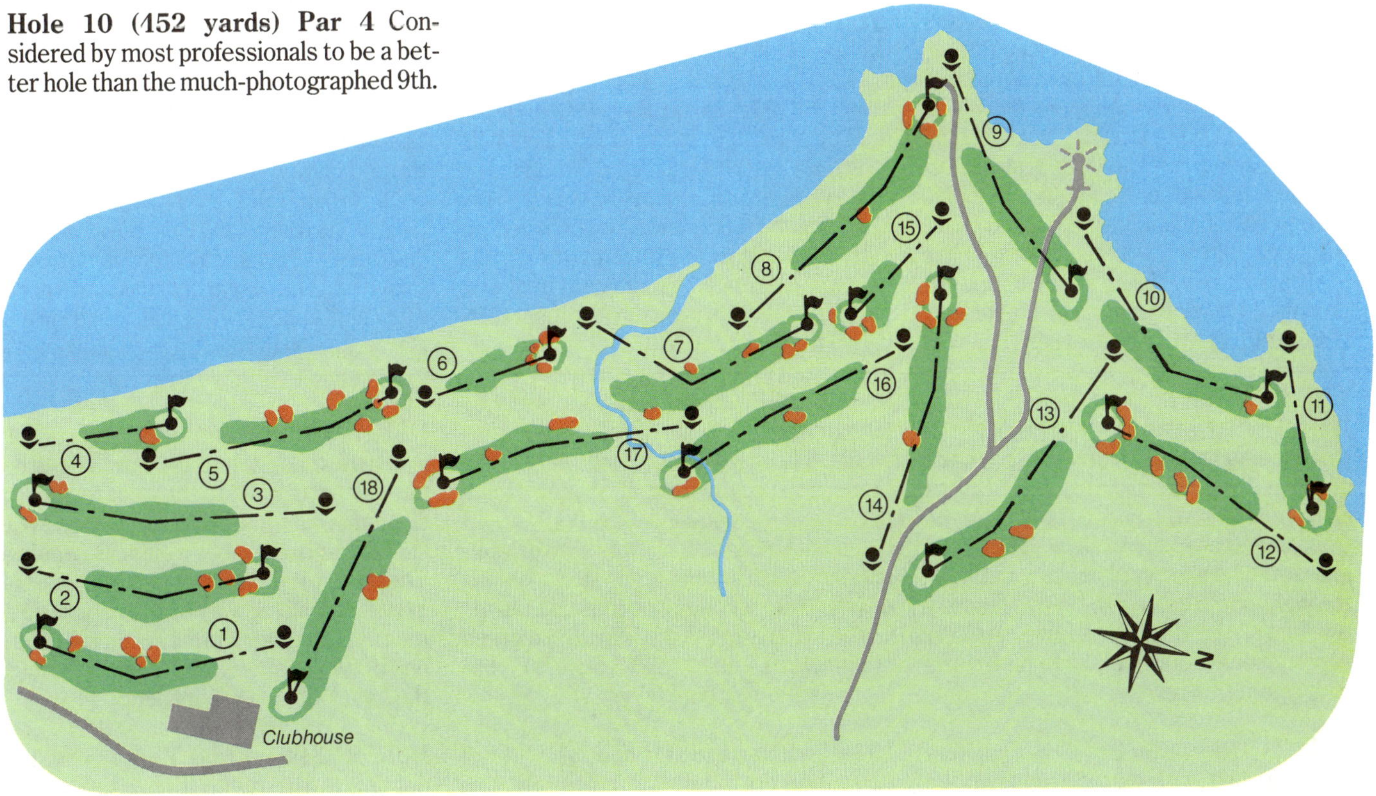

WALTON HEATH

Bill Elliott, Golf Correspondent of
The Daily Star

Walton Heath, in the heart of Surrey, is set 700 feet above sea-level. The original 18 holes were designed by Herbert Fowler in 1904 who used the natural sweep of the land with its heather, bracken and wonderfully dry turf to create a course on the grand scale. Walton Heath is recognised as one of the finest inland courses in England. One year after the course opened in 1904 *The News of the World* Matchplay Championship was staged there, making it the oldest professional event in the world. A further 18 holes have been added since and it is a composite of the Old and New Courses that has been used for the 1981 Ryder Cup and the present European Open which is held at Walton Heath every other year.

THE COURSE

Hole 1 (410 yards) Par 4 The key to this opening hole is the drive, which must be long enough to reach the bottom of the slope otherwise the second shot is played from an awkward downhill lie. The green is guarded by a forward bunker, rough on the right and trees on the left, with only the top of the flagstick visible. A fairly gentle opener, but one not to be treated with complacency.

Hole 2 (513 yards) Par 5 Six bunkers litter this hole with out of bounds on the left and thick heather on the right. The hole dog-legs to the right so a brave drive is called for if par or better is to be achieved. The second shot is threatened by bunkers flanking the fairway, which narrows as it approaches the green. The green itself, like all the greens on this course, is full of subtle borrows.

Hole 3 (391 yards) Par 4 One of the finest par fours in the country. This hole calls for a perfectly placed drive and then a very demanding approach shot. Any deviation from line and a bogey is inevitable, for the green is raised and guarded by two horrendously difficult bunkers. The green itself is probably the most testing on the course.

Hole 4 (422 yards) Par 4 A perfectly straight hole but far from straightforward. The prevailing wind here (and there is usually a wind at Walton Heath because of the course's elevation) is right to left with a cunning fairway bunker waiting on the left to trap even good looking drives. The second shot must be played so the ball carries all the way to the green otherwise a ridge will deflect the ball towards another bunker.

Hole 5 (174 yards) Par 3 The first of three wonderful short holes on this course. Again the prevailing wind is right to left and when the pin is sited close to the right-hand greenside bunker this hole calls for genuine shot-making. Usually a high fade off the tee (for right-handers) will encourage the ball to finish anywhere near the hole and set up the possibility of a birdie.

Hole 6 (489 yards) Par 5 The shortest of the long holes. This one relies on three fairway bunkers, two greenside bunkers and the ever-present Walton Heath heather and bracken for its defences. The fairway, too, is narrower than usual and only truly struck and accurate shots are rewarded. The green always seems in reach in two; however, it rarely is.

Hole 7 (390 yards) Par 4 The 7th hole is a severe dog-leg to the left. The drive must be struck out to the right to afford a clear approach shot. Overhit it, however, and the most vicious rough is waiting. The green itself is elevated and the ball must carry all the way or the natural lie of the land will carry a timid second shot into one of two bunkers. Not a hole to indulge the golfer lacking in confidence.

Hole 8 (395 yards) Par 4 This is a dog-leg to the right. It also sets up the most intimidating drive of the round with a thicket of thorns on the left and a fairway bunker and a thick copse of trees on the right. The second shot has to be hit over a deep valley to make the green, thus calling for accurate club selection.

Hole 9 (189 yards) Par 3 Club selection is all important at this most attractive looking short hole. The ball must be struck far enough to fly the two front greenside bunkers and accurately enough to avoid the other two bunkers to the left and right of the green. Once safely on the green, the danger continues. Hitting the ball above the hole leaves a tricky downhill putt, and anything more than a few feet from the pin can borrow tremendously on this undulating surface.

Hole 10 (341 yards) Par 4 This dog-leg to the right is one of the many holes in Britain known as Cotton's Hole (after Henry Cotton). This time because the great man once won the hole from South Africa's Bobby Locke, by driving over the trees on the right to reach the front edge of the green. Today most of the trees have gone but the ball must still be struck with authority and power out to the right if the green is to be attacked and the hole threatened.

Hole 11 (521 yards) Par 5 Another dog-leg to the right. The ideal drive should be hit centre right. Too far right and the ball will run across the fairway and into heather. Too far left and the player has no sight of the next target area. The green itself slopes away and an over-struck approach leaves a difficult recovery from heavy rough behind the green. By Walton Heath standards, a fairly simple hole.

Hole 12 (462 yards) Par 4 Sheer length makes this a very difficult hole for an average golfer, and even the best have come to grief here. Drive into the right-hand rough and a dropped shot is guaranteed. Drive into the left-hand heather and although there is a chance of recovery, it is not much of one. The green is notoriously tricky, sloping to the right and guarded by bunkers to the front and left.

Hole 13 (470 yards) Par 4 The simple rule here is to play conservatively and drive short of the right-hand fairway bunker, at the same time keeping the ball out to the left. Having achieved this, the next shot should be struck towards the right-hand side of the green where the natural lie of the land will turn the ball towards the flag's usual position.

Hole 14 (465 yards) Par 4 Once the longest hole on the course, a new forward tee has turned this hole into a par four, but a fiendishly long one. There are five fairway bunkers to avoid, the safest route being towards the left-hand side. The green slopes dramatically and any approach must be struck well-up towards the flag.

Hole 15 (404 yards) Par 4 Three fairway bunkers on the right dictate the tee-shot. They are set at varying distances so as to threaten any golfer, no matter what their handicap or strength. The green slopes wildly to the right where another bunker is set. Wherever the ball lands on this green, putting is always difficult to judge both in line and distance.

Hole 16 (475 yards) Par 4 One of the great gems in the Walton Heath crown. This hole demands a player's best drive, both in accuracy and in length, if the green is to be attacked at all. Even then the single cavernous bunker to the right of the green, rather than the green itself, is more often than not the destination of the ball. This is because the green runs left to right and the slightest cut on an approach shot will send the ball skipping towards this most exactly sited trap.

Hole 17 (165 yards) Par 3 A great par three. Because of the moat-style bunker protecting the front of the green there is simply no 'bale out' shot to be played. Each golfer must assess distance in relation to wind conditions and then hit the ball sweetly if the green is to be found. Once on this green 'island' the back-to-front slope must be considered always or even the shortest putt can frustratingly take an unexpected borrow.

Hole 18 (432 yards) Par 4 The drive must be struck over a deep valley of heaviest gorse to make the fairway. The perfect shot should finish right of centre to afford the best approach. The green is two-tiered and any golfer who comes up short, with both severe slope and borrow to battle against, will be hard-pressed to make par. All great courses have a marvellous finishing hole. This hole is a fine test of anyone's nerve and ability.

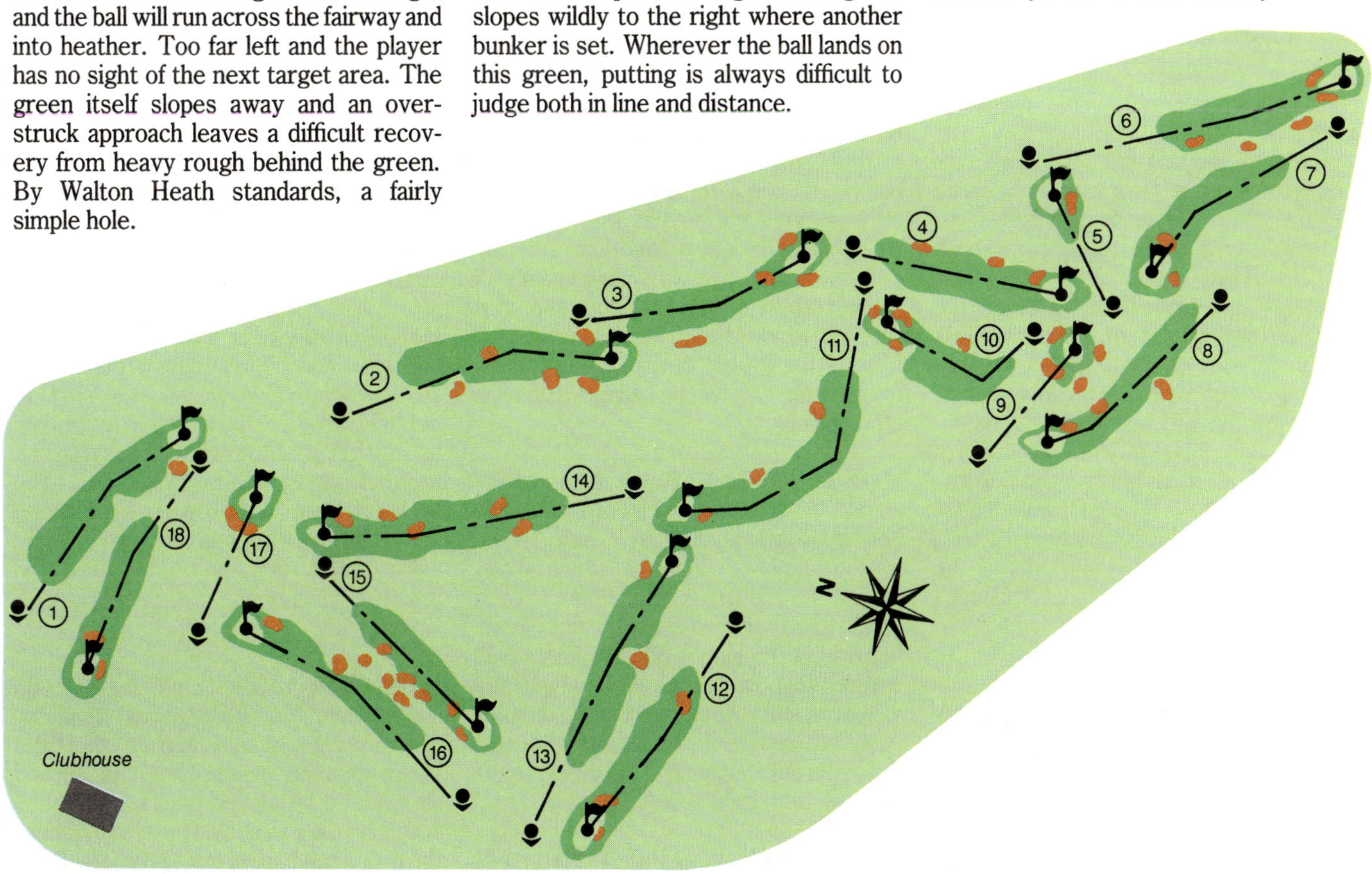

WENTWORTH (West Course)

Bill Elliott, Golf Correspondent of
The Daily Star

Set in Surrey's Virginia Water, the West Course at Wentworth is the best-known golf course in Britain after St. Andrews. The course was completed shortly after the lesser-known, but equally commendable East Course, in 1925 by Harry S. Colt. The West Course has earned its fame through the worldwide televising of the World Matchplay Championship that has been staged there since the early sixties.

Every major star has competed over the West Course during the last three decades and the two closing par fives are as familiar to golf fans as their own back gardens. This stretch of testing golf is known as The Burma Road because at the end of World War Two the course was restored by prisoners of war after it was used as a centre for army operations. Nowadays the only sound of battle is the crash of ball against tree, for Wentworth is a golf complex cut out of a genuine forest. The course is a magnificent sight at any time of the year, but particularly so in the autumn when the colours dazzle the eye and Harry S. Colt's genius challenges the talent of all classes of player.

THE COURSE

Hole 1 (471 yards) Par 4 A desperately challenging opening hole. Although the fairway is generous, the second shot to a crowned green must carry over a valley and avoid each of three bunkers guarding the hole. Rough to the left and trees to the right threaten this shot.

Hole 2 (155 yards) Par 3 Three bunkers surround the kidney-shaped green with a large tree adding danger to the right. The drive is struck from an elevated tee across a valley and up onto a green that tends to be among the quickest on the course.

Hole 3 (452 yards) Par 4 Even the very best players have struggled on this hole. Most drives tend to stray out towards the right to avoid a fairway bunker on the left. But waiting on the right is rough and beyond that there are trees packed tightly together, offering only a chip out sideways as a means of making progress. A long second shot, not only has to avoid the two bunkers at the front of the green, but, must also carry towards the flag, or the ball may run back off the green.

Hole 4 (501 yards) Par 5 A blind drive should be hit down the left to leave the best approach shot. The green can be reached in two assuming there are no disasters. In the right conditions a good drive to the left will run many yards because of the slope. But any successful second shot has to be well-judged and well-struck for there is a large bunker guarding the green, which foreshortens the apparent distance. The green tends to break from right to left.

Hole 5 (191 yards) Par 3 With trees on the left, the natural tendency is to drive to the right of the green. However, an accurate shot to the left is the one to aim for because the natural shape of the land should take such a shot in towards the flag. The bottom of the flag incidentally is never visible from the tee because of the large humps in front of the green.

Hole 6 (344 yards) Par 4 A short par four but a great one. The green is tucked in to the right so the ideal tee-shot favours the left-hand side of a tight fairway. Even then the green is elevated with three bunkers guarding it and a short second shot has to be judged well to stay on the putting surface.

Hole 7 (399 yards) Par 4 A dog-leg to the right, and Wentworth's professional, and now Ryder Cup captain, Bernard Gallacher's favourite hole. The drive should be shot left of centre where it will gain distance from the downhill slope. The approach shot is then played to an elevated and two-tiered green with the prevailing wind urging the ball to drift to the left. It is always one club nearer than it looks.

Hole 8 (398 yards) Par 4 A wonderful looking hole. The drive should be aimed down the right-hand side, from where the green is most accessible. The second shot has to be played over a large pond and again the ball should be aimed right as the green tends to break to the left. But if the shot is mishit, then this approach becomes one of the most difficult shots to play on the course.

Hole 9 (450 yards) Par 4 Probably the toughest hole on the course. No matter what tee is in play, there is a long carry of heather to overcome, with the green out of reach in two for all but the longest hitters. The green itself is much smaller than usual with a narrow entrance made narrower by a bunker and encroaching trees.

Hole 10 (186 yards) Par 3 A superb short hole with the green all but obscured by a line of fir trees on the right from the tee. This hole requires a high tee-shot over the edge of these trees if the ball is to hold on a green that is kidney-shaped and slopes from left to right, falling away towards rough.

Hole 11 (376 yards) Par 4 A deceptively easy-looking dog-leg left hole. The drive should be aimed towards the centre, but it is the second shot that confuses many golfers for the green is elevated and usually fools players into taking a club less than they need. The clue to this trap is the three cross-bunkers straddled across the entrance to the green.

Hole 12 (483 yards) Par 5 Another spectacular driving hole. The tee-shot must carry over a line of tall fir trees that bestrides the fairway some 150 yards from the tee. Once safely over this obstacle, the hole dog-legs to the left and is reachable in two on most days. But care is needed to avoid the out-of-bounds fence that runs immediately to the left and behind the green.

Hole 13 (441 yards) Par 4 This is one of the toughest holes on the course. A decent drive is essential otherwise the fairway contours will drag the ball to the left and leave the player stymied by tall trees. Long and to the right is the way to tee-off here. There is a ditch across the fairway, some 50 yards short of the green, waiting to catch any mishit approach shot. The green is protected to the front by three bunkers.

Hole 14 (179 yards) Par 3 Easily the steepest hole on the course and frequently played into the wind, this is a genuinely challenging par three. The green slopes severely and is two-tiered with the flag usually on the top tier. Out of bounds on the left and thick woodland on the right mean that, above all, accuracy is called for.

Hole 15 (466 yards) Par 4 A long left-to-right dog-leg hole where the drive should be aimed to the left but where, naturally, there is a fairway bunker. The second shot is a long iron to a green that has bunkers either side and which, though appearing level, actually falls away dramatically from right to left. Most professionals are content with a par at this hole.

Hole 16 (380 yards) Par 4 A dog-leg to the left. The perfect drive is aimed left and manages to fly the fairway bunker set there. But the ground slopes from right to left and the prevailing wind also blows in this direction so that any slightly hooked shot can end up in very dense woodland. Three bunkers guard the right-hand side of the green, while shots going left land out of bounds. But once the drive is accomplished there are few real problems.

Hole 17 (571 yards) Par 5 Easily the longest of the par fives with out of bounds all the way down the left-hand side. The fairway falls away from the tee and also slopes to the right where there is light rough and, beyond that, trees. The second shot must be played with extreme caution to avoid the out of bounds on the left while on the right thick rough and trees may cause problems. The green is slightly tilted and high approach shots tend to stop suddenly. There is also a lot of trouble on the right if you miss the green.

Hole 18 (502 yards) Par 5 This severe dog-leg right demands a tee-shot to the left otherwise the second shot will be blocked by trees and overhanging branches. But the perfect drive brings a great reward, for the green is then reachable in two – as long as the fairway shot of some 220 yards or so does not go astray. The green is defended by a large oak tree and three bunkers, while the putting surface itself is as subtle as Wentworth is challenging. Right to left putts are always quicker.

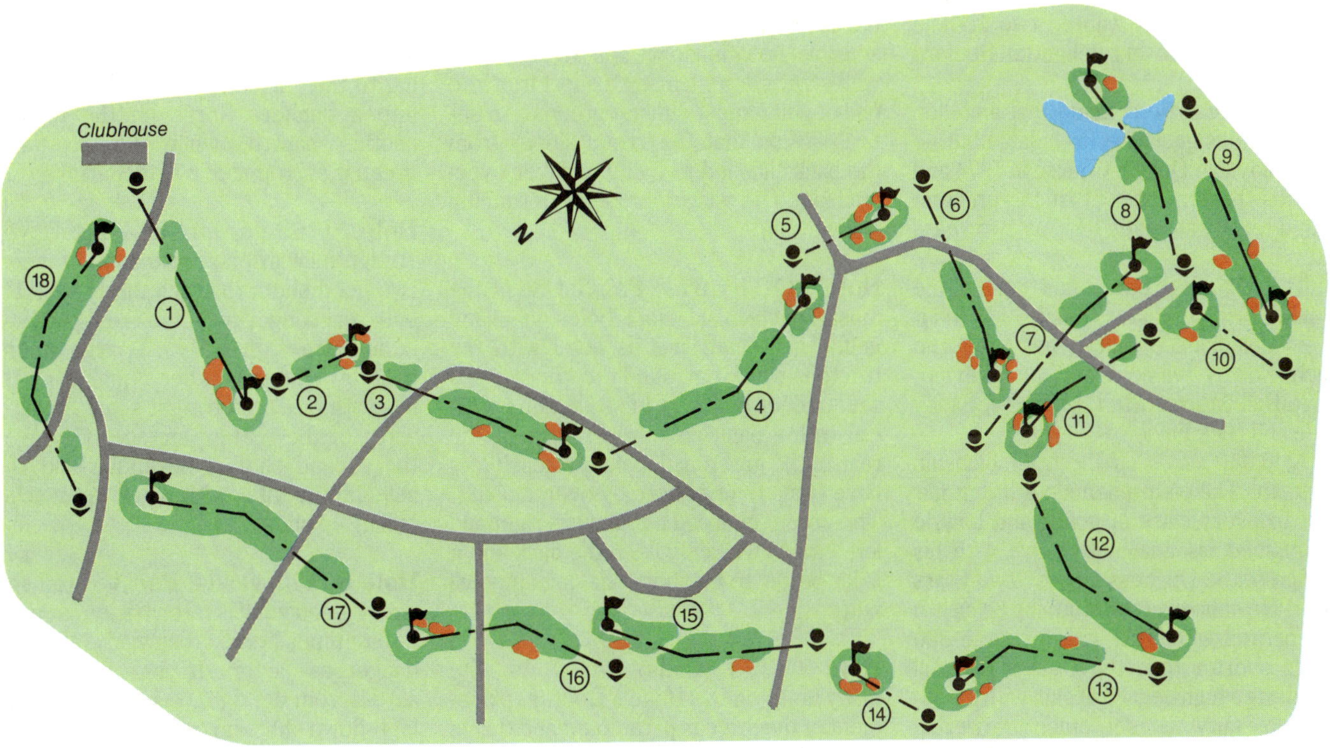

WOBURN

Bill Blighton, Golf Correspondent of
Today

Woburn is rich in pine, beech, oak and silver birch and must surely rank as any golf course designer's dream. Add heather, bracken and a superb rolling landscape and it is easy to appreciate why the Marquess of Tavistock wanted two 18-hole courses to adorn his delightful Bedford estate.

Charles Lawrie realised that ambition when he designed the formidable but no less enjoyable Duke's Course in 1974 and what has become one of Britain's greatest inland tests was ready for play two years later.

The Duke's Course has hosted the Dunhill British Masters since 1985 and it is no coincidence that it has produced such worthy winners as Lee Trevino, Seve Ballesteros, Mark McNulty, Sandy Lyle and Nick Faldo.

At 6,940 yards off the Championship tees, the Duke's presents a stiff but fair test to every class of golfer and Lawrie maintained his imaginative eye with his design of the Duchess Course two years later. He enhanced the stunning beauty of the natural woodland with a course 300 yards shorter than the Duke's but still requiring a high degree of skill with its ribbon-like fairways set among towering pines.

THE COURSE

Hole 1 (385 yards) Par 4 The temptation for the big hitters is to try to cut the left-hand dog-leg. One does so at one's peril with pine and fir ready to block out the second shot The cautious, and usually sensible line, is down the right with a well-struck drive leaving a short iron into one of golf's most difficult greens. An optical illusion that the green slopes from the back, has led to many a player overpitching. The wise approach is a running second shot.

Hole 2 (134 yards) Par 3 One of the most spectacular short holes in inland golf. The teeing area is level with the treetops which surround the green, itself set in a deep hollow. Club selection is crucial with a bank covered in ferns at the rear of the green and many professionals have come to grief here by overclubbing. The green, guarded by bunkers right and left, slopes wickedly from the back and it is far better to be short, leaving an uphill putt.

Hole 3 (395 yards) Par 4 As with many holes on the Duke's Course, placement of the drive is paramount and that is the case at this challenging hole. Six pine trees encroach on the right of the fairway and the line is just to the left of them. A drive struck too far to the left will necessitate a blind second shot over a high bank to a sloping green, heavily guarded by bunkers. Another factor is the wind which can appear deceptively calm in the valley.

Hole 4 (510 yards) Par 5 A genuine birdie chance for the professional. The chief feature is a huge gully on the left which is situated 270 yards from the tee. Again, a drive up the right is advocated and it is wise to stay on that side of the fairway, even though the flag may be hidden by trees for the third shot to the green. It is a large target area – some 34 yards deep – with the only real danger a huge bunker on the left.

Hole 5 (207 yards) Par 3 An intimidating tee-shot across a deep valley with high trees on the right. This tempts the player to aim left where a cavernous bunker awaits. The least of the troubles lies at the back of the green, so it is better to aim straight and long. An overhit shot will leave a tricky downhill chip or putt, but this is by far the lesser of two evils.

Hole 6 (464 yards) Par 4 A monster par four and rightly awarded the honour of stroke index one. The hole dog-legs left and again it pays to be conservative with rhododendrons poised to gather the over ambitious drive. A long and difficult second shot awaits with the fairway sloping to the left and ready to kick the ball into a bunker. Gorse on the right is another hazard, while the two-tiered green is surrounded by steep banks.

Hole 7 (409 yards) Par 4 A relatively straightforward hole although it needs two good shots to reach the green. The only real danger from the tee is a cluster of birch trees on the left. A large green's main protection is a deep bunker on the left with one on the right some 25 yards short of the putting surface. However, the second shot is deceptive and club selection is vital with many approaches pulling up short.

Hole 8 (177 yards) Par 3 A tee-shot over a deep gully is often tricky, although a sometimes fierce crosswind is the most dangerous factor. It normally sweeps across from the right, ready to gather the high-flown shot and carry the ball into the only bunker, a large trap on the left of the green. It is worthwhile taking an extra club to carry the ball all the way to a receptive green which will hold the well-struck shot.

Hole 9 (404 yards) Par 4 At first glance this appears an easy hole but first impressions can be misleading and they certainly are in this case. Tall trees await to stymie the ball on the right and left, while even a well-struck drive can leave an awkward stance in two hollows which dissect the fairway. There is dead ground ahead so it is wise to fly the ball to the green, which has only one hazard, a bunker on the left.

Hole 10 (502 yards) Par 5 A fade from the tee is a distinct advantage at this hole with the favoured drive finishing on the right-hand side of the fairway. This is a superb long hole with the second shot being threaded between huge fir trees on the right and a bunker on the left. Once safely negotiated all that remains is a simple pitch to the green to set up the chance of a birdie.

Hole 11 (193 yards) Par 3 Another testing par three and it is folly to be short with the ball likely to kick into a bunker. With the green sloping steeply from the back to the front it's much better to be long. This does pose some danger, however. Although the green is at its widest at the back, an overhit shot may trundle down the slope at the rear. But it is still possible to get a decent shot at the flag even from that position.

Hole 12 (419 yards) Par 4 A huge gully stretching 130 yards to the right of the green leaves an intimidating second shot. But the preferred drive is aimed to the right and one that carries the gully at its deepest point. A strategically placed bunker awaits the other side of the gully but if both are safely negotiated the ball will reach a receptive green. The danger of driving to the left is that balls are kicked into the pines with the only option to chip back onto the fairway. Whatever, the approach shot must be bold, because short spells danger.

Hole 13 (565 yards) Par 5 The longest hole on the course and an accurate drive is essential with a cunningly placed bunker sited 236 yards from the tee. Worse, a gully lies behind so it is vital to by-pass these dangers. Hit the drive left and the second shot can be played to avoid a deep fairway bunker 80 yards from the green. Positional play is the requirement at this hole.

Hole 14 (432 yards) Par 4 The most generous landing area from the tee on the course. There is a small grove of trees to the right of the fairway but the most compelling danger lies with the second shot. Out of bounds skirts the left of the green where an awkward bunker is also likely to gather the wayward approach.

Hole 15 (449 yards) Par 4 A truly demanding hole which requires common sense and nerve to come away with a par or better. Two bunkers, the first 230 yards from the tee, lay in wait on the left, while thick woods line the right of the fairway. Beyond the bunkers there are two tall pines blocking progress to the green. Although a longer route, the right-hand side of the fairway is the line to a generous green 39 yards deep.

Hole 16 (425 yards) Par 4 Yet another hole where the drive determines success or failure. The line is a tall pine on the right, with the ball likely to bounce into the centre of the fairway. Beware of hooking the drive because a huge fir tree blocks the view of the putting surface, where a bunker swings from the left to the front of the green. Another encroaches on the right so make sure you are up with the second shot.

Hole 17 (329 yards) Par 4 Several big-hitting professionals have driven this green but if the ball is leaked to the right, it is in deep trouble. In addition, an overhit shot can outrun the fairway, leaving a player struggling for his par. The safest route for this right-hand dog-leg is to aim slightly left, which should leave a short iron onto a green bunkered to the left with another trap cutting across the front.

Hole 18 (514 yards) Par 5 Out of bounds on the left and a deep gully on the right of the fairway make this a superb driving hole. A bold drive to the left leaves a clear view of the green but the safer shot is to the right. But this also has its dangers with the ball likely to nestle in a valley, requiring an awkward stance with bunkers ready to swallow the second shot. This hole is played as the 18th in the Dunhill Masters and it was here that Lee Trevino narrowly missed an albatross two, his eagle being sufficient to capture the inaugural title in 1985.

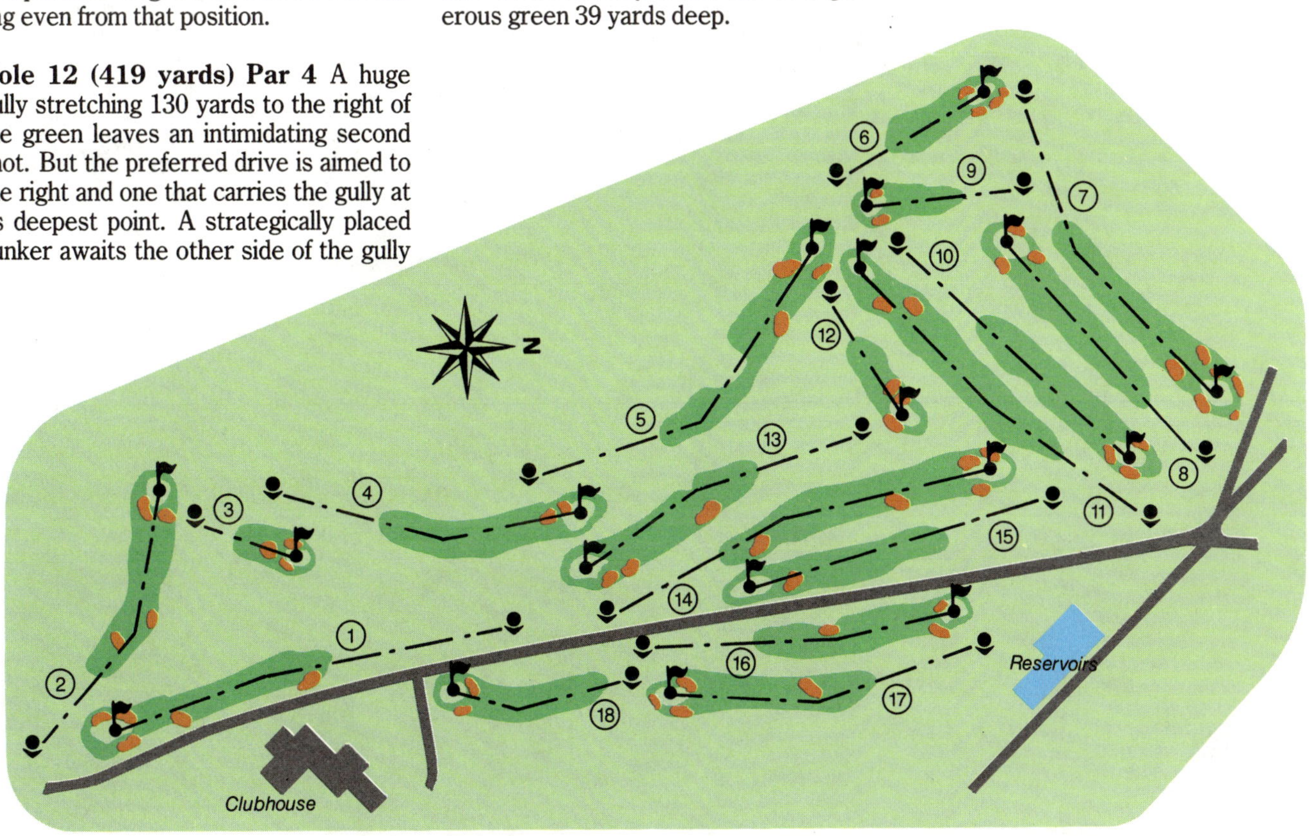

GOLF HOLIDAYS ABROAD

David Davies, *The Guardian*

For the travelling golfer there is no greater pleasure than throwing the sticks in the boot and setting off. Golf clubs, which prove such a pain when flying, fit well into the rear of a car and even if the principal object of the exercise is a family holiday and not purely golf, well, they are there lest one happens across an irresistable gem.

Of course, with a little prior planning, the cunning spouse can ensure that you do just 'happen' on a course that must not be bypassed, and while this is a little more difficult abroad than it is in the United Kingdom, it is by no means impossible.

Northern, Spain

Take, for instance, the seemingly innocent trip to Santander aboard one of Brittany Ferries' excellent ships. That particular port is the starting point for many wonderful holidays: so much so it hardly matters which direction you take as you leave the terminal. But the clever golfer will, before the ferry reaches port, have started a conversation which goes something like this:

'Have you got the map, darling? I've got a feeling that that Pedrena place isn't far from Santander.'

'What place?'

'You know, where Seve Ballesteros learned his golf.'

'Well?'

'Well, it'd be silly to come all this way and not see it. . . .'

And so it would, just as it would be silly to drive directly out of Santander and not spend some time in a town that deserves an attentive few hours. Pedrena, the village that gave the golfing world one of its few authentic geniuses, is best reached by another ferry, a much smaller one, which takes 15 minutes to cross the estuary to Pedrena. The ferry berths, walk 200 yards and you're in the clubhouse, which of course, is more than Seve was for a great many years. He was a caddie at Pedrena and very strictly confined to the caddie shack. In fact he had won the Open Championship before he was made an honorary member of the club that nurtured him.

But Pedrena is more than just the home course of one of golf's greats. It is a picturesque place, hilly, and with views from the top part of the course that are worth any detour. You see the estuary, the town of Santander in the distance and then the eye swivels out to sea, taking in the dramatic headlands that frame the waters. It can be quite distracting.

The course itself is on the short side. When the European Tour played the Spanish Open there, Mark James had two rounds of 63 and won with a total of 18 under par. However, Pedrena will test the hacker with its continual demands for accuracy.

One of the loveliest cities in Spain is San Sebastian and if you turn left out of Santander, it is likely that you'll come across it. San Sebastian has a lovely cathedral, a magnificent bay right in the middle of town and, as a bonus in the evening, a selection of very good tapas bars. Time for the map again.

'You know, darling, I've got a feeling that that Fuenterrabia place isn't far from here.'

'What Fuenterrabia place. . . .' But you know the rest.

The Basque region

Fuenterrabia is the fishing village in which Spain's other world class golfer was brought up. Jose-Maria Olazabal seems certain to be the next superstar from Europe and he learned his golf on the Royal San Sebastian course. He could hardly have done otherwise, in fact, for he was born in a lovely 250-year-old Basque farmhouse which overlooks the 9th green, where he still lives with his mother, father, sister and grandparents. His father works as a greenkeeper, his mother works in the clubhouse and the whole family are literally surrounded by golf.

The course is less picturesque than Pedrena, but it is nevertheless a good test of golf and well worth playing. It would be sensible, too, to arrange to stay in the nearby parador at Fuenterrabia, for it is one of the best in the country. The fishing village itself is fascinating, with more to see than can be accomplished in one day. This is a marvellous, unsuspected, part of Spain (only just, too, for France is only an estuary away) and the eating, Basque-style, is fabulous. Olazabal is deeply reluctant to go to America to stay and play, and one visit to his homeland makes you understand why.

By now you are in the heart of the Basque country. Olazabal is himself a Basque and his name contains what seems to be the almost compulsory 'z', common to names from this part of the world. If it's not 'z', it's 'x', and the language is near to 'unpronounxeable.' Basques, of course, recognise no borders, and even if you cross from Spain into France, you will still find a profusion of Basque names.

Le golf?

This southwest corner is the part of France that first took to golf and you are guaranteed a point in almost any sports quiz if you can answer the question: 'Who was the first Continental golfer to win the Open Championship?' It was not, of course, Seve, it was Arnaud Massy, who came from these parts and won the Open in 1907 at Hoylake, breaking up two wins by James Braid. Massy, it is said, set sail for North Berwick on his first visit to the United Kingdom as a left-handed golfer, but arrived as a right-hander. He had left his own clubs at home and the only ones available on board were right-handed!

He was a good player though, having finished joint fifth in 1905, sixth in 1906 and losing a play-off, over 36 holes, to Harry Vardon in 1911 at Royal St. George's. He conceded at the 35th when he could not possibly win. There is a long history of golf in the southwest of France, and not only are there some lovely, old established courses, there are also some new ones that match the best.

One of the first was Biarritz, which came into existence in 1888 when there was a large British presence in this corner of the world. It was built by Willie Dunn, who then went on to create Shinnecock Hills, host of the 1986 US Open. A description of the Biarritz countryside ran as follows, 'The scenery is very fine – to the northeast the hundred-mile forests of the Landes; to the north the Bay of Biscay; to the south, the Pyrenees and the west coast of Spain.' That was written over 100 years ago and is still true today. The course has been extended and improved since those days and is now a match for any touring golfer in search of a good holiday round. Like Pedrena, it has hosted a professional tournament in the recent past, and in 1988 the Welsh World Cup player, David Llewellyn, had the chance to break a golf record that is proving as difficult to beat as the first four-minute mile. He came to the last green in the third round of the event needing two putts for a 59 to become the first man on the European Tour to break 60. He three-putted, of course.

The good old days

Competitive golf has a long history at Biarritz, going back over 100 years when there used to be matches between the Biarritz club and the oldest club on the Continent, at Pau. The members at the latter club used to catch a coach and journey for 10 or more bone-shaking hours to get to Biarritz, but even then they often used to win. This was because, for a while, Pau had the strongest team of golfers anywhere in the world. The course had been created by officers of the Duke of Wellington's army who found the climate beneficial and retired there.

In those days, of course, all the best golfers were amateurs and Pau could boast three members who had won the Amateur Championship. They were in the habit of wintering there, although a contemporary account makes it clear that the weather was not always perfect. One report ran, 'The winter climate is not to be trusted. Sharp, cold snaps are apt to be enlivened by terrible 'tempetes'. But after the first of February, the climate is to be relied upon.'

Pau is still there, worth a diversion because of its antiquity and because of one quite remarkable aspect of the clubhouse. There is a revolving bookcase in one corner, filled with ancient books. They are all in English, remnants of the days, up until 1935, when all the members were British. Now there are only a handful.

But before leaving the Biarritz area there are other courses that demand to be played. The very upmarket Chantaco, set in a beautifully wooded area is probably the best of them. The former Prime Minister of France, M. Chaban Delmas, is a member and if you are lucky, and speak sufficient French, the caddiemaster, Kiki Larretche, will reminisce with you. He used to carry for Catherine Lacoste, a member and the best woman player the Continent has ever produced. He will tell you how she could hit a two iron under the wind. . . .

Home from home

Chiberta is another course that should not be missed, with a lovely mixture of seaside and inland holes. Throughout your golfing experience in this part of the world there is a feeling as you play this course, of being more at home than you would expect to feel in an exotic part of France. It's due to the fact that there is such a long tradition of the golf in the area; it is not just an activity for the 'nouveau golfeur' keen to impress the neighbours.

Nowhere on the Continent is golf booming more than in France. By the end of 1991 there will be more than 400 courses in the country and while that may not be a lot in an overall context, it represents a quadrupling in the last decade. It would be possible now to play your way through France until you reached the Channel coast where, there have been courses for many years. On your way you would be wise to try and take in two little-known, but nevertheless superb courses in the Paris area, Chantilly and Morfontaine. The former hosts the French Open from time to time, and is high on any list of good courses. The latter does not have room for the French Open, and is not really long enough anyway, but it is high on the list of good courses. In the matter of getting on, however, it helps to know a member.

Not so on the coast, where they welcome visitors, indeed thrive on them. They are, of course, used to Britons pouring over La Manche to Calais and Boulogne, usually going on into deepest France, but often enough stopping to play on some of the superb courses hereabouts. It may be that of all the courses in this area, Hardelot is the best. It is certainly one of the few anywhere in the world that has its own travel company, Hardelot Holidays, based in Brentwood, which specialises in things Hardelottian.

The course was designed by Tom Simpson, one of the great architects and the man who laid down the two 18-hole courses at The Berkshire. There are, indeed, similarities, as Hardelot winds its way through pine forest on a largely sand-based soil. I once broke a putter at Hardelot. Well, how many times in your life do you have a six-foot uphill, straight putt for an eagle, and then leave it short? Nevertheless, if someone gave me a week in which to play golf for the last time, Hardelot could well be one of the courses I'd choose.

French links

The coast has several other attractive courses on which to play, such as the genuine links of Wimereux, just down the road from Boulogne, and Etretat, a cliff top course where has some dizzying views over the Channel. These are all combined, of course, with dozens of attractive places to eat and drink, which is the additional factor which makes golf in France more than just a game.

Few places, nowadays, are far away by car. To go back to the beginning, it is possible to penetrate deep into Spain and Portugal, to the delights of the Costas and the Algarve, by simply heading south-east or south-west from Santander. Be warned, though, the distances in those two countries are vast and the journey times are much longer than you might think, even if you keep to the big roads. The problem is that because there are so few good roads, all the traffic concentrates itself on the major arteries, and it can take a lot of time to get anywhere.

Be warned, also, that wherever you take the car, it will need to be emptied completely at night time, and parked where you can see it during the day. Robbery is rife these days and even an apparently empty car is not guaranteed to be safe.

As always, a little preplanning goes a long way when it comes to deciding where to go and where to play. The London-based French Government Tourist Office in Piccadilly will be helpful, as will the Spanish Tourist people in St. James's, and all the cross-channel companies know about, and cater for, the golfing holiday trade.

EQUIPMENT

Colin Callander, Deputy Editor, *Golf Monthly*

There is little doubt that over the centuries the equipment used in the game of golf has changed much more than in many other sports. Indeed it might be argued that the modern game bears little resemblance to the primitive sport that our ancestors developed on the eastern seaboard of Scotland in the 14th century and which later spread to other areas in the British Isles and elsewhere.

To begin with this process of change might have been slow, but over the last 100 years or so, it has accelerated at an incredible rate. Entering the 'nineties the golfer hardly has time to remove the wrappers from his latest hi-tech, club or ball before it is rendered obsolete through the arrival of yet another new product.

We may be no closer to discovering the elusive secret which has enabled us to record rounds in the 50s and 60s with ease, but that is due to human fallibility rather than the fault of the manufacturers, whose ingenuity seems to have no bounds.

The early game

Clues to the sort of equipment used by golfers in the 14th and 15th centuries are hard to find, but there is documented evidence to show that there were a number of clubmakers in existence at that time. In the late 16th century it is recorded that one William Mayne was producing clubs for the nobility in Scotland. A bowmaker by trade, in 1603 Mayne was appointed, among other things, clubmaker to King James VI of Scotland, shortly before his accession to the throne of England. Even earlier it was recorded that James IV of Scotland purchased some golf clubbes in Perth. These were also bought from a bower or bowmaker, then a flourishing trade and one which possessed all the tools required to produce a rudimentary golf club.

Unfortunately, nothing survives which tells us about the construction of such clubs, but it is fair to assume that they were primitive objects with rough heads hewn from ash or hazel and simple shafts crafted from beech, apple or pear. Certainly, at that time, most golfers would have been content to use just one club to hit all shots. It was some time later, when special clubs were introduced to deal with difficult lies or short approaches, and not until the 1890s, that golfers found it necessary to use a bag to carry their clubs. Until then, as photographs of old golf matches show, the golfers or their caddies marched around the course with their clubs held under their arms or attached to a simple leather strap hanging loosely around their necks.

In earliest times golf was a simple game contested on rugged courses set out on rough land beside the sea. It was to remain so for centuries until the charms of the game attracted a wider audience.

The gutta-percha

The modern era can be said to have started during the 1840s when the traditional 'featherie' golf ball was replaced with the gutta-percha ball, a ball made out of a latex compound from the percha tree. This change was to have large implications for club design and was also to bring the sport to a much wider audience.

Until the 1840s it had been the featheries that golfers had used since the game was first developed. Come the middle of the 19th century there were hundreds of craftsmen and their apprentices toiling to produce such balls. Large numbers of them were to be reduced to destitution with the advent of the 'guttie'.

Producing a featherie was a time consuming process which required considerable expertise. The craftsmen themselves vied with each other for contracts from the richest patrons of the game and were sometimes scathing about the results which their competitors achieved. To produce a featherie, a piece of leather had to be cut into three pieces, softened with alum and water, and then sewn together leaving a small hole into which feathers were pressed until the ball was hard. The hole was then stitched up and the ball given three coats of paint before being sold. Each craftsman could produce no more than three or four featheries a day, with the result that each cost as much as 4 shillings, throughout the early 19th century – a considerable amount of money. Nor was a featherie liable to last the duration of a round. In wet weather, in particular, the seams tended to split, which meant that a golfer was required to carry six or eight balls when he set out for a game.

Contrary to popular opinion, however, the featheries didn't disappear overnight once gutties appeared. Some of the leading craftsmen, such as David Gourlay soon realised that their livelihood was under threat and so dispatached huge consignments of featheries to their major clients in the hope of cutting their losses. Others were less pragmatic. Such luminaries as Allan Robertson derided the new inventions and were vehement in support of the featherie. It was one of the most turbulent eras in the history of the game of golf, but in the end it was inevitable that the gutties would prevail.

The economical ball

When it came to the crunch the gutta-percha ball succeeded its traditional rival for the simple reason that it was both more durable and less expensive than the featherie. A skilled workman could roll a guttie in a matter of minutes whereas it required a craftsman to spend hours of endless toil to produce a featherie. Hundreds of gutties could be produced during a single shift with the result that each cost no more than 8 old pence or less than a quarter the price of a featherie. On the negative side, its detractors noted that a new guttie was much more difficult to control than a featherie, but this problem was solved once the manufacturers started to scar their products at the production stage. This was done because it soon became clear that a smooth ball didn't perform as consistently as a scarred one. Before long it became the practice to use a hammer to hack all new gutties in a random fashion before they were allowed to leave the factory. Later, moulds were made which put uniform markings on them.

The rise of modern equipment

As is often true, one change soon led to another. The arrival of the guttie meant that clubs had to be strengthened to cope with the harder ball. It became the prescribed practice to use hickory rather than ash for shafts, because the former was much more supple than the latter. Another important change in club design, brought about by the appearance of the guttie, was that the practice of splicing a clubhead and a shaft together was abandoned in favour of inserting the end of the shaft into a hole bored into the head of the club. The arrival of the guttie even led to a change in the golf swing itself. In the 1860s golfers used more upright swings than their predecessors had done in the 1850s and before. The simple reason for this was that the guttie had to be hit whereas the featherie was swept away.

The arrival of the gutta-percha ball might have led to the first major revolution in the game of golf, but it was not to be the last. The game was to witness a similar transformation with the appearance of the rubber core ball (circa 1900) and again in the 1930s when the Royal & Ancient Golf Club of St. Andrews and the United States Golf Assocation (USGA) acted to introduce strict rules to regulate the modern golf ball.

Modern golf – skill v. technology?

Thus far it should be clear that the golf ball manufacturers have played a unique role in the development of the game of golf through the centuries. Such manufacturers have been the leading lights behind all the major changes we have witnessed in the last 100 years or so and should continue to occupy a prominent role as we head towards the 21st century.

Nevertheless, it is debatable whether the ball manufacturers themselves will continue to transform the game in the future as much as they have done in the past. Entering the 1990s, science has advanced enough to suggest that manufacturers could come up with a ball which would have as much impact as the guttie had in the 1840s. But such a ball would never be permissible under the current rules. In the short term we will never see a golf ball which the average golfer can hit 350 yards because the existing rules would not permit it. In time we might be able to purchase such a product, but only if the R & A and the USGA either decide to alter their rules, or relinquish their right to govern the game altogether under a hail of lawsuits from other interested parties. Such a scenario might be welcome to some, but to others it would be an anathema which would lead to the ruination of the game.

In the interests of preserving the mass appeal of a game which has stood the test of time, let us assume that there is to be no dramatic change in the rules in the foreseeable future. The manufacturers will continue to refine their products but there will be no sweeping changes brought about as a result of a major upheaval among the governors of the game.

Under this scenario there is still much to encourage the golfer who believes that it is possible to purchase a better game.

Metal success

In recent times one of the big success stories in the world of golf equipment has been the rise of metal woods. Metal woods, however, are nothing new. Such clubs were available in the 1930s, but it is only in the last decade that sales have boomed. Recent research done by *Golf Monthly*, in the British Isles, and *Golf Magazine*, in the USA, found that no less than 46.8 per cent of golfers on the USPGA Tour now use metal woods. The figures are much the same in the realm of amateur golf.

Although there still exists a group of purists who would rather be seen dead than clutching a metal wood, their numbers are dwindling and will continue to do so as we approach the year 2000.

One result of this phenomenon, which is sometimes referred to as 'Metal Mania', is that the manufacturers themselves are now confident enough to experiment with a whole range of new metarials to be used in both shafts and clubheads. Graphite and boron have both become popular and titanium is also starting to catch on.

It is inevitable that further materials will be developed for use in the future. Certainly there will continue to be a place in the golf bag for traditional Persimmon woods and cast and forged steel irons, but the 'nineties may see the demise of the laminated wood, once so popular in the 'sixties and 'seventies, but which have since been pushed aside in the race to acquire a metal replacement. Research has found that only 33 per cent of British amateur golfers still use laminated woods. In the United States the corresponding figure is less than 20 per cent and is dropping at a rate close to 5 per cent per annum.

One of the factors which has attracted the customer to metal woods is that they are much more forgiving than traditional woods. In a metal wood the weight in its head is situated around its perimeter, with the result that the sweetspot is larger than on a more conventional wooden club. Shots hit from the toe or heel with a metal wood might not sail to the desired target but at least they will finish less far offline than a similar shot hit with a wooden club.

Perimeter weighting is also a common feature on the Game Improvement irons which most manufacturers produce and which are now selling well, both in Europe and the USA. The manufacturers themselves must adhere to strict rules which govern the specification of clubs, but even while following these parameters many manufacturers have spent millions of dollars in their goal to transform the amateur golfer into a more consistent animal.

Human nature is such that golfers will continue to search for the secret which will transform their games overnight. It is a desire which the manufacturers are pleased to pander to. Indeed their livelihood depends upon it.

GOLF COURSES IN BRITAIN AND IRELAND

A county by county guide of where to play and where to stay

Key to Map Sections

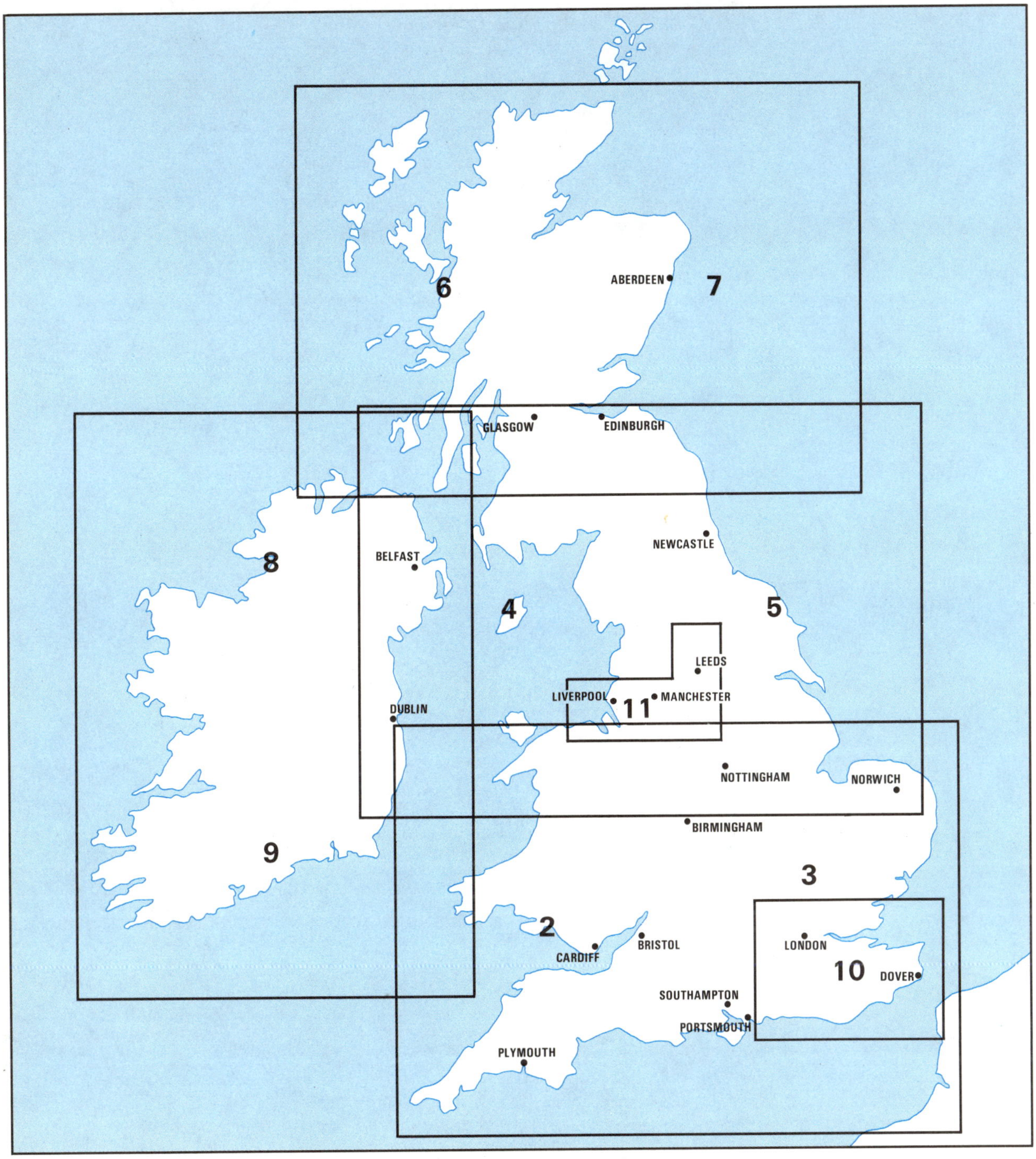

LEGEND

Uckfield — Entry in Guide

Motorway and Motorway Junction

51 — Primary Route

565 — Other Route

RAC — RAC Office

Scale 20 miles to 1 inch approx.

0 20 40 60 80 Kilometres

0 10 20 30 40 50 Statute Miles

MAP 10: Scale 11 miles to 1 inch approx.

0 20 40 60 80 Kilometres

0 10 20 30 40 50 Statute Miles

MAP 11: Scale 14 miles to 1 inch approx.

0 10 20 30 40 50 60 Kilometres

0 10 20 30 40 Statute Miles

1. Broadstone
2. Ferndown
3. Knighton Heath
4. Meyrick Park
5. Boscombe
6. Christchurch
7. Highcliffe Castle
8. Barton-on-Sea
9. Freshwater Bay
10. Ventnor
11. Shanklin & Sandown
12. Newport
13. Ryde
14. Cowes
15. Osborne
16. Lee-on-the-Solent
17. Gosport & Stokes Bay
18. Southsea
19. Hayling
20. Portsmouth
21. Southwick Park
22. Waterlooville
23. Burley
24. Brockenhurst Manor
25. New Forest
26. Dibden
27. Bramshaw
28. Southampton
29. Stoneham
30. Meon Valley G & CC
31. Romsey
32. Fleming Park
33. Dunwood Manor
34. Ampfield
35. Hockley
36. Corhampton
37. Brynhill
38. Wenvoe Castle
39. Dinas Powis
40. Glamorganshire
41. Llantrisant & Pontyclun
42. Creigiau
43. Llanishen
44. Cardiff
45. Caerphilly
46. Radyr
47. Whitchurch
48. St Mellons
49. Tredegar Park
50. Llanwern
51. Rhondda
52. Pontypridd
53. Bryn Meadows G & CC
54. Newport
55. Whitehall
56. Blackwood
57. Pontnewydd
58. Aberdare
59. Mountain Ash
60. Bargoed
61. Tredegar & Rhymney
62. West Monmouthshire
63. Monmouthshire
64. Pontypool
65. Long Ashton
66. Shirehampton Park
67. Henbury
68. Filton
69. Bristol & Clifton
70. Mangotsfield
71. Tracy Park G & CC
72. Knowle
73. Mendip
74. Saltford
75. Lansdown
76. Bath
77. Rose Hill
78. Blackwell
79. Redditch
80. Ladbrook Park
81. North Worcestershire
82. Kings Norton
83. Fulford Heath
84. Shirley
85. Copt Heath
86. Halesowen
87. Warley
88. Harborne
89. Harborne Church Farm
90. Edgbaston
91. Moseley
92. Cocks Moor Woods
93. Gay Hill
94. Robin Hood
95. Olton
96. Hatchford Brook
97. North Warwickshire
98. Forest of Arden G & CC
99. Maxstoke Park
100. Himley Hall
101. Dudley
102. Sandwell Park
103. Hill Top
104. Penn
105. Dartmouth
106. Handsworth
107. Pype Hayes
108. Patshull Park
109. South Staffordshire
110. Oxley Park
111. Bloxwich
112. Walsall
113. Druids Heath
114. Great Barr
115. Little Aston
116. Calderfields
117. Sutton Coldfield
118. Boldmere
119. Walmley
120. Moor Hall
121. Drayton Park
122. Tamworth
123. Belfry
124. Purley Chase
125. Nuneaton
126. Grange
127. Hearsall
128. City of Coventry (Brandon Woods)
129. Kenilworth
130. Rugby
131. Coventry
132. Newbold Comyn
133. Leamington & County
134. Warwick
135. Breadsall Priory G & CC
136. Ormonde Fields G & CC
137. Ilkeston Borough
138. Erewash Valley
139. Beeston Fields
140. Wollaton Park
141. Bulwell Forest
142. Nottingham City
143. Mapperley
144. Edwalton Municipal

LINCOLNSHIRE
DERBYSHIRE
NOTTINGHAMSHIRE
NORFOLK
LEICESTERSHIRE
WEST MIDLANDS
CAMBRIDGESHIRE
NORTHANTS
WARWICKSHIRE
SUFFOLK
BEDFORDSHIRE
ENGLAND
HERTS
BUCKINGHAMSHIRE
ESSEX
OXFORDSHIRE
GREATER LONDON
LONDON
BERKSHIRE
KENT
SURREY
HAMPSHIRE
WEST SUSSEX
EAST SUSSEX
The Wash
Strait of Dover
Isle of Wight
Lincoln
Nottingham
Derby
Leicester
Coventry
Norwich
Peterborough
Cambridge
Northampton
Ipswich
Milton Keynes
Luton
Colchester
Chelmsford
Reading
Southend-on-Sea
Southampton
Portsmouth
Brighton
Bournemouth
CHANNEL ISLANDS
Alderney
Guernsey
St. Peter Port
Sark
Jersey
St. Helier
FRANCE

Islay
Port Askaig
Portnahaven
Machrie
Port Ellen
Tarbert
Loch Fyne
Kennacraig
Carradale
Kilbrannan Sound
Machrihanish
Campbeltown
Dunaverty
Mull of Kintyre
Lochranza
Arran
Corrie
Brodick
Lamlash
Shiskine
Blackwaterfoot
Firth of Clyde
Helensburgh
Greenock
Gourock
Cowal
Dunoon
Rothesay
Largs
Millport
West Kilbride
Ardrossan
Irvine
Kilmarnock
Troon
Prestwick
Ayr
Turnberry Hotel
Maybole
Girvan
GLASGOW
STRATHCLYDE
Cumbernauld
Falkirk
EDINBURGH
LOTHIAN
Middleton
West Linton
Lanark
Carnwath
Peebles
Biggar
Leadhills
Abington
Lauder
Galashiels
Melrose
Selkirk
Hawick
BORDERS
Moffat
Beattock
Strathaven
Hollandbush
Muirkirk
Cumnock
New Cumnock
Douglas Water
Sanquhar
Dalmellington
Thornhill
GALLOWAY FOREST PARK
DUMFRIES AND GALLOWAY
New Galloway
Dumfries
Lochmaben
Lockerbie
Langholm
Gretna
Longtown
Powfoot
Castle Douglas
Dalbeattie
Colvend
Southerness
Kirkcudbright
Gatehouse
Newton Stewart
Wigtown
Glenluce
Cairnryan
Stranraer
Portpatrick
Luce Bay
Port William
Drummore
Isle of Whithorn
Mull of Galloway
Solway Firth
SOLWAY COAST
Silloth on Solway
Carlisle
Maryport
Workington
Cockermouth
Whitehaven
St. Bees Head
Egremont
Keswick
Derwent Water
Ullswater
CUMBRIA
LAKE DISTRICT NATIONAL PARK
Glenridding
Ambleside
Windermere
Kendal
Coniston
Coniston Water
Broughton in Furness
Seascale
Ravenglass
Silecroft
Ulverston
Barrow-in-Furness
Grange-over-Sands
Silverdale
ARNSIDE AND SILVERDALE
Morecambe Bay
Morecambe
Heysham
Lancaster
Knott End
Fleetwood
Garstang
Blackpool
Lytham St. Annes
Preston
Southport
Skelmersdale
MERSEYSIDE
LIVERPOOL
Wallasey
Hoylake
Birkenhead
Bebington
Liverpool Bay
Ellesmere Port
Chester
Mold
Wrexham
Ruabon
Llangollen
Ellesmere
Oswestry
Whittington
Shrewsbury
SHROPSHIRE
Welshpool
WALES
Lake Bala
Bala
SNOWDONIA NATIONAL PARK
Blaenau Ffestiniog
Porthmadog
Portmadoc
Criccieth
Pwllheli
Abersoch
LLEYN
Nefyn & District
Penygroes
GWYNEDD
Caernarfon
Menai Strait
Caernarfon Bay
Bangor
Conwy
Llandudno
Colwyn Bay
Abergele
Rhyl
Prestatyn
Denbigh
CLWYD
Ruthin
Betws-y-Coed
Pentrefoelas
Dolgellau
Barmouth
Tywyn
Machynlleth
Anglesey
ANGLESEY
Holyhead
Amlwch
Bull Bay
Great Orme's Head
Isle of Man
Point of Ayr
Ramsey
Peel
Douglas
Castletown
Calf of Man
IRISH SEA
Giant's Causeway
Portrush
Coleraine
Bushfoot
Ballycastle
Ballymoney
Cushendall
Carnlough
ANTRIM
Ballymena
Larne
Island Magee
Whitehead
Carrickfergus
Magherafelt
Lough Neagh
Antrim
BELFAST
Holywood
Bangor
Donaghadee
Newtownards
Lisburn
Dungannon
Portadown
Lurgan
Armagh
ARMAGH
Banbridge
DOWN
Ballynahinch
Downpatrick
Strangford
Portaferry
Ardglass
Newcastle
Newry
Warrenpoint
Kilkeel
Greenore
Castleblayney
Dundalk
LOUTH
Ardee
Dunleer
Drogheda
Slane
Boyne
Navan
Laytown and Bettystown
Balbriggan
Skerries
Rush
Donabate
Malahide
Portmarnock
Howth
DUBLIN
Dun Laoghaire
Killiney
Bray
Greystones
Delgany
WICKLOW
Wicklow
Wicklow Head
Woodenbridge
Arklow
Gorey
Courtown

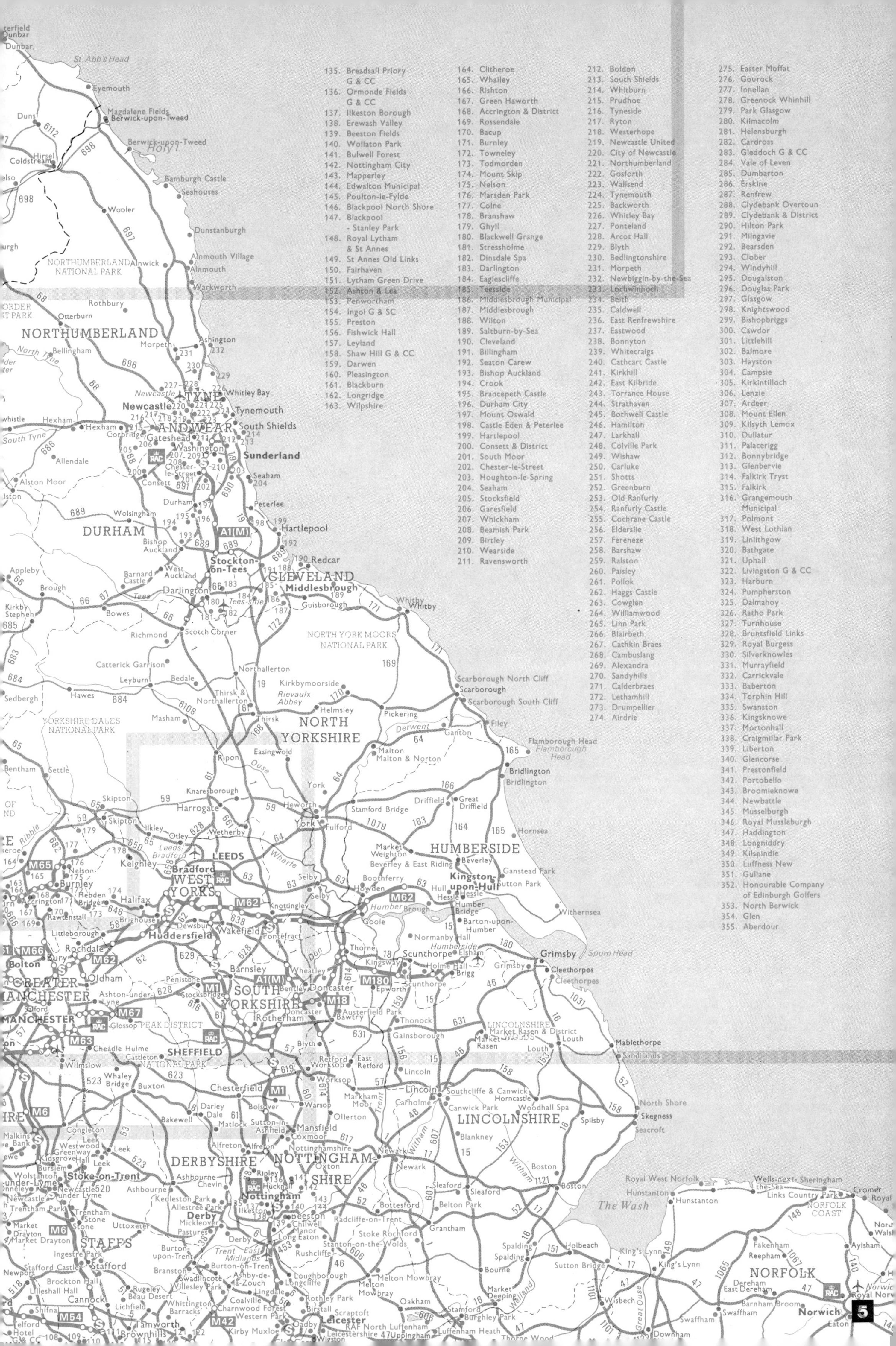

135. Breadsall Priory G & CC
136. Ormonde Fields G & CC
137. Ilkeston Borough
138. Erewash Valley
139. Beeston Fields
140. Wollaton Park
141. Bulwell Forest
142. Nottingham City
143. Mapperley
144. Edwalton Municipal
145. Poulton-le-Fylde
146. Blackpool North Shore
147. Blackpool - Stanley Park
148. Royal Lytham & St Annes
149. St Annes Old Links
150. Fairhaven
151. Lytham Green Drive
152. Ashton & Lea
153. Penwortham
154. Ingol G & SC
155. Preston
156. Fishwick Hall
157. Leyland
158. Shaw Hill G & CC
159. Darwen
160. Pleasington
161. Blackburn
162. Longridge
163. Wilpshire
164. Clitheroe
165. Whalley
166. Rishton
167. Green Haworth
168. Accrington & District
169. Rossendale
170. Bacup
171. Burnley
172. Towneley
173. Todmorden
174. Mount Skip
175. Nelson
176. Marsden Park
177. Colne
178. Branshaw
179. Ghyll
180. Blackwell Grange
181. Stressholme
182. Dinsdale Spa
183. Darlington
184. Eaglescliffe
185. Teesside
186. Middlesbrough Municipal
187. Middlesbrough
188. Wilton
189. Saltburn-by-Sea
190. Cleveland
191. Billingham
192. Seaton Carew
193. Bishop Auckland
194. Crook
195. Brancepeth Castle
196. Durham City
197. Mount Oswald
198. Castle Eden & Peterlee
199. Hartlepool
200. Consett & District
201. South Moor
202. Chester-le-Street
203. Houghton-le-Spring
204. Seaham
205. Stocksfield
206. Garesfield
207. Whickham
208. Beamish Park
209. Birtley
210. Wearside
211. Ravensworth
212. Boldon
213. South Shields
214. Whitburn
215. Prudhoe
216. Tyneside
217. Ryton
218. Westerhope
219. Newcastle United
220. City of Newcastle
221. Northumberland
222. Gosforth
223. Wallsend
224. Tynemouth
225. Backworth
226. Whitley Bay
227. Ponteland
228. Arcot Hall
229. Blyth
230. Bedlingtonshire
231. Morpeth
232. Newbiggin-by-the-Sea
233. Lochwinnoch
234. Beith
235. Caldwell
236. East Renfrewshire
237. Eastwood
238. Bonnyton
239. Whitecraigs
240. Cathcart Castle
241. Kirkhill
242. East Kilbride
243. Torrance House
244. Strathaven
245. Bothwell Castle
246. Hamilton
247. Larkhall
248. Colville Park
249. Wishaw
250. Carluke
251. Shotts
252. Greenburn
253. Old Ranfurly
254. Ranfurly Castle
255. Cochrane Castle
256. Elderslie
257. Fereneze
258. Barshaw
259. Ralston
260. Paisley
261. Pollok
262. Haggs Castle
263. Cowglen
264. Williamwood
265. Linn Park
266. Blairbeth
267. Cathkin Braes
268. Cambuslang
269. Alexandra
270. Sandyhills
271. Calderbraes
272. Lethamhill
273. Drumpellier
274. Airdrie
275. Easter Moffat
276. Gourock
277. Innellan
278. Greenock Whinhill
279. Park Glasgow
280. Kilmacolm
281. Helensburgh
282. Cardross
283. Gleddoch G & CC
284. Vale of Leven
285. Dumbarton
286. Erskine
287. Renfrew
288. Clydebank Overtoun
289. Clydebank & District
290. Hilton Park
291. Milngavie
292. Bearsden
293. Clober
294. Windyhill
295. Dougalston
296. Douglas Park
297. Glasgow
298. Knightswood
299. Bishopbriggs
300. Cawdor
301. Littlehill
302. Balmore
303. Hayston
304. Campsie
305. Kirkintilloch
306. Lenzie
307. Ardeer
308. Mount Ellen
309. Kilsyth Lennox
310. Dullatur
311. Palacerigg
312. Bonnybridge
313. Glenbervie
314. Falkirk Tryst
315. Falkirk
316. Grangemouth Municipal
317. Polmont
318. West Lothian
319. Linlithgow
320. Bathgate
321. Uphall
322. Livingston G & CC
323. Harburn
324. Pumpherston
325. Dalmahoy
326. Ratho Park
327. Turnhouse
328. Bruntsfield Links
329. Royal Burgess
330. Silverknowles
331. Murrayfield
332. Carrickvale
333. Baberton
334. Torphin Hill
335. Swanston
336. Kingsknowe
337. Mortonhall
338. Craigmillar Park
339. Liberton
340. Glencorse
341. Prestonfield
342. Portobello
343. Broomieknowe
344. Newbattle
345. Musselburgh
346. Royal Musselburgh
347. Haddington
348. Longniddry
349. Kilspindie
350. Luffness New
351. Gullane
352. Honourable Company of Edinburgh Golfers
353. North Berwick
354. Glen
355. Aberdour

Port of Ness
Barvas
Carloway
Stornoway
Lewis
North Minch
Tarbert
Harris
Rodel
North Uist
Lochmaddy
Benbecula
Little Minch
South Uist
Askernish
Lochboisdale
Barra
Castlebay
Uig
Dunvegan
Portree
Skye
Inner Sound
Sconser
Broadford
Elgol
Armadale
Rhum
Mallaig
Lochailort
Salen
Coll
Tiree
Vaul
Western Isle
Tobermory
Lochaline
Craignure
Mull
Fionnphort
Firth of Lorn
Colonsay
Jura
Port Askaig
Islay
Portnahaven
Machrie
Port Ellen
Malin Head
Ballyliffin
Portsalon
Durness
Tongue
Bettyhill
Laxford Bridge
Kylestrome
Unapool
Lochinver
Loch Shin
Ledmore
Lairg
Ullapool
Bonar Bridge
Dornoch
Golspie
Royal Dornoch
Dornoch Firth
Tain
Alness
Invergordon
Cromarty
Gairloch
Loch Maree
Loch Fannich
Kinlochewe
Gorstan
Achnasheen
Strathpeffer Spa
Conon
Fortrose and Rosemarkie
Nairn
Shieldaig
Muir of Ord
Beauly
Inverness
Torvean
Daviot
Loch Monar
Farrar
Lochcarron
Stromeferry
Kyle of Lochalsh
Cannich
Drumnadrochit
HIGHLAND
Shiel Bridge
Invermoriston
Loch Ness
Moriston
Carrbridge
Boat of Garten
Fort Augustus
Kingussie
Newtonmore
Garry
Invergarry
Caledonian Canal
Spey
Loch Laggan
Spean Bridge
Spean
Dalwhinnie
Fort William
Loch Ericht
Corran
Glen Coe
S. Ballachulish
Loch Linnhe
Loch Rannoch
Tummel
Pitlochry
Taymouth Castle
Aberfeldy
Loch Tay
Bridge of Orchy
Killin
Loch Etive
Connel
Glencruitten
Oban
Dalmally
Tyndrum
Crianlarich
Loch Earn
Lochearnhead
St Fillans
Comrie
Muthill
Auchterarder
Gleneagles Hotel
Loch Awe
Inveraray
Loch Katrine
Callander
Aberfoyle
Teith
Ardgartan
Strachur
Dunblane
CENTRAL
Loch Lomond
Forth
Stirling
STRATHCLYDE
Lochgilphead
Buchanan Castle
SCOTLAND
Helensburgh
Blairmore & Strone
Cowal
Dunoon
Greenock
Gourock
Dumbarton
Falkirk
Kyles of Bute
Innellan
Port Glasgow
Cumbernauld
Loch Fyne
Tarbert
Port Bannatyne
Wemyss Bay
Skelmorlie
Airdrie
Rothesay
Kennacraig
Routenburn
Largs
Millport
GLASGOW
Lochranza
Kilbirnie Place
West Kilbride
Corrie
Ardeer
Fenwick
Clyde
Lanark
Ardrossan
Irvine
Ravenspark
Annanhill
Kilmarnock
Strathaven
Carradale
Kilbrannan Sound
Machrie Bay
Brodick
Lamlash
Arran
Shiskine
Blackwaterfoot
Western Gailes
Glasgow (Ayr)
Kilmarnock (Barassie)
Troon
Caprington
Loudoun
Darvel
Hollandbush
Royal Troon & Portland
Prestwick
Troon Municipal
Ballochmyle
Muirkirk
Machrihanish
Campbeltown
Prestwick St Cuthbert
Prestwick St Nicholas
Ayr
Ayr Dalmilling
Cumnock
Ayr Belleisle
Ayr Seafield
Douglas Water
Firth of Clyde
New Cumnock
Dunaverty
Turnberry Hotel
Maybole
Sanquhar
Giant's
M9
M80

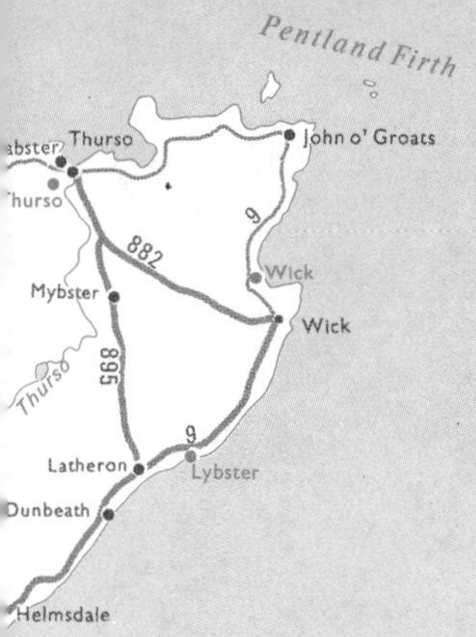

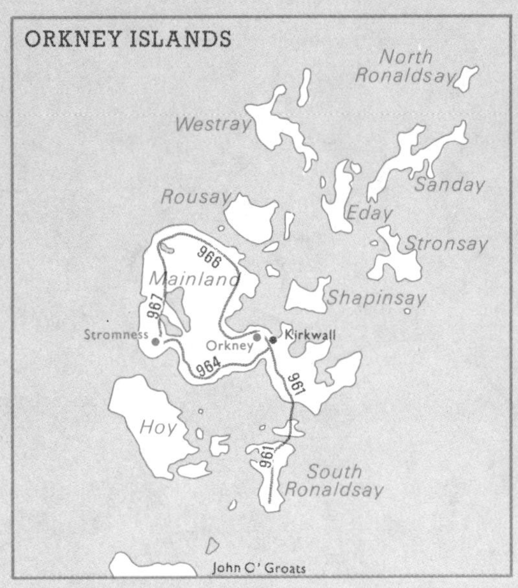

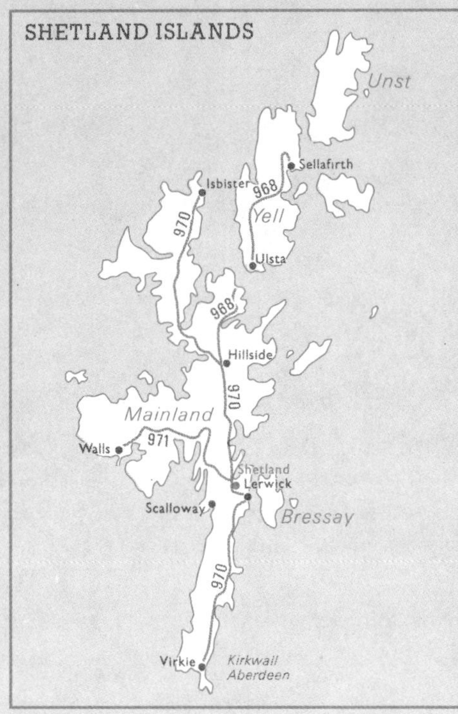

233. Lochwinnoch
234. Beith
235. Caldwell
236. East Renfrewshire
237. Eastwood
238. Bonnyton
239. Whitecraigs
240. Cathcart Castle
241. Kirkhill
242. East Kilbride
243. Torrance House
244. Strathaven
245. Bothwell Castle
246. Hamilton
247. Larkhall
248. Colville Park
249. Wishaw
250. Carluke
251. Shotts
252. Greenburn
253. Old Ranfurly
254. Ranfurly Castle
255. Cochrane Castle
256. Eldersile
257. Fereneze
258. Barshaw
259. Ralston
260. Paisley
261. Pollok
262. Haggs Castle
263. Cowglen
264. Williamwood
265. Linn Park
266. Blairbeth
267. Cathkin Braes
268. Cambuslang
269. Alexandra
270. Sandyhills
271. Calderbraes
272. Lethamhill
273. Drumpellier
274. Airdrie
275. Easter Moffat
276. Gourock
277. Greenock
278. Greenock Whinhill
279. Park Glasgow
280. Kilmacolm
281. Helensburgh
282. Cardross
283. Gleddoch G & CC
284. Vale of Leven
285. Dumbarton
286. Erskine
287. Renfrew
288. Clydebank Overtoun
289. Clydebank & District
290. Hilton Park
291. Milngavie
292. Bearsden
293. Clober
294. Windyhill
295. Dougalston
296. Douglas Park
297. Glasgow
298. Knightswood
299. Bishopbriggs
300. Cawdor
301. Littlehill
302. Balmore
303. Hayston
304. Campsie
305. Kirkintilloch
306. Lenzie
307. Crow Wood
308. Mount Ellen
309. Kilsyth Lemox
310. Dullatur
311. Palacerigg
312. Bonnybridge
313. Glenbervie
314. Falkirk Tryst
315. Falkirk
316. Grangemouth Municipal
317. Polmont
318. West Lothian
319. Linlithgow
320. Bathgate
321. Uphall
322. Livingston G & CC
323. Harburn
324. Pumpherston
325. Dalmahoy
326. Ratho Park
327. Turnhouse
328. Bruntsfield Links
329. Royal Burgess
330. Silverknowles
331. Murrayfield
332. Carrickvale
333. Baberton
334. Torphin Hill
335. Swanston
336. Kingsknowe
337. Mortonhall
338. Craigmillar Park
339. Liberton
340. Glencorse
341. Prestonfield
342. Portobello
343. Broomieknowe
344. Newbattle
345. Musselburgh
346. Royal Musselburgh
347. Haddington
348. Longniddry
349. Kilspindie
350. Luffness New
351. Gullane
352. Honourable Company of Edinburgh Golfers
353. North Berwick
354. Glen
355. Aberdour
356. Tulliallan
357. Stirling
358. Dunblane New
359. Bridge of Allan
360. Braehead
361. Alva
362. Alloa
363. Tillicoultry
364. Dollar
365. Saline
366. Dunfermline
367. Canmore
368. Pitreavie (Dunfermline)
369. Muckhart
370. Milnathort
371. Green Hotel
372. Lochgelly
373. Auchterderran
374. Leslie
375. Glenrothes
376. Dunnikier Park
377. Kirkcaldy
378. Burntisland
379. Kinghorn
380. Thornton
381. Ladybank
382. Cupar
383. Lundin
384. Scoonie
385. Leven
386. Elie
387. Elie Sports Club
388. Anstruther
389. Crail
390. St Andrews Balgrove Course
391. St Andrews Eden Course
392. St Andrews Jubilee Course
393. St Andrews New Course
394. St Andrews Old Course
395. Murcar
396. Royal Aberdeen
397. Kings Links
398. Northern
399. Bon-Accord
400. Caledonian
401. Balnagask
402. Nigg Bay

NORTHERN IRELAND
DONEGAL
DERRY
ANTRIM
TYRONE
FERMANAGH
ARMAGH
DOWN
MONAGHAN
CAVAN
LEITRIM
SLIGO
MAYO
ROSCOMMON
LONGFORD
LOUTH
MEATH
Londonderry
BELFAST
Islay
Port Askaig
Portnahaven
Machrie
Port Ellen
Tarbert
Kennacraig
Lochranza
Carradale
Campbeltown
Machrihanish
Dunaverty
Kilbrannan Sound
Mull of Kintyre
Malin Head
Giant's Causeway
Donegal Bay
Erris Head
Achill Head
Achill Island
Clew Bay
Slyne Head
Connemara
Lough Foyle
Lough Neagh
Lower Lough Erne
Upper Lough Erne
Lough Allen
Lough Conn
Lough Mask
Lough Corrib
Lough Ree
Ballyliffin
Portsalon
Greencastle
Moville
Buncrana
Rosapenna
Dunfanaghy
Gweedore
Bunbeg
Dungloe
Otway
North West
Letterkenny
Lifford
Strabane
Sion Mills
Stranorlar
Ballybofey
Ballybofey & Stranorlar
Narin & Portnoo
Killybegs
Donegal
Rossnowlagh
Bundoran
Ballyshannon
Limavady
City of Derry
Dungiven
Garvagh
Maghera
Coleraine
Castlerock
Portstewart
Royal Portrush
Bushfoot
Ballycastle
Ballymoney
Cushendall
Carnlough
Cairndhu
Larne
Ballymena
Moyola Park
Magherafelt
Ballyclare
Greenisland
Carrickfergus
Whitehead
Island Magee
Antrim
Massereene
Helen's Bay
Carnalea
Bangor
Donaghadee
Royal Belfast
Holywood
Fortwilliam
Cliftonville
Ormeau
Dunmurry
Balmoral
Lisburn
Malone
Belvoir Park
Shandon Park
The Knock
Clandeboye
Newtownards
Scrabo
Mahee Island
Kirkistown Castle
Portaferry
Strangford
Downpatrick
Ardglass
Royal County Down
Newcastle
Ballynahinch
Spa
Banbridge
Tandragee
Lurgan
Portadown
Armagh
County Armagh
Newry
Warrenpoint
Kilkeel
Greenore
Dundalk
Newtownstewart
Omagh
Cookstown
Killymoon
Dungannon
Dromore
Fintona
Irvinestown
Aughnacloy
Monaghan
Rossmore
Castleblayney
Enniskillen
Lisnaskea
Clones
Belturbet
County Cavan
Cootehill
Bailieborough
Virginia
Nuremore
Ardee
Dunleer
County Louth
Drogheda
Laytown and Bettystown
Balbriggan
Skerries
Slane
Navan
Headfort
Royal Tara
Trim
Mullingar
Castlepollard
Granard
Edgeworthstown
Longford
County Longford
Ballinamore
Carrick-on-Shannon
Carrick on Shannon
Mohill
Boyle
Roscommon
Castlerea
Ballyhaunis
Ballyhawnis
Claremorris
Tuam
Swinford
Castlebar
Westport
Mallaranny
Mulrany
Clifden
Ballina
Belmullet
Enniscrone
Sligo
Strandhill
County Sligo
Moy
Bann
Foyle
Boyne
M1
M2
M22

REPUBLIC OF IRELAND
DUBLIN
WICKLOW
KILDARE
OFFALY
LAOIS
CARLOW
WEXFORD
KILKENNY
TIPPERARY
WATERFORD
LIMERICK
CLARE
CORK
KERRY
St. George's Channel
PEMBROKESHIRE COAST NATIONAL PARK
St. David's Head
St. David's
Haverfordwest
Milford Haven
South Pembrokeshire
Newport
Malahide
Portmarnock
Sutton
Howth
Dun Laoghaire
Killiney
Bray
Greystones
Wicklow
Wicklow Head
Arklow
Gorey
Courtown
Enniscorthy
Rosslare
Rosslare Harbour
Carnsore Point
Wexford
New Ross
Waterford
Tramore
Dungarvan
Youghal
Middleton
Cork
East Cork
Monkstown
Ringaskiddy
Kinsale
Bandon
Clonakilty
Skibbereen
Cape Clear
Mizen Head
Bantry
Bantry Bay
Glengarriff
Berehaven
Kenmare
Waterville
Skellig Mhicil
Ring of Kerry
Dingle Bay
Dingle
Brandon Head
Dooks
Killorglin
Killarney
Tralee
Loop Head
Mouth of the Shannon
Ballybunion
Listowel
Abbeyfeale
Kilkee
Kilrush
Spanish Point
Lahinch
Ennistimon
Ballyvaughan
Galway Bay
Aran Is.
Galway
Oranmore
Athenry
Loughrea
Gort
Ennis
Shannon
Dromoland Castle
Limerick
Castletroy
Adare Manor
Newcastle West
Charleville
Rath Luirc
Doneraile
Mallow
Muskerry
Blackwater
Macroom
Lee
Dunmanway
Fermoy
Mitchelstown
Lismore
Cappoquin
Tipperary
Cahir
Cahir Park
The Nire Valley Drive
Suir
Clonmel
Carrick-on-Suir
Cashel
Thurles
Rathdowney
Urlingford
Callan
Kilkenny
Castlecomer
Abbeyleix
Portlaoise
Mountrath
Roscrea
Nenagh
Borrisokane
Lough Derg
Portumna
Birr
Ballinasloe
Ferbane
Tullamore
Garryhinch
Portarlington
Heath
Edenderry
Athy
Carlow
Muine Bheag (Bagenalstown)
Borris
Barrow
Nore
Bunclody
Tullow
Baltinglass
Kilcullen
The Curragh
Cill Dara
Naas
Blessington
Maynooth
Liffey
Lucan
Hermitage
Woodenbridge
Slaney
Delgany

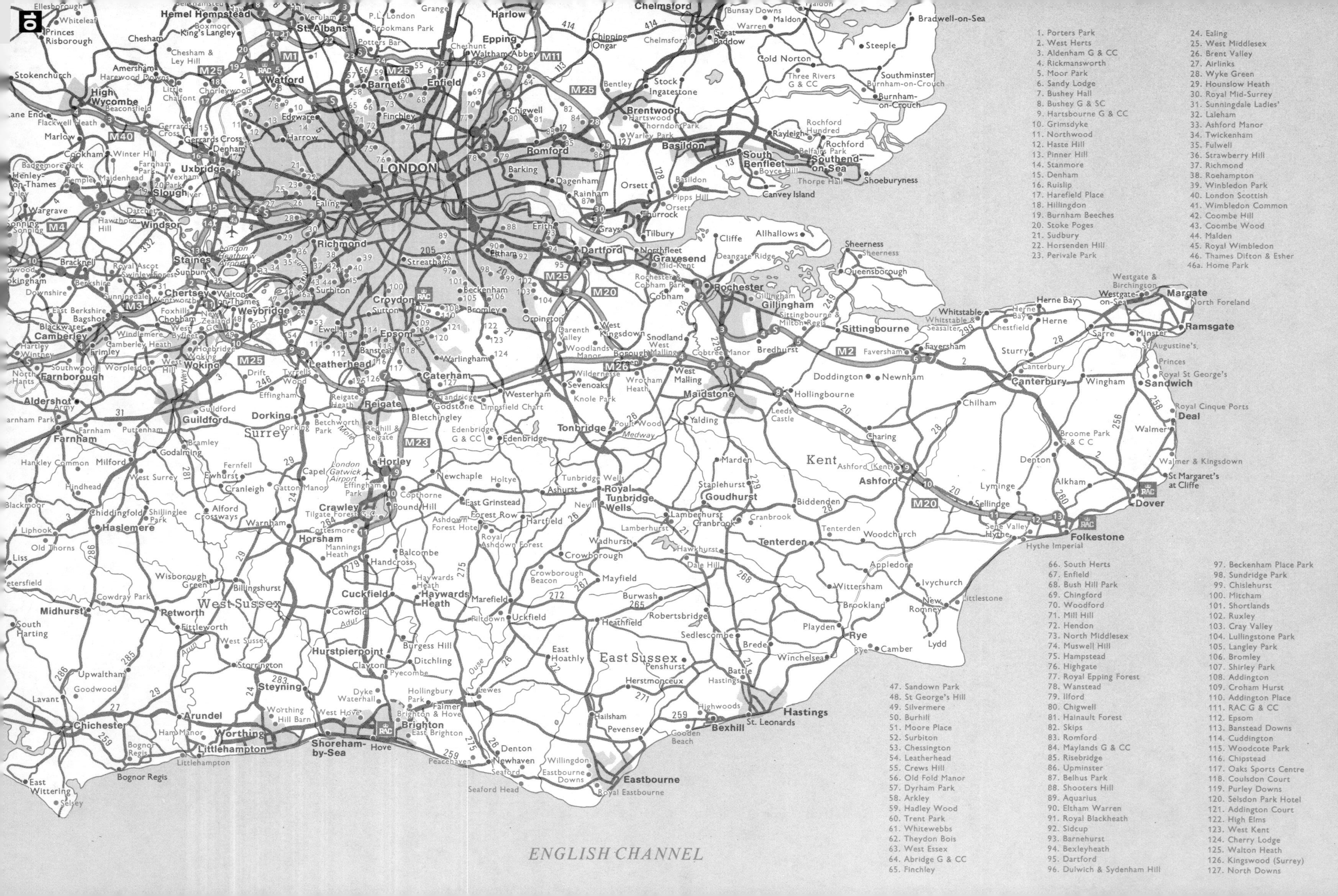
LONDON
Surrey
Kent
West Sussex
East Sussex
ENGLISH CHANNEL
1. Porters Park
2. West Herts
3. Aldenham G & CC
4. Rickmansworth
5. Moor Park
6. Sandy Lodge
7. Bushey Hall
8. Bushey G & SC
9. Hartsbourne G & CC
10. Grimsdyke
11. Northwood
12. Haste Hill
13. Pinner Hill
14. Stanmore
15. Denham
16. Ruislip
17. Harefield Place
18. Hillingdon
19. Burnham Beeches
20. Stoke Poges
21. Sudbury
22. Horsenden Hill
23. Perivale Park
24. Ealing
25. West Middlesex
26. Brent Valley
27. Airlinks
28. Wyke Green
29. Hounslow Heath
30. Royal Mid-Surrey
31. Sunningdale Ladies'
32. Laleham
33. Ashford Manor
34. Twickenham
35. Fulwell
36. Strawberry Hill
37. Richmond
38. Roehampton
39. Winbledon Park
40. London Scottish
41. Wimbledon Common
42. Coombe Hill
43. Coombe Wood
44. Malden
45. Royal Wimbledon
46. Thames Ditton & Esher
46a. Home Park
47. Sandown Park
48. St George's Hill
49. Silvermere
50. Burhill
51. Moore Place
52. Surbiton
53. Chessington
54. Leatherhead
55. Crews Hill
56. Old Fold Manor
57. Dyrham Park
58. Arkley
59. Hadley Wood
60. Trent Park
61. Whitewebbs
62. Theydon Bois
63. West Essex
64. Abridge G & CC
65. Finchley
66. South Herts
67. Enfield
68. Bush Hill Park
69. Chingford
70. Woodford
71. Mill Hill
72. Hendon
73. North Middlesex
74. Muswell Hill
75. Hampstead
76. Highgate
77. Royal Epping Forest
78. Wanstead
79. Ilford
80. Chigwell
81. Hainault Forest
82. Skips
83. Romford
84. Maylands G & CC
85. Risebridge
86. Upminster
87. Belhus Park
88. Shooters Hill
89. Aquarius
90. Eltham Warren
91. Royal Blackheath
92. Sidcup
93. Barnehurst
94. Bexleyheath
95. Dartford
96. Dulwich & Sydenham Hill
97. Beckenham Place Park
98. Sundridge Park
99. Chislehurst
100. Mitcham
101. Shortlands
102. Ruxley
103. Cray Valley
104. Lullingstone Park
105. Langley Park
106. Bromley
107. Shirley Park
108. Addington
109. Croham Hurst
110. Addington Place
111. RAC G & CC
112. Epsom
113. Banstead Downs
114. Cuddington
115. Woodcote Park
116. Chipstead
117. Oaks Sports Centre
118. Coulsdon Court
119. Purley Downs
120. Selsdon Park Hotel
121. Addington Court
122. High Elms
123. West Kent
124. Cherry Lodge
125. Walton Heath
126. Kingswood (Surrey)
127. North Downs

1. Rhyl
2. Prestatyn
3. St Melyd
4. Rhuddlan
5. Denbigh
6. Holywell
7. Flint
8. Mold
9. Old Padeswood
10. Padeswood & Buckley
11. Hawarden
12. Chester
13. Upton-by-Chester
14. Vicars Cross
15. Ellesmere Port
16. Heswall
17. Bromborough
18. Eastham Lodge
19. Caldy
20. Arrowe Park
21. Brackenwood
22. Prenton
23. Wirral Ladies'
24. Royal Liverpool
25. Hoylake
26. Leasowe
27. Bidston
28. Wallasey
29. Warren
30. Formby
31. Formby Ladies'
32. Southport & Ainsdale
33. Royal Birkdale
34. Hillside
35. Hesketh
36. Southport Municipal
37. Southport Old Links
38. West Lancashire
39. Bootle
40. Breightmet
41. Ormskirk
42. Beacon Park
43. Gathurst
44. Dean Wood
45. West Derby
46. Grange Park
47. Sherdley Park
48. Ashton-in-Makerfield
49. Haydock Park
50. Leigh
51. Huyton & Prescot
52. Childwall
53. Bowring
54. Allerton Municipal
55. Woolton
56. Lee Park
57. Widnes
58. Poulton Park
59. Birchwood
60. Runcorn
61. Walton Hall
62. Warrington
63. Lymm
64. Helsby
65. Delamere Forest
66. Sandiway
67. Duxbury Park
68. Chorley
69. Wigan
70. Haigh Hall
71. Horwich
72. Bolton
73. Old Links
74. Dunscar
75. Turton
76. Harwood
77. Greenmount
78. Lowes Park
79. Walmersley
80. Springfield Park
81. Rochdale
82. Lobden
83. Whittaker
84. Todmorden
85. Castle Hawk
86. Manchester
87. Crompton & Royton
88. Hindley Hall
89. Westhoughton
90. Great Lever & Farnworth
91. Brackley
92. Ellesmere
93. Worsley
94. Swinton Park
95. Stand
96. Whitefield
97. Bury
98. Prestwich
99. Heaton Park
100. New North Manchester
101. Blackley
102. Pike Fold
103. Brookdale
104. Werneth (Oldham)
105. Saddleworth
106. Oldham
107. Ashton-unde-Lyne
108. Stamford
109. Davyhulme Park
110. William Wroe
111. Flixton
112. Ashton on Mersey
113. Sale
114. Chorlton cum Hardy
115. Northenden
116. Withington
117. Didsbury
118. Heaton Moor
119. Houldsworth
120. Reddish Vale
121. Denton
122. Fairfield G & Sailing C
123. Dukinfield
124. Werneth Low
125. Romiley
126. Glossop & District
127. Dunham Forest G & CC
128. Altrincham
129. Hale
130. Ringway
131. Gatley
132. Cheadle
133. Bramall Park
134. Bramhall
135. Mirrlees
136. Stockport
137. Davenport
138. Marple
139. Hazel Grove
140. Disley
141. Mellor & Townscliffe
142. New Mills
143. Chapel-en-le-Frith
144. Mere G & CC
145. Knutsford
146. Wilmslow
147. Alderley Edge
148. Prestbury
149. Macclesfield
150. Cavendish
151. Buxton & High Peak
152. Sandbach
153. Astbury
154. Congleton
155. Bakewell
156. Sickleholme
157. Marsden
158. Meltham
159. Crosland Heath
160. Longley Park
161. Woodsome Hall
162. Halifax Bradley Hall
163. Outlane
164. Elland
165. Bradley Park
166. Huddersfield
167. Halifax
168. West End
169. Lightcliffe
170. Headley
171. Clayton
172. Queensbury
173. South Bradford
174. Cleckheaton & District
175. West Bowling
176. East Bierley
177. Phoenix Park
178. Bradford Moor
179. Woodhall Hills
180. West Bradford
181. Northcliffe
182. Shipley
183. Bingley St Ives
184. Baildon
185. Bradford
186. Keighley
187. Riddlesden
188. Otley
189. Silsden
190. Ben Rhydding
191. Ilkley
192. Ripon City
193. Easingwold
194. Knaresborough
195. Oakdale
196. Harrogate
197. Pannal
198. Wetherby
199. Pike Hills
200. Rawdon
201. Headingley
202. Moortown
203. Scarcroft
204. Sand Moor
205. Moor Allerton
206. Alwoodley
207. Horsforth
208. Roundhay
209. Leeds
210. Gott's Park
211. Temple Newsam
212. Garforth
213. South Leeds
214. Middleton Park
215. Howley Hall
216. Hanging Heaton
217. Dewsbury District
218. Low Laithes
219. City of Wakefield
220. Normanton
221. Pontefract & District
222. Painthorpe House
223. Wakefield
224. Barnsley
225. Silkstone
226. Hickleton
227. Stocksbridge & District
228. Wortley
229. Tankersley Park
230. Wath
231. Doncaster Town Moor
232. Hillsborough
233. Concord Park
234. Grange Park
235. Tinsley Park
236. Phoenix
237. Rotherham
238. Sitwell Park
239. Hallamshire
240. Beauchief
241. Abbeydale
242. Dore & Totley
243. Lees Hall
244. Hallowes
245. Renishaw Park
246. Lindrick
247. Stanedge
248. Chesterfield
249. Tapton Park
250. Matlock
251. Sherwood Forest

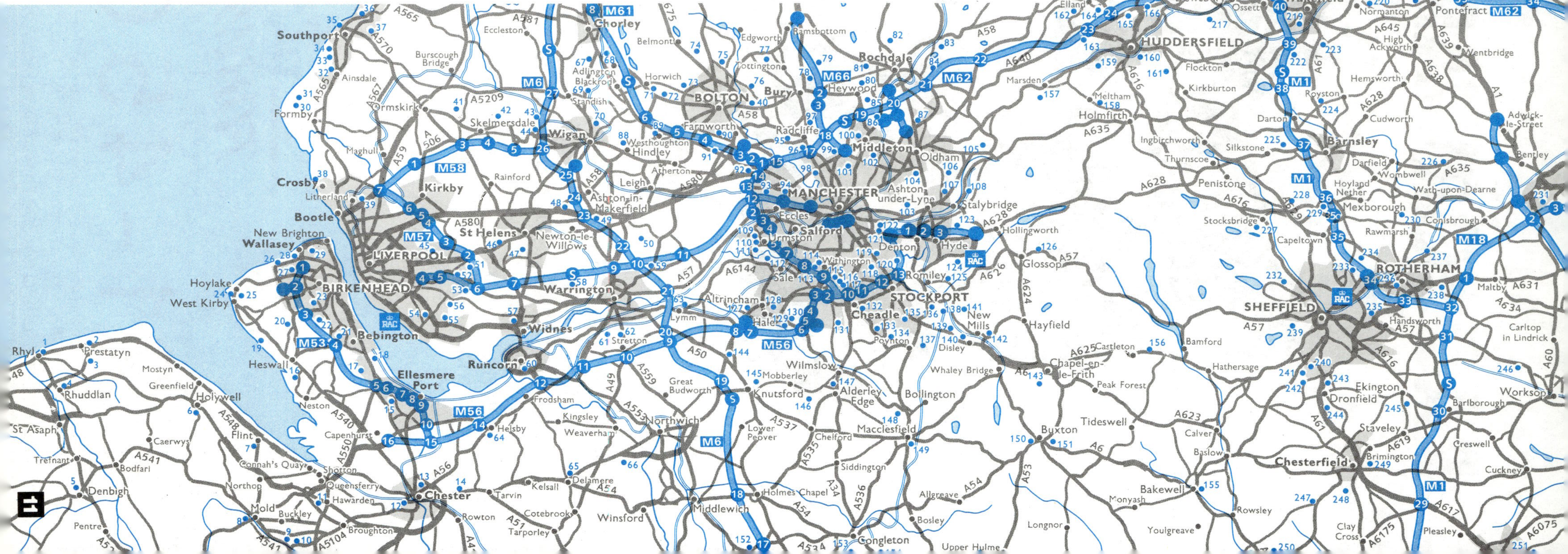

ENGLAND

AVON

BATH
(0225) 25182
An attractive 18-hole downland course (6369 yards, SSS 70). Founded in 1880. Visitors are welcome on both weekdays and weekends providing the course is free, but you must have a handicap certificate. Green fees are £12 on weekdays, £15 at weekends and Bank Holidays. Meals every day except Thursday, when snacks only are available. Local interests include the historic city of Bath, and the American Museum with its fine collection of patchwork quilts.
Location
Sham Castle, North Road, Bath, Avon BA2 6JG
Situated 1½ miles south east of the city. Turn off the A36 Bath-Warminster road, into North Road. The clubhouse is about half a mile on the left.

RAC recommended hotels
Francis ★★★★ (0225) 424257 Traditional hotel built of Bath stone. Looking onto Queen's Square.
Hilton National ★★★★ (0225) 463411 Large purpose-built hotel offering modern accomodation. Near to city centre.
Royal Crescent ★★★★ (0225) 319090 This luxuriously furnished hotel is located at the centre of the famous Georgian Royal Crescent.
Dukes ★★★ (0225) 463512 A four-storey, gracious Georgian town house in a wide boulevard in the city centre.
Lansdown Grove ★★★ (0225) 448092 Elegant Georgian hotel set in own grounds on hilltop overlooking Bath.
Pratt's ★★★ (0225) 460441 Georgian stone terrace hotel in quiet area. Once home of Sir Walter Scott.
Priory ★★★ (0225) 331922 Georgian building of Bath stone in country house style. Lovely garden. Swimming pool.
Redcar ★★★ (0225) 469151 Bath stone terrace hotel in quiet area. Easy walk to town centre.
Royal York ★★★ (0225) 461541 Bath stone terrace hotel on corner site. Near city centre.
Berni Royal ★★ (0225) 463134 Four-storey Victorian building close to city centre and railway station.
Fernley ★★ (0225) 461603 Privately-owned building of historic interest. Two minutes from Pump Room.
Gainsborough ★★ (0225) 311380 In a residential area about a mile from the city centre, this mellow Bath stone Victorian house has a large, attractive garden.
Old Mill ★★ (0225) 858476 Small riverside hotel in attractive surroundings. Off A4 in outskirts.
Ashley Villa ★ (0225) 423645 Small villa hotel run by proprietor. Off the A4. Swimming pool.
Bath Spa (0225) 444424 Luxury hotel in newly refurbished historic building.

BRISTOL & CLIFTON
(0272) 393474
An 18-hole parkland course (6270 yards, SSS 70). Provided you have a handicap certificate, visitors are welcome, but telephone ahead for weekend games. Green fees are £15 on weekdays, £20 at weekends. Catering is available. Local interests include Bristol Zoo and the magnificent Clifton Suspension Bridge.
Location
Beggar Bush Lane, Failand, Bristol, AvonBS8 3TH
From the M5, junction 19, take the A369 towards Bristol for 4 miles. At the traffic lights turn right into Beggar Bush Lane and you will find the club after about 1½ miles.

RAC recommended hotel
Redwood Lodge and Country Club ★★★
(0272) 393901 A hotel and country club with modern accommodation close to Clifton Suspension Bridge. Indoor and outdoor swimming pools, tennis, squash, sauna, solarium, gymnasium and billiards.

CHIPPING SODBURY
(0454) 319042
A particularly attractive downland course situated close to Bristol. There are actually two courses; an 18-hole (6912 yards, SSS 73), and a 9-hole (6194 yards, SSS 69). Visitors are welcome, but after midday at weekends when a handicap certificate is required. Green fees are £11 on weekdays, £15 at weekends and Bank Holidays, but there are reductions if you are with a member. Meals are available.
Location
Chipping Sodbury, Bristol, Avon BS16 6PU
Take the Wickwar Road from Chipping Sodbury (nearest motorway exits: M4, junction 18; M5, junction 14) and turn first right, signposted Horton.

CLEVEDON
(0272) 874057
An 18-hole parkland course in a splendid location overlooking the Severn estuary (5887 yards, SSS 69). Visitors are welcome every day except Monday and Wednesday, but you must be playing members of a golf club and hold a handicap certificate. Green fees are £12 on weekdays, £15 at weekends and Bank Holidays. There are full catering facilities every day, apart from Tuesday when sandwiches only are served.
Location
Castle Road, Clevedon, Avon BS21 7AA
From the M5 (junction 19) take the A369 and the B3124 signposted Clevedon. As you approach Clevedon turn right into Hodly Lane, go to the top of the hill before turning right into a private lane leading to the golf club.

RAC recommended hotels
Walton Park ★★★ (0272) 874253 A converted house with pleasant gardens and fine views of the Bristol Channel.
Highcliffe ★★ (0272) 873250 A charming Victorian stone building overlooking the Severn estuary.

ENTRY HILL
(0225) 834248
A 9-hole public golf course (4206 yards, SSS 61). Visitors of all levels are welcome daily but it is necessary to book at weekends. Green fees £3.30 for 9 holes, £5.30 for 18 holes. Light refreshments are available. Close to historic city of Bath.
Location
Entry Hill, Bath, Avon BA2 5NA
South of Bath on the A367.

RAC recommended hotels see Bath

FILTON
(0272) 694169
An 18-hole parkland course (6277 yards, SSS 70). Visitors are welcome on weekdays provided you have a handicap certificate, and at weekends with a member. Green fees are £11 on weekdays. Lunch and dinner are available by arrangement. The club is close to the Clifton Suspension Bridge and Bristol Zoo.
Location
Golf Course Lane, Filton, Bristol, Avon BS12 7QS
From the Almondsbury Interchange (M4/M5) take the A38 towards Bristol. After 2 miles turn right at a roundabout and right again at the traffic lights.

RAC recommended hotels in Bristol.
Crest Hotel ★★★★ (0272) 564242 Purpose-built modern hotel offering conference facilities. Convenient for M32. Indoor swimming pool, sauna, solarium, gymnasium.
Grand ★★★★ (0272) 291645 Large traditional Victorian hotel with modern facilities. Near city centre.
Holiday Inn ★★★★ (0272) 294281 Purpose-built modern hotel in pleasant location. Indoor swimming pool, sauna, solarium, gymnasium.
Hilton International ★★★★ (0272) 260041 Purpose-built six-storey modern hotel with spacious public areas. Convenient for station. Indoor swimming pool, sauna, solarium, gymnasium.
Avon Gorge ★★★ (0272) 738995 A traditional large Victorian terraced hotel overlooking Gorge.
Henbury Lodge ★★★ (0272) 502615 A gracious white-painted, half Georgian house in a quiet residential suburb. Converted stable block with sauna, solarium, gymnasium.
St Vincent's Rocks ★★★ (0272) 739251 Modernised Regency building with fine views of Clifton Suspension Bridge.
Stakis Leisure Lodge ★★★ (0454) 201144 Modern low-built hotel to north of the city, convenient for the motorway network. Indoor swimming pool, sauna, solarium, gymnasium.
Clifton ★★ (0272) 736882 Large stone-built terrace residence set in attractive part of Clifton.
Parkside ★★ (0272) 711461 Stone-built, part Georgian building with an attractive conservatory in residential suburb. Separate night club. Billiards.
Rodney ★★ (0272) 735422 Elegant, recently refurbished, Georgian terrace house in Clifton village.
Seeley's ★★ (0272) 738544 Terraced houses in Clifton converted to privately-owned hotel. Sauna, solarium.
Westbury Park ★ (0272) 620465 Two-storey building with garden in a residential area on the edge of Downs.

FOSSEWAY
(0761) 412214
A 9-hole parkland course (4246 yards, SSS 61). Visitors of all levels of playing ability are welcome any time except Sunday morning, and Wednesday after 5pm. Green fees on application. A full a la carte restaurant, Table d'hote and bar meals are available in the Country Club. There is an abundance of local interest including Cheddar Gorge, Wookey Hole and Longleat.
Location
Charlton Lane, Midsomer Norton, Bath, Somerset

BA3 4BD
Take the A367 south of Bath, through Radstock and turn left at the Charlton roundabout.

RAC recommended hotel
Centurion ★★★ (0761) 417711 A modern hotel built in farmhouse style in the grounds of the Country Club. Other facilities include indoor swimming pool, squash, sauna and billiards.

HENBURY
(0272) 500044
A very mature 18-hole parkland course partly set in the beautiful Blaise Castle woods (6039 yards, SSS 70). Visitors with a handicap certificate are welcome on weekdays. Green fees on application. A full range of catering facilities is available. Close to Bristol and its surrounding countryside.
Location
Henbury Hill, Westbury-on-Trym, Bristol, BS10 7QB
Turn off the M5 (junction 17). Henbury is in the suburb of Westbury-on-Trym about 3 miles N of Bristol.

RAC recommended hotel
Henbury Lodge ★★★ (0272) 502615 A gracious, part Georgian house in a quiet residential suburb. Converted stable block with sauna, solarium and gymnasium.

KNOWLE
(0272) 770660
An 18-hole parkland course (6016 yards, SSS 70). Visitors are welcome both on weekdays and at weekends, but a handicap certificate is required. Green fees are £12 on weekdays, £15 at weekends. Lunch is available daily and evening meals by arrangement. Many interesting places to visit in the surrounding Bristol area.
Location
Fairway, Brislington, Bristol, BS4 5DF
Take the A4 south of Bristol city centre for about 3 miles to the junction with West Town Lane. The entrance to the club is 800 yards along on the left.

RAC recommended hotels in Bristol see Filton

LONG ASHTON
(0272) 392316
An attractive, undulating 18-hole moorland/parkland course (6051 yards, SSS 70). Visitors are welcome but you must have an official club handicap. Green fees are £15 on weekdays, £18 at weekends. Full catering facilities are available daily until 6pm with evening meals by arrangement. The club is close to Bristol and the Clifton Suspension Bridge.
Location
Long Ashton, Bristol, Avon BS18 9DW
Leave the M5 at junction 19 and take the A369 to Bristol. Turn right onto the B3129 at the traffic lights and then left onto the B3128. The club is about half a mile on the right.

RAC recommended hotels see Bristol and Clifton

LANSDOWN
(0225) 22138
An 18-hole parkland course adjacent to Bath Racecourse (6267 yards, SSS 70). Visitors with a handicap certificate are welcome at all times, but the course closes on racing days. Green fees £12 on weekdays, £16 at weekends and Bank Holidays. Catering facilities are available.
Location
Lansdown, Bath, Avon BA1 9BT
Turn off the M4 (junction 18) onto the A46 towards Bath. The golf course is next to Bath Racecourse.

RAC recommended hotels see Bath

MANGOTSFIELD
(0272) 565501
An easy 18-hole hilly meadowland course (5337 yards, SSS 66). Visitors of all levels are welcome. Green fees £6 on weekdays, £9 at weekends. Meals are served.
Location
Carsons Road, Mangotsfield, Bristol, Avon BS17 3LW.
Take the M32 and leave at the junction for Filton and Downend. Follow the sign for Downend and Mangotsfield.

RAC recommended hotels, see Filton

SALTFORD
(022 17) 3220
An 18-hole meadowland course with easy walking (6081 yards, SSS 69). Visitors are welcome but you must have a handicap certificate. Green fees £12 on weekdays, £14 at weekends. Meals are served daily.
Location
Golf Club Lane, Saltford, Bristol, Avon BS18 3AA
The club is off the A4 between Bath and Bristol.

RAC recommended hotels see Bath

SHIREHAMPTON PARK
(0272) 822083
An attractive 18-hole undulating parkland course (5493 yards, SSS 67) with views over the Portway beside the River Avon. Visitors are welcome on weekdays, but only with a member at weekends. A handicap certificate is required. Green fees are £13 per round/day (£8 with member). Snacks and lunches are always available and evening meals by arrangement with the Stewardess (823059). Places of local interest include the SS Great Britain.
Location
Park Hill, Shirehampton, Bristol, Avon BS11 0UL
Turn off the M5 at junction 18 onto the B4018 through the village of Shirehampton. The club is about 1½ miles from the junction.

RAC recommended hotels see Filton

TRACY PARK GOLF AND CRICKET CLUB
(027 582) 2251
A 9-hole and an 18-hole parkland course with fine views of the Cotswolds (6800 yards, SSS 73 & 5200 yards). Visitors are welcome, but a preliminary telephone arrangement is recommended. Green fees are £12 per round, £16 per day (£8 with member) on weekdays, £15 per round and £22 per day (£10 with member) at weekends. Lunch, dinner and bar snacks are available in the clubhouse, which dates back to 1600. Other facilities include squash, tennis, outdoor swimming pool, croquet and snooker. Close to Bath.
Location
Bath Road, Wick, Bristol, Avon BS15 5RN
Turn off M4 at junction 18 and turn south on A46 for 4 miles. Then turn right onto the A420 for 2 miles.

RAC recommended hotels see Bath

WESTON-SUPER-MARE
(0934) 621360
An 18-hole seaside course (6225 yards, SSS 70). Visitors welcome except on competition days. Green fees £9 on weekdays, £12 at weekends. Snacks and meals are available daily.
Location
Uphill Road North, Weston-super-Mare, Avon BS23 4NQ
Take the M5 or A370 from Bristol.

RAC recommended hotels
Berni Royal ★★★ (0934) 623601 Regency-style hotel in attractive garden. Overlooks the promenade.
Commodore ★★★ (0934) 415778 Traditional hotel by unspoilt bay.
Grand Atlantic ★★★ (0934) 626543 A large conventional stone-built hotel in dominant position overlooking the estuary. Fine views.
Rozel ★★★ (0934) 415268 Bay-windowed Victorian building well positioned at western end of town with good views of bay. Swimming pool.
Albert ★★ (0934) 621363 Family-run hotel overlooking bay. Near to promenade and town centre.
Arosfa ★★ (0934) 419523 Centrally situated four-storey white building, close to shops and sea front.
Beachlands ★★ (0934) 621401 Substantial former residence extended into hotel. Set in pleasant well-cared-for garden.
Dauncey's ★★ (0934) 621144 Family-run, terraced hotel with sea views and pleasant gardens.
Dorville ★★ (0934) 621522 Spacious modern hotel offering fine sea views. Near town centre. Billiards.
Old Manor ★★ (0934) 515143 Charming farmhouse in village, now a family-run hotel. Sauna, solarium, gymnasium, billiards.
Queenswood ★★ (0934) 416141 Attractive privately-run hotel with modern facilities and sea views.

WORLEBURY
(0934) 623214
An 18-hole seaside meadowland course with easy walking (5945 yards, SSS 68). Visitors are welcome on weekdays provided you have a handicap certificate. Green fees £7.50 on weekdays (£4.50 with a member), £17 at weekends (£7 with a member). Snacks, lunch and evening meals are available. Places of interest locally include the Cheddar Caves and Wookey Hole.
Location
Worlebury, Weston-super-Mare, Avon BS22 9SX.
Off the A370 from Bristol about 2½ miles from Weston-super-Mare.

RAC recommended hotels see Weston-super-Mare

BEDFORDSHIRE

BEADLOW MANOR
(0525) 60800
Two 18-hole parkland courses (3021 yards, SSS 35 and 6238 yards, SSS 70). Visitors are welcome on weekdays and at weekends provided you have a handicap certificate. Green fees are £12 per round, £17 per day weekdays; £15 per round, £20 per day weekends. There are catering facilities in the golf bar from 7am to 6pm, with a restaurant on site after 6pm.
Location
Beadlow, Shefford, Beds. SG17 5PH
Take the A6 from Luton towards Bedford, turn off onto the A507 at Clophill towards Shefford. The golf club is about 1 mile down the road before Shefford.

RAC recommended hotel
Beadlow Manor ★★ (0525) 60800 A single storey extension to golf and country club. Bars and restaurant in the club. Golf, putting, sauna, solarium, gymnasium.

BEDFORD & COUNTY
(0234) 52617
An 18-hole parkland course (6347 yards, SSS 70). A pleasant course overlooking Bedford and surrounding countryside. Visitors with a handicap certificate are welcome on weekdays, although booking is advisable, and with a member at weekends. Green fees are £15. Party catering is available at all times but please telephone in advance. Local places of interest include the John Bunyon Centre and Woburn Abbey.
Location
Green Lane, Clapham, Beds. MK41 6ET
Turn off the A6 north of Bedford before you reach Clapham village.

RAC recommended hotel
Woodlands Manor ★★★ (0234) 63281 A late Victorian manor house in several acres of woods and gardens. 2½ miles north of Bedford.

BEDFORDSHIRE
(0234) 261669
An 18-hole parkland course (6172 yards, SSS 69). Visitors with a handicap certificate are welcome on weekdays. Green fees are £15 per day. Lunch is served every day. Local places of interest include Elstow Abbey, the John Bunyon Centre and the Higgins Art Gallery.
Location
Bromham Road, Biddenham, Bedford MK40 4AF
Take the A428 north west out of Bedford. The golf club is about 1½ miles from the town centre.

RAC recommended hotels
Barns ★★★ (0234) 270044 A hotel developed from a 17th century manor house with extensions and an impressive 13th century tythe barn, overlooking the Great Ouse river. Sauna and solarium.
Bedford Moat House ★★★ (0234) 55131 A modern hotel on the bank of a river, overlooking the market square. Sauna and solarium.
Woodlands Manor ★★★ (0234) 63281 A late Victorian manor house in several acres of wood and gardens. 2½ miles north of the town.
Bedford Swan ★★ (0234) 46565 A historic hotel standing on the riverside, near the town centre. Indoor swimming pool, sauna, solarium and gymnasium.
De Parys ★★ (0234) 52121 Two converted adjoining large Victorian residences in the suburbs.
Knife and Cleaver ★★ (0234) 740387 A country inn with a charming conservatory restaurant and bedrooms in a modern bungalow extension.
Queen's Head ★★ (0234) 272822 Modernised and extended village inn on the A6. 5 miles north of the city.
Embankment ★ (0234) 261332 A Victorian residence in mock Tudor style, located in a residential suburb overlooking the river.

DUNSTABLE DOWNS
(0582) 604472
An 18-hole downland course (6184 yards, SSS 70) laid out on high ground, with remarkably extensive views. Visitors are welcome on weekdays if they are a member of a recognised club. Green fees on application. Full catering facilities are available every day except Monday. The club is close to Whipsnade Zoo and Dunstable Downs.
Location
Whipsnade Road, Dunstable, Beds. LU6 2NB.
Take the Whipsnade road out of Dunstable and turn left at the third mini-roundabout.

RAC recommended hotel.
Highwayman ★★ (0582) 601122 A two-storey modern hotel conveniently situated on the main A5.

GRIFFIN
(0582) 415573
A 9-hole meadowland course (5354 yards, SSS 66). Visitors are welcome on weekdays and with a member at weekends and Bank Holidays. Green fees are £3.50 on weekdays and £5.50 at weekends and Bank Holidays. Catering is by arrangement. Local places of interest include Whipsnade Zoo, Woburn Abbey and Luton Hoo (Faberge Collection).
Location
c/o 3 Hillcrest Avenue, Luton, LV2 7AB.
Leave M1 at junction 11 and take the A505 to Dunstable. The club is 3 miles west of Luton between Dunstable and Ivinghoe.

RAC recommended hotel
Luton Crest ★★★ (0582) 575955 A modern purpose-built hotel adjacent to junction 11 of M1.

IVINGHOE
(0296) 668881
A 9-hole meadowland course (4508 yards, SSS 62) with easy walking. Visitors of all playing abilities welcome after 9am on weekdays and 8am at weekends. Green fees are £4.50 on weekdays and £6 at weekends. Lunch is served every day except Monday. The club is close to Ashridge Park (NT) and Tring Zoological Museum.
Location
Wellcroft, Ivinghoe, Nr Leighton Buzzard, Beds. LU7 9EP
Take the B489 from Dunstable or the B488 from Tring to Ivinghoe. The club is in Ivinghoe village, 4 miles from Tring and 6 miles from Dunstable.

RAC recommended hotel
Rose & Crown ★★★ (0442) 824071 A 20th century inn built in Tudor style in nearby Tring.

JOHN O'GAUNT
(0767) 260360
Two undulating parkland courses; the John O'Gaunt (18 holes, 6513 yards, SSS 71) and the shorter Carthagena (18 holes, 5869 yards, SSS 68). Visitors with a handicap certificate are welcome but you are advised to contact the club beforehand. Green fees are £20 per day (£10 with a member) on weekdays and £30 per day (£15 with a member) at weekends. Meals are served every day. Places of interest locally include the Cambridge colleges, Wimpole Hall (NT) and the Old Warden Air Museum.
Location
Sutton Park, Sandy, Beds. SG19 2LY
Turn off the A1 at Biggleswade on to the A6001 then on to the B1040 towards Potton. The club is on the right just past John O'Gaunts Hill.

LEIGHTON BUZZARD
(0525) 373811/2
An 18-hole parkland course (5454 yards, SSS 68). Easy walking. Visitors with a handicap certificate are welcome on weekdays except Tuesday. Green fees are £15 per round or £20 per day (£10 with a member). Catering is available. The club is close to Whipsnade Zoo and Woburn Abbey.
Location
Plantation Road, Leighton Buzzard, Beds. LU7 7JF
Turn off the A418 1 mile north from Leighton Buzzard and take left fork at the Stag Inn.

RAC recommended hotel
Swan ★★★ (0525) 370444 A carefully restored 18th century posting house in the centre of the market town of Leighton Buzzard.

MILLBROOK
(0525) 404683
An 18-hole course (6473 yards, SSS 72). The course is hilly with some water hazards. Visitors of all playing abilities are welcome on any day except Thursday. Green fees are £12 or £8 if accompanied by a member. Juniors are half price. Bar snacks are available. Local interests include Woburn Abbey.
Location
Millbrook, Ampthill, Bedford. MK45 2GB
Turn off M1 at junction 12 onto A5120 through Flitwick, then take A507 to Millbrook. The club is in Millbrook village.

RAC recommended hotel
Flitwick Manor C/H ★★★ (0525) 712242 A Substantial 18th century house attractively set in a 50 acre park. Putting, tennis, and fishing.

MOWSBURY
(0234) 771041
An 18-hole municipal parkland course (6514 yards, SSS 71). Visitors of all playing abilities are welcome. Green fees on application. Snacks and meals are available.
Location
Cleat Hill, Kimbolton Road, Bedford. MK41 8DQ
Take the B660 out of Bedford towards Kimbolton. The golf course is about 2 miles north of the city centre just past Cleat Hill.

RAC recommended hotels see Bedfordshire

SOUTH BEDFORDSHIRE
(0582) 591500
An 18-hole undulating downland course (6342 yards, SSS 70) and a 9-hole course (2490 yards, SSS 64). Visitors are welcome on weekdays but it is advisable to telephone ahead. A handicap certificate is required. Green fees are £14 per round (£10 with a member), £20 per day (£12 with a member). Snacks are available daily and a la carte lunch and dinner by arrangement. Places of interest locally include Luton Hoo (Faberge Collection) and Woburn Abbey.
Location
Warden Hill Road, Luton, Beds.
Take the A6 north from Luton. Warden Hill is on the right, about 2½ miles from the centre of Luton.

RAC recommended hotels
Strathmore Thistle ★★★★ (0582) 34199 A modern purpose-built centre of town hotel adjacent to the shopping centre.
Chiltern ★★★ (0582) 575911 Near the M1, a large wooden hotel with some executive rooms.
Luton Crest ★★★ (0582) 575955 A modern purpose-built hotel adjacent to junction 11 of the M1.
Red Lion ★★★ (0582) 413881 A refurbished town-centre inn with a rear courtyard. Near the Arndale Centre.
Leaside ★★ (0582) 417643 A small, owner managed hotel close to the town-centre. Billiards.

STOCKWOOD PARK
(0582) 23612
An 18- hole meadowland municipal course (5964 yards, SSS 69). Visitors of all playing abilities are welcome at any time. Green fees are £3.40 on weekdays and £5.10 at weekends. Lunch is served daily. Local places of interest include the nearby Arts and Crafts Museum.
Location
Stockwood Park, London Road, Luton, Beds.
Turn off the M1 at junction 10, then left towards the town centre, and left at the first set of traffic lights into Stockwood Park.
Recommended RAC hotels
Luton hotels see South Bedfordshire.

TILSWORTH
(0525) 210722
A 9-hole moorland course (5443 yards, SSS 67). Visitors of all playing levels are welcome at any time except on Sunday between 7.30am and 11.30am. Green fees are £3.75 per 18 holes on weekdays and £4.75 per 18 holes at weekends. Hot and cold home-cooked food is served every lunchtime and on Thursday, Friday and Saturday evenings. The club is close to Whipsnade Zoo and Woburn Abbey and Park.
Location
Dunstable Road, Tilsworth, Leighton Buzzard, Beds.
Take the A5 north of Dunstable to Tilsworth.

Recommended RAC hotels see Leighton Buzzard.

WYBOSTON LAKES
(0480) 212501
An 18-hole parkland course around lakes and the River Ouse (5721 yards, SSS 69). Visitors of all playing abilities are welcome every day. Green fees are £7 per 18 holes and £3.50 per 9 holes on weekdays; £10 per 18 holes and £5 per 9 holes at weekends. Full catering facilities are available. Places of interest locally include Ely Cathedral. There is also a nature trail on site.
Location
Wyboston Lakes, Wyboston, Beds. MK44 3AL.
The club is off the A1 and A45 junction south of St Neots.

RAC recommended Hotel
Wyboston Lakes ★★★ (0480) 219949 A modern motel by the golf and leisure park alongside the River Ouse, 3 miles south of the town. Putting and fishing.

BERKSHIRE

BEARWOOD
(0734)760060
An 18-hole parkland course (2814 yards, SSS 67). There is also a 9-hole pitch and putt course. Visitors with a handicap certificate are welcome on weekdays before 4pm, but must be accompanied by a member at weekends. Limited catering facilities are available.
Location
Mole Road, Sindlesham, RG11 5DB
Leave the M4 at junction 10 for the B3030. The club is about 1½ miles north of Arborfield Cross.

BERKSHIRE
(0990) 21495
Two splendid 18-hole heathland courses with glorious tree-lined fairways; the 'Red' e (6356 yards, SSS 70) and the 'Blue' (6258 yards, SSS 70). Visitors are welcome but it is necessary to apply to the Secretary first. Green fees are £37 per day or £24 per round. Lunch is available. Close to Windsor Castle.
Location
Swinley Road, Ascot, Berks. SL5 8AY
If travelling from the SW, leave the M3 at junction 3 or the M4 at junction 10. The club is situated on the A330 about half a mille north of Ascot.

RAC recommended hotels
Berystede ★★★★ (0344) 23311 A large luxury mansion in woodland setting. Swimming pool and putting.
Royal Berkshire C/H ★★★★ (0990) 23322 A Queen Anne mansion with later additions, in 15 acres of lawns, gardens and woods. Indoor swimming pool, putting, tennis, squash and sauna.

CALCOT PARK
(0734) 427124
An 18-hole parkland course presenting many interesting challenges (6283 yards, SSS 70). Visitors are welcome on weekdays only except Bank Holidays. Green fees on application. Lunch is served daily except Monday.
Location
Bath Road, Calcot, Reading, RG3 5RN
From junction 12 on the M4 take the A4 to Reading. The club is about 1 mile on the left.

RAC recommended hotels
Caversham ★★★★ (0734) 391818 A well designed modern hotel with landscaped gardens and terraces, beside the river. Indoor swimming pool, sauna, solarium, gymnaseum, and snooker.
Ramada ★★★★ (0734) 586222 A purpose-built modern town centre hotel. Indoor swimming pool, sauna solarium and gymnasium.
Reading Moat House ★★★★ (0734) 351035 A modern hotel based on a 19th century mill beside the River Loddon 4 miles south east of Reading. Fishing, sauna, solarium and gymnasium.
Post House ★★★ (0734) 875485 A modern red brick hotel constructed around a central garden. Indoor swimming pool, sauna, solarium and gymnasium.
Rainbow Corner ★★★ (0734) 588140 Four Victorian terrace houses make up this family-run hotel, 100 yards from the river and not far from the city centre.
George ★★ (0734) 573445 Centrally placed former coaching inn with a charming Georgian cobbled courtyard.
Ship ★★ (0734) 583445 Four-storey hotel with Georgian features situated in the town centre.

DOWNSHIRE
(0344) 424066
A municipal 18-hole parkland course with easy walking (6382 yards, SSS 70). Visitors are welcome daily but it is advisable to book in advance. Green fees are £6.50 on weekdays and weekends. Bar and catering facilities are available. The club is close to the Sports Centre in Bracknell.
Location
Easthampstead Park, Wokingham, Berks. RG11 3DH
Take the M3 or M4 to Bracknell and then follow the signs to Easthampstead Park. The course is 2 miles from Bracknell.

RAC recommended hotel
Hilton National ★★★★ (0344) 424801 A large modern hotel on the edge of woodland. Indoor swimming pool, sauna.

EAST BERKSHIRE
(0344) 772041)
A very attractive 18-hole heathland course (6315 yards, SSS 70). A testing course but with easy walking. Visitors with a handicap certificate are welcome during the week. Green fees are £20 on weekdays or £8 with a member. Lunch and snacks are available every day. Local attractions include Windsor Castle.
Location
Ravenswood Avenue, Crowthorne, Berks. RG11 6BD
Take the M3 or M4 to Bracknell. Then the A3095 south west out of Bracknell and turn off on the right onto the B3348.

RAC recommended hotel
Waterloo ★★★ (0344) 777711 In a tree-lined corner of the village, this period hotel has a modern extension.

GORING & STREATLEY
(0491) 873229
An 18-hole park and moorland course (6255 yards, SSS 70). Visitors are welcome Monday to Friday but only with a member at weekends. Green fees are £16 per day. The restaurant with full a la carte and table d'hote menu is open daily. Places of local interest include Basildon Park (NT).
Location
Rectory Road, Streatley-on-Thames, Berks. RG8 9QA
The club is situated 10 miles north west of Reading, just past Goring.

RAC recommended hotel
Swan Diplomat ★★★ (0491) 873737 A lovely 300 year old building right beside the Thames, this hotel has extensive riverside terraces, lawns and gardens. Indoor swimming pool, fishing, sauna, solarium and gymnasium.

HAWTHORN HILL
(0626) 75588
An undulating 18-hole parkland course (6212 yards, SSS 70). Visitors are welcome at all times. Green fees on application. Bar snacks, lunch and dinners are available. Places of local interest include Windsor Castle, the Stanley Spencer Gallery at Cookham and Boulters Lock.
Location
Drift Road, Nr Maidenhead, Berks.
Leave the M4 at exit 8/9 and take the A330 towards Bracknell for 2½ miles. The course is on the right, 1 mile from the ICI Research Centre at Jealotts Hill.

HURST
(0734) 345143
A 9-hole public course (3013 yards, SSS70 men; 2906 yards, SSS 72 ladies). Visitors of all abilities are welcome at any time. Green fees £3.25. Bar snacks are available daily. The course is within a leisure park and close to Dinton Pastures Country Park.
Location
Sandford Lane, Hurst, Wokingham
From the A329 west of Wokingham take the B3030 north. The course is 3 miles from Wokingham and 5 miles from Reading.

LAVENDER PARK
(0344) 884074
A 9-hole public golf centre with a parkland course (1104 yards, SSS 27). The centre includes a driving range which is floodlit until 10pm. Visitors of all playing abilities are welcome. Green fees £1.20 weekdays and £1.40 at weekends; £2.10 per round weekdays and £2.25 at weekends. Full catering facilities are available. The centre is close to Windsor Great Park and Safari Park.
Location
Swinley Road, Ascot, SL5 8BD
The centre is 3½ miles south west of Ascot on the A332.

RAC recommended hotels
See Berkshire.

MAIDENHEAD
(0628) 24693
An attractive 18-hole parkland course with easy walking (6360 yards, SSS 70). Visitors are welcome before midday Monday to Friday but it is advisable to telephone first. A handicap certificate is required. Green fees £20 per round or day. Light lunches and tea, and full lunches and dinners by arrangement, are available daily except Monday. Local attractions include Windsor Castle and Great Park.
Location
Shoppenhangers Road, Maidenhead, Berks. SL6 2PZ
Take the A4 or M4 to Maidenhead. The club is off the A308, adjacent to Maidenhead station.

RAC recommended hotels
Crest ★★★★ (0628) 23444 A modern hotel with restaurant and conference facilities in 13th century manor house, Shoppenhangers Manor. Swimming pool, squash, sauna, solarium, gymnasium and billiards.
Fredrick's ★★★★ (0628) 35934 A former private house with modern extension in 2 acres of attractive landscaped gardens.
Monkey Island ★★★★ (0628) 23400 This famous hotel in an extended 18th century 'temple', is an island in the Thames reached by a footbridge. Fishing.
Boulter's Lock ★★★ (0628) 21291 Built as a mill in 1726, an enchanting lock on the Thames. All bedrooms are in the riverside cottages.
Taplow House ★★★ (0628) 70056 A former Georgian manor house in 6 acres of attractive grounds. Putting and billiards.
Norfolk House ★★ (0628) 23687 A Georgian listed building in 3 acres of wooded grounds close to the river on the A4. Swimming pool.
Thames ★★ (0628) 28721 A Victorian red-brick building overlooking the Thames near Maidenhead Bridge.

NEWBURY & CROOKHAM
(0635) 40035
An 18-hole parkland course (5880 yards, SSS 68). Visitors who are members of a golf club are welcome on weekdays and at weekends with a member. Green fees £15, or £7.50 with a member. Lunch, snacks and evening meals are available. Local places of interest include Littlecote House, Highclere Castle, and locks on the Avon and Kennet Canal.
Location
Bury's Bank Road, Greenham, Newbury, Berks. RG15 8BZ
The club is 2 miles south east of Newbury off the A34.

RAC recommended hotels
Foley Lodge ★★★★ (0635) 528770 A Victorian hunting lodge, modernised and extended, in

landscaped grounds off the B4000 between Newbury and Hungerford. Indoor swimming pool, solarium and snooker.
Regency Park ★★★★ (0635) 71555 A four-storey mansion with a large modern extension giving spacious and tastefully furnished accommodation. Set in 5 acres of parkland.
Chequers ★★★ (0635) 38000 A former three-storey coaching inn with a later wing,near the town centre.
Millwater Grange ★★ (0635) 528838 A charming two-storey Georgian house in lovely grounds with the river running by. Fishing.
Enborne Grange ★★ (0635) 40046 A family-run hotel converted from a private house in a 5 acres of attractive gardens.
Hare and Hounds ★★ (0635) 521152 Conveniently situated on the A4 west of the town, a red-brick 17th century former coaching inn.

READING
(0734) 472909
An 18-hole meadowland course (6212 yards, SSS 70). Visitors may play from Monday to Thursday, unless accompanied by a member, when they are welcome any time. Green fees £19 per day or round. Full catering facilities are available daily except Monday. The surrounding countryside holds many attractions.
Location
17 Kidmore End Road, Emmer Green, Reading, Berks. RG4 9SG.
Emmer Green is 2 miles north of Reading off Peppard Road (B481).

RAC recommended hotels
See Calcott Park.

ROYAL ASCOT
(0990) 25175
An 18-hole heathland/moorland course in the centre of Royal Ascot Racecourse (5653 yards, SSS 67). Visitors are welcome on weekdays. Green fees on application. Catering is available by arrangement. Close to Windsor Castle and Great Park.
Location
Winkfield Road, Ascot, Berks. SL5 7LJ
Leave the M3 at junction 3 and take the A322 north through Bagshott to Ascot.

RAC recommended hotels
See Berkshire.

THE ROYAL HOUSEHOLD
(071) 930 4832
A 9-hole parkland course (4560 yards, SSS 62). Visitors can play strictly by invitation of a member. The course is set in the Home Park, Windsor Castle.
Location
Contact Buckingham Palace, London SW1

SONNING
(0734) 693332
A good 18-hole parkland course with wide fairways (6345 yards, SSS 70). Visitors with a handicap certificate are welcome on weekdays. Green fees on application. Full catering facilities are available. The club is close to Windsor Great Park and the River Thames.
Location
Duffield Road, Sonning-on-Thames, Berks. RG4 0GJ
Take the A4 north from Reading to Maidenhead, the course is 1½ miles out of Reading.

RAC recommended hotel
Great House at Sonning ★★★ (0734) 692277 A former 16th century inn with converted cottages. Beautiful riverside gardens.

SUNNINGDALE
(0990) 21681
Two splendid heather and pine courses with gorse bordering the fairways; the 'Old' (6586 yards, SSS 71) and the 'New' (6676 yards, SSS 71). Visitors are welcome on weekdays by prior arrangement. A handicap certificate is required. Green fees £47 per day. Full catering facilities are available. Local attractions include Ascot, Virginia Water and Windsor Castle.
Location
Ridgemount Road, Sunningdale, Ascot, Berks. SL5 9RR
Off the A30, about 28 miles west of London. Leave the M3 at junction 3 or the M4 at junction 10. If you are coming from the north, both the A332 and the A330 pass through nearby Ascot. The club is 50 yards west of Sunningdale Station.

RAC recommended hotels
See Berkshire.

SUNNINGDALE LADIES'
(0990) 20507)
An 18-hole heathland course (3622 yards, SSS 60). Visitors are welcome but it is advisable to telephone first. Green fees £11 ladies, £14 men weekdays; £13 ladies, £16 men weekends and Bank Holidays. Lunch and tea is provided daily except Sunday.
Location
Cross Road, Sunningdale, Berks. SL5 9RX
Leave the M3 at junction 3 or the M4 at junction 10. If you are coming from the north, both the A332 and the A330 pass through nearby Ascot. The club is the second turning on the left on the A30 going west from Sunningdale level crossing.

RAC recommended hotel
See Berkshire.

SWINLEY FOREST
(0990) 20197
An outstanding 18-hole heathland course (6011 yards, SSS 69). Visitors with a handicap certificate are welcome but as guests of members only. Green fees on application. Lunch is served daily. Nearby Virginia Water and Windsor Castle are local attractions.
Location
Coronation Road, South Ascot, Berks. SL5 9LE
Take the M3 or M4 to Ascot. Turn S at Ascot Station, through South Ascot village, right into Coronation Road and then take the fourth right to the club. About 1½ miles from Ascot station.

RAC recommended hotels
See Berkshire.

TEMPLE
(062 882) 4795
A fine undulating parkland course, 18 holes (6206 yards, SSS 70). Visitors are welcome on weekdays but you must have a handicap certificate. Green fees £20. Full catering facilities are available except on Monday. The course is close to Henley, Windsor and Cookham.
Location
Henley Road, Hurley, Maidenhead, Berks. SL6 5LH
Leave the M4 at junction 9 and take the A423 Maidenhead-Henley road. The club is about 1 miles east of Hurley.

RAC recommended hotel
Bell ★★★ (062882) 5881 A white-faced, gabled building dating from the 12th century. Large attractive garden.

WEST BERKSHIRE
(048 82) 574
A splendid 18-hole downland course (7053 yards, SSS 74). Visitors of all playing abilities are welcome. Green fees £15 weekdays, £20 weekends. A full catering service is available.
Location
Chaddleworth, Newbury, Berks.
The club is situated just south of the village of Chaddleworth. Leave the M4 at junction 14, take the A338 north towards Wantage and then turn right for 1 mile. Follow the signs to RAF Welford.

WINTER HILL
(062 85) 27613
An 18-hole parkland course with views of the River Thames (6408 yards, SSS 71). Visitors are welcome on weekdays and after noon at weekends by prior arrangement. Green fees £13 for weekdays and £16 at weekends. Full catering facilities are available. Local attractions include Clivedon House (NT) and nearby Marlow.
Location
Grange Lane, Cookham, Maidenhead, Berks. SL6 9RP.
The club is situated 4 miles from Maidenhead via the M4 (junction 9) and then following the signs to Cookham, or 6 miles from Marlow via the M40 (junction 4) and then taking the A404 to Marlow.

RAC recommended hotel
Taplow House ★★★ (0628) 70056 A former Georgian manor house in 6 acres of attractive grounds. Putting, billiards.

BUCKINGHAMSHIRE

ABBEY HILL
(0908) 562408
An 18-hole municipal meadowland course (6193 yards, SSS 69). Visitors of all playing abilities are welcome at any time. Green fees on application. Snacks and meals are available daily. The course is close to the new town of Milton Keynes, and local attractions include Woburn Abbey and Safari Park.
Location
Monks Way, Two Mile Ash, Stony Stratford, Milton Keynes, MK8 8AA
Take the A5 north from Milton Keynes and you will find the club 2 miles south of Stony Stratford.

RAC recommended hotels
Cock ★★ (0908) 567733 A historic former coaching inn, rebuilt in Georgian times and famed in folklore.

ASPLEY GUISE AND WOBURN SANDS
A good 18-hole undulating heathland course (6248 yards, SSS 70). Visitors are welcome on weekdays and with a member at weekends, provided you have a handicap certificate. Green fees are £10 after 1pm and £14 before 1pm. Local attractions include Woburn Abbey and Safari Park, and the nearby shopping centre of Milton Keynes.
Location
West Hill, Aspley Guise, Milton Keynes, MK17 8DX
Turn off the M1 at junction 13 and take the A507 or A421 west and then the A5130 to Woburn Sands. The club is halfway between Aspley Guise and Woburn Sands.

RAC recommended hotel
Bedford Arms ★★★★ (0525) 290441 A modernised Georgian coaching inn with much old world charm.
Moore Place ★★★ (0908) 282000 A Georgian mansion with a restaurant and bedroom extension at rear.

BEACONSFIELD
(0494) 676545
A varying 18-hole parkland course with easy walking (6469 yards, SSS 71). Visitors with a handicap certificate are welcome on weekdays. Green fees are £20 per round or £25 a day. Full catering facilities are available. Local attractions include the model village at Beaconsfield.
Location
Seer Green, Beaconsfield, Bucks. HP9 2UR
Leave the M40 at junction 2 and take the A355 towards Amersham. Turn right at Jordans signs, adjacent to the Seer Green and Jordans railway halt.

RAC recommended hotels
The Bell House ★★★ (0753) 887211 A modern hotel set in peaceful countryside. Indoor swimming pool, sauna, solarium, gymnasium, squash and billards.
White Hart Osprey ★★ (04946) 71211 An attractive former coaching inn with a modern extension, in the town centre.

BUCKINGHAM
(0280) 815566
An 18-hole undulating parkland course (6082 yards, SSS 69). Visitors are welcome on weekdays and as guests of a member at weekends, provided you are a member of a recognised golf club. Green fees are £16. Lunch and dinner is available daily. The club is within easy access of Milton Keynes, Blenheim Palace and Warwick Castle.
Location
Tingewick Road, Buckingham, MK18 4AE
You will find the club 2 miles from Buckingham on the A421 towards Oxford.

BURNHAM BEECHES
(0628) 661448
An 18-hole parkland course in the beautiful surroundings of Burnham Beeches (6415 yards, SSS 71). Visitors with a handicap certificate are welcome Monday to Friday and as guests of a member at weekends. Full catering facilities are available except Monday. Green fees are £18.50 per round, £27 per day. Local attractions include Windsor, Burnham Beeches, Runnymede and the Beaconsfield Model Village.
Location
Green Lane, Burnham, Bucks. SL1 8EG
Take the M40 to Beaconsfield and turn onto the A355 road towards Slough. Turn right and follow the Burnham signs not Burnham Beeches to Green Lane.

RAC recommended hotel
Burnham Beeches Moat House ★★★ (0628) 603333 A former Royal hunting lodge in 10 acres of attractive grounds. Indoor swimming pool, tennis, sauna, solarium and gymnasium.

CHESHAM & LEY HILL
(0494) 784541
A 9-hole heathland course with easy walking (5240 yards, SSS 66). Visitors of all playing levels are welcome on weekdays except Tuesday and Friday after 1pm, and only with a member at weekends. Green fees on application. Light meals and snacks are available except on Monday.
Location
Ley Hill. Chesham. Bucks. HP5 1UZ
Take the A41 and turn off at Boxmoor onto the B4505 through Bovingdon and follow the signs. The club is on the left.

CHILTERN FOREST
(0296) 630899
A 9-hole forestland course on two levels (6038 yards, SSS 70). Visitors of all playing abilities are welcome on weekdays and as a guest of a member at weekends. Green fees £10 weekdays, £7 with a member and £9 at weekends. Full catering facilities are available. The club is surrounded by Forestry Commission land.
Location
Aston Hill, Halton, Aylesbury, HP22 5NQ
The club is 5 miles south east of Aylesbury off the A41.

RAC recommended hotel
Bell Inn ★★★ (0296) 630252 A charming 18th century mellow brick building with cobbled courtyard and lovely roses.

DATCHET
(0753) 43887
A 9-hole parkland course with easy walking (5978 yards, SSS 69). Provided you have a handicap certificate, visitors are welcome on weekdays before 3pm. Green fees £10 per round, £15 per day. Full catering facilities are available. Local attractions include Windsor Castle and Runnymede.
Location
Buccleuch Road, Datchet, Slough, Berks. SL3 9BP
With easy access from the M4 (junction 5), 2 miles from Slough and Windsor.

RAC recommended hotel
The Manor ★★ (753) 43442 A gabled, half-timbered building, part 18th century; in Datchet village overlooking the Green.

DENHAM
(0895) 832022
An 18-hole slightly hilly parkland course in a quiet setting (6451 yards, SSS 71). Visitors are welcome from Monday to Thursday. Green fees £35 per(36 holes), £14 per(18 holes). Lunch is served daily. The club is surrounded by some glorious countryside.
Location
Tilehouse Lane, Denham, Bucks. UB9 5DE
Leave the M40 at the Uxbridge/Gerrards Cross exit and take the A40 towards Gerrards Cross. Turn right onto the A412 towards Watford and then take the second turning on the left to the club.

RAC recommended hotel
The Bell House ★★★ (0753) 887211 A modern hotel set in peaceful countryside near Beaconsfield. Indoor swimming pool, sauna, solarium, gymnasium, squash and billards.

ELLESBOROUGH
(0296) 622114
An 18-hole undulating downland course (6271 yards, SSS 71). Visitors with a handicap certificate are welcome on weekdays although it is advisable to telephone first. Green fees on application. Full catering facilities are available. A rather hilly course situated on part of the property of Chequers with extensive views across the Buckinghamshire countryside.
Location
Butlers Cross, Aylesbury, Bucks. HP17 0TZ
Take the A413 to Wendover and the club is 1 mile west of Wendover on the A4010.

FARNHAM PARK
(0628) 61521
An attractive 18-hole parkland municipal course (5787 yards, SSS 68). Visitors are welcome at all times. Green fees are £4, £2.50 OAP, £2.70 juniors on weekdays, and £6, juniors £4 at weekends. There is a grill restaurant. Local attractions include Windsor Castle.
Location
Park Road, Stoke Poges, Bucks. SL2 4EP
Turn off the A4 at Slough and take the A355 to Farnham Royal roundabout. From there take B416 Farnham road and proceed for about ½ mile, turn right and the course is on your left.

RAC recommended hotels
See Burnham Beeches.

FLACKWELL HEATH
(062 85) 20929
An 18-hole undulating parkland course (6150 yards, SSS 69). overlooking Loudwater. Visitors are welcome on weekdays although a handicap certificate is required. Green fees are £16 per day. Full catering facilities are available but they are limited on Monday. Places to visit locally include Windsor, Aylesbury and Oxford.
Location
Treadaway Road, Flackwell Heath, High Wycombe, Bucks. HP10 9PE
Take the A40 High Wycombe-Beaconsfield road and leave it at the Loudwater roundabout. Go up Treadaway Hill and you will reach the golf club before the apex of the hill.

RAC recommended hotel
Crest ★★★ (0494) 442100 A modern purpose built hotel in the outskirts of the town.

GERRARDS CROSS
(0753) 885300
A pleasant 18-hole parkland course (6021 yards, SSS 69). Visitors are welcome on weekdays but you must have a handicap certificate. Green fees £23 per day, £17 after 3pm. Bar snacks and lunch are available by arrangement. The club is within easy access of Windsor Castle and Safari Park.
Location
Chalfont Park, Gerrards Cross, Bucks. SL9 0QA
Leave the A40 at the A413 and continue for about 1 mile to the first roundabout. Leave by the third exit onto a private road.

RAC recommended hotels
The Bull ★★★ (0753) 885995 A delightful 17th century coaching inn.
Ethorpe ★★ (0753) 882039 A Georgianmansion standing in landscaped gardens close to the town.

HAREWOOD DOWNS
An 18-hole downland/meadowland course (5448 yards, SSS 69). Visitors with a handicap certificate are welcome on weekdays and with members at weekends. Green fees are £18 a day, £12 per round (£8 if accompanied by a member) and £10 at weekends. Catering facilities are available daily. Local attractions include Taplow(NT) and Milton's Cottage.
Location
Cokes Lane, Chalfont St Giles, Bucks. HP8 4TA
You will find the club off the A413 about 3 miles south of Amersham.

RAC recommended hotel
Crown ★★ (0494) 721541 A half-timbered 16th century inn with an attractive courtyard in the centre of Amersham.

HAZLEMERE GOLF AND COUNTRY CLUB
An 18-hole undulating parkland course (6039 yards, SSS 69). Visitors are welcome at all times although it is necessary to book at weekends. Green fees are £14 on weekdays and £18 at weekends. Full catering facilities are available. Buggies can be hired. Interesting local places to visit include Bekonscot Model Village.
Location
Penn Road, Hazlemere, High Wycombe, HP15 7LR
Take the A404 north east from High Wycombe towards Amersham. You will find the club 3 miles from High Wycombe on the B474.

RAC recommended hotel
See Flackwell Heath.

IVER
(0753) 655615
A 9-hole parkland course (6214 yards, SSS 70). Visitors are always welcome. Green fees £3.60 per 9 holes, £5 per 18 holes on weekdays and £4.60 per 9 holes, £8 per 18 holes at weekends. There are reductions for juniors and OAPs. Full catering facilities are available. Local attractions include Windsor Great Park, Runnymede and Eton College.
Location
Hollow Hill Lane, Langley Park Road, Iver, Bucks. SL0 0JJ
Take the A4 to Slough and turn off onto the B470 towards Iver. The green is near Langley station just outside Slough.

RAC recommended hotels
Holiday Inn ★★★★ (0753) 44244 A purpose built modern hotel in Langley with indoor swimming pool, tennis, sauna, solarium, gymnasium and billiards.
King William ★★ (0753) 44253 A traditional hotel in Langley, with a substantial modern extension for bedrooms.

LITTLE CHALFONT
(024 04) 4877
A flat parkland 9-hole course surrounded by trees (2926 yards, SSS 68). Visitors of all playing abilities are welcome at any time. Green fees are £7 midweek and £9 at weekends. Buggies can be hired. Full catering facilities are available. The course is well situated for country walks.
Location
Lodge Lane, Little Chalfont, Bucks. HP8 4AJ
Take the A404 from Amersham and the club is about 200 yards from the road at Little Chalfont.

RAC recommended hotel
Bedford Arms Thistle ★★★ (09278) 3301 An Elizabethan-style former coaching inn in the historic village of Chenies.

STOKE POGES
(0753) 26385
A fine 18-hole parkland course (6654 yards, SSS 72). Provided you have a handicap certificate, visitors are welcome on weekdays by arrangement, and at weekends and Bank Holidays as a guest of a member. Green fees are £25 per day or £18 per round. A full catering service is available. Local places of interest include the churchyard where Thomas Gray wrote his 'Elegy'.
Location
Stoke Park, Park Road, Stoke Poges, Slough, Bucks. SL2 4PG
Turn off the A4 at Slough into Stoke Poges Lane, (B416) and you will find the club 1½ miles on the left.

RAC recommended hotels
See Iver.

STOWE
(0280) 813650
A 9-hole course set in National Trust property (4573 yards, SSS 63). Visitors with a handicap certificate are welcome if accompanied by a member. Green fees are £5 per round, juniors £2.50. Catering is by arrangement.
Location
Stowe, Buckingham, MK18 5EH
The club is 4 miles from Buckingham on the A413.

WESTON TURVILLE
(0296) 24084
An 18-hole lengthy parkland course with easy walking (6782 yards, SSS 72). Visitors of all playing abilities are welcome except on Sunday morning. Green fees are £8 weekdays and £10 at weekends and Bank Holidays. Cooked lunches and evening snacks are available. Local attractions include Waddesdon Manor (NT) and Hartwell House.
Location
New Road, Weston Turville, Aylesbury, Bucks. HP22 5QT
Leave Aylesbury by the A413 and turn off to the left for Weston Turville.

RAC recommended hotels
Hartwell House C/H ★★★★ (0296) 747444 A superb new hotel in a lovely part Jacobean, part Georgian mansion, beautifully restored and furnished in keeping, set in a landscaped parkland. Fishing.
Bell ★★ (0296) 89835 Originally a coaching inn this fine Georgian buildings is situated in the market square at Aylesbury.
Forte ★★★★ (0296) 393388 A newly built hotel in landscaped grounds in a rural area. Indoor swimming pool, sauna, solarium and gymnasium.

WREXHAM PARK
(0753) 663271
Two gentle undulating parkland courses, a 9-hole course (2383 yards, SSS 32) and an 18-hole course (5836 yards, SSS 68). Visitors are welcome at any time. Green fees £5.60 on weekdays, and £8 at weekends(18 holes), and £3.60 weekdays, £4 at weekends(9 holes). A full catering service is available. On Thursday, veterans can play for £1.50 before 1pm. Local attractions include Burnham Beeches, Black Park and the Slough Sports Centre.
Location
Wexham Street, Wexham, Slough, Bucks. SL3 6ND
Leave Slough by the A412 towards Gerrards Cross and follow the signs to Wexham Park Hospital. The club is ½ mile further on.

RAC recommended hotels
See Iver and Gerrards Cross.

WHITELEAF
(08444) 3097
A delightful 9-hole parkland course with fine views of the Chilterns (5391 yards SSS 66). Visitors with a handicap are welcome on weekdays. Green fees £12.50 per 18 holes and £10 per 36 holes, or £20 per day. Lunch is served daily except Monday. Close to Princes Risborough Manor(NT) and Butler's Cross (NT).
Location
The Clubhouse, Whiteleaf, Aylesbury, Bucks.
Take the A4010 High Wycombe-Aylesbury road and 1½ miles north east from Princes Risborough turn right for Whiteleaf.

RAC recommended hotel
Rose and Crown ★★ (08444) 5299 In a rural setting, two-storey white Georgian inn, with a modern extension.

WINDMILL HILL
(0908) 20263
An 18-hole public meadowland course (6773 yards, SSS 72). Visitors are welcome at all times. Green fees £3.75 on weekdays and £5.30 at weekends. There is also a 23-bay floodlit driving range. Full catering facilities are available. The club is convenient for Milton Keynes shopping centre and leisure plaza.
Location
Tannenhoe Lane, Bletchley, Milton Keynes, Bucks. MK3 7RB
From exit 13 on the M1 take the A421 towards Bletchley and follow the signs for Windmill Hill golf course.

RAC recommended hotels
Post House ★★★★ (0908) 667722 A modern hotel with stylish open plan public areas. Facilities include an indoor swimming pool, sauna, solarium and gymnasium.
Broughton ★★★ (0908) 667726 A well furnished, red-brick hotel in country surroundings, but close to junction 14 of M1.
Friendly Lodge ★★★ (0908) 561666 A modern red-brick complex in landscaped grounds, next to the golf course on the A5.
Moorings Toby ★★★ (0908) 691515 A modern low-built brick hotel on the east side of the city overlooking the Marina and the Grand Union Canal.

WOBURN GOLF AND COUNTRY CLUB
(0908) 70756
Two fine 18-hole courses set within the beautiful grounds of the Woburn Abbey estate, the Duke's (6913 yards, SSS 74) and the Duchess (6641 yards, SSS 72). Visitors are welcome Monday to Friday although prior booking is essential and you must have a handicap certificate. Green fees available on application. The clubhouse offers a range of catering, and dinners can be arranged. The Abbey itself and the Safari Park are particular attractions .
Location
Bow Brickhill, Milton Keynes, MK17 9LJ
Leave the M1 at junction 13 into Woburn Sands, turn left for Woburn and after half a mile turn right at the club sign. The A5 also passes close by.

RAC recommended hotel
Bedford Arms ★★★★ (0525) 290441 A modernised Georgian coaching inn with much old world charm in Woburn.

CAMBRIDGESHIRE

ABBOTSLEY
(0480) 215153
A pleasant 18-hole undulating meadowland course (6150 yards, SSS 71). Visitors are welcome every day. Green fees are £10 on weekdays, juniors £6, and £15 at the weekend, juniors £7. The club has a residential golf school and a floodlit driving range. There is a bar and restaurant where snacks and meals are served daily. Other facilities at the club include squash courts, snooker and pool, solarium and sauna, and there are two public swimming pools in nearby Cambridge.
Location
Eynesbury Hardwicke, St Neots, Cambs. PE19 4XN
The club is 3 miles east of the A1. From Cambridge take the A45 to St Neots and turn off at the signpost to Eynesbury, St Neots.

RAC recommended hotels
See St Neots.

CAMBRIDGESHIRE MOAT HOUSE HOTEL
(0954) 80555
An 18-hole undulating parkland course, challenging but with easy walking (6734 yards, SSS 72). Visitors are welcome but you must have a letter of introduction or membership card from a recognised golf club. This rule is waived for hotel residents. It is advisable to telephone first to check course availability. Green fees are £16 on weekdays and £25 at weekends and Bank Holidays. There are full catering facilities. Cambridge is close by and the club is within easy access of Anglesey Abbey and Wimpole Hall.
Location
Bar Hill, Cambs. CB3 8EU
Take the A604 from Huntingdon or the A45 and then the A604 north west. The club is 4 miles from Cambridge.

RAC recommended hotel
Cambridgeshire Moat House ★★★★ (0954) 80555 A large modern hotel set in parkland. Indoor swimming pool, solarium, golf, gymnasium, squash, tennis and putting.

ELY CITY
(0353) 662751
An 18-hole parkland course (6686 yards, SSS 72). Visitors of all playing abilities are welcome on weekdays, but you must have a handicap certificate to play at the weekend unless accompanied by a member. Green fees are £14 on weekdays and £20 at the weekend and Bank Holidays. There is a restaurant with full facilities and bar snacks are available. Local attractions include Ely Cathedral.
Location
Cambridge Road, Ely, Cambs. CB7 4HX
The club is situated on the A10, on the southern outskirts of Ely.

RAC recommended hotels
Fenlands Lodge ★★★ (0353) 667047 An attractively converted farm set 2 miles outside the city. Tennis.
Lamb ★★★ (0353) 663574 A centrally situated former coaching inn with a pleasant courtyard, close to the Cathedral.

GIRTON
(0223) 276169
An 18-hole flat open course with easy walking (6085 yards, SSS 69). Visitors of all playing abilities are welcome on weekdays. Green fees are £14 per day during the week. Lunch and dinner is served every day except Monday.
Location
Dodford Lane, Girton, Cambs. CB3 0QE
Take the A604 from Cambridge and you will find the club 3 miles N on the right.

RAC recommended hotel
Post House ★★★★ (0223) 23700 A modern hotel with many facilities including indoor swimming pool, sauna, solarium, gymnasium and snooker.

GOG MAGOG
(0223) 247626
Two undulating high ground courses with some fine views of the Ural Mountains! an 18-hole (5354 yards, SSS 70) and a 9-hole (5833 yards, SSS 68). Visitors are welcome on weekdays if introduced by a member or in possession of a handicap certificate. Practice ground is available. Green fees on application. Lunch is served daily. The club is close to Cambridge with its magnificent colleges.
Location
Shelford Bottom, Cambridge, CB2 4AB
Leave Cambridge by the A13107 (Hills Rd.) the club is on the left 2 miles south of Cambridge.

RAC recommended hotels
Garden House ★★★★ (0223) 63421 A luxurious modern hotel, set in secluded riverside gardens near the city centre. Fishing.
University Arms ★★★★ (0223) 351241 A Victorian building in the 'Grand Hotel' style with modern extensions.
Gonville ★★★ (0223)66611 A Victorian hotel situated opposite Parkers Place.
Arundel House ★★ (0223) 67701 An elegant Victorian building beautifully located by the River Cam.

MARCH
(0354) 52364
A 9-hole parkland course (6200 yards, SSS 70). Visitors of all playing abilities are welcome on weekdays. Green fees are £8. Local attractions include Cambridge, Peterborough and Wisbech.
Location
Frogs Abbey, Grange Road, March, Cambs.
The club is on the A141, west of the March by-pass. It is signposted.

RAC recommended hotel
Olde Griffin (0354) 52517.

ORTON MEADOWS
(0733) 237478
An 18-hole course (5800 yards, SSS 68). There is a 12-hole pitch and putt course. Visitors are welcome at any time but please book in advance. Green fees are £4.40 on weekdays and £6.50 at the weekend. Meals are available from 'The Granary' Steakhouse, which is adjacent to the club. Local attractions include the facilities at the Ferry Meadows Country Park, including fishing, sailing and riding.
Location
Ham Lane, Peterborough, PE2 0UU
Take the A605 Peterborough-Oundle road and you will find the club 2 miles west of Peterborough at the entrance to the Ferry Meadows Country Park.

RAC recommended hotels
See Peterborough.

OUNDLE
(0832) 73267
An 18-hole undulating parkland course (5507 yards, SSS 67). Visitors of all playing abilities are welcome on weekdays. Green fees on application. A full catering service is available. Local attractions include Barnwell Country Park.
Location
Benefield Road, Oundle, Peterborough, Cambs. PE8 4EZ

RAC recommended hotel
Talbot ★★★ (0832) 272621 A 17th century stone building with a modern extension.

PETERBOROUGH MILTON
(0733) 380489
An 18-hole parkland course with easy walking (6431 yards, SSS 71). Provided you have a handicap certificate, visitors are welcome on weekdays, but you must arrange it with the Secretary beforehand. Green fees on application. There are full catering facilities except on Monday. Local attractions include the Cathedral and the Nene Valley Steam Railway.
Location
Milton Ferry, Peterborough, PE6 7AG
Take the A47 from Peterborough and you will find the club 2 miles west of the city.

RAC recommended hotels
Swallow ★★★★ (0733) 371111 A long low hotel with indoor swimming pool, sauna, solarium and gymnasium.
Peterborough Moat House ★★★ (0733) 260000 A luxury hotel situated well outside the city. Indoor swimming pool. sauna, solarium and gymnasium.
Bull ★★★ (0733) 61364 A much enlarged and extensively altered old coaching inn in the city centre.

RAMSEY
(0487) 813573
An 18-hole parkland course (6136 yards, SSS 70). Visitors with a handicap certificate are welcome between Monday and Friday. Green fees are £12. Full catering facilities are available. Places of local interest include the Ramsey Abbey Ruins and the Rural Museum.
Location
4 Abbey Terrace, Ramsey, Huntingdon, Cambs. PE17 1DD
Take the A141 north east from Huntingdon and turn onto the B1040 at Warboys to Ramsey. The club is 12 miles south east of Peterborough.

RAC recommended hotel
George ★★★ (0480) 432444 An historic old posting inn with attractive galleried inner courtyard.
Old Bridge Inn ★★★ (0480) 52681 A renovated 18th century Georgian hotel on the river bank. Fishing.
Alconbury House ★★ (0480) 891259 Three-storey grey-brick hotel in rural area on A1. Squash, sauna, solarium and snooker.

ST IVES
(0480) 64459
A pretty 9-hole course (6052 yards, SSS 69). Provided you have a handicap certificate, visitors are welcome on weekdays and with a member at weekends. Green fees are £10 on weekdays and £15 at weekends. Catering facilities are available daily except Monday. The club is not far from Huntingdon where there is a statue of Oliver Cromwell.
Location
Westwood Road, St Ives, Cambs. PE17 4RS
Take the A604 Cambridge-Huntingdon road and turn off at the B104 to St Ives. The club is 5 miles east of Huntingdon.
Slepe Hall ★★★ (0480)63122 An elegantly adapted Victorian mansion near the town centre.

ST NEOTS
(0480) 72363
An 18-hole parkland/meadowland course with easy walking (6027 yards, SSS 69). Visitors are welcome during the week and with a member at weekends and Bank Holidays. Green fees on application. There are full catering facilities in the clubhouse. The club is within easy access of Cambridge.
Location
Crosshall Road, St Neots, Huntingdon, Cambs. PE19 4AE
The club is 1½ miles west of St Neots off the A1 or take the A45 from Cambridge through St Neots.

RAC recommended hotels
Old Falcon ★★ (0480) 72749 An inn since the 15th century, this riverside hotel was a stagecoach stop on the Great North Road.
Wyboston Lakes ★★ (0480) 219949 A modern motel by a golf and leisure park alongside the River Ouse 3 miles south of the town.

THORPE WOOD
(0733) 267701
A municipal 18-hole parkland course (6595 yards, SSS 74). Visitors are welcome at any time but it is preferable to book in advance. Green fees are £4.20 on weekdays and £6.50 at the weekend and Bank Holidays. There are catering facilities at The Greenkeeper. Local attractions include the facilities at the Ferry Meadows Country Park, including fishing, sailing and riding.
Location
Thorpe Wood, Peterborough, PE3 6SE

RAC recommended hotels
See Peterborough.

CHESHIRE

ALDERLEY EDGE
(0625) 585583
An undulating 9-hole parkland course (5839 yards, SSS 68). Visitors are welcome without reservation but proof of handicap is required. Green fees £10 weekdays and £13 weekends and Bank Holidays. Full catering facilities are available except on Monday. The club is not far from Knutsford and Tatton Park(NT). There are fine views of the Derbyshire hills.
Location
Brook Lane, Alderley Edge, Cheshire SK9 7RU
Take the A34 to Alderley Edge and turn left opposite the Tower Garage onto the B5085 towards Mobberley. The golf course is on the right.

RAC recommended hotel
De Trafford Arms ★★★ (0625) 583881 A charming black and white country hotel in village setting.

ASTBURY
(0260) 272772
An 18-hole parkland course divided by the Macclesfield Canal (6277 yards, SSS 70). Visitors who are members of a recognised golf club are welcome but must be accompanied by a member at weekends. A handicap certificate is required. Green fees are £12 per day. Catering can be made available by prior arrangement. There are many local attractions including Congleton, Gawsworth Hall, Little Moreton Hall, Jodrell Bank telescope and Chatley Whitefield mining museum.
Location
Peel Lane, Astbury, Nr Congleton, Cheshire CW12 4RE
On leaving the outskirts of Congleton, take the A34 road towards Newcastle-under-Lyme. The club is on the right at Astbury village.

RAC recommended hotel
See Congleton.

AVRO
061-439 2709
A 9-hole meadowland course on British Aerospace land (5735 yards, SSS 68). Visitors are welcome but you must be accompanied by a member. A handicap certificate is required. Green fees are £4 per day and £6 at weekends. Local attractions include Alderley Edge with its fine view of the Derbyshire Hills.
Location
British Aerospace, Woodford, SK7 1QR
Take the A5102 to Woodford from Wilmslow and the Aerodrome is on the right.

RAC recommended hotel
Bramhall Moat House ★★★ 061-439 8116 Purpose-built modern hotel with conference

facilities. Sauna and solarium.

BIRCHWOOD
(0925) 818819
An 18-hole challenging parkland course (6808 yards, SSS 73). The course is based on the Pilgrim's Progress, the 11th hole, Valley of Humiliation, crosses water three times and the 18th is Deliverance. Visitors are welcome on weekdays provided you have a handicap certificate. Green fees are £11 to £15. A restaurant with a la carte menu and bar snacks is open daily.
Location
Kelvin Close, Risley, Warrington, Cheshire WA3 7PB
Leave the M62 at junction 11 and follow the A574 towards Risley/Birchwood. The entrance is opposite Data-General.

RAC recommended hotels
See Warrington.

CHAPEL-EN-LE-FRITH
(0298) 813943
A gentle 18-hole parkland course (6065 yards, SSS 69). A friendly club which welcomes visitors who have a handicap certificate. Green fees are £8 weekdays, £12 weekends and Bank Holidays. Meals are available every day except Monday. There are many local attractions including Chatsworth House, Blue John Mines, Buxton, and walks in the Peak District.
Location
The Cockyard, Manchester Road, Chapel-en-le-Frith, Stockport, SK12 6UH.
Take the A6 south through Disley and onto the A5002 for Whaley Bridge. Turn left at the second set of traffic lights and continue towards Chapel-en-le-Frith for 2 miles. The club is on the right- hand side, almost opposite the Hanging Gate Public House.

RAC recommended hotels
Buckingham ★★★ (0298) 70481 A stone-built hotel overlooking the Pavilion Gardens, Buxton.
Lee Wood ★★★ (0298) 23002 A fully modernised building of Georgian splendour situated in its own ground
Palace ★★★ (0298) 2001 Stately hotel with elegant public rooms and sun lounge. Indoor swimming pool, sauna, solarium, gymnasium and billiards.
Grove ★★ (0298) 3804 Proprietor-run central hotel in 18th century building.
Portland ★★ (0298) 22462 Family-run, stone-built hotel facing the park near the centre of town.
Sandringham ★★ (0298) 72257 A hotel in attractive setting with views of Pavillion Gardens and lake.
Hartington ★ (0298) 22638 A small privately-owned hotel in attractive residence overlooking gardens and lake.

CHESTER
(0244) 677760
An 18- hole parkland course (6487 yards, SSS 71). Visitors are welcome but it is necessary to make arrangements in advance. A handicap certificate is required. Green fees are £10 on weekdays and £13 at weekends. Full catering facilities are available.
Location
Curzon Park North, Chester, CH4 8AR
You will find the club 1 mile from the centre of Chester, off the A55, behind Chester Racecourse.

RAC recommended hotels
Chester Grosvenor ★★★★ ((0244) 324024 An elegant half-timbered mid-Victorian hotel with individually decoorated luxury suites. Sauna, solarium and gymnasium.
Crabwell Manor ★★★★ (0244) 851666 A Gothic-style country mansion set in attractive grounds with helipad, 2 miles north of city. Snooker.
Mollington Banastre ★★★★ (0244) 851471 Set in gardens, a three- storeyVictorian building on the A540. Indoor swimming pool, sauna, solarium, gymnasium, squash, tennis, riding and putting.
Abbots Well ★★★ (0244) 332121 Modern purpose-built hotel with spacious gardens enjoying fine views.
Blossoms ★★★ (0244) 323186 Large 300 year old city centre building of character.
Hoole Hall ★★★ (0244) 350011 Rambling Georgian-cum-Victorian building with sympathetic modern extension and a conservatory, in landscaped grounds.
Penguin ★★★ (0244) 851551 Large modern hotel only a short drive out of the city centre. Fishing.
Plantation Inn ★★★ (0244) 374100 Attractive modern hotel with a leisure centre. Just north of the city. Sauna, solarium and gymnasium.
Post House ★★★ (0244) 680111 Modern purpose-built hotel in extensive grounds.
Queen ★★★ (0244) 328341 Hotel combining Victorian elegance and modern facilities. Secluded gardens.
Rowton Hotel ★★★ (0244) 335262 Georgian manor house in attractive grounds. Indoor swimming pool, sauna, solarium and gymnasium.
Royal Oak ★★★ (0244) 301391 Attractive hotel building with motel extension. 1 mile from the city centre.
Chester Court ★★ (0244) 20779 Black and white gabled building with purpose-built chalets.
Dene ★★ (0244) 321165 Family-run hotel in its own grounds adjacent to Alexandria Park.
Green Bough ★★ (0244) 326241 Small privately-owned and run hotel in residencial district 1 mile from city centre.
City Walls ★ (0244) 313416 Overlooking the city walls, a red-brick period building close to the city centre. Sauna.
Curzon ★ (0244) 678581 Converted Victorian private house situated in quiet residential area.
Ye Olde King's Head ★ (0244) 24855 Historic black and white building (1520) near the famous old Rows.

CONGLETON
(0260) 273540
An 18-hole parkland course (5704 yards, SSS 65). Visitors are welcome daily but telephone first in case it is a competition day. Green fees on application. Snack meals are available but book in advance if you require a full meal. The club is close to the magnificent Peak District.
Location
Biddulph Road, Congleton, Cheshire SW12 3LZ
Leave the M6 at junction 17 (Sandbach) and take the A534 to Congleton. The club is on the main Congleton-Biddulph road (A517) 1 mile south east of Congleton station.

RAC recommended hotel
Lion and Swan ★★ (0260) 273115 An attractive 16th century coaching inn with a timber frame and an impressive porchway.

CREWE
(0270) 584099
A pleasant undulating 18-hole parkland/ meadowland course (6181 yards, SSS 69). Visitors with a handicap certificate are welcome on weekdays but must be accompanied by a member at weekends. Green fees are £12 for visitors on weekdays (£5 with a member) and £6 with a member at weekends. Bar snacks, lunch and dinner is available every day. Places of local interest include Stapley Water Gardens, Bridgmere Nurseries and Nantwich.
Location
Fields Road, Haslington, Crewe, Cheshire CW1 1TB
Take the A534 from the Sandbach junction of the M1 (junction 17) to Crewe and the club is 1 mile south east of Haslington, on the B5077.

RAC recommended hotel
Crewe Arms ★★★ (0270) 213204 An imposing Victorian style hotel.

DAVENPORT
(0625) 876951
An undulating 18-hole parkland course (6066 yards, SSS 69). Some wonderful views over the Cheshire Plain. Visitors with a handicap certificate are welcome on most days but it is advisable to telephone ahead. Green fees are £12 on weekdays and £16 at weekends. There are reductions if you are with a member. Meals are available by arrangement with the Steward. Interesting places to visit locally include the Silk Weaving Museum at Macclesfield, and the splendid countryside of the Peak District.
Location
Worth Hall, Middlewood Road, Higher Poynton, Stockport, SK12 1TS
From Stockport take the A6 to the Rising Sun at Hazel Grove, then take the A523 Macclesfield road. When you come to the traffic lights at Poynton turn left into Park Lane, then take the left-hand fork into Middlewood Road. The club is approximately 1½ miles from here.

DELAMERE FOREST
(0606) 882807
A good, undulating 18-hole heathland course (6287 yards, SSS 70). Visitors of all playing abilities are welcome but can play 2 balls only at weekends and Bank Holidays. Green fees £15 weekdays, £20 weekends and Bank Holidays. Bar snacks are available daily and the restaurant can be booked in advance. Local attractions include the historic city of Chester and the nearby Sandstone Trail.
Location
Station Road, Delamere, Northwich, Cheshire, CW8 2JE
Take the A556 Manchester-Chester road west from Northwich, then the B5152 towards Frodsham. The club is on the right, approximately 1 mile from the A556, by Delamere station.

RAC recommended hotels
Hartford Hall ★★★ (0606) 75711 A 17th century building set in beautiful gardens in Northwich.
Nunsmere Hall ★★★ (0606) 889100 Spacious Victorian mansion beautifully set on a wooded peninsular in a lake.
Blue Cap ★★ (0606) 883006 White painted, part 18th century inn with distinctive diamond leaded windows. On the A559.
Woodpecker ★★ (0606) 45524 Victorian country residencs. 20 minutes from the motorway and Chester city centre.

DUKINFIELD
061-338 2340
A challenging 16-hole hillside course (5544 yards, SSS 67). Visitors are welcome on weekdays except on Wednesday afternoon. A handicap certificate is necessary. Green fees on application. Meals are served by prior arrangement. The club is located close to Manchester City Centre and the magnificent scenery of the Pennines and Peak District.
Location
Yew Tree Lane, Dukinfield, Gtr. Manchester, SK16 5DF
Take the A635 from Manchester through Ashton-Under-Lyne and on for 1 mile, then turn right into Yew Tree Lane. The club is 1 mile on the right, on the hill.

EATON
(0244) 680474
A testing 18-hole parkland course (6446 yards, SSS 71). Visitors with a handicap certificate are welcome but it is necessary to make prior arrangements. Green fees are £13 per round on weekdays and £15 per round at the weekend, or half price if you are with a member. There are full

catering facilities. Local attractions include the historic city of Chester.

Location

Eaton Park, Eccleston, Chester
Take the A483 Wrexham road from Chester and the club is about 2 miles south of the city.

RAC recommended hotels

See Chester.

ELLESMERE PORT
051-339 7689

An 18-hole municipal parkland/meadowland course (6432 yards, SSS 71). Visitors can play at any time and beginners are particularly welcome. Clubs can be hired. Green fees are £2.90 on weekdays and £3.60 at weekends and Bank Holidays. Catering facilities are available. Local attractions include the Boat Museum and the North Western Museum of Inland Navigation, and also the nearby historic city of Chester.

Location

Chester Road, Hooton, S Wirral L66 1QH
The club is situated approximately 9 miles north of Chester on the main A41 road to Birkenhead. The clubhouse is at the rear of St Paul's Church, Hooton, just opposite the Burleydam Nurseries.

RAC recommended hotel

Woodhey ★★ 051-339 5121 Extended Georgian residence in 4½ acres of grounds.

HAZEL GROVE
061-483 3978

An 18-hole moorland course (6300 yards, SSS 70). Visitors of all playing abilities are welcome on weekdays. Green fees on application. There are full catering facilities every day except Monday. The club has easy access to Manchester and the Peak District.

Location

Buxton Road, Hazel Grove, Stockport, Cheshire SK7 6LU
Take the A6 from Manchester to Hazel Grove and the club is on the left.

HELSBY
(09282) 2021

A tranquil 18-hole parkland course (6262 yards, SSS 70). Visitors of all playing abilities are welcome on weekdays. Green fees are £12 per day or £10 per round. Full catering facilities are available except on Wednesday. Places of interest locally include the historic town of Chester and Delamere Forest.

Location

Towers Lane, Helsby, Warrington, Cheshire WA6 0JB
Leave the M56 at junction 14 to Helsby. Then turn into Primrose Lane and take the first right into Towers Lane.

RAC recommended hotels

See Chester.

KNIGHTS GRANGE
(06065) 52780

A 9-hole municipal parkland course with kidney-shaped greens, water hazards and a very difficult 7th hole over trees (6210 yards, SSS 69). Visitors are welcome but it is necessary to book at the weekend. Green fees are £1.65 weekdays, £2.10 weekends (9 holes) and £2.10 weekdays, £2.80 weekends (18 holes).
All day pub catering is provided by the Golf Club 'Knights Grange' Hotel. The course is part of a leisure complex also providing tennis and bowling greens. Other local attractions include the Salt Museum at Northwich, boat trips with jazz sessions on the River Weaver, and Delamere Forest.

Location

Grange Lane, Winsford, CW7 2PT
Leave the M6 at junction 18 and take the A54 west through Middlewich to Winsford then follow the signposts from the town centre to the Knights Grange Sports Complex.

KNUTSFORD
(0565) 3355

A good 9-hole parkland course surrounded by a beautiful deer park (6288 yards, SSS 70). Visitors are welcome on weekdays by arrangement with the Secretary. Green fees on application. Catering is available by prior arrangement with the Steward. Local attractions include Tatton Park (NT).

Location

Mereheath Lane, Knutsford
Leave the M6 at junction 19 for the A5033 to Knutsford. The entrance to Tatton Park Club is a few yards on the right down Mereheath Lane.

RAC recommended hotels

Cottons ★★★ (0565) 50333 A beautifully designed hotel reminiscent of New Orleans. Indoor swimming pool, tennis, sauna, solarium and gymnasium.
Royal George ★★★ (0565) 4151 Historic Georgian-fronted hotel with panelled interior and minstrel gallery.

LEIGH
(092576) 3130

An 18-hole parkland course (6861 yards, SSS 68). Visitors are welcome at any time except during club competitions, but you must have a handicap certificate. Green fees are £10 on weekdays and £15 on weekends and Bank Holidays. Bar snacks and full catering facilities are available.

Location

Kenyon Hall, Broseley Lane, Culcheth, Warrington, WA3 4BG
Leave the M62 at junction 10 for the A574 to Culcheth. The club is about 5 minutes from Culcheth village centre.

LYMM
(092575) 5020

An 18-hole parkland course (6319 yards, SSS 70). Visitors are welcome provided you have a handicap certificate. Green fees are £11 on weekdays and £13.50 at weekends and Bank Holidays. Meals are available. Local attractions include Jodrell Bank and the historic town of Chester, and Liverpool.

Location

Whitbarrow Road, Lymm, Cheshire WA13 9AM
Leave the M6 at exit 20 and take the 5158 to Lymm, about 5 miles south east of Warrington.

RAC recommended hotels

Lymm ★★★ (092 575) 2233 A quiet hotel in the village.

MACCLESFIELD
(0625) 23227

A hilly 9-hole parkland course with extensive views over the Pennines (5974 yards, SSS 69). Visitors of all levels are welcome on weekdays although a handicap certificate is preferred. Green fees are £10, or £5 if you are with a member. Lunch is served daily except Tuesday. The club is pleasantly situated in the heart of the Peak District.

Location

The Hollins, Macclesfield, Cheshire SK11 7EA
You will find the club off Windmill Street in Macclesfield (the A523 Macclesfield-Leek road).

RAC recommended hotel

Shrigley Hall C/H ★★★★ (0625) 75757 Early 19th century mansion restored to former elegance, set in 260 acres of parkland. Indoor swimming pool, golf, putting, tennis, fishing, riding, squash, sauna, solarium, gymnasium and snooker.

MALKINS BANK
(0270) 767878

An 18-hole undulating meadowland municipal course with easy walking (6071 yards, SSS 69). Visitors are welcome at all times. Green fees are £3.40 weekdays and £4.10 at weekends. You can also buy an unlimited season ticket for £90, or Monday-Friday only for £50. There is a bar and meals are available daily. Local attractions include Sandbach Crosses, the Norman church of St Mary's and Morton Great Hall.

Location

Betchton Road, Sandbach, Cheshire
Leave the M6 at junction 17 and take the A534 to Sandbach. The club is about 1½ miles further on.

RAC recommended hotels

See Sandbach.

MERE GOLF AND COUNTRY CLUB
(0565) 830155

An 18-hole parkland course (6849 yards, SSS 73). Set in tranquil surroundings, Mere is one of the finest inland courses in the north west of England. Visitors who have a handicap certificate are welcome by prior arrangement on Monday, Tuesday and Thursday. Green fees are £30. Breakfast, lunch and dinner is served daily. Places of local interest include Tatton Park (NT) and Knutsford.

Location

Chester Road, Mere, Knutsford, Cheshire WA16 6LJ
From junction 19 on the M6 take the A556 for 2 miles. If you are coming from the M55 leave at junction 7 and take the A556 past the Swan at Bucklow Hill.

RAC recommended hotel

Swan ★★★ (0565) 830295 A coaching inn which is steeped in history and a lot of local charm.

MIRRLEES

A 9-hole parkland course (6102 yards, SSS 69). Visitors are welcome if they are accompanied by a member. Green fees on application. Bar snacks are available daily.

Location

Bramhall Moor Lane, Hazel Grove, Stockport, SK7 5AH. From Stockport follow the A6 to Hazel Grove, then turn right into New Moor Lane and the course is 400 yards on the right- hand side.

RAC recommended hotels

See Avro.

NEW MILLS
(0663) 43485

A 9-hole moorland course with fine views (5707 yards, SSS 67). Visitors of all playing abilities are welcome on weekdays and Saturdays except when there is a competition. Green fees on application. Snacks and meals are available daily. Local attractions include Lyme Park (NT).

Location

Shaw Marsh, New Mills, Stockport, Cheshire
Take the A6 to Newtown and then the A6015 to New Mills. Follow the St Mary Road from the centre of New Mills and you will find the golf course about 800 yards away.

ONNELEY
(0782) 750577

An attractive 9-hole undulating meadowland course (5584 yards, SSS 67). Visitors are welcome on Monday, Wednesday, Thursday and Friday. You can also play on Saturday if you are with a member. Green fees are £10 per day, or £5 with a member. Catering can be arranged by prior arrangement with the Stewardess. The club is within easy access of Stapely Water Gardens and Bridgemere Wildlife Park.

Location

Onneley, Crewe, Cheshire CW3 5QF
Take the A51 from Nantwich and the club is about 1 mile from Woore.

RAC recommended hotel

Wheatsheaf Inn (0782) 751581 18th century country inn next to the golf course, 6 miles west of Newcastle-under-Lymne.

POULTON PARK
(0925) 812034

A fine 9-hole meadowland course (4918 metres, SSS 66). Visitors of all abilities are welcome at any

time. Green fees are £8 on weekdays, £3.50 with a member, and £10 at weekends, £3.50 with a member. Juniors can play on weekdays. Lunch is served daily except Monday.
Location
Dig Lane, Cinnamon Brow, Warrington.
Take the A574 from Warrington and turn into Crab Lane. The club is 3 miles from Warrington.

RAC recommended hotel
See Warrington.

PRESTBURY
(0625) 82824
An 18-hole well-maintained undulating meadowland course with extensive views (6359 yards, SSS 71). Visitors are welcome on weekdays and with a member at weekend but it is advisable to telephone in advance. You are required to have a handicap certificate. Green fees are £16 per day/round. Lunch, dinner and bar snacks are served daily. Local attractions include Lyme Park (NT).
Location
Macclesfield Road, Prestbury, Macclesfield, Cheshire, SK10 4BJ

QUEENS PARK
(0270) 666724
A 9-hole parkland course (5370 yards, SSS 68). Visitors are welcome and no handicap certificate is necessary. Green fees are £1.80 weekdays, £2.50 weekends for 9 holes, and £2.50 weekdays, £3 weekends for 18 holes. Bar snacks are available until 3pm and from 6.30pm-11.30pm daily. The club is convenient for fishing and walking.
Location
Queens Park Gardens, Crewe, CW2 7SB
You will find the club 1¼ miles from Crewe centre.

RAC recommended hotels
See Crewe.

RUNCORN
(09285) 72093
An 18-hole high parkland course with easy walking (6035 yards, SSS 69). Visitors are welcome on weekdays provided they have a handicap certificate. Green fees are £10 per round on weekdays, £12 per round at weekends and Bank Holidays. Catering is available by arrangement. Local attractions include the Northern Priory Complex.
Location
Clifton Road, Runcorn, Cheshire WA7 4SU
Take the A557 from Runcorn signposted Runcorn Heath and you will find the golf course on the left.

RAC recommended hotels
Crest ★★★ (09280) 714000 A modern hotel near the M62. Indoor swimming pool, sauna, solarium and gymnasium.

ST MICHAEL JUBILEE (WIDNES MUNICIPAL)
051-424 0989
An 18-hole municipal parkland course which has been recently extended (5612 yards, SSS 67). Visitors of all levels are welcome but you should telephone ahead for a game at the weekend. Green fees are £2.70 on weekdays (and concessions) and £3.20 at weekends. There is a cafeteria and bar service where snacks are available between 11am and 11pm every day except Monday. The club is close to the Leisure Centre and the Shopping Centre.
Location
Dundark Road, Widnes, WA8 8BS
Leave the M56 at junction 12 or the M62 at junction 21. The club is about 2 miles from each.

RAC recommended hotel
See Widnes.

SANDBACH
(0270) 762117
A 9-hole undulating meadowland course with easy walking (5614 yards, SSS 67). Visitors are welcome on weekdays the club prefers you to have a handicap certificate. Weekends and Bank Holidays are by invitation only. Green fees are £10 per round, or £5 if you are with a member. A catering service is available daily except on Monday and Thursday. Places of local interest include the historic towns of Chester and Crewe.
Location
117 Middlewich Road, Sandbach, Cheshire CW11 9EA
Leave the M6 at junction 17 and you will find the club 1 mile north of the town centre on the A533 Middlewich road.

RAC recommended hotels
Saxon Cross ★★★ (0270) 763281 A modern hotel in quiet countryside.
Old Hall ★★ (0270) 761221 A Jacobean hotel of character offering all modern comforts.
Chimney House ★★★ (0270) 764141 An attractive converted Tudor-style country vicarage.

SANDIWAY
(0606) 883247
An attractive 18-hole undulating heath and woodland/parkland course (6435 yards, SSS 72). Visitors are welcome but it is necessary to arrange it first. A handicap certificate is required. Meals are served every day by arrangement. The club is within easy reach of Delamere Forest.
Location
Chester Road, Sandiway, Northwich, Cheshire CW8 2DJ
Leave Northwich by the A556 and the club is 14 miles east of Chester, 4 miles from Northwich.

RAC recommended hotels
See Northwich.

TYTHERINGTON
(0625) 34562
An 18-hole parkland course (6717 yards, SSS 72).
Location
Macclesfield, SK10 2JP
Near Macclesfield on the Manchester road.

RAC recommended hotels
See Macclesfield.

UPTON-BY-CHESTER
(0244) 381183
An 18-hole parkland course (5875 yards, SSS 68). A pleasant course with tree-lined fairways. Visitors are welcome a handicap certificate is preferred. Green fees are £10 on weekdays and £13 at weekends and Bank Holidays. There are full restaurant facilities daily except Monday. Local attractions include Chester town centre, Chester Zoological Gardens and the River Dee.
Location
Upton Lane, Upton-by-Chester, Chester, CH2 1EE
The club is 1½ miles north of Chester off the A5116.

RAC recommended hotels
See Chester.

VICARS CROSS
(0244) 335174
An 18-hole undulating meadowland course (5876 yards, SSS 68). Visitors are welcome at all times. Green fees are £10 per day onweekdays and £13 per day at weekends and Bank Holidays. Full catering facilities are available on Tuesday and Thursday. Local attractions include Chester Cathedral and town centre, amphitheatre and Heritage Centre.
Location
Tarvin Road, Littleton, Chester, CH3 7HN
Follow the A51 east from Chester for 2 miles and the club is on the left.

RAC recommended hotel
See Chester.

WALTON HALL
(0925) 66775
An 18-hole undulating parkland course (6801 yards, SSS 73). Visitors of all playing abilities are welcome. Green fees on application. Bar snacks are available during licensed hours and meals available by arrangement with the Steward. Local attractions include Walton Gardens.
Location
Warrington Road, Higher Walton, Warrington, WA4 5LU
Leaving the M56 at exit 11, take the A56 towards Higher Walton. The club is 4 miles south west from Warrington, about half a mile from the M56.

RAC recommended hotels
See Warrington.

WARRINGTON
(0925) 61775
An undulating varied parkland course, with a long 18 holes (6217 yards, SSS 70) and a short 18 holes (5890 yards, SSS 68). Visitors are welcome and a handicap certificate is preferred. Green fees are £12 on weekdays and £18 at weekends and Bank Holidays. Meals and snacks are available daily except Monday. The historic town of Chester is 13 miles away.
Location
London Road, Appleton, Warrington, Cheshire, WA4 5HR
The club is on the A49 between junction 10 of the M56 and Warrington.

RAC recommended hotel
Fir Grove ★★★ (0925) 67471 Well-appointed small hotel in former private residence in wooded surroundings.
Old Vicarage ★★ (0925 73) 706 A former vicarage which has been modernised and extended to include tennis, fishing, sauna and billiards.
Paddington House ★★ (0925) 816767 Former large residence with modern wing in landscaped garden with sweeping lawn.
Patten Arms ★★ (0925) 36602 Yellow brick Victorian building close to town centre. Convenient for railway station.
Ribblesdale ★★ (0925) 601197 Conveniently placed hotel in ¼ acre of grounds.
Rockfield ★★ (0925) 62898 Small quietly situated hotel with pleasant garden. 2 miles froOm town centre.

WIDNES
051-424 2995
An 18-hole parkland course with easy walking (5688 yards, SSS 68). Visitors are welcome on weekdays but a handicap certificate is required. Green fees on application. Meals are served by prior arrangement.
Location
Highfield Road, Widnes, Cheshire
The club is near the town centre.

RAC recommended hotel
Hillcrest ★★★ 051-424 1616 A modernised hotel which includes a restaurant and buttery bar.

WILMSLOW
(056587) 2148
A well-kept 18-hole parkland course formerly used for championship golf (6611 yards, SSS 72). Visitors are generally welcome during the week although it is necessary to telephonefirst. Green fees on application. Catering facilities are available.
Location
Great Warford, Mobberley, Knutsford, Cheshire WA16 7AY
Take the B5085 from Knutsford. The club is 2 miles from Wilmslow.

RAC recommended hotels
Stanneylands ★★★★ (0625) 525225 Family-run luxury hotel in red-brick building of character. Attractive grounds.
Valley Lodge ★★★ (0625) 529201 Purpose-built

hotel in Tyrolean style. Set in rural area. Indoor swimming pool, sauna, solarium, gymnasium and billiards.

CLEVELAND

BILLINGHAM
(0642) 554494
An undulating 18-hole parkland course with hard walking (6034 yards, SSS 71). Visitors are welcome. Green fees are £12 a day on weekdays, £6 with a member, and £16 at the weekend, £8 with a member. Catering facilities are available daily except Monday. The club is close to the interesting town of Middlesbrough.
Location
Sandy Lane, Billingham, Cleveland, TS22 5NA
Take the A19 north from Middlesbrough to Billingham. The club is near the town centre.

RAC recommended hotel
Billingham Arms ★★★ (0642) 553661 In the town square. Facilities include a solarium.

CASTLE EDEN & PETERLEE
(0429) 836220
An attractive 18-hole parkland course with hard walking (6293 yards, SSS 70). Visitors are welcome at all times. Green fees are £9 per day (£4.50 with a member) on weekdays, and £15 (£4.50 with a member) at weekends and Bank Holidays. There are full catering facilities daily. The course is next to a nature reserve and local attractions include Beamish Museum, Durham Cathedral and the Metro Centre in Newcastle.
Location
Castle Eden, Hartlepool, Cleveland TS27 4SS
Take the A19 and follow the signs for Castle Eden. The golf course is at the junction of A19 with the A181, Durham Road opposite the Whitbread Brewery.

RAC recommended hotels
Crossways ★★ (0429) 266345 A small hotel standing at the road junction in the rural area of Thornley. Facilities include solarium and billiards.
Norseman ★★★ 091-586 2161 A modern hotel in a recently developed area of the town of Peterlee.
Hardwicke Hall C/H ★★ (0429) 836326 An historic mansion set in 8 acres of grounds.

CLEVELAND
(0642) 471798
A links championship course (6707 yards, SSS 72). Visitors are welcome provided you have a handicap certificate. Green fees are £8 on weekdays and £12.50 at the weekends. There are reductions if you are accompanied by a member. Catering facilities are available.
Location
Queen St, Redcar, Cleveland, TS10 1BT
Take the A174 from Middlesbrough and then the A1042 to Redcar. You will find the course through Coatham.

RAC recommended hotel
Hotel Royal York ★★★ (0642) 486221 A modern hotel close to Redcar sea front.

EAGLESCLIFFE
(0642) 780098
An interesting 18-hole undulating parkland course (6045 yards, SSS 69) with marvellous views of the Cleveland Hills. Visitors are welcome on weekdays but are restricted on Tuesday and Friday which are Ladies Days. Green fees are £10 on weekdays and £12.15 at weekends. If you are with a member it is half price. There are full catering facilities available. Local attractions include Preston Park Museum.
Location
Yarm Road, Eaglescliffe, Stockton on Tees, Cleveland TS16 0DQ
Take the A135 (Tees-Yarm road) out of Stockton and the club is on the left-hand side of the road.

RAC recommended hotels
Swallow ★★★★ (0642) 679721 A modern luxury hotel in the centre of Stockton town redevelopment area.
Claireville ★ (0642) 780378 Large three-storey late Victorian villa set in own grounds.

HARTLEPOOL
(0429) 274398
An 18-hole seaside half links course overlooking the North Sea (6215 yards, SSS 70). Visitors can play at any time except onSunday but the club prefers you to have a handicap certificate. Green fees are £10 on weekdays and £14 at weekends and Bank Holidays. It is half price if you are with a member. Catering facilities can be arranged with the Steward.
Location
Hart Warren, Hartlepool, Cleveland TH24 9QE
Take the A1086 to the north end of Hartlepool and the club is off King Oswy Drive.

RAC recommended hotels
Grand ★★★ (0429) 266345 A large sandstone Victorian hotel in the town centre, overlooking the sea.

MIDDLESBROUGH
(0642) 311515/316430
An 18-hole undulating parkland course (6106 yards, SSS 69). Visitors are welcome on weekdays except Tuesday. A handicap certificate is not required but you must be a member of a golf club. Green fees are £12.50 (£5 with a member) on weekdays, and £15 (£7 with a member) at weekends and Bank Holidays. There are full catering facilities except on Monday. Local attractions include the Captain Cook Museum, Preston Park, Stockton, the nearby beaches at Whitby, the Yorkshire Moors and the Cleveland Hills.
Location
Brass Castle Lane, Marton, Middlesbrough, Cleveland, TS8 9EE
Take the A172 from Middlesbrough and the club is 5 miles south of the town about 1 mile wset of the road.

RAC recommended hotels
Hospitality Inn ★★★★ (0642) 232000 Ten-storey modern hotel in the centre of Middlebrough. Solarium.
Marton ★★★ (0642) 317141 A large hotel situated on the main road, south.
Post House ★★★ A modern motel-style hotel near the outskirts of Middlesbrough. Sauna and solarium.
Marton Way ★★★ (0642) 817651 Modern hotel in motel style on main road south of town.
Highfield ★★ (0642) 817638 Turn-of-the-century private residence with modern extensions. On outskirts.

MIDDLESBROUGH MUNICIPAL
(0642) 315361
An 18-hole undulating parkland course divided by a stream (6314 yards, SSS 70). Visitors are welcome but you need to telephone in advance to book a game. Green fees are £3.75 on weekdays and £5 at weekend, and Bank Holidays. There is a floodlit driving range open to 9pm on weekdays and 5pm at the weekend. Lunch and evening meals are available. Places of interest locally include the Captain Cook Museum and Monument.
Location
Ladgate Lane, Middlesbrough, Cleveland T95 7YZ
You can reach the club by taking the A19 via the A174 to Acklam.

RAC recommended hotels
See Middlesbrough.

SALTBURN-BY-SEA
(0287) 22812
An 18-hole undulating wooded meadowland course with fine views of the Cleveland Hills (5803 yards, SSS 68). Visitors are welcome if they are a member of a recognised club. Green fees on application. There are full catering facilities daily except Monday. The club is convenient for the East coast resorts and close to Herriot Country
Location
Guisborough Road, Hobb Hill, Saltburn-by-Sea, Cleveland TS12 1NJ
Take the A174 to Saltburn and the club 1 mile from the centre of the town on the B1268.

RAC recommended hotel
Grinkle Park C/H ★★★ (0287) 40515 Stone-built manorial style building in tranquil parkland with extensive gardens. Tennis, fishing and billiards.

SEATON CAREW
(0429) 266249
A championship links course (6802 yards, SSS 72). Visitors are welcome but you must be a member of a recognised golf club. Green fees are £12 on weekdays and £15 at weekends. Catering facilities are available. Local attractions include Durham Cathedral, and the local beaches.
Location
Tees Road, Seaton Carew, Hartlepool.
Take the A178 from Hartlepool and the club is 3 miles south of the town.

RAC recommended hotels
See Hartlepool.

TEESSIDE
(0642) 616516
An 18-hole meadowland course with easy walking (6472 yards, SSS 71). Visitors are welcome on weekdays before 4.30pm and after 11am on Bank Holidays unless they are with a member. Green fees are £8 per day, £6.50 with a member during the week and £12 per day (£7 with a member) at the weekend. The club is close to the Cleveland Hills.
Location
Acklam Road, Thornaby, Cleveland TS17 7JS
Turn off the A19 from Stockton onto the A1130 at Thornaby. The course is situated 1 mile from the A19 on the right.

RAC recommended hotels
See Middlesbrough.

WILTON
(0642) 465265
An 18-hole parkland course with fine views (6019 yards, SSS 69). Visitors are welcome on weekdays, Sunday and Bank Holidays, but not on Saturday. Green fees are £10 on weekdays and £10 at weekends. If you are with a member it is £6 per day. Lunches are available Monday to Saturday. Local attractions include Captain Cook's monument, museum and park and Roseberry Topping, the smallest mountain in England.
Location
Wilton Castle, Redcar, Cleveland, TS10 4DQ
The club is 4 miles west of Redcar off the A174. Take the road for Wilton village and follow the signs to the castle.

RAC recommended hotels
See Cleveland.

CORNWALL

BUDE AND N CORNWALL
(0288) 2006
An 18-hole seaside links course with excellent greens and sand bunkers (6202 yards, SSS 70). Visitors are welcome, but during seasonal times the first tee is reserved for members until 9.30am and between 12-30pm-2.00pm and 5.00pm-6.30pm on weekday and before 2.30pm on Sundays. Green fees are £10 per round and £15 a day. A wide selection of meals is available at lunchtimes and

evenings. Local attractions include Clovelly and the North Devon holiday area.

Location
Burn View, Bude, Cornwall EX23 8DA
The club is about 1 minute from Bude town centre on the A39.

RAC recommended hotels
Camelot ★★ (0288) 352361 A small hotel close to the town and beach. Solarium
Burn Court ★★ (0288) 352872 A modern hotel on the edge of the golf course. Countryside views.
Hartland ★★★ (0288) 55661 Modern hotel on private road overlooking beach. Short walk to town. Swimming pool.
Strand ★★★ (0288) 353222 Modern hotel near river and a short walk from beach. Billiards.

BUDOCK VEAN
(0326) 250281
A 9-hole undulating parkland course with plenty of challenges (5007 yards, SSS 65). The course is attached to the Budock Vean hotel (C/H ★★★) Visitors are welcome at any time. Green fees on application. There is a restaurant where snacks, lunch and table d'hote or an a la carte dinner is available. The hotel, which is in easy access of the many National Trust properties in the area, has its own private beach.

Location
Mawnan Smith, Falmouth, Cornwall TR11 5LG
The club is on the main road between Falmouth and Helston(A394) about 7 miles from Helston.

CARLYON BAY HOTEL
(072 681) 2304
An 18-hole clifftop/parkland course in a glorious setting with magnificent views (6463 yards, SSS 71). Visitors of all playing abilities are welcome if you are a member of another club, but telephone for starting times. Green fees are £12.50 on weekdays and £14 at weekends and Bank Holidays. Company golf days can be catered for. Bar snacks are available and lunch and dinner by prior arrangement with the hotel (★★★★). The club is convenient for the many attractions of Cornwall including St Michael's Mount and Land's End.

Location
Carlyon Bay, St Austell, Cornwall PL25 3RD

FALMOUTH
(0326) 311262
An 18-hole seaside parkland course with fine views over the bay (5581 yards, SSS 67). Visitors are welcome if you are a member of a recognised club. Green fees are £10 per round or £12 per day. Juniors under 18 are half price all week. Lunch and tea is available daily with evening meals by arrangement. Close to the harbour of Falmouth.

Location
Swanpool Road, Falmouth, Cornwall TR11 5BQ
The club is 1 mile W of Swanpool Beach just outside Falmouth.

RAC recommended hotels
Green Lawns ★★★ (0326) 312734 Set in lovely gardens, this hotel has distinctive French chateau features. Indoor swimming pool, tennis, squash. sauna, solarium and gymnasium.
Penmere Manor C/H ★★★ (0326) 211411 A white-faced fine Georgian mansion in secluded gardens. Indoor swimming pool, tennis, sauna, solarium and gymnasium.
Royal Duchy ★★★ (0326) 313042 Surrounded by its own garden this hotel has fine views of the Bay. Indoor swimming pool, sauna, and solarium.
St Michaels ★★★ (0326) 312707 A Substantial hotel in exception gardens enjoying fine sea views. Indoor swimming pool, tennis, sauna, solarium and gymnasium.
Meudon C/H ★★★ A country-house hotel in 10 acres of subtropical gardens descending to a private beach and the sea. Fishing and riding. Open Mar-Dec.
Bay ★★★ (0326) 312094 Large three-storey Edwardian hotel in lovely gardens, sun terrace with sea view. Swimming pool, putting, sauna, solarium and billiards.
Greenbank ★★★ (0326) 312440 Historic building with nautical flavour. Right on thr quayside. Fishing and solarium.
Gyllyngdune ★★★ (0326) 312978 Old Georgian manor house in 2 acres of gardens. Indoor swimming pool, sauna, solarium and gymnasium.
Carthion ★★ (0326) 313669 Small family-managed hotel with panoramic view over the sea.
Crill ★★ (0326) 312994 Small family-run hotel in quiet countryside with attractive garden. Swimming pool.
Somerdale ★★ (0326) 312566 An attractive Edwardian hotel with secluded rear garden. Closed January.

LAUNCESTON
(0566) 3442
An 18-hole undulating parkland course with fine views towards Bodmin and Dartmoor (6357 yards, SSS 70). Provided you have a handicap, visitors are welcome. Green fees are £10 on weekdays and £12 at weekends. Bar snacks are available at lunchtime, other meals by arrangement.

Location
St Stephens, Launceston, Cornwall PL15 8HF
Take the Bude road from Launceston (B3254) and 1 mile N of the town centre turn left opposite St Stephen's Church. The club is 300 yards on the right.

RAC recommended hotels
Eagle House ★★★ (0566) 772036 Attractive Georgian house in town centre.
White Hart ★★ (0566) 2013 A former coaching inn in the town centre. Billiards.

LOOE BIN DOWN GOLF AND COUNTRY CLUB
(05034) 571
An 18-hole moorland/meadowland course with easy walking (6104 yards, SSS 69). Situated on high ground, this course can get exceptionally windy. Visitors are welcome at any time. Green fees are £10 per day. Bar snacks are available and meals can be arranged. The club is within easy access of Bodmin Moor and Whitesand Bay.

Location
Widegates, Looe, Cornwall
The course is midway between Liskeard and Looe. Take the A38 from Liskeard, turn off onto the B3252, and then the A387. The club is on the right. Alternatively take the B3253 from Looe and the club is on the left.

RAC recommended hotels
Commonwood Manor ★★ (050 36) 2929 A manor house set in 3 acres of grounds with lovely views of the river valley and town. Swimming pool. Open Mar-Oct.
Hannafore Point ★★★ (050 26) 3273 Modern hotel with unspoilt views of glorious coastline. Indoor swimming pool, squash, sauna, solarium and gymnasium.
Talland Bay ★★★ (0503) 72667 Attractive country house in lovely garden with sea view Swimming pool, putting, sauna, solarium and gymnasium.
Fieldhead ★★ (05036) 2689 In elevated position with good sea views, an attractive Victorian building in gardens. Swimming pool.
Klymiarven C/H ★★ (050 36) 2333 Originally the manor house of East Looe set in extensive gardens. Swimming pool and solarium.

MULLION
(0326) 240276
An 18-hole undulating seaside course (5616 yards, SSS 67) on the cliff edges overlooking the sands and with distant views of St Michael's Mount. Visitors with a handicap certificate are welcome. Green fees are £12 per day and £40 per 5 days. Bar snacks are available and there is a restaurant. The club is close to the lovely beaches of Polurrian and Mullion Cove.

Location
Cury, Helston, Cornwall TR12 7BP
About 5 miles from Helston, taking the A3081 Lizard road and leaving it at the B3296. Then follow the signs for Mullion.

RAC recommended hotels
Polurrian ★★★ (0326) 240421 An impressive white building in 12 acres with panoramic sea views. Indoor/outdoor swimming pool, putting, tennis, squash, riding, sauna, solarium, gymnasium and billards.
Mullion Cove ★★ (0326) 240328 A large hotel overlooking Mount Bay. Swimming pool, tennis, sauna and solarium.

NEWQUAY
(0637) 872091
An 18-hole seaside links course with outstanding views of the sea (6140 yards, SSS 69). Visitors are

welcome at all times. Green fees on application. Lunch is served daily.

Location

Tower Road, Newquay, TR17 1LT

The club is about ½ mile from the town centre of Newquay in the direction of Fistral beach.

RAC recommended hotels

Bristol ★★★ (0637) 875181 A family-run hotel overlooking the beach. Indoor swimming pool, sauna, solarium and billiards.

Windsor ★★★ (0637) 875188 A large hotel with a modern extension. Secluded sun trap garden. Indoor and outdoor swimming pools putting, squash, sauna, solarium and gymnasium.

Barrowfield ★★★ (0637) 878878 Large four-storey modern hotel just of the seafront. Indoor and outdoor swimming pool, sauna, solarium, gymnasium and billiards.

Edgcumbe ★★★ (0637) 872061 Four-storey white hotel with fine sea views. Offers entertainment programme. Indoor and outdoor swimming pools, sauna, solarium and billiards.

Kilbirnie ★★★ (0637) 875155 Three-storey building with excellant sea views. Easy access to beach. Indoor swimming pool, sauna, solarium and billiards.

Riveria ★★★ (0637) 874251 Owner-run cliff-top hotel set in grounds. Swimming pool, squash, sauna and billiards.

St Brannocks ★★★ (0637) 872038 Four-storey hotel in commanding position with magnificent seaviews. Indoor swimming pool, sauna and solarium.

Trebarwith ★★★ (0637) 872288 Cliff-top hotel with sub-tropical secluded gardens and commanding sea views. Indoor swimming pool fishing, sauna, solarium and billiards.

Windsor ★★★ (0637) 875188 Large hotel with modern extension Secluded sun-trap garden. Indoor and outdoor swimming pool, putting, squash, sauna, solarium and gymnasium.

Beachcroft ★★ (0637) 873022 Large hotel in 2½ cliff-top acres, private steps to beach. Swimming pool, putting, tennis, sauna and solarium,

Bewdley ★★ (0637) 872883 Modern owner-run hotel in outskirts. Overlooks Fistral Beach. Swimming.

Corrisande Manor ★★ (0637) 872042 Hotel of unique turreted design, in secluded groundsby tidal estuary. Solarium and putting.

Cross Mount ★★ (0637) 872669 Charming two-storey white-painted 17th century building with beamed restaurant.

Great Western ★★ (0637) 872010 Imposing white building convenient for town and enjoying fine sea views. Indoor swimming pool, sauna and solarium.

Newgarth ★★ (0637) 873250 A four-storey, stone-built hotel, recently refurbished a short way from the town centre.

Porth Veor Manor ★★ (0637) 873274 Small hotel with manor house appearance. Fine sea views. Putting and tennis.

Sandy Lodge ★★ (0637) 872851 Owner-run pleasant hotel conveniently situated by the sea front. Indoor and outdoor swimming pool, sauna, solarium and billiards.

Tregurrian ★★ (0637) 860280 Attractive white building 100 yards from a mile-long sandy beach. Swimming pool and solarium.

Waters Edge ★★ (0637) 872048 Small hotel in own grounds. Picture windows give panoramic sea views.

PERRANPORTH
(0872) 573701

An 18-hole links course with outstanding sea views (6208 yards, SSS 72). Provided you have a handicap certificate, visitors are welcome, but it is advisable to telephone before arrival. Green fees are £12 on weekdays and £15 at weekends and Bank Holidays. There is a resident Steward and Stewardess who can arrange meals.

Location

Budnick Hill, Perranporth, Cornwall TR6 0AB

Leave Newquay on the A3075 and turn onto the B3285. The club is on the fringe of the town adjacent to the beach.

PRAA SANDS
(0736) 763445

A 9-hole seaside course (4036 yards, SSS 60). Visitors are welcome except on Friday evenings and Sunday mornings. The club prefers you to have a handicap certificate. Green fees £5 per day/round (£3 with a member), Juniors £3 and from £7 per round for 18 holes. Breakfast, lunch and dinner is available. Places of local interest include the beach, Minack Theatre, Flambard Theme Park and Land's End.

Location

Germoe Crossroads, Penzance, Cornwall T20 9TQ

Take the A394 from Helson towards Penzance and the club is about halfway between the two towns.

RAC recommended hotels

Prah Sands ★★ (0736) 762438 Set in two acres of attractive grounds, 300 yards from the sea. Swimming pool, tennis and billiards.

ST AUSTELL
(0726) 74756

An challenging 18-hole heathland/parkland course (5725 yards, SSS 68). Visitors are welcome but you must be a member of a recognised club and hold a handicap certificate. Green fees are £10 per round or day and £12 at weekends. Hot meals and bar snacks are available from midday until 2pm daily and evening meals can be provided by arrangement. The club is within easy access of St Austell Bay.

Location

Tregongeeves Lane, St Austell, Cornwall PL26 7DS

Take the A390 St Austell-Truro road for 1 mile W of St Austell. The Tregongeeves Lane junction is clearly signposted just below the St Mewan school.

RAC recommended hotels
Carlyon Bay ★★★★ (072 681) 2304 A large 1930s hotel with lovely cliff-top views. Indoor and outdoor swimming pool, tennis and billiards.
Cliff Head ★★★ (072 681) 2345 Set in its own pleasant grounds this is a family-run hotel enjoying fine sea views. Swimming pool.
Porth Avallen ★★★ (072 681) 2802 Overlooking the bay, an attractive mid-20th century building.
Boscundle Manor C/H ★★ (072 681) 3557 Charming stone-built 18th century house in secluded grounds. Swimming pool.
White Hart ★★ (0726) 72100 Georgian hotel conveniently situated in town centre.

ST ENODOC
(020886) 3216
Two 18-hole seaside links courses with massive sandhills, including the 'Himalayas', supposed to be the highest in Britain; the Church course (6207 yards, SSS 70) and the Holywell course (4165 yards, SSS 61). Visitors are welcome but you must have a handicap of 24 or below for the Church course. There are no restrictions on when you can play. Green fees on application. Lunch is available every day at the Cornish Arms, Pendogget. There are good beaches and sailing facilities locally.
Location
Rock, Wadebridge, Cornwall PL27 6LB
From Wadebridge take the B3314 Port Isaac road for 3 miles and turn left for Rock.

RAC recommended hotels
St Moritz ★★ (020 886) 2312 A family hotel in 8 acres of grounds enjoying fine sea views.
Mariners ★★ (020 886) 2312 Modern hotel with motel-style bedrooms in two seperate buildings; overlooking the Camel Estuary.
Roskarnon House ★★ (020 886) 2329 Overlooking the sea, attractive Edwardian house set in gardens.
Molesworth Arms ★★ (020 881) 2055 16th century inn of attractive design. Conveniently situated.

ST MELLION COUNTRY CLUB
(0579) 50101
Two fine 18-hole parkland courses; the Nicklaus, a challenge with its splendid greens (6626 yards, SSS 72) and the more 'friendly' Old (5927 yards, SSS 68). Visitors are welcome but you need a handicap certificate to play on the Nicklaus. Green fees are £30 per round on the Nicklaus and £14 on the Old course. There is a hotel, restaurant, grill room and coffee shop. Squash, badminton, swimming and tennis are available at the hotel, which is within access of Cotehele House (NT).
Location
St Mellion, Saltash, Cornwall PL12 6SD
Take the A388 south for 3 miles from Callington.

TEHIDY PARK
(0209) 842208
A well-maintained 18-hole parkland course set amongst pine trees and rhododendrons (6222 yards, SSS 70). Provided you have a handicap certificate, visitors are welcome. Green fees are £10 on weekdays and £15 at the weekend. A full range of bar snacks is available and there is an a la carte restaurant open in the mornings and evenings.
Location
Camborne, Cornwall TR14 0HH
You will find the club off the A30, 2 miles north east of Camborne on the Portreath road (B3300)

TREGENNA CASTLE HOTEL
(0736) 796254
An 18-hole course (3549 yards, SSS 58). Visitors of all playing abilities are welcome. Green fees are £7 on weekdays and £8 at weekends. There is a bar. The hotel is close to the seaside resort of St Ives.
Location
St Ives, TR26 2DE
1 mile from the centre of St Ives on the A3074.

TREVOSE COUNTRY CLUB
(0841) 520208
Two particularly attractive seaside links courses; 18-hole (6608 yards, SSS 72) and 9-hole (1357 yards). Visitors are welcome at any time but are restricted to 3 and 4 ball matches. It is advisable to telephone first. A handicap certificate is required for the 18-hole course, but beginners are welcome on the 9 hole course. Green fees vary according to the season. There is a good restaurant where all meals are available. The club is close to the quaint port of Padstow and is an ideal spot for a holiday.
Location
Constantine Bay, Padstow, Cornwall PL28 8JB
Taking the B3276 you will find the club 4 miles W of Padstow.

RAC recommended hotels
Metropole ★★★ (0841) 532486 Hotel above the town overlooking the Camel Estuary. Swimming pool and putting.
Old Custom House ★★ (0841) 532359 Delightful inn with views of busy harbour and Camel Estuary.

TRURO
(0872) 72640
An 18-hole undulating parkland course (5357 yards, SSS 66). Visitors are welcome provided you have a handicap certificate. Green fees are £12 on weekdays (£6.50 with a member) and £15 at weekends and Bank Holidays (£7.50 with a member). Lunch and evening meals are served daily. Local attractions include St Michael's Mount (NT) and Padstow.
Location
Treliske, Truro, Cornwall TR1 3LG
Take the A390 W out of Truro and the golf club is signposted just off the roundabout. It is about 1½ miles on the right.

RAC recommended hotels
Brookdale ★★★ (0872) 73513 A large impressive looking hotel set in its own grounds.
Carlton ★★ (0872) 72450 An attractive Victorian

building with large modern bedroom extension. Sauna, solarium and gymnasium.
Royal ★★ (0872) 70345 Established hotel in the old tradition, a dignified city centre building.

WEST CORNWALL
(0736) 753401
A beautiful 18-hole natural seaside links course (5854 yards, SSS 68). Visitors with handicap certificates are welcome but it is a good idea to telephone ahead. Green fees are £10 per round, £12 per day, £45 per week, and £12 per round, £14 per day at the weekend. Lunch and dinner is available daily except Monday. Places of interest include Land's End and the nearby resort of St. Ives.
Location
Lelant, St Ives, Cornwall TR26 3DZ

RAC recommended hotels
Chy-an-Drea ★★★ (0736) 795076 Extended granite buildings overlooking Porthminster Beach. Solarium and gymnasium.
Porthminster ★★★ (0736) 795221 Large and imposing building with views across the bay. Indoor and outdoor swimming pools, sauna, solarium and gymnasium.
Chy-an-Albany ★★ (0736) 796759 Privately-owned three-storey hotel with fine views over the bay.
Chy-an-Dour ★★ (0736) 796436 Fine granite building with extension, enjoying panoramic views of the bay.
Pedn Olva ★★ (0736) 796222 Attractive white building almost surrounded by sea. Sun terraces overlooking beach. Swimming pool.

WHITSAND BAY HOTEL GOLF CLUB
(0503) 30276/30470
An 18-hole clifftop course with easy walking (5367 yards, SSS 67). Visitors are welcome by arrangement. Green fees are £10 on weekdays and £11.50 at weekends and Bank Holidays. Catering facilities can be arranged. There is a leisure complex and an RAC approved hotel on site, with a swimming pool and sauna and the club is central to the Cornish holiday area.
Location
Portwinkle, Crafthole, Torpoint, Cornwall PL11 3BU
Take the A38 from Liskeard or Saltash and turn onto the A374 at Budge's Shop roundabout following this road until you reach the B3247 at Haye. The club is just past Crafthole.

CUMBRIA

ALSTON MOOR
(0498) 81675
A 9-hole meadowland course (6450 yards, SSS 66). Visitors are welcome at any time. Green fees are £3.50 on weekdays and £4.50 at weekends and Bank Holidays. Catering facilities can be arranged.
Location
The Hermitage, Alston, Cumbria CA9 3DB
Take the A686 from Penrith and turn right onto the B6277 in Alston. The club is about 1½ miles S.

RAC recommended hotels
Lowbyer Manor ★★ (0498) 81230 An attractive 300 year old manor house in a quiet area of outstanding natural beauty.
Lovelady Shield C/H ★★ (0498) 81203 Charming Regency country house in 2½ acres of sheltered, secluded gardens. Tennis.

APPLEBY
(0930) 51432
An 18-hole moorland course (5895 yards, SSS 68). Visitors of all playing abilities are welcome at any time. Green fees are £6 during the week and £8 at weekends and Bank Holidays. Catering facilities can be arranged. The club is close to the Wild Rose Caravan Park at Ormside. Local attractions include Appleby Castle and Conservation Centre.
Location
Brackenber Moor, Appleby-in-Westmorland, Cumbria CA16 6LP
Take the A66 from Penrith to Appleby-in-Westmorland. The club is 2 miles south of Appleby on the A66.

RAC recommended hotels
Appleby Manor ★★★ (076 83) 51571 A Victorian country house in extensive grounds with panoramic views. Indoor swimming pool, sauna, solarium and gymnasium.
Tufton Arms ★★★ (076 83) 51593 A town centre 16th century posting house in the market square.
Royal Oak ★★ (076 83) 51463 A two-storey coaching inn with beams. The hotel dates back to the 17th century.
White Hart ★★ (076 83) 51598 Family-managed hotel, close to castle and town centre.

BARROW
(0229) 25444
An attractive 18-hole undulating meadowland course with some fine views of the Lakes (6209 yards, SSS 70). Visitors who are members of a recognised golf club are welcome. Green fees are £8, or £6 if playing with a member. Catering facilities are available by arrangement. Local attractions include Furness Abbey.
Location
Blakesmoor Lane, Hawcoat, Barrow-in-Furness, Cumbria LA154 4QB
Take the A590 towards Barrow-in-Furness and turn right to Hawcoat just after entering the boundary of Barrow. You will find the club a little way ahead.

RAC recommended hotel
Abbey House ★★★★ (0229) 38282 Lutyens-designed mansion in 14 acres of gardens and wood, on A590 north of town. Putting.

BRAMPTON
(06977) 2255
A testing 18-hole moorland course with exceptional views from its hilltop position (6420 yards, SSS 71). Visitors are welcome but the club prefers you to have a handicap certificate. Green fees are £7 on weekdays and £10 at weekends. Full catering facilities are available but it is advisable to arrange this in advance. Local attractions include Talkin Tarn.
Location
Brampton, Cumbria CA8 1HN
Take the A69 from Carlisle to Brampton and turn right onto the B6413 Castle Carrock road. You will find the course about 2 miles S on the right.

RAC recommended hotels
Tarn End ★★ (06977) 2340 An 18th century farmhouse overlooking a lake in quiet grounds. Fishing. Open from 1 Mar-31 Jan.
Farlam Hall C/H ★★ (069 76) 234 Lovely 17th century manor with lake in ground.
Kirby Moor C/H ★★ Small, owner-run hotel just off A6071 north west of town.

CARLISLE
(0228) 513303
A particularly attractive 18-hole parkland course with fine turf and natural hazards (6278 yards, SSS 70). Visitors are welcome by application as there are some restrictions at weekends. All levels of players are welcome. Green fees on application. Snacks, lunches, dinners and high teas are served daily. Local attractions include Carlisle Castle and Hadrian's Wall.
Location
Aglionby, Carlisle CA4 8AG
The club is 3 miles E of Carlisle. You should leave the M6 at Exit 43 and take the A69 for about three quarters of a mile.

RAC recommended hotels.
Queens Arms (0228) 60699 A white-painted inn close to the River Eden in a quiet village. The bedrooms are in an adjoining modern building.
Crown ★★★ (0228) 61888 An attractive Georgian building situated in its own grounds. Facilities include a swimming pool, fishing, squash, sauna, solarium, gymnasium and billiards.
Central ★★★ (0228) 20256 Tall Victorian brick-built hotel in the city centre.
Crest ★★★ (0228) 31201 A large modern hotel in Carlisle with a 'travel' theme decor. Billiards.
Crown and Mitre ★★★ (0228) 25491 Edwardian period hotel in centre of Carlisle, near the cathedral. Indoor swimming pool
Cumbrian ★★★ (0748) 850445 Four-storey elegant Victorian building in the city centre.
Cumbria Park ★★★ (0228) 22887 Family-managed hotel set in beautiful gardens, between city centre and M6. Hadrian's Wall runs through grounds.
Hayton Castle C/H ★★★ (0228) 70651 Castle-style mansion set in 68 acres of park and woodland. Putting.
String of Horses ★★★ (0228) 70297 17th century coaching inn at Faugh to east of city. Easy access to M6. Swimming pool, sauna, solarium and gymnasium.
Swallow Hilltop ★★★ (0228) 29255 Modern two-storey in own grounds by A6 link road. Indoor swimming pool, putting, tennis, sauna, solarium and gymnasium.
Carrow House ★★ (0228) 32073 Traditional detached red sandstone building with single storey extension.
Pinegrove ★★ (0228) 24828 Small traditional stone-built house set in own grounds; convenient for town centre.
Woodlands ★★ (0228) 45643 Family-run hotel in converted stone-built houses on A6, 2 miles south of town centre.

COCKERMOUTH
(059681) 223
An 18-hole fell-land course with some challenging holes but wonderful views (5496 yards, SSS 67). Visitors are always welcome. Green fees are £6 a day and £8 at the weekend. Snacks and meals are available by arrangement with the Stewardess. Local attractions include Wordsworth's birthplace, Cockermouth and Bassenthwaite Lake.
Location
Embleton, Cockermouth, Cumbria CA13 9SG
Take the A66 from Keswick to Cockermouth and you will come to the club 4 miles before Cockermouth, about 1 mile E of the road.

RAC recommended hotels
Broughton Craggs C/H ★★★ (0900) 824400 19th century manor house in acres overlooking river to west of town. Fishing.
Trout ★★★ (0900) 823591 White-painted 17th century building with lovely garden running to river. Fishing.
Globe ★★ (0900) 822126 A handsome Georgian red brick hotel in the centre of the market town of Cockermouth.

DUNNERHOLME
(0229) 62675
A unique 10-hole links course with good views of the Lake fells (6101 yards, SSS 69). Visitors are welcome at any time, except onSunday when you can play after 4.30pm. Green fees are £5 on weekdays, £6 at weekends and Bank Holidays. It is £2.50 on weekdays if you are with a member. Catering facilities can be arranged.
Location
Duddon Road, Askam-in-Furness, Cumbria LA16 7AW
Follow the A590 to Barrow-in-Furness and turn right onto the A595 towards Askam-in-Furness. Go over the Askam railway crossing towards the seashore then turn right at the cattle grid.

FURNESS
(0229) 41232
An 18-hole links course with extensive views of the Lake District (6418 yards, SSS 71). Visitors of all playing abilities are always welcome. Green fees are £10 on weekdays or £8 with a member. You can also buy a weekly ticket for £40. Full catering facilities are available but you need to arrange it in advance. The club is very handy for a holiday in the Lake District.
Location
Central Drive, Walney Island, Barrow-in-Furness, Cumbria LA14 3LN
Take the A590 to Barrow-in-Furness and go through the town, following the signs to the Isle of Walney. Go straight ahead at the traffic lights onto the bridge over the channel. The club is to the right of the road.

RAC recommended hotels
See Barrow.

GRANGE FELL
(05395) 32536
A 9-hole hillside course with some glorious views of the surrounding hills (4826 metres SSS 66). Visitors are welcome provided you have a bag of clubs and proper dress. A handicap certificate is not required. Green fees are £6 on weekdays and £7 at weekend and Bank Holidays. Local attractions include Cartmel Village race-course, Holker Hall and the seawater swimming pool at Grange-over-Sands.
Location
Fell Road, Grange-over-Sands, Cumbria LA11 6HB
Take the A590 and at, the roundabout, turn onto the B5278 signposted Grange-over-Sands. The club is situated on the main road towards Cartmel.

RAC recommended hotels
See Grange-over-Sands.

GRANGE-OVER-SANDS
(05395) 33180
An 18-hole flat parkland course with easy walking (5660 yards, SSS 68). Visitors are welcome at any time and a handicap certificate is not required, although you must be a member of a recognised golf club. Green fees are £8 a day during the week and £10 at weekends and Bank Holidays. The fees are half price if you are with a member. Full catering facilities are available, except on Tuesday. Places of local interest include Haverthwaite Railway at Bowness and the local leisure centre and beaches.
Location
Meathop Road, Grange-over-Sands, Cumbria LA11 6QX
Follow the A590, leaving it at the roundabout signposted Grange-over-Sands. The course is on the left-hand side just before you enter Grange itself.

RAC recommended hotels
Cumbria Grand ★★★ (04484) 2331 A grand grey-stone Victorian hotel with breathtaking views and extensive grounds. Facilities include putting, tennis and billiards.
Grange ★★★ (053 95) 33666 A spacious stone-built mid-Victorian hotel in a prominent position overlooking the sea.
Graythwaite Manor C/H ★★ (053 95) 32001 Attractive well-appointed country house hotel. Delightful gardens. Putting, tennis and billiards.
Netherwood ★★ (053 95) 32552 Lovely Victorian house, in Jacobean style with oak panelling.

KENDAL
(0539) 724079
A fine 18-hole undulating moorland course with a difficult first hole (5483 yards, SSS 67). Provided you have a handicap certificate, visitors are welcome at any time, but it is advisable to telephone first. The club requires smart dress. There are full catering facilities except on Monday.
Location
The Heights, Kendal, Cumbria
Take the A6 to Kendal and turn off onto the B5284, following the signs to the golf course.

RAC recommended hotels
County ★★★ (0539) 22461 A classic early 19th century building near the station and town centre.
Riverside ★★★ (0539) 724707 A sympathetic conversion of a 17th-century tannery.
Woolpack ★★★ (0539) 723852 A coaching inn in the centre of Kendal, retain its 'old worlde' charm.
Garden House ★★ (0539) 731131 Attractive Regency house in acres of formal grounds.

KESWICK
(07687) 83324
An 18-hole undulating moorland/parkland course with tree-lined fairways and several streams (6175 yards, SSS 72). Visitors are always welcome even at weekends and Bank Holidays. Green fees are £6 a day or £4 with a member. Catering facilities are available by arrangement. The club is situated in the heart of the Lake District and all its many attractions.
Location
Threlkeld Hall, Keswick, Cumbria CA12 4HH
Take the A66 E out of Keswick and you will find the course about 4 miles along the road.

RAC recommended hotels
Stakis Lodore Swiss ★★★ (059 684) 285 A modernised, largely Victorian impressive granite hotel with grounds overlooking the lake. Indoor and outdoor swimming pools, tennis, squash, fishing, sauna, solarium and gymnasium.
Keswick ★★★ (076 87) 72020 A majestic, turreted Victorian hotel in a quiet situation within its own grounds.
Brundholme C/H ★★★ (076 87) 74495 Regency villa described by Coleridge as being in a delicious situation.

Derwentwater ★★★ (076 87) 72538 Pleasant white-painted three-storey hotel in 15 acres of grounds by lake. Putting and fishing.
Queen's ★★★ (076 87) 71144 Modernised early 19th century posting house pleasantly situated in town centre.
Chaucer ★★ (076 87) 72318 Four-storey stone-built family-managed hotel in quiet street near town centre.
Crow Head ★★ (076 87) 72208 Tall Lakeland stone 19th century building enjoying panoramic views of Derwentwater.
Daleview ★★ (076 87) 72666 Small family-run hotel near town centre.
Grange Country House C/H ★★ Attractive small hotel set in gardens, perched on hill top.
Hazeldene ★★ (076 87) 72106 Three-storey stone terrace houses at south end of town. Lovely views to Derwentwater.
Highfield ★★ (076 87) 72508 Enjoying magnificent hill views, a three-storey building of local slate and stone, to south of town.
Lairbeck ★★ (067 87) 73373 Fine house of Lakeland stone in secluded garden with mountain views.
Lyzzick C/H ★★(067 87) 72277 In spacious grounds on southern foot of Skiddaw, a country house with fine views. Swimming pool.
Red House C/H ★★ (076 87) 72211 Country mansion (1840) of red-stone and brick with lawns and woodland. Swimming pool and putting.

KIRKBY LONSDALE
(0468) 71429
A 9-hole meadowland links course (4058 yards, SSS 60). Visitors are welcome at any time except Sunday mornings. Green fees are £4 on weekdays and Saturdays, and £7 on Sundays. Local attractions include country walks in South Lakeland, Kendal, and Lancaster Castle.
Location
Casterton Road, Kirkby Lonsdale LA6 2JN
You will find the club about 1 mile out of the town centre on the Sedbergh Road (the A683).

RAC recommended hotels
Royal ★★★ (052 42) 71217 Attractive old stone-built three-storey hotel overlooking the town square. Billiards.
Whoop Hall ★★ (052 42) 71284 A beamed 17th century inn sympathetically modernised to retain its character.

MARYPORT
(0900) 812605
An 18-hole seaside links course with good views over the River Solway (6272 yards, SSS 71). There is some 'back' running through a few holes. Visitors are welcome and a handicap certificate is not required. Green fees are £6 on weekdays and £8 at weekends and Bank Holidays (£4 with a member). Catering facilities are available by prior arrangement. Local attractions include Maryport Harbour Museum, Roman remains, sea fishing in Solway Firth and the Lake District.
Location
Bank End, Maryport, Cumbria CA15 6PA
Leave the A6 at Penrith for the A66 to Workington. Then turn right onto the A596 and then left onto the B5300 (Silloth) road. The course is about 1 mile along the road.

RAC recommended hotels
Ellenbank ★★ (0900) 815233 A fine sandstone building set in its own grounds north of the town.
Waverley ★★ (0900) 812115 A corner terraced family-run hotel on the main street.

PENRITH
(0768) 62217
A lovely 18-hole parkland course with some challenging holes (6026 yards, SSS 69). Visitors are welcome provided you have a handicap and are members of a golf club. It is very busy between April and October, so it is advisable to telephone first as there are some restrictions, especially at weekends. Green fees are £10 on weekdays and £12 at weekends and Bank Holidays (£5 and £6 respectively if you are with a member). Lunch and evening meals are available except on Monday and Tuesday. Situated in the heart of the Lake District, the club is very convenient for walking and touring.
Location
Salkeld Road, Penrith, Cumbria CA11 8SP
Follow the A6 NE of Penrith and the club is about ½ a mile on the right.

RAC recommended hotels
George ★★★ (0768) 92696 A substantial former coaching house-stone built in Georgian style.
North Lake Gateway ★★★★ (0768) 68111 Modern stone-built three-storey hotel near M6. Impressive foyer-lounge featuring massive fireplace. Indoor swimming pool, squash, sauna, solarium, gymnasium and billiards.
Clifton Hill ★★ (0768) 62717 Modernised hotel in charming Edwardian style building south of the town.
Glen Cottage ★★ (0768) 62221 Attractive cottage-style building situated close to town centre.
Mill Inn ★★ (076 87) 79632 Picturesque 16th-century inn beside a river. Fishing.

SEASCALE
(09467) 28202
A testing 18-hole seaside links course with some wonderful views of Wasdale Screes and Scafell (6416 yards, SSS 71). Visitors of all playing abilities are welcome. Green fees are £10 on weekdays and £12 at weekends and Bank Holidays. Full catering facilities are available by prior arrangement, except on Monday and Tuesday when there are some restrictions.
Location
The Banks, Seascale, Cumbria CA20 1QL
Leave the M6 at junction 36 or the A6 at Levens Hall and follow the A590 to Barrow-in-Furness. At

the junction of Greenodd take the A5092 and then the A595 towards Workington. Turn off onto the B5344 at Holmrook and the course is on the coast just north of the village.

RAC recommended hotel
Pennington Arms ★ (0229) 717222 Country inn in small village close to sea.

SEDBERGH
(0587) 20993
A 9-hole fell-land course with some hilly terrain (4134 yards, SSS 61). Visitors are always welcome with no restrictions, but there are limited facilities and it is advisable to telephone the Secretary first. Green fees are £2 a day on an honesty box system.
Location
The Riggs, Millthrop, Sedbergh, Cumbria
Leave the M6 at junction 37 and turn onto the A684 E towards Sedbergh. The course is 1 mile from Sedbergh on the Dent road, via the hamlet of Millthrop.

RAC recommended hotel
Oakdene ★★ (053 96) 20280 Victorian stone-built house of character with views of Yorkshire dales.

SILECROFT
(0657) 4250
A 9-hole seaside course with easy walking (5712 yards, SSS 68). Visitors are welcome on weekdays but are often restricted between midday and 5.30pm at weekends and Bank Holidays. Green fees are £5 a day. A £10 weekly ticket is available from the caravan site which is adjacent to the club. Local attractions include Millom Castle and Millom Folk Museum.
Location
Silecroft, Millom, Cumbria LA18 4AG
Take the A590 towards Barrow-in-Furness and leave at the junction of Greenodd onto the A5092 and A595. Turn off the road onto the A5093 at Hallthwaites towards the village of Millom. The course is 3 miles north of Millom, through Silecroft village and towards the seashore.

SILLOTH ON SOLWAY
(0965) 31304
An 18-hole undulating seaside championship course (6343 yards, SSS 70). Visitors are welcome but the club prefers you to have a handicap certificate. Green fees are £10 a day on weekdays and £16 at weekends and Bank Holidays, and half price if you are with a member. A full range of catering services is available daily except Monday. Attractions include the local beaches.
Location
Silloth on Solway, Carlisle, Cumbria CA5 4AT
Take the A595 from Carlisle and turn onto the A596 at Thursby. Follow the road to Wigton and then take the B5302 to Silloth. The club is about 18 miles W of Carlisle.

RAC recommended hotels
Golf ★★★(069 73) 31438 A pleasant 19th century building overlooking grass and trees to sea.
Skinburness ★★★ (069 73) 32332 A refurbished hotel in a peacefully situated large Victorian house. Sauna, solariumn, gymnasium and billiards.

ST BEES SCHOOL
(0946) 82295
A 9-hole seaside course with fine sea views (5082 yards, SSS 65). Visitors are welcome except on competition days during the summer. Green fees on application.
Location
Rhoda Grove, Rheda, Frizington
Take the A595 to Whitehaven. The club is 4 miles S of Whitehaven on the B5345.

STONYHOLME MUNICIPAL
(0228) 34856
An 18-hole flat meadowland course (5600 yards, SSS 68). The rivers Eden and Petrel flowing through and around the course affect 7 holes, and there are additional water hazards. Visitors of all playing abilities are welcome. Green fees are £3.90 per round. There is a full catering service. Local attractions include Carlisle Castle, the Lake District and Hadrian's Wall.
Location
St Aidans Road, Carlisle
The club is 1 mile north east of Carlisle. Leave the M6 at junction 43, and take A69 for 1 mile west.

RAC recommended hotels
See Carlisle.

ULVERSTON
(0229) 52824
A quiet 18-hole parkland course (6142 yards, SSS 69). Visitors are welcome both as individuals or as parties of bona fide golfers. A handicap certificate or membership of a recognised club is necessary. From March to October, green fees are £12 on weekdays and £15 at weekends and Bank Holidays, and there is a weekly rate of £30 for any 3 days in 5. From November to February, fees are £8 on weekdays and £10 at weekends and half price if you are with a member. Tuesday is Ladies Day. Full meals and bar snacks are provided daily except Monday. Local attractions include Holker Hall with its car museum and deer park, Wordsworth's Cottage, and Beatrix Potter's Cottage at Hawkeshead.
Location
Bardsea Park, Ulverston, Cumbria
Follow the A590 to Ulverston and leave it for the B5087 to Bardsea. The club is in Bardsea Park on the right of the road.

RAC recommended hotel
Sefton House ★★ (0229) 52190 A small pleasant hotel in a Georgian town house.
Lonsdale House ★★★ (0229) 52598 Three-storey 18th century building in quiet street. Pleasant garden at rear.

WINDERMERE
(09662) 3123
A pleasant 18-hole undulating parkland course with glorious views of the Lake District (5006 yards, SSS 65). The course is commonly known as the 'mini Gleneagles'. Visitors are welcome provided you have a handicap certificate. Green fees are £12 on weekdays and £14 at weekends and Bank Holidays. There is a restaurant which has very good English food. The club is situated in splendid area of the Lake District National Park.
Location
Cleaharrow, Windermere, Cumbria LA23 3NB
Leave the M6 at junction 36/37 for Kendal and then take the A591 to Windermere. The course is 9 miles from Kendal.

RAC recommended hotels
Low Wood ★★★ (05394) 33338 A large hotel of character with lake and mountain views. Indoor swimming pool, putting, fishing, squash, sauna, solarium, gymnasium and billiards.
Wild Boar ★★★ (096 62) 5225 A well-appointed hotel just outside Windermere.
Old England ★★★★ (096 62) 2444 Imposing four-storey Victorian hotel (modern extension). Fine views from garden. Swimming pool and billiards.
Belmont Manor C/H ★★★ (05394) 33316 Stone-built villa, completely refurbished, with modern extension in 7 acres of delightful gardens.
Beech Hill ★★★ (096 62) 2137 Light modern hotel with terrace garden offering fine lake views. Indoor swimming pool, sauna, solarium and gymnasium.
Belsfield ★★★ (096 62) 2448 Elegant early 19th century hotel in lovely grounds overlooking lake. Indoor swimming pool, putting, tennis, sauna and solarium.
Burn How ★★★ (096 62) 6226 Modern chalets adjoining 19th century building in peaceful, secluded gardens.
Burnside ★★★ (096 62) 2211 Attractive white-faced Victorian building with extensive lake view from garden. Swimming pool, squash, sauna, solarium, gymnasium and snooker.
Dawson Dene Cottage ★★★ (044 88) 676 Charming two-storey white-painted stone building set in country. Swimming pool, squash, sauna, solarium, gymnasium and snooker.
Langdale Chase C/H ★★★ (05394) 32201 A stone-built Victorian country house with superb lake views from gardens. Putting, tennis and fishing.
Merewood C/H ★★★ (096 62) 6484 Impressive Lakeland country house standing in 20 acres of grounds on a hill overlooking Lake Windemere.
Royal ★★★ (096 62) 3045 Elegantly furnished white-faced Georgian 19th century building in town centre.
Windermere Hydro ★★★ (096 62) 4455 Large modernised Victorian hotel overlooking the Lakeside village.
Bordriggs Country House C/H ★★ (096 62) 3567 A two-storey white-faced house in 1½ acres of gardens. Swimming pool.
Cedar Manor ★★ (096 62) 3192 Pretty, Victorian stone-built house in 1½ acres of garden in residential area.
Ellerthwaite Lodge ★★ (096 62) 5115 Town centre hotel with garden, a Victorian residence.
Grey Walls ★★ (096 62) 3741 Family-managed hotel in stone-built Victorian house set in attractive grounds.
Hideaway ★★ (096 62) 3070 A 19th century stone-built small house quietly set in oen grounds.
Hillthwaite House ★★ (096 62) 3636 Family-run hotel on hill above Bowness with marvelous views of lake and hills. Indoor swimming pool, sauna and solarium.
Holbeck Ghyll C/H ★★ (053 94) 32375 Hotel in delightful hillside position outside town. Good lake views. Putting and billiards.
Lindeth House C/H ★★ (096 62) 5759 Small country house, once home of Beatrix Potter; in beautiful grounds.
Linthwaite C/H ★★ (096 62) 3688 Two-storey country house with lake views from grounds. Putting and fishing,
Ravensworth ★★ (096 62) 3747 Family-managed hotel in three-storey 19th century stone-building.

WORKINGTON
(0900) 603460
An undulating 18-hole meadowland course with magnificent views of the Solway Firth and the Lake District (6100 yards, SSS 70). Visitors are welcome but you must be a member of a golf club and hold a current handicap certificate. Green fees are £8 on weekdays (£8 if you are with a member) and £10 at weekends and Bank Holidays (£5 with a member). There are reductions for parties of 12 or more. A full catering service is available. The club is situated within 20 minutes of the Lake District.
Location
Branthwaite Road, Workington, Cumbria CA1 4NW
The club is off the A595 2 miles SE of Workington town centre. Leave the M6 or A6 at Penrith and take the A66, or from the south leave the M6 at junction 36 for Kendal and take the A590 and then the A595.

RAC recommended hotels
Cumberland Arms ★★★ (0900) 64401 Hotel in town centre, convenient for railway station.
Washington Central ★★★ (0900) 65772 Four-storey purpose-built modern hotel in town centre with public rooms on first floor.
Westland ★★★ (0900)64544 A modern hotel just south of the town.
Crossbarrow ★★ (0900) 61443 A lovely old stone farm building with adjoining motel units.

DERBYSHIRE

ALLESTREE PARK
(0332) 55061
A rather hilly 18-hole parkland course (5749 yards, SSS 68). Visitors are welcome at all times except during competition days or Sunday mornings. Green fees on application. Catering facilities are available by prior arrangement. The club is very handy for parkland walks.
Location
Allestree Hall, Allestree, Derbys DE3 2EU
Leave Derby on the A6 going north; about 4 miles from the city centre you will see the club signposted.

ASHBOURNE
(0335) 42078
A 9-hole undulating parkland course (5388 yards, SSS 66). Visitors are welcome, and green fees are £6 on weekdays and £8 at weekends and Bank Holidays. Catering facilities can be arranged with the Stewards (no catering facilities on Thursdays).
Location
Clifton, Nr Ashbourne, Derbys DE6 4BN
The club is situated 2 miles west of Ashbourne on the A515 towards Sudbury and Lichfield.

BAKEWELL
(062981) 2307
A 9-hole hilly parkland course with tremendous views over the Wye Valley (4804 yards, SSS 64). Visitors of all playing abilities are welcome. Green fees are £8 on weekdays and £12 at weekends, £4 and £8 respectively if you are the guest of a member. There is a bar and meals are available daily except Monday. Local attractions include the Peak District National Park, Chatsworth House and Haddon Hall.
Location
Station Road, Bakewell, Derbys DE4 1GB
Take the A6 from Buxton to Matlock. Bakewell is about midway between the two towns and the club is just under 1 mile from Bakewell Square. Cross the bridge over the River Wye on the A619 Sheffield Chesterfield road, then turn left up Station Road, and after about 1/2 mile, turn right before the Industrial Estate.

RAC recommended hotels
Rutland Arms ★★★ (062 981) 2812 An imposing Georgian building in local stone, well-situated overlooking the town square.
Milford House ★★ (0629) 812130 Georgian residence standing in own grounds yet only 300 yards from town centre.

BLUE CIRCLE
(0433) 20317
A 9-hole parkland course (5252 yards, SSS 66). Although set within the cement works, this is a very scenic part of the Peak District National Park. Visitors are welcome but you must be accompanied by a member. Green fees are £2 on weekdays and £3 at the weekend. There is a works canteen, and a bar which is open during usual licensing hours. Local attractions include the Peak District National Park and Castleton Blue John Mines and Caverns which are 1 1/2 miles away.
Location
Cement Works, Hope, S30 2RP
Leave Sheffield on the A625 and the club is about 10 miles west in Hope Valley.

BREADSALL PRIORY GOLF AND COUNTRY CLUB
(0332) 832235
A pleasant 18-hole undulating parkland course (6402 yards, SSS 71). Visitors of all playing abilities are welcome. Green fees are £10 a day and £14 at the weekend and Bank Holidays. Lunch and dinner is available daily. The local Agricultural College, which is open to the public, is an interesting place to visit.
Location
Moor Road, Morley, Derbys DE7 6DL
Take the A61 from Derby, and 3 miles north east, turn off onto the A608 towards Breadsall. Turn left into Rectory Lane and then right onto Moor Road.
Breadsall Priory ★★★ (0332) 832235 A large stone-built mansion in a parkland setting. Indoor swimming pool, golf, putting, tennis, squash, sauna, solarium, gymnasium and billiards.

BUXTON & HIGH PEAK
(0298) 23453
A good 18-hole meadowland course (5954 yards, SSS 69). Visitors are welcome, and green fees are £10 on weekdays and £12 at weekends. There are full catering facilities and a supper licence. Local attractions include the Pavilion Gardens with its swimming pool.
Location
Waterswallows Road, Fairfield, Buxton, Derbys SK17 7EN
The club is 1 mile from Buxton station, heading north on the A6.

RAC recommended hotels
Buckingham ★★★ (0298) 70481 A substantial stone-built hotel overlooking the Pavilion Gardens.
Portland ★★ (0298) 22462 A family-run, stone-built hotel facing the park near the centre of Buxton.
Lee Wood ★★★ (0298) 23002 Fully modernised building of Georgian splendour situated in own grounds.
Palace ★★★ (0298) 2001 Stately hotel with elegant public rooms and sun lounge. Indoor swimming pool, sauna, solarium, gymnasium, billiards.
Grove ★★ (0298) 3804 Proprietor-run central hotel in 18th century building.
Sandringham ★★ (0298) 72257 Hotel in attractive setting with views of Pavilion Gardens and lake.

CAVENDISH
(0298) 25052
An 18-hole parkland/downland course with excellent greens (5833 yards, SSS 68). Visitors are welcome provided you have a handicap certificate. Green fees are £12 per round or £14 per day on weekdays and £16 per round only at weekends. Fees are half price if you are with a member. Snacks are available at all times and meals by arrangement. The club is in the heart of the Peak District National Park and handy for visiting nearby Chatsworth House.
Location
Gadley Lane, Buxton, Derbys SK17 6XD
Drive for little under 1 mile west from the town centre of Buxton on the A53 St John's Road to Leek road. Turn right in to Carlisle Road and then left in to Watford Road.

RAC recommended hotels see Buxton

CHESTERFIELD
(0246) 279256
An interesting 18-hole parkland course (6326 yards, SSS 70). Visitors are welcome on weekdays and at the weekend if you are accompanied by a member but you must be an established player with a handicap certificate. Green fees on application. Lunch and dinner is available every day. Local attractions include Chatsworth House and the wonderful scenery of the Peak District.
Location
Walton, Chesterfield, Derbyshire S42 7LA
The club is 2 miles south west of Chesterfield town centre on the Matlock road (A632).

RAC recommended hotels
Chesterfield ★★★ (0246) 271141 A town centre Victorian hotel refurbished in 1920s art deco style. Swimming pool, sauna, solarium and gymnasium.
Ringwood Hall ★★★ (0246) 280077 Recently refurbished hotel.
Abbeydale ★★ (0246) 277849 Family-run hotel in a recently converted three-storey Victorian house.
Portland ★★ A 19th century medium-sized hotel.

CHEVIN
(0332) 841864
An interesting 18-hole undulating parkland/moorland course with some hard walking (6043 yards, SSS 69). Visitors are welcome on weekdays and with a member at weekends, provided you have a handicap certificate. Green fees are £15. Meals are served daily except Monday. Local attractions include the Crich Museum, and the club is in the heart of the Peak District.
Location
Golf Lane, Duffield, Derby DE6 4EE
Take the A6 north of Derby for about 5 miles to Duffield.

DERBY
(0332) 766462
An 18-hole parkland municipal course (6183 yards, SSS 69). Visitors of all playing abilities are welcome. Green fees are £3.50 on weekdays and £4.60 at weekends and Bank Holidays. There is a full catering service available daily.
Location
Shakespeare Street, Sinfin, Derby DE2 9HD
The club is 1 mile off the A5111 at Normanton.

RAC recommended hotels
Crest ★★★ (0332) 514933 Traditional hotel with modern bedrooms. In country setting yet handy for town.
Gables ★★ (0332) 40633 Brick-built city hotel near to station.
International ★★ (0332) 369321 Privately owned hotel in well-modernised Victorian residence close to city centre.
Midland ★★★ (0332) 45894 Dignified and spacious three-storey mid-19th century hotel next to station.
Pennine ★★ (0332) 41741 Large modern hotel in city centre with conference facilities. Billiards.
Aston Court ★★ (0332) 42716 Medium-sized hotel adjacent to station to south of city centre.
Clarendon ★★ (0332) 365235 Pleasant city-centre hotel constructed at the end of the Victorian era.
Kedleston ★★ (0332) 559202 A mid-18th century listed building situated in delightful countryside north west of Derby.

EREWASH VALLEY
(0602) 323258
An 18-hole meadowland/parkland course with some interesting quarry holes but splendid views (6487 yards, SSS 71). Visitors are welcome on weekdays but the club prefers you to have a handicap certificate. Green fees are £12 on weekdays and £16 at weekends and Bank Holidays. Lunch is served daily and evening meals can be arranged. Local attractions include the American Adventure.
Location
Stanton-by-Dale, Ilkeston, Derbys DE7 4QR
Leave the M1 at junction 25 and follow the signs to Stanton Ironworks Co Ltd through Sandiacre.

RAC recommended hotel at Sandiacre
Post House ★★★ (0602) 397800 Modern hotel strategically placed at M1/A52 junction.

GLOSSOP & DISTRICT
(04574) 3117
An 11-hole moorland course with some good natural hazards (5726 yards, SSS 68). Visitors are welcome, and green fees are £7 per round on weekdays and £10 at weekends and Bank Holidays. If you are with a member, fees are £5 and there is a £15 weekly rate. Meals are available by arrangement. The club is only ½ mile from the Peak District National Park.
Location
Hurst Lane, off Sheffield Road, Glossop, Derbys SK13 8RH
The club is 1 mile out of town on the A57.

RAC recommended hotel
Wind in the Willows (04574) 68001 (Highly Acclaimed).

ILKESTON BOROUGH
(0602) 3004550
A 9-hole meadowland municipal course (4000 yards, SSS 60). Visitors of all playing abilities can play and beginners are particularly welcome. Green fees are £4. Local attractions include Nottingham Castle and the Peak District.
Location
Peewit West End Drive, Ilkeston, Derby
Leave the M1 at junction 25 and take the A52 west to the roundabout, then the A6007 north to Ilkeston. The club is ½ mile west of Ilkeston market place.

KEDLESTON PARK
(0332) 840035
A beautiful 18-hole parkland course with a stunning view of Kedleston Hall (6611 yards, SSS 72). Provided you have a handicap certificate, visitors are welcome on weekdays and with a member at weekends. Only spike shoes are allowed on the course. Green fees are £20 a day or £15 per round. Full catering facilities are available. The club is well situated for visits to Kedleston Hall and Chatsworth House.
Location
Kedleston, Quarndon, Derby DE6 4JD
Take the A6 north from Derby and follow the RAC signs to Kedleston Hall. The club is 4 miles north west of Derby off the A5111.

RAC recommended hotel
Kedleston (0332) 559202 A mid-18th century listed building situated in delightful countryside north west of Derby.

MATLOCK
(0629) 582191
An 18-hole moorland/parkland course with splendid views of the Peak District (5989 yards, SSS 69). Visitors are welcome on weekdays but not at weekends. Green fees are £12.50 on weekdays and £16 at weekends and Bank Holidays. Snacks are always available and meals can be arranged except on Monday. Local attractions include Chatsworth House and Haddon Hall.
Location
Chesterfield Road, Matlock, Derbyshire DE4 5LF
The club is off the A632 Matlock-Chesterfield road, 1½ miles north of Matlock, to the left of the road.

RAC recommended hotels
New Bath ★★★ (0629) 583275 Elegant Georgian white-faced spa hotel with gardens. Swimming pool, tennis, sauna, solarium and billiards.
Riber Hall C/H ★★★ (0629) 580475 A luxurious Elizabethan house with antique four-poster beds. Superb views. Tennis.

Temple ★★★ (0629) 2911 A small hotel in attractive Georgian building in own grounds.

MICKLEOVER
(0332) 512092
An attractive 18-hole meadowland course (5701 yards, SSS 68). Visitors of all playing abilities are welcome. Green fees are £11 on weekdays and £13 at weekends and Bank Holidays. A society rate can be arranged at £10 a day. There are catering facilities available. Local attractions include the Tramway Museum and the lovely Peak District.
Location
Uttoxeter Road, Mickleover, Derbys DE3 5AD
Take the A516 out of Derby and join the B5020 to Mickleover. The club is 3 miles west of Derby.

RAC recommended hotels see Derby.

ORMONDE FIELDS GOLF AND COUNTRY CLUB
(0773) 42987
An 18-hole undulating parkland course (6011 yards, SSS 69). Visitors are welcome at any time during the week but you must arrange weekend games with the Secretary beforehand. Green fees on application. There are full catering facilities available. The club is in a good position for visits to the Peak District.
Location
Nottingham Road, Codnor, Ripley, Derbys DE5 9RL
Leave the M1 at junction 26 and take the A610 towards Ripley for 7½ miles to Codnor.

PASTURES
(0332) 513921
A 9-hole undulating meadowland course (5005 yards, SSS 64) with fine views across the Trent valley. Visitors are welcome but you must be accompanied by a member. Green fees on application. Local attractions include Chatsworth House and the Peak District.
Location
Pastures Hospital, Mickleover, Derby DE3 3DQ
Take the A516 west of Derby and then the B520 to Mickleover.

RAC recommended hotels see Derby.

SHIRLAND
(0733) 834935
A hilly 18-hole parkland course with fine views (5948 yards, SSS 68). Visitors are welcome but it is necessary to book through the Secretary first. Green fees are £7 on weekdays and £10 at weekends. There is a restaurant and bar. A bowling green is planned.
Location
Lower Delves, Shirland DE5 6AU
Take the A61 north of Alfreton and the club is 1 mile off the road by Shirland Church.

SICKLEHOME
(0433) 51506
An 18-hole hilly grassland course with fine views (6064 yards, SSS 69). Visitors are welcome before 10.30am and after 2.30pm on Saturday and after 2pm on Sunday. Green fees are £12.50 on weekdays and £15 at weekends. There is a bar which serves bar snacks, and evening meals can be arranged. The club is in some very picturesque countryside.
Location
Bamford, Sheffield S30 2BH
Take the A625 west from Sheffield; the club is between Hathersage and Hope.

RAC recommended hotels in Hathersage
George ★★★ (0433) 50436 Modernised 16th century coaching inn with Bronte connections
Hathersage ★★ (0433) 50259 Hotel of character built in local stone by the village squire.

STANEDGE
(0246) 566156
A 9-hole undulating moorland course with narrow fairways (4867 yards, SSS 64). Visitors are welcome on Monday to Friday morning and in the afternoons if you are with a member. You must be with a member on Saturday and Bank Holidays, and no visitors may play on Sundays. Green fees are £7 on weekdays (£3 with a member) and £5 on Saturdays and Bank Holidays. Catering facilities can be provided for parties by prior arrangement. Local attractions include Chatsworth House, Hardwicke House and Chesterfield Crooked Spire.
Location
Walton Hay Farm, Walton, Chesterfield, Derbys S45 0LW
Leave Chesterfield and, 5 miles south west, at the top of the long hill on the A632, turn onto the B5057. The road leading to the club is 300 yards west of the Red Lion Inn.

RAC recommended hotels see Chesterfield.

TAPTON PARK
(0246) 273887
An 18-hole parkland course with some hard walking (6013 yards, SSS 69). Visitors are welcome but you must arrange it with the Pro, J. Delaney, first. Green fees are £3.50 on weekdays and £4.50 at weekends. There are full bar and catering facilities available. The club is pleasantly situated in the heart of the Peak District.
Location
Murray House, Crow Lane, Chesterfield S41 0EQ
The club is ½ mile from Chesterfield station.

RAC recommended hotels see Chesterfield

DEVON

AXE CLIFF
(0287) 20499
An 18-hole undulating seaside course with some lovely sea views (5000 yards, SSS 65). Visitors are welcome on weekdays but there are restrictions at weekends. Green fees are £8 on weekdays and £10 on Saturdays and Bank Holidays. Snacks and meals are available. The club is situated within easy reach of some good beaches.
Location
Axmouth, Seaton, Devon EX12 4AB
Take the A35 to Axminster and then turn off onto the A358 and then the B3172 to Seaton; the club is about 1 mile east of the town.

RAC recommended hotel
Mariners (Acclaimed) (0297) 20560.

BIGBURY
(0548) 810207
An 18-hole undulating seaside course with easy walking (6076 yards, SSS 69). Visitors are welcome provided you have a handicap certificate. Green fees are £12 a day but half price after 5pm. There is a full catering and bar service available. Local places of interest are Bigbury-on-Sea, and Beach and Burgh Island.
Location
Bigbury-on-Sea, Kingsbridge, Devon TQ7 4BB
Take the A379 Plymouth to Kingsbridge road. About 2 miles from Modbury, at Harraton Cross, turn right onto the B3392, signposted Bigbury-on-Sea. The golf club is a further 5 miles from here.

RAC recommended hotels
Thurlestone ★★★★ An impressive white building set in gardens and parkland. Indoor and outdoor swimming pools, golf, putting, tennis, squash, sauna, solarium, gymnasium and billiards.
Henley ★ (0548) 810240 Small cliff-top hotel with terraced garden and steps to beach. Superb views over Bigbury Bay.

CHULMLEIGH
(0769) 80519
A testing, short 18-hole meadowland course (1450 yards, SSS 54). In winter, December to March, there is also a 9-hole course (2360 yards, SSS 56). Visitors of all playing abilities are welcome. Green fees are £2 per round or £4.50 a day. There is a licensed terrace bar where light snacks are available. Local attractions include the village of Chulmleigh with its 15th-century church. There are riding stables and tennis courts nearby.
Location
Leigh Road, Chulmleigh, N Devon EX18 7BL
Take the A377 Exeter-Barnstaple road. Chulmleigh is about midway between the two towns about 1 mile off the main road.

CHURSTON
(0803) 842751
A spectacular clifftop 18-hole downland course (6219 yards, SSS 70) with some glorious views over Brixham and Tor Bar. Visitors who are members of a recognised golf club are welcome at all times but handicap proof is required. Green fees on application. Catering facilities are available daily but opening hours depend on the time of the year. The local steam railway runs close by the club house. The course is very handy for those holidaying in the Torbay area, and a particular attraction is Brixham old village.
Location
Churston, Nr Brixham, Devon TQ5 0LA
Take the A379 south from Paignton and the club is about 3 miles along the road.

RAC recommended hotels
Quayside ★★★ (080 45) 55751 On Inner Harbour with views over Torbay, converted 17th-century fishermens cottages.
Ranscombe House ★ (0803) 882337 Charming 18th-century building with attractive wrought-iron balconies; overlooking the outer harbour.

DOWNES CREDITON
(03632) 4464
A particularly attractive 18-hole parkland/meadowland (5868 yards, SSS68) course with some water hazards and splendid views. Visitors are welcome if they are members of a recognised club, but it is advisable to telephone the club first. Club hire can be arranged on request. Green fees are £10 on weekdays and £14 at weekends and Bank Holidays. Coffee, lunch and dinner are available. The club is within easy access of Exeter city centre and trips to the moors.
Location
Hookway, Crediton, Devon EX17 3PT
The club is 8 miles north west of Exeter on the A377 Exeter-Crediton road. Turn off at Crediton station.

RAC recommended hotels
Coombe House ★★ (0363) 84487 A family-run hotel in a Georgian manor house set in 5 acres of grounds. Swimming pool, putting, tennis.

EAST DEVON
(03954) 8370
An 18-hole heathland seaside course with panoramic views over the sea (6214 yards, SSS 70). Visitors who have a handicap certificate are welcome with a letter of introduction. Green fees are £12. Full catering facilities are available daily from 10am.
Location
North View Road, Budleigh Salterton, Devon EX9 6DQ
Take the A376 from Exmouth to Budleigh Salterton and the club is 5 miles along the road.

RAC recommended hotels
Long Range (Acclaimed) (039 54) 3321.
Tidwell House (Acclaimed) (039 54) 2444.

ELFORDLEIGH
(0752) 336428
A pleasant 9-hole undulating parkland course with some hard walking (5609 yards, SSS 67). Visitors are welcome at any time on weekdays, but it is necessary to telephone ahead for a weekend game. Green fees are £10. Bar snacks are always

available and meals can be arranged. Local attractions include Dartmoor Park and the nearby hotel Leisure Centre with its swimming pool gymnasium and tennis court.
Location
Cobrook, Plympton, Plymouth, Devon PL7 5EB
The club is off the A38, 5 miles north east of Plymouth. Go through Plympton and the club is to the north.

RAC recommended hotels
Elfordleigh C/H ★★ (0752) 336428 Privately owned country hotel set in gardens, lawns and woodland. Indoor and outdoor swimming pools, golf, putting, tennis, fishing, squash, sauna, solarium, gymnasium, billiards.

EXETER GOLF AND COUNTRY CLUB
(039287) 4139
An 18-hole very flat parkland course with some challenging holes and beautifully maintained greens (6061 yards, SSS 69). Visitors are welcome on weekdays provided you have a handicap certificate. Green fees are £15 per day. Lunch and evening meals are always available. The area is surrounded by National Trust land and the club is close both to Dartmoor and the coast.
Location
Countess Wear, Exeter, Devon EX2 7AE
Leave the M5 at junction 30 and take the A379 to Exmouth. The club is to the left of the road.

RAC recommended hotel
Countess Wear Motor Lodge ★★★ (039 287) 5441 A modern hotel with purpose built accommodation in annexe. Tennis.

GREAT TORRINGTON
(02372) 22229
A 9-hole undulating commonland course with some hard walking, although the views are spectacular (4418 yards, SSS 62). Visitors of all playing abilities are welcome except on Sunday mornings. Green fees are £6 per round and £3 for juniors on weekdays and weekends. There is a bar and light meals can be provided by arrangement. Nearby local attractions include Westward Ho!
Location
Weare Trees, Torrington, N Devon EX38 7EZ
Take the A386 from Okehampton to Great Torrington and continue through the town for 1 mile north on the Weare Giffard road.

RAC recommended hotel
Castle Hill ★★ (0805) 22339 On site of castle, stone-built hotel with pleasant dining room.

HOLSWORTHY
(0409) 253177
An 18-hole parkland course (5935 yards, SSS 68). Visitors are welcome at any time except on Sunday mornings. Green fees are £7 daily or £28 for a week. Light meals can be provided by arrangement with the club.
Location
Kilatree, Holsworthy, N Devon
Take the A388 from Launceston to Holsworthy and turn west towards Bude on the A3072. The club is 1½ miles west of Holsworthy on the left.

RAC recommended hotel
Coles Mill (Acclaimed) (0409) 253313.

HONITON
(0404) 44422
An 18-hole parkland course with some easy walking (5931 yards, SSS 68). Visitors are welcome at any time, unless there is a competition, provided they are members of a recognised golf club and have a handicap certificate. Green fees are £11 a day and £14 at weekends and Bank Holidays. Full catering facilities are available.
Location
Middlehills, Honiton, Devon EX14 8RT
You will find the club 2 miles south of Honiton.

RAC recommended hotel
Deer Park C/H ★★★ (0404) 41266 A Georgian mansion in 26 acres of beautiful countryside. Swimming pool, putting, tennis, fishing, squash, sauna, solarium and billiards.

ILFRACOMBE
(0271) 62176
An 18-hole undulating cliff-top course with fine sea views from every tee (5857 yards, SSS 68). Visitors are welcome provided you have a handicap certificate. Green fees are £10 per round or day, or £35 for a 5 day ticket (Mon-Fri). There are full bar and dining room facilities available. The course is handy for North Devon beaches.
Location
Hele Bay, Ilfracombe, N Devon EX34 9RT
Take the A399 from Ilfracombe to Combe Martin and the club is 2 miles along the road past Hele.

RAC recommended hotels
Trimstone Manor C/H ★★★ (0271) 62841 Two-storey manor house with adjacent leisure centre set in 50 acres of grounds, 3 miles south of Ilfracombe. Tennis, putting.
Arlington ★★ (0271) 62002 Bay-windowed, five-storey hotel overlooking harbour and coast. Family-run. Swimming pool, sauna, solarium.
Carlton ★★ (0271) 62446 Large Victorian building in own grounds close to sea.
Elmfield ★★ (0271) 63377 Brick-built Victorian mansion with a terraced garden. Indoor swimming pool, sauna, solarium.
Imperial ★★ (0271) 62536 Privately-owned Victorian building on main road with Bay views.
Longleigh ★★ (0271) 62629 In very attractive garden with stream, a substantial former manor house. Solarium.
St Helier ★★ (0271) 64906 A modern family-run hotel in a terrace overlooking the sea.
Tracy House ★★ (0271) 63933 In quiet area, stone-built Victorian residence in acre of walled garden. Putting.

MANOR HOUSE HOTEL
(0647) 40355
A beautiful 18-hole parkland course with stunning views across the moorland (6016 yards, SSS 69). Visitors of all playing abilities are welcome by arrangement, although the course is not suitable for absolute beginners. Green fees are £12 per round or £15 per day. There is a full catering service available including cream teas. Local attractions include the miniature pony centre, and Exeter Cathedral.
Location
Moretonhampstead, Newton Abbot TQ13 8RE
Take the A382 from Newton Abbot to Moretonhampstead and then turn left onto the B3212. The club is about 1½ miles down the road on the left.

RAC recommended hotel
WhiteHart ★★ (0647) 40406 A listed building, a Georgian stone-built posting house in village centre. Billiards.

NEWTON ABBOT(STOVER)
(0626) 52460
An 18-hole parkland course dissected by a brook (5834 yards, SSS 68). Visitors are welcome but you must be introduced or have proof that you are a member of a recognised club. A handicap certificate is necessary. Green fees are £14. Full catering facilities are available daily. The club is close to Dartmoor National Park.
Location
Bovey Road, Newton Abbot, S Devon TQ12 6QQ
You will find the club on the A382 Bovey Tracey road from Newton Abbot. Before you come to the junction with the A38 turn off to the west.

RAC recommended hotels
Passage House ★★★ (0626) 55515 New hotel, cream-painted with a pitched, in a stunning position overlooking the Teign estuary. Inddor swimming pool, fishing, sauna, solarium, gymnasium.
Queen's ★★ (0626) Privately-owned, stone-built Victorian hotel opposite station and motorail terminus.

OKEHAMPTON
(0837) 2113
An 18-hole undulating moorland course with some interesting holes (5163 yards, SSS 67). Visitors are welcome, but no athletes' shorts, ankle socks, denims or trainers may be worn. Green fees are available on application but they are modest. Lunch is served daily and others meals are available by arrangement. The club is actually within the Dartmoor National Park.
Location
Okehampton, Devon EX20 1EF
Take the A30 to Okehampton town centre from where the club is clearly signposted. Turn towards Dartmoor at the traffic lights and take the third right, then the right fork, and the club is the second on the right. The name is on the entrance post.

RAC recommended hotel
Collaven Manor C/H ★★★ (083 786) 522 A mellow stone country manor with some parts dating back to the 15th century. The hotel stands in 5 acres of grounds. Putting.

ROYAL NORTH DEVON
(02372) 73817
A championship 18-hole links course (6662 yards, SSS 72). Provided you have a handicap certificate, visitors are welcome. Green fees are £12 on weekdays and £14 at weekends and Bank Holidays. Full catering facilities are available. The course is well located for the beaches and coastal walks.
Location
Westward Ho!, Bideford, Devon EX39 1HD
Take the A386 to Northam village and then take the road down Bone Hill, going past the post office and keeping to the left. The club-house is visible as you come down the hill.

RAC recommended hotels
Durrant House ★★★ (0237) 472361 Purpoe-built large hotel in own grounds. Within easy reach of the coast. Swimming pool, sauna, solarium.
Royal ★★★ A recently refurbished Victorian building at the East end of the bridge.
Riversford ★★ (0237) 474239 Family-run hotel in 3 acres of secluded gardens sloping down to river. Putting, solarium.
Sonnenheim ★★ (023 72) 74989 Stone-built former private house in an acre of grounds just off A39, north of town.
Yeolden House C/H ★★ (023 72) 74400 Georgian country residence in attractive grounds with panoramic view. Putting.

SAUNTON
(0271) 812436
Two traditional links courses with natural hazards; the 'East' 18-hole course (6703 yards, SSS 73) and the 'West' (6356 yards, SSS 71). Visitors who have a handicap certificate are welcome. On weekdays green fees are £15 a day on the 'East' course (£17 at weekends and public holidays) and £15 on the 'West' course. There is a restaurant which is open all day. Local attractions include the beaches and Arlington Court.
Location
Saunton, Nr Braunton, N Devon EX33 1LG
Take the A361 from Barnstaple and turn onto the B3231 at Braunton towards Croyde Bay. The club is 7 miles from Barnstaple.

RAC recommended hotel
Saunton Sands ★★★★ (0271) 890212 An hotel with fine views of the sands. Indoor swimming pool, putting, tennis, squash, sauna, solarium and billiards.

SIDMOUTH
(0395) 513023
A cliff-top 18-hole undulating parkland course on a cliff-top with springy turf and panoramic views over the sea (5166 yards, SSS 66). Provided you have a handicap certificate, visitors are welcome, although it is necessary to book beforehand. Green fees are £10 on weekdays and £12 at weekends. Meals are served daily except Tuesday. The club is within easy access both Exeter and Exmoor.
Location
Peak Hill, Cotmaton Road, Sidmouth EX10 8SX
From Sidmouth take the Exeter Station Road to the Woodlands Hotel, then turn right to Cotmaton Road.

RAC recommended hotels
Riviera ★★★ (0395) 515201 A promenade hotel with fine sea views. Within easy walking distance to the town centre.
Belmont ★★★★ (0395 512555 Large hotel, near to Promenade;easy walk to town centre. Putting.
Victoria ★★★★ (0395) 512651 Large hotel with fine sea views; quiet surroundings. Indoor and outdoor swimming pools, putting, tennis, sauna, solarium and billiards.
Bedford ★★★ (0395) 513047 Terraced hotel, situated on the Promenade.Easy walk to town centre.
Fortfield ★★★ (0395) 512403 Large brick-built hotel in extensive grounds overlooking sea. Indoor swimming pool, putting, sauna andsolarium
Royal Glen ★★★ (0395) 513221 Privately run country house style hotel near sea. Convenient for town centre. Indoor swimming pool and putting.
Salcombe Hill House ★★★ (0395) 514 697 Spacious Georgian house in secluded surroundings. Swimming pool, putting and tennis.
Westcliff ★★★ (0395) 513252 Brick-built hotel with spacious gardens and sea views. Swimming pool, puting,solarium and gymnasium.
Abbeydale ★★ (0395) 512060 Brick-built hotel in sheltered garden.Fine views of the sea.
Brownlands C/H ★★(0395) 513053 Country house hotel in delightful grounds with fine sea views. Putting and tennis.
Byes Links ★★ (0395) 513129 Brick-built hotel in own grounds.Few minutes from local ammenities.
Elizabeth ★★ (0395) 513503 Right on the sea front, a white-painted late Victorian building with lovely sea views. Family run.
Little Court ★★ (0395) 515279 Regency hotel with secluded garden. Easy walk to sea and town. Swimming pool.
Royal York and Faulkner ★★ (0395) 513043 Large terraced hotel on the promenade withfine sea views. Saune, solarium and gymnasium.
Torbay ★★ (0395) 513456 Privately owned terraced hotel, near to promenade; Easy walk to town.
Westbourne ★★ (0395) 513774 A Victorian residence set in pleasant garden in a residential area.
Woodlands ★★ (0395) 513120 Privately-owned period hotel with attractive garden. Convenient for sea. Putting.

STADDON HEIGHTS
(0752) 402475
An 18-hole seaside links course which can be windy, but with easy walking (5861 yards, SSS 68). Visitors are welcome on weekdays but the club prefers you to have a handicap certificate. Green fees are £9 a round (£6 with a member) or £11 on weekdays, £12 a round or £14 at weekends. Local attractions include Plymouth shopping centre, Dartmoor National Park and the local beaches.
Location
Staddon Heights, Plymstock, Plymouth, Devon PL9 9SP
Leave Plymouth on the Plymstock road (A379) and the clubhouse is 5 miles S of the city near the Royal Navy aerial towers.

RAC recommended hotel
Langdon Court C/H ★★ (0752) 862358 A lovely stone-built Elizabethan manor set in gardens, with lovely country views. 4 miles south east of Plymouth.

TAVISTOCK
(0822) 612049
An 18-hole moorland course with easy walking and splendid views into Cornwall (6250 yards, SSS 70). Provided you have a handicap, certificate visitors are welcome, but it is advisable to telephone in advance. Green fees are £12 on weekdays (with a member) and £15 at weekends and Bank Holidays. Local places to visit include Tavistock and the Ancient Pannier Market.
Location
Down Road, Tavistock, Devon, PL19 9AQ
From Tavistock take the Whitchurch road, turning into Down Road and onto Whitchurch Down, and the club house is ahead of you.

RAC recommended hotel
Bedford ★★★ (0822) 613221 A castle-like hotel with parts dating from the Middle Ages. In the centre of town.

TEIGNMOUTH
(0626) 774194
A high 18-hole moorland course, 6142 yards, SSS 69, which can be shrouded in fog in the winter, but very pleasant in the summer . Visitors are welcome, but you must be a member of a club and in possession of a current handicap certificate, as the course can be a 'good test of golf'. Green fees are £13 on weekdays and £16 after 4pm at weekends. Full catering facilities are available daily.
Location
Exeter Road, Teignmouth, Devon TQ14 9NY
The club house is 2 miles from Teignmouth on the B3192 (leading to the A380) road to Exeter. The clubs is 900 feet above Teignmouth on Haldon Moor

THURLESTONE
(0548) 560405
A superb 18-hole downland clifftop course with expansive coastal views (6303 yards, SSS 70). Visitors are welcome provided you are a member of a recognised club. A handicap certificate is required. Green fees are £15 a day. Catering facilities are available throughout the day.
Location
Thurlestone, Nr Kingsbridge, S Devon TQ7 3NZ
Take the A379 Plymouth-Salcombe road, turn right at the signposts for Thurlestone. The club is situated 4 miles south of Kingsbridge.

RAC recommended hotel
Thurlestone ★★★★ (0548) 560382 An impressive white building set in gardens and parkland. Indoor and outdoor swimming pools, golf, putting, tennis, squash, sauna, solarium, gymnasium and billiards.

TIVERTON
(0884) 252187
An 18-hole parkland/meadowland course with some interesting holes (6263 yards, SSS 71). Provided you have a handicap certificate, visitors are welcome, but it is advisable to telephone first in case there are competition reservations. Green fees are £12 a day on weekdays and £16 at weekends. Lunch and teas are available daily. Local attractions include Tiverton Castle and Knightshayes Court (NT).
Location
Post Hill, Tiverton, Devon EX16 4NE
Leave the M5 at junction 27 for Tiverton. Drive for 5 miles towards Tiverton on the A373 and then take the first exit left on the dual carriageway through Samford Peverell-Halberton. From there you should see the golf course.

RAC recommended hotel
Tiverton ★★★ (0884) 256120 A modern hotel on the edge of the town.

TORQUAY
(0803) 37371
An 18-hole parkland course with a meandering brook and abundant heather and woods to provide plenty of challenge (6192 yards, SSS 69). Visitors with a handicap certificate are welcome. Green fees are £14 on weekdays and £16 at weekends and public holidays. Full catering facilities are available except on Monday. The club is very handy for those holidaying in the Torbay area.
Location
Petitor Road, St Marychurch, Torquay TQ1 4QF
The club is north of Torquay on the A379 Teignmouth road. It is signposted on the outskirts of the town.

RAC recommended hotels
Imperial ★★★★★ (0803) 294301 A luxury hotel in sub-tropical gardens and with period decor in the public rooms. Indoor and outdoor swimming pools, putting, tennis, squash, sauna, solarium, gymnasium and billiards.
Grand ★★★★ (0803) 296677 Spacious and imposing Victorian building at Western end of seafront.Indoor and outdoor swimming pools, tennis, sauna, solarium and gymnasium.
Palace ★★★★ (0803) 200200 A large hotel with spelndid decor. Extensive Italian grounds leading to the sea. Indoor and outdoor swimming pools, golf, putting, tennis(indoor and outdoor), squash, sauna and billiards.
Many other hotels in Torquay.

WARREN
(0626) 862255
An 18-hole flat links course (5968 yards, SSS 69). Visitors are welcome on weekdays but the club prefers you to have a handicap certificate. Green fees are £12.80 on weekdays and £14 at weekends. Bar snacks and meals are served daily. The club is situated within easy access of Dartmoor National Park.
Location
Dawlish Warren, Dawlish, Devon EX7 0NF
Leave Exeter by the A379 to Dawlish. Dawlish Warren and golf club are to the east of Dawlish, about 1 mile along the coast.

RAC recommended hotel
Langstone Cliff ★★★ (0626) 865155 A rambling, white-painted hotel overlooking the sea, set in 12 acres of lawns and woods north of Dawlish. Indoor and outdoor swimming pools, tennis, solarium, snooker.

WRANGATON
(03647) 3229
A 9-hole moorland course in Dartmoor National Park (5790 yards, SSS 68). The course has many natural hazards including sheep and ponies! Visitors are welcome on weekdays and Saturday, but not onWednesday afternoons or Sunday between March and October. Green fees on application. Snacks are available at lunchtimes. The course has some spectacular views over the sea and the moors.
Location
Wrangaton, South Brent, S Devon TQ10 9HJ
Turn off the A38 Exeter-Plymouth at Wrangton post office, between South Brent and Bittaford.

YELVERTON
(0822) 852824
An 18-hole moorland course with fine greens (6288 yards, SSS 70). Visitors who are accredited golfers are welcome. Green fees are £12 on weekdays (£6 with a member) and £15 at weekends and Bank Holidays (£7.50 with a member). Full catering facilities are available, except on Tuesday when bar snacks only are served. Local attractions include Princetown, Tor Reservoir and the moors.

Location
Golf Links Road, Yelverton, Devon PL20 6BN
Yelverton is 8 miles north of Plymouth and 5 miles S of Tavistock on the A386.

RAC recommended hotel
Moorland Links C/H ★★★ (0822) 852245 A purpose built hotel in 9 acres of grounds. Putting and tennis.

DORSET

ASHLEY WOODS
(0258) 452253
A 9-hole undulating downland course (6227 yards, SSS 70). Visitors are welcome on weekdays and after midday at on weekends. Green fees are £10 for 18 holes during the week (£15 for 36 holes), and £12 for 18 holes at weekends and Bank Holidays (£18 for 36 holes). Catering facilities are available by arrangement. The course is situated in the middle of Hardy country and close to Blandford Forum.
Location
Wimborne Road, Blandford Forum, Dorset DT11 9HN
From Blandford Forum take the B3082 south east to Wimborne Minster.

RAC recommended hotels
Crown ★★★ (0258) 456626 A well-modernised Georgian hotel overlooking the water meadows. Fishing.
Anvil ★★ (0258) 53431 Privately- owned thatched inn in Pimperne village adjoining Blandford.

BRIDPORT AND WEST DORSET
(0308) 22597
A pleasant 18-hole seaside course with splendid views over Lyme Bay (5246 yards, SSS 66). Visitors are welcome but the club prefers you to have a handicap certificate. Green fees are £10 on weekdays and £15 at weekends. Full catering facilities are available daily except Monday, and there is also a licensed bar. Local attractions include Parnham House at Beminster, and Bridport.
Location
East Cliff, West Bay, Bridport, Dorset DT6 4EP
Take the A35 from Bridport and turn onto the B3157. You will find the club 1½ south of Bridport at West Bay.

RAC recommended hotels
Eype's Mouth ★★★ (0308) 23300 Family-run Georgian hotel with spectacular views. Easy walking distance to sea.
Haddon House ★★★ (0308) 23626 Family-run hotel in elegant Regency style building. Easy walking distanc to sea.
Roundham House ★★ (0308) 421145 Mellow stone-built residence with pleasant secluded garden few minutes from sea.

BROADSTONE
(0202) 692595
A beautiful 18-hole heathland course with plenty of gorse and pine trees and well-maintained greens (6151 yards, SSS 70). Visitors are welcome on weekdays after 9.30am and at weekends and Bank Holidays after 10am. A handicap certificate is required. Green fees are £16 per round, £19 a day on weekdays, and £18 per round, £22 a day at weekends. There are full catering facilities available by prior arrangement. The club is located in the middle of Hardy country, and other local attractions include the Puddletown Martyrs, Bradbury Rings and Poole Harbour.
Location
Wentworth Drive, off Station Approach, Broadstone, Dorset BH18 8DQ
The club is situated about halfway between Wimborne and Poole on the A349.

RAC recommended hotel
Fairlight (Acclaimed) (0202) 694316

CAME DOWN
(030581) 3494
An undulating 18-hole downland course (6224 yards, SSS 71). Provided you have a handicap certificate, visitors are welcome, there are some restrictions on Sundays. Green fees are £12.50 on weekdays and £16 at weekends and Bank Holidays. There are full catering facilities available. Interesting local places to visit include the Hardy monument and museum in Dorchester.
Location
Came Down, Dorchester, Dorset DT2 8NR
Take the A354 from Dorchester towards Wimborne, and the club is about 2 miles south on the left-hand side of the road.

RAC recommended hotel
Kings Arms ★★★ (0305) 65353 An 18th century coaching inn with distinctive bow windows.
Yalbury Cottage ★★★ (0305) 62382 Beautifully kept, thatched cottage with sympathetic bedroom extension to rear.

FERNDOWN
(0202) 874602
Two beautiful heathland links courses; the 'Old' 18-hole course (6442 yards, SSS 71) and the 'New' 9-hole course (5604 yards, SSS 68). Visitors who have a handicap certificate are welcome to play, but prior permission is necessary. Green fees are £20 on weekdays, £27 at weekends on the 'Old' course, and £10 on weekdays, £16 at weekends on the 'New'. There are full catering facilities except on Monday. The course is within easy access of Poole, Bournemouth and the New Forest.
Location
119 Golf Links Road, Ferndown, Dorset BH22 8BU
Take the A31 south to Tricketts Cross and turn onto the A348. The club is to the left of the road at Ferndown.

RAC recommended hotel
Dormy ★★★★ (0202) 872121 A country house style hotel in 12 acres of landscaped grounds next to the golf course. Indoor swimming pool, putting, tennis, squash, sauna, solarium, gymnasium and billiards.

HIGHCLIFFE CASTLE
(04252) 72210
An 18-hole seaside course with easy walking (4732 yards, SSS 63). Visitors are welcome if they are members of a recognised golf club. A handicap certificate is required. Green fees are £11 on weekdays and £13 at weekends and Bank Holidays. There is a bar and restaurant. Bournemouth and Lymington are nearby.
Location
107 Lymington Road, Highcliffe on Sea, Dorset BH23 4LA
Take the A35 from Bournemouth to Hinton Admiral and then follow the signposts to Highcliffe. It is approximately 1 mile on the A337, 3 miles east of Christchurch.

ISLE OF PURBECK
(092944) 361
Two courses with splendid views across the Channel, Poole Harbour and the Purbeck Hills. Both are undulating heathland courses, one 18-hole (6248 yards, SSS 71) and one 9-hole (2022 yards, SSS 30). Visitors are welcome but a handicap certificate is necessary for the 18-hole course. Green fees are £16 on weekdays, £18.50 at weekends and Bank Holidays on the 18-hole and £7.50 a day, £10 at weekends and Bank Holidays on the 9-hole course. Lunch and evening meals are available daily. Local attractions include Poole town and harbour, Brownsea Island and the Isle of Purbeck.
Location
Studland, Dorset BH19 3AB
The club is situated between Studland and Swanage on the B3351, overlooking Poole Harbour.

RAC recommended hotels
Knoll House C/H ★★★ (092 944) 251 A modern country house hotel with direct access to the beach. Swimming pool, golf, tennis, sauna, solarium and gymnasium.
Manor House ★★★ (092 944) 288 A stone-built manor house overlooking the sea. Attractive garden. Tennis.

KNIGHTON HEATH
(0202) 572633
An 18-hole heathland course (6206 yards, SSS 70). Visitors are welcome after 9.30am on weekdays and after 10.30am at weekends. A handicap certificate is required. Green fees are £15 on

weekdays and £17 at weekends. Lunch is available daily except Monday. The club is close to Bournemouth and Poole.
Location
Francis Avenue, Bournemouth, Dorset BH11 8NX
Take the A348 Poole-Ringwood road 4 miles north of Bournemouth. The club is signposted at the junction of the A3049.

RAC recommended hotels
Many hotels in Bournemouth.

LAKEY HILL
(0929) 471776
An 18-hole parkland course set amongst some splendid rhododendrons (6108 yards, SSS 69). There is a fine floodlit driving range which is open all year from 8am to 10pm daily. Visitors are welcome on weekdays and after 9.30am at weekends, provided there are no tee reservations. Green fees are £10 on weekdays and £12 at weekends and Bank Holidays. There is a club restaurant which serves lunch and evening meals, and also a club bar. Local attractions include Cloudshill, home of Lawrence of Arabia, Corfe Caste (NT) and Kingston Lacey.
Location
Hyde, Wareham, Dorset BH20 7NT
The club is situated 3 miles west of Wareham off Worgret Road.

RAC recommended hotels
See Wareham.

LYME REGIS
(02974) 2963
An 18-hole undulating meadowland course with some dramatic views over Lyme Bay (6262 yards, SSS 70). Provided you have a handicap certificate, visitors are welcome except on Thursday and Sunday morning. However, it is advisable to confirm the booking by telephone first. Green fees are £15 on weekdays and £18 at weekends. Lunch, tea and dinner is served every day. Local places to visit include Lyme Regis with its famous fossils, and Cobb.
Location
Timber Hill, Lyme Regis, Dorset DT7 3HQ
Take the A3052 Charmouth road from Lyme Regis and the club is 1 mile E of the town.
Lyme Regis

RAC recommended hotels
Alexandra ★★★ (029 74) 2010 A large white 18th century building with fine sea views from the gardens.
Devon ★★★ (029 74) 3231 Originally an old rectory this hotel has very attractive grounds. Swimming pool, putting. Open 30 march to 4 November.
Mariners ★★★ (029 74) 2753 An hotel with old world charm in delightful gardens.
Bay ★★ (029 74) 2059 Purpose-built hotel on Marin Parade with fine sea views. Privately owned.
Buena Vista ★★ (029 74) 2494 Privately owned Regency house with garedn and sea views. On main street.
Dorset ★★ (029 74) 2482 An extended Georgian building in quiet residential area. Privately owned.
Dower House ★★ (0297) 21047 Substantial country residence in rural surroundings at Rousdon. Privately owned. Putting
Kersbrook ★★ (029 74) 2596 An attractive stone-built hotel with thatched roof. Pleasant garden to rear.
Orchard Country ★★ (029 74) 2972 Pleasant hotel set in gardens in the countryside.
Royal Lion ★★ (029 74) 5622 Privately-owned coaching inn of character; in main street. Indoor swimming pool, sauna, gymnasium and billiards.
St Michael ★★ (029 74) 2503 Pleasantly modernised family-run Regency hotel in central location.

MEYRICK PARK
(0202) 290871
An 18-hole parkland public course (5885 yards, SSS 69). Visitors are welcome, but the course is closed after 11am on Sundays. Bournemouth Club plays here. Green fees are £7.50 per round on both weekdays and weekends. There is a bar and snacks are available.
Location
Parks Department, Bournemouth BH2 6LH

PARKSTONE
(0202) 707138
A particularly beautiful 18-hole undulating heathland course (6250 yards, SSS 70). Provided you have a handicap certificate visitors are welcome on weekdays, but it is advisable to book in advance. Green fees are £16 per round, £20 a day on weekdays, and £18 per round, £22 a day at weekend, and Bank Holidays. Lunch is available daily. The club is handy for visits to Bournemouth and Poole Harbour.
Location
Links Road, Parkstone, Poole, Dorset BH14 9JU
Take the A35 Bournemouth-Poole road and turn S at St Osmonds Church.

QUEEN'S PARK
(0202) 396198
An 18-hole undulating parkland municipal course often described as the best public course in the country (6505 yards, SSS 72). Boscombe Club plays here. Visitors are welcome but the last tee-off is at 10.30am on Sundays. Green fees are £7.50 per round and £11 a day. Juniors can play for £4.30. There is a bar and meals are available. The club is convenient for the seaside resort of Bournemouth.
Location
Queen's Park, South Drive, Bournemouth BH8 9BY
The club is situated 2 miles north east of Bournemouth.

SHERBORNE
(0963) 814431
A particularly pretty 18-hole parkland course with good fairways and some panoramic views (5758 yards, SSS 68). Visitors are welcome on weekdays after 10am and also at weekends, depending on the Club Diary. Green fees are £12 on weekdays and £15 at weekends. Full catering facilities are available. Local attractions include Sherborne Old and New Castles and the Abbey.
Location
Higher Clatcombe, Sherborne, Dorset DT9 4RN
Take the B3145 Wincanton road north of Sherborne and the club is on the left.

RAC recommended hotels
Eastbury ★★★ (0935) 813131 Georgian town house in a quiet street. Pleasant garden.
Post House ★★★ (0935) 813191A modern hotel situated on the outskirts of the town.
Half Moon ★★ (0935) 812017 A substantial brick and stone building with attractive high gables, situated near to the Abbey.

WAREHAM
(09295) 54147
An 18-hole undulating meadowland course (5332 yards, SSS 66). Visitors are welcome on weekdays and at weekends and Bank Holidays, if you are the guest of a member. Green fees are £10 on weekdays or £6 with a member. Bar snacks are available.
Location
Sandford Road, Wareham, Dorset BH20 4DH
Take the A351 north from Wareham and the club is about half a mile mile along the road.

RAC recommended hotels
Priory C/H ★★★★ (0929) 552772 Privately-owned 16th century stone building witha lovely garden on River Frome. Fishing.
Springfield Country ★★★ (092 95) 2177 Attractive two-storey house in secluded grounds. Swimming pool, tennis, riding, solarium and billiards.
Worgret Manor ★★ (092 95) 2957 A privately-owned attractive manor house converted into an hotel.

WEYMOUTH
(0305) 773981
An 18-hole seaside course (5979 yards, SSS 69). Visitors are welcome provided you have proof of membership of a recognised golf club. Green fees are £12 on weekdays and £14 at weekends and Bank Holidays. Full catering facilities are available. Local attractions include Abbotsbury Swannery and Botanical Gardens, and Weymouth Sea World.
Location
Links Road, Westham, Weymouth, Dorset DT4 0PF
The club is situated off the main Dorchester road via Radipole Lane.

RAC recommended hotels
Prince Regent ★★ (0305) 771313 An hotel in a

Regency terrace with fine sea views.
Central ★★ (0305) 760700 Modernised hotel conveniently placed for town centre and the beach.
Crown ★★ (0305) 760800 Centre of town, imposing purpose-built hotel. Convenient for the harbour.
Glenburn ★★ (0305) 832353 Small family-run hotel extended modern residence. Near to sea.
Rex ★★ (0305) 760400 Georgian terraced hotel near to the sea. Easy walk to shops.
Streamside ★★ (0305) 833121 Two-storey black and white modern hotel with considerable charm.

Co DURHAM

AYCLIFFE
(0325) 310820
A 9-hole parkland course (6054 yards, SSS 69). There is a floodlit driving range which is undercover and open all hours. There are no restrictions on visitors who are welcome at any time. Green fees are £2.75 on weekdays and concessions and £3.75 at the weekend. The club is attached to the Leisure/Sports Complex where there is a cafeteria and bar.
Location
School Aycliff Lane, Newton Aycliff DL5 6QZ
Leave the A1 for the A68 N of Darlington and then take right form onto the A6072. The Sports complex is 1½ miles away.

RAC recommended hotel
Rose and Crown ★★ A stone-built pub and restaurant in the centre of Romaldkirk.

BARNARD CASTLE
(0833) 38355
An undulating parkland course (5838 yards, SSS 68). Visitors are welcome except on competition days. Green fees on application. There are catering facilities where meals and bar snacks are served. Places of local interest include the Bowes Museum.
Location
Harmire Road, Barnard Castle, Co Durham DL12 8QN
The club is situated on the north edge boundary of the town on the B6278 Barnard Castle-Eggleston road.

BEAMISH PARK
091-3701133
An 18-hole parkland course laid out in a former deer park (6000 yards, SSS70). Visitors who have a handicap certificate are welcome except on Sunday and before 9am on any weekday. Green fees are £8 (£4 with a member) on weekdays and £12 (£6 with a member) at weekends. There are reductions for parties. Full catering facilities are available every day except Monday. Local attractions include the Beamish Open Air Museum.
Location
Beamish, Stanley, Co Durham DH9 0RH
From Chester-le-Street follow the signs for Beamish Open Air Museum.

BIRTLEY
091-4102207
A 9-hole parkland course (5154 yards, SSS 67). Visitors are welcome on weekdays. Green fees are £5 (£3 with a member) on weekdays and £5 at the weekends with a member only. You can buy a weekly ticket for £20. Snacks and meals are available daily. Local places of interest worth visiting include Lumley Castle and Lamston Castle.
Location
Portobello Road, Birtley, Co Durham
Take the A6127 off the A1 6 miles south of Newcastle upon Tyne. The club is between Birtley and Whitelands.

RAC recommended hotels
Post House ★★★ 091-415 3371 A modern hotel in Washington, convenient for the A1(M)
Washington Moat House ★★★ 091-417 2626 Modern purpose-built hotel in red brick, in own landscaped grounds. Indoor swimming pool, golf, putting, squash, sauna, solarium, gymnasium and billiards.

BISHOP AUCKLAND
(0388) 602198
A pleasant 18-hole parkland course (6420 yards, SSS 71). There is a good view of the Bishop of Durham's Palace from the fairway in the winter. Visitors of all playing abilities are welcome. Green fees are £12 per round or £15 a day on weekdays, or £15 a round at weekends. If you are with a member, the prices are reduced by half. Lunch and evening meals are available. Local attractions include the City of Durham.
Location
High Plains, Durham Road, Bishop Auckland, Co Durham DL14 8DL
You will find the course on the left side of the road going north, just outside the town.

RAC recommended hotel
Queens Head ★★ (0388) 603477 A traditional style hotel in the market square.
Helme Park Hall C/H ★★★ (0388) 730970 Modernised 17th century house with Victorian additions in 5 acres of gardensand woodlands beside A68. Lovely views.

BLACKWELL GRANGE
(0325) 464464
A well-maintained 18-hole undulating parkland course with a variety of trees (5587 yards, SSS 67). Visitors are welcome except on Wednesday afternoons which is Ladies Day. Green fees are £9 on weekdays and £11 at weekends, or £5 if you are the guest of a member. Lunch is served daily except Monday. The course is close to the moors.
Location
Briar Close, Blackwell, Darlington, Co Durham DL3 8QX
Take the A66 south from Darlington for 1 mile and

the club is a quarter of a mile east of the road.

RAC recommended hotel
Blackwell Grange Moat House ★★★★ (0325) 380888 An imposing 17th century mansion with later extensions in pleasant grounds. Indoor swimming pool, golf, putting, tennis, sauna, solarium and gymnasium.

BRANCEPETH CASTLE
091-3780075
An attractively situated 18-hole parkland course (6300 yards, SSS 70) in a former deer park. Visitors are welcome on weekdays only and it is advisable to have a handicap certificate. Green fees are £14 on weekdays. Lunch and bar snacks are available daily but prior booking is necessary for dinner. The course is overlooked by the 13th-century Brancepeth Castle and Church. Other local attractions include Durham Cathedral.
Location
Brancepeth, Durham DH7 8EH
The club is situated 4½ miles south west of Durham City on the A690 Durham-Crook road.

CHESTER-LE-STREET
091-3883218
An 18-hole parkland course with easy walking (6054 yards, SSS 69). Visitors who have a letter of introduction are welcome at any time on weekdays, but not before 10am or between midday and 2pm at weekends. Green fees on application. Bar snacks, lunch and evening meals are served daily. The course is set in Lumley Castle grounds and close to the Beamish Open Air Museum.
Location
Lumley Park, Chester-le-Street, Co Durham DH3 4NS
Leave the A1(M) to Chester-le-Street and then follow the A167 signposted Durham. The course is a quarter of a mile east of Chester-le-Street.

CONSETT AND DISTRICT
(0207) 502186
An undulating 18-hole parkland course (6001 yards, SSS 69). Visitors are welcome at weekends and when there are competitions although the club prefers you to have a handicap certificate. Green fees are £7 or £3.50 with a member on weekdays, and £10, or £5 with a member at weekends. Lunch and high tea is available every day by arrangement. Local attractions include Beamish Open Air Museum.
Location
Elmfield Road, Consett, Co Durham DH8 5MM
Take the A691 from Durham or A694 from Newcastle upon Tyne towards Castleside. The club is off the A691 on the left-hand side of the road towards Shotley Bridge.

CROOK
(0388) 762429
An 18-hole meadowland/parkland course with natural hazards (6016 yards, SSS 69). Visitors are welcome at all times. Green fees are £6, on weekdays, £5 with a member, and £7 at weekends and Bank Holidays, £6 with a member. Full catering facilities are available daily except Thursday. Interesting places to visit locally include Durham Cathedral and Castle, Raby Castle and the Beamish Open Air Museum.
Location
Low Jobs Hill, Crook, Co Durham DL15 9AA
Crook is 6 miles west of Durham city off the A690.

RAC recommended hotels
See Bishop Auckland.

DARLINGTON
(0325) 463936
An attractive 18-hole parkland course with easy walking (6032 yards, SSS 70). Visitors who are members of a recognised golf club are welcome on weekdays. Green fees are £10 on weekdays and £15 on Bank Holidays, (half price with a member). There are full catering facilities.
Location
Haughton Grange, Darlington, Co Durham DL1 3JD
You will find the club situated north east of the town on the A1150 (between the A167 and A66).

RAC recommended hotels
Blackwell Grange Moat House ★★★★ (0325) 380888 Imposing brick-built 17th century mansion with later extension in pleasent grounds. Indoor swimming pool, golf, putting, tennis, sauna, solarium and gymnasium.
St George ★★★ (0325) 332631 Modern building conveniently set just 200yards from airport.
Stakis White Horse ★★★ (0325) 382121 A former inn with modern accommodation extensions.
Swallow Kings Head ★★★ (0325) 380222 A Victorian building of character in the centre of Darlington.

DINSDALE SPA
(0325) 332297
An 18-hole parkland course with good views of the Cleveland Hills (6078 yards, SSS 69). Visitors are welcome on weekdays. Green fees are £8 per round or £9.50 a day. Catering facilities are available.
Location
Middleton St George, Darlington, Co Durham DL2 1DW
From the A66 or A19 follow the signs for Teesside Airport until the village of Middleton St George. The clubhouse is 1½ miles from Middleton St George on Neasham road.

DURHAM CITY
091-3780069
An 18-hole meadowland course (6211 yards, SSS 70). Visitors are welcome on weekdays. Green fees are £8 on weekdays and £12 at weekends and Bank Holidays, and £4 and £6 respectively if you are with a member. Full catering facilities are available except on Monday. Local attractions include Durham Cathedral and Castle.
Location
Littleburn Farm, Langley Moor, Durham DH7 8HL
The course is off the A690 2 miles south west of Durham.

RAC recommended hotels
Royal County ★★★★ 091-386 6821 A luxury hotel in the centre of Durham. Indoor swimming pool, sauna and solarium
Three Tuns ★★★ 091-386 4326 An historic hotel with many Tudor features. It is situated in the centre of Durham and guests may use the facilities at the Royal County Hotel.
Bridge ★★★ 091-378 0524 Two-storey hotel with modern accommodation units around it.
Hallgarth Manor C/H ★★★ Grade II listed Victorian country house set in grounds of 4 acres on edge of village.
Ramside Hall ★★★ 091-386 5282 Large Victorian (part Tudor) castle-like mansion, in extensive grounds.

HOBSON MUNICIPAL
(0207) 71605
An 18-hole municipal parkland course (6582 yards, SSS 71). Visitors are welcome at any time. Green fees are £4.50 on weekdays and £6 at weekends. There is a restaurant and bar open daily. Local attractions include the Beamish Open Air Museum.
Location
Hobson, Nr Burnopfield, Newcastle upon Tyne NE16 6BZ
The club is situated between Gateshead and Consett on the A692.

HOUGHTON-LE-SPRING
091-5841198
An 18-hole undulating moorland course (6450 yards, SSS 71). Visitors who are members of other clubs are welcome, you must be the guest of a member. There may be some restrictions on competition days. Green fees are £8 on weekdays and £12 at weekends and Bank Holidays. It is £5 at all times if you are with a member. There are catering facilities available on most days.
Location
Copt Hill, Houghton-le-Spring DH5 8LU
Take the A690 and then the A19 from Houghton-le-Spring towards Seaham and then take the B1404 road from Seaton. The club is on the B1404 Houghton-le-Spring-Seaham Harbour road.

MOUNT OSWOLD
091-3867527
An 18-hole parkland course (6101 yards, SSS 69). Visitors are welcome at any time, either as individuals or in groups. Green fees are £8 a day, £5.50 a round on weekdays and £10 a day £6.50 a round at weekends. Meals are available from 9.30am-2.30pm and 6.00pm-9.30pm. Coffee, tea and sandwiches are always available until the club closes. Sunday lunch can be arranged by booking in advance. Local attractions include the city of Durham and Beamish Open Air Museum.
Location
South Road, Durham DH1 3TQ
The club is south west of Durham on the A1050.

RAC recommended hotels
See Durham.

ROSEBERRY GRANGE
091-3700670
An 18-hole parkland course (5628 yards, SSS 68). Visitors are welcome between 8am and 7pm daily. Green fees are £4.25 per round on weekdays and £5.30 at weekends. Day tickets can be bought for £5.30 on weekdays and £6.50 at weekends. There is a restaurant, and bar snacks are always available. Local attractions include the Beamish Open Air Museum.
Location
Grange Villa, Chester-le-Street DH2 3NF
The club is 3 miles west of Chester-le-Street on the A693

SEAHAM
091-5812354
An 18-hole undulating heathland course (5972 yards, SSS 69). Visitors of all playing abilities are welcome on weekdays and most weekends depending on competitions etc. No jeans or training shoes are allowed. Green fees are £5 (£4 with a member) on weekdays and £12 (£6 with a member) at weekends and Bank Holidays. Bar snacks are available. The club is convenient for the local beaches.
Location
Dawdon, Seaham, Co Durham SR7 7R
The club is 6 miles south of Sunderland off the A19. Take the road to Seaham.

SOUTH MOOR
(0207) 232848
An 18-hole moorland course (6445 yards, SSS 72). Visitors are welcome but you must be a member of a recognised golf club. Green fees on application. Full catering facilities are available. Local attractions include the Beamish Open Air Museum.
Location
The Middles, Craghead, Stanley, Co Durham DH9 6AG
Take the B6313 from Chester-le-Street and the club is 2 miles from Stanley.

RAC recommended hotels see Birtley.

STRESSHOLME
(0325) 461002
A very pretty 18-hole parkland municipal course (6511 yards, SSS 71). Visitors of all playing abilities are welcome. Green fees are £5 on weekdays and £6 at the weekends. There are reductions after are 2pm during the winter and 4pm in the summer. Lunch is available daily. There are many parks and museums locally, including the Arts Centre.

Location
Snipe Lane, Darlington, Co Durham
Take the A66 south from Darlington to the junction with the A167 and you will see the club on the left towards Snipe House. It is about 8 miles north of Scotch Corner..

RAC recommended hotel
Blackwell Grange Moat House ★★★★ (0325) 380888 An imposing 17th century mansion with later extensions in pleasant grounds. Indoor swimming pool, golf, putting, tennis, sauna, solarium and gymnasium.

WOODHAM GOLF AND COUNTRY CLUB
(0325) 320574
An attractive 18-hole parkland course with views over the Cleveland Hills and lakes. (6727 yards, SSS 72). Visitors are welcome but it is advisable to book at weekends. Green fees are £7 per round and £10 a day on weekdays and £9 per round and £12 a day at weekends. There is a restaurant and bar meals are available. Local attractions include Durham, Bishop Auckland and Barnard Castle, and the club is within reasonable access of the Yorkshire Dales.
Location
Burnhill Way, Newton Aycliffe DH5 4PM
The club is 1 mile north of Newton Aycliffe; turn off the A167 on to the B6443.

RAC recommended hotels
See Newton Aycliffe.

ESSEX

ABRIDGE GOLF AND COUNTRY CLUB
(04028) 396
A fine parkland course with easy walking (6703 yards, SSS 72). Visitors are welcome on weekdays by arrangement provided you have a handicap certificate. Green fees are £17. Catering facilities are available daily except Friday, and there are the country clubhouse facilities which include an indoor heated pool and snooker.
Location
Epping Lane, Stapleford Tawney, Abridge, Essex RM4 1ST
From London leave the M11 at junction 5 via Abridge, or if coming from the north leave it at junction 7 via Epping, and take the A414 and then the A113 to Stapleford Tawney. If you are travelling on the M25 leave it at junction 26.

RAC recommended hotel in Epping
Post House ★★★ (0378) 73137 A modernised 16th century former coaching inn with residential annexes.

BALLARDS GORE
(07022) 58917
An 18-hole course (7062 yards, SSS 74). Visitors are welcome on weekdays, and with members after 12.30pm during the summer (11.30am in the winter).
Location
Gore Road, Canedon, Rochford, Essex SS4 2DA
Take the A127 towards Southend-on-Sea and turn off onto the A1159 at Prittlewell. Then take the B1073 to Rochford and the club is ½ mile east of the town.

BASILDON
(0268) 533297
An undulating 18-hole parkland course (6122 yards, SSS 69). Visitors are welcome at all times. Green fees on application. The club is close to the East Gate Shopping Centre.
Location
Clay Hill Lane, Basildon, Essex
If you are travelling on the A127, go through Basildon to the Kingswood roundabout, or from the A13 turn left at the Five Bells roundabout to the Kingswood roundabout.

RAC recommended hotel
Crest ★★★ (0268) 533955 A modern hotel in its own picturesque lakeside gardens. Putting and billiards.

BELFAIRS PARK
(0702) 525345
An 18-hole municipal parkland course with easy walking (5871 yards, SSS 68). The club is private but plays on the undernoted public course. Visitors are welcome but it is necessary to book for Thursdays mornings, weekends and public holidays. Green fees are £6 on weekdays and £9 on public holidays. There is a public restaurant which offers light refreshments.
Location
Eastwood Road North, Leigh-on-Sea, Essex SS9 4LR
Take the A127 from London to Southend-on-Sea and turn onto the A13, or take the A13 from Dagenham to Leigh-on-Sea. The club is on the north of the A13..

BELHUS PARK
(0708) 854260
A flat parkland course with easy walking (5900 yards, SSS 68). Visitors of all playing abilities are welcome. Green fees are £3.65 on weekdays and £6.35 at weekends. There is a bar and restaurant.
Location
Belhus Park, South Ockendon, Essex RM15 4QR
Leave the M25 at junction 30 on to the A13 at Aveley and take the B186 to South Ockendon.

RAC recommended hotels
Royal ★★ (0708) 865432 A riverside inn with a more recently built residential annexe, in Purfleet.
Ye Olde Plough House ★★★ (0375) 891592 A reconstructed 16th century barn in Bulphan. Indoor swimming pool, putting, tennis, sauna, solarium and gymnasium

BENTLEY
(0277) 73179
An 18-hole parkland course (6709 yards, SSS 72). Visitors are welcome on Monday to Friday provided you have a letter of introduction or a handicap certificate. Green fees on application. There are snacks available at all times and hot food at lunchtimes. Evening meals can be provided by arrangement.
Location
Ongar Road, Brentwood, Essex CM15 9SS
Leave the M25 at junction 28 on to A1023 to Brentwood and turn onto the A128 Ongar road. The club is 4 miles north of Brentwood.

RAC recommended hotel
Brentwood Moat House ★★★ 0277) 217974 Well-preserved hunting lodge of Henry VIII, with modernised residential wings.
Post House ★★★ (0277) 260260 A modern hotel in an attractive residential area. Indoor swimming pool, sauna, solarium and gymnasium.

BIRCH GROVE
(0206) 34276
A picturesque 9-hole meadowland course with plenty of challenges (4076 yards, SSS 62). Visitors of all playing abilities are welcome except on Sunday morning. Green fees are £6 (18 holes) on weekdays and £8 at weekends and Bank Holidays. Meals are available during opening hours and parties can be catered for by prior arrangement. Local attractions include the historic town of Colchester and the Castle and Museum.
Location
Layer Road, Colchester CO2 0HS
The club is 2 miles south of Colchester.

RAC recommended hotels see Colchester

BOYCE HILL
(0268) 793625
An 18-hole hilly parkland course (5882 yards, SSS 68). Visitors are welcome on weekdays and weekends if you are the guest of a member. Green fees are £15 per round or day. There are full catering facilities available daily.
Location
Vicarage Hill, South Benfleet, Essex SS7 1PD
Take the A13 towards South Benfleet and the club is south of the town between the B1006 and B1014, 7 miles west of Southend-on-Sea.

BRAINTREE
(0376) 24117
An 18-hole parkland course surrounded by many rare trees (6026 yards, SSS 69). Visitors of all playing abilities are welcome except on Saturday when you must have a handicap certificate, and on Sunday which is for members only. Green fees are £12 per round, £16 a day on weekdays, and £13 per round, £25 a day at weekends and Bank Holidays. If you are with a member, fees are £6.50 per round or £12.50 a day.

Location
Kings Lane, Stisted, Braintree, Essex CM7 8DA
Take the A120 or A131 to Braintree and the club is 1½ miles north east of the town on the A120.

RAC recommended hotels
White Hart ★★★ (0376) 21401 A charming 15th century, half-timbered coaching inn near the town centre.
Old Court ★★ (0376) 21444 Ancient half-timbered building with a Georgian facade.

BUNSAY DOWNS
(024541) 2648
A 9-hole gently undulating meadowland course (2913 yards, SSS 68). Visitors are welcome and teeing-off times may be prebooked up to 7 days in advance. Green fees are £5 on weekdays, £5.50 at weekends (18 holes) and £4 and £4.50 at weekends(9 holes). Breakfast, lunch and evening meals are available from 10am(8am at weekends) to 10pm daily.
Location
Little Baddow Road, Woodham Walter, Nr Maldon, Essex CM9 6RW
From Chelmsford take the A414 and leave it at Danbury, signposted Woodham Walter. The course is ½ mile west of the village.

RAC recommended hotel in Maldon
Blue Boar ★★ (0621) 852681 Old coaching inn in town centre, modernised yet retains much originality.

BURNHAM-ON-CROUCH
(0621) 782282
A 9-hole undulating meadowland course with easy walking(5350 yards, SSS 68). Visitors who are members of bona fide clubs are welcome on weekdays but not at weekends or Bank Holidays. Green fees are £12. Bar snacks are available daily except Monday and evening meals by arrangement. There is a good local museum and the club is convenient for yachting.
Location
Ferry Road, Creeksea, Burnham-on-Crouch, Essex CM0 8PQ
Leave the A130 at the Battlesbridge roundabout and turn east onto the A132. At the roundabout at Woodham Ferrers take the B1012 to Althorne and then turn left onto the B1010 for Burnham-on-Crouch.

RAC recommended hotel
Ye Olde White Harte ★ (0621) 782106 An attractive waterside inn of character.

CANONS BROOK
(0279) 21482
An 18-hole parkland course (6462 yards, SSS 72). Visitors are welcome on weekdays but at weekends you have to be the guest of a member. Green fees are £15. Full catering facilities are available except on Sunday.
Location
Elizabeth Way, Harlow, Essex CM19 5BE
Take the M11 to Harlow and turn onto Edinburgh Way and then Elizabeth Way.

RAC recommended hotels
Churchgate Manor ★★★ (0279) 420246 An enlarged Jacobean chantry house of great charm. Indoor swimming pool, sauna, solarium and gymnasium.
Green Man ★★★ (0279) 442521 Much modernised old coaching inn with added residential wing.
Harlow Moat House ★★★ (0279) 22441 A large modern hotel situated in the New Town.

CHANNELS
(0245) 440005
An 18-hole undulating meadowland course with several lakes (6100 yards, SSS 69). Visitors who have a handicap certificate are welcome on weekdays. Green fees are £16.50. A pitch and putt course is available on weekdays. The superb Elizabethan clubhouse has an excellent restaurant with table d'hote and a la carte menus.
Location
Belsteads Farm Lane, Little Waltham, Chelmsford, Essex CM3 3PT

RAC recommended hotels see Chelmsford

CHELMSFORD
(0245) 256483
An 18-hole undulating parkland course (5912 yards, SSS 68). Visitors are welcome on weekdays if you are a member of a recognised club, and at weekends with a member. Green fees are £15 per round or £20 a day. Lunch is served daily except Monday, and dinner on Friday and Saturday. Bar snacks are available every day. Local attractions include Hylands Park and House.
Location
Widford Road, Chelmsford, Essex CM2 9AP
From London take the A12 to the Wood Street roundabout in Chelmsford and turn right and then right again.

RAC recommended hotels
South Lodge ★★★ (0245) 264564 An attractive Georgian town residence with a small garden and mature trees.
Pontlands Park C/H (0245) 76444 19th-century manor house in 4 acres of grounds. Comprehensive fitness centre with two swimming pools, sauna and solarium.
County ★★ (0245) 491911 Traditional 'county town' hotel close to railway station.
Saracen's Head ★★ (0245) 262368 Sympathetically restored Victorian hotel set in town centre.

CHIGWELL
081-500 2059
An 18-hole parkland course with splendid greens (6279 yards, SSS 71). Provided you have a handicap certificate, visitors are welcome on weekdays by prior arrangement. Green fees are £15 per round or £20 a day. From Monday to Saturday, lunch is served and dinner is available by arrangement. The club is close to Epping Forest.
Location
High Road, Chigwell, Essex IG7 5BH
The club is 13½ miles north east of London. Leave the M11 at junction 5 for the A113 to Chigwell.

CLACTON-ON-SEA
(0255) 421919
An 18-hole undulating, somewhat windy, seaside course (6244 yards, SSS 70). Visitors of all playing abilities including beginners are welcome midweek subject to availability and, provided you have a handicap certificate, visitors can play at weekends and Bank Holidays. Green fees are £12 per round on weekdays and £18 at weekends and Bank Holidays. Full catering facilities are available except on Monday.
Location
West Road, Clacton-on-Sea, Essex CO15 1AG
Take the A133 from Colchester to Clacton and you will find the club 1 mile west of the pier, 16 miles from Colchester.

RAC recommended hotel
King's Cliff ★★★ (0255) 812343 A modern hotel standing right on the seafront.

COLCHESTER
(0206) 853396
An 18-hole parkland course in very pretty surroundings (6319 yards, SSS 70). Visitors are welcome on weekdays and at weekends if you are with a member. Green fees are £15 a day and £12 per round. Catering facilities are available. The course is in the middle of Constable country.
Location
Braiswick, Colchester, Essex CO4 5AU
The club is about 1 mile north west on the Bergholt road, B1508, from the A134 at Colchester North station.

RAC recommended hotels
George ★★★ (0206) 761732 An ancient town centre inn which has been modernised without loss of charm. Sauna, solarium and gymnasium.
Marks Tey ★★★ (0206) 21001 A modern 2-storey hotel situated well outside the town. Tennis and gymnasium.
Red Lion ★★★ (0206) 577986 Historic town-centre coaching inn recently refurbished to a high standard.

FORRESTER PARK
(0621) 891903
A 9-hole undulating parkland course with easy walking and some fine views over the Blackwater estuary (2675 yards, SSS 66). The club is soon to have 18 holes. Visitors are welcome on weekdays and after midday on Sunday. Green fees are £8 on weekdays and £10 at weekends. Full catering facilities are available.
The **Location**
Beckingham Road, Great Totham, Maldon CM9 8EA
From Maldon take the Tiptree road and the club is about 3 miles north.

RAC recommended hotel see Maldon.

FRINTON
(0255) 674618
A pleasant 18-hole seaside course though somewhat windy (6259 yards, SSS 70). Visitors are welcome on weekdays but a handicap certificate is required for the main course. Green fees are £18. Full catering facilities are available except on Monday.
Location
Esplanade, Frinton-on-Sea, Essex CO13 9EP
Take the A133 from Colchester to Weeley village and then take the B1033 for Frinton. Turn right at the seafront for the golf course.

RAC recommended hotels
Maplin ★★ (0255) 673832 An hotel with bow windows overlooking the sea.
Rock ★★ (0255) 675173 A large Victorian hotel situated in its own grounds on the sea front.

HAINAULT FOREST
081-500 2097
Two 18-hole parkland courses (5754 yards, SSS 67 and 6600 yards, SSS 71). The course is a public one and visitors of all playing abilities are welcome. Green fees on application. Meals are served daily. Local attractions include Havering-atte-Bower, an old Norman village.
Location
Chigwell Row, Hainault, Essex IG7 4QW
From junction 4 of the M11 at Woodford, take the A113 north then the B173 east to Hainault Forest. Chigwell Row is on the left off the A1112.

HARTSWOOD
(0277) 217128
An 18-hole municipal parkland course with easy walking (6238 yards, SSS 70). Visitors of all playing abilities are welcome, but it is necessary to telephone first as there is a booking system in operation. Green fees are £5 on weekdays and £7.50 at weekends. Lunch and bar snacks are available daily except on Sunday and Friday.
Location
King George's Playing Fields, Ingrave Road, Brentwood, Essex
From junction 28 on the M25, the club is 1 mile south of Brentwood.

RAC recommended hotels see Bentley.

HARWICH AND DOVERCOURT
(0255) 503616
A flat 9-hole meadowland course with easy walking (5692 yards, SSS 68). Visitors who have a handicap certificate are welcome. Green fees on application. Full catering facilities including bar snacks are available daily. Local attractions include the nature

reserve at 'Wrabness Woods' and the historic town of Harwich.
Location
Station Road, Parkeston, Harwich, Essex CO12 4NZ
Keep on the A120 for Harwich towards Parkeston Quay and the club is after the last roundabout, 200 yards on the left.

RAC recommended hotels
Cliff ★★ (0255) 503345 An attractive white-faced Victorian hotel in a seafront position overlooking the bay.
Pier at Harwich ★★ (0255) 241212 Right onthe waterfront, a turn-of -the-century building with stunning views of the Stour and Orwell estuaries.
Tower ★★ (0255) 504952 An hotel featuring Grade 1 listed Italian ceilings and friezes.

HAVERING
(0708) 741429
An 18-hole municipal parkland course (5237 yards, SSS 70). There is also a pitch and putt course. Risebridge Club plays here. Visitors are welcome but it is necessary to book for weekend games. Green fees are £4.50 on weekdays and £5.90 at weekends. There are snacks available daily.
Location
Risebridge Chase, Lower Bedfords Road, Romford, Essex RM1 4DG
The club is off the A12 2 miles from Gallows Corner and Romford station.

ILFORD
081-554 2930
An 18-hole parkland course (5414 yards, SSS 68) where the Barking Creek river crosses the green five times . Visitors of all playing abilities are welcome at any time. Green fees are £8 per round. There is a restaurant which is open daily.
Location
291 Wanstead Park Road, Ilford, Essex IG1 3TR
The course is 1/2 mile from Ilford station.

MALDON
(0621) 853212
A 9-hole meadowland course (6197 yards, SSS 69). Provided they have a handicap certificate, visitors are welcome on weekdays only. Green fees are £10 per round or £12 a day. Catering facilities are by arrangement.
Location
Beeleig, Langford, Maldon, Essex CM9 7SS
The club is 2 miles north west of Maldon on the B1019. Turn off the road at the Essex Waterworks in Langford.

RAC recommended hotel
Blue Boar ★★ (0261) 852681 An old coaching inn in the town centre. It has been modernised yet retains much of its originality.

MAYLANDS GOLF AND COUNTRY CLUB
(04023) 73080
A pretty 18-hole undulating parkland course (6182 yards, SSS 69, Ladies SSS 72). Visitors are welcome at any time if you are with a member, or on weekdays only if you are a member of another club. Green fees are £10 on weekdays and £16 per round or £25 a day at weekends. There is a bar and lunch is available daily.
Location
Colchester Road, Harold Park, Romford, Essex RM3
The club is on the A12 between Romford and Brentwood. Leave the M25 at exit 28 and turn east towards Harold Hill.

ORSETT
(0375) 891352
An 18-hole heathland course with easy walking (6614 yards, SSS 72). Provided they have a handicap certificate, visitors are welcome by arrangement on weekdays. Green fees are £17 per round or day. There is a restaurant which is open from 8.30am until 8.30pm.
Location
Brentwood Road, Orsett, Essex RM16 3DS
From the A13 towards Southend-on-Sea turn south on the A128, the course is about 400 yards on the left.

PIPPS HILL COUNTRY CLUB
(0268) 523456
A 9-hole meadowland course with several ditches (2829 yards, SSS 67). Visitors are welcome. Green fees on application. Full catering facilities are available.
Location
Pipps Hill Country Club, Cranes Farm Road, Basildon, Essex SS14 3DG
Take the A127 or A13 to Basildon.

RAC recommended hotels see Basildon.

QUIETWATERS
(0621) 868829
The links course is an 18-hole parkland one (6450 yards, SSS 71). Visitors are welcome on weekdays and, if you book in advance, at weekends and Bank Holidays. Green fees are £10 per round during the week and £14 at the weekend. Full catering facilities are available. A new championship course is being developed at Quietwaters, to be called Quietwaters Lakes (6793 yards, SSS 72) and play is expected to start on it in spring 1991. A hotel and conference centre are also under construction here.
Location
Colchester Road, Tolleshunt D'Arcy, Nr Maldon CM9 8HX
The club is on the B1026 Maldon-Colchester road about 8 miles south of Colchester.

ROCHFORD HUNDRED
(0702) 544302
An 18-hole parkland course with some ponds (6255 yards, SSS 69). Provided they have a handicap certificate, visitors are welcome on weekdays and with a member at weekends. Green fees are £14 per round and £18 a day. Lunch is available between Monday and Friday. Local attractions include the Historic Aircraft Museum.
Location
Rochford Hall, Hall Road, Rochford, Essex SS4 1NW
The club is off the Rochford-Southend road adjacent to the Airport, 4 miles north of Southend.

RAC recommended hotel
Airport Moat House ★★★ (0702) 546344 A modern hotel with all the rooms on the ground floor. Tennis, squash, gymnasium and billiards.

ROMFORD
(0708) 40007
An attractive, well-bunkered 18-hole parkland course with easy walking (6365 yards, SSS 70). There are also practice facilities. Provided you have a handicap certificate and are a member of a golf club, visitors are welcome on weekdays. Green fees are £13 per round or £20 a day. Catering facilities are available. The course is handy for Romford and Basildon shopping centres.
Location
Heath Drive, Gidea Park, Romford, Essex RM2 5QE
You will find the club 1 1/2 miles from Romford town centre, off the A12.

SAFFRON WALDEN
(0799) 22786
An 18-hole undulating parkland course set in very pretty surroundings and with beautiful views (6608 yards, SSS 72). Visitors who have a handicap certificate are welcome on weekdays, but only as a guest of a member at weekends and Bank Holidays. Green fees are £17 per round. Lunch is available daily during the week and evening meals can be arranged for societies. Interesting places to visit locally include Audley End House.
Location
Windmill Hill, Saffron Walden, Essex CB10 1BX
Leave the M11 at junction 9 and take the B184 from Stump Cross roundabout. The entrance to the club is just before you enter the town of Saffron Walden.

RAC recommended hotel
Saffron ★★ (0799) 22676 Family-run former coaching inn with many delightfully developed features.

SKIPS
(04023) 48234
A flat 18-hole meadowland course which can be testing (6146 yards, SSS 71). Visitors have to be season ticket holders. Green fees on application. There are no catering facilities.
Location
Horsemanside, Tysea Hill, Stapleford Abbots, Essex RM4 1JU
Leave the A12 at Romford and turn onto the B175 to Stapleford Abbots. The club is on the left off Tysea Hill.

STOKE-BY-NAYLAND
(0206) 262836
Two 18-hole undulating meadowland courses; the Gainsborough (6471 yards, SSS 71) and the Constable (6498 yards, SSS 71). Visitors are unrestricted during the week and can play after 10.30am at weekends, provided you have a handicap certificate and are members of a recognised club. Green fees are £15 a day on weekdays and £18 at weekends. Full catering facilities are available.
Location
Keepers Lane, Leavenheath, Colchester, Essex CO6 4PZ
Take the A134 north from Colchester for 7 miles and then turn off onto the B1068 to Stoke-by-Nayland.

THEYDON BOIS
(0378) 3054
An 18-hole undulating woodland course with the original holes within the forest and the nine new ones in open hillside (5472 yards, SSS 68). Provided you have a handicap certificate and are a member of a club or recognised golf society, visitors are welcome. Green fees are £14 on weekdays and £20 at weekends. Full catering facilities are available. The club is situated on the edge of the Forest, and is particularly attractive in the autumn.
Location
Theydon Road, Epping, Essex CM16 4EH
The club is off the B172 1 mile south of Epping.(Junctions 6 (M11) or 27 (M25).

THORNDON PARK
(0277) 810345
A fine 18-hole parkland course (6455 yards, SSS 71). Visitors are welcome on weekdays and with a member at weekends. Green fees are £20 per round or £30 a day. Meals are served daily except Monday.
Location
Ingrave, Brentwood, Essex CM13 3RH
Take the A12 to Brentwood and the club is 2 miles south east on the A128.

RAC recommended hotels see Bentley.

THORPE HALL
(0702) 582205
An 18-hole parkland/meadowland course (6286 yards, SSS 71). Provided they have a handicap certificate, visitors are welcome on weekdays. Green fees are £17 per day or round. Lunch is served daily except Monday.
Location
Thorpe Hall Avenue, Thorpe Bay, Essex SS1 3AT
Take the A127 or A13 to Southend-on-Sea. Thorpe Hall Avenue joins the seafront about 2 miles east of the pier.

RAC recommended hotels in Southend
Airport Moat House ★★★ (0702) 546344 Modern purpose-built hotelwith all rooms on ground floor. Tennis, squash, gymnasium, billiards.
Tower ★★ (0702) 348635 Large house with distinctive tower, in corner position. Recently refurbished and redecorated.
Balmoral ★★ (0702) 342947 Owner-managed pleasant hotel in converted residential buildings.

THREE RIVERS GOLF AND COUNTRY CLUB
(0621) 828631
Two fine parkland courses. The Kings course, 18 holes (6609 yards, SSS 72) and the Queens course, 9-hole x 2 (2142 yards, Par 27). Provided you have a handicap certificate, visitors are welcome on weekdays, but only in the morning at weekends unless you are with a member. It is advisable to check for competition days. Green fees are £12 (£7.50 with a member) on weekdays and £12 (£10 with a member) at weekends. Full catering facilities are available. Club facilities include tennis, swimming, squash, snooker, sauna, solarium and gymnasium. Local attractions include Burnham-on-Sea for the sailing.
Location
Stow Road, Purleigh, Nr Chelmsford, Essex CM3 6RR
From London, take the A127 and turn onto the A130; at Battlebridge take the A132 east and continue on the B1012 to Cold Norton and follow the signs for Purleigh. From Chelmsford, take the A12 to the A130 and then follow the same route.

RAC recommended hotels see Maldon

TOWERLANDS
(0376) 26802
Two undulating meadowland courses, 9 holes (2698 yards, SSS 66) and 18 holes (5406 yards, SSS 66). Visitors are welcome at any time except before 12.30pm at weekends or after 4.30pm on Wednesday. Green fees are £5 (9 holes) and £6.50 (18 holes) on weekdays and £9 (18 holes) at weekends and Bank Holidays. There are full bar and restaurant facilities.
Location
Panfield Road, Braintree, Essex CM7 5BJ
Take the A120 or A131 to Braintree and the club is on the B1053 out of the town.

RAC recommended hotels see Braintree.

UPMINSTER
(040220) 22788
An 18-hole parkland course near the Ingrebourne river (5926 yards, SSS 68). Visitors who have some playing experience are welcome on weekdays if you are a member of a recognised club. Green fees are £9 per round or £15 a day on weekdays and £12 per round and £18 a day at weekends. Meals are served daily except Monday. Local attractions include an old windmill.
Location
114 Hall Lane, Upminster, Essex
Take the A127 towards Southend-on-Sea and turn off at Upminster.

WARREN
(024541) 3258
An 18-hole undulating parkland course with some fine views (6211 yards, SSS 70). Visitors are welcome on weekdays. Green fees are £14 per round or £17 a day. Full catering facilities are available daily.
Location
Woodham Walter, Maldon, Essex CM9 6RW
The club is on the A414, 6 miles east of Chelmsford going towards Maldon.

RAC recommended hotels see Maldon.

WEST ESSEX
081-529 0928
An challenging 18-hole parkland course within Epping Forest (6289 yards, SSS 70). Visitors are welcome on weekdays and, if you are with a member, at weekends and Bank Holidays. A handicap certificate is necessary. Green fees are £18 per round. Full catering facilities are available. Local attractions include the forest itself and Queen Elizabeth's Hunting Lodge.
Location
Sewardstonebury, Chingford, London E4 7QL
From junction 26 of M25 take the A121 east, then A104 and A1069 to Chingford. Turn north on Bury Road for ½ mile.

WOODFORD
081-504 0553
A 9-hole forest land course with natural hazards including grazing cows (5806 yards, SSS 68). There are some panoramic views of London from the course. Visitors are welcome on weekdays, except on Tuesday and Thursday mornings, and at the weekend if you are with a member. Green fees are £9 per round or £12 a day. Snacks are available daily except Monday and meals can be served by arrangement. Local attractions include Epping Forest.
Location
2 Sunset Avenue, Woodford Green, Essex IG8 0ST
The course is 10 miles from London by taking any road to Woodford Green. The club is near the Castle public house.

RAC recommended hotels
Prince Regent ★★★ 081-505 9966 Georgian mansion with outbuildings converted to a luxury small hotel.
Woodford Moat House ★★★ 081-505 4511 Large modern hotel situated at the edge of Epping Forest.

GLOUCESTERSHIRE

CLEEVE HILL MUNICIPAL
(024267) 2592
An 18-hole undulating heathland course situated on high ground (6217 yards, SSS 70). Visitors of all playing abilities are welcome, including beginners, except on Sunday mornings. Green fees are £5.50 on weekdays and £6 at weekends and Bank Holidays. OAPs and juniors can play for £3. Full catering facilities are available daily. Places of interest locally include Sudeley Castle, Broadway, and Cleeve Hill with its ancient earthworks.
Location
Cleeve Hill, Nr Prestbury, Cheltenham, Glos GL52 3PN
Take the A46 from Cheltenham and the club is 3 miles north.

RAC recommended hotel
Rising Sun ★★★ A refurbished stone-built inn on the edge of the Cotswolds affording outstanding views over the Severn Vale. Sauna.

CIRENCESTER
(0285) 2465
An undulating 18-hole course (6100 yards, SSS 69). Provided you have a handicap certificate, visitors are welcome, but you must arrange it beforehand. Green fees are £14 (£7 with a member) on weekdays and £20 (£10 with a member) at weekends and Bank Holidays. Lunch and evening meals are available every day except Monday. Local attractions include the Corinium Museum and the Cornhall.
Location
Cheltenham Road, Bagendon, Cirencester, Glos GL7 7BH
The course is 1½ miles from Cirencester on the A435 Cheltenham road.

RAC recommended hotels
Fleece ★★★ (0285) 568507 A coaching inn in the town centre.
King's Head ★★★ (0285) 653322 A 14th century former coaching inn in the square facing the Parish Church.
Stratton House C/H ★★★ (0285) 651761 Attractive Georgian manor house of Cotswold stone. Delightful walled garden.
Corinium Court ★★ (0285) 69711 Originally a wool merchant's house (1695) converted to a small hotel.

COTSWOLD EDGE
(0453) 844167
An 18-hole course (5897 yards, SSS 69). Visitors of all playing abilities are welcome on weekdays. Green fees are £10 a day. Full catering facilities are available daily. The club is situated in the heart of the beautiful Cotswold countryside.
Location
Rushmire, Wotton Under Edge, GL12 7PT
You will find the course 2 miles north east of Wooton Under Edge, on the B4058 Tetbury road.

RAC recommended hotel
Swan ★★ (0453) 842329 Traditional coaching inn with attractive period features. In town centre.

COTSWOLD HILLS
(0242) 515264
A gently undulating course with some fine views of the Cotswolds (6716 yards, SSS 72). Provided you have a handicap certificate, visitors are welcome, but you must also be a member of a recognised club. Green fees on application. Lunch and dinner is served daily together with bar snacks, except on Monday when sandwiches only are available. The course is close to Cheltenham.
Location
Ullenwood, Cheltenham, Glos GL53 9QT
The club is situated 3 miles south of Cheltenham between the A435 and B4070.

RAC recommended hotel
Royal George ★★★ (0452) 862506 A traditional Cotswolds coaching inn with a modern extension, in Birdlip. Sauna and solarium.

GLOUCESTER GOLF AND COUNTRY CLUB
(0452) 411331
A pleasant 18-hole undulating wooded parkland course (6135 yards, SSS 69) with some splendid views over Gloucester and the surrounding Cotswolds. There is also a 9-hole course par 27. Provided you have a handicap certificate, visitors are welcome at any time but you must telephone for a reservation first. Golfing attire is compulsory. Green fees are £14 on weekdays and £18 at weekends and Bank Holidays. The club is attached to the hotel and full catering facilities are available. Local attractions include Gloucester Cathedral, Broadway, Cheltenham and Prinknash Abbey.
Location
Matson Lane, Robinswood Hill, Gloucester GL4 9EA
You will find the course 2 miles south of Gloucester city centre on the B4073 to Painswick.

RAC recommended hotel
Gloucester Hotel and Country Club ★★★ (0452) 25653 A converted 16-17th century farmhouse with a modern leisure complex added. Swimming pool, golf, putting, tennis, squash, sauna, solarium, gymnasium and billiards.

LILLEY BROOK
(0204) 526785
An 18-hole undulating parkland course with commanding views of the Gloucestershire countryside (6226 yards, SSS 70). Provided you have a handicap certificate, visitors are welcome, but you must also be a bona fide member of a club. Green fees are £15 on weekdays and £20 at weekends, or £6 if you are with a member. Lunch

and dinner is served daily except Monday. The club is handy for the Cotswolds and is not far from Tetbury.
Location
Cirencester Road, Charlton Kings, Cheltenham, Glos GL53 8EG
Take the A435 Cirencester road and you will find the course 3 miles from the centre of Cheltenham.

RAC recommended hotels
Queens ★★★★ (0242) 514724 An elegant Regency building overlooking the Imperial Gardens.
Carlton ★★★ (0242) 514453 A fine Regency building centrally but quietly situated.
Golden Valley Thistle ★★★★ (0242) 232691 Modern hotel in own grounds on the western outskirts of town. Indoor swimming pool, sauna, solarium, gymnasium.
White House ★★★ (0452) 713226 Recently refurbished hotel on the outskirts of town, close to junction 11 of the M5.
George ★★ (0242) 235751 Gracious Georgian building, a landmark close to the town centre.
Lansdown ★★ (0242) 522700 White stone Regency building with attractive gardens; a shortway from town centre.
Savoy ★★ (0242) 527788 Elegant three-storey white Regency building on tree-lined avenue.
Wellesley Court ★ (0242) 580411 Pleasant Regency house hotel situated in a quiet square.

LYDNEY
(0594) 842614
A 9-hole flat parkland course (5382 yards, SSS 66). Visitors are welcome at weekends but they must be accompanied by a member unless you have made prior arrangements. Green fees are £6 a day. Light snacks are available daily.
Location
off Lakeside Avenue, Lydney, Glos
As you come into Lydney on the A48 from Gloucester, turn left at the bottom of Highfield Hill and look for Lakeside Avenue. It is the 7th turning on the left.

MINCHINHAMPTON
(045383) 3866
An 18-hole meadowland course in attractive surroundings (6675 yards, SSS 72). Provided you have a handicap certificate visitors, are welcome at all times, subject to availability of the course. Green fees are £12 on weekdays and £15 at weekends, or £7 if you are with a member. Full catering facilities are available. Local attractions include Chavinedge House.
Location
New Course, Minchinhampton, Stroud, Glos GL6 9BE
Leave the M5 at junction 13 and the course is 5 miles south east of Stroud on the Minchinhampton-Avening road.

RAC recommended hotels
Bear of Rodborough ★★★ (0453) 878522 A Cotswold stone bujilding in its own attractive grounds enjoying fine views.
Burleigh Court ★★★ (0453) 883804 A large country house of local Cotswold stone set in pleasant grounds. Swimming pool and putting.
Alpine Lodge ★★ (045 36) 4949 Situated near town centre. A three-storey building with some 'Alpine' features.
Imperial ★★ (045 36) 4077 Stone-built hotel in town centre; close to railway station.
London ★★ (0453) 759992 Attractive small hotel close to town centre. Well furnished rooms.

PAINSWICK
(0452) 812180
An 18-hole commonland course (4780 yards, SSS 64)situated on Painswick Beacon, with some splendid views over the Cotswold Hills . Visitors are welcome on weekdays and at weekends if you are with a member. Green fees are £5 (£4 with a member) on weekdays and £7 (£6 with a member) at weekends. Catering facilities can be arranged with the Steward, but snacks are normally available at all times.
Location
Painswick, Stroud, Glos GL6 6TL
The club is situated 1 mile north of Painswick village on the A46.

RAC recommended hotels
Painswick ★★★ (0452) 812160 Georgian house with well-furnished rooms. In town centre. Billiards.
Falcon ★★ (0452) 812189 16th-century former inn built in Queen Anne's time.

ROYAL FOREST OF DEAN
(0594) 32583
A good 18-hole parkland course surrounded by some lovely countryside (5519 yards, SSS 67). Visitors of all playing abilities are welcome. Car hire is £10 per round or £15 a day. Green fees are £8 per round, £10 a day on weekdays and £9 per round, £11 a day at weekends. There is a restaurant which serves table d'hote and a la carte dinners daily, and snacks are always available. There is also a hotel in the grounds, and other facilities include tennis, outdoor heated swimming pool and bowling green. The club is situated in the heart of the Forest of Dean and close to the Wye Valley.
Location
Lords Hill, Coleford, Glos GL16 8BD
Leaving the M50 at Ross, take the A40 towards Monmouth (14 miles south) and then turn onto the A466 for Coleford. The club is 1½ miles from the town on the Parkend road.

RAC recommended hotels
Bells ★★ (0594) 32583 A modern hotel next to the golf course, Swimming pool, putting, tennis and billiards.
Speech House ★★ (0594) 22607 17th-century Court House adapted to a hotel of great character.

STINCHCOMBE HILL
(0453) 2015
An 18-hole downland meadowland course (5710 yards, SSS 68) with amazing views of the Cotswolds, River Sever and the Welsh hills . Visitors of all playing abilities are welcome on any weekday, but there are some restrictions at weekends and Bank Holidays unless you are with a member. Golfing attire is required. Green fees are £12 on weekdays (£7 with a member) and £14 at weekends and Bank Holidays (£7 with a member). Full catering facilities are available daily. Local attractions include Slimbridge Wildfowl Trust and Berkeley Castle.
Location
Stinchcombe Hill, Dursley, Glos GL11 6AQ
You can approach the club either directly from Dursley town centre and find it ½ mile up the hill past the bus station, or, if you take the A4135 from Tetbury the club is 1 mile along a narrow lane which is signposted off the main road.

TEWKESBURY PARK HOTEL
(0684) 295404
An 18-hole parkland course close to the River Severn (6533/6197 yards, SSS 72/70). Provided you have a handicap certificate, visitors are welcome. Green fees are £14 on weekdays and £18 at weekends. Snacks and meals are available daily. Local attractions include Sudeley Castle and the club is within reasonable access of Warwick and Stratford-upon-Avon.
Location
Lincoln Green Lane, Tewkesbury GL20 7DN
Leave the M5 at junction 9 and the club is half a mile south of the town on the A38, about 3 miles from the motorway.

RAC recommended hotel
Tewkesbury Park ★★★ (0684) 295405 An 18th century mansion with outstanding recreational facilities and sports complex. The hotel enjoys panoramic views. Indoor swimming pool, putting, tennis, squash, sauna, solarium, gymnasium and billiards.

WESTONBIRT
(0666) 88242
A 9-hole parkland course with some fine views (4504 yards, SSS 61). Visitors are welcome, and green fees are £3.50. Meals are available at the Holford Arms. The club is situated in the heart of the Cotswolds and is close to Westonbirt Aboretum, 150 acres of forest, trees and shrubs.
Location
Tetbury, Glos GL8 8QG

RAC recommended hotel
Hare & Hounds ★★★ (066 688)An early 19th century building of Cotswold stone in Tetbury. It is set in ten acres of garden and woodland. Tennis and squash.

GREATER MANCHESTER

ACRE GATE
061-748 1226
An 18-hole municipal parkland course (4395 yards, SSS 60). Visitors of all playing abilities are welcome at any time. Green fees are £3 on weekdays and £4.50 at weekends. Catering facilities are available at weekends.
Location
Pennybridge Lane, Flixton, Manchester
From Urmston take the Flixton Road, then turn left at the Bird in Hand public house.

ALTRINCHAM
061-928 0761
An undulating 18-hole parkland course with easy walking (6162 yards, SSS 69). Visitors of all playing abilities are welcome. Green fees are £3 on weekdays and £4.50 at weekends. There are no catering facilities at the club but there is a restaurant next door. Local attractions include Dunham Park and Deer Park(NT).
Location
Stockport Road, Timperley, Altrincham, Cheshire WA15
The club is situated on the A560 1 mile east of Altrincham.

RAC recommended hotels
Cresta Court ★★★ 061-927 7272 A large modern purpose-built hotel within easy reach of Manchester.
Woodlands Park ★★★ 061-928 8631 A pleasant white faced hotel in a residential area, conveniently situated for Manchester Airport.
Ashley ★★★ 061-928 3794 Modern hotel set in Cheshire village of Hall, 9 miles south of Manchester city centre.
Bowdon ★★★ 061 928 7121 Large Vistorian building with modern extensions; in residential area convenient for motorway network.
George and Dragon ★★ 061 928 9933 Attractive hotel only minutes from motorway, airport and city centre.
Pelican ★★ 061 962 7414 Black and white inn with quiet courtyard motel bedrooms.

ASHTON-IN-MAKERFIELD
(0942) 724229
A wooded 18-hole parkland course (6169 yards, SSS 69). Visitors who are members of a recognised golf club are welcome on weekdays except Wednesday and with a member at weekends. Green fees on application. Meals are available daily except Monday. Local places of interest include Wigan Pier, and the course is close to Haydock Racecourse.

Location
Garswood Park, Liverpool Road, Ashton-in-Makerfield WN4 8QU
The course is situated on the A58, off the M6 at the Haydock roundabout (junction 24).

ASHTON ON MERSEY
061-973 3220
A 9-hole parkland course with easy walking (6202 yards, SSS 69). Provided you have a handicap certificate, visitors are welcome on weekdays except Tuesday after 3pm, as that is Ladies Day. Snacks and lunches are available daily except Monday. There are some good working museums in the vicinity.
Location
Church Lane, Sale, Cheshire M33 5QQ
The course is situated 2 miles from Sale station.

RAC recommended hotels
See Sale

ASHTON-UNDER-LYNE
061-330 1537
A challenging 18-hole moorland course with large greens (6209 yards, SSS 70). Visitors of all playing abilities are welcome during the week but only with a member at weekends. Green fees are £11. Full catering facilities are available daily except Monday. Stamford Park is close by.
Location
Gorsey Way, Ashton-under-Lyne, Greater Manchester OL6 9HT
From Ashton, take the Mossley Road and turn left at Queens Road then right at Kings Road.

RAC recommended hotel
York House ★★★ 061-330 5899 A fine Victorian terrace house in a tree lined street near the town centre

BLACKLEY
061-643 2980
An 18-hole parkland course (6237 yards, SSS 70). Visitors are welcome during the week but must be the guest of a member at weekends and Bank Holidays. Green fees are £8 a day. Full catering facilities are available. The city of Manchester is only 5 miles away.
Location
Victoria Ave East, Blackley, Manchester M9 2HW
Take the A664 from Middleton towards Blackley.

BOLTON
(0204) 43067
An 18-hole parkland course (6215 yards, SSS 69). Visitors who are members of a bona fide golf club are welcome any day, but it is best to arrange it beforehand. Green fees are £12 on Monday, Tuesday, Thursday and Friday, and £15 on Wednesday, Saturday, Sunday and Bank Holidays. Lunches and evening meals are served daily.
Location
Lostock Park, Chorley New Road, Bolton BL6 4AJ
Leave the M61 at junction 6 and the club is off the main road halfway between Bolton and Horwich.

RAC recommended hotels
Crest ★★★ (0204) 615511 A modern hotel which is situated conveniently for Junction 5 M61.
Egerton House C/H ★★★ (0204) 57171 Attractive country house amongst 4½ acres of lawns, trees and shrubs; fine views.
Last Drop Village ★★★ (0204) 591131 Unique stone-built hotel of character; hub of beautifully restored village.
Pack Horse ★★★ (0204) 27261 Traditional Georgian hotel in centre. Public car park adjacent. Billiards.

BOLTON MUNICIPAL
(0204) 42336
An 18-hole municipal parkland course (6012 yards, SSS 69). Visitors of all playing abilities are welcome at any time. Green fees are £3 on weekdays and £4 at weekends. There is a bar, restaurant and cafe which are open daily. The course is close to some beautiful countryside and there are some interesting local museums including Smith Halls, a Spinning Jenny Museum.
Location
Links Rd, Bolton, Lancs BL6 4AF
The club is situated on the A673 3 miles west of Bolton. Leave the M61 at junction 6.

RAC recommended hotels
See Bolton

BRACKLEY
061-790 6076
A flat 9-hole parkland course (3003 yards, SSS 69). Visitors are welcome, and the course is particularly good for beginners. Green fees are £2.30 during the week and £2.30 for 9 holes, £3.50 for 18 holes at weekends and Bank Holidays.
Location
Bullows Rd, Little Hulton, Worsley, Manchester
Leave Manchester on the A6 and 9 miles along the road turn right at the White Lion Hotel into Highfield Road. Turn left into Captain Fold Road, then left into Bullows Road.

BRAMHALL
061-439 4057
A wooded 18-hole meadowland course with some wonderful views of the Pennines (6293 yards, SSS 70). Visitors who are members of a bona fide golf club are welcome, but it is best to check beforehand in case there is a member's competition taking place. Green fees are £10 on weekdays and £12 at weekends and Bank Holidays. There is a restaurant where an a la carte menu is served, and bar snacks are always available.
Location
Ladythorn Rd, Bramhall, Stockport, Cheshire SK7 2EY
The course is situated three quaters of a mile from Bramhall station, 8 miles south of Manchester on the A5102.

RAC recommended hotel
Bramhall Moat House ★★★ 061-439 8116 A purpose-built modern hotel with conference facilities. There is a sauna and solarium avilable.

BRAMALL PARK
061-485 3119
An 18-hole parkland course (6214 yards, SSS 70). It is a very pretty course and one of the best in the vicinity. Visitors of all playing abilities are welcome. Green fees are £12 on weekdays and £15 at weekends. There is a restaurant and bar which is open daily except Friday. Local attractions include Bramall Hall, built in the 15th/16th century, and Lyme Park Hall.
Location
20 Manor Rd, Bramhall, Stockport SK7 3LY
Take the A6 8 miles south of Manchester to Bramhall Lane, then take the A5102 to Carr Wood Road.

RAC recommended hotels
See Bramhall

BREIGHTMET
(0204) 27381
A long 9-hole parkland course (6448 yards, SSS 71). Visitors are welcome on weekdays except Wednesday and also at weekends if you are with a member. Green fees are £6 (£3 with a member) on weekdays and £8 (£4 with a member) at weekends and Bank Holidays. Full catering facilities are available except on Monday.
Location
Red Bridge, Ainsworth, Bolton, Lancs
Leave Bolton on the main road to Bury and turn left after 3 miles for the Milnthorpe Road and Red Bridge.

RAC recommended hotels
See Bolton

BROOKDALE
061-681 4534
An 18-hole parkland course (5878 yards, SSS 68). Visitors who are members of a bona fide golf club are welcome. Green fees are £8 (£5.50 with a member) on weekdays and £12 (£6.50 with a member, at weekends. Catering facilities are available daily except Monday. Local attractions include 'Daisy Nook' Park and Garden Centre(NT).
Location
Ashbridge, Woodhouse, Failsworth, Manchester M35 9WM
The course is situated 5 miles north east of Manchester.

RAC recommended hotels
See Oldham

BURY
061-766 4897
An 18-hole undulating moorland course with some hard walking (5953 yards, SSS 69). Visitors of all levels are welcome providing you have a reservation. Green fees are £10 on weekdays (£4 with a member) and £12 at weekends. Full catering facilities are available except on Monday. Heaton Park with its zoo and attractive lakes is nearby.
Location
Unsworth Hall, Blackford Bridge, Bury BL9 9TH
The course is situated on the A56 7 miles north of Manchester.

RAC recommended hotels
Bolholt ★★ 061-764 5239 Historic building set in 3 acres of grounds, within 55 acres of parkland. Tennis, fishing, sauna and gymnasium.
Woolfield House ★ 061-797 9775 A privately-owned hotel situated in the centre of town conveniently placed for the M66.

CASTLE HAWK
(0706) 40841
An 18-hole undulating parkland/meadowland course (3158 yards, SSS 65). Visitors of all playing abilities are welcome. Green fees on application. Snacks and lunches are normally available and evening meals by arrangement. Local attractions include Hollingworth Lake.
Location
Heywood Road, Castleton, Rochdale
Leave Rochdale on the Castleton road. In Castleton, turn right directly before the railway station, and then follow the road until you reach Heywood Road (a dirt track).

CHEADLE
061-428 2160
A 9-hole undulating parkland course (5006 yards, SSS 65). Visitors are welcome every day except Tuesday and Saturday, but you must be a member of a golf club and hold an official handicap certificate. Green fees are £8 (£4 with a member) on weekdays and £10 a day on Sundays and Bank Holidays. Lunches are provided daily except Thursday and other meals by arrangement with the Stewardess.
Location
Shiers Drive, Cheadle, Cheshire SK8 1HW
Leave the M63 at junction 11 and the club is situated 1 mile south of Cheadle village, 1 mile north of Cheadle Hulme station.

RAC recommended hotels
See Stockport

CHORLTON-CUM-HARDY
061-881 3139
An 18-hole meadowland course (6003 yards, SSS 69). Visitors of all playing abilities are welcome but you must telephone the Pro beforehand. Green fees are £12 on weekdays and £15 at weekends. Evening meals are served daily by arrangement except on Monday when only sandwiches and bar snacks are available. Local attractions include Dunham Hall and Park, Tatton Hall, Granada Studios tour and the Castlefield Museum.

Location
Barlow Hall Road, Chorlton, Manchester M21 2JJ
The club is near the junction of A5145 and A5103 (M63 junction 9). The course is 3 miles from the city centre near Southern Cemetery.

CROMPTON & ROYTON
061-642 2154
An 18-hole moorland course (6212 yards, SSS 70). Visitors are welcome at any time and a handicap certificate is not required. Green fees are £9 on weekdays (£5 with a member) and £12 at weekends (£7 with a member). Local attractions include Tandle Hill Park.
Location
Highbarn, Royton, Oldham, Lancs OL2 6RW
The course is situated off the A627 north of Oldham at Royton centre.

RAC recommended hotels
See Oldham

DAVYHULME PARK
061-748 2260
An 18-hole wooded parkland course (6237 yards, SSS 70). Visitors who are members of a bona fide golf club are welcome except on competition days. Green fees are £9.50 per round, £11.50 a day on weekdays and £14.50 per round, £14 a day at weekends and Bank Holidays. Full catering facilities are available daily except Monday. The course is close to Tatton Park and Sale Leisure Park.
Location
Gleneagles Road, Davyhulme, Urmston, Manchester M31 2SA
The course is located 8 miles south of Manchester, adjacent to Trafford General Hospital, Moorside Road.

DEANE
(0204) 61944
An 18-hole inland meadowland course (5511 yards, SSS 67). A deep gorge runs through the course which makes it rather tricky. Visitors are welcome although the club prefers you to have a handicap certificate. It is advisable to book beforehand. Green fees are £10 a day on weekdays and £15 at weekends. Full meals are available by arrangement except on Monday when only bar snacks are served. The course is close to Bolton, and the beautiful countryside of the West Pennines and Lake District. Blackpool and Southport are 30 miles away.
Location
off Junction Road, Deane, Bolton
You will find the club 4 miles west of Bolton. Leave the M61 at junction 5 and the club is 2 miles from there.

RAC recommended hotels
See Bolton

DENTON
061-336 3218
An easy 18-hole flat parkland course with a stream running through (6290 yards, SSS 70). Visitors are welcome on weekdays and at weekends subject to members competitions. A handicap certificate is necessary. Green fees are £10 on weekdays and £12 at weekends. Lunch is served daily except Monday. The course is within easy access of the Peak District and surrounding countryside.
Location
Manchester Road, Denton, Manchester M34 2NU
Take the A57 east from Manchester and the club is 5 miles from the city centre.

DIDSBURY
061-998 9278
An 18-hole parkland course (6273 yards, SSS 70). There are two practice grounds. Visitors who have a handicap certificate are welcome on weekday but you must arrange it beforehand if you wish to play at the weekend. Tuesday is Ladies Day. Green fees are £10 (£5 with a member) on weekdays and £12 (£6 with a member) at weekends. There is a restaurant and snacks are also normally available.
Location
Ford Lane, Northendon, Manchester M22 4NQ
The club is located off the M63 at junction 9, near Northenden Church. There is a club sign on the wall.

RAC recommended hotels
Post House ★★★ (061) 998 7090 A modern hotel with well-equipped bedrooms and easy access to the motorway.
Britannia Ringway ★★★ 061-434 3411 A bustling hotel with two bedroom wings leading off central public areas.

DISLEY
(0663) 63266
An 18-hole moorland/meadowland course with lots of trees (6015 yards, SSS 69). A handicap certificate or proof of membership of a recognized club is necessary, but visitors are welcome to play during the week except on Bank Holidays. Full catering facilities are available except Monday. Local attractions include Lyme Park (NT).
Location
Stanley Hall Lane, Jackson's Edge, Disley, Stockport, Cheshire SK12 2JX
Take A6 for 6 miles south of Stockport.

RAC recommended hotel
Moorside ★★★ (0663) 64151 A spacious, elegant hotel on open moorland commanding superb views.

DUNHAM FOREST
061-928 2605
An 18-hole parkland course (6800 yards, SSS 72). Visitors are welcome but the club prefers you to have a handicap certificate. Green fees on application. Full catering facilities are available daily. Local attractions include Dunham Massey Park and Hall, and Tatton Hall and Gardens.
Location
Oldfield Lane, Altrincham, Cheshire WA14 4TY
Leave the M56 at junction 7 and proceed in the direction of Manchester for 2 miles north. The golf course is on the left of the main road.

RAC recommended hotels
See Altrincham

DUNSCAR
(0204) 51090
An 18-hole parkland/moorland course (5957 yards, SSS 70). Visitors are welcome on weekdays and at weekends by special invitation. Lunch and dinner is available daily except Monday. Places worth visiting locally include Last Drop Village, Market Hall and the Octagon Theatre.
Location
Longworth Lane, Bromley Cross, Bolton BL7 9QY
The course is situated 3 miles north of Bolton off the A666 Blackburn road. The golf course is signposted to the left at Dunscar Bridge.

RAC recommended hotels
See Bolton

ELLESMERE
061-790 2122
A wooded 18-hole undulating parkland course (5957 yards, SSS 69). Visitors with a handicap certificate who are members of a recognised club are welcome by arrangement with the Pro, except during club competitions. Green fees are £9 (£4 with a member) on weekdays and £8.50 at weekends and Bank Holidays. Full catering facilities are available at all times by arrangement with the Steward's wife.
Location
Old Clough Lane, Worsley, Manchester M28 5HZ
The course is situated 5 miles west of Manchester on the A580, adjacent to junction 14 of the M62.

FAIRFIELD GOLF AND SAILING CLUB
061-370 2292
An 18-hole meadowland course (5654 yards, SSS 68) between two reservoirs where there is sailing. Six holes are affected by water. Visitors of all playing abilities are normally welcome except Wednesday afternoons, and there maybe restrictions at times on Thursday and on weekend mornings, and when there are club competitions being played. Full catering facilities are available by arrangement.
Location
Booth Road, Audenshaw, Manchester M34 5GA
The course is situated off the A635/Manchester road 4 miles from the city centre.

FLIXTON
061-748 2116
A 9-hole parkland course (6441 yards, SSS 71). Visitors are welcome during the week but you must be the guest of a member to play at weekends. Green fees are £8. There is a bar and snacks and meals are served daily. Dunham Park and Salford Quays are close by, and the course is within easy access of the centre of Manchester.
Location
Church Road, Flixton, Manchester
6 miles S of Manchester. Leave the M63 at junction 4 (Lostock).

GATHURST
(02575) 2861
A challenging 9-hole meadowland course with easy walking (6308 yards, SSS 70). Visitors who are bona fide members of a recognised club are welcome on Monday, Tuesday, Thursday and Friday. Green fees are £10 (£3 with a member). Lunch is served daily except on Monday and Tuesday. The course is close to Rufford Hall and Grounds, and Mere Wild Fowl Trust.
Location
Miles Lane, Shevington, Wigan WN6 8EW
The course is situated 1 mile south of junction 27 on the M6.

RAC recommended hotels
Almond Brook ★★★ (0257) 425588 Modern purpose-built family-owned and managed hotel.
Beeches ★★ (0257) 426432 Victorian mansion set in own grounds, 1½ miles from M6, junction 27.

GATLEY
061-437 2091
A 9-hole parkland course (5934 yards, SSS 68). Visitors of all handicap levels are welcome on weekdays except Tuesday. Green fees on application. Full catering facilities are available but societies should book in advance. Local attractions include Styal Mill.
Location
Waterfall Farm, Styal Road, Heald Green, Gatley, Cheshire SK8 3TW
The course is off Yew Tree Grove, and Styal Road 2 miles from Cheadle, 1 mile from Manchester Airport.

RAC recommended hotels
Excelsior ★★★★ 061-437 5811 A large modern hotel with spacious bedrooms. Facilities include indoor swimming pool, sauna, solarium and gymnasium.
Hilton International ★★★★ 061-436 4404 A large modern hotel, 5 minutes walk from the airport. Facilities include indoor swimming pool, sauna and gymnasium.
Post House ★★★ 061-998 7090 A modern purpose built hotel with well equipped bedrooms and easy access to the motorway.
Belfry ★★★★ 061-437 0511 A family run luxury modern hotel with small beamed buildings attached.
Britannia Ringway ★★★ 061-434 3411 A bustling hotel with two bedroom wings leading off the central public areas.

GREAT LEVER & FARNWORTH
(0204) 62582
An 18-hole meadowland course (5958 yards, SSS 69). Visitors of all playing abilities are welcome on

weekdays. Green fees are £4.50 (£3.50 with a member) on weekdays and £6.50(£5.50 with a member) at weekends and Bank Holidays. Lunch is served daily except Monday. Hall's Wood with its picnic area is nearby.
Location
Lever Edge Lane, Bolton BL3 3EN
You will find the club $1^1/_2$ miles from Bolton town centre.

RAC recommended hotels see Bolton

HAIGH HALL
(0942) 831107
A municipal 18-hole parkland course (6400 yards, SSS 71). Visitors of all playing abilities including beginners are welcome at any time, but it is best to telephone first for a tee-off time. Green fees are £2.75 on weekdays and £4.50 at weekends. There is a cafe run by Wigan Metro. Local attractions include Wigan Pier, Park Hall and Camelot.
Location
Haigh Country Park, Haigh, Wigan WN2 1PE
Leave the M6 at junction 27 and follow the B5106 through Standish, following the signs for the country park.

RAC recommended hotels
Brocket Arms ★★★ (0942) 46283 A well-appointed modern purpose built red-brick hotel in pleasant suburban surroundings.
Kilhey Court ★★★ (0257) 423083 Victorian mansion of character set in 10 acres of grounds with many rhododendrons.
Bel Air ★★ (0942) 41410 Privately-owned and run former private house.
Bellingham ★★ (0942) 43893 On A49, in a residential area, a former private house.
Grand ★★ (0942) 43471 Black and white commercial hotel near town centre. Privately-owned.

HALE
061-980 4225
A beautiful 9-hole undulating parkland course with the River Bolin running through (5780 yards, SSS 68). Visitors of all playing abilities are welcome during the week except on Thursday, and at weekends and Bank Holidays if you are the guest of a member. Lunch is served daily by arrangement with the Steward, except on Tuesday and Thursday. Local attractions include Dunham Park.
Location
Rappax Road, Hale, Altrincham, Cheshire
The course is situated 2 miles south east of Altrincham.

RAC recommended hotel
Ashley ★★★ (061) 928 3794 A modern hotel situated in Cheshire village of Hale, 9 miles south of Manchester city centre.

HEATON MOOR
061-432 2134
An 18-hole parkland course with easy walking (5876 yards, SSS 68). Visitors of all playing abilities are welcome daily except on Tuesday and Wednesday. Green fees are £7.50 (£3.50 with a member), £2.50 after 5pm on weekdays, and £9 (£4 with a member) at weekends. Meals are served daily except Monday.
Location
Heaton Mersey, Stockport, Cheshire SK4 3NX
You will find the club 2 miles north west of Stockport between A6 and A5145.

HEATON PARK
061-798 0295
An 18-hole undulating parkland course (5849 yards, SSS 68). Visitors of all playing abilities are welcome but you must book in advance. Green fees are £4 per round on weekdays and £6 at weekends. Catering facilities are available by arrangement. Local attractions include Heaton Park and Manor House with its zoo and bowling green.
Location
Prestwich, Manchester
Leave the M62 at junction 18 onto M66 southbound and turn right at the roundabout junction with the A576. The park entrance is 200 yards on the right.

HINDLEY HALL
(0942) 55131
An 18-hole moorland course with easy walking (5875 yards, SSS 68). Visitors are welcome if you are a member of a recognised club but it is advisable to check with the Pro in advance. Green fees on application. Full catering facilities are available daily except Monday. Local attractions include Hay Hall.
Location
Hall Lane, Hindley, Wigan, Lancs WN2 2SQ
Leave the M61 at junction 6 and turn onto the A6. Turn into Dicconson Lane and then, after 1 mile, turn left at the church into Hall Lane. The club is just after the lake.

RAC recommended hotels see Wigan.

HORWICH
(0204) 696980
A 9-hole parkland course with natural hazards and some hard walking (5404 yards, SSS 67). Visitors of all playing abilities are welcome but you must be accompanied by a member. Green fees on application. Bar snacks are available daily. The course is near some good walking country, including and Rivington Pike.
Location
Victoria Road, Horwich, Bolton, Greater Manchester
The course is situated $1^1/_2$ miles from the M61 junction 6.

HOULDSWORTH
061-224 5055
A flat 18-hole parkland course with tree-lined fairways and water hazards (6078 yards, SSS 69). Visitors of all playing abilities are welcome on weekdays. Ladies Day is on Tuesday between 1.30pm and 3.30pm. Green fees are £6 on weekdays and £8 at weekends, or half price if you are with a member. There is a restaurant and bar snacks are also available. Prior notice for large parties is required.
Location
Wingate House, Higher Levenshulme, Manchester M19 3JW
Leave the M63 at junction 12 and turn left onto the A6 main Stockport-Manchester road. Turn right at the traffic lights at Barlow Road.

LOBDEN
(0706) 343228
A 9-hole course with hard walking and one which can be prone to winds (5750 yards, SSS 68). Visitors of all playing abilities are welcome on weekdays and Sundays. Green fees on application. Meals can be provided by arrangement with the Steward.
Location
Lobden Moor, Whitworth, Rochdale
Take the A671 4 miles north of Rochdale to Whitworth and the club is half a mile from the centre of the village.

LOWES PARK
061-764 1231
An exposed 9-hole moorland course with easy walking (6035 yards, SSS 69). Visitors who are members of a bona fide golf club are welcome on weekdays, except on Wednesday which is Ladies Day, and by invitation on Sunday. Green fees are £6 on weekdays and £7 at weekends. Full catering facilities are available daily except Monday.
Location
Hill Top, Bury, Lancashire
Take the A56 north from Bury and turn right into Lowes Road at Bury General Hospital into Lowes Road. Follow the road until the course is signposted.

RAC recommended hotels see Bury.

MANCHESTER
061-643 3202
An 18-hole undulating moorland course (6540 yards, SSS 72). There is a large practice ground. Visitors are welcome on weekdays but the club prefers you to have a handicap certificate. Green fees are £13 a day. There is a first-class restaurant which is open daily. The course is convenient for Manchester city centre.
Location
Hopwood Cottage, Rochdale Road, Middleton, Manchester M24 2QP
The course is situated 7 miles north of the city on the A665, 2 miles from exits 19 and 20 of the M62.

MARPLE
061-427 2311
An 18-hole parkland/meadowland course (5700 yards, SSS 67). Visitors who are members of a recognised club are welcome, but not on competition days. Green fees are £9 on weekdays and £11 at weekends. There is a reduction if you are with a member. Full catering facilities are available daily. Local attractions include Lyme Park(NT) and the lovely Peak District countryside.
Location
Hawk Green, Marple, Stockport, Cheshire SK6 7EL
Turn off the A6 at High Lane and then turn left at Hawk Green.

RAC recommended hotel
West Tower ★★ (061) 427 7133 A family-owned hotel converted and extended, in a quiet semi-rural area.

MELLOR & TOWNSCLIFFE
061-427 2208
An 18-hole undulating parkland/moorland course with hard walking (5925 yards, SSS 69). There are some fine views. Visitors of all playing abilities are welcome except Saturday when you must be accompanied by a member. Green fees are £10 per round, £12 a day (£3 with a member) on weekdays and £15 a day (£4 with a member) at weekends and Bank Holidays. Full catering facilities are available daily except on Tuesday when you must book in advance. The club is on the fringe of the Peak District.
Location
Tarden, Gibb Lane, Mellor, Stockport, Cheshire SK6 5NA
Leave the A626 7 miles south east of Stockport, opposite the Devonshire Arms on Longhurst Lane, Mellor.

RAC recommended hotel
West Tower ★★ 061-427 7133 A family-owned hotel converted and extended, in a quiet semi-rural area.

NEW NORTH MANCHESTER
061-643 9033
An 18-hole moorland/parkland course (6527 yards, SSS 72) with some panoramic views of Manchester and Oldham. Four holes are affected by water . Provided you have a handicap certificate, visitors are welcome on weekdays. Green fees on application. There is a restaurant which is open daily except Tuesday, and bar snacks are normally available. The course is conveniently situated for Manchester city centre, and Heaton Hall(NT) is nearby.
Location
Rhodes House, Manchester Old Road, Middleton, Manchester M24 4PE
Leave the M62 at exit 18 on the M" southbound. At the roundabout junction with A576, turn left and the course is 300 yards towards Middleton.

RAC recommended hotel
Bower ★★★ 061-682 7254 A former private house with picturesque gardens, near some local beauty spots.

NORTHENDEN
061-998 4738
An 18-hole parkland course (6469 yards, SSS 71). There is also a practice net. Provided you have a handicap certificate, visitors are welcome by arrangement except on Saturday. Green fees are £13.50 on weekdays and £17 at weekends. Snacks are available daily, and lunches and evening meals by arrangement.
Location
Palatine Road, Northenden, Manchester M22 4FR
Leave the M63 at exit 9. The course is 1 mile through Northenden.

RAC recommended hotel
Britannia Ringway ★★★ 061-434 3411 A bustling hotel with two bedroom wings leading off the central public areas.
Post House ★★★ 061-998 7090 Modern purpose-built hotel with well-equipped bedrooms. Easy access to motorways.

OLDHAM
061-624 4986
An 18-hole moorland/parkland course with no bunkers and some hard walking (5045 yards, SSS 65). Visitors of all playing abilities are welcome but you should telephone ahead in case there is a competition being played. Green fees are £6 on weekdays and £7 at weekends and Bank Holidays. Full catering facilities are available daily.
Location
Lees New Road, Oldham OL4 5EN
The course is situated off the B6194 between Oldham and Ashton-under-Lyne or from the A669, turn south at Lees.

RAC recommended hotels
Bower ★★★ 061-682 7254 Former private house with picturesque gardens, near local beauty spots.
Smokies Park ★★★ 061-624 3405 Recently built, almost 'E' shaped, two-storey hotel, elegantly decorated in Art Nouveau style. Sauna, solarium, gymnasium.
High Point ★★ 061-624 4130 Large Victorian mansion within easy reach of the town centre.

OLD LINKS
(0204) 43089
A championship 18-hole moorland course with practice facilities (6406 yards, SSS 72). Visitors of all handicap levels are welcome except on competition days. Green fees are £10 (£5 with a member) on weekdays and £15 (£7.50 with a member) at weekends and Bank Holidays. There is a bar and restaurant which is open daily except Monday.
Location
Chorley Old Road, Bolton BL1 5SU
You will find the club on the B6226 just north of the A58 ring road.

RAC recommended hotels see Bolton.

PIKE FOLD
061-740 1136
A wooded 9-hole undulating meadowland course (5789 yards, SSS 68). Visitors of all playing abilities are welcome on weekdays at any time. Green fees are £5 per round or day on weekdays (£3.50 with a member) and £7.50 per round at weekends (£5 with a member). Full catering and bar facilities are available daily. Local attractions include Heaton Park with its zoo, pitch and putt course and bowling green.
Location
Cooper Lane, Victoria Avenue, Blackley, Manchester M9 2QQ
The course is situated 4 miles north of the city centre off Rochdale Road.

PRESTWICH
061-773 4578
An 18-hole parkland course (4712 yards, SSS 63). Provided you have a handicap certificate, visitors are welcome at all times. Green fees on application. Snacks and meals are available daily except on Monday, by arrangement with the Steward. The course is close to Manchester city centre.
Location
Hilton Lane, Prestwich, Manchester M25 8SB
The course is situated on the A6044 1 mile from the junction with the A56.

REDDISH VALE
061-480 2359
A varied 18-hole undulating course (6086 yards, SSS 69) situated in a valley with the River Tame running across 5 holes. A handicap certificate is preferred, but visitors are welcome on weekdays, except between 12.30pm and 1.30pm, and with a member at weekends. Green fees on application. There is a bar and catering facilities are available during normal opening hours. Local attractions include Lyme Park(NT).
Location
Southcliffe Road, Reddish, Stockport, Cheshire SK5 7EE
The club is 1 mile north of Stockport, off Reddish Road.

RINGWAY
061-980 2630
An interesting 18-hole parkland course with natural hazards and some fine views (6494 yards, SSS 71). Visitors are welcome but the club prefers you to have a handicap certificate. Green fees are £16 (£6 with a member) on weekdays and £20 (£6 with a member) at weekends. Full catering facilities are available by arrangement with the Caterer. Local attractions include Style Mill, Tatton Hall(NT) and Dunham Hall(NT).
Location
Hale Mount, Hale Barns, Altrincham, Cheshire WA15 8SW
Leave the M56 at junction 6 and follow the signs for Hale. The course is just through Hale Barns village, 8 miles south of Manchester.

RAC recommended hotel
Ashley ★★★ 061-928 3794 Modern hotel situated in Cheshire village of Hale, 9 miles south of Manchester city centre.

ROMILEY
061-430 2392
A wooded 18-hole undulating parkland course with a practice area (6335 yards, SSS 70). Visitors of all playing abilities are welcome at any time, except on Thursday which is Ladies Day. Green fees are £11 on weekdays and £16 at weekends and Bank Holidays. Full catering facilities are available by arrangement except on Monday. Tatton Park and Dunham Park, both National Trust properties, are close by.
Location
Goosehouse Green, Romiley, Stockport SK6 4LJ
The course is situated on the B6101 and is signposted from Romiley village.

SADDLEWORTH
(0457) 7872059
An 18-hole moorland course with splendid views (5976 yards, SSS 69). Provided you have a handicap certificate, visitors are welcome at any time. Green fees are £12 on weekdays (£4 with a member) and £15 at weekends (£5 with a member). Full catering facilities are available daily. Local attractions include Upper Mill with its museum and arts and crafts shops.
Location
Mountain Ash, Ladcastle Road, Uppermill, Oldham
The course is situated 5 miles from Oldham, and is signposted off the A670 Ashton-Huddersfield road, at the bend where the road crosses the railway bridge.

SALE
061-973 3404
An 18-hole parkland course (6346 yards, SSS 70). Visitors who are members of a bona fide golf club are welcome any time but you should telephone first to confirm it. Green fees are £12 on weekdays and £18 at weekends and Bank Holidays. There is a bar where snacks are available and main meals are served daily except Monday. Tatton Park(NT), Dunham Park(NT) and Manchester are all within easy access.
Location
Sale Lodge, Golf Road, Sale, Cheshire M33 2LU
The course is situated on the edge of Sale, 1 mile from Sale station.

RAC recommended hotel
Amblehurst ★★★ 061-973 8800 Brick-built gabled building on A56. Modern bedroom extension round an attractive sunken garden.

STAMFORD
(04575) 2126
An 18-hole undulating moorland course (5619 yards, SSS 67). Visitors of all playing abilities are welcome on weekdays. Ladies Day is Tuesday afternoon, Green fees are £8 (£4 with a member) on weekdays and £12.50 (£6 with a member) at weekends. Lunches and evening meals are served daily except Monday. Local attractions include Tame Valley Nature Reserve.
Location
Oakfield House, Huddersfield Road, Heyheads, Stalybridge, Cheshire SK15 3ET
The course is situated on the B6175, off the A6018 3 miles from Ashton-under-Lyne.

RAC recommended hotel
York House ★★★ 061-330 5899 This hotel is a fine Victorian terraced house in a tree-lined street within reach of the town centre.

STAND
061-766 2388
A challenging 18-hole undulating parkland course with a difficult finish (6425 yards, SSS 71). Provided you have a handicap certificate, visitors are welcome on weekdays. Green fees are £10 (£4 with a member) on weekdays and £14 (£6 with a member) at weekends and Bank Holidays. Lunch and snacks are served daily except Monday, but it is advisable to order in advance. The club also has snooker and fishing. Local attractions include Peel's Monument and birthplace, and the Pennines are within easy access.
Location
The Dales, Ashbourne Grove, Whitefield, Manchester M25 7NL
The course is situated 1 mile north of the M62 exit 17, and 1 mile from the A56/A665.

STOCKPORT
061-427 2001
An attractive 18-hole parkland course with excellent greens (6319 yards, SSS 71). If you are a member of a recognised club, visitors of all playing abilities are welcome. Green fees are £12 a day on weekdays and £14 at weekends. There is an excellent restaurant, which is closed Monday. Lyme Park and grounds(NT) is within easy access.
Location
Offerton Road, Offerton, Stockport SK2 5HL
Take A262 from Stockport towards Marple, then proceed down the A627 towards Hazel Grove.

RAC recommended hotels
Alma Lodge ★★★ 061-483 4431 On the A6, a red-brick building with purpose-built extension.
Rudyard Toby ★★ 061-432 2753 Off the A6, pleasant hotel in converted residences with attractive pillared and stepped entrances.

SWINTON PARK
061-794 1785
An 18-hole parkland course which is one of the area's longest courses (6675 yards, SSS 72). Visitors who are members of a bona fide golf club are welcome on weekdays. Green fees are £12 (£6 with a member). There is a bar where snacks are served and meals are usually available throughout the day, except on Monday.
Location
East Lancashire Road, Swinton, Manchester M27 1LX
The course is situated on the A580 Manchester-Liverpool Road, 5 miles from Manchester city centre.

TURTON
(0204) 852235
A 9-hole moorland course with panoramic views (5805 yards, SSS 68). Players of all abilities are welcome except on Wednesday between 12.30pm and 4pm, Saturday, and competition days. The course is not really suitable for beginners. Green fees are £6 a day on weekdays and £8 at weekends (£3 with a member). There is a resident Steward and Stewardess and meals are normally served daily except Monday. Local attractions include Turton Towers and Hall'ith Wood Country Park.
Location
Wood End Farm, Chapeltown Road, Bromley
The course is situated 3 miles north of Bolton on the A666/A676, adjacent to the Last Drop Hotel.

RAC recommended hotel
Last Drop ★★★ (0204) 591131 A unique, stone-built house situated in a beautifully restored village. Facilities include an indoor swimming pool, squash courts, sauna, solarium, gymnasium and billards.

WALMERSLEY
061-764 0018
A 9-hole moorland course with wide fairways and good greens (3057 yards, SSS 70). Visitors of all playing abilities are welcome on Wednesday, Thursday and Friday, and on Sunday if you are with a member. Green fees are £6 (£4 with a member). Lunches and evening meals are served daily except Monday. The East Lancashire Railway Museum is close by.
Location
Garretts Close, Walmersley, Bury
The course is situated on the A56 about 2½ miles north of Bury.

RAC recommended hotel
Old Mill ★★★ (070 682) 2991 A unique black and white timbered hotel incorporating a mill wheel. Facilities include an indoor swimming pool, sauna, solarium and a gymnasium.

WERNETH (OLDHAM)
061-624 1190
An 18-hole semi-moorland course with a stream crossing the fairways (5363 yards, SSS 66). Visitors of all playing abilities are welcome on weekdays. Green fees are £6. Lunch is served daily except Monday.
Location
Green Lane, Garden Suburb, Oldham, Lancashire OL8 3AZ
The course is situated 5 miles from Manchester. Take the A62 to Hollinwood and then the A6104.

RAC recommended hotels see Oldham

WERNETH LOW
061-368 2503
An exposed 9-hole undulating course (5734 yards, SSS 68) with hard walking excellent greens. There are some lovely views. Visitors of all playing abilities are welcome daily except on Sunday. Green fees are £9 (£3.75 with a member) on weekdays and £14 (£5 with a member) on Saturday. Light refreshments are normally available except on Wednesday. The course is situated on the outskirts of Werneth Low Country Park.
Location
Werneth Low Road, Hyde, Cheshire SK14 3AF
The course is situated 2 miles from Hyde town centre via Gee Cross and Joel Lane.

RAC recommended hotel
Needhams Farm (Acclaimed) 061-368 4610.

WESTHOUGHTON
(0942) 811085
A 9-hole downland/meadowland course (5834 yards, SSS 68). Visitors of all playing abilities are welcome on weekdays and with a member at weekends. Green fees on application. Snacks and meals are available daily except Monday. Local attractions include Hall'ith Wood and Rivington Country Park.
Location
Long Island, Westhoughton, Bolton, Lancashire
The course is situated 4 miles south west of Bolton on the A58.

RAC recommended hotels see Bolton.

WHITEFIELD
061-766 2904
A fine, sporty 18-hole parkland course (2580 yards, SSS 68). Provided you have a handicap certificate, visitors are welcome at any time. Green fees on application. There is a restaurant which is open daily.
Location
81/83 Higher Lane, Whitefield, Manchester M25 7EZ
Leave the M62 at exit 17 then take the road to Radcliffe for one mile.

WHITTAKER
(0706) 78310
A 9-hole undulating moorland course (5576 yards, SSS 67). Visitors who are members of a bona fide golf club are welcome except on Sunday and Tuesday afternoons. Green fees are £6 (£4 with a member) on weekdays and £5 at weekends. Local attractions include Hollingworth Lake.
Location
Whittaker Lane, Littleborough, Lancashire OL15 OLH
The course is situated 1 mile from the town centre along Blackstone Edge Old Road.

WILLIAM WROE
061-748 8680
An 18-hole municipal parkland course with easy walking (4395 yards, SSS 61). Visitors are welcome but booking is advisable. Green fees are £3 on weekdays and £4.50 at weekends.
Location
Penny Bridge Lane, Flixton, Manchester M31
Leave the M63 at exit 4 and join the B5124 to Davyhulme
Circle and then, after 1 mile on the B5158, left the at Bird-in-Hand Hotel, Flixton.

WITHINGTON
061-445 9544
An 18-hole parkland course (6411 yards, SSS 71). Visitors are welcome but the club prefers you to have a current handicap certificate. Green fees on application. Snacks are available at all times except on Monday, and lunch and evening meals can be ordered. The club has a snooker room. Manchester is only 3 miles away.
Location
243 Palatine Road, West Didsbury, Manchester M20 8UD
The course is situated 3 miles from Manchester city centre, adjacent to the M56 and M63.

WORSLEY
061-789 4202
A wooded 18-hole parkland course (6217 yards, SSS 70). Visitors who are members of a golf club and have an official handicap are welcome. Green fees are £11 a day. Snacks, lunches and evening meals are available from midday daily. The club is situated near Salford Quays development area.
Location
Stableford Avenue, Monton, Eccles, Manchester M30 8AP
Leave the M62 at junction 13 and proceed for one mile east. The club is signposted.

HAMPSHIRE

ALRESFORD
(0962) 733746
A testing 11 hole undulating wooded parkland course (6038 yards, SSS 69). Visitors are welcome on weekdays. Green fees are £10.30 per round, £15 a day on weekdays and £20 per round at weekends and Bank Holidays. Full catering facilities are available daily except Monday. Local attractions include Northington Grange, and some beautiful walking country.
Location
Cheriton Road, Alresford, Hants SO24 0PN
The club is situated 1 mile south of the A31 Winchester to Alton road, 2 miles north of the A272 Winchester-Petersfield road, and 1 mile south of Alresford.

ALTON
(0420) 82042
A 9 hole undulating wooded meadowland course (5744 yards, SSS 68). Visitors of all playing abilities are welcome except on competition days, when the course is closed until 5.30pm. Green fees are £8 on weekdays and £12 at weekends and Bank Holidays. Catering facilities can be provided by arrangement. Local places of interest include Jane Austen's house.
Location
Old Odiham Road, Alton, Hants GU34 4BU
Leave Alton by the B3349 towards Odiham, and after 2 miles turn right at the Gold Pot public house. Take the next right immediately and the club is half a mile on the right.

RAC recommended hotels
Swan ★★★ (0420) 83777 Attractive coaching inn dating from 16th century; in High Street.
Alton House ★★ (0420) 80033 A Regency hotel in 2½ acres of gardens, close to the town centre. facilities include swimming pool, tennis and billiards.
Grange ★★ (0420) 865465 Two-storey country house style building located at edge of town. Putting.

AMPFIELD PAR 3
(0794) 68480
A picturesque 18 hole parkland course with easy walking (2478 years, SSS 53). Visitors of all playing abilities are welcome, but it is advisable to telephone first to avoid the busy times. A handicap certificate is required for weekend play. Green fees are £5 per round and £8 a day on weekdays and £10 per round at weekends. Light meals and snacks are available except on Tuesday. Local attractions include Romsey Abbey.
Location
Winchester Road, Ampfield, Romsey, Hants SO5 9BQ
The club is situated on the A31, 2½ miles west of Hursley village, next door to the White Horse public house.

RAC recommended hotel
Potters Heron ★★★ (0703) 266611 Thatched, two-storey, cosy old inn with modern extensions, elegantly furnished and set in countryside. Sauna, gymnasium.

ARMY
(0252) 540638
A pretty 18 hole heathland course (6579 yards, SSS 71). Visitors are welcome on Monday,

Thursday and Friday, and also at the weekend if you are the guest of a member. A handicap certificate is required. Green fees on application. A range of catering is available between 8.30am and 6.00pm.
Location
Laffans Road, Aldershot, Hants GU11 2HF
Access to the club is reach by the Eelmoor Bridge off the A323 Aldershot Fleet Road.

RAC recommended hotels
Queen's ★★★ An imposing hotel with an Edwardian facade on the A325. Facilities include indoor swimming pool, sauna, solarium and gymnasium.
Falcon ★★ (0252) 545378 Modernised hotel on A325 south of town opposite the aerospace centre, 3 miles from M3 junction 4.

BARTON-ON-SEA
(0425) 615308
An exposed 18 hole seaside course (5565 yards, SSS 67) situated on the cliff edge with some excellent views over the Isle of Wight and Christchurch Bay . Provided you have a handicap certificate, visitors are welcome on weekdays after 8.30am and at weekends and Bank Holidays after 11.15am. It is advisable to telephone the club first to ascertain the programme for the day. Green fees are £15 per round on weekdays and £18 at weekends and Bank Holidays. Snacks and teas are available daily and evening meals are available for societies by arrangement. The course is well situated for some lovely coastal walks.
Location
Marine Drive, Barton-on-Sea, New Milton, Hants BH25 7DY
The course is off the A337 at the extreme east end of Marine Drive at Barton, about 1 mile from New Milton.

RAC recommended hotels
Chewton Glen C/H ★★★★ (0425) 72310 Elegant country house-a luxury hotel surrounded by woodland. Swimming pool, golf, putting, tennis, billiards.
Cliff House ★★ (0425) 619333 Former country residence standing in 16 acres of lawns and woodlands. Swimming pool, tennis, putting.

BASINGSTOKE
(0256) 465990
A well-kept 18 hole parkland course (6284 yards, SSS 70) built on an old deer park with some lovely beech trees. Visitors who have a handicap certificate are welcome on weekdays and at weekends, as the guest of a member. Green fees are £14 per round, £20 a day on weekdays. Lunches and teas are served daily except Monday. Local attractions include Winchester Cathedral.
Location
Kempshott Park, Basingstoke, Hants RG23 7LL
The club is situated on the A30, 3 miles west of the town on the road to Winchester. If you are travelling from Winchester leave the M3 at exit 7.

RAC recommended hotels
Crest ★★★ (0256) 468181 Beside A30, modern two-storey hotel in own gardens. On outskirts of town. Billiards.
Hilton National ★★★ (0256) 20212 Large modern red brick hotel with open plan public areas. I mile from centre. Indoor swimming pool, sauna, gymnasium.
Hilton Lodge ★★★ (0256) 460460 Long modern one and two-storey hotel prominently placed on outer edge of town near M3. Indoor swimming pool, sauna, gymnasium, snooker.
Red Lion ★★ (0256) 28525 Town centre traditional coaching inn with beams. Large, modern extensions.

BASINGSTOKE HOSPITALS
(0256) 20347
A 9 hole meadowland course (5455 yards, SSS 67). Visitors are welcome on weekdays before 4.30pm and at weekends by arrangement. Green fees are £6.50 on weekdays and £9 at weekends. There is a bar. Local attractions include 'The Vine', a historic house with grounds.
Location
Aldermaster Road, Basingstoke RG24 9NB
The course is 1½ miles north of Basingstoke town centre.

BISHOPSWOOD
(0734) 815213
A 9 hole wooded parkland course (6474 yards, SSS 71 with water hazards There is a floodlit driving range which is open seven days a week. Visitors are welcome on Tuesday, Thursday and Friday only. Green fees are £4.50 per 9 holes, £8 per 18 holes. There is a restaurant which is open daily except Monday and bar snacks are normally served.
Location
Bishopswood Lane, Tadley, Basingstoke, Hants RG26 6AT
You will find the club 6 miles north of Basingstoke, off the A340 west out of Tadley.

BLACKMOOR
(04203) 2775
A fine 18 hole parkland/heathland course (6232 yards, SSS 70) with tree lined-fairways. Provided you have a handicap certificate visitors are welcome on weekdays, but you must be with a member to play at weekends. Green fees are £23 a day or £15 after 2pm on weekdays. Full catering facilities are available daily.
Location
Golf Lane, Whitehill, Bordon, Hants GU35 9EH
From the A325 between Petersfield and Farnham, turn into Firgrove Road at Whitehill crossroads.

BRAMSHAW
(0703) 813433
Two 18 hole courses; the Manor, a parkland course (6233 yards, SSS 70) and the Forest, an easy walking course (5774 yards, SSS 69) with streams situated in the New Forest. Green fees are £17 a day. There is a club house and restaurant which provide full catering facilities daily. There is also the Bell Inn next door where, as a resident, you are entitled to free golf.
Location
Brook, Lyndhurst, Hants SO4 7HE
Leave the M27 at Cadnam and take the B3078 for 1 mile.

RAC recommended hotel
Bartley Lodge C/H ★★★ (0703) 812248 Red-brick, 18th century hunting lodge in 11 acres of mature grounds.

BROCKENHURST MANOR
(0590) 23332
A splendid 18 hole parkland course (6212 yards, SSS 70). Visitors who have a handicap certificate of 24 or better are welcome, but you are advised to contact the Secretary beforehand. There is restricted play at the weekend. Green fees are £10 a day and £25 at weekends and Bank Holidays. Full catering facilities are available daily except Monday and Tuesday, when only lunches and teas are served. The club is situated on the edge of the New Forest and it has been known to see a rare white buck frequent the surrrounding woods.
Location
Sway Road, Brockenhurst, Hants SO42 7SG
Leaving the M27, take the A337 to Brockenhurst and then the B3055 for New Milton. The course is 1 mile outside Brockenhurst village on Sway Road, 5 miles from Lymington.

RAC recommended hotels
Balmer Lawn ★★★★ (0590) 23116 A splendid country house set in the heart of the New Forest but convenient for road and rail. Facilities include indoor/outdoor swimming pool, tennis, squash, sauna and gymnasium.
Carey's Manor ★★★ (0590) 23551 An elegant manor house in the heart of the forest. Facilities include indoor swimming pool, putting, sauna, solarium and gymnasium.
Forest Park ★★★ (0590) 22844 Compact half-timbered hotel with immediate access to New Forest. Swimming pool, tennis, riding, sauna, solarium.
Rhinefield House C/H ★★★ (0590) 22922 Grand Victorian mansion set in lovely gardens, restored to their former glory. Indoor and outdoor swimming pool, putting, tennis, sauna, solarium, gymnasium.
Watersplash ★★ (0590) 22344 Family-run, quietly situated Victorian house with a pleasant garden. Swimming pool.

BURLEY
(04253) 2431
A 9 hole undulating downland course (6149 yards, SSS 69). Visitors are welcome on weekdays and most Sundays, but not until after 1.30pm on Wednesday afternoons. Green fees are £10 on weekdays and weekends, and £5 if you are with a member. Snacks are served at lunchtime between Monday and Saturday.
Location
Burley, Ringwood, Hants BH24 4BB
Take the A31 from Ringwood, turn right at Picket Post and go through Burley Street and Burley. The club is on the left at the top of the hill.

RAC recommended hotels
Burley Manor ★★★ (04253) 3522 A 19th century country house surrounded by gardens and parkland. There is a swimming pool, fishing and riding.
Moorhill House ★★★ (04253) 3285 A gabled Victorian house in 3 acres of well-tended garden in the Forest.

CORHAMPTON
(0489) 877279
An 18 hole undulating downland course (6088 yards, SSS 69). Visitors are welcome on weekdays and with a member at the weekends, although a handicap certificate is required. Green fees are £12 per round or £18 a day on weekdays (£6 with a member). Lunches, teas and dinners are served daily except Tuesday.
Location
Sheeps Pond Lane, Droxford, Southampton, Hants SO3 1QZ
The club is situated off the A32 1 mile from Corhampton on the Bishops Waltham-Corhampton road (B3135).

RAC recommended hotel
Little Uplands (Highly Acclaimed) (0489) 878507 A motel with a swimming pool, sauna and gymnasium.

DIBDEN
(0703) 845596
A municipal 18 hole parkland course (6206 yards, SSS 70) with views over Southampton Water. Visitors are welcome at all times. Green fees are £3.90 on weekdays and £5.70 at weekends. Full catering facilities are available. The course is situated close to the New Forest, and other local attractions include Hythe Village and the Applemore Recreation centre.
Location
Dibden, Southampton, Hants SO4 5TB
From the A326 Totton-Fawley road, follow the Hythe sign at Dibden roundabout. The course entrance is half a mile at the bottom of the hill on the right-hand side.

DUNWOOD MANOR
(0794) 40549
A wooded 18 hole undulating parkland course (6004 yards, SSS 69) with some good views. There is a large practise area. Visitors are welcome on weekdays by arrangement with the club. There is

also a snooker room. Green fees are £10 per round or £15 a day on weekdays and £15 per round at weekends and Bank Holidays. Bar meals are served between 12pm-2pm and 7pm-9.30pm. The course is situated close to the New Forest.
Location
Shootash Hill, Romsey, Hants SO5 0GF
Leave Romsey on the A27 towards Salisbury, and after 2 miles turn right at Shootash crossroads into Danes Road. The club is on the left.

RAC recommended hotel
White Horse ★★★ (0794) 512431 Town-centre hotel with traces of Mummers' Gallery and Tudor wall-paintings.

FLEMING PARK
(0703) 61297
A municipal 18 hole parkland course (4402 yards, SSS 62) with a stream running through. The club has a particular interest in teaching young players. Visitors are welcome but it is advisable to book first. Green fees on application. Bar snacks and meals are available daily. The Fleming Park Sports Centre is next to the golf course.
Location
Magpie Lane, Eastleigh, Hants SO5 PLH
From the A27/M27, turn off at the Eastleigh Airport turning. The course is 1 mile north.

RAC recommended hotels seeSouthampton.

GOSPORT AND STOKES BAY
(0705) 527941
A challenging 9 hole seaside course with lots of gorse (5806 yards, SSS 69). Visitors of a reasonable playing standard are welcome except on Sunday. Green fees are £6 a day on weekdays and £8 a day at weekends and Bank Holidays. There is a bar where food is served. There is a good view from the beach across to the Isle of Wight.
Location
Military Road, off Fort Road, Haslar, Gosport

RAC recommended hotel
Anglesey ★★ (0705) 582157 A Regency building in an attractive quiet terrace.

GREAT SALTERNS
(0705) 664549
A municipal 18 hole meadowland course (5970 yards, SSS 68). There is a floodlit driving range. Visitors of all playing abilities are welcome. The Southsea Golf Club plays here. Green fees are £5.40 between April and September, and £4.00 between October and March. There is a bar where snacks are available.
Location
Portsmouth Golf Centre, Eastern Road, Portsmouth PO3 6QB

RAC recommended hotels see Portsmouth.

HARTLEY WINTNEY
(025126) 4211
A 9 hole parkland course with easy walking (6096 yards, SSS 69). Visitors are welcome on weekdays and with a member at weekends and Bank Holidays. There are some restrictions on Wednesday. Green fees are £10 per round (£4.50 with a member) on weekdays, and £15 a day (£8 with a member) or £12 per round (£7 with a member) at weekends and Bank Holidays. Jeans and trainers are not permitted. Full catering facilities and snacks are available daily. Local attractions include Stratfield Saye House, the home of the Duke of Wellington, and The Vyne at Sherborne St John.
Location
London Road, Hartley Wintney, Hants RG27 8PT

RAC recommended hotel
Lismoyne C/H ★★★ (0252) 62855 A substantial Victorian country house set in attractive gardens and grounds.

HAYLING
(0705) 464446
An attractive 18 hole seaside links course (6489 yards, SSS 71) with views across to the Isle of Wight. Visitors are welcome but a private club handicap certificate is required, and a letter of introduction from the home club is appreciated. Green fees are £18 a day on weekdays and £25 at weekends and Bank Holidays. Lunches and afternoon teas are available by arrangement except on Monday. There is a lake to the rear of the club house and the beach, and fairground are close by.
Location
Ferry Road, Hayling Island, Hants PO11 0BX

RAC recommended hotels
Post House ★★★★ (0705) 465011 A modern hotel located close to the bridge linking Havant to the Island. Facilities include an indoor swimming pool, sauna, solarium and gymnasium.
Newtown House ★★ (0705) 466131 Attractive early 19th century farmhouse in own grounds, a quarter of a mile from the sea. Swimming pool, tennis, sauna, billiards.

HOCKLEY
(0962) 713165
A high 18 hole downland course with some fine views (6279 yards, SSS 70). Visitors are welcome on weekdays and at weekends if you are the guest of a member, or by arrangement with the Secretary. Green fees on application. Lunch is served daily. The course is handy for Winchester city centre.
Location
Twyford, Winchester, Hants SO21 1PL

RAC recommended hotels
Wessex ★★★★ (0962) 61611 A modern hotel facing the Cathedral.
Lainston House C/H ★★★ (0962) 63588 Fine 17th century red-brick mansion with attractive furnishings. Tennis, fishing.
Saxon Court ★★★ (0962) 68102 Long, low, red-brick modern hotel in a quiet road about half a mile from city centre. Indoor swimming pool, sauna, solarium, gymnasium.

LECKFORD AND LONGSTOCK
(0264) 810710
A challenging 9 hole downland course with good views (3251 yards, SSS 71). Visitors are welcome by invitation only. Green fees on application.
Location
Leckford, Stockbridge, Hants SO20 65G

RAC recommended hotel
Grosvenor ★★★ (0264) 810606 An attractive inn, popular with fishermen. Facilities include sauna and billiards.

LEE-ON-THE-SOLENT
(0705) 551170
An 18 hole meadowland course (6022 yards, SSS 69) with some testing holes. Visitors are welcome on weekdays. Green fees are £14 per round or day on weekdays and £16 per round or day at weekends. If you are with a member it is £7. Lunch and snacks are served daily except Mondays. Local attractions include Portsmouth Dockyard with the 'Mary Rose' and the 'Victory'. There is a ferry from Gosport.
Location
Brune Lane, Lee-on-the-Solent, Hants PO13 9PB

RAC recommended hotel
Belle Vue ★★★ (0705) 550258 Two-storey, white-painted hotel on seafront with lovely views over the Solent.

LIPHOOK
(0428) 723271
An 18 hole heathland course (6250 yards, SSS 70) with easy walking and some good views. Provided you have a handicap certificate or proof of membership from a recognised golf club, visitors are welcome on weekdays and after 1pm on Sunday. Golf clothing must be worn. Green fees are £15 per round, £25 a day on weekdays and £25 per round, £30 a day at weekends. Lunches are normally available but you should order in advance, and bar snacks are served every day. Local attractions include Forest Mere Health Farm, Wagonners Well (NT) and Frensham Ponds (NT).
Location
Wheatsheaf Enclosure, Liphook, Hants GU30 7EH

RAC recommended hotels
Milland Place C/H ★★★ (042 876) 633 Gabled Edwardian house, elegantly furnished and with lovely public rooms.

MEON VALLEY GOLF AND COUNTRY CLUB
(0329) 833455
An attractive 18 hole parkland course with lots of tree hazards (6519 yards, SSS 71). Visitors of all playing abilities are welcome. Green fees are £16 on weekdays and £20 at weekends and Bank Holidays. Meals and snacks are available daily. The club is part of the Hotel and Country Club complex, and other facilities include squash, tennis, snooker, gymnasium, indoor swimming pool, solarium, sauna, steam room and spa bath.
Location
Sandy Lane, Shedfield, Southampton SO3 2HQ

NEW FOREST
(042128) 2450
A pretty 18 hole heathland course (5748 yards, SSS 68) set on high ground in the New Forest with many natural hazards, including ponies. Visitors are welcome any time between Monday and Saturday and on Sunday after 1.30pm. Green fees are £7 per round or day on weekdays and £9 at weekends. Full catering facilities are available between 11am and 5pm. Local attractions include Beaulieu Motor Museum.
Location
Lyndhurst, Hants SO4 7BU

RAC recommended hotels
Crown ★★★ (042128) 2922 A fine black and white building set in the town centre.
Forest Lodge ★★★ (0703) 283677 Modernised and extended 1830s former Royal hunting lodge. Swimming pool, putting.
Lyndhurst Park ★★★ (042128) 3019 An imposing Georgian building set in its own grounds. facilities include swimming pool, tennis, snooker, sauna and solarium.
Evergreens ★★ (042 128) 2175 Samll hotel with attractive garden, in a rural setting. Swimming pool.

NORTH HANTS
(0252) 616443
An attractive 18 hole tree-lined heathland course with lots of heather close to the fairways (6251 yards, SSS 70). Provided you have a handicap certificate, visitors are welcome by prior application to the secretary and with a letter of introduction. Lunches, teas and dinners are available but you must book beforehand.
Location
Minley Road, Fleet, Hants GU13 8RE

RAC recommended hotel
Lismoyne C/H ★★★ (0252) 628555 Substantial Victorian country house set in attractive gardens.

OLD THORNS
(0428) 724555
A testing 18 hole rapidly maturing championship course with some magnificent trees (5629 yards, SSS 72). Visitors are welcome at all times. Green fees are £16 per round or £24 a day on weekdays and £22 per round or day at weekends and Bank Holidays. There is a restaurant which offers a range of French, English and Japanese food. Other facilities include a heated swimming pool, sauna solarium, tennis, and a Japanese masseur! The

course is within easy access of Portsmouth, and Bird World is close by.
Location
London Kosaido Golf and Country Club, Longmoor Road, Liphook, Hants GU30 7PE

RAC recommended hotel see Liphook.

PETERSFIELD
(0730) 62386
An 18 hole heath and meadowland course with a lake and some fine views (5720 yards, SSS 68). Visitors are welcome daily but not before 10.30am at weekends. Green fees are £10 per round, £15 a day on weekdays and £15 per round, £20 a day at weekends. Lunch is available between Tuesday and Saturday, and evening meals can be provided for parties of 12 or more. The Queen Elizabeth Country Park is near by.
Location
Heath Road, Petersfield, Hants GU31 4EJ

PORTSMOUTH
(0705) 372210
A municipal 18 hole undulating parkland course (6259 yards, SSS 70) located on the hill overlooking Portsmouth Harbour. There is a practice area. Visitors are welcome at any time. Green fees are £4.50 between October and March, and £5.80 a round or £9 a day at other times. Full catering facilities are available. The course is close to Portsmouth Harbour.
Location
Crookhorn Lane, Widley, Portsmouth, Hants PO7 5QL

RAC recommended hotels
Holiday Inn ★★★★ (0705) 383151 Modern 'Holidome' hotel. Leisure and conference facilities. Indoor swimming pool, squash, sauna, solarium, gymnasium.
Crest ★★★ (0705) 827651 Modern purpose-built hotel overlooking Southsea Common. Centrally situated. Indoor swimming pool, sauna, solarium, gymnasium.
Pendragon ★★★ (0705) 823201 Traditional hotel facing Southsea Common and near front.
Hospitality Inn ★★★ (0705) 731281 Large white seafront hotel with superb views across the Solent.
Keppel's Head ★★ (0705) 833231 A hotel with a maritime flavour set on the Portsmouth Hard.

ROMSEY
(0703) 734637
An 18 hole undulating woodland course with some lovely views (5759 yards, SSS 68). Provided you have a handicap certificate, visitors are welcome on weekdays. Green fees on application. Full catering facilities are available. Local attractions include Beaulieu House and National Motor Museum.
Location
Nursling, Southampton SO1 9XW

RAC recommended hotel
White Horse ★★★ (0794) 512431 A town-centre hotel with traces of Mummers' Gallery and Tudor wall-paintings.

ROWLANDS CASTLE
(0705) 412784
A testing 18 hole parkland course in a peaceful setting (white tees, 6627 yards, SSS 72; yellow tees, 6381 yards, SSS 70). Visitors are welcome on weekdays but not on Saturday and visiting is limited on Sunday. It is advisable to telephone prior to arriving at weekends, especially during the summer season. Green fees are £16 per round or day on weekdays and £20 at weekends and Bank Holidays. A full catering service is available until 6pm except on Monday.
Location
Links Lane, Rowlands Castle, West Sussex PO9 6AE

RAC recommended hotel
Brookfield ★★★ (0243) 373363 A modern conversion with landscaped gardens.

ROYAL WINCHESTER
(0962) 52462
A notable 18 hole downland course (6218 yards, SSS 70). Provided you have a handicap certificate, visitors are welcome on weekdays. Green fees are £17 per round or day. Full catering facilities are available every day except Thursday, but it is best to liaise with the Steward. The course is close to Winchester and the Cathedral.
Location
Sarum Road, Winchester, Hants SO22 5QE

RAC recommended hotel see Hockley.

SOUTHAMPTON
(0703) 768407
A lovely municipal 18 hole parkland course which guarantees a good game (6218 yards, SSS 70). There is also a separate 9 hole course (2391 yards, SSS 33). Visitors are welcome at any time. Green fees on application. Breakfasts, lunches and bar snacks are always available.
Location
Golf Course Road, Bassett, Southampton, Hants

RAC recommended hotels
Polygon ★★★★ (0703) 330055 Modern hotel near Watts Park in town centre. Near station.
Dolphin ★★★ (0703) 339955 Charming city centre Georgian building with bay windows.
Post House ★★★ (0703) 330777 Tall traditional hotel near the Docks. Indoor swimming pool, sauna, solarium, gymnasium.
Southampton Moat House ★★★ (0703) 559555 Modern purpose-built hotel of three-storeys situated in Portswood area.
Southampton Park ★★★ (0703) 223467 City centre hotel overlooking park. Convenient for station. Indoor swimming poool, sauna, solarium, gymnasium.
Avenue ★★ (0703) 229025 Seven-storey modern hotel set back from main road and city to North.
Elizabeth House ★★ (0703) 224327 Elegant modernised Victorian house close to the common and city centre.
Star ★★ (0703) 339939 Former coaching inn, modernised into pleasant hotel. Close to station.

SOUTHWICK PARK
(0705) 380131
An 18 hole parkland course (5855 yards, SSS 69). There is also a practice area and a pitch and putt course. Visitors are welcome during the week, and as guests of a member at weekends. Green fees are £8. There is a bar and snacks are available. Local attractions include Portsmouth Dockyard with the 'Mary Rose'.
Location
Pinsley Drive, Southwick, Fareham, Hants PO17 6EL

RAC recommended hotels
Maylings Manor ★★ (0329) 286451 Attractive Georgian building set in 3 acres of landscaped gardens.

SOUTHWOOD
(0252) 548700
A flat 18 hole parkland public course with a stream running through (5553 yards, SSS 67). Visitors are welcome on a pay as you play scheme but you must book to play at weekends. Green fees on application. There is a bar and a good range of food is available.
Location
Ively Road, Cove, Farnborough, Hants GU14 0LJ

RAC recommended hotels see Army

STONEHAM
(0703) 768151
A hilly, heathery 18 hole parkland course with woodland separating the fairways (6310 yards, SSS 70). Visitors are welcome on weekdays but it is advisable to telephone in advance. A handicap certificate is requested. Green fees are £18 per round of 36 holes on weekdays. The bar is open all day and full catering facilities are available. Local attractions include Broadlands House.
Location
Bassett Green Road, Bassett, Southampton SO2 3NE

TIDWORTH GARRISON
(0980) 42301
A superb 18 hole downland course with good turf and some lovely views over Salisbury Plain (5990 yards, SSS 69). The beech and fir trees protect players from the winds. Visitors are welcome but it is advisable to book first. Green fees are £12 per day, (£7 with a member) on weekdays and £15 at weekends (£7 with a member). Full catering facilities are available by prior arrangement except on Monday, but bar snacks are normally available every day. Local attractions include Stonehenge.
Location
Bulford Road, Tidworth, Hants SP9 7AF

TYLNEY PARK
(0256) 762079
An 18 hole parkland course (6138 yards, SSS 70) with a practice area available. Visitors of all playing abilities are welcome but a handicap certificate is required. Green fees are £13 on weekdays (£6.50 with a member), and £20 at weekends (£9.50 with a member). Full catering facilities are available. Local attractions include Windsor Castle (20 miles) and Maidenhead (15 miles).
Location
Rotherwick, Basingstoke, Hants

RAC recommended hotel
Tylney Hall ★★★★ A large well-kept parkland, fine ornate Victorian mansion built in Elizabethan style. Facilities include an indoor swimming pool, tennis, sauna, gymnasium and billiards.

WATERLOOVILLE
(0705) 263388
An 18 hole parkland course (6647 yards, SSS 72) with some easy walking. Visitors of all playing abilities are welcome from Monday to Friday but a handicap certificate is required. Green fees are £14 per round or £17 per day. Full catering facilities are available from 10am to 5pm daily. Local attractions include Hayling Island and the Leisure Centre at Havant.
Location
Cherry Tree Avenue, Cowplain, Portsmouth PO8 8AP

RAC recommended hotel
Post House ★★★★ (0705) 46511 A modern hotel located close to the bridge linking Havant to the Island. Facilities include an indoor swimming pool, sauna, solarium and gymnasium.

HEREFORDSHIRE

BELMONT
(0432) 35266
An attractive 18-hole undulating meadowland course with some wooded areas (6448 yards, SSS 71). Visitors are welcome at all times. Green fees on application. There is a restaurant, and bar snacks are also available, but it is closed on Sunday evenings and Mondays. Local attractions include Hereford, the Cathedral, The Old House, Museum and Art Gallery.
Location
Belmont House, Belmont, Hereford HR2 9SA
Leave Hereford on the Abergavenny Road(A465) and the club is 1½ miles south

RAC recommended hotels
Green Dragon ★★★ (0432) 272506 Large former coaching inn in city centre near Cathedral.
Hereford Moat House ★★★ (0432) 354301 A

modern hotel on outskirts of city. Bedrooms set in quiet garden.
Castle Pool ★★ (0432) 356321 Quietly placed city centre Georgian building with lawned garden overlooking castle moat.
Merton ★★ (0432) 265925 Three-storey Georgian building of character, conveniently near town centre.
Netherwood ★★ (0432) 272388 An attractive early Victorian house in 2 acres of grounds on eastern edge of the city.
New Priory ★★ (0432) 760264 In 3½ acres of lawns, a charming red-brick Victorian building with mock Tudor features.

HEREFORDSHIRE
(0432) 71219
An 18-hole undulating parkland course with some wonderful views (6200 yards, SSS 69). Visitors of all playing abilities are welcome on weekdays, but are limited at the weekend, so it is advisable to telephone first. Green fees are £10 on weekdays and £14 at the weekend. Fees are reduced by £4 if you are playing with a member. Local attractions include Hereford Cathedral, the Wye Valley and the Welsh Mountains.
Location
Ravens Causeway, Wormsley, Hereford HR4 8LA
Leave Hereford by the A4110 road and six miles north west turn left at the Three Elms Inn,

RAC recommended hotels
New Priory ★★ (0432) 760264 A charming Victorian hotel situated in 3½ acres of lawns. In village of Stretton Sugwas.
Red Lion ★★ (0544) 318220 Attractive black and white inn with well appointed bedrooms.

KINGTON HEREFORDSHIRE
(0544) 230340
An 18-hole moorland course with easy walking (5726 yards, SSS 68). It is the highest in England and Wales, with views over seven counties. Visitors are welcome at all times. Green fees are £5.50 on weekdays and £7 at weekends. Lunch and dinner is available daily except Monday, when snacks only are served. Local places of interest include Offa's Dyke Gardens and a 15th-century farmhouse.
Location
Bradnor Hill, Kington, Herefordshire HR5 3RE
Take the A44 from Leominster and the club is 1 mile north of Kington on the B4355.

RAC recommended hotel
Burton ★★ (0544) 230323 A refurbished Vistorian building with modern extensions, in the town centre.

LEOMINSTER
(0568) 2863
A 9-hole undulating meadowland course (5250 yards, SSS 66). Visitors of all playing abilities are welcome on weekdays but you must arrange beforehand in order to play at the weekend. Green fees on application. Full catering facilities are available daily except Monday.
Location
Ford Bridge, Leominster, Herefordshire HR6 0LE

RAC recommended hotels
Royal Oak ★★ (0568) 2610 A Georgian coaching inn in the town centre.
Talbot ★★ (0568) 6347 An old coaching inn dating from the 15th century.

ROSS-ON-WYE
(098982) 267
A beautiful 18-hole parkland course cut into a silver birch forest (6500 yards, SSS 73). Provided you have a handicap certificate, visitors are welcome, but you must be a member of a golf club. Tuesday is Ladies Day. Green fees are £15 on weekdays and £18 at the weekend. Full catering facilities are available, although these are limited on Monday when only bar snacks are served. Local attractions include Goodridge Castle, River Wye and the Forest of Dean.
Location
Two Park, Gorsley, Ross-on-Wye, Hereford HR9 7UT
The club is situated on the B4421, just 100 yards from junction 3 of the M50.

RAC recommended hotels
Chase ★★★ (0989) 763161 A lovely Georgian house with extensions in pleasant grounds.
Royal ★★★ (0989) 65105 A modernised Victorian hotel in an elevated situation which provides fine views over the river.
Castle Lodge ★★ (0989) 62234 Historic house in rural setting. Family-run hotel enjoying wonderful views.
Chasedale C/H ★★ (0989) 62423 Small country house, quietly situated on outskirts of town.
Hunsdon Manor ★★ (0989) 62748 Stone-built Victorian manor house carefully modenised to retain its character. Sauna, solarium.
King's Head ★★ (0989) 763174 14th-century coaching inn in town centre. Attractive rear courtyard.
Orles Barn ★★ (0989) 762155 Small family-run hotel set in a pleasant garden. Swimming pool.

HERTFORDSHIRE

ALDENHAM GOLF AND COUNTRY CLUB
(0923) 853929
An 18 hole undulating parkland course (6344 yards, SSS 71). There is a practice area. Visitors are welcome on weekday, and after 1pm on Saturday and Sunday. Green fees are £12 on weekdays and £18.50 at weekends. There is a bar, snack bar and restaurant which are all open daily. The course is close to both St Albans and Watford.
Location
Radlett Road, Aldenham, Watford, Hertfordshire WD2 8AL
Take the A41 south from the M25 or leave the M1 at junction 5.

RAC recommended hotel
Dean Park ★★★ (0923) 229212 Modern high rise block close to station and town centre.

ARKLEY
081-449 0394
Two 9 hole parkland courses situated on high ground with some fine views (6045 yards, SSS 69). Provided you have a handicap certificate, visitors are welcome on weekdays and with a member at weekends. Tuesday is Ladies Day. Green fees are £10 per round, £15 a day. Snacks are available daily, except on Monday, by arrangement with the Steward.
Location
Rowley Green Road, Barnet, Hertfordshire
Leave the A1 at Stirling Corner. The club is signposted at Rowley Lane on the left. Alternatively, take the A1000 from London and turn by the Elstree Moat House, two miles from Barnet.,

ASHRIDGE
(044284) 2244
An 18 hole parkland course situated in a particularly peaceful spot (6508 yards, SSS 71). Visitors are welcome but you should telephone the Secretary to make a booking. Green fees are £15 per round, £25 a day. Morning coffee, lunches, afternoon tea and sandwiches are always available, and dinners can be arranged. Local attractions include Whipsnade Zoo, and Ashridge House.
Location
Little Gaddesden, Berkhamsted, Hertfordshire HP4 1LY
Take the A41 to Berkhamsted and turn north at Northchurch onto the B4506.

BATCHWOOD HALL
(0727) 52101
A municipal 18 hole parkland course (6463 yards, SSS 71). Visitors are welcome at all times. Green fees are £5 on weekdays and £6 at weekends. There are no catering facilities. The course is situated close to St Albans city centre and Verularium.
Location
Batchwood Drive, St Albans, Hertfordshire, AL3 5XA
The course is situated in the north west part of the town.

RAC recommended hotels see Verulam

BERKHAMSTED
(0442) 865832
An 18 hole heathland course well known for its lack of sand bunkers (6568 yards, SSS 72). Visitors are welcome but you must have a handicap certificate and be a member of a golf club. Visitors may not play on Tuesday before 12.30pm, or on Sunday and Bank Holidays before 11.30am. Green fees are £25 a day, £17.50 per round on weekdays and £35 per day or round at weekends and Bank Holidays. Full catering facilities are available except on Monday when it is limited. The course is near Champneys Health Farm.
Location
The Common, Berkhamsted, Hertfordshire, HP4 2QB
Leave the M1 at junction 8 for Hemel Hempstead and at the roundabout take the Leighton Buzzard road. After about 3 miles take the Potten End road and turn and follow the road until you come to the club. Alternatively, take the A41 to Berkhamsted, go up Raven's Lane to the top of the hill and turn left.

RAC recommended hotel
Swan Inn ★ (04427) 71451 A lovingly restored 15th century coaching inn which retains most of its originally.

BISHOP'S STORTFORD
(0279) 54715
A flat parkland course (6449 yards, SSS 71). Provided you have a handicap certificate, visitors are welcome on weekdays and with a member at weekends. Green fees are £13 per round, £15 a day. Lunches and dinners are available by arrangement, and bar meals until 9.30pm.
Location
Dunmow Road, Bishop's Stortford, Hertfordshire CM23 5HP
Leave the M11 at exit 8 and follow the signs to the town centre and the hospital. The golf course is on the left next to the Nags Head public house on the east edge of the town.

RAC recommended hotel
Foxley ★★★ (0279) 654977 A large hotel set in a quiet location.

BOXMOOR
(0442) 42434
A testing 9 hole undulating moorland course with some fine views but hard walking (4854 yards, SSS 64). Children are welcome. Visitors can play on weekdays but not on Sunday. Players of all abilities are welcome, but the course is unsuitable for beginners. Green fees are £6 on weekdays and £7 on Saturday. Limited catering facilities are available.
Location
18 Box Lane, Hemel Hempstead, Hertfordshire
The club is 2 miles from Hemel Hempstead, three-quarters of a mile from the railway station on the A41.

RAC recommended hotel
Post House ★★★ (0442) 51122 Modern purpose-built hotel with pleasant motel-style bedrooms.

BRICKENDON GRANGE
(099 286) 258
An 18 hole undulating parkland course with some specimen trees (6315 yards, SSS 70). Visitors who have handicap certificates are welcome on weekdays. Green fees are £16 per round or £20 a day. A snack lunch is served daily.
Location
Brickendon, Nr Hertford, Hertfordshire SG13 8PD
The club is 3 miles south of Hertford, 1 mile from Bayford Station.

RAC recommended hotels
White Horse Inn ★★★ (0992) 586791
Beautifully-preserved coaching inn situated off the Hertford/Hatfield road. Pleasant garden.
Salisbury Arms ★★ (0992) 583091 Attractive old town centre hotel – three-storey building of ornate design. Solarium.

BROOKMANS PARK
(0707) 52487
A popular 18 hole undulating parkland course with a difficult hole across a lake (6454 yards, SSS 71 (white)). There is also a practice ground and putting green. Green fees on application. Snacks are served at lunchtimes and evening meals are available for societies. Local attractions include Hatfield House.
Location
Golf Club Road, Hatfield, Hertfordshire AL9 7AT
The club is situated between the A1 and A1000, also just off the M25, Potters Bar junction.

RAC recommended hotel
Comet ★★★ (0707) 265411 Red-brick hotel situated on A1 on the edge of town.

BUSHEY GOLF AND COUNTRY CLUB
081-950 2283
A semi-private 9 hole parkland course with a driving range (3000 yards, SSS 69). Visitors are welcome on weekdays before 5.30pm and at weekends and Bank holidays after 2.30pm. No visitors may play on Wednesday. Green fees are £6 on weekdays and £7 at weekends for 9 holes, and £10 and £13 respectively for 18 holes. Meals are served daily. The area is good for nature walks, and Watford town centre and Brent Cross are within easy access.
Location
High Street, Bushey, Hertfordshire
The course is on the A411, 1½ miles from the M1/A411 junction.

RAC recommended hotels
Hilton National ★★★★ (0923) 35881 A large modern hotel convenient for the M1. Facilities include indoor swimming pool.
Spider's Web ★★★ 081-950 6211 A modern motor hotel with a health centre, indoor swimming pool, tennis, sauna, solarium and gymnasium.

BUSHEY HALL
(0923) 225802
An 18 hole undulating parkland course (6071 yards, SSS 69). Visitors who have a handicap certificate are welcome on weekdays. Green fees are £13 per round or £20 a day. Full catering facilities are available
Location
Bushey Hall Drive, Bushey, Hertfordshire WD2 2EP
You will find the club 1 mile south east of Watford. Take the Bushey Hall Road at the Aldenham Road roundabout, 1 mile from the M1.

CHADWELL SPRINGS
(0920) 463647
A 9 hole parkland course on high ground and subject to wind (3209 yards, SSS 71). Visitors are welcome on weekdays and at weekends with a member, but it is advisable to telephone first to check on competition times. Green fees are £12 a round (18 holes) or £18 a day. Food is available in the bars at lunchtime. Local attractions include Hatfield House.
Location
Hertford Road, Ware, Hertfordshire SG12 9LE
The club is situated midway between Ware and Hertford on the A119.

RAC recommended hotel
Ware Moat House ★★★ (0920) 465011
Medium-sized modern hotel, on the northern edge of the town.

CHESHUNT
(0992) 24009
A municipal 18 hole flat parkland course which is well bunkered with ponds (6608 yards, SSS 71). There is a practice area. Green fees are £4.50 on weekdays and £6 at weekends, and booking is not necessary. There is a public café which is open daily. The course is within easy access of Epping Forest and Brookfield Farm shopping mall.
Location
Park Lane, Cheshunt, Hertfordshire EN7 6QD
Leave the M25 at junction 25 and take the A10 towards Hertford. Turn off to Flanstead End at the second set of traffic lights. The club is signposted.

CHORLEYWOOD
(09278) 2009
A 9 hole parkland course with natural hazards and some fine views (2838 yards, SSS 67). Visitors are welcome on weekdays except on Tuesday and Thursday mornings. Green fees are £6 on weekdays and £7.50 at weekends.
Location
Common Road, Chorleywood WD3 5LN
The club is situated off the A404, 3 miles west of Rickmansworth.

DYRHAM PARK
081-440 3361
An 18 hole parkland course (6369 yards, SSS 70 white, SSS 69 yellow). Visitors are welcome but only as a guest of a club member. Green fees are £12.50 on weekdays and £15 at weekends. Full restaurant facilities are available.
Location
Galley Lane, Barnet, Hertfordshire
The club is off the A1, 2 miles outside Barnet, Near Arkley.

EAST HERTS
(0920) 821978
A picturesque 18 hole undulating parkland course with splendid specimen trees (6449 yards, SSS 71). Provided you have a handicap certificate or are a member of a golf society, visitors are welcome on weekdays. Green fees are £18 per round, £23 a day. Catering facilities are available.
Location
Hamels Park, Buntingford, Hertfordshire SG9 9NA
The club is 1 mile north of Puckeridge on the A10, between Buntingford and Ware. Turn off a quarter of a mile north of the Puckeridge roundabout.

ELSTREE
081-953 6115
An 18 hole parkland course (6100 yards, SSS 69). There is a floodlit driving range with 40 bays. It is a pay and play course, and green fees are £12 a day on weekdays and £25 at weekends. Full catering facilities are available. Local attractions include St Albans Cathedral and Roman ruins.
Location
Watling Street, Elstree WD6 3AA
Leave the M1 at junction 4 and the club is 1 mile north of Elstree on the A5183.

RAC recommended hotel
Edgwarebury ★★★ 081-953 8227 Tudor-style mansion with modern extension set in 10 acres of woodland, lawns and gardens. Tennis, sauna, solarium, gymnasium.

HADLEY WOOD
081-449 4486
A particularly beautiful, gently undulating 18 hole parkland course with some very attractive wooded areas (6473 yards, SSS 71). Provided you have a handicap certificate or you are a club member, visitors are welcome on weekdays, and at weekends, if you are playing with a member. Green fees are £20 per round or £25 a day. Morning coffee, lunches and dinners are available for functions and societies. The club has a snooker room.
Location
Beech Hill, Barnet, Hertfordshire EN4 0JJ
Leave the M25 at junction 24 and take the A111 towards Cockfosters. The club entrance is 400 yards on the left.

RAC recommended hotel
West Lodge Park ★★★★ 081-440 8311 A luxurious Georgian country house hotel in 35 acres of grounds with a small lake.

HARPENDEN
(05827) 2580
A gently undulating 18 hole parkland course with easy walking (6363 yards, SSS 70). Visitors are welcome on weekdays but a handicap certificate is required. Green fees on application. Lunches are available at the club, but you must order in advance. Local attractions include St Albans Abbey, Hatfield House and Knebworth House.
Location
Hammonds End, Redbourn Lane, Harpenden, Herts AL5 2AX
Take the A1081 4 miles north of St Albans towards Harpenden and turn off at the B487.

RAC recommended hotels
Harpenden Moat House ★★★★ (058 27) 69858
A 300 year old, red-brick building overlooking Harpenden Common.
Glen Eagle ★★★ (058 27) 60271 An attractive former country house with additional wings, at the edge of the town centre.

HARPENDEN COMMON
(05827) 2856
An 18 hole commonland course with good greens (5659 yards, SSS 67). Visitors are welcome on Monday, Wednesday, Thursday and Friday. Green fees are £15 a day or £11 a round. Lunch is served every day. Local attractions include Luton Hoo, Knebworth House, Woburn Abbey and Safari Park, and St Albans.
Location
East Common, Harpenden, Herts AL5 1BL
Take the A1081 between Harpenden and St Albans and turn onto the B487.

HARTSBOURNE GOLF AND COUNTRY CLUB
081-950 1133
Two parkland courses with some fine views; an 18 hole course (6305 yards, SSS 70) and a 9 hole course (5432 yards, SSS 66). Visitors are welcome but you must be accompanied by a member. Lunch is served daily except on Monday and Friday. Places of interest worth visiting locally include Cassiobury Park at St Albans.
Location
Hartsbourne Avenue, Bushey Heath, Herts WD2 1JW
Take the A411 from Watford 5 miles south east towards Bushey and turn south at the entrance to Bushey Heath village.

RAC recommended hotels see Bushey.

LONDON COUNTRY CLUB
(0707) 42624
A varied 18 hole undulating meadowland course with pond, stream and ditch hazards (6878 yards, SSS 72). There is also a 9 hole pitch and putt course. Visitors are welcome at all times as the course is open to the public. Green fees are £9 on weekdays, £18 on Saturday and £19 on Sunday and Bank Holidays. Bar snacks are served at lunchtimes except on Monday. The clubhouse is a 19th-century manor house. Local attractions

include Hatfield House.
Location
Bedwell Park, Essendon, Hatfield, Herts AL9 6JA
Take the A1000 from Potters Bar and then the B158 towards Essendon.

KNEBWORTH
(0438) 812752
An 18 hole parkland course with easy walking (6428 yards, SSS 71). Visitors with a handicap certificate are welcome on weekdays, and at weekends and Bank Holidays if they are accompanied by a member. Full catering facilities are available daily. Local attractions include Hatfield House and Knebworth House.
Location
Deards End Lane, Knebworth, Herts SG3 6NL
The course is situated on the B197, 1 mile south of Stevenage.

RAC recommended hotels see Stevenage.

LETCHWORTH
(0462) 683203
An exciting 18 hole parkland course with a variety of hazards and an unpredictable wind (6181 yards, SSS 69). Visitors who are members of a bona fide golf club and who hold a current handicap certificate are welcome on weekdays, and at weekends with a member. Green fees are £16 a day. Full meals and snacks are available except on Monday. The course is 18 miles from Cambridge and 20 miles from Woburn.
Location
Letchworth Lane, Letchworth, Herts SG6 3NQ
Take the A1(M) from Letchworth and turn onto the A505. The club is situated near the village of Willian, adjacent to Letchworth Hall Hotel.

RAC recommended hotel
Broadway Toby ★★★ (0462) 685651 Modern hotel in 'georgian' style, part of original Garden City development.

LITTLE HAY
(0442) 833798
An 18 hole semi-parkland inland links course (6610 yards, SSS 72). There is also a 9 hole pitch and putt course and an 18 hole putting green. All members of the public are welcome. Green fees on application. Full catering facilities are available daily.
Location
Box Lane, Hemel Hempstead, Herts HP3 0DT
The club is off the A41, and off the Chesham Road from Hemel Hempstead. Turn off the road at the Box Lane traffic lights.

MID-HERTS
(058283) 3385
A short and tight 18 hole heathland/parkland course with gorse-lined fairways (6060 yards, SSS 69). Visitors are welcome, but not before 1pm on Tuesday, or after 1pm on Wednesday, and you must be accompanied by a member at weekends and Bank Holidays. Green fees on application. Full catering facilities are available daily except Sunday.
Location
Gustard Wood, Wheathampstead, St Albans, Herts AL4 8RS
Take the B651 6 miles north of St Albans to the club.

MOOR PARK
(0923) 773146
Two 18 hole parkland courses; The High (6713 yards, SSS 72) and The West (5815 yards, SSS 68) and High Championship tees (6903 yards, SSS 73). Visitors who have a handicap certificate are welcome on weekdays by prior arrangement. Green fees on request. Snacks and meals are served daily.
Location
Moor Park Mansion, Moor Park, Rickmansworth, WD3 1QN
The club is on the A404 between Rickmansworth and Northwood, three quarters of a mile from Moor Park station.

OLD FOLD MANOR
081-440 9185
A challenging 18 hole parkland course (6449 yards, SSS 71). Visitors are welcome on weekdays and with a member at weekends. Green fees are £22 a day. Meals are served daily except on Monday and Wednesday.
Location
Hadley Green, Barnet, Herts EN5 4QN
The club is on the Potters Bar road, a quarter of a mile from Barnet.

PANSHANGER
(0707) 333350
A municipal 18 hole undulating parkland course (6538 yards, SSS 72). There is also a 9 hole pitch and putt course and a practice area. Visitors are unrestricted but it is advisable to book in advance. Green fees are £5.50 on weekdays and £6 at weekends and Bank Holidays. Lunch is served every day.
Location
Herns Lane, Welwyn Garden City, Herts
Leave the A1(M) at the Clock Motel exit at Welwyn and turn onto the B1000, 1 mile north east of the town.

RAC recommended hotels see Welwyn.

PORTERS PARK
(0923) 854127
An interesting 18 hole undulating parkland course with fine trees and a brook (6313 yards, SSS 70). There is a putting green and also two practice areas. Provided you have a handicap certificate, visitors are welcome on weekdays but you must book in advance. Green fees are £22 per round or £30 a day. Full catering facilities are available. . The club has its own chef and full catering is available for societies. Bar snacks are served on other day unless meals have been specially ordered. Local attractions include the historic city of St Albans and Salisbury Hall.
Location
Shenley Hill, Radlett, Herts WD7 7AZ
Leave the M25 at junction 22, or the M1 at junction 5. Turn off the A5183 on to Shenley Road at the railway station, go half a mile to the top of the hill and the club is on the bend of the road.

POTTERS BAR
(0707) 52020
An 18 hole undulating parkland course (6273 yards, SSS 70). There is a small practice ground, nets and putting green. Visitors who have a handicap certificate are welcome on weekdays. Green fees on application. Lunch is served daily. The course is conveniently situated on the outskirts of London.
Location
Darkes Lane, Potters Bar, Herts EN6 1DE
Take the A1000 north of Barnet and the club entrance is opposite Tesco's.

REDBOURN
(058285) 3493
A challenging 18 hole parkland course (6407 yards, SSS 71) and a shorter 9 hole public course (1361 yards, Par 27). Visitors are welcome on weekdays. Green fees are £7.50 (£6.50 with a member) on weekdays and £9 as a member's guest at weekends and Bank Holidays. There is a fully licensed bar with bar snacks, and restaurant meals are served daily by arrangement. Functions are also catered for. The course is close to St Albans.
Location
Moor Lane, Rickmansorth, Herts WD3 1QL
Leave the M1 south at junction 9 and turn onto the A5, turn left, and the club is 1 mile down Luton Lane.

RAC recommended hotel
Aubrey Park ★★★ (058 285) 2105 A peaceful hotel set in 7 acres of grounds with a swimming pool.

RICKMANSWORTH
(0923) 773163
A municipal 18 hole undulating parkland course (4412 yards, SSS 62). There is also a 9 hole course (644 yards). Green fees are £4.40 on weekdays and £6.30 at weekends for the 18 hole course, and it is necessary to book one week in advance. The fees for the 9 hole course are £1 for adults and 50p for OAPs and juniors. Meals are served all day. Local attractions include Moor Park Mansion and the Aquadrome.
Location
Moor Lane, Rickmansworth, Herts WD3 1QL
Leave the town centre by the A404 towards the waterworks, turn left along the B4504, then first right to the club.

RAC recommended hotel
Bedford Arms Thistle ★★★ (09278) 3301 An Elizabeth-style former coaching inn in an historic village.

ROYSTON
(0763) 242696
An 18 hole undulating heathland course (6032 yards, SSS 69). Visitors are welcome during the week and with a member at weekends. Green fees are £12 on weekdays. Full catering facilities are available.
Location
Baldock Road, Royston, Herts SG8 5BG
The club is situated on the A505 on the outskirts of the town, between Royston and Baldock. The golf course is actually on Therfield Heath.

STEVENAGE
(043888) 424
A municipal 18 hole parkland/meadowland course (6451 yards, SSS 71). There is a 20-bay driving range also. Visitors are welcome every day but it is necessary to book in advance. Green fees are £4.50 on weekdays and £6 at weekends. Full meals and bar snacks are normally available.
Location
Aston Lane, Aston, Stevenage, Herts SG2 7EL
Take the A602 to Hertford from the A1 and the course is signposted after about 1 mile.

RAC recommended hotels
Blakemore Thistle ★★★ (0438) 355821 Georgian-style mansion with modern wing, in 5 acres of attractive gardens. Swimming pool, sauna, solarium.
Hertford Park ★★★ (0438) 350661 Modern tower block hotel on edge of the new town shopping centre.
Roebuck Inn ★★★ (0438) 365444 A thoroughly modernised period country inn with up-to-date residential wing.
Stevenage Moat House ★★★ (0438) 359111 17th-century building in old high street. Modernised but retains much charm.

VERULAM
(0727) 53327
An 18 hole parkland course (6432 yards, SSS 71). Visitors are welcome on weekdays. Green fees are £8 per round, £12 a day on Monday and £12 per round, £15 a day on Tuesday to Friday. Full catering facilities are available daily except Monday, when bar snacks only are served. The course is close to St Albans Abbey and the city centre.
Location
London Road, St Albans, Herts AL1 1JG
Leave the M25 at junction 22 and take the A1081 to St Albans.

RAC recommended hotels
Lake Holidays ★★★ (0727) 40904 Modern brick-built, mostly two-storey hotel set back from the main road into the city from the south.
Noke Thistle ★★★ (0727) 54252 Elegant country-house style hotel outside St Albans.

St Michael's Manor ★★★ (0727) 64444 A Elizabethan manor house in 5 acres of attractive gardens.
Sopwell House ★★★ (0727) 64477 A beautifully maintained elegant country residence, set in parkland.

WELWYN GARDEN CITY
(0707) 325243
An undulating 18 hole parkland course with a ravine (6200 yards, SSS 69). Visitors are welcome on weekdays, and green fees are £16.50 a day or £14 per round. Bar snacks, lunches and dinners are normally served daily. The historic city of St Albans is close.
Location
Mannicotts, High Oaks Road, Welwyn Garden City, Herts AL8 7BP.
Turn off the A1 at Stanborough and follow the B197 to Welwyn Garden City centre.

RAC recommended hotels
Crest ★★★ (0707) 324336 A modern hotel in the centre of Welwyn Garden City.
Clock ★★★ (04387) 4065 A one time roadhouse converted to a large motel alongside the A1(M).

WEST HERTS
(0923) 224264
A very dry 18 hole parkland course with a most severe finish (6488 yards, SSS 71). Visitors are welcome on weekdays provided you have a handicap certificate, and at weekends with a member. Green fees on application. Lunch and tea is served daily except on Monday. The city of St Albans is nearby.
Location
Cassiobury Park, Watford, Herts WD1 7SL
The club is situated 2 miles south of Watford on the A412.

WHIPSNADE PARK
(044284) 2330
An 18 hole parkland course (6735 yards, SSS 72) situated on the downs next to Whipsnade Zoo. . Visitors are welcome at any time during the week. Green fees are £14 per round or £18 a day. There is a restaurant, and bar snacks are also served daily except Monday. As well as Whipsnade Zoo, the Downs are a lovely place for walks.
Location
Studham Lane, Dagnall, Herts HP4 1RH
Leave the M1 south at junction 11, or the M1 north at junction 9. Follow the signs to Whipsnade Park, between the villages of Dagnall and Studham.

HUMBERSIDE

BEVERLEY AND EAST RIDING
(0482) 868757
A pretty 18 hole undulating parkland course with some hard walking (6164 yards, SSS 69). The course is a challenging one and there are many natural hazard, including grazing cattle and sheep, and early-morning horse riders. Visitors are welcome on weekdays. Green fees are £6 (£4 with a member) on weekdays and £8.50 (£8.50) on weekends and Bank Holidays. Lunch is served daily. Local attractions include The Minster at Beverley, and Hull is only 8 miles away.
Location
Anti Mill, The Westwood, Beverley HU17 8RG
The course is situated on the Beverley-Walkington road, the B1230, 1 mile from Beverley town centre.

RAC recommended hotels
Beverley Arms ★★★ (0482) 869241 A refurbished 18th century coaching inn situated in a quiet area.
Tickton Grange C/H ★★★ (0964) 543666 Georgian building – a country house in 4 acres of lawns and rose gardens.
Lairgate ★★ (0482) 882141 A stone built Georgian listed building in a narrow street in the older part of town.

BOOTHFERRY
(0430) 430364
An 18 hole meadowland course with lots of bunkers, ponds and several dykes (6651 yards, SSS 72). There are two large practice areas. Visitors of all playing levels are welcome on weekdays, weekends and Bank Holidays. Green fees are £4 per round, £6 a day on weekdays and £7 per round, £10 a day at weekends and Bank Holidays. Snacks and meals are served every lunchtime, and, during the summer season, every evening also. There is a leisure centre in Goole and a museum in Howden.
Location
Spaldington, Howden, Goole DN14 7NG
Leave the M62 at junction 12 then take the B1228 for Howden towards Bubwith for 3 miles.

RAC recommended hotel
Bowmans ★★★ (0430) 430805 A three storey stone built former coaching inn in the town centre.

BRIDLINGTON
(0662) 672092
An 18 hole meadowland seaside course (6320 yards, SSS 70) situated on a cliff top which can be windy. Visitors of all playing abilities are welcome and parties can be booked with the Hon. Secretary. Green fees are £5 per round, £8 a day on weekdays and £7 per round, £10 a day at weekends and Bank Holidays. Full catering facilities are available daily except Tuesday, but you should book in advance.
Location
Belvedere Road, Bridlington, N Humberside YO15 3NA
The course is situated $1^1/_2$ miles south of Bridlington station, off the A165.

RAC recommended hotels
Expanse ★★★ (0262) 675347 Modern family-run hotel in splendid situation with fine sea views.
Monarch ★★ (0262) 674447 A medium sized hotel overlooking beaches and bay.
New Revelstoke ★★ (0262) 672362 Two well-appointed large buildings on the north side of town.

BROUGH
(0472) 667291
An 18 hole parkland course (6035 yards, SSS 69). There are practice facilities. Visitors who have a handicap certificate are welcome on weekdays only, and only after 2.30pm on Wednesday. Green fees are £20 on weekdays (£10 with a member). Snacks are normally available. The Hull Marina is only 15 minutes away by car.
Location
Cave Road, Brough, N Humberside HU15 1HB
From the A63 12 miles west of Hull, turn off towards Brought. The course is on the western edge of the village.

CLEETHORPES
(0472) 812059
An 18 hole meadowland seaside course with a stream running through (6015 yards, SSS 69). There is a restricted practice area. Provided you are a member of a recognised golf club, visitors are welcome. Ladies Day is Wednesday afternoon. Green fees are £10 on weekdays (£7 with a member) and £13 at weekends, (£10 with a member). Bar snacks are always available, and evening meals by arrangement with the Steward. Cleethorpes offers the full facilities of a seaside resort.
Location
Kings Road, Cleethorpes, S Humberside DN35 0PN
The club is situated off the A1031 1 mile south of Cleethorpes.

RAC recommended hotels
Kingsway ★★★ (0472) 601122 A lovely three storey hotel with a pleasant roof garden overlooking the sea.
Wellow ★★ (0472) 695589 A small modern hotel situated on the fringe of town.

DRIFFIELD
(0377) 43116
A 9 hole parkland course with easy walking (6227 yards, SSS 70). The course is soon to be extended to 18 holes. Visitors of all playing abilities are welcome. Green fees are £6 per round on weekdays and £10 a day or round with a member at weekends. There is a bar and meals are available except on Monday. Local attractions include Burton Agnes Hall.
Location
Sunderlandwick, Driffield, N Humberside
The course is 1 mile from Driffield town centre towards Hull on the A164.

RAC recommended hotels
Bell ★★★ (0377) 46661 Situated in a market place this 18th century coaching inn has modern bedrooms built on. Facilities include an indoor swimming pool, squash, solarium and billiards.
Wold House C/H ★★ (0377) 44242 Large country house on hillside; fine views over open countryside. Swimming pool, putting, billiards.

FLAMBOROUGH HEAD
(0262) 850333
An 18 hole undulating seaside course (5438 yards, SSS 66). Visitors who are members of a bona fide golf club are welcome daily except before midday on Sunday. Green fees are £7 on weekdays and £9 at weekends and Bank Holidays. A weekly ticket can be bought for £28. Full catering facilities are available daily except Monday. There is a bird sanctuary on the cliffs and the club is close to the lighthouse.
Location
Lighthouse Road, Flamborough, Bridlington, N Humberside YO15 1AR
Leave Bridlington for 5 miles north east on the B1255 and the club is near the lighthouse on the headland at Flamborough.

GANSTEAD PARK
(0482) 811280
An 18 hole parkland course with easy walking (6495 yards, SSS 71). Visitors who are of a reasonable standard, with a handicap of 28 for men and 36 for ladies, are welcome on any day except Wednesday and on Sunday mornings. Green fees are £8 (£5 with a member) on weekdays and £12 (£6 with a member) at weekends. Lunch and evening meals are served daily. Local attractions include Burton Constable Hall and the magnificent Humber Bridge.
Location
Longdales Lane, Coniston, Hull HU11 4LB
The club is on the A165 east of Hull, 2 miles from the city boundary.

RAC recommended hotels see Hull.

GRIMSBY
(0472) 42630
An 18 hole undulating parkland course with easy walking (6058 yards, SSS 69). Visitors who are members of a recognised golf club are welcome. Ladies Day is Tuesday. Green fees are £10 on weekdays and £13 at weekends. There is a £3 reduction if you are introduced by a member. Bar snacks are available and other meals can be provided by arrangement with the Steward. The club is close to Cleethorpes seaside resort, Grimsby fish docks and the magnificent Humber Bridge.
Location
Littlecoates Road, Grimsby, S Humberside DN34 4LU
Turn left off the A46 at the first roundabout in Grimsby, and the club is three quarters of a mile on the left, next to the Humber Royal Hotel.

RAC recommended hotel
Humber Royal Crest ★★★★ (0472) 350295 A medium-sized modern hotel, in a quiet area overlooking the golf course.

HAINSWORTH PARK
(0964) 542362
A 9 hole parkland course with mature trees and easy walking (5360 yards, SSS 66). Visitors are welcome at any time. Green fees are £5 on weekdays and £7.50 at weekends. Bar snacks are available daily except on Monday. Local attractions include Beverley with its Minster and museum, and the course is close to the Yorkshire coast.
Location
Brandesburton, Driffield YO25 8RT
The club is on the A165 between Beverley and Bridlington, 8 miles north of Beverley.

HESSLE
(0482) 650171
A wooded 18 hole undulating meadowland course which can be windy (6638 yards, SSS 72). Provided you have a handicap certificate, visitors are welcome on any day except Tuesday between 9.15am and 1pm. Green fees are £12 per round, £14 a day on weekdays and £18 per round or day at weekends. Full catering facilities are available daily. Local attractions include the splendid Humber Bridge, Hull Marina and Hull Ice Rink.
Location
Westfield Road, Cottingham, Hull, N Humberside HU16 5YL
4 miles west of Hull city centre off the A1105.

RAC recommended hotels see Hull.

HOLME HALL
(0724) 862078
A championship 18 hole parkland course with easy walking (6475 yards, SSS 71). Visitors who are members of a bona fide golf club are welcome on weekdays and with a member at weekends. Green fees are £8 per round, £12 a day, or half price if you are with a member. Bar snacks are served daily except Friday and meals by arrangement. There is a snooker room. Local attractions include Normanby Hall, Elsham Park, Wrawby Mill and the magnificent Humber Bridge.
Location
Holme Hall, Bottesford, Scunthorpe, S Humberside DN16 3RF
Take the A159 south from Scunthorpe. Turn east to Bottesford and continue on to the course on the left.

RAC recommended hotels see Scunthorpe.

HORNSEA
(04012) 2020
A beautiful 18 hole parkland/moorland course with outstanding greens (6450 yards, SSS 71). There is a large practice area and also a snooker room. Visitors are welcome daily except on Tuesday, but you should telephone the Pro or the Secretary first. Green fees are £8 per round or £12 a day. Full catering facilities are available daily except Tuesday.
Location
Rolston Road, Hornsea, N Humberside HU18 1XG
Follow the sign for Hornsea Pottery in Hornsea, and the club house is approximately 600 yards past the entrance to the pottery, on the road to Withernsea.

HULL
(0482) 658919
An 18 hole parkland course with easy walking (6242 yards, SSS 70). Visitors are welcome on weekdays only and you must be a member of a recognised golf club and preferably have a handicap certificate. Green fees are £15 per round or day. Lunches are served on weekdays but you are advised to book in advance.
Location
The Hall, 27 Packman Lane, Kirk Ella, Hull HU10 7TJ
The club is situated 5 miles west of Kingston-upon-Hull off the A164.

RAC recommended hotels
Marina Post House ★★★★ (0482) 225221 Four-storey hotel overlooking the yacht marina in the old dock area. Indoor swimming pool, sauna, solarium, gymnasium.
Crest Hull-Humber Bridge ★★★ (0482) 645212 Modern hotel in own grounds overlooking river and Humber Bridge.
Grange Park ★★★ (0482) 656488 A substantial early Victorian house in a large garden. Facilities include an indoor swimming pool, sauna, solarium and gymnasium.
Pearson Park ★★★ (0482) 43043 Large Victorian building situated in public park north of city centre.
Rowley Manor C/H ★★★ (0482) 848248 Attractive Georgian country house set in lawns and rose gardens. Solarium.
Stakis Paragon ★★★ (0482) 26462 A modern six-storey hotel situated near station in centre.
Waterfront ★★★ (0482) 227222 Fine Victorian warehouse, successfully converted into luxury hotel of character. Solarium.
Willerby Manor ★★★ (0482) 652616 A large attractive memorial hotel among 3 acres of gardens.
Maxim's ★★ (0482) 509660 Victorian building in Dutch colonial style on main road, west of city centre.

IMMINGHAM
(0469) 75298
An 18 hole parkland course (5809 yards, SSS 68). There is a practice area. Visitors are welcome on weekdays but you must be accompanied by a member at weekends. Green fees are £8 on weekdays (£6.50 with a member) and £12 at weekends. There is a bar and light meals and snacks are available. Local attractions include the port of Grimsby, Cleethorpes and the starting point of the Pilgrim Fathers' voyage on the 'Mayflower'.
Location
Church Lane, Immingham, Grimsby DN40 2EN
From the A180, turn north to Immingham. The club is near the Civic Centre, half a mile behind St Andrews Church.

KINGSWAY
(0724) 840945
A pretty 9 hole undulating parkland course (1915 yards, SSS 59). The course is a municipal one and visitors of all playing abilities are welcome daily. Green fees are £1.60 for adults, 80p for children on weekdays and £2 for adults, £1 for children at weekends and Bank Holidays. Snacks are available daily. Local attractions include Normanby Hall.
Location
Kingsway, Scunthorpe, S Humberside DN15 7ER
The club is south of the A18 between Berkeley and Queensway roundabouts. The entrance to the club is off Scotter Road.

NORMANBY HALL
(0724) 720252
An 18 hole parkland course (6548 yards, SSS 71). Visitors are welcome at any time. Green fees are £5.50 per round, £7 a day on weekdays and £7 at weekends. There is a fully licensed club house with a restaurant which is open daily. The club is adjacent to Normanby Hall.
Location
Normanby Park, Normanby, Scunthorpe, S Humberside DN15 9HU
Turn right off the B1430 5 miles north of Scunthorpe and follow the signs for Normanby Hall Country Park. The club is adjacent to the Hall.

SCUNTHORPE
(0724) 866561
A tight 18 hole wooded parkland course (6281 yards, SSS 71). Visitors are welcome on weekdays but you must be a member of a recognised golf club and have a current handicap certificate. Green fees are £10 a day. Full catering facilities are available between Monday and Thursday but are limited on Friday. The country parks at Elsham and Normanby Hall are close by.
Location
Burringham Road, Scunthorpe, S Humberside DN17 2AB
The club is situated on the B1450, adjoining the Mallard Hotel, opposite the Asda Superstore.

RAC recommended hotel
Royal ★★★ (0724) 282233 A modernised traditional hotel on the western fringe of town.
Wortley House ★★★ (0724) 842223 Large brick building on fringe of town. Banqueting suite and ballroom.

SPRINGHEAD PARK
(0482) 656309
A municipal 18 hole parkland course with undulating fairways (6439 yards, SSS 71). Visitors are welcome but you should book first if you wish to play on Sunday. Green fees are £2.85 on weekdays and £4 at weekends. There is a bar and restaurant. The course has some splendid views of the Humber Bridge, and Beverley Minster is only 5 miles away.
Location
Willerby Road, Hull HU5 5JE
From Hull centre take the A1105 to Willerby, or the A164 north from the Humber Bridge.

SUTTON PARK
(0482) 74242
A municipal 18 hole parkland course (6251 yards, SSS 70). There is also a snooker room. Visitors are welcome without restriction, and green fees are £2.85 on weekdays and £4 at weekends. Bar snacks are available at lunchtime and full meals can be provided by arrangement. There are many leisure and sports facilities in Hull.
Location
Salthouse Road, Sutton, Hull, N Humberside HU8 9HF
The club is 4 miles east of the city centre on the A165 (B1237).

RAC recommended hotels see Hull.

WITHERNSEA
(0964) 612258
A 9 hole exposed seaside links course with bunkers (5112 yards, SSS 64). Visitors are welcome at all times but there are certain restrictions on some weekends, so it is advisable to telephone first. Green fees are £5 a day, juniors £2.50. There is a bar, and meals are available by arrangement at lunchtime and on some evenings. Withernsea is a good seaside resort.
Location
Chestnut Avenue, Withernsea, N Humberside HU19 2QD
Withernsea is 17 miles east of Kingston-upon-Hull and the club is at the south end of the town.

ISLE OF WIGHT

COWES
(0983) 292303
A 9-hole parkland course (2940 yards, SSS 68). Visitors are welcome by arrangement. Green fees are £10 a day. Bar snacks are available from 11.30am to 1pm except on Sunday. The course is close to the seafront.
Location
Crossfield Avenue, Cowes PO31 8HN
Make for Cowes High School and the course is at

the far end of the school playing fields.

RAC recommended hotels
Fountain ★★ (0983) 292397 A Georgian inn in a narrow street near the waterfront, An archway leads to the hotel's restaurant and bar and the ferry concourse.
Cowes Hotel ★★ (0983) 291541 Two-storey former inn with good views of Marina and River Medina. Swimming pool, sauna, solarium.

FRESHWATER BAY
(0983) 752955
An 18-hole downland seaside links course (5662 yards, SSS 68) with some wonderful views over the Solent and the Channel . The club also has a separate 18-hole pitch and putt course. Visitors with golfing experience are welcome at all times. Green fees are £10 a day on weekdays and £12 at weekends and Bank Holidays. There is a licensed bar, and lunch and snacks are normally served.
Location
Afton Down, Freshwater Bay, Isle of Wight PO40 9TZ
The course is situated at the western end of the island, approximately 1/2 mile east of Freshwater, 2 miles from Yarmouth on the A3055.

RAC recommended hotels
Albion ★★★ (0983) 753631 An attractive white building on the water's edge. Most rooms have sea views and balconies.
Farringford ★★★ (0983) 752500 Gothic style mansion, once belonging to Tennyson, set in lovely grounds. Swimming pool, golf, tennis, billiards.

NEWPORT
(0983) 525076
A 9-hole undulating parkland course which is partly wooded (5704 yards, SSS 68). Practice grounds are available. Visitors who have a handicap certificate are welcome at all times except when there are major club competitions. Green fees are £9 a day. There is a bar, and meals are available by request from the Stewardess before your round. Local attractions include Carisbrooke Castle and Osborne House.
Location
St George's Down, Newport, Isle of Wight PO30 3BA
Take the A3056 Newport-Sandown road and the club is half a mile from Newport.

OSBORNE
(0983) 295421
A 9-hole undulating parkland course situated in the grounds of Osborne House (6304 yards, SSS 70). Provided you have a handicap certificate, visitors are welcome before midday except on Sunday, and between 11.30am and 3pm on Tuesday. Green fees are £10 on weekdays and £12 at weekends and Bank Holidays. Bar snacks are always available and restaurant meals by arrangement.
Location
Osborne, East Cowes, Isle of Wight PO32 6JX
Take the A3052 Newport-East Cowes road or the A3027 south of East Cowes and follow the signs for Osborne House.

RYDE
(0983) 614809
A 9-hole parkland course with wide views over the Solent (5200 yards, SSS 68). There is also a practice area. Visitors who have a handicap certificate or are members of another golf club are welcome, except on Wednesday afternoons and Sunday mornings. Green fees on application. Meals and snacks are served daily.
Location
Binstead Road, Ryde, Isle of Wight PO33 3NF
The course is situated on the A3054 very close to the town.

RAC recommended hotel
Yelf's ★★ (0983) 64062 A former coaching inn in a busy street near the ferry, pier and beach.
Ryde Castle ★★★ (0983) 63755 Attractive building on seafront enjoying good views of Solent.

SHANKLIN AND SANDOWN
(0983) 403217
An 18-hole seaside links course (5980 yards, SSS 69). Provided you have a handicap certificate, visitors are welcome. Green fees are £15 per round or day on weekdays and at weekends. 5-day tickets can also be bought for £60 for use between Monday and Friday. Bar snacks are available throughout the day and there is also a restaurant which provides lunches and evening meals.
Location
The Fairway, Sandown, Isle of Wight PO36 9PR
The club is readily accessible by car and is 12 minutes walk from Sandown station.
Broadway Park ★★★ (0983) 405214 Charming country house set in 7 acres of gardens and parkland. Swimming pool, putting, tennis, billiards.
Melville Hall ★★★ (0983) 406526 Large former residence in attractive gardens. Swimming pool, putting.

VENTNOR
(0983) 853326
A 9-hole undulating downland course which is prone to winds but which has some superb views over the sea (5752 yards, SSS 68). Visitors are welcome at all times except Sunday mornings. Green fees are £7 on weekdays and £8 at weekends and Bank Holidays. There is a bar and snacks are served.
Location
Steephill Down Road, Ventnor, Isle of Wight
The course is situated on the north west boundary of Ventnor on the A3055.

RAC recommended hotels
Royal ★★★ (0983) 852186 Hotel stands in beautiful gardens in elevated position facing the sea. Swimming pool, billiards.
Ventnor Towers ★★★ (0983) 852277 Fine Victorian white-faced house in 4 acres of cliff top gardens. Swimming pool, putting, tennis, billiards.
Madeira Hall C/H ★ (0983) 852624 Lovely country house built of local stone (1800) in 2 acres of gardens. Swimming pool, putting.

KENT

ASHFORD (KENT)
(0233) 622655
A challenging 18-hole undulating heathland course with fine views and easy walking. Provided you have a handicap certificate, visitors are welcome any day except before midday at weekends and Bank Holidays. Green fees are £16 a day or £8 if you are with a member. There is a bar and full catering facilities are available. Local attractions include Canterbury Cathedral.
Location
Sandyhurst Lane, Ashford, Kent TN25 4NT
The club is just off the A20, 1 1/2 miles north of Ashford.

RAC recommended hotels
Eastwell Manor ★★★★ (0233) 35751 A superbly furnished, restored Tudor building with some commanding fine views over parkland Facilities include tennis and billards.
Post House ★★★ (0233) 625790 A much extended, 15th century manor house with adjacent 17th century timber-clad barn; on the A28 close to the M20.
Master Spearpoint ★★★ (0233) 636863 On outskirts of town, hotel in 5 acres of natural parkland with Downland views.

BARNEHURST
(0322) 523746
A 9-hole moorland course with easy walking (5320 yards, SSS 66). Visitors of all levels are welcome on Monday, Wednesday and Friday. Green fees on application. There is a bar where snacks are served, and lunch can be arranged.
Location
Mayplace Road East, Barnehurst, Kent DA7 6JU
Go to Bexleyheath Clock Tower then on to Mayplace Road East. The golf club is on the left.

BEARSTED
(0622) 38198
A secluded 18-hole undulating parkland course with splendid views of the North Downs (6253 yards, SSS 70). There is also a practice ground and a putting green. Visitors who are members of a bona fide golf club and have a current handicap certificate are welcome on weekdays. Green feese flat parkland course (4356 yards, SSS 61). Visitors are welcome at all times. Green fees are £2 per 9 holes, £2.75 per 18 holes on weekdays and £2.75 per 9 holes, £4 per 18 holes at weekends. Light snacks are available at lunchtimes. The club is attached to the leisure complex and other facilities include swimming, squash, indoor bowls, sauna, solarium, badminton and snooker.
Location
Mill Lane, Enderby, Leicester LE9 5LH
Leave the M1/M69 at the junction 21 roundabout and Enderby is 2 miles south.

BECKENHAM PLACE PARK
081-650 2292
A pretty 18-hole municipal parkland course (5722 yards, SSS 68). The first 9 holes can be played separately. There is also a practice ground, nets and putting green. Green fees are £5.90 for 18 holes or £3.60 for 9 holes on weekdays and £8.40 for 18 holes, £4.60 for 9 holes at weekends and Bank Holidays. There is a cafe.
Location
Beckenham Hill Rd, Beckenham, Kent, BR3 2BP
1 mile from Catford, towards Bromley.

BEXLEYHEATH
081-303 6951
A 9-hole hilly parkland course (5239 yards, SSS 66). Visitors of all playing abilities are welcome between 8am and 4pm on Monday to Friday. Green fees are £8, or £4 with a member. Lunches, snacks and evening meals are available except on Monday. Local places of interest include Danson Park, and Hall Place with its gardens.
Location
Mount Row, Mount Rd, Bexleyheath, Kent DA6 8JS
The course is situated 1 mile from Bexleyheath station, off Upton Road, adjacent to the A2.

RAC recommended hotel
Crest ★★★ (0322) 526900 A modern three-storey moter hotel with all rooms en suite. Conveniently situated for the M2. Facilities include billards.

BROMLEY
081-462 7014
A short 9-hole flat parkland course with easy walking (2745 yards, SSS 69). Visitors of all playing abilities are welcome. No booking is required as it is considered to be a public course. Green fees on application. Snacks are available daily.
Location
Magpie Hall Lane, Bromley, Kent BR2 8JF
Take the A21 south from the Bromley-Farnborough road and the club is on the left.

RAC recommended hotels
Bromley Court ★★★ 081-464 5011 Large detached hotel with conference facilities. Short walk from centre.
Grianan 081-460 1795
Villa St Philomena 081-460 6311 Hotel

BROOME PARK GOLF AND COUNTRY CLUB
(0227) 831701
An 18-hole parkland course (6610 yards, SSS 72) situated in a valley in the grounds of Lord

Kitchener's country house. Visitors are welcome but you must hold a valid handicap certificate, to be presented on arrival, and starting times must be booked in advance. Green fees are £14.50 per round on weekdays and £17.50 per round on Saturday. There are no fees on Sunday. There are two bars and two restaurants all of which are open daily. Local attractions include Canterbury Cathedral.

Location
Barham, Canterbury, Kent CT4 6QX
Leave the M2 for the A2 and then turn onto the Folkestone road (A260). The club is 700 yards on the right hand-side, 8 miles from Canterbury.

CANTERBURY
(0227) 453532
An undulating 18-hole parkland course with some natural hazards (6249 yards, SSS 70). The course has been much improved and is now one of the best in the country. Provided you have a handicap certificate, visitors are welcome on weekdays. Green fees are £13 per round, £17.50 for 36 holes, and £20 after 10am on Saturday. Full catering facilities are available between Monday and Saturdays. The course is close to the city centre and the Cathedral.

Location
Scotland Hills, Canterbury, Kent CT1 1TW
The course is situated 1 mile from the town centre on the A257 road to Sandwich.

RAC recommended hotels
County ★★★★ (0227) 766266 Gabled 16th century building on historic site. Luxury city centre hotel.
Chaucer ★★★ (0227) 464427 Detached red-brick Regency building near town centre and Cathedral.
Falstaff ★★★ (0227) 462138 18th century inn with well-matched extension. In city centre.
Slatters ★★★ (0227) 463271 16th century building with modern block added. In shopping centre.
Canterbury ★★ (0227) 450551 Large detached Georgian-style house, half a mile from the city centre.
Victoria ★★ (0227) 459333 Detached red brick residence with modern extension in attractive garden.

CHERRY LODGE
(0959) 72250
An 18-hole undulating downland course with some fine views (6908 yards, SSS 73). There is a practice ground. Visitors are welcome on weekdays only. The course is not suitable for beginners. Green fees are £16 per round, £22 a day. As the guest of a member it is £7.50 on weekdays and £8.50 at weekends. There is a bar which provides snacks, and also a restaurant which serves an à la carte menu on Tuesday to Saturday. The course is close to Biggin Hill airfield.

Location
Jail Lane, Biggin Hill, Kent TN16 3AX
Leave Bromley on the A233 to Westerham. Jail Lane is on the left.

CHESTFIELD WHITSTABLE
(022 779) 2365
An 18-hole parkland seaside course (6080 yards, SSS 69). Visitors of all playing abilities are welcome on weekdays, subject to other tee reservations. Green fees are £10.50 per round, £13.50 a day on weekdays. Light meals are normally available daily and dinners by arrangement. The club is near Canterbury.

Location
103 Chestfield Road, Whitstable, Kent CT5 3LU
Take the A299 to roundabout near Chestfield station. Turn south through Chestfield village to golf course.

CHISLEHURST
081-467 2782
A pleasant undulating parkland course with some wooded areas (5128 yards, SSS 65). Provided you have a handicap certificate, visitors are welcome on weekdays. Green fees are £20 (£8 with a member). Lunch is served daily. Local attractions include Chislehurst Caves and Bromley.

Location
Camden Park Road, Chislehurst, Kent BR7 5HJ
The club is between Bromley and the junction of the A222 and Sidcup by-pass, half a mile from Chislehurst station.

COBTREE MANOR
(0622) 753276
An 18-hole undulating parkland course with trees and an interesting 6th hole over a lake (5701 yards, SSS 68). The course is a municipal one and visitors of all levels are welcome. There is a practice ground and putting green, and tuition is available by arrangement. Green fees are £5 on weekdays and £7.50 at weekends and Bank Holidays. There is a bar where food is served and meals are available by arrangement. The course is within the grounds of Cobtree Manor Museum.

Location
Maidstone, Kent ME14 3AZ
Take the M2 or M20 and turn off at the A229 where you will find the club.

CORINTHIAN
(04747) 7559
A 9-hole course with artifical greens (3118 yards, SSS 36). Visitors who have a handicap certificate are welcome on weekdays and at weekends and Bank Holidays with a member. Green fees are £7.50 daily (£5 with a member). There is a bar and meals are available by arrangement.

Location
Gaydawn Farm, Fawkham, Nr Dartford DA3 8L2
The course is situated 4 miles south of the Dartford Tunnel, 1 mile east of Brands Hatch, along Fawkham Valley Road.

RAC recommended hotel
Brandshatch Place ★★★ (0474) 872239 Red-brick Georgian mansion with good views and 12 acres of parkland. Indoor swimming pool, tennis, squash, sauna, solarium, gymnasium, billiards.
Brands Hatch Thistle ★★★★ (0474) 854900 Recently built, two-storey hotel with a motoring theme in park-like gardens.

CRAY VALLEY
(0689) 39677
An 18-hole undulating meadowland course with man-made lakes and open ditches (5624 yards, SSS 67). Visitors can play at any time during the week and beginners are particularly welcome. There are some visitors, restrictions at weekends. Green fees are £7.50 on weekdays and £10 at weekends. Catering facilities are available by arrangement. Local attractions include Hever Castle, Chartwell, and Scotney Castle.

Location
Sandy Lane, St Pauls Cray, Orpington, Kent BR5 3HY
Take the A20 to Ruxley roundabout and turn off into Sandy Lane, half a mile on the left.

DARENTH VALLEY
(09592) 2944
An 18-hole parkland course (6356 yards, SSS 71) situated in a lovely valley. Visitors of all playing abilities are welcome but you need to book at weekends and Bank Holidays. Green fees are £6 for 18 holes, £3.75 for 9 holes on weekdays and £8.75 for 18 holes, £5.50 for 9 holes at weekends. There is a restaurant and a bar where meals are served. The course is close to Sevenoaks and Lullingston Castle.

Location
Station Road, Shoreham, Kent TN14 7SA
Take the A225 Sevenoaks-Dartford road and the club is 4 miles north of Sevenoaks, 50 yards from Shoreham station.

RAC recommended hotel
Royal Oak ★★ (0732) 451109 A pleasant mellow stone hotel of medium size. The hotel is situated in the old part of the town.
Sevenoaks Park ★★ (0732) 454245 Quiet hotel with pleasant gardens in side road. Swimming pool.

DARTFORD
(0322) 23616
An 18-hole flat heathland course (5914 yards, SSS 68). Provided you have a handicap certificate and are a member of a recognised club, visitors are welcome on weekdays and at weekends with a member. Green fees are £20 on weekdays (£10 with a member). Snacks are always available, lunches by arrangement, and evening meals on Wednesday and Friday by arrangement. The club is near Brands Hatch.

Location
Dartford Heath, Dartford, Kent DA1 2TN
The course is situated on Dartford Heath, backing on to the A2, 1 mile from the Dartford Tunnel and the M25. It is 2 miles from the town centre.

DEANGATE RIDGE
(0634) 251180
A municipal 18-hole wooded parkland course (6300 yards, SSS 70). Visitors of all playing abilities are welcome at any time but it is necessary to book at weekends. There is also an 18-hole pitch and putt course. Green fees are £3.30 on weekdays and £4.65 at weekends. Lunches and dinners are served but booking is essential at weekends. Local attractions include Upnor Castle and Rochester.

Location
Hoo, Rochester, Kent ME3 8RZ
Take the A228 from Rochester to the Isle of Grain and then the road is signposted to Deangate Ridge. The club is 4 miles north east of Rochester.

EDENBRIDGE GOLF AND COUNTRY CLUB
(0732) 865097
An 18-hole gently undulating meadowland course (6643 yards, SSS 73). There is also a 9-hole beginners course and a 16-bay floodlit driving range. Visitors of all playing abilities are welcome at any time although it is advisable to book at weekends. Green fees are £10 on weekdays and £12 at weekends and Bank Holidays. Lunches and bar snacks are served daily. Other facilities at the club include fishing. Nearby attractions include Hever Castle, Penshurst Place and Chartwell.

Location
Crouch House Road, Edenbridge, Kent TN8 5LQ
From the A25 at Westerham take the B2026 to Edenbridge. As you travel north along Edenbridge High Street, 30 yards before Edenbridge Town station, turn left into Stangrove Road. At the end of the road turn right and the course will be found a short distance on the left.

FAVERSHAM
(079589) 561
A lovely 18-hole parkland course (5979 yards, SSS 69) situated in a most tranquil setting and with some superb views. During the autumn the fairways are often covered with strolling pheasants. Visitors are welcome at all times but you should be the guest of a member at the weekends. Green fees are £12 per round, £17.50 a day on weekdays and £15 per round, £20 a day at weekends. Catering facilities are available by arrangement with the Steward. Local attractions include Belmont House.

Location
Belmont Park, Faversham, Kent ME13 0HB
Leave the M2 at junction 6 and take the A251 to Faversham. Follow the A2 to Sittingbourne for half a mile and then turn left at Brogdale Road, and follow the golf club signs.

RAC recommended hotel
Thorley House C/H ★★★ (0795) 539168 Charming Georgian manor house with Regency additions standing in 16 acres of parkland close to M2 junction 6. Indoor swimming pool, putting, riding, sauna.

GILLINGHAM
(0634) 53017
An 18-hole seaside/meadowland links course (5863 yards, SSS 68). Visitors are welcome but, unless you are playing with a member, you must hold a current handicap certificate or be a member of a recognised golf club. You must be the guest of a member at weekends. Green fees are £11 per round, £16.50 a day on weekdays(£7 per round or £11 a day with a member), and £7 per round, £11 a day at weekends. Lunches and evening meals are served between Wednesday and Sunday. The course is close to Rochester with its cathedral and castle.
Location
Woodlands Road, Gillingham, Kent ME7 2BX
Take the M2 to junction 4 and turn north to the A2. Turn left towards Gillingham and the course is on the right-hand side of the road.

RAC recommended hotel
Park Hotel ★ (0634) 37737 A public house with a restaurant conveniently situated.

HAWKHURST
(05805) 2396
A 9-hole undulating parkland course (5769 yards, SSS 68). Visitors are welcome, and green fees are £8 on weekdays and £10 at weekends. Snacks are normally available. Other facilities at the club include squash.
Location
High Street, Hawkhurst, Cranbrook, Kent TN18 4JS
The course is situated on the A268 2 miles from the A21 at Flimwell, half a mile from the junction with the A229.

RAC recommended hotel
Tudor Court ★★ (0580) 752312 Georgian building situated in pleasant rural setting. Lovely garden. Putting, tennis.

HERNE BAY
(0227) 373964
An 18-hole parkland course (5466 yards, SSS 67). Visitors are welcome at all times but there are some restrictions at weekends and Bank Holidays. A handicap certificate is required at weekends. Green fees on application. Full catering facilities are available at the club, but prior notice is required by the Steward if you would like a full meal. The club is within easy access of Canterbury.
Location
Eddington, Herne Bay, Kent CT6 7PG
Take the A291 Thanet Way road to Herne Bay and the club is near the railway station.

HIGH ELMS
(0689) 59175
A municipal 18-hole parkland course (5626 yards, SSS 69). Visitors of all playing abilities are welcome at any time. Green fees are £4.40 on weekdays and £6.80 at weekends. Juniors and senior citizens pay £2.65 on weekdays and after 5pm at weekends. Full catering facilities are available.
Location
High Elms Road, Downe, Kent
Take the A21 from Bromley and, 2 miles from Farnborough Hospital, turn right at Shire Lane and then take the second left for the club.

HOLTYE
(034286) 635
A 9-hole undulating heathland course with tree-lined fairways and alternative tees (5289 yards, SSS 66). There is a large practice ground. Visitors of all playing abilities are welcome on weekdays but there are restrictions on Thursday mornings and weekend mornings. Green fees are £10 on weekdays and £12 at weekends. Snacks are normally available and meals by arrangement. Local attractions include Sheffield Park, Standen Park and Hever Castle.
Location
Holtye Common, Cowden, Edenbridge, Kent TN8 7ED
The club is on the A264 between East Grinstead and Tunbridge Wells, 5 miles from East Grinstead.

HYTHE IMPERIAL
(0303) 67554
A well-bunkered 2 x 9-hole flat seaside course (5511 yards, SSS 67). Visitors who have a handicap certificate are welcome. Green fees are £8 on weekdays (£7 with a member) and £10 at weekends (£7 with a member). The course is adjacednt to the hotel, with facilities including tennis, indoor swimming pool, squash, snooker, sauna, solarium and gymnasium. Light snacks are available at the clubhouse.
Location
Princes Parade, Hythe, Kent CT21 5RN
Turn off the M20 for Hythe and the course is at the east end of the seafront.

RAC recommended hotels
Hythe Imperial ★★★★ (0303) 67441 An impressive seafront hotel set in 52 acres, with some splendid sea views. Facilities include an indoor swimming pool, golf, putting, tennis, squash, sauna, solarium, gymnasium and billards.
Fredericks ★★★ (0303) 67279 Elegant small hotel in a beamed and gabled Edwardian building overlooking the sea. On A259 between Hythe and Folkestone.
Stade Court ★★★ (0303) 68263 A modernised hotel with some dramatic sea views. Sport facilities are shared with the Hythe Imperial hotel.

KNOLE PARK
(0732) 452150
A tough 18-hole parkland course in stately surroundings (6249 yards, SSS 70). Provided you have a handicap certificate, visitors are welcome on weekdays by appointment only. Green fees are £15 per round, £26 a day. Lunches and teas are available daily and dinners by arrangement. Local attractions include Knole House (NT).
Location
Seal Hollow Road, Sevenoaks, Kent TN15 0HJ
The club is on the north east side of Sevenoaks, down Seal Hollow road towards A25 and village of Seal.

RAC recommended hotels
Royal Oak ★★ (0732) 451109 A pleasant mellow stone hotel of medium size, situated in the old part of the town.
Sevenoaks Park ★★ (0732) 454245 A quiet hotel with pleasant gardens in a side road. This hotel is conveniently situated near Knole. Facilities include a swimming pool.

LAMBERHURST
(0892) 890241
An 18-hole undulating parkland course which crosses the river twice (6277 yards, SSS 70). Visitors are welcome at any time during the week and after midday at weekends and Bank Holidays, unless you are with a member. Green fees are £20 per round or day on weekdays and £25 per round or day at weekends. Lunches, dinners and snacks are served daily except on Monday, when only sandwiches are available.
Location
Church Road, Lamberhurst, Kent TN3 8DT
Take the A21 south from Tonbridge towards Hastings. Turn left at Church Road prior to descending the hill to Lamberhurst. The entrance to the course is immediately left on the outskirts of the village.

LANGLEY PARK
081-658 6849
An 18-hole gently undulating wooded parkland course with a lake (6488 yards, SSS 71). Visitors are welcome during the week but it is advisable to book with the Pro beforehand. Green fees are £20 per round, £25 a day. Full catering facilities are available daily. The course is within easy access of Bromley town centre.
Location
Barnfield Wood Road, Beckenham, Kent BR3 2SZ
From Bromley South station, turn left at the traffic lights into Westmoreland Road, and the clubhouse is 1½ miles on the left.

LEEDS CASTLE
(0622) 765400
A most beautiful 9-hole parkland course (2910 yards, SSS 34) situated in the grounds of Leeds Castle. There are also practice nets and a putting green. Visitors of all playing abilities are welcome at any time. Green fees are £6.95 for 9 holes. You need to book 6 days in advance. Full catering facilities are available daily. The setting is quite idyllic.
Location
Maidstone, Kent ME17 1PL
Take the M20 from Maidstone towards Ashford and turn onto the A20 at Hollingbourne. Go towards the Castle and the golf course is on the right, actually in the grounds of the Castle.

RAC recommended hotel
Great Danes ★★★ (0622) 30022 A large hotel built around a Georgian Manor house, set in 20 acres of parkland.

LITTLESTONE
(0679) 63355
A varied 18-hole seaside links course (6424 yards, SSS 71). There is also a 9-hole course (3996 yards, SSS 63). Visitors with a handicap of 20 or less are welcome on weekdays by arrangement with the Secretary, and after 3pm at weekends. Full catering facilities are available daily except Tuesday.
Location
St Andrews Road, Littlestone, New Romney, Kent TN28 8RB
Take the A20 to Ashford and turn onto the B2070 to New Romney. The club is 1 mile from New Romney.

RAC recommended hotel
Broadacre ★ (0679) 62381 Small hotel in a Georgian house set in a quiet street.

LULLINGSTONE PARK
(0959) 34542
A municipal 18-hole parkland course (6674 yards, SSS 72), and a 9-hole course (2432 yards). There is also a practice ground, putting nets and pitch and putt. Visitors of all playing abilities are welcome. Green fees are £6 on weekdays and £7.50 at weekends for 18 holes, £3.50 for 9 holes. There is a cafeteria and bar and meals are served by arrangement.
Location
Park Gate, Chelsfield, Orpington, Kent
Take the A20 to Swanley and then the B258 Daltons Road to Park Gate. The course is signposted.

MAGPIE HALL LANE
081-462 7014
A flat 9-hole public course (5538 yards, SSS 66). Visitors of all playing abilities, particularly beginners, are welcome. Bromley Club plays here. Green fees are £2.10 for 9 holes, OAPs and juniors are £1.40 on weekdays, and £3.40 for everyone at weekends. There is a bar where snacks are served.
Location
Magpie Hall Lane, Bromley BR2 8JF

The course is situated on the A21 off Bromley Common.

RAC recommended hotels see Bromley.

MID-KENT
(0474) 52387
A well-kept 18-hole parkland course with easy walking (6206 yards, SSS 70). Provided you have a handicap certificate visitors are welcome on weekdays and at weekends with a member. Green fees on application. Lunches are served daily except Monday and dinners by arrangement.
Location
Singlewell Road, Gravesend, Kent DA11 7R?
The club is off the A2 south of Gravesend, at the A227 turn-off by the Tollgate Motel.

RAC recommended hotels
Clarendon Royal ★★ (0474) 363151 Typical Georgian building overlooking Thames estuary.
Tollgate Manor ★★ (0474) 357655 Modern motel units adjoin restaurant and bars.

NEVILL
(0892) 25818
A well-wooded 18-hole open parkland course with lots of heather and gorse (6336 yards, SSS 70). Visitors with a handicap certificate are welcome on weekdays. Green fees are £18 per day on weekdays, £24 a day at weekends. Lunch is served at the club daily. The course is close to Tunbridge Wells and other attractions include Chartwell and Scotney Castle (NT).
Location
Benhall Mill Road, Tunbridge Wells, Kent TN2 5JW
The course is situated 1 mile south east of Tunbridge Wells off Forest Road. The club is signposted.

RAC recommended hotels
Spa ★★★★ (0892) 20331 An impressive Georgian hotel in its own grounds. Facilities include an indoor swimming pool, tennis, sauna, solarium and a gymnasium.
Calverley ★★★ (0892) 26455 A fine early 19th-century hotel overlooking Caverley Gardens at rear.
Royal Wells Inn ★★★ (0892) 511188 Small detached hotel in lovely listed building. Overlooks the town.
Mount Edgcumbe House ★★ (0892) 26823 Attractive Victorian house built on an outcrop of Sandstone on the Common.
Russell ★★ (0892) 544833 Well-appointed small hotel, situated close to the shopping centre.
Wellington ★★ (0892) 542911 Regency style hotel overlooking the Common. Sauna, solarium, gymnasium.

NORTH FORELAND
(0843) 62140
A pretty 18-hole downland seaside championship course (6382 yards, SSS 70). Visitors are welcome on weekdays but not at weekends or Bank Holidays. A handicap certificate is required. Green fees are £13 per round, £17 a day on weekdays and £7 per round at weekends (summer), and £8 per round, £16 a day on weekdays and £13 per round at weekends (winter). There is a bar and dining room and meals are available during the day.
Location
Convent Road, Broadstairs, Kent CT10 3PU
The club is 1 mile from Broadstairs station, near North Foreland Lighthouse.

RAC recommended hotels
Castle Keep ★★★ (0843) 65222 A hotel standing in its own grounds situated on the cliff edge. Facilities include a swimming pool and snooker.
Castlemere ★★★ (0843) 61566 Large detached red brick building overlooking Western Esplanade.
Royal Albion ★★ (0843) 6807 A family-run terraced Georgian hotel overlooking Broadstairs Bay.

POULT WOOD
(0732) 364039
A municipal 18-hole wooded parkland course with some water hazards (5569 yards, SSS 67). There is also a practice ground. Visitors are welcome on a pay as you play scheme, but if you are registered at the golf shop you can book in advance. Green fees are £4.75, juniors and OAPs £2.70 on weekdays, and £7 at the weekend. There is a bar and restaurant with views over the course.
Location
Higham Lane, Tonbridge, Kent TN11 9QR
The club is 2 miles north of Tonbridge town centre off the A227.

RAC recommended hotel
Rose and Crown ★★★ (0732) 357966 A modernised coaching inn with original oak beams.

PRINCES
(0304) 611118
A championship seaside links course with 27 holes (3 loops of 9, 'Dunes', 'Himalayas', 'Shore') (6599-7000 yards, SSS 72, 71, 73). Visitors of all playing abilities are welcome. Green fees are £18 per round, £20 a day on weekdays, and £24 per round, £26 a day at weekends. Breakfast, lunch and dinner available every day although prebooking is advisable. There is also a bar where a buffet is served at lunchtime and in the evening. Light snacks are served throughout the day. The course is near the Cinque Ports, Sandwich and Deal.
Location
Sandwich Bay, Sandwich, Kent CT13 9QB
The club is 4 miles from Sandwich through the town centre.

RAC recommended hotels
Bell ★★★ (0304) 613388 A 17th-century brick-built hotel with a modern extension, picturesquely situated by the Quay.
Beachcomber (0843) 221616 Hotel overlooking Westbrook Bay near Margate.
Sutherland House (0304) 362853 Victorian

house on A258 Deal to Sandwich Road.

ROCHESTER AND COBHAM PARK
(047 482) 3411
A challenging 18-hole undulating parkland course (6467 yards, SSS 71). Provided you have a handicap certificate, visitors are welcome during the week, and at weekends before 5pm with a member. Green fees are £18 per round, £25 per 2 rounds. Lunch, tea, dinner and snacks are available, although lunch should be ordered in advance. Local attractions include the Medway towns, Rochester, 'Dickens' Country, and Cobham village.
Location
Park Lane by Rochester, Kent ME2 3UL
From the A2, three miles west of Rochester turn south on the B2009 towards Sole Street and follow signs to the clubhouse.

ROYAL CINQUE PORTS
(0304) 374007
An 18-hole seaside links course (Championship 6744 yards, Medal 6407 yards, SSS 71). Visitors are welcome on weekdays although a handicap certificate of 22 is required. Green fees are £15 per round, £22 a day. Hot bar snacks are available between Monday and Saturday, and meals on Sunday by arrangement. The course is close to Canterbury.
Location
Sandwich, Kent CT13 9PB
Take the A258 from Sandwich, and in Upper Deal take the Middle Deal Road. Then turn left into Albert Road, then Western Road and onto Golf Road. If you are travelling from Dover, take the A258 via the seafront and Godwin Road.

ROYAL ST GEORGE'S
(0304) 613090
An 18-hole links course (6857 yards, SSS 74). Visitors are welcome between Monday and Friday but a handicap certificate is required. Green fees are £25 per round or £35 a day. There is a snack bar and dining room where dinners can be arranged. The course is convenient for Canterbury.
Location
Sandwich, Kent CT13 9PB
The club is 1 mile from Sandwich on the road to Sandwich Bay.

RAC recommended hotel see Princes.

RUXLEY
(0689) 71490
An open 18-hole undulating parkland course with man-made lakes (4885 yards, SSS 65). The course is public and visitors of all playing abilities are welcome on weekdays from 7am and at weekends after 11.30am. There is a floodlit driving range. Green fees are £6 on weekdays and £9 at weekends. Breakfast and lunch are served daily.
Location
Sandy Lane, St Pauls Cray, Orpington, Kent BR5 3HY
Follow the A20 to Ruxley roundabout and turn off into Sandy Lane.

RAC recommended hotel
Crest ★★★ (0322) 526900 A modern motor hotel with all rooms en suite. It is conveniently situated for the M2 and facilities include billards.

ST AUGUSTINE'S
(0843) 590333
An 18-hole parkland course with dykes running across the course (5138 yards, SSS 65). Visitors who have a handicap certificate are welcome on weekdays and after 10.30am at weekends. Green fees are £14 on weekdays and £16 at weekends and Bank Holidays. Full catering facilities are available daily except Monday, but prior booking is essential. Local attractions include Sandwich, Deal Castle and Dover.
Location
Cottingham Road, Cliffsend, Ramsgate, Kent CT12 5JN
The club is 2 miles south west of Ramsgate. Take the B2048 road to Sandwich and turn right at the hoverport. Then turn left at Viking Caravan Club and right at the Post Office. The entrance is next to the railway bridge.

RAC recommended hotel
Savoy ★★ (0843) 592637 Small hotel in former terraced houses; offers modern amenities.

SENE VALLEY
(0303) 268513
An 18-hole undulating downland course on two levels overlooking the sea (6320 yards, SSS 70). Visitors are welcome but it is advisable to telephone ahead to check availability. The course is 'appreciated by experts'. Green fees are £16 on weekdays and £20 at weekends and Bank Holidays. There is a bar and restaurant and catering is available daily except Monday. Local attractions include Saltwood Castle.
Location
Sene, Folkestone, Kent CT18 8BL
Take the A20 from Ashford or Folkestone and turn south at the B2065 by the Channel Tunnel works. The club is signposted.

RAC recommended hotels in Hythe.
Hythe Imperial ★★★★ (0303) 67441 An impressive seafront hotel set in 52 acres, with some splendid sea views. Facilities include an indoor swimming pool, golf, putting, tennis, squash, sauna, solarium, gymnasium and billards.
Fredericks ★★★ (0303) 67279 Elegant small hotel in a beamed and gabled Edwardian building overlooking the sea.
Stade Court ★★★ (0303) 68263 A modernised hotel with some dramatic sea views. This hotel shares sport facilities with Hythe Imperial hotel.

SHEERNESS
(0795) 662585
An 18-hole seaside course with easy walking but with several water hazards (6500 yards, SSS 71). There is also a practice area. Provided you have a handicap certificate visitors are welcome on weekdays and at weekends with a member. Green fees are £10 on weekdays and £15 at weekends. Full catering facilities are available daily except Monday. The bird reserve is close by.
Location
Power Station Road, Sheerness, Kent ME12 3AE
The club is 9 miles from Sittingbourne. Follow the A249 then the A250 towards Sheerness.

SHORTLANDS
081-460 2471
A 9-hole meadowland course with a brook (5261 yards, SSS 66). Visitors are welcome if invited by a member at weekends. Green fees are £7 on weekdays, and £10 with a member. Full catering facilities are available daily.
Location
Meadow Road, Shortlands, Bromley BR2 0PB
The car park and entrance to the club are in Ravensbourne Avenue, off the main Beckenham-Bromley Road.

RAC recommended hotel see Bromley.

SIDCUP
081-300 2150
A 9-hole parkland course (yards, SSS) with easy walking and some natural water hazards. Provided you have a handicap certificate, visitors are welcome. Green fees are £10 per round. Meals and snacks are available during bar opening hours or by arrangement at other times.
Location
7 Hurst Road, Sidcup, Kent DA15 9AE
Take the A20 and then the A211 to the centre of Sidcup. Turn north on A222; the club is 400 yards north of Sidcup station.

SITTINGBOURNE AND MILTON REGIS
(0795) 842261
An 18-hole undulating wooded course with some good views (6121 yards, SSS 69). Visitors who have a handicap certificate or a letter of introduction from another golf club are welcome except on Wednesday and at weekends. Green fees are £13 per 18 holes and £23 per 36 holes. Full catering facilities are available between Tuesday and Saturday. Local attractions include the Barge Museum at Sittingbourne.
Location
Wormdale, Newington, Sittingbourne, Kent ME9 7PX
Leave the M2 at junction 5 for the A249. The club is approximately 1 mile north of here.

RAC recommended hotel
Coniston ★★★ (0795) 72131 A red-brick hotel with a modern extension, conveniently situated on the A2.

SUNDRIDGE PARK
081-460 278
Two 18-hole courses; the East, a wooded parkland course (6410 yards, SSS 71) and the hillier West

course with some fine views (6028 yards, SSS 69). Provided you have a handicap certificate, visitors are welcome on weekdays only. Green fees are £25 a day. There is a dining room and full catering facilities are available. Snacks are also served.

Location

Garden Road, Bromley, Kent BR1 3NE

Take the A2212 from Bromley and the club is approximately 1 mile along the road.

RAC recommended hotel see Bromley.

TENTERDEN
(05806) 3987

A pretty 9-hole undulating parkland course (5141 yards, SSS 65). Visitors are welcome on weekdays, and green fees are £10 per round or £15 a day. Light meals are served daily and other meals by arrangement. Local attractions include the Kent & East Sussex Railway, Bodiam Castle and Sissinghurst Gardens.

Location

Woodchurch Road, Tenterden, Kent PN30 7DR

The club is 1 mile east of Tenterden on the B2067, off the A28.

RAC recommended hotel

White Lion ★★ (05806) 2921 An attractive old inn, situated in the centre of a picturesque market town.

TUDOR PARK GOLF AND COUNTRY CLUB
(0622) 35891

An 18-hole parkland course (6000 yards, SSS 69). Visitors who have a handicap certificate are welcome on weekdays. Green fees are £20 on weekdays and £25 at weekends. The club is attached to the Country Club and there are two restaurants and bars which offer a full service. Other facilities include accommodation, swimming pool, squash, snooker and tennis. Leeds Castle is only 2 miles away.

Location

Ashford Road, Bearsted, Maidstone, Kent ME14 4NQ

Leave the M20 at junction 8 and turn right onto the Ashford Road (A20) 3 miles from Maidstone centre.

TUNBRIDGE WELLS
(0892) 23034

An open undulating 9-hole course with plenty of heather and gorse (4684 yards, SSS 62). Visitors who are accredited handicap certificate holders are welcome on weekdays. Green fees are £15 per round (£5.50 with a member) or £20 a day.

Location

Langton Road, Tunbridge Wells TN4 8XH

The club is adjacent to the Spa Hotel and garage.

RAC recommended hotels

Spa ★★★★ (0892) 20331 An impressive Georgian hotel in its own grounds. Facilities include an indoor swimming pool, tennis, sauna, solarium and a gymnasium.

Royal Wells Inn ★★★ (0892) 511188 A small detached hotel in a lovely listed building overlooking the town.

Mount Edgcumbe House ★★ (0892) 26823 Attractive Victorian house built on an outcrop of sandstone on the Common.

Russell ★★ (0892) 544833 Well-appointed small hotel; situated close to shopping centre.

Wellington ★★ (0892) 542991 A Regency style hotel overlooking the Common. Facilities include a sauna, solarium and a gymmnasium.

WALMER AND KINGSDOWN
(0304) 373256

An 18-hole undulating downland course situated on the cliff top with some lovely views (6465 yards, SSS 71). There is also an 18-hole pitch and putt course. Visitors are welcome on weekdays and after midday at weekends. Green fees on application. Full catering facilities are available. Local attractions include Walmer Castle and Dover Castle.

Location

The Leas, Kingsdown, Deal, Kent CT14 8EP

The club is situated off the A258, 2 miles south of Deal.

WESTGATE AND BIRCHINGTON
(0843) 31115

A flat 18-hole seaside links course with good walking (4926 yards, SSS 64). Visitors of all playing abilities are welcome but you must be a member of a recognised club. Green fees are £10 on weekdays and £12 at weekends. There is a bar and catering facilities can be arranged. Canterbury is 10 miles away and the club is convenient for both the seaside resort at Broadstairs and the Channel ports.

Location

Domneva Road, Westgate-on-Sea, Kent CT8 8LT

The course is on the A28 between Westgate-on-Sea and Birchington, a mile from Westgate station.

RAC recommended hotel

Ivyside ★★ (0843) 31082 A family seaside hotel attractively situated on seafront. Facilities include indoor and outdoor swimming pools, squash, sauna, solarium, billiards.

WEST KENT
(0689) 51323

An 18-hole undulating meadowland course (6392 yards, SSS 70). Visitors are welcome on weekdays if you have a letter from the Secretary or a current handicap certificate. Green fees are £17.50 per round, £23 a day. Full catering facilities are available daily except Monday. Biggin Hill airfield is next door to the club and other local attractions include Charles Darwin's house and a Wild Life Trust area.

Location

West Hill, Downe, Orpington, Kent BR6 7JJ

Take the A21 to Orpington and head for Downe village.

WEST MALLING
(0732) 844785

There are two parkland courses here, both with streams running through; the 'Spitfire' (6142 yards, SSS 70) and the 'Hurricane' (6011 yards, SSS 70). Visitors are welcome mid-week and after midday at weekends. Green fees are £12 per round, £16 a day on weekdays and £16 at weekends. Full catering facilities available. Other facilities at the club include snooker, squash and table tennis. The club is within easy access of Leeds Castle.

Location

London Road, Addington, Maidstone, Kent ME19 5AR

Take the A20 from London and, 8 miles west of Maidstone, turn left at the Greenaway Hotel.

WHITSTABLE AND SEASALTER
(0227) 272020

A 9-hole seaside links course (5276 yards, SSS 63). Visitors of all playing abilities are welcome on weekdays and also at weekends with a member. Green fees are £10 (£5 with a member). Bar snacks are available. The course is close to the seafront of this resort.

Location

Collingwood Road, Whitstable, Kent CT51 1EB

From the A299 Thanet Way turn off at Long Reach roundabout and drive down Borstal Hill. Pass under the railway bridge and take the second left into Nelson Road, and second left again along an unmade road.

WILDERNESSE
(0732) 61199

A tight, heavily wooded parkland course (6478 yards, SSS 72). Visitors who have a recognised handicap certificate are welcome on weekdays by prior arrangement. Green fees are £20 per round, £27.50 a day on weekdays. Lunches and teas are available except on Tuesday. Local attractions include Knole House and the lovely surrounding Kent countryside.

Location

Seal, Sevenoaks, Kent TN15 OJE

Take the A25 from Sevenoaks towards Maidstone and turn right at the sign in the village of Seal.

RAC recommended hotels see Knole.

WOODLANDS MANOR
(09592) 3806

A varied 18-hole undulating parkland course (5858 yards, SSS 69). There is also a 6-acre practice ground. Visitors are welcome on weekdays and at weekends after 1pm if you have a handicap certificate. The course is not suitable for complete beginners. Green fees on application. There is a restaurant and bar which is open daily. The many local attractions include Knole House (NT) Chartwell, Hever Castle, Leeds Castle and

Ightham Moat. Brands Hatch is only 3 miles away.
Location
Tinkerpot Lane, Sevenoaks, Kent TN15 6AB
Leave the M25 at junction 3 and take the 'Brands Hatch' sign on the A20. Turn off the A20 at Portobello Inn, West Kingsdown, or alternatively take the A225 4 miles north east of Sevenoaks.

RAC recommended hotels
Brands Hatch Place ★★★ (0474) 872239 A red brick Georgian mansion with good views and 12 acres of parkland. Facilities include an indoor swimming pool, tennis, squash, sauna, solarium, gymnasium and billiards.
Brands Hatch Thistle ★★★★ (0474) 854900 Recently built, two-storey hotel with a motoring theme in park-like gardens.

WROTHAM HEATH
(0732) 884800
A 9-hole hilly heathland course with lots of woods and heather (5959 yards, SSS 68). Provided you have a handicap certificate, visitors are welcome on weekdays and also at weekends if you are with a member. The course is not suitable for beginners. Green fees are £15 per round or £20 a day. There is a bar, and light lunches, teas and dinners are served by arrangement. Leeds Castle is within easy access.
Location
Seven Mile Lane, Comp, Sevenoaks, Kent TN15 8QZ
The club is on the B2016 south of the junction with the A20.

RAC recommended hotel
Post House Hotel ★★★★ (0732) 883311 A modern hotel of distinctive design at junction of M20 and M26. Facilities include an indoor swimming pool, sauna, solarium and a gymnasium.

LANCASHIRE

ACCRINGTON AND DISTRICT
(0254) 32734
An 18-hole moorland course (5954 yards, SSS 69). Visitors are welcome at any time. Green fees are £8 (£5 with a member) on weekdays and £10(£8 with a member) at weekends. There is a newly extended clubhouse with good facilities, and lunches and evening meals are served.
Location
New Barn Farm, Devon Avenue, West End, Oswaldtwistle, Accrington, Lancs BB5 4LR
The course is situated on the A679, 5 miles from Blackburn.

ALT
(0704) 530435
An 18-hole links parkland course (5939 yards, SSS 69). The course is a public one and visitors are welcome at all times, but you should book first. Green fees are £5 on weekdays and at weekends. There is a bar and restaurant with full facilities.
Location
Park Road, West Southport PR9
The course is north of Marine Lake.

RAC recommended hotels
Prince Of Wales ★★★★ (0704) 36688 A large gracious Victorian hotel.
Royal Clifton ★★★ (0704) 33771 A striking white faced hotel in a central position. Well-equipped bedrooms. Facilities include an indoor swimming pool, sauna, solarium and a gymnasium.
Scarisbrick ★★★ (0704) 43000 Centrally-placed hotel with attractive arcade frontage. Facilities include disco bars.
Balmoral Lodge ★★ (0704) 544298 Edwardian residence with well-equipped bedrooms. Close to town centre. Sauna.
Bold ★★ (0704) 32578 Victorian commercial hotel set on attractive tree-lined Lord Street.
Lockerbie House ★★ (0704) 65298 Converted brick-built villa in quiet residential area. Billiards.
Metropole ★★ (0704) 36836 Attractive former private house under proprietor's personal supervision.
Stutelea ★★ (0704) 44220 Pleasant three-storey Victorian building with half acre garden. Indoor swimming poool, sauna, solarium, gymnasium.

ASHTON AND LEA
(0772) 726480
An 18-hole semi-parkland course with water features and some pleasant walking (6289 yards, SSS 70). There is a practice ground. Visitors of all playing abilities are welcome on weekdays, but you should telephone beforehand if you wish to play at weekends. Green fees are £10 on weekdays and £15 at weekends. Full catering facilities are available daily. Local attractions include Houghton Towers.
Location
Tudor Avenue, off Blackpool Road, Lea, Preston, Lancs PR4 0XA
Take the A583 from Preston towards Blackpool and turn right opposite the Pig and Whistle, 3 miles from Preston.

RAC recommended hotels see Preston.

BACUP
(0706) 873170
A 9-hole mainly flat meadowland course (5652 yards, SSS 67). Visitors of all playing abilities are welcome on weekdays except Tuesday and also at weekends after competitions have been played. Green fees on application. Full catering facilities are available.
Location
Maden Road, Bacup, Lancs OL13 8HY
Take the A671 south from Burnley and the club is half a mile from Bacup centre.

BAXENDEN AND DISTRICT
(0254) 34555
A 9-hole moorland course (5740 yards, SSS 68). Visitors are welcome at all times. Green fees are £6 on weekdays and £8 at the weekends. There is a dining room where bar snacks and meals are served daily except Tuesday. Helmshore Textile Museum is 3 miles away and the surrounding moorland countryside is lovely for walks.
Location
Top o th'Meadow, Baxenden, Nr Accrington BB5 2EA
The course is situated off the A680 via Langford Street, about 2 miles south east of Accrington.

BEACON PARK
(0695) 622700
An 18-hole undulating hilly parkland course (5996 yards, SSS 69) situated on the side of Ashurst Beacon Hill overlooking Skelmersdale . There is also a large practice ground. Visitors are welcome at any time. Green fees are £2.90 on weekdays and £3.95 at weekends. Bar meals are served during normal opening times and other meals by arrangement.
Location
Beacon Lane, Dalton, Up Holland, Wigan, Lancs WN8 7RU
Leave the M6 at junction 26 and take the A577. The club is signposted from the centre of Up Holland.

RAC recommended hotel
Holland Hall ★★ (0695) 624426 Attractive building offering all the comforts of a country hotel.

BENTHAM
(0468) 61018
A 9-hole undulating meadowland course (5752 yards, SSS 69) with some magnificent views of the Yorkshire Peaks and Lake District Hills. Visitors of all playing levels are welcome at any time. Green fees are £6.50 per day (£3.25 with a member) on weekdays and £5 (£4.50 with a member) at weekends and Bank Holidays. There are limited catering facilities, by arrangement. Ingleton waterfalls and the Lake District are within easy access for walking.
Location
Robin Lane, Bentham, Lancaster LA2
Leave the M6 at junction 34 and the club is 13 miles east on the B6480, between Lancaster and Settle.

RAC recommended hotel see Lancaster.

BLACKBURN
(0254) 51122
An 18-hole undulating meadowland course with superb views (6100 yards, SSS 70). Provided you have a handicap certificate, visitors are welcome on weekdays. There is a practice ground. Green fees are £12 (£3.50 with a member) on weekdays and £15 (£4 with a member) at weekends and Bank Holidays. Full catering facilities are available daily except Monday.
Location
Beardwood Brow, Blackburn, Lancs BB2 7AX
The course is situated in the west end of the town, off Revidge Road. From the Moat House Hotel on the A677, proceed to the traffic lights and turn left at the Dog Hotel, and then left again to the clubhouse.

RAC recommended hotels
Blackburn Moat House ★★★ (0254) 64441 An attractive modern gabled building surrounded by lawns.
Mytton Fold Farm ★★★ (0254) 240662 Attractively built in local stone, a country hotel in delightful surroundings.

BLACKPOOL NORTH SHORE
(0253) 51017
An 18-hole undulating parkland course (6442 yards, SSS 71). Visitors of all playing abilities can play at most times although there are some restrictions on Thursday and at weekends. Green fees are £14 on weekdays and £16 at weekends. Full catering facilities are available.
Location
Devonshire Road, Blackpool FY2 0RD
You will find the club on the A587 north of the town centre, just behind the North Promenade.

RAC recommended hotels
Imperial ★★★★ (0253) 23971 Majestic hotel in commanding promenade position; elegant public rooms. Indoor swimming pool, sauna, solarium.
Pembroke ★★★★ (0253) 23434 A large modern hotel on the seafront in 5 acres of its own grounds. Facilities include an indoor swimming pool, sauna and a solarium.
Savoy ★★★ (0253) 52561 Large and impressive well-equipped hotel on promenade.
Brabyns ★★ (0253) 54263 Brick-built hotel with mullioned windows and a sun loggia. Close to North Shore Promenade.
Carlton ★★ (0253) 28966 Prominent Victorian hotel overlooking quieter North Promenade; family run.
Claremont ★★ (0253) 293122 Largely modernised family-run hotel on seafront. Many facilities.
Cliffs ★★ (0253) 52388 Well-positioned on promenade, an updated 1930s hotel. Indoor swimming pool, squash, sauna, gymnasium, billiards.
Gables Balmoral ★★ (0253) 45432 Family-run hotel with distinctive facade. Conveniently near Promenade.
Headlands ★★ (0253) 41179 Privately-owned hotel on prominent corner site near beach with coastal views. Solarium, billiards.
Kimberley ★★ (0253) 41184 Well-appointed, attractive terrace building with sun loggia in quiet area. Billiards.
Revill's ★★ (0253) 25768 Privately-owned family-run hotel on North Promenade. Near town centre. Billiards.

Ruskin ★★ (0253) 24063 Well-run hotel with elegant 'art-deco' style public rooms; close to Winter Gardens.
Sheraton ★★ (0253) 52723 Red-brick four-storey hotel in central position on Queens Promenade; panoramic sea views. Indoor swimming pool, sauna, solarium.
Stretton ★★ (0253) 25688 Three-storey building with glass sun lounge overlooking sea near Tower. Solarium.
Warwick ★★ (0253) 42192 Modern hotel enjoying panoramic sea views. Indoor swimming pool, solarium.
Sunray (0253) 51937 Owner-run hotel just off Queen's Promenade.

BLACKPOOL-STANLEY PARK
(0253) 33960
An 18-hole parkland course (6060 yards, SSS 69). Visitors are welcome at any time. Green fees are £4.25 on weekdays and £5 at weekends. Full catering facilities are available daily except Tuesday.
Location
North Park Drive, Blackpool, Lancs FY3 8LS
The course is situated 1½ miles east of the town centre.

BURNLEY
(0282) 21045
An 18-hole moorland meadowland course (5891 yards, SSS 69). Visitors are welcome midweek and on Sunday but there are restrictions on Saturday. Green fees are £8 on weekdays and £10 at weekends and Bank Holidays. Snacks and full meals are available daily.
Location
Glen View, Burnley BB11 3RW
From the junction of the A56 and A646, turn right after 300 yards into Glen View Road.

RAC recommended hotels
Keirby ★★★ (0282) 27611 A centrally placed modern purpose built hotel with ballroom, banqueting and conference facilities. There is also a gymnasium.
Oaks ★★★ (0282) 414141 A modernised Victorian mansion in landscaped gardens. Facilities include an indoor swimming pool, squash, sauna, solarium, gymnasium and billiards.
Rosehill House ★★ (0282) 53931 A secluded elegant stone-built manor retaining many interesting original features.

CHORLEY
(0257) 480263
A municipal 18-hole undulating course (6277 yards, SSS 71). Provided you have a handicap certificate, visitors are welcome but it is advisable to ring the Pro beforehand. Green fees are £11 (£5.50 with a member) on weekdays and £20 (£5 with a member) at weekends and Bank Holidays. Full catering facilities are available. From the clubhouse, there are some panoramic views over seven counties.
Location
Hall o'th'Hill, Heath Charnock, Chorley, Lancashire PR6 9HX
The course is situated on the A673, 100 yards south of the junction with the A6, at the Skew Bridge traffic lights.

RAC recommended hotel
Hartwood Hotel ★★ (025 72) 69966 A privately owned Georgian style hotel situated one mile from the town centre

COLNE
(0282) 863391
A flat 9-hole scenic moorland course (5961 yards, SSS 69). Visitors of all playing abilities, including beginners, are welcome at any time except on competition days, and it is advisable to telephone first. Green fees are £7 on weekdays and £9 at weekends and Bank Holidays. Catering facilities are available by arrangement. The club is close to Pendle Witch country and Brontë country.
Location
Law Farm, Skipton Old Road, Colne, Lancashire BB8 7EB
The club is 1½ miles east of Colne, between the A56 and the A6068 on the Lothersdale road, three quarters of a mile from Colne Cricket Club.

DARWEN
(0254) 701287
An 18-hole moorland course (5752 yards, SSS 68). Visitors are welcome on weekdays and, if you book in advance, also at weekends. Green fees are £6.90 (£4.60 with a member) on weekdays and £9.20 (£5.75 with a member) at weekends. Full catering facilities are available daily except Monday. Local attractions include Darwen Tower.
Location
Winter Hill, Darwen, Lancashire BB32 OLB
The course is situated 1½ miles from Darwen town centre, off the A666 Bolton-Blackburn road.

RAC recommended hotel
Whitehall ★★★ (0254) 71595 An attractive stone-built hotel in secluded grounds one mile from the town centre. Facilities include an indoor swimming pool, sauna, solarium and snooker

DEAN WOOD
(0695) 622219
A varied 18-hole undulating parkland course (6129 yards, SSS 70). Visitors of all playing abilities are welcome on weekdays, and also at weekends if you are introduced by a member. Green fees are £12 on weekdays and £15 at weekends. Full catering facilities are available daily. Local attractions include Wigan Pier.
Location
Lafford Lane, Up Holland, Skelmersdale, Lancashire WN8 0QZ
Leave the M6 at exit 26, signposted for Southport, and follow the A577 to Up Holland. The club is on the first right after the church.

DUXBURY PARK
(02572) 65380
An 18-hole wooded parkland course with some water hazards (6390 yards, SSS 70). As this is a municipal course, visitors of all playing abilities are welcome. Telephone bookings are accepted. Green fees are £2.70 on weekdays and £4.80 at weekends. Dining facilities can be arranged. The club is close to Ashley Hall. The club is within easy access of Fleetwood and Blackpool.
Location
Wyreside, Knott End, Blackpool FY6 0AA
Leave the M55 at exit 3 and take the A585 road towards Fleetwood, turning off at the B2588 to Knott End. Alternatively you can take the passenger ferry from Fleetwood across the River Wyre to Knott End.

LANCASTER
(0524) 751247
An attractive 18-hole undulating parkland course (6422 yards, SSS 72) with natural hazards and easy walking, situated on the Lune estuary Provided you have a handicap certificate, visitors are welcome but there are restrictions at weekends. Green fees on application. Full catering facilities are available. Local attractions include Lancaster Castle.
Location
Ashton Hall, Ashton-with-Stodday, Lancaster LA2 0AJ
The club is 2½ miles south west of Lancaster on the A588.

RAC recommended hotel
Post House ★★★★ (0524) 65999 A modern hotel standing in 10 acres of grounds. Facilities include an indoor swimming pool, sauna, solarium and a gymnasium.

LANSIL
(0524) 39269
An 18-hole meadowland/parkland course (5608 yards, SSS 67). Visitors who have a handicap certificate are welcome but not before 1pm on Sunday. Green fees are £4 on weekdays and £6 at weekends. Light refreshments are served. Local attractions include fishing and the bowling greens.
Location
Caton Road, Lancaster, Lancashire LA1 3PE
The club is 1 mile east of Lancaster town centre on the A683.

LEYLAND
(0772) 421359
A flat 18-hole meadowland course (6105 yards, SSS 69). Visitors can play at any time on weekdays and also at weekends if you are the guest of a member. Green fees are £8. Full catering facilities are available daily except Monday.
Location
Wigan Road, Leyland, Lancashire PR2 5UD
Leave the M6 at exit 28 and turn right to the traffic lights, then right onto the A49. The course is located 1 mile on the left.

RAC recommended hotel
Penguin ★★★ (0772) 422922 A luxurious modern motorway hotel.

LONGRIDGE
(077478) 3291
An 18-hole moorland course (5800 yards, SSS 68) with some wonderful views of the Ribble valley, The Fylde, Trough of Bowland and the Welsh Mountains. Visitors of at least intermediate standard are welcome at all times. Green fees are £10 on weekdays and £12 at weekends and Bank Holidays. Full catering facilities are available daily except Monday.
Location
Fell Barn, Jeffrey Hill, Longridge, Preston, Lancashire PR3 3TU
Take the B6243 from Preston to Longridge. Climb through the village and continue climbing for $1^1/_2$ miles. The club is situated on the fell.

LYTHAM GREEN DRIVE
(0253) 737390
An attractive 18-hole parkland course (6159 yards, SSS 69). Provided you have a handicap certificate visitors are welcome mid week. Green fees are £15 on weekdays (£6 with a member). Full catering facilities are available. The club is close to the holiday resort of Blackpool.
Location
Ballam Road, Lytham, Lancashire FY8 4LE
The club is three-quarters of a mile from Lytham town centre.

RAC recommended hotels
Clifton Arms ★★★★ (0253) 739898 A handsome building, largely 19th century, overlooking the green and with fine sea views. Facilities include sauna and solarium.
Chadwick ★★★ (0253) 720061 Converted dwelling houses, modernised with extensive sun lounges facing estuary. Indoor swimming pool, sauna, solarium.
Dalmeny ★★★ (0253) 712236 An ultra-modern glass-fronted extension to this hotel overlooks the sea. Indoor swimming pool, squash, sauna, solarium, billiards.
Grand Osprey ★★★ (0253) 721288 Splendidly restored impressive hotel situated on South Promenade overlooking bay.
Bedford ★★ (0253) 724636 Three converted residences form pleasant family-run hotel enjoying central position. Sauna, solarium, gymnasium.
Fernlea ★★ (0253) 726726 Spacious three-storey modern hotel on seafront. Indoor swimming pool, squash, sauna, solarium, gymnasium, billiards.
Glendower ★★ (0253) 723241 Privately-owned Victorian style building situtaed on North Promenade. Indoor swimming pool, solarium, gymnasium.
St Ives ★★ (0253) 720011 Light modern two-storey family hotel, offering entertainment. Indoor swimming pool, sauna, solarium, billiards.
Lindum ★ (0253) 721534 Pleasant family hotel situated on the promenade. Sauna, solarium.

MARSDEN PARK
(0282) 67525
A hilly 18-hole meadowland course (5806 yards, SSS 68). The course is a municipal one and visitors of all playing abilities are welcome. Green fees are £3.85 on weekdays and £4.95 at weekends. There is a bar and snacks are served on Tuesday and Friday evening, and all day at weekends.
Location
Townhouse Road, Nelson, Lancashire BB9 8GD
The club is just off the M65 or A56, 4 miles north of Burnley heading towards Colne.

MORECAMBE
(0524) 412841
An 18-hole seaside/parkland course with some splendid views over Morecambe Bay (5766 yards, SSS 67). Visitors who are members of a bona fide golf club are welcome by arrangement. Green fees on application. Full catering facilities are available daily except Monday, when bar snacks only are served. The club is conveniently situated at the 'Gateway to the Lake District'.
Location
Bare, Morecambe, Lancashire LA4 6AJ
Leave the M6 at junctions 34 or 35, Lancaster or Carnforth, and follow the signs to Morecambe. The course is on the seafront.

RAC recommended hotels
Elms ★★★ (0524) 411501 A white-painted hotel with a spacious lounge and dining-room. Situated in its own pleasant grounds.
Headway ★★★ (0524) 412525 On promenade with sea view, attractive hotel specialising in family holidays.
Midland (0524) 417180 Hotel of outstanding 1930s architecture, commanding panoramic view of bay.
Strathmore ★★★ (0524) 421234 An attractive hotel overlooking Morecambe Bay and facing the Lakeland Hills.
Clarendon ★★ (0524) 410180 19th century building of character in central position overlooking bay.

NELSON
(0282) 64583
A windy 18-hole moorland course with trees and some good views (5967 yards, SSS 69). Visitors are welcome on weekdays except Thursday afternoons and also at weekends and Bank Holidays by prior application. Green fees are £10 (£5 with a member) on weekdays and £12 (£6 with a member) at weekends. Lunches and evening meals are served daily except Monday. The club is within easy access of the Yorkshire Dales.
Location
King's Causeway, Brierfield, Nelson, Lancashire BB9 0EU
The course is situated on the A682, 2 miles north of Burnley and 1 mile from junction 12 of the M65.

RAC recommended hotels see Burnley.

ORMSKIRK
(0695) 72112
A quietly situated 18-hole parkland course with lots of silver birch (6333 yards, SSS 70). Provided you have a handicap certificate, visitors are welcome but advanced booking is advised. Green fees are £16 on Monday, Tuesday, Thursday and Friday, and £19 on Wednesday, Sunday and Bank Holidays. Full catering facilities are available except on Mondays. Local attractions include Marton Mere Nature Reserve.
Location
Cranes Lane, Lathom, Ormskirk, Lancashire L40 5UJ
The course is situated 2 miles east of Ormskirk.

PENWORTHAM
(0772) 744630
A fine 18-hole parkland course with tree-lined fairways (5915 yards, SSS 68). Visitors of all playing abilities are welcome on weekdays except Tuesday. Green fees are £12 (£5 with a member) on weekdays and £14.50 (£6.05 with a member) at weekends and Bank Holidays. Lunches and evening meals are served daily except Monday. The club is on the banks of the River Ribble.
Location
Blundell Lane, Penwortham, Preston, Lancashire PR1 0AX
The club is off the A59, 1 mile west of Preston on the main Southport-Liverpool Road, at the Penwortham traffic lights.

RAC recommended hotels see Preston.

PLEASINGTON
(0254) 22177
A secluded and scenic 18-hole undulating woodland/parkland course (6417 yards, SSS 71) situated in some lovely moorland country . Visitors who have a handicap certificate are welcome on Monday, Wednesday and Friday by prior arrangement. Green fees are £15 on weekdays and £20 at weekends and Bank Holidays. Full catering facilities are available daily. Local attractions include Houghton Towers.
Location
Pleasington, Blackburn, Lancashire BB2 5JF
Leave Blackburn south west on the A674 until you come to a crossroads, then turn right to Pleasington.

RAC recommended hotels see Blackburn.

POULTON-LE-FYLDE
(0253) 892444
A 9-hole meadowland course with easy walking (5958 yards, SSS 69). Visitors are welcome at all times. Green fees are £2.50 on weekdays and £3.50 at weekends and Bank Holidays. Lunches are served daily. The club is situated near the old village of Poulton.
Location
Myrtle Farm, Breck Road, Poulton-Le-Fylde, Lancashire FY6 7HT
The course is situated 3 miles east of Blackpool, 2 miles from Poulton via Breck Road.

PRESTON
(0772) 700011
A pleasant 18-hole undulating parkland course with groups of trees (6233 yards, SSS 71). Provided you have a handicap certificate, visitors are welcome by arrangement on weekdays and occasionally at weekends. Green fees are £12 on weekdays and £15 at weekends. The prices are reduced if you are with a member. There is a good dining room where breakfasts, lunches, dinners and snacks are served daily. The course is close to the town centre.
Location
Fulwood Hall Lane, Fulwood, Preston, Lancashire PR2 4DD
You will find the club north of Preston off Watling Street Road.

RAC recommended hotels
Broughton Park ★★★★ (0772) 861727 An Edwardian country house with a purpose built extension including a leisure complex.
Barton Grange ★★★ (0772) 862551 A unique combination of a modern hotel with an international garden centre. Facilities include an indoor swimming pool.
Crest ★★★ (0772) 59411 Centrally placed modern hotel with conference facilites.
Novotel Summit ★★★ (0772) 31333 Modern purpose-built hotel (French chain) conveniently near motorway junction. Swimming pool, billiards.
Swallow Trafalgar ★★★ (0772) 877351 Modern hotel situated in open countryside close to Ribble valley. Indoor swimming pool, squash, sauna, solarium, gymnasium.
Tickled Trout ★★★ (0772) 877671 Modern purpose-built hotel halfway between London and Glasgow. Indoor swimming pool, sauna, solarium.
Dean Court ★★ (0772) 35114 Well-maintained hotel in a converted private house with an attractive Italian patio garden.

RISHTON
(0254) 884442
A 9-hole undulating meadowland course (6094 yards, SSS 69). Visitors are welcome on weekdays and also at weekends and Bank Holidays if you are with a member. Green fees are £6, or £3 if you are with a member. Full catering facilities are available by arrangement.
Location
Eachill Links, Rishton, Blackburn, Lancashire BB1 4HG
The club is 3 miles east of Blackburn. Take the A679, and halfway to Accrington, turn off at the roundabout near the Red Lion public house.

ROCHDALE
(0706) 43818
An 18-hole parkland course which provides some good golf (5981 yards, SSS 69). Visitors of all playing abilities are welcome. Green fees on application. Coffee, lunches and evenings meals are served daily except Monday. Local attractions include the original Co-op shop in Rochdale and working textile mills in Helmshaw, Rossendale.
Location
Edenfield Road, Bagslate, Rochdale OL11 5YR
Leave the M62 at exit 20 for the A680 and the club is approximately 3 miles from here.

RAC recommended hotels
Norton Grange ★★★ (0706) 30788 Turreted and gabled Victorian building standing in 14 acres of pleasant grounds. New bedroom extension.

ROSSENDALE
(0706) 213056
A challenging 18-hole moorland/meadowland course (6267 yards, SSS 70). Visitors of all playing abilities are welcome on weekdays and Sunday. Green fees are £9 on weekdays and £11 on Sunday. There is a bar and full catering facilities are available daily except Monday.
Location
Edwood Lane Head, Haslingden, Rossendale, Lancashire BB4 6LH
The club is approximately 16 miles north of Manchester off the A56, or via the M66.

ROYAL LYTHAM & ST ANNE'S
(0253) 724206
A famous 18-hole championship links course (6673 yards, SSS 73). Visitors are welcome on weekdays only, and a handicap certificate and letter of introduction are required. Green fees are £30 per round or £40 a day. There is a restaurant and bar and also accommodation for men only in Dormy House.
Location
Links Gate, St Anne's on Sea, Lytham St Anne's, Lancashire FY8 3LQ
The club is 1 mile from the centre of St Anne's on Sea.

ST ANNE'S OLD LINKS
(0253) 723597
A fine 18-hole seaside links course (6616 yards, SSS 72) which has staged the Open Championship It is a testing course with a famous 9th hole. There is also a practice ground. Visitors are welcome on weekdays but there are some restrictions on Tuesday and Sunday. No visitors may play on Saturday. A handicap certificate is required. Green fees are £15 on weekdays and £18 at weekends. The club facilities are particularly good, and lunch, tea and dinner is served daily.
Location
Highbury Road, St Annes, Lytham St Anne's, Lancashire FY8 2LD
The club is on the A584 coastal road towards St Annes. Turn left at the traffic lights just past the holiday camp and the club is 400 yards on the left.

RAC recommended hotels
Clifton Arms ★★★★ (0253) 739898 Handsome building overlooking sea.
Dalmeny ★★★ (0253) 712236 Well-extended hotel overlooking sea. Indoor swimming pool, squash.
St Ives ★★ (0253) 720011 A light modern family hotel offering entertainment. Indoor swimming pool, sauna, solarium and billiards.
Lindum ★ (0253) 721534 Pleasant hotel on the Promenade.

SHAW HILL GOLF AND COUNTRY CLUB
(02572) 69221
A picturesque 18-hole parkland course with seven lakes (6467 yards, SSS 71). Provided you have a handicap certificate, visitors are welcome at any time. Green fees are £14 on weekdays and £18 at weekends. The course is attached to the hotel with all its facilities, including a restaurant with full à la carte menu and a bar where snacks are served.
Location
Whittle-Le-Woods, Chorley, Lancashire PR6 7PP
The club is on the A6, 1½ miles north of Chorley.

RAC recommended hotel
Shaw Hill Golf & Country Club ★★★ (025 72 69221) A magnificent Georgian mansion set in 110 acres of rolling parkland. A full range of leisure activities are available include putting, sauna, solarium and billiards.

SILVERDALE
(0524) 701300
A 9-hole hilly heathland course with some rock outcrops providing the hazards (5262 yards, SSS 67). Visitors are welcome at all times except when there are competitions. No handicap certificate is required but players are expected to dress correctly. Sunday is Men's day and Wednesday is Ladies Day. Green fees are £6 on weekdays (£4 with a member) and £10 at weekends and Bank Holidays (£6 with a member). Catering facilities are available by arrangement with the Secretary.
Location
Red Bridge Lane, Silverdale, Carnforth, Lancashire LA5 0SP
Leave the M6 at junction 35. The course is opposite Silverdale station via Carnforth and Warton.

SPRINGFIELD
(0706) 49801
An 18-hole parkland course with the River Roch flowing through (5209 yards, SSS 66). Visitors of all playing abilities are welcome at any time. Green fees are £2.80 on weekdays and £3.20 at weekends and Bank Holidays.
Take the A58 out of Rochdale and continue along Bolton Road. The club is on the left.
Location
Springfield Park, Bolton Road, Rochdale, Lancashire

RAC recommended hotel see Rochdale.

TODMORDEN
(0706) 812986
An excellent 9-hole moorland course with good greens, narrow fairways and a testing 9th (5818 yards, SSS 68). There are some good views of the Pennines. Visitors are welcome on weekdays and on Sunday. Green fees on application. Full catering facilities are available daily except Monday. The course is situated on a Celtic burial ground and the clubhouse itself was built in 1764. Other attractions are Calderdale Way, Hebden Bridge and Brontë Castle.
Location
Rive Rocks, Cross Stone Road, Todmorden, Lancashire
Turn off the A646 Halifax road, climb Cross Stone Road and bear left at the top the hill, three quarters of a mile from the town centre.

TOWNELEY
(0282) 38473
An 18-hole parkland/meadowland course (5862 yards, SSS 68). Visitors of all playing abilities are welcome at any time. Green fees are £3.50 on weekdays and £4 at weekends and Bank Holidays. There is a café where lunch and bar snacks are available daily except on Monday.
Location
Todmorden Road, Burnley, Lancashire BB11 3ED
Leave Burnley town centre, following the Halifax and Todmorden signs. Turn right at the traffic lights near Burnley football ground and the club is approximately 1 mile on the left.

RAC recommended hotel see Burnley.

TUNSHILL
(0706) 342095
A challenging 9-hole moorland course (2902 yards, SSS 68). Visitors of all playing abilities are welcome on weekdays except Tuesday evenings and, with special permission, at weekends. Green fees on application. Catering facilities are available by prior arrangement.
Location
Kiln Lane, Milnrow, Lancashire
The club is situated alongside the M62 near junction 21. Follow Kiln Lane out of Milnrow town centre and continue along a narrow lane to the clubhouse.

WHALLEY
(025482) 2236
A 9-hole parkland course (5953 yards, SSS 69). Visitors are welcome at all times except Tuesday between 12.30pm and 4pm (Ladies Day), and Saturday between April and September. Green fees are £7 on weekdays and £10 at weekends and Bank Holidays. There is a bar, and lunches, teas and dinners are served daily except Monday.

Location
Portfield Road, Whalley, Blackburn, LancashireBB6 9DR
Take the A59 to Whalley and turn south of the town towards Accrington.

RAC recommended hotel see Blackburn.

WIGAN
(0257) 421360
A 9-hole parkland course with hard walking (6058 yards, SSS 69). Visitors are welcome on weekdays except Tuesday, which is Ladies Day. Full catering facilities are available. Snack lunches and evening meals are available daily. The club is adjacent to Haigh Country Park.
Location
Arley Hall, Haigh, Wigan WN1 2UH
The club is situated on the B5239, 3½ miles north of Wigan. Go through Standish and turn left at the traffic lights on Canal Bridge, opposite the Crawford Arms public house.

RAC recommended hotels
Brockett Arms ★★★ (0942) 46283 A well-appointed modern hotel in pleasant suburban surroundings.
Kilhey Court ★★★ (0257) 423083 Victorian mansion of character set in 10 acres of grounds with many rhododendrons.
Bel Air ★★ (0942) 41410 Privately-owned and run former private house.
Bellingham ★★ (0942) 43893 A former private house in a residential area on the A49.
Grand ★★ (0942) 824583 Black and white commercial hotel near town centre. Privately-owned.

WILPSHIRE
(0254) 48260
An 18-hole moorland course overlooking the Ribble Valley (5911 yards, SSS 69). Provided you have a handicap certificate, visitors are welcome on weekdays. Green fees are £12 (£4 with a member) on weekdays and £15 (£5 with a member) at weekends. Lunches are served daily except on Monday. There is a snooker room at the club.
Location
72 Whalley Road, Wilpshire, Blackburn, Lancashire BB1 9LF
The club is on the A666, 4 miles east of Blackburn.

RAC recommended hotels see Blackburn.

LEICESTERSHIRE

BIRSTALL
(0533) 674322
An 18-hole parkland course (5988 yards, SSS 69). Provided you have a handicap certificate, visitors are welcome on weekdays. Green fees are £15. There is a bar and catering facilities are normally available except on Monday. Local attractions include Leicester Cathedral and Leicester Castle remains.
Location
Station Road, Birstall, Leicester LE4 3BB
The course is situated 3 miles north of Leicester, just off the A6.

CHARNWOOD FOREST
(0509) 890259
A 9-hole undulating heathland course with hard walking (6202 yards, SSS 70). There are no bunkers but there are some granite outcrops which can cause problems. Visitors who have a handicap certificate are welcome. Green fees are £9 on weekdays and £12 at weekends and Bank Holidays. Full catering facilities are available on most days except Monday and Thursday when snacks only are served.
Location
Breakback Lane, Woodhouse Eaves, Loughborough, Leics LE12 8TA
Leave the A6 south east for the B591 at Quorndon and follow the signs to Woodhouse Eaves.

RAC recommended hotels
Cedars ★★★ (0509) 214459 Attractive two storey building with modern bedroom wing. Situated off A6. Swimming pool, sauna, solarium.
Great Central ★★ (0509) 263405 Victorian hotel of character-'railway hotel' furnished with railway memorabilia.
King's Head ★★★ (0509) 233222 A large Georgian style hotel of brick and stone in town centre.

COSBY
(0533) 864759
An 18-hole parkland course (6277 yards, SSS 70). Visitors are welcome on weekdays and with a member at weekends, although you must have a current handicap certificate. Green fees on application. There is a bar and full catering facilities are available except on Monday. There is a snooker room at the club house.
Location
Chapel Lane, Cosby, Leics LE9 5RG
Take the A546 or A426 out of Leicester and in Cosby village take the Broughton road.

RAC recommended hotel
Charnwood ★★ (0533) 8622 A detached Victorian building with two upper storeys situated in residential village of Warborough.

ENDERBY
(0533) 849388
A 9-hole flat parkland course (4356 yards, SSS 61). Visitors are welcome at all times. Green fees are £2 per 9 holes, £2.75 per 18 holes on weekdays and £2.75 per 9 holes, £4 per 18 holes at weekends. Light snacks are available at lunchtimes. The club is attached to the leisure complex and other facilities include swimming, squash, indoor bowls, sauna, solarium, badminton and snooker.
Location
Mill Lane, Enderby, Leicester LE9 5LH
Leave the M1/M69 at the junction 21 roundabout and Enderby is 2 miles south.

GLEN GORSE
(0533) 714159
A pretty 18-hole parkland course with some interesting holes and a stream running through (6641 yards, SSS 72). Visitors are welcome on weekdays and at weekends if you are with a member. The club does prefer visitors to have a handicap certificate. Snack meals, sandwiches and full meals are normally available except on Monday.
Location
Glen Road, Oadby, Leicester LE2 4RRF
Take the A6 from Leicester towards Market Harborough. The club is on the right-hand side just past Oadby.

RAC recommended hotel see Oadby.

HINCKLEY
(0455) 615124
An 18-hole parkland course with several lakes and gorse-lined fairways (6592 yards, SSS 71). There is a practice ground for members. Visitors who have a handicap certificate are welcome on weekdays except Tuesday, and on Sunday after 4pm. Green fees on application. Lunch is served daily and evening meals are available every day except Sunday.
Location
Leicester Road, Hinckley, Leics LE10 3DR
The club is situated 1 mile north east of Hinckley on the A47.

RAC recommended hotels
Fernleigh ★★ (0455) 47011 Modern hotel set beside A47 right in the middle of Earl Shilton.
Sketchley Grange ★★★ (0455) 634251 A former private residence in a quiet situation in 4 acres of parkland.
Hinckley Island ★★★ (0455) 61512 A modern hotel with a leisure complex situated beside a small lake. Facilities include indoor swimming pool, fishing, sauna, solarium, gymnasium and billiards.

HUMBERSTONE HEIGHTS
(0533) 761905
An 18-hole municipal parkland course (6444 yards, SSS 71) with some scenic views over Leicester . There is also a practice area and a 9-hole pitch and putt course. Visitors are welcome at any time. Green fees are £3.50 on weekdays and £4.50 at weekends. Juniors can play for £2. There is a bar where snacks are served, and also a restaurant. Local attractions include Bradgate Park.
Location
Gipsy Lane, Leicester LE5 0TV
The club is 3 miles east of the city centre on the A47, opposite Towers Hospital.

RAC recommended hotels see Leicester.

KIBWORTH
(0533) 792301
A flat, wooded 18-hole parkland course (6282 yards, SSS 70) with easy walking. A brook crosses a number of fairways . Visitors are welcome on weekdays and at weekends if you are accompanied by a member. Green fees are £11 a day (£4 with a member) and £12 a day (£5 with a member) at weekends and Bank Holidays. Full catering facilities are available daily.
Location
Weir Road, Kibworth Beauchamp, Leics LE8 0LP
Leave Leicester on the A6 south east for 8 miles until you come to Kibworth.

KIRBY MUXLOE
(0533) 393457
An 18-hole undulating parkland course with a lake (6303 yards, SSS 70). Visitors are welcome on weekdays only and at weekends with the Captain's permission only. A current handicap certificate is required. Green fees on application. There is a bar and catering facilities are available daily except Monday.
Location
Station Road, Kirby Muxloe, Leicester LE9 9EN
The club is 4 miles west of Leicester on the A47. Leave the M1 at exit 21.

RAC recommended hotels see Leicester.

LEICESTERSHIRE
(0533) 738825
An attractive 18-hole undulating parkland course with a stream running through (6312 yards, SSS 70). Visitors of all playing abilities are welcome. Green fees are £15 (£6 with a member) on weekdays and £17 at weekends and Bank Holidays. Lunch and tea is served daily during the summer months.
Location
Evington Lane, Leicester LE5 6DJ
Leave Leicester on the A6 and make for Evington village in the SE district of the city. It is 2 miles from the city centre.

RAC recommended hotels in Leicester
Grand ★★★★ (0533) 555599 Traditional city centre hotel with large foyer and modern decorations.
Holiday Inn ★★★★ (0533) 531161 Modern purpose-built hotel with eight storeys. Indoor swimming pool, sauna, gymnasium.
Belmont ★★★ (0533) 544733 In quiet tree-lined street, several houses combined into an imposing hotel.
Leicester Forest Moat House ★★★ (0533) 394661 Modern hotel of brick construction. Set in own grounds in suburbs.
Leicestershire Moat House ★★★ (0533) 719441 Light modern four storey hotel attached to older building near racecourse.
Penguin ★★★ (0533) 620471 A large modern purpose-built hotel in the city centre.
Post House ★★★ (0533) 630500 A modern hotel situated south of Leicester city centre.
St James ★★★ (0533) 510666 Modern city centre above public car park. Sauna, solarium, gymnasium.

LINGDALE
(0509) 890035
A 9-hole undulating parkland course with a trout stream flowing through (6114 yards, SSS 72). Visitors of all playing abilities are welcome. Green fees are £9 per day and £12 at weekends. There is a clubhouse and full catering facilities are available daily.
Location
Joe Moores Lane, Woodhouse Eaves, Leics LE12 8TF
Leave Loughborough S on the A6 and turn off at the B591 for Woodhouse Eaves. Alternatively leave the M1 at exit 23 for the B5300.

RAC recommended hotels see Charnwood.

LONGCLIFFE
(0509) 239129
A wooded 18-hole undulating heathland course (6551 yards, SSS 71) with some granite outcrops which form natural hazards, and plenty of gorse and bracken. The course has recently been redesigned and a particularly testing 9th hole introduced. Provided you have a handicap certificate, visitors are welcome on weekdays and at weekends with a member. Green fees are £17 a day (£5 with a member). Meals are available by arrangement with the Stewardess except on Monday.
Location
Shell's Nook Lane, Nanpantan, Loughborough, Leicester LE11 3YA
Leave the M1 at junction 23 and follow the A512 towards Loughborough. After a quarter of a mile turn right into Snells Nook Lane and the golf course is three quarters of a mile on the right.

RAC recommended hotels see Charnwood.

LUTTERWORTH
(0455) 552532
A hilly 18-hole parkland course with open fairways and the River Swift running through (5570 yards, SSS 67). Visitors of all playing abilities are welcome on weekdays and with a member at weekends. Green fees are £10. Full catering facilities are available daily. The club is situated close to Leicester.
Location
Rugby Road, Lutterworth, Leics LE17 5HN
Leave the M1 at exit 20 for the A426 and the club is a half mile from the motorway.

RAC recommended hotels
Denbigh Arms ★★★ (0455) 553537 A completely refurbished old building of great character set in the centre of town.
Moorbarns ★★ (045 55) 2237 Modern complex with motel style bedrooms, lounges and restaurant. Swimming pool.

MARKET HARBOROUGH
(0858) 463684
A 9-hole parkland course with extensive views across the surrounding countryside (6080 yards, SSS 69). There is a practice ground. Visitors of all playing levels except beginners are welcome on weekdays and with a member at weekends. Green fees are £8. Full catering facilities are available daily.
Location
Oxendon Road, Market Harborough, Leics LE16 9HB
Take the A508 from Market Harborough for 1 mile south.

RAC recommended hotels
Three Swans ★★★ (0858) 66644 A 16th century hotel in the town centre, recently enlarged and refurbished.
Grove ★★ (0858) 64082 On southern fringe of town. Modern motel with large function room.

MELTON MOWBRAY
(0664) 62118
A fine 9-hole flat downland course with easy walking (6200 yards, SSS 70). Visitors who are members of a bona fide golf club are welcome. Green fees are £9 on weekdays and £12 at weekends. Bar meals are available by arrangement. Local attractions include Ann of Cleves' House and the Carnegie Museum.
Location
Waltham Road, Thorpe Arnold, Melton Mowbray, Leics LE14 4SD
The club is on the A607 between Melton Mowbray and Grantham, 2 miles north west of Melton Mowbray.

RAC recommended hotels
Stapleford Park C/H ★★★★ (057 284) 522 An elegant hotel in a large, mainly 18th century country house set in 500 acres of park with a lake. Marvellous views. Tennis, fishing, riding.
Sysonby Knoll ★★ (0664) 63563 Large early 20th century red-brick house with modern bedroom wing. Swimming poool
Westbourne House (0664) 63556

OADBY
(0533) 700215
A municipal 18-hole moorland course (6228 yards, SSS 70). There is a practice ground and coaching is available. Visitors of all playing abilities are welcome at all times. Green fees are £4 on weekdays (£3 for OAPs and juniors) and £3 at weekends (£2.50 for OAPs and juniors). Catering facilities are available on application to the Steward.
Location
Leicester Road, Oadby, Leicester LE2 4AB
Take the A6 south from Leicester and the club is 1 mile from the City boundary, near Leicester Racecourse.

RAC recommended hotel
Leicestershire Moat House ★★★ (0533) 719441 Light modern four storey hotel attached to older building near racecourse.

RAF NORTH LUFFENHAM
(0780) 720041
A 9-hole meadowland course (5998 yards, SSS 69). Visitors are welcome but you must be accompanied by a member. Green fees are £4 on weekdays and £5 at weekends and Bank Holidays. Light refreshments are available. Local attractions include Rutland Water and Stamford.
Location
North Luffenham, Oakham, Leics LE15 8RL
To reach the club follow the signposts for RAF North Luffenham from the A606. The RAF station is close to Rutland Water.

RAC recommended hotels in Oakham
Normanton Park C/H ★★★ (0780) 720315 Elegant hotel in converted Georgian Clock Tower, Coach House and stables in 4 acres of grounds leading down to Rutland Water.
Boultons ★★ (0572) 722844 Once a medieval hunting lodge and part Georgian, a listed building in a pleasant garden on south side of town. Hotel being extended; new bedrooms, bar, restaurant and function room.

ROTHLEY PARK
(0533) 302809
A particularly picturesque 18-hole parkland course (6487 yards, SSS 71). Visitors who have a handicap certificate are welcome but you must be a member of a recognised club. Players must wear smart dress. Green fees are £16 on weekdays and £19 at weekends and Bank Holidays. Full catering facilities are available except on Monday.
Location
Westfield Lane, Rothley, Leicester LE7 7LH
Take the A6 6 miles north of Leicester and the club is situated to the west of the road.

RAC recommended hotel
Rothley Court ★★★ (0533) 374141 A medieval manor set in parkland with a temple. There are modern rooms in an annexe.

SCRAPTOFT
(0533) 419000
A pleasant 18-hole meadowland course (6146 yards, SSS 70). Provided you have a handicap certificate, visitors are welcome. Green fees are £12 on weekdays and £16 at weekends and Bank Holidays. Meals are served daily except on Monday during the winter season. The club is within easy access of Leicester.
Location
Beeby Road, Scraptoft, Leicester LE17 9SJ
Turn off the main A47 Leicester-Peterborough road, towards Scraptoft, at Thurnby.

RAC recommended hotels in Leicester.

ULLESTHORPE
(0455) 209023
An 18-hole meadowland course (6206 yards, SSS 70). Provided you have a handicap certificate, visitors are welcome on weekdays. Green fees are £9.50. There is a bar where snacks are available,and also a restaurant. The club is within easy access of Coventry, Leicester and Stratford on Avon.
Location
Frolesworth Road, Ullesthorpe, Lutterworth, Leics LE17 5BZ
Take the A5 N and turn off at the B577 to Claybrooke and Ullesthorpe and follow the signs to the course.

RAC recommended hotels see Lutterworth.

WESTERN PARK
(0533) 872339
A flat, wooded 18-hole parkland course with open fairways (6532 yards, SSS 71). Visitors are welcome and clubs may be hired. Green fees are £3.50 on weekdays and £4.50 at weekends. It is advisable to book at the weekend. Full catering facilities are available daily.
Location
Scudmore Road, Braunstone Frith, Leicester LE3 1UQ
Take the A47 from Leicester and the club is 2 miles west of the city centre.

RAC recommended hotels
Leicester Forest Moat House ★★★ (0533) 394661 Modern hotel of brick construction. Set in grounds in suburbs.
Post House ★★★ (0533) 630500 A modern hotel situated south of Leicester city centre.

WHETSTONE
(0533) 861424
A small, flat 18-hole meadowland course (5795 yards, SSS 68). There is also a driving range and putting green. Visitors are welcome but not on Saturday and Sunday mornings. Green fees are £6 on weekdays and £7.50 at weekends. There is a bar which serves snacks.
Location
Cambridge Road, Cosby, Leicester LE8 3NW
The club is situated near the south boundary of Leicester. If you are travelling on the M1 leave it at junction 21.

RAC recommended hotel see Leicester.

WILLESLEY PARK
(0530) 414596
An 18-hole undulating parkland/heathland course (6304 yards, SSS 70). Provided you have a handicap certificate visitors are welcome, but you must also be a member of a bona fide club. Green fees are £15 on weekdays and £18 at weekends. Full catering facilities are available except on Monday. Local attractions include Calke Abbey.
Location
Tamworth Road, Ashby-de-la-Zouch, Leics LE6 5PF
The club is on the A453, approximately 1½ miles from the centre of Ashby-de-la-Zouch south towards Tamworth.

RAC recommended hotel
Royal Osprey ★★★ (0530) 412833 A charming Regency-styled hotel situated on A453 near the centre of town.

LINCOLNSHIRE

BELTON PARK
(0476) 67399
A wooded 18-hole parkland course situated in a deer park (6420 yards, SSS 71). It is a 27-hole championship course made up of three 9-hole combinations. There are also two large practice areas. Visitors of all playing abilities are welcome. Green fees are £12 per round, £16 a day on weekdays and £15 per round, £19 a day at weekends. Snacks, lunches and dinners are available daily. The club is adjacent to Belton House (NT), Isaac Newton's birthplace and, as well as the Deer Park, there is a Canadian Geese Reserve.
Location
Belton Lane, Londonthorpe Road, Grantham, Lincs NG31 9SH
The club is 2 miles from Grantham. Take the A607 from Grantham and follow the signposts to Sleaford and Lincoln. Turn right at the traffic lights at the Park signposted Londonthorpe, and the golf club is 1 mile on the left.

RAC recommended hotels
Angel & Royal ★★★ (0476) 65816 A 13th century building with unique stonework in the bar, situated in the town centre.
George ★★★ (0476) 63286 An imposing historic hotel(1760) situated in a main thoroughfare.
Kings ★★★ (0476) 590800 A pleasant brick building set back from the road.
Garden (acclaimed) (0476) 62040

BLANKNEY
(0526) 20263
A quiet 18-hole parkland course (6402 yards, SSS 70). There is a large practice area. Visitors are welcome on weekdays with no restrictions but you should book ahead for weekend play. Green fees are £13 a day, £11 per round. Full catering facilities are available and bar snacks are also served.
Location
Blankney, Lincoln, Lincs LN4 3AZ
To reach the club take the B1188 10 miles south from Lincoln, 1 mile past Metheringham.

BOSTON
(0205) 350589
An 18-hole parkland course with water hazards (5825 yards, SSS 68). Visitors of all playing abilities are welcome. Green fees are £10 on weekdays and

£15 at weekends and Bank Holidays. Full catering facilities are available daily except Wednesday, when only bar snacks are served.
Location
Cowbridge, Horncastle Road, Boston, Lincs PE22 7EL
The club is situated 2 miles north of Boston on the B1183. Look for the sign on the right when crossing the first bridge.

RAC recommended hotels
New England ★★★ (0205) 65255 A well maintained hotel in the town centre.
White Hart ★★★ (0205) 64877 A Regency building close to the centre of the town and overlooking the River Whitham.

BURGHLEY PARK
(0780) 53789
A short, flat 18-hole parkland course with fine greens (6200 yards, SSS 70). There is also a generous practice ground and lessons are available. Visitors of all playing abilities are welcome on weekdays and after 3pm at weekends and Bank Holidays. Green fees are £15, or £6 if you are with a member. Lunches and teas are served daily and dinners can be arranged for societies. The course is in the grounds of Burghley House.
Location
St Martins Without, Stamford, Lincs PE9 3JX
Leave the A1 at the roundabout south of Stamford and the course is the first gateway on the right.

RAC recommended hotels
Crown ★★ (0780) 63136 A stone-built hotel situated in the centre of this ancient town.
Garden House ★★★ (0780) 63359 18th century terraced hotel with spacious accommodation. Refurbished.
George of Stamford ★★★ (0780) 55171 A famouse 16th-century coaching inn offering modern amenities.
Lady Anne's ★★★ (0780) 53175 A dignified stone built house situated in residential area of town. Tennis, billiards.

CANWICK PARK
(0552) 22166
An 18-hole parkland course (6257 yards, SSS 70). Visitors are welcome on weekdays. Green fees are £5 on Monday, £7 on other weekdays and £10 at weekends. Lunches and evening meals are served daily except Monday. Local attractions include Lincoln Cathedral.
Location
Canwick Park, Washingborough Road, Lincoln LN4 1EF
Leave Lincoln on the A158 and the course is 2 miles S of the city centre.

RAC recommended hotels see Lincoln.

CARHOLME
(0522) 23725
An 18-hole parkland course with some good views. The prevailing winds can make the course interesting (6114 yards, SSS 69). Visitors are welcome on weekdays and Saturday. Green fees on application. Lunches, snacks and sandwiches are served daily except on Monday. Local attractions include Lincoln Cathedral and Castle.
Location
Carholme Road, Lincoln LN1 1SE
Leave Lincoln on the A57 north and the club is 1 mile from the city centre.

RAC recommended hotels see Lincoln.

GAINSBOROUGH
(0427) 3088
An attractive 18-hole flat parkland course (6504 yards, SSS 71). There is a putting green and a floodlit driving range. Visitors are welcome at any time but it is advisable to book for the weekend. Green fees are £10 per round on weekdays, £15 at weekends. You can also buy a £12 day ticket. There is a restaurant with carvery, bar and coffee shop. Places of local interest include Clumber Park (NT), Sherwood Forest and Gainsborough Old Hall, an Elizabethan house.
Location
Thonock, Gainsborough DN21 1PZ
The club is situated 1 mile north east of Gainsborough between the A159 and A631.

RAC recommended hotel
Hickman Hill ★★ (0427) 3639 An interesting 16th-century former school building in own grounds. Facilities include a solarium.

LINCOLN
(042 771) 721
An 18-hole undulating meadowland course with easy walking (6400 yards, SSS 70). Provided you have a handicap certificate and a letter of introduction, visitors are welcome. Green fees are £10 per round, £14 a day on weekdays and £12 per round, £15 a day at weekends. Meals are served by arrangement. Local attractions include Lincoln Cathedral.
Location
Torksey, Lincoln LN1 2EG
The club is situated off the A156, 12 miles north west of Lincoln.

RAC recommended hotels
White Hart ★★★★ Historic hotel, dating to c1750, and boasting charming modern orangery.
Eastgate Post House ★★★ (0522) 20341 Modern hotel in old city in elevated position near to Cathedral.
Four Seasons ★★★ (0673) 60108 Modern hotel situated in rural area 5½ miles north east of Lincoln.
Moor Lodge ★★★ (0522) 791366 Medium-sized early 20th century hotel in attractive village setting. 4½ miles south east of city.
Washingborough Hall C/H ★★★ (0522) 790340 Dignified Georgian mansion standing in 3 acres of fine grounds near to Lincoln. Swimming pool.
Barbican ★★ (0522) 543811 An early Victorian city-centre hotel furnished in period style.
Castle ★★ (0522) 538801 17th century stone built hotel situated on elevated ground adjacent to castle.
Hillcrest ★★ (0522) 510182 High up, close to the Cathedral, a Victorian former rectory with splendid views over the lower town.
Loudor ★★ (0522) 680333 Conveniently situated on A1434 in North Hykeham, West of Lincoln, a large house pleasantly converted into a hotel.

LOUTH
(0507) 603681
An 18-hole undulating parkland course with fine views (6502 yards, SSS 71). Visitors who are members of a bona fide club are welcome. Green fees are £8 per round, £10 a day on weekdays and £10 per round, £12 a day at weekends. Lunches and bar snacks are served daily.
Location
Crowtree Lane, Louth, Lincs LN11 9LJ
Travelling from Lincoln or Gainsborough, turn right at the Trout Farm on the outskirts of Louth. From Sleaford turn left by the Grammar School and the course is situated in Hubbard Hills, 1 mile outside Louth.

RAC recommended hotel
Priory (Acclaimed) (0507) 602930

LUFFENHAM HEATH
(0780) 720205
An 18-hole undulating heathland course (6254 yards, SSS 70) with plenty of bushes and gorse, situated in a conservation area for flora and fauna. Visitors who have a handicap certificate are welcome by prior arrangement. Green fees are £20 on weekdays and £25 at weekends and Bank Holidays. Full catering facilities are available by arrangement.
Location
Ketton, Stamford, Lincs PE9 3UU
Turn off the A47 at Morcott for the B6121 and the club is situated 6 miles south west of Stamford, by Fosters Bridge.

RAC recommended hotel
Normanton Park C/H ★★★ (0780) 720315 Elegant hotel in converted Georgian Clock Tower, Coach House, and stables in 4 acres of grounds leading down to Rutland Water.

MARKET RASEN AND DISTRICT
(0673) 842416
A pretty 18-hole wooded moorland course (6043 yards, SSS 69). There is also a practice ground. Visitors of all playing abilities are welcome on weekdays and with a member at weekends. Green fees on application. Lunch is available daily except Monday. The club is near the racecourse.
Location
Legsby Road, Market Rasen, Lincs LN8 3DZ
Take the A46 to Market Rasen and, at the junction, continue in the same direction on the A631 the racecourse. The golf course is 1 mile south.

RAC recommended hotel
Limes C/H ★★★ (0673) 842357 Victorian building with modern extension for bedrooms; pleasant gardens. Squash.

MILLFIELD
(042771) 255
An 18-hole inland meadowland links course (5583 yards, SSS 67). There is also a floodlit driving range. Visitors are welcome at all times. Ladies Day is Wednesday. Green fees are £3 for 18 holes, £1 for 9 holes and £1 for the driving range. There is a bar and light refreshments are served. The club also has 10 self-catering golf apartments. The club is within easy access of Doddington Hall, Lincoln Cathedral and Castle, Newark and the Medieval Hall at Gainsborough.
Location
Laughterton, Lincoln LN1 2LB
Take the A57 west from Lincoln and turn right at the A156 to Laughterton.

NORTH SHORE
(0754) 3298
An 18-hole half seaside (6134 yards, SSS 69) half parkland links course overlooking the sea Visitors who are bona fide members of a recognised club are welcome. Green fees are £12 on weekdays and £14 at weekends and Bank Holidays. There is a hotel on site with normal catering facilities. Local attractions include Fun Coast World.
Location
North Shore Road, Skegness, Lincs PE25 1DN
The course is 1 mile north of the town on the seaward side of Ingoldmells Road.

RAC recommended hotels
County ★★ (0754) 2461 A large, modernised hotel in commanding position overlooking beach. Sauna.
Vine ★★ (0754) 3018 Building of character in pleasant residential area with gardens to rear.

RAF WADDINGTON
(0552) 720271
An 18-hole heavily bunkered parkland course (5223 yards, SSS 66). Some holes must give way to taxiing aircraft. Visitors are welcome but you must book with the Secretary first. Green fees are £3. Catering is available by arrangement. There is plenty of plane-spotting available on the airfield, and Lincoln Cathedral is only 4 miles away.
Location
Waddington, Lincoln LN5 9NB
The course is off the A607 Lincoln-Grantham Road, 4 miles from Lincoln.

SANDILANDS
(0521) 41432
An 18-hole flat seaside course next to the sea (5995 yards, SSS 69). Provided you have a handicap certificate, visitors are welcome at any time. Green fees are £8 per round, £10 a day on weekdays and £10 per round, £12 a day at weekends and Bank Holidays. Bar meals are normally available except on Wednesday. There are some good local beaches and fine seaside walks.
Location
Sea Lane, Sandilands, Sutton-on-Sea, Mablethorpe, Lincs LN12 2JR
The course is 4 miles south of Mablethorpe on the A52 coast road. The course actually runs next to the sea wall.

RAC recommended hotel
Grange and Links ★★★ (0521) 41334 A 1930s style building situated in a quiet suburb. Facilities include golf, putting, tennis, billiards.

SEACROFT
(0754) 3741
An 18-hole moderately undulating links course (6478 yards, SSS 71). Visitors who have a handicap certificate and are members of a bona fide club are welcome. However, there are some restrictions at weekends, and ladies cannot play before 11am, so it is advisable to check first. Green fees are £12 per round, £15 a day on weekdays and £15 per round, £20 a day at weekends. The course is close to the Gibraltar Point Bird Sanctuary.
Location
Drummond Road, Skegness, Lincs PE25 3AU
The club is 1 mile S of Skegness on the road to the Gibraltar Point Bird Sanctuary.

SLEAFORD
(05298) 273
An inland 18-hole links-type heathland course which is fairly flat and lightly wooded (6443 yards, SSS 71). Visitors who have a handicap certificate are generally welcome. There is also a practice field. Green fees are £11.50 on weekdays, £18 at weekends and holidays, and there are reductions when you are with a member. There is a bar where meals and snacks are available.
Location
South Rauceby, Sleaford, Lincs NG34 8PL
Take the A153 west from Sleaford and the club is on the left after the crossroads.

RAC recommended hotel
Whichcote Arms (052 95) 239

SPALDING
(077585) 234
A very pretty 18-hole meadowland course with the River Glen running through (5847 yards, SSS 68). Visitors who are a member of a recognised club are welcome but you are advised to telephone first. Green fees are £10 on weekdays and £12 at weekends and Bank Holidays. Full catering facilities are available daily except on Tuesday. Local attractions include a good fishing area, and Burghley House.
Location
Surfleet, Spalding, Lincs PE11 4DG
The club is 4 miles north of Spalding off the A16.

RAC recommended hotels
Cley Hall ★★ (0775) 710785 A ship-owner's Georgian house of character on banks of River Welland near town centre.
Woodlands ★★ (0775) 769933 A large Victorian house converted into well-appointed hotel.

STOKE ROCHFORD
(047 683) 275
An 18-hole parkland course (6204 yards, SSS 70). There is a small practice ground. Provided you have a handicap certificate visitors are welcome on any day, but you cannot tee-off before 10.30am on Saturday or Sunday unless you are with a member. Green fees are £12 (£6 with a member) on weekdays and £20 (£10 with a member) at weekends and Bank Holidays. Lunch and evening meals are served daily on request. Lincoln is within easy access.
Location
Stoke Rochford, Grantham, Lincs NG33 5EW
Leave Grantham on the A1 south for 5 miles and the entrance to the club is by the 'AJS' service station.

SUTTON BRIDGE
(0406) 350323
A 9-hole parkland course (5804 yards, SSS 68). Visitors who have a handicap certificate are welcome on weekdays. Green fees are £12. Meals and sandwiches are normally served except on Mondays. Local attractions include the new dock on the River Nene.
Location
New Road, Sutton Bridge, Spalding, Lincs PE12 6RG
The club is situated on the A17 10 miles west of Kings Lynn.

WOODHALL SPA
(0526) 52511
A flat 18-hole wooded heathland course with easy walking (6866 yards, SSS 73). There is also a practice ground and driving net. Provided you have a handicap certificate, visitors are welcome all week by prior arrangement with the Secretary. Green fees are £16 per round, £20 a day on weekdays and £18 per round, £22 a day at weekends and Bank Holidays. Full catering facilities are available daily. Local attractions include the magnificent Humber Bridge, and the club is 18 miles from Boston.
Location
The Broadway, Woodhall Spa, Lincs LN10 6PU
The club is on the B1191, 6 miles south west of Horncastle.

RAC recommended hotels
Golf ★★★ (0526) 53535 A hotel in a picturesque situation in own grounds adjacent to golf course.
Petwood ★★★ (0526) 52411 Superb Edwardian building in black and white timber. Extensive grounds. Putting.

LONDON

AQUARIUS
081-693 1626
A 9-hole course situated on and around a reservoir with hazards including vents and bollards (5078 yards, SSS 65). Provided you have a handicap certificate, visitors are welcome. Green fees on application. A limited catering service is available. Local attractions include the Horniman Museum.
Location
Marmora Road, Honor Oak, London SE22
The course is situated off Forest Hill Road.

BRENT VALLEY
081-567 1287
A municipal 18-hole meadowland course (yards, SSS) with easy walking and the River Brent running through. Visitors of all playing abilities are welcome at any time. Green fees are £4.50 on weekdays and £6.20 at weekends. There is a restaurant which is open daily. Brent Lodge Park is close by, incorporating an animal centre, playground and tennis courts.
Location
Church Road, Cuckoo Lane, Hanwell, London W7 3BE
Take the A4020 Uxbridge Road at Hanwell, and then turn onto Church Road by Brent Lodge Animal Centre.

BUSH HILL PARK
081-360 5738
An attractive 18-hole parkland course surrounded by trees (5809 yards, SSS 67). Visitors of all playing abilities are welcome on weekdays. Green fees are £14 per 18 holes and £17 per 36 holes. There is a bar where snacks are served and lunch is normally available. Local attractions include Hatfield House and Waltham Abbey.
Location
Bush Hill, Winchmore Hill, London N21 2BU

RAC recommended hotel
Royal Chase ★★★ (081) 366 6500 A three-storey gabled hotel with helipad. It adjoins the open countryside and facilities include a swimming pool.

CHINGFORD
081-529 2107
An 18-hole parkland course (6336 yards, SSS 70). Visitors are welcome but a red outer garment must be worn. Green fees on application. Snacks are available daily.
Location
158 Station Road, Chingford, London E4
The club is just off Station Road.

DULWICH AND SYDENHAM HILL
081-693 3961
A hilly 18-hole parkland course with narrow fairways and good views over London (6051 yards, SSS 69). Provided you have a handicap of 22 or under, visitors are welcome on weekdays by arrangement. Green fees are £16 per round. Lunches are served daily and dinners by arrangement. Local attractions include Dulwich Village, Dulwich Picture Gallery and the Horniman Museum.
Location
Grange Lane, College Road, London SE21 7LH
The course is off the South Circular Road at the junction of Dulwich College and College Road.

ELTHAM WARREN
081-850 1166
A 9-hole parkland course with easy walking (5840 yards, SSS 68). Provided you have a handicap certificate and are a member of a recognised club, visitors are welcome on weekdays. Green fees are £14 (£4 with a member). Full catering facilities are available every day except Monday, and Friday, when only bar snacks are served.
Location
Bexley Road, Eltham, London SE9 2PE
The course is situated a few minutes walk from Eltham station, on the continuation of Eltham High Street, half a mile east.

FINCHLEY
081-346 2436
A wooded 18-hole parkland course with easy walking (6411 yards, SSS 71). Visitors are welcome on weekdays and in the afternoons at weekends. Green fees are £18 per round on weekdays and £25 at weekends. Full catering facilities are available every day except Monday. Local attractions include the RAF Museum at Hendon.
Location
Nether Court, Frith Lane, Mill Hill, London NW7 1PU
The nearest main junction to the club is the A1/A41. Mill Hill East Underground station (Northern line) is within 5 minutes walk.

HAMPSTEAD
081-455 7089
A 9-hole undulating parkland course with some very individual holes (5812 yards, SSS 68). Provided you have a handicap certificate, visitors are welcome on weekdays but prior booking with the Pro is requested. There are restrictions at weekends. Green fees are £15 per round (18 holes) or £12.50 a day on weekdays and £20 per round (18 holes) £20 a day at weekends and Bank Holidays. Lunch is served but you should reserve it with the Stewardess beforehand. Bar snacks are always available. Local attractions include Kenwood House, Hampstead Heath, Highgate

Cemetery and Waterlow Park.
Location
Winnington Road, Hampstead, London N2 0TU
Follow the A41 from Highgate Village, 1 mile down Hampstead Lane, and the course is adjacent to the Spaniards Inn.

HENDON
081-346 6023
An 18-hole parkland course with lots of trees and easy walking (6241 yards, SSS 70). Visitors who are members of a recognised club are welcome between Tuesday and Friday, but there are restrictions, on Monday and, at weekends. Green fees on application. Lunches, snacks and high teas are served until 6pm daily except Monday when only snacks are served.
Location
off Sanders Lane, Mill Hill, London NW7 1DG
From central Hendon take Queens Road through Brent Street, andcontinue to the roundabout. Take the first exit on your left and the club is half a mile on the left in Devonshire Road.

HIGHGATE
081-340 1906
An 18-hole parkland course (5982 yards, SSS 69). Visitors who have a handicap certificate are welcome on weekdays except onWednesday mornings. No visitors may play at weekends. Green fees are £25 per round, £30 a day. Catering facilities are available between midday and 2.30pm, and 4.30pm and 6.30pm. Local attractions include Kenwood House, Highgate Cemetery and Hampstead Heath.
Location
Denewood Road, London N6 4AH
The course is situated off Hampstead Lane near Kenwood House. Turn into Sheldon Avenue then first turning into Denewood Road.

HOME PARK
081-977 2423
An 18-hole flat parkland course with easy walking (6519 yards, SSS 71). The course is public and visitors are welcome at all times. Green fees are £8/£12 on weekdays (£5/£4 with a member) and £12/£22 at weekends(£4/£16 with a member). Lunch is served daily. The golf course is actually in the grounds of Hampton Court Palace and there are some lovely walks along the River Thames.
Location
Hampton Wick, Richmond-uon-Thames, Surrey KT1 4AS

RAC recommended hotel
Lion Gate ★★★ 081-977 8121 Attractive Georgian building with later annexe, near Hampton Court Palace.

LONDON SCOTTISH
081-789 7517
An 18-hole heathland/parkland course with no bunkers (5436 yards, SSS 67). Visitors are welcome on weekdays but the club prefers you to have a handicap certificate. All players must wear a pillar-box red top which can be hired. Green fees are £10 a round or £16 a day. Lunch is served daily and evening meals can be ordered except on Monday. The course is on the outskirts of London near Wimbledon Lawn Tennis Club.
Location
Windmill Enclosure, Wimbledon Common, London SW19 5NQ
The course is situated 2 miles from Wimbledon station, and is next to the windmill on Wimbledon Common.

MILL HILL
081-959 2339
A flat, wooded 18-hole parkland course with easy walking (6286 yards, SSS 70). There is also a practice ground. Visitors are welcome on weekdays, and green fees are £16 per round or £20 a day. Lunch is served daily. Local attractions include the RAF Museum at Hendon.
Location
100 Barnet Way, Mill Hill, London NW7 3AL
The course is approximately 500 yards from the A1/A41 junction at Apex Corner, 1 mile south of Stirling Corner.

MUSWELL HILL
081-888 1764
An excellent 18-hole undulating parkland course providing a stiff test of golf (6474 yards, SSS 71). Visitors are welcome on weekdays, but you should book with the Pro beforehand to play at weekends and Bank Holidays, as play is limited. A handicap not exceeding 24 is required. Fees are £15 per round, £20 a day on weekdays and £25 at weekends and Bank Holidays; £5 at all times if you are with a member. There is a bar and full catering facilities are available daily. Local attractions include Alexandra Palace.
Location
Rhodes Avenue, Wood Green, London N22 4UT
The club is situated 1 mile from Bounds Green Underground station and 1½ miles from the north Circular Road.

NORTH MIDDLESEX
081-445 1604
A short 18-hole undulating parkland course with some challenging greens (5611 yards, SSS 71). Green fees on application. Lunches are served daily except on Monday.
Location
Friern Barnet Lane, Whetstone, London N20 0Nl
The course is on the A1000, 5 miles north of Finchley.

PICKETTS LOCK
081-803 3611
A public 9-hole parkland course (2496 yards, SSS 64). The River Lea borders the course and provides a natural hazard. There is also a putting green, and a practice ground with a floodlit driving range. Visitors of all playing abilities are welcome at any time. Green fees are £2.50 on weekdays and £3 at weekends. Full catering facilities are available daily.
Location
Picketts Lock Lane, Edmonton, London N9 0AS
The course is in north east London, near the north Circular Road and the A10.

ROEHAMPTON
081-876 5505
An 18-hole parkland course (6011 yards, SSS 69). Visitors are welcome if they are introduced by a member. Green fees are £10 on weekdays and £12 at weekends. Full catering facilities are available daily. Other sports facilities are available.
Location
Roehampton Lane, London SW15 5LR

ROYAL BLACKHEATH
081-850 1795
An attractive 18-hole parkland course (6214 yards, SSS 70). It was the first London club to move from common land. Provided you have a handicap certificate, visitors are welcome. Green fees are £25 a day for 1 round and £30 a day for 2 rounds. The clubhouse dates from 1787 and has an excellent dining room and 2 bars. Local attractions include Eltham Palace.
Location
Court Road, Eltham, London SE9 5AF
The course is 5 minutes walk from Mottingham station, off Court Road.

ROYAL EPPING FOREST
081-529 2195
A wooded 18-hole parkland course (6620 yards, SSS 70). Visitors are welcome but the club prefers you to have a handicap certificate. It is compulsory to wear either a red coat or red trousers in order to distinguish players from other users of the common. Green fees are £4.50 on weekdays and £6.50 at weekends. There is a bar and catering can be provided by arrangement. Local attractions include Epping Forest and Queen Elizabeth's Hunting Lodge.
Location
Forest Approach, Chingford, London E4 7AZ
The course is 300 yards south of Chingford station.

ROYAL WIMBLEDON
081-946 2125
An 18-hole parkland course (6300 yards, SSS 70) built on an old Roman encampment. Visitors with a handicap of 18 are welcome by arrangement with the Secretary, but at least 2 days notice is necessary. Green fees are £20 per round or day. Snacks are always available but lunch is not available regularly. The club is close to Wimbledon Lawn Tennis Club.
Location
29 Camp Road, Wimbledon, London SW19 4UW
The club is 1 mile west of the War Memorial in Wimbledon village.

SHOOTERS HILL
081-854 6368
A hilly 18-hole parkland course with some fine views (5718 yards, SSS 68). Visitors who are members of a bona fide golf club and have a handicap certificate are welcome on weekdays only. Green fees are £19. Catering facilities are available. Local attractions include Greenwich Park and Observatory, the Cutty Sark, the Maritime Museum and trips on the River Thames.
Location
'Lowood', Eaglesfield Road, London SE18 3DA
The club is within 2 miles of the A2, 1 mile from Welling and 2 miles from Woolwich.

SOUTH HERTS
081-445 2035
An open, pleasant parkland course (6432 yards, SSS 71). Provided you have a handicap certificate, visitors are welcome on weekdays. Tuesday is Ladies Day. Green fees on application. Lunches, snacks and teas are served daily.
Location
Links Drive, Totteridge, London N20 8QU
Leave the A1000 for 400 yards at Whetstone to Totteridge Lane, and it is another 400 yards to Links Drive. The nearest station is Totteridge.

RAC recommended hotel
Crest ★★★ (0707) 43311 A purpose built hotel in the M25 motorway service area. Facilities include indoor swimming pool, sauna, solarium and gymnasium.

TRENT PARK
081-366 7432
An 18-hole parkland course (6008 yards, SSS 69) with some testing holes, set in the Green Belt area. There is a large practice area. Visitors are welcome at any time although it is necessary to book at weekends and Bank Holidays. Green fees are £3.80 on weekdays and £5.10 at weekends and Bank Holidays. Snacks are always available and meals by arrangement. The course is actually in Trent Park and there are many nature trails.
Location
Bramley Road, Southgate, London N14 4XS
The course is opposite Oakwood Underground station (Piccadilly line).

WANSTEAD
081-989 3938
A pretty 18-hole parkland course with lots of trees and shrubs (6211 yards, SSS 69). Provided you have a handicap certificate, visitors are welcome on Monday, Tuesday, and Friday, but you should telephone first. Green fees are £15 per round or day. Lunches and teas are served at the club.
Location
Overton Drive, Wanstead, London E11 2LW
Leave the A12 at Wanstead station and turn right at 'The Green' for St Mary's Avenue. Then turn

left at the T-junction at St Mary's Church.

WEST ESSEX
081-529 7558
A challenging 18-hole parkland course (6342 yards, SSS 70) situated in Epping Forest. Visitors who have a handicap certificate or are members of another club are welcome on weekdays. Green fees are £15 per round, £18 a day. Lunch is served by arrangement. There is the additional attraction of the beautiful Epping Forest.
Location
Bury Road, Sewardstonebury, Chingford, London E4 7QL
The club is off the A11, 1 mile from Chingford station.

WIMBLEDON COMMON
081-946 7571
A wooded 18-hole moorland links-type course (5486 yards, SSS 66). Visitors are welcome on weekdays. Green fees on application. Lights meals are served daily. Local attractions include Wimbledon Common, Cannizaro Park and Gardens, and the Lawn Tennis Club.
Location
Camp Road, Wimbledon Common SW19 4UW
The club is 1 mile north west of the War Memorial in Wimbledon village, just past the Fox and Grapes plublic house on the left in Camp Road.

WIMBLEDON PARK
081-946 1250
An 18-hole parkland course with easy walking (5465 yards, SSS 67). Provided you have a handicap certificate and have a letter of introduction from your own club, visitors are welcome. Green fees are £20 a day on weekdays and £20 per round at weekends. Full catering facilities are available daily except Monday. The club is near the Lawn Tennis Club and Wimbledon Common.
Location
Home Park Road, Wimbledon, London SW19 7HR
From Wimbledon High Street, the club is reached via Church Road, Arthur Road and Home Park Road. The club is also signposted from Wimbledon Park station (District line).

RAC recommended hotel
Cannizaro House ★★★★ 081-879 1464 A Georgian mansion, luxuriusly furnished and equipped in garden and parkland on the edge of Wimbledon Common.

MERSEYSIDE

ALLERTON MUNICIPAL
051-428 4074
An 18 hole undulating parkland course (5494 yards, SSS 67) . There is also a 9 hole course (1845 yards, SSS 34). Visitors of all playing abilities are welcome. Green fees are £1.60 adults, 80p juniors and OAPs (9 holes) and £2.20 adults, £1.10 juniors and OAPs (18 holes). Snacks are served daily.
Location
Allerton, Liverpool L18
Take the Allerton road from the city centre.

RAC recommended hotels
Atlantic Tower ★★★★ 051-227 4444 Distinctive modern hotel with luxury suites. Fine river views.
Liverpool Moat House ★★★★ 051-709 0181 Modern nine-storey city centre hotel. Indoor swimming pool, sauna, solarium, gymnasium.
St George's ★★★★ 051-709 7090 High rise purpose-built central hotel with all modern facilities.
Trials ★★★★ 051-227 1021 A luxury hotel in a fine Victorian city centre building originally a bank.
Cherry Tree ★★★ 051-546 7531 Purpose-built two-storey hotel with modern wings to rear.
Crest ★★★ 051-709 7050 Centrally situated modern hotel with modern amenities. Billiards.
Park ★★★ 051-525 7555 Modern purpose-built hotel with well-equipped bedrooms. Near Aintree.
Royal ★★★ 051-928 2332 Cream-faced historic Georgian building offering modern facilities. Views of Mersey.
Alicia ★★ 051-727 4411 A Victorian cotton merchant's lane overlooking Sefton Park.
Grange ★★ 051-427 2950 An extended large and elegant cream-faced building set in own grounds.
Green Park ★★ 051-733 3382 Well-equipped privately-run hotel 2 miles form city centre. Attractive frontage.

ARROWE PARK
051-677 1527
An attractive 18 hole parkland course (6377 yards, SSS 70). There is also a 9 hole pitch and putt course and a putting green. The course is a public one and visitors are welcome at any time, but you should telephone first to check tee-off times. Green fees are £3.20. There is a fishing lake in the park, and some lovely walks. The course is also close to Birkenhead Priory Ruins and the Williamson Art Gallery.
Location
Arrowe Park, Woodchurch, Birkenhead, Merseyside
The club is 3 miles from the town centre. Take Borough Road then Woodchurch Road and head for the Arrowe Park roundabout. Bear left after approximately 400 yards and turn right into Arrowe Park, opposite the Landicon Cemetery.

RAC recommended hotels
Bowler Hat ★★★ 051-652 4931 A large converted period residence, attractively gabled, overlooking the Wirral Peninsula.
Riverhill ★★ 051-653 3773 Former private house set in own grounds in quiet residential areas.

BIDSTON
051-638 3412
An 18 hole parkland course with a practice ground (6207 yards, SSS 70). Visitors of all playing abilities are welcome at any time. Green fees are £7. Full catering facilities are available daily.
Location
Scoresby Road, Leasowe, Wirral, Merseyside L46 1QQ
Take the A551 from Wallasey and the club is about three quarters of a mile at Leasowe.

BOOTLE
051-928 6196
An 18 hole seaside links course (6362 yards, SSS 70). Visitors of all playing abilities are welcome. Green fees are £2.55 on weekdays and £3.75 at weekends. Full catering facilities are available by arrangement.
Location
Dunnings Bridge Road, Bootle, Merseyside L30 2PP
The club is about 5 miles north of Liverpool on the A565.

BOWRING
051-489 1910
A 9 hole flat parkland course (2500 yards, SSS 66). Visitors of all playing abilities are welcome at any time. Green fees are £2.50 for adults and £2.25 for juniors and OAPs.
Location
Bowring Park, Roby Road, Huyton, Liverpool L36 4HD
The club is approximately 4½ miles east of the city centre.

BRACKENWOOD
051-608 3093
An 18 hole parkland course with easy walking (6285 yards, SSS 70). All visitors are welcome. Green fees are £3.20 for adults and £1.60 for juniors and OAPs. Local attractions include the garden village of Port Sunlight, and Lady Lever Hume Art Gallery.
Location
Bracken Lane, Bebington, Wirral, Merseyside
Leave the M56 at junction 4 and the club is signposted from here.

BROMBOROUGH
051-334 2155
An 18 hole parkland course (6650 yards, SSS 73). Visitors of all playing abilities are welcome on weekdays but it is advisable to book at weekends. Green fees are £12 (£6 with a member) on weekdays and £15 (£6 with a member) at weekends and Bank Holidays. Snacks and lunches are available every day and other meals by arrangement. Local attractions include Lady Lever Hume Art Gallery.
Location
Raby Hall Road, Bromborough, Wirral, Merseyside L63 0NW
Leave the M53 Wirral Motorway at junction 4. The club is half a mile from Bromborough station and three quarters of a mile from the A41 Birkenhead-Chester road.

RAC recommended hotels
Cromwell ★★★ 051-334 2917 A modern brick-built hotel on the A41 in centre of village. Sauna, solarium, gymnasium.
Dibbinsdale ★★ 051-334 5171 An hotel with a purpose-built extension, situated in a quiet area.

CALDY
051-625 5660
An 18 hole undulating seaside/parkland course (6665 yards, SSS 73) situated on the cliff top, with excellent views across the Dee to the North Wales hills. There is a practice ground. Visitors are welcome on weekdays but only at weekends if you are accompanied by a member. Green fees are £15 a day or £13 after 2pm (£5 if you are with a member). Lunch is served daily and dinner by arrangement. The club house has particularly good facilities including snooker.
Location
Links Hey Road, Caldy, Wirral, Merseyside L48 1NB
Take the A540 from Chester and turn left at the Caldy crossroads.

CHILDWALL
051-487 0654
A testing 18 hole parkland course (6425 yards, SSS 71). Visitors of all playing abilities are welcome every day except Tuesday. Green fees are £10.50 a day. Lunches and evening meals are served daily.
Location
Naylor's Road, Liverpool, Merseyside L27 2YB
Leave Liverpool via Childwall Valley Road, and turn left at the Bridge Inn into Naylors Road. If you are travelling from Huyton, take Tarbock Road into Wheathill Road at the traffic lights.

EASTHAM LODGE
051-327 3003
A 15 hole parkland course (6444 yards, SSS 68). Provided you have a handicap certificate, visitors are welcome on weekdays. Green fees are £10 per round or day or £5 if you are with a member. Bar snacks are normally served and full meals can be arranged. The course is close to the historic city of Chester.
Location
117 Ferry Road, Eastham, Wirral L62 0AP
The club is off the A41 towards Eastham Country Park, 6 miles from Birkenhead. Leave the M53 at junction 5.

FORMBY
(07048) 72164
A wooded 18 hole seaside links course (6781 yards, SSS 73). Visitors who have an official handicap are welcome on weekdays but advance reservation is advisable. Green fees are £21 on

weekdays and £24 at weekends and Bank Holidays. Lunch is served daily except Monday. Local attractions include Southport holiday centre.
Location
Golf Road, Formby, Liverpool L37 1LQ
The course is situated 6 miles south of Southport off the A565.

RAC recommended hotel
Blundellsands ★★★ 051-924 6515 Striking Edwardian mansion in quiet area of Crosby.

FORMBY LADIES
(07048) 73493
An 18 hole seaside links course with some tricky holes (5374 yards, SSS 71). It is one of the few independent ladies courses in the country. There is also a practice area. Provided you have a handicap certificate, visitors are welcome but it is advisable to telephone first. Green fees are £17 on weekdays and £20 at weekends. Bar snacks and salads are served daily. Local attractions include Freshfield Nature Reserve.
Location
Golf Road, Formby, Liverpool L37 1LQ
The club is 6 miles south of Southport off the A565.

GRANGE PARK
(0744) 26318
A fairly flat 18 hole parkland/meadowland course with some splendid views (6429 yards, SSS 71). There is a practice area. Visitors of all playing abilities are welcome on weekdays and by arrangement at weekends. Tuesday is Ladies Day. Green fees are £14 on weekdays and £20 at weekends. There is a dining room with full facilities, and two bars.
Location
Prescot Road, St Helens, Merseyside WA10 3AD
The club is on the A58 approximately 1 mile from St Helens towards Prescot.

HAYDOCK PARK
(09252) 224389
A flat, well-wooded 18 hole parkland course (6043 yards, SSS 69) in a lovely setting next to the famous racecourse. There is a large practice area. Visitors are welcome on weekdays except Tuesday. Green fees are £10 per round or day. There is a restaurant and two bars, and meals are available by arrangement.
Location
Golbourne Park, Newton-Le-Willows, Merseyside WA12 0HX
Leave the M6 at junction 23 for the A580. The course is 1 mile east of the junction.

HESKETH
(0704) 36897
A championship 18 hole seaside links course (Yellow-6193 yards, SSS 70 and White-6478 yards, SSS 72). There is a practice ground. Provided you have a handicap certificate, visitors are welcome on weekdays and occasionally at weekends. Societies need to book in advance. Green fees are £15 per round, £20 a day on weekdays and £20 per round, £25 a day at weekends. There are two bars where snacks are always available, and a dining room where you can order meals. Local attractions include the Botanical Gardens and Hesketh Park.
Location
Cockle Dicks Lane, off Cambridge Road, Southport, Merseyside PR9 9QQ
The club is 1 mile north of Southport town centre on the main A565 Preston road.

RAC recommended hotels see Southport.

HESWALL
051-342 1237
A beautiful 18 hole undulating parkland course (6472 yards, SSS 72) on the banks of the River Dee, overlooking the Welsh coast and hills. The course offers an outstanding challenge of golf. Visitors who have an accredited handicap certificate are welcome at any time but a telephone call beforehand is advisable. There is a large practice area. Green fees are £14 a day on weekdays (£5 with a member) and £18 a day (£6 with a member) at weekends and Bank Holidays. Full catering facilities are available daily except Monday, and bar snacks every day. The historic city of Chester is only 8 miles away.
Location
Cottage Lane, Gayton Heswall, The Wirral, Merseyside L60 8PB
Leave the M53 at junction 4 and at the roundabout turn into Well Lane. This leads into Cottage Lane.

RAC recommended hotel
Hill House ★★ 051-342 5535 A converted and extended former mill owner's house with attractive views over River Dee.

HILLSIDE
(0704) 67169
An 18 hole parkland links course with natural hazards (6850 yards, SSS 74). Provided you have a handicap certificate, visitors are welcome by appointment. Green fees on application. Full catering facilities are available. The club is convenient for the Southport shopping centre.
Location
Hastings Road, Hillside, Southport PR8 2LU
Take the A565 south from Southport and in Birkdale turn right before you come to Hillside station. The club is situated at the end of Hastings Road.

HOYLAKE
051-632 2956
A flat 18 hole links course with some difficult fairways (6330 yards, SSS 70). Visitors of all playing abilities are welcome at any time, but if you wish to play at weekends you should telephone one week in advance. Green fees are £3.20 per round. There is a bar where hot snacks and meals are served. Local attractions include West Kirby and Thurstaston Nature Reserve.
Location
Carr Lane, Hoylake, Merseyside
Leave the M53, at junction 2 and take A551 and A553 to Hoylake. The club is 100 yards from Hoylake station.

HUYTON AND PRESCOT
051-489 3948
An 18 hole parkland course with easy walking (5738 yards, SSS 68). There is also a driving range. Visitors who are members of a bona fide golf club are welcome on weekdays and at weekends with a member. Green fees are £12 a day. Full catering facilities are available daily. Knowsley Safari Park is within easy access.
Location
Hurst Park, Huyton Lane, Huyton, Liverpool L36 1UA
Take the A57 from Liverpool through Huyton to Prescot or leave the M57 at junction 2. The club is off the B5199.

KIRKBY (LIVERPOOL MUNICIPAL)
051-546 5435
An 18 hole meadowland course (6571 yards, SSS 71). There is a practice ground. Visitors who have a handicap certificate are welcome every day. Green fees are £2.50 on weekdays and at weekends. Juniors and OAPs can play for £1.25. Lunches are available at weekends.
Location
Ingoe Lane, Kirkby, Liverpool L32 4SS
Leave the M57 at junction 6.

LEASOWE
051-677 5852
An 18 hole seaside course (6204 yards, SSS 71). Provided you have a handicap certificate, visitors are welcome on weekdays and also at weekends by prior arrangement. Green fees are £10 on weekdays and £14 at weekends. There is a restaurant and bar snacks are also served. The course is situated in the heart of the Wirral.
Location
Leasowe Road, Moreton, Wirral L46 3RD
Take the Wallasey turn-off from end of the M53. The club is 1 mile west of Wallasey village.

LEE PARK
051-487 3882
An 18 hole parkland course with some ponds (6024 yards, SSS 69). Visitors of all playing abilities are welcome with a reservation. Green fees are £9 on weekdays (£4.50 with a member) and £12 at weekends (£6 with a member), or £4 after 4pm on weekdays and £6 after 5.30pm at weekends. Bar snacks are available at all times and there is a dining room where meals are served by arrangement.
Location
Chidwall Valley Raod, Gateacre, Liverpool L27 3YA
Take the A562 from Liverpool and turn onto the B5171, next to Netherley Comprehensive School.

PRENTON
051-608 1053
An 18 hole flat parkland course with easy walking (6411 yards, SSS 71). There are some fine views of the Welsh hills from the green. Visitors of all playing abilities are welcome at all times except on competition days, which are normally held on Saturday in the summer months. Green fees are £12 on weekdays (£6 with a member) and £15 at weekends and Bank Holidays. There is also a £50 weekly rate (Mon-Fri). Full catering facilities are available daily.
Location
Golf Links Road, Prenton, Birkenhead, Wirral L42 8LW
The club is 2 miles west of Birkenhead off the A552. Leave the M53 at junction 3.

RAC recommended hotels see Arrowe Park.

ROYAL BIRKDALE
(0604) 67920
An 18 hole classic championship links course (6703 yards, SSS 73). This course has the distinction of staging all the major championships, the only course in Great Britain to have done so. Visitors who have a letter of introduction from their home club together with a handicap certificate are welcome. Green fees are £25 on weekdays, £45 at weekends in the winter, and £30 per round, £45 a day on weekdays and £45 per round at weekends during the summer. Light lunches and afternoon teas are served daily and full lunches and dinners by arrangement for parties of 20 or more. The course is near the historic city of Chester and the Albert Docks in Liverpool.
Location
Waterloo Road, Birkdale, Southport, Merseyside PR8 2LX
The club is situated 1½ miles south of Southport on the A565.

RAC recommended hotels see Southport.

ROYAL LIVERPOOL
051-632 3101
An 18 hole seaside championship links course (6737 yards, SSS 74). There is a large practice area. Provided you have a handicap certificate, visitors are welcome on weekdays, and if you wish to play at weekends you also need a letter of introduction from your home club. Green fees are £25 on weekdays (£8 with a member) and £30 at weekends (£10 with a member). Bar snacks are served daily, and lunches on Sunday. The course is within easy access of the historic city of Chester and the Albert Docks in Liverpool.
Location
Meols Drive, Hoylake, Wirral, Merseyside L47 4AL
Take the A553 to Hoylake on the Wirral Peninsula, 10 miles west of Liverpool.

SHERDLEY PARK
(0744) 813149
An 18 hole undulating parkland course with some ponds (5941 yards, SSS 69). Visitors of all playing abilities are welcome at any time. Green fees on application.
The club is situated 2 miles from town centre on the A570 Warrington road.
Location
Elton Head Road, St Helens, Merseyside

SOUTHPORT AND AINSDALE
(0704) 78000
An 18 hole championship links course (6612 yards, SSS 73). Visitors who are members of a bona fide golf club are welcome on weekdays, and advance booking is recommended. Green fees are £25 a day, £11 per round. Full catering facilities are available. There is a snooker room at the club house. Local attractions include Rufford Old Hall (NT).
Location
Bradshaws Lane, Ainsdale, Southport, Merseyside PR8 3LG
The club is 3 miles south of Southport on the A565, approximately half a mile from Ainsdale station.

RAC recommended hotel
Prince Of Wales ★★★★ A large, gracious Victorian classic hotel.
Royal Clifton ★★★ (0704) 33771 Striking white-faced hotel in central position. Well equipped bedrooms. Indoor swimming pool, sauna, solarium, gymnasium.
Scarisbrick ★★★ (0704) 43000 A centrally-placed hotel with an attractive arcade frontage. Facilities include disco bars.
Balmoral Lodge ★★ (0704) 544298 Edwardian residence with well-equipped bedrooms. Close to town centre. Sauna.
Bold ★★ (0704) 32578 Victorian commercial hotel set in aatractive tree-lined Lord Street.
Lockerbie House ★★ (0704) 65298 Converted brick-built villa in quiet residential area. Billiards.
Metropole ★★ (0704) 65298 Attractive former private house under proprietor's personal supervision.
Stutelea ★★ (0704) 44220 Pleasant three-storey Victorian building with half acre garden. Indoor swimming pool, sauna, solarium, gymnasium.

SOUTHPORT MUNICIPAL
(0704) 35286
An 18 hole flat seaside course with some fine sea views from the 12th and 13th holes (6139 yards, SSS 70). Visitors are welcome. Green fees are £2.75 adults, £1.35 juniors on weekdays and £3.50 at weekends, when booking is required. There is a licensed café where meals are served.
Location
Park Road West, Southport, Merseyside
The course is situated at the north end of the Promenade near Marine Lake.

SOUTHPORT OLD LINKS
(0704) 28207
A 9 hole seaside course with easy walking (6486 yards, SSS 72). Visitors are welcome on weekdays but preferably not on Wednesday or at weekends. Green fees are £7.50 on weekdays and £10 at weekends. Snacks and light meals are available by arrangement with the Steward.
Location
Moss Lane, Southport, Merseyside PR9 7QS
From the town centre, take Lord Street to the roundabout at the Law Courts, turn right into Manchester Road, then into Roe Lane and finally into Moss Lane where you will find the club.

WALLASEY
051-691 1024
An 18 hole seaside links course (6607 yards, SSS 73). Visitors who have a handicap certificate are welcome on weekdays but there are some restrictions at weekends. Green fees are £16 (£8 with a member) on weekdays and £20 (£10 with a member) at weekends and Bank Holidays. Full catering facilities are available daily. The club is near to the New Albert Dock Complex.
Location
Bayswater Road, Wallasey, Merseyside L45 8LA
You can reach the club either via the M53 through the Wirral or, from the centre of Liverpool, take the Wallasey Tunnel.

WARREN
051-639 5730
A 9 hole municipal links course with fine greens (2945 yards, SSS 34 (68)). Visitors of all playing abilities are welcome on weekdays but you should telephone first if you want a game at weekends. Green fees are £3 per 18 holes and £1.50 per 9 holes. Lunches and teas are served daily in the club house café. Local attractions include New Brighton Promenade.
Location
The Grange, Grove Road, Wallasey, Merseyside
The course is situated 500 yards up Grove Road, just beyond Grove Road station.

WEST DERBY
051-254 1034
An excellent 18 hole parkland course with wooded fairways (6333 yards, SSS 70). Visitors of all playing levels are welcome between Monday and Friday. Green fees are £12 a day on weekdays and £16 at weekends. Catering facilities are available.

The club is within easy access of Croxteth Hall Park and Knowsley Safari Park.
Location
Yew Tree Lane, Liverpool L12 9HQ
Take the A57 for 4 miles east of the centre of Liverpool and the club is 1 mile south of West Derby village.

WEST LANCASHIRE
051-924 1076
A challenging 18 hole seaside links course (6756 yards, SSS 73). Provided you have a handicap certificate, visitors are welcome at all times except on competition days. Green fees are £17 on weekdays and £20 at weekends. Lunches are served between Tuesday and Sunday and other meals by arrangement.
Location
Hall Road West, Blundellsands, Liverpool L23 8SZ
From the end of the M57, take the A5207 and then the A565 to Crosby and follow the signposts for the club or the Waterlooo Rugby Club by Hall Road station.

WIRRAL LADIES'
051-652 1255
An 18 hole heathland course (Ladies 6966 yards, SSS 70 and Men 5170 yards, SSS 66). Visitors who have a handicap certificate are welcome at any time by arrangement. Green fees are £10 per round. Meals are served at all times by arrangement. The club is within easy access of the New Albert Dock with all its amenities.
Location
93 Bidston Road, Oxton, Birkenhead, Merseyside L43 6TS
The club is on the boundary of the town, in the Bidston Hill area. Leave the M53 at junction 3 for the A41.

RAC recommended hotels see Arrowe Park.

WOOLTON
051-486 2298
An 18 hole parkland course providing some good golf (5706 yards, SSS 68). Visitors of all playing abilities are welcome. Green fees are £10 on weekdays and £16 at weekends. Catering facilities are available by arrangement. There is a snooker room at the club. Local attractions include the historic Speke Hall.
Location
Doe Park, Speke Road, Woolton, Liverpool L25 7TZ
The club is situated 6 miles from the city centre, 1 mile from Woolton village.

MIDDLESEX

AIRLINKS
081-561 1418
An 18 hole meadowland/parkland course with three lakes (5883 yards, SSS 69). Visitors are welcome between Monday and Friday and also at weekends if you book in advance. Green fees are £5.50 per round on weekdays and £7 at weekends. There is a licensed bar where hot and cold snacks are served.
Location
Southall Lane, Hounslow, Middx TW5 9PE
Leave the M4 at junction 3 for the A312 and A4020. The golf club has the same entrance as David Lloyd Tennis Centre.

RAC recommended hotel see Hounslow.

ASHFORD MANOR
(0784) 257687
A deceptively difficult 18 hole parkland course (6343 yards, SSS 70). Provided you are a member of a recognised golf club and hold a handicap certificate, visitors are welcome on weekdays and at weekends by prior arrangement. Green fees are £20 on weekdays. Lunches are served daily except Monday and high teas every day. Local attractions include Hampton Court, Windsor Castle and Heathrow Airport.
Location
Fordbridge Road, Ashford, Middx TW15 3RT
Take the A308 Staines by-pass and turn onto the B377, 2 miles east of Staines.

CREWS HILL
081-363 6674
An 18 hole parkland course surrounded by countryside (6230 yards, SSS 70). Visitors who have a handicap certificate are welcome at weekends and Bank Holidays with a member. If you are a member of a recognised golf club you can also play on weekdays by prior arrangement. Green fees on application. There is a restaurant and lunch is served daily except Monday. Local attractions include Theobalds Park and Capel Manor (NT).
Location
Cattlegate Road, Crews Hill, Enfield, Middx EN2 8AZ
Leave the M25 at junction 24 and follow the signs to Enfield Chase station. Alternatively take the A1005 Enfield-Potters Bar road into East Lodge Lane and turn right into Cattlegate Road.

RAC recommended hotel see Enfield.

EALING
081-997 0937
A flat 18 hole parkland course (6216 yards, SSS 70) with the River Brent flowing through, affecting 9 of the 18 holes. Provided you have a handicap certificate, visitors are welcome on weekdays only. Green fees are £19 (£10 with a member). Lunches are served every day and evening meals by arrangement. There is also a bar where snacks are served. The canal and basin are nearby.
Location
Perivale Lane, Greenford, Middx UB6 8SS
The club is off the A40 Western Avenue, half a mile from Hanger Lane Gyratory System.

RAC recommended hotel see Hillingdon.

ENFIELD
081-363 3970
An 18 hole parkland course (6137 yards, SSS 70) with a brook crossing 7 holes. Visitors who have a handicap certificate and are members of another club are welcome on weekdays by giving 24 hours notice. Full catering facilities are available. There is a bar and restaurant where meals are available daily. The course is situated on a Saxon Moat ancient monument.
Location
Old Park Road South, Enfield, Middx EN2 7DA
The course is situated 1 mile north east of Enfield, near Enfield Chase station. It is on the bus route 107.

RAC recommended hotel
The Royal Chase ★★★ 081-366 6500 A three-storey gabled hotel with helipad. The hotel adjoins the open countryside and facilities include a swimming pool.

FULWELL
081-977 2733
A championship 18 hole flat meadowland course (6490 yards, SSS 71). Provided you have a handicap certificate, visitors are welcome on weekdays. Green fees are £20 a day. Lunches and teas are served and other meals by arrangement. Local attractions include Hampton Court, the River Thames, Twickenham, Kempton Park and Sandown.
Location
Wellington Road, Hampton Hill, Middx TW12 1JY
The club is opposite Fulwell station and bus garage, 2 miles south of Twickenham on the A311.

GRIM'S DYKE
081-428 4539
An 18 hole parkland course with tree-lined fairways and testing greens (5598 yards, SSS 67). There is also a practice area. Visitors are welcome on weekdays but a handicap certificate is required. Green fees are £18 on weekdays. Lunch is served daily except Monday and dinners by arrangement. Harrow School and Church are close by, and also The Mansion House, the home of Gilbert of Gilbert & Sullivan.
Location
Oxhey Lane, Hatch End, Pinner, Middx HA5 4AL
The club is situated on the A4008 Watford-Harrow road, 2 miles west of Harrow.

HAREFIELD PLACE
(0895) 31169
An 18 hole public parkland course (5753 yards, SSS 68). Visitors can play by arrangement with the London Borough of Hillingdon, and beginners are welcome. Green fees are £4.50 on weekdays and £7 at weekends. Full catering facilities are available.
Location
The Drive, Harefield Place, Uxbridge, Middlesex
The club is 2 miles north of Uxbridge off the A40.

HASTE HILL
(09274) 26485
An 18 hole parkland course with a stream running through (5787 yards, SSS 68). Visitors of all playing abilities are welcome. Green fees are £4.50 on weekdays and £7 at weekends. Full catering facilities are available daily.
Location
The Drive, Northwood, Middx HA6 1HN
The club is situated on the A404.

HILLINGDON
(0895) 33956
A 9 hole undulating parkland course sloping down to the river (5459 yards, SSS 67). Visitors are welcome on Monday, Tuesday, Wednesday and Friday, and must hold a handicap certificate and also be a member of a golf club. If you wish to play at weekends and Bank Holidays you must be the guest of a full member. Green fees are £10 per 18 holes. Sandwiches are served at lunchtime and other meals by arrangement.
Location
18 Dorset Way, Hillingdon, Middx UB10 0JR
Turn off the A40 to Uxbridge, go past the RAF Station, up Hillingdon Hill and turn off to your left at the Vine public house into Vine Lane. The club gates are three quarters of a mile on your left.

RAC recommended hotel
Master Brewer ★★★ (0895) 51199 A motel-type hotel set in attractive gardens.

HORSENDEN HILL
081-902 4555
A well-maintained 9 hole undulating wooded parkland course (3236 yards, SSS 56). There is a practice area and nets and also a putting green. Visitors of all playing abilities are welcome. Green fees are £2.50, juniors and OAPs £1.25 on weekdays and £4, juniors and OAPs £2 at weekends. Snacks are available and restaurant meals by arrangement. The course is within easy access of Wembley Stadium.
Location
Woodland Rise, Greenford, Middx UB6 0RD
The club is signposted off Whitton Avenue, running alongside Sudbury Golf Club.

HOUNSLOW HEATH
081-570 5271
An 18 hole parkland course in a conservation area with the River Crane running through (5820 yards, SSS 68). Visitors of all playing abilities are welcome. Green fees are £4 per 18 hole round, £2.35 for 9 holes on weekdays. Fees are £2.50 on Sunday and there is a special price of £1.85 for juniors and OAPs. Snacks are available. There is a nature trail attached to the golf course and the club is within easy access of Heathrow Airport.

Location
Staines Road, Hounslow, Middx
Take the M4 out of London and then the main road from Hounslow town to Bedfont. The club is on the left-hand side of the road by Hounslow Heath.

RAC recommended hotel
Master Robert ★★★ 081-570 6261 Hotel with extensive modern motel-type accommodation. Near Heathrow.

LIME TREES PARK
081-845 3180
A 9 hole undulating parkland course with varied water hazards (5789 yards, SSS 69). The course is public and visitors of all playing abilities are welcome. There is also a driving range. Green fees on application. There is a bar and restaurant where full facilities are available, and a facility room.
Location
Ruislip Road, Northolt, UB5 6QZ
The club is off the A40 Western Avenue, near the Polish War Memorial.

NORTHWOOD
(09274) 25329
An 18 hole wooded parkland course with a stream flowing through affecting a number of holes (6493 yards, SSS 71). Provided you have a handicap certificate, visitors are welcome on weekdays. Green fees are £16 per round or £24 a day. Lunches are served daily.
Location
Rickmansworth Road, Northwood HA6 2QW
The course is situated on the main A404 road between Northwood Hills and Rickmansworth.

PERIVALE PARK
081-578 1693
A 9 hole parkland course (2667 yards, SSS 65 men, SSS 67 women). There is an excellent practice ground. Visitors are welcome. Green fees are £1.95 on weekdays and £2.75 at weekends. Snacks are served daily.
Location
Ruislip Road East, Greenford, Middx
The club is on Ruislip Road East between Greenford and Perivale.

PINNER HILL
081-866 0963
An 18 hole parkland course (6293 yards, SSS 70). Visitors are welcome on weekdays and by previous arrangement on Saturday afternoons. Green fees on application. Light refreshments are served at the club at all times and full meals by arrangement.
Location
South View Road, Pinner Hill, Middx HA5 3YA
Leave the A404 at the Northwood Hills roundabout and the club is 1 mile west of Pinner Green.

RUISLIP
(0895) 638835
An 18 hole municipal parkland course with lots of trees (5500 yards, SSS 68). There is also a 40-bay driving range. Visitors of all playing abilities are welcome. Green fees are £4.50 on weekdays and £7 at weekends. There is a bar and a restaurant which serves an à la carte menu, breakfasts, lunches and snacks daily.
Location
Ickenham Road, Ruislip, Middx
The course is 1 mile N of the A40 to Hillingdon, near Ruislip Underground station (Central line).

RAC recommended hotel see Hillingdon.

STANMORE
081-954 2599
An 18 hole undulating parkland course (5881 yards, SSS 68). Visitors who have a handicap certificate are welcome on Tuesday, Wednesday and Thursday, and at weekends and Bank Holidays with a member. The course is open to the public on Monday and Friday. Green fees are £6 per round on weekdays and £15 per round at weekends. Full catering facilities are available daily except Monday and Friday. Local attractions include Harrow Leisure Centre.
Location
Gordon Avenue, Stanmore, Middlesex HA7 2RL
Approach Stanmore from Harrow and turn right at St John's Church, Stanmore. Gordon Avenue is the first on the right from here.

STRAWBERRY HILL
081-894 0165
A 9 hole parkland course (2381 yards, SSS 62). Visitors are welcome on weekdays and with a member at weekends. Green fees are £10. Bar snacks are available daily except Monday. Local attractions include Syon Park.
Location
Wellesley Road, Twickenham, Middlesex
The club is situated adjacent to Strawberry Hill station.

SUDBURY
081-902 3713
An 18 hole undulating parkland course (6282 yards SSS 70). Provided you have a handicap certificate or are a member of a recognised golf club, visitors are welcome on weekdays, and at weekends with a member. Green fees are £16 per round, (£24 for two rounds) on weekdays and £20 per round (£30 for two rounds) at weekends. Full catering facilities are available except on Monday. Club facilities include a snooker room. The club is within easy reach of Wembley Stadium and the Grand Union Canal.
Location
Bridgewater Road, Wembley, Middlesex HA0 1AL
Leave the A40 and the club is situated at the junction of the A4005 Bridgewater Road and the A4090 Whitton Avenue East. Sudbury Town Underground station (Piccadilly line) is within 5 minutes walk.

RAC recommended hotel
Hilton National ★★★★ 081-902 8839 Modern tower block building, part of the Wembley Stadium complex.

TWICKENHAM
081-892 5579
A tight 9 hole municipal commonland course (6014 yards, SSS 69). Visitors of all playing abilities are welcome. Green fees are £4 on weekdays and £7 at weekends. Full catering facilities are available daily. Local attractions include Hampton Court, Kew Gardens and the River Thames.
Location
Staines Road, Twickenham, Middx
The club is situated on the A305 near the Hope and Anchor roundabout.

WEST MIDDLESEX
081-574 3450
An 18 hole gently undulating parkland course (6242 yards, SSS 70). Visitors are welcome on weekdays, and Monday and Friday are public days. Green fees are £6.50, on Monday and Wednesday, and £9.50 per round on Tuesday, Thursday and Friday. Full catering facilities are available daily but 3-course meals should be booked in advance. Other facilities include three squash courts. Local attractions include Osterley Park.
Location
Greenford Road, Southall, Middx UB1 3EE
Take the A40 from Central London to Greenford, and take the left junction off the roundabout. The club is 2 miles straight down the road.

WHITEWEBBS
081-363 4458
An 18 hole parkland course (5881 yards, SSS 68). Visitors of all playing abilities are welcome. Green fees on application. Full catering facilities are available. Local attractions include Capel Manor.
Location
Beggars Hollow, Clay Hill, Enfield, Middx
The course is 1 mile north of Enfield. Turn 1 mile past the Civic Centre and take the left turn off Baker Street.

RAC recommended hotel see Enfield.

WYKE GREEN
081-560 8777
An 18 hole fairly flat wooded parkland course (6242 yards, SSS 70). Provided you have a handicap certificate, visitors are welcome by arrangement. Green fees are £20 on weekdays. Bar snacks, light lunches and full meals including Sunday lunch are available. Local attractions include Syon Park, Osterley Park and Thorpe Park.
Location
Syon Lane, Isleworth, Middlesex TW7 5PT
The golf course is located in Syon Lane, off the A4, just north of Gillette Corner.

RAC recommended hotel
Osterley ★★★ 081-568 9981 A Tudor-style converted pub with bedroom accommodation in a separate block.

NORFOLK

BARNHAM BROOM GOLF AND COUNTRY CLUB
(060 545 393
A pretty 18-hole meadowland course situated in a river valley (6603 yards, SSS 72). Visitors of all playing levels are welcome mid-week, hotel residents every day. Green fees are £17.50 for residents or £20 per round, £25 a day. There is a leisure centre attached to the hotel which has a restaurant, and a snack bar, open daily. The club is within easy reach of Norwich, the Norfolk Broads and the windmill at Dereham.
Location
Norwich, Norfolk NR9 4DD
The course is 8 miles south west of Norwich between the A11 and A47.

RAC recommended hotel
Barnham Broom ★★★ (060 545) 393 A modern hotel complex with a leisure and conference centre. Facilities include an indoor swimming pool, golf, tennis, squash, sauna and snooker.

BAWBURGH
(0603) 746390
A 9-hole meadowland course (5278 yards, SSS 66). Visitors are welcome on weekdays and Saturday but not before midday on Sunday. Green fees are £5 for 9 holes, £8 for 18 holes on weekdays and £7 for 9 holes, £10 for 18 holes at weekends. There is a bar where snacks are served.
Location
Long Lane, Bawburgh, Norwich NR9 3LX
Take the A47 ring road 1 mile south of Norwich and turn left at the Roundwell public house. The course is at the rear of the Royal Norfolk Showground.

RAC recommended hotels see Norwich.

COSTESSEY PARK
(0603) 746333
An 18-hole meadowland/parkland course situated in a river valley (5853 yards, SSS 68). The River Tud actually meanders through the course. There is also a practice area. Visitors are welcome but not before 11.30am at weekends. Green fees are £9 on weekdays and £12 at weekends. There is a dining room and also a bar where snacks are served. The course is close to Norwich where attractions include the Castle, Cathedral and market. The Norfolk Broads are within easy access.
Location
Costessey Park, Costessey, Norwich NR8 5AL
The club is 3 miles west of Norwich. Turn off the A47 ring road at the Roundwell public house.

DEREHAM
(0362) 695900
A 9-hole wooded parkland course (6225 yards, SSS 70). Provided you have a handicap certificate, visitors are welcome on weekdays, and also at weekends if you are with a member. Green fees are £12.50 on weekdays and £12 at weekends. Catering facilities are by arrangement but lunches and sandwiches are normally served. Dereham Town is nearby.
Location
Quebec Road, Dereham, Norfolk NR19 2DS
You will find the course three quarters of a mile from the town centre on the B1110.

RAC recommended hotels
Phoenix ★★★ (0362) 692276 A hotel quietly situated just off the town centre.
George ★★ (0362) 696801 A picturesque 17th-century coaching inn with original oak panelling.
Kings Head ★★ (0362) 693842 An attractive 2-storey 18th-century hotel which has been thoroughly modernised.

DISS
(0379) 642847
A 9-hole commonland course with some natural hazards (5900 yards, SSS 68). Visitors are welcome on weekdays before 4pm and at weekends after 4pm in the summer. There are no restrictions between October and March. Green fees are £6 on weekdays and £8 at weekends. It is half price if you are with a member. Lunches, teas and evenings meal are served daily.
Location
Stuston Road, Stuston Common, Diss, Norfolk IP21 4AA
Diss is 2 miles west of the A140 Norwich-Ipswich road. Turn off at Scole onto the B1077. The club is half a mile from Diss station, 1 mile from the town centre.

RAC recommended hotel
Park ★★ (0379) 642244 A low-built modern hotel situated near the centre of town.

EATON
(0603) 51686
An 18-hole undulating woodland/parkland course (6125 yards, SSS 69). Visitors are welcome on weekdays but there are some restrictions at weekends so it is best to telephone ahead. There is a practice area available. A handicap certificate is required. Green fees are £14 on weekdays and £18 at weekends. Lunch and teas are served on weekdays. The club is close to Norwich and the Cathedral.
Location
Newmarket Road, Norwich NR4 6SF
From Norwich, take the right-hand exit from the A11 into Sunningdale. The club is signposted.

RAC recommended hotels **see Norwich.**

FAKENHAM
(0328) 2867
A 9-hole parkland course (5879 yards, SSS 68). Visitors are welcome at all times. Green fees are £8 on weekdays and £12 at weekends. There is a bar and full catering facilities are available. The club has the additional facilities of a sports centre including squash, tennis, table tennis, indoor bowls, archery and a rifle club. Local attractions include Blickling Hall, Sheringham Park and Penthorpe Wildlife Park.
Location
Sports Centre, The Racecourse, Fakenham, Norfolk
Take the A1067 from Norwich or the B1146 from Dereham to Fakenham and the course is half a mile south of the town off the A1065.

RAC recommended hotel
Crown ★★ (0328) 51418 A 17th-century town-centre inn with many beams and a 'listed' fireplace.

GORLESTON
(0493) 661911
An 18-hole seaside course overlooking the North Sea (6400 yards, SSS 71). Visitors are welcome at all times but it is best to telephone first. A handicap certificate is required. Green fees are £7.50 on weekdays and £12 at weekends and Bank Holidays. A weekly ticket can be bought for £30. Full catering facilities are available daily except Monday. Local attractions include Great Yarmouth and Pleasure Wood Hills, an American theme park.
Location
Warren Road, Gorleston, Great Yarmouth, Norfolk NR31 6JT
The course is located off the A12, three miles south of Great Yarmouth. At the Yarmouth end of the dual carriageway, follow the signs down Links Road to the squash club, and the club entrance is 200 yards on the left.

RAC recommended hotels
Cliff ★★★ (0493) 662179 A three-storey white building with some attractive balconies, situated on a cliff-top.
Pier ★★ (0493) 662631 Small owner-managed hotel, standing between beach and harbour mouth.

GREAT YARMOUTH & CAISTER
(0493) 728699
A fine 18-hole seaside links course (6235 yards, SSS 70). Visitors of all playing abilities are welcome but it is advisable to telephone in advance. Green fees on application. Coffee, lunches and evening meals are available.
Location
Beech House, Caister-on-Sea, Great Yarmouth, Norfolk NR30 5DT
The club is on the A149 coast road, approximately 2 miles north of Great Yarmouth. About 1 mile north of the town take a right turn at the roundabout. Turn right into a signposted lane almost immediately.

RAC recommended hotels
Carlton ★★★ (0493) 855234 A large hotel of traditional style in a prominent seafront position.
Imperial ★★ (0493) 851113 A fine Victorian-style building in own grounds overlooking the sea.
Linwood ★★ (0493) 852427 Prominent yellow-brick 19th century building in town centre.
Star ★★ (0493) 842294 400 year-old building overlooking River Yare and quays in town centre.
Two Bears ★★ (0493) 603198 Just across the River Yare from the business centre of town, an early 20th century building, once a station hotel.

HUNSTANTON
(04853) 2811
A magnificent 18-hole seaside links course (6670 yards, SSS 72). There is also a practice ground. Provided you have a handicap certificate visitors are welcome, but booking is advisable. Three-quarters ball play is restricted. Green fees are £20 a day, £15 after 4pm on weekdays and £25 a day, £18 after 4pm at weekends and Bank Holidays. Local attractions include Sandringham House.
Location
Golf Course Road, Old Hunstanton, Norfolk PE36 6JQ
From King's Lynn, take the A149 north east to Hunstanton and the club is signposted off the road in Old Hunstanton village.

RAC recommended hotels
Le Strange Arms ★★★ (048 53) 34411 By the sea, a large 19th century building with fine views across the Wash. Tennis, billiards.
Lodge ★★ (048 53) 2896 Owner-run 17th century former Dower House, 2 miles from town centre.

KING'S LYNN
(055387) 656
A superb 18-hole undulating wooded parkland course (6646 yards, SSS 72). Visitors who have a handicap certificate are welcome on weekdays. Green fees are £20 on weekdays and £25 at weekends, or half price if you are with a member. Lunch is served daily on weekdays and evening meals by arrangement. The course is close to Sandringham.
Location
Castle Rising, King's Lynn, Norfolk PE31 6BD
Take the A149 from King's Lynn-Hunstanton and turn left at the Castle Rising sign. The club is about three quarters of a mile on the left-hand side.

RAC recommended hotels
Dukes Head ★★★ (0553) 774996 A hotel with beautifully preserved Regency facade on 'Tuesday Market' place.
Knights Hill Village ★★★ (0553) 675566 A hotel complex containing accommodation ranging from a country house to a motel, a restaurant, conference rooms and a sports centre which has

facilities including an indoor swimming pool, tennis, sauna, solarium, gymnasium and billiards.
Butterfly ★★★ (0553) 771707 Ultra modern two-storey hotel on the eastern outskirts of town on the A47/A10 junction.
Globe ★★ (0553) 772617 A georgian-style building overlooking the River Ouse and close to town centre.
Grange ★★ (0553) 673777 Refurbished Edwardian house quietly set on edge of town with some bedrooms in a separate modern block.
Stuart House ★★ (0553) 772169 Set back from the residential road, two-storey house in own grounds.
Tudor Rose ★★ (0553) 762824 Town centre hotel formed from three attractive period houses.

LINKS COUNTRY PARK
(026375) 691
A 9-hole undulating downland course with some narrow fairways (2407 yards, SSS 32). Visitors of all playing abilities are welcome. Green fees are £10 on weekdays and £12 at weekends and Bank Holidays. There is a grill room at the club which serves snacks, and the hotel has a restaurant with full à la carte and table'hôte menus. Other facilities include an indoor swimming pool, sauna and solarium. Local attractions include the Shire Horse Centre and Felbrigg Hall (NT).
Location
West Runton, Norfolk NR27 9QH
The course is midway between Cromer and Sheringham on the A149. In West Runton village, 2 miles from Sheringham, turn left opposite the village inn towards the railway station. Go over the bridge and the club is 100 yards on the left.

MUNDESLEY
(0263) 720095
A 9-hole undulating seaside course with some good views (5410 yards, SSS 66). Visitors of all playing abilities are welcome except between 12.30pm and 3.30pm on Wednesday (Ladies Day) and before midday on Sunday. Green fees are £10 a day on weekdays and £16 at weekends and Bank Holidays. Full catering facilities are available daily except Tuesday. The beach is only half a mile away.
Location
Links Road, Mundesley, Norwich, Norfolk NR11 8ES
Turn off the Mundesley-Cromer road (B1159 coast road) by Mundesley Church. The club is signposted as you enter the village, 1 mile from the village centre.

RAF MARHAM
(0760) 337261
A 9-hole meadowland/heathland course (5244 yards, SSS 66). Visitors are welcome but prior permission must be granted and you must be accompanied by a member. Green fees are £5 on weekdays and £7 at weekends. There are limited bar facilities. Local attractions include King's Lynn, the Wildlife Reserves and the Norfolk Broads.
Location
RAF Marham, King's Lynn PE33 9NP
The club is near Narborough, 11 miles south east of King's Lynn.

ROYAL CROMER
(0263) 512884
A particularly attractive 18-hole undulating seaside course (6508 yards, SSS 71) situated on the cliff edge with a famous 'Lighthouse Hole'. There is a large practice ground. Provided you have a handicap certificate, visitors are welcome on weekdays and after 11am on most weekdends. Green fees are £15 on weekdays and £20 at the weekends. Full catering facilities are available and bar snacks are also served. Local attractions include Blickling Hall (NT), Sandringham and Langham Hall.
Location
145 Overstrand Road, Cromer, Norfolk NR27 0JH
The club is situated 1 miles east of Cromer on the B1159, where the main coast road adjoins the Cromer lighthouse.

RAC recommended hotel
Cliftonville ★★ (0263) 512543 Imposing Victorian building-traditional style hotel overlooking sea. Billiards.

ROYAL NORWICH
(0603) 45712
An 18-hole undulating parkland/heathland course (6603 yards, SSS 72). Visitors who have a handicap certificate are welcome during the week and also at weekends if you are with a member. Green fees are £20 per round or day and £25 at weekends. Fees are half price if you are with a member. There are full restaurant facilities. Local attractions include Sport Village.
Location
Drayton High Road, Hellesdon, Norwich NR6 5AH
Take the ring road from the city centre and turn onto the A1067 Fakenham road. The club is 500 yards along the road.

RAC recommended hotels
Arlington ★★★ (0603) 617841 Expanded building in residential suburbs. Extensive non-residents facilities.
Maid's Head ★★★ (0603) 761111 The Maid's Head is an example of 13th century architecture.
Nelson ★★★ (0603) 760260 Modern hotel with garden beside the River Wensum. Near station. Sauna.
Norwich ★★★ (0603) 787260 Large modern hotel on the city ring road.
Norwich Sport Village ★★★ (0603) 788898 Modern, Swiss-designed village incorporating hotel, sports and leisure centre. Indoor swimming pool, tennis, squash, sauna, solarium, gymnasium, billiards.
Post House ★★★ (0603) 56431 Typical Post House with an all-day coffee shop. Indoor swimming pool, sauna, solarium, gymnasium.
Annesley ★★ (0603) 624553 Two Georgian-style buildings joined by a fully glazed covered way. Situated on the A11 in a residential area.
Lansdowne ★★ (0603) 620302 Three-storey modern hotel, outside city centre.
Oaklands ★★ (0603) 34471 Privately-owned hotel sited in pleasant outskirts of city overlooking River Yare.

ROYAL WEST NORFOLK
(0485) 210223
A very traditional 18-hole links course situated in a range of sand hills between the marshland and the sea (6428 yards, SSS 71). Visitors are welcome by arrangement except at weekends during July, August and September, when you can only play only if accompanied by a member. A handicap certificate is appreciated at all times. Green fees are £20 on weekdays and £25 at weekends. Snacks are served daily and lunches by arrangement. The course is close to Sandringham and Holkam.
Location
Brancaster, King's Lynn, Norfolk PE31 8AX
Take the A149 from King's Lynn to Hunstanton and from there take the beach road to Brancaster village.

RYSTON PARK
(0366) 383834
A 9-hole parkland course (6292 yards, SSS 70). Visitors are welcome on weekdays and also at weekends if you are with a member. Green fees are £8 or £4 with a member. Only one visitor per member is allowed at the weekend. Full catering facilities are available except on Monday.
Location
Denver, Downham Market, Norfolk PE38 0HH
The club is on the A10, just before turning into the village of Denver, 1 mile south of Downham Market.

RAC recommended hotel
Castle ★★ (0366) 384311 A stone-built 17th-century coaching inn situated near the town centre.

SHERINGHAM
(0263) 823488
Another fine 18-hole seaside course situated on the cliff top (6464 yards, SSS 71). Provided you have a handicap certificate, visitors are welcome but it is advisable to telephone first. Green fees on application. Full catering facilities are available daily. Local attractions include Blickling Hall (NT), Felbrigg Hall (NT), Sheringham Park (NT) and the Cley Marshes Bird Reserve.
Location
Weybourne Road, Sheringham, Norfolk NR26 8HG
Take the A149 from Cromer to Sheringham and the club is 1 mile from the town centre.

SWAFFHAM
(0760) 721611
A 9-hole moorland course (6252 yards, SSS 70). There is a practice ground. Visitors are welcome on weekdays and also at weekends with a member, but only after 12.30pm on Sunday. Green fees are £12. Snacks are always available and meals by arrangement.
Location
Cley Road, Swaffham, Norfolk PE37 8AE
The club is situated 2 miles south west of Swaffham Market Place, 1 mile out of town. It is signposted in the market place.

RAC recommended hotels
George ★★★ (0760) 721238 A charming William and Mary period building with a modern luxury residential wing.
Grady's Country House ★★ (0760) 23355 Attractive red-brick Georgian building in pleasant grounds close to town centre.

THETFORD
(0842) 2169
A beautiful 18-hole wooded heathland course with a difficult finish (6879 yards, SSS 73). Provided you have a handicap certificate, visitors are welcome on weekdays and at weekends with a member. Green fees are £12.50 on weekdays and £15 at weekends. Lunches are served daily and dinners every day except Monday and Tuesday. The course is within easy access of Cambridge and Norwich and other attractions include the Cluniac Priory ruins and the Ancient House Museum.
Location
Brandon Road, Thetford, Norfolk IP24 3NE
The course is 1 mile from the junction of the A11 and B1107 to Brandon.

RAC recommended hotels
Bell ★★★ (0842) 755552 A well-preserved coaching inn with a modern bedroom wing.
Anchor ★★ (0842) 763925 Traditional old coaching inn beside the river in centre of town.

NORTHAMPTONSHIRE

COLD ASHBY
(0604) 7400548
An 18-hole undulating meadowland course with some fine views (5898 yards, SSS 69). Visitors of all playing abilities are welcome on weekdays and after 2pm at weekends. Green fees are £8.50 per round, £12 a day on weekdays and £10 per round at weekends. A full range of bar snacks and restaurant meals is available daily. Local attractions include Stanford Hall and Althorp House.
Location
Cold Ashby, Northampton NN6 7EP
Take the A428 east from junction 18 of the M1 and then turn north on the B4036 for Cold Ashby. The club is approximately 5 miles from the motorway.

DAVENTRY & DISTRICT
(0327) 702829
A 9-hole hilly meadowland course with hard walking (5582 yards, SSS 67). Visitors of all playing abilities are welcome at all times except before 11am on Sunday. Green fees are £6 on weekdays and £8 at weekends and Bank Holidays. Catering facilities are only available for societies. The club is close to Daventry Country Park and Althorp House.
Location
Norton Road, Daventry, Northamptonshire NN11 4AA
The club is situated 1 mile north east of the town, next to the BBC transmitter.

RAC recommended hotels
Heyford Manor ★★★ (0327) 349022 Long, low modern hotel in rural surroundings 1 mile from M1, junction 16. Sauna, gymnasium.
Stanton Park ★★★ New hotel in rural surroundings, 1 mile west of Daventry.

DELAPRE PARK
(0604) 763957
A public 18-hole parkland course which is actually two 9-hole par 3 courses (6293 yards, SSS 70). There is also a pitch and putt course and a covered floodlit driving range with 35 bays. Visitors of all playing abilities are welcome. Green fees are £4.60 on weekdays and £5.75 at weekends. Meals are available daily between 9am and 9.30pm. Local attractions include Stanford Hall, Stoke Bruerne Waterways Museum, Althorp House, and Abington Park with aviary and museum.
Location
Eagle Drive, Nene Valley Way, Northampton NN4 0DU
The club is on the southern outskirts of Northampton; leave the M1 at junction 15 north on the A508.

RAC recommended hotels see Northampton.

KETTERING
(0536) 512074
An attractive 18-hole meadowland course with easy walking (6036 yards, SSS 69). Provided you have a handicap certificate, visitors are welcome on weekdays and also at weekends and Bank Holidays if you are with a member. Green fees are £12 (£6 with a member). Lunches and evening meals are served daily except Monday. Interesting local places to visit include Boughton House.
Location
Headlands, Kettering, Northamptonshire NN15 6XA
The course is situated at the south end of Headlands, which is a continuation of the High Street where it joins Bowling Green Road, just past the Council offices. Continue along Headlands for about ½ mile, past the Fire Station on the left, and the golf club is over the railway bridge on the right.

RAC recommended hotels
Kettering's Royal Hotel ★★★ (0536) 520732 A former 18th century stone built coaching inn situated in the market square.
George Hotel ★★ (0536) 518620 A 16th century coaching inn near the town centre.

KINGSTHORPE
(0604) 710610
An 18-hole undulating meadowland course (6006 yards, SSS 69). Visitors are welcome on weekdays by arrangement provided you have a handicap certificate. Green fees are £15 per round or day or £6 if you are with a member. There is a bar where snacks are available and lunches and dinners are served daily except Monday. Local attractions include the Saxon Church at Brixworth, Abingdon Park Museum, The Boot and Shoe Museum and the Guildhall.
Location
Kingsley Road, Northampton NN2 7BU
The club is situated 2 miles from the town centre, just off the A508. It is signposted.

RAC recommended hotels see Northampton.

NORTHAMPTON
(0604) 711054
An 18-hole meadowland course with pleasant walking (6002 yards, SSS 69). Provided you have a handicap certificate, visitors are welcome on weekdays and with a member at weekends. Green fees are £12 a day or £3.50 with a member. Full catering facilities are available. Althorp House is within easy access.
Location
Kettering Road, Northampton NN3 1AA
The course is located on the north east outskirts of the town centre on the A43.

RAC recommended hotels
Weststone Moat House ★★★ (0604) 406262 A large handsome house with modern extensions. Facilities include putting, sauna, solarium and a gymnasium.
Swallow ★★★★ (0604) 768700 An ultra-modern hotel in landscaped grounds overlooking a lake. Facilities include an indoor swimming pool, sauna, solarium and a gymnasium.
Northampton Moat House ★★★ (0604) 22441 A large modern hotel situated in the town centre. Facilities include a conference centre, sauna, solarium and gymnasium.
Grand ★★★ (0604) 250511 Red-brick building situated in town centre. Privately-owned.
Lime Trees ★★ (0604) 32188 Originally two Victorian terrace houses; additional accommodation in converted mews. On A508 not far from city centre.
Queen Eleanor ★★ (0604) 762468 A refurbished 1930s pub with modern bedroom accommodation set in a large garden. 1 mile from M1, junction 15.

NORTHAMPTONSHIRE COUNTY
(0604) 843025
An 18-hole undulating heathland/parkland course with woods and a stream (6503 yards, SSS 71). There is also a practice ground and an indoor net. Visitors who have a handicap certificate can play by arrangement on weekdays, after 3.30pm on Saturday and after 11.15am on Sunday. Green fees are £15 per round, £17 a day on weekdays and £20 per round or day at weekends (£7 with a member). There is a snack menu which is available between 11am and 6pm and other meals can be arranged. Local attractions include Althorp House, (Lord Spencer is President of the club).
Location
Sandy Lane, Church Brampton, Northampton NN6 8AZ
The club is situated off the A50 Northampton-Leicester road, 4½ miles from Northampton.

PRIORS HALL
(0536) 60756
An 18-hole parkland course (6677 yards, SSS 72). Visitors can play at any time and players of all abilities are welcome. Green fees are £2.90 on weekdays and £4.10 at weekends. Snacks and meals are available daily. East Carlton Leisure Park is within easy reach.
Location
Stamford Road, Weldon, Northampton
The club is just off the A43 Corby-Stamford Road, 2 miles east of Weldon.

RUSHDEN AND DISTRICT
(0933) 312581
A 9-hole undulating meadowland course (6381 yards, SSS 70). There is also a small practice area. Provided you have a handicap certificate, visitors are welcome on weekdays except Wednesday afternoons, and also at weekends with a member. Green fees are £10 (£5 with a member). There is a bar and restaurant with full facilities. Local attractions include Rockingham Castle, Wicksteed Park and Stoke Bruerne Waterways Museum.
Location
Kimbolton Road, Chelveston, Wellingborough, Northants NN9 6AN
Take the A6 or A45 east to Higham Ferrers and the club is 2 miles from here.

RAC recommended hotels
Rilton ★★ (0933) 312189 Small hotel conveniently situated a short distance from town centre.
Tudor Gate ★★ (0933) 68408 A family-run hotel in a fine converted 17th century farmhouse with a modern extension.

STAVERTON PARK
(0327) 705911
A testing 18-hole undulating meadowland course (6204 yards, SSS 70). There is also a driving range. Visitors of all playing abilities are welcome. Green fees are £10 per round, £15 a day on weekdays and £19.50 at weekends. Full catering facilities are available.

Location
Staverton, Daventry, Northants NN11 6JT
The club is 1 mile south from Daventry on the A425 to Leamington Spa. There is easy access from the M1, junctions 16 or 18.

WELLINGBOROUGH
(0933) 677234
An 18-hole undulating parkland course with lots of trees (6604 yards, SSS 72). There is also a practice ground. Provided you have a handicap certificate, visitors are welcome on weekdays. Green fees are £16 per day or £12 per round. There are two bars and excellent dining facilities where lunches and dinners are available. Other facilities at the club include an outdoor heated swimming pool, fishing and snooker. Northampton is within easy reach.
Location
Horrowden Hall, Great Horrowden, Wellingborough, Northants NN9 5AD
Take the A509 Wellingborough-Kettering road and the club is on the A509. The club is signposted from Great Horrowden crossroads. You should turn right at the church.

RAC recommended hotels
Hind ★★★ (0933) 222827 A 17th century stone-built hotel located in the town centre.
Columbia ★★ (0933) 229333 Two houses joined by a modern extension in pleasant tree-lined road.
High View ★★ (0933) 278733 Attractive well maintained Victorian building in quiet situation.

WOODLANDS VALE
(032736) 291
A particularly scenic 18-hole undulating parkland course (6330 yards, SSS 71). Visitors of all playing abilities are welcome at all times. Green fees are £9 per round, £15 a day on weekdays and £12 per round, £20 a day at weekends. There is a hotel on site and an extensive leisure complex is planned. There is a restaurant and carvery and bar snacks are also available. The club is conveniently situated for visits to Stratford-upon-Avon, Northampton, Milton Keynes and other attractions include the Waterways Museum at Stoke Bruerne, Silverstone and the ancestral home of George Washington, Sulgrave Manor.
Location
Woodlands Vale, Farthingstone, Towester, Northants NN12 8MA
Leave the M1 at junction 16 and the club is 3 miles west of the A5 at Weedon on the Farthingstone to Everdon Road.

RAC recommended hotels
Crossroads ★★★ (0327) 40849 Originally a 19th century toll house, with modern well-appointed annexe. Tennis.
Globe ★★ (0327) 349058 An old posting house at A5/A45 junction now refurbished to a family-run hotel.
Heart of England ★★ (0327) 40335 White-faced 18th century coaching inn with attractive gardens. On A45.

NORTHUMBERLAND

ALLENDALE
(091) 267 5875
A 9-hole meadowland course in a rural situation with some fine views (4410 yards, SSS 61). Visitors are welcome at any time, except August Bank Holiday. Green fees are £2.50 on weekdays and £3.50 at weekends and Bank Holidays. There are reductions for juniors. A weekly ticket can be bought for £16.50. There are catering facilities available.
Location
Thornley Gate, Allendale, Hexham, Northumberland NE47 9LG
Take the B6301 south west of Hexham and turn onto the B6295 at Langley, approximately 10 miles along the road, and the club is situated near Allendale Town.

ALNMOUTH
(0665) 830368
An 18-hole seaside meadowland course with some breathtaking views (6414 yards, SSS 71, Par 71). All visitors are welcome but a handicap certificate is preferred. Green fees are £11 a day (£5 with a member) on weekdays and £14 a day (£7 with a member) at weekends and Bank Holidays. Full catering facilities are available at all times. There are some good beaches in the vicinity, and the castles at Alnwick, Bamburgh, Dunstanburgh and Walkworth are within easy reach.
Location
Foxton Hall, Alnmouth, Alnwick, Northumberland NE66 3BE
Take the A1068 Alnmouth road from Alnwick and, once in Alnmouth, turn left, and Foxton is 1 mile on the right.

ALNMOUTH VILLAGE
(0665) 830370
A 9-hole undulating seaside course with some good coastal views (6078 yards, SSS 70). Visitors are welcome at all times. Green fees are £6 on weekdays and £10 at weekends and Bank Holidays. A weekly ticket can be bought for £25. Catering facilities are available by arrangement. There are several castles in the surrounding area including Alnwick, Bamburgh, Dunstanburgh and Walkworth.
Location
Marine Road, Alnmouth, Northumberland
Leave the A1 at Alnwick for the A1068 to Alnmouth.

RAC recommended hotel
Marine House (Highly Acclaimed) (0665) 830349

ALNWICK
(0665) 602632
A mature, wooded 9-hole parkland course which can provide a good test of golf (5379 yards, SSS 66). Visitors of all playing abilities are welcome except on competition days. Green fees on application. There is a bar and full catering facilities are available.
Location
Swansfield Park, Alnwick, Northumberland
Turn off the A1 at Alnwick and take the first left into Willowburn Avenue. Follow the road to Swansfield crossroads and turn left into Swansfield Park Road, to the park gates. Then you should take the next left and the first right.

RAC recommended hotel
White Swan ★★★ (0665) 601109 A former coaching inn situated in the centre of Alnwick near the castle.
Hotspur ★★ (0665) 510101 Sandstone former coaching inn with modern extension standing by main road.

ARCOT HALL
091-2362794
An 18-hole wooded parkland course in a tranquil setting (6389 yards, SSS 70). Visitors are welcome on weekdays and at non-competition weekends. Green fees are £12 on weekdays and £15 at weekends. Lunches and high teas are served daily. There are several good beaches in the area.
Location
Dudley, Cramlington, Northumberland NE23 7QP
Turn off the A1 onto the A1068 for Ashington and follow the signs.

BAMBURGH CASTLE
(06684) 321
An 18-hole seaside course with spectacular coastal views (5465 yards, SSS 67). Visitors who are members of a bona fide golf club are welcome but there are restrictions on Bank Holiday weekends. Green fees are £12 per day or round (£3 with a member) on weekdays between April and October, and £16 a day, £12 per round (£3 with a member) at weekends and Bank Holidays. There are reduced rates during the winter months. Buggies are available for hire. Lunches, teas and evening meals are available daily except Tuesday. Local attractions include Bamburgh Castle, Holy Island and the Farne Islands.
Location
The Wynding, Bamburgh, Northumberland NE69 7DE
Turn off the A1 between Alnwick and Berwick, and take the B1341 or B1342 to Bamburgh. On reaching the village, turn left opposite the Lord Crewe Arms and travel along The Wynding.

RAC recommended hotels
Waren House ★★★ (066 84) 211 18th century country house on the edge of Budle Bay.
Lord Crewe Arms ★★ (06684) 243 A late 18th-century 2 storey stone-built hotel situated near the village green.
Victoria ★★ (06684) 431 A Victorian hotel built in the traditional style.

BEDLINGTONSHIRE
(0670) 822457
An 18-hole meadowland/parkland course with easy walking (6224 metres, SSS 73). Visitors are welcome on weekdays from 9am to sunset, and at weekends from 9.30am to sunset except on competition days. The course is a public one and no handicap certificate is necessary. Trolleys are available for hire. There is also a practice ground and a putting green. Green fees are £5 per round on weekdays and £7 per round at weekends. Catering facilities are available by arrangement. There are some large sports centres within easy reach, and the surrounding National Trust area is very good for walking.
Location
Acorn Bank, Bedlington, Northumberland
Turn off the A1 for the A1068, just north of Dudley, and continue along the road towards Bedlington. The club is about half a mile west of the town.

BELLINGHAM
(0660) 20530
A 9-hole undulating meadowland course with natural hazards (5245 yards, SSS 66). Visitors are welcome but there are some limitations on Sunday. Green fees are £5 on weekdays and £5 at weekends, £3 after 5pm. Catering facilities are available for parties and for individuals by arrangement. Local attractions include Hadrian's Wall and Kielder Water and Forest.
Location
Boggle Hole, Bellingham, Hexham, Northumberland NE48 2DT
The club is situated off the B5245, 16 miles north of Hexham, with easy access from the A68.

RAC recommended hotel
Riverdale Hall ★★ (0660) 20254 A stone-built spacious 19th century mansion in 5 acres of grounds. Facilities include indoor swimming pool, putting, fishing, solarium, sauna.

BERWICK-UPON-TWEED
(0289) 87256
An 18-hole seaside links course (6399 yards, SSS 71). Visitors are welcome on weekdays but not between 10am and 2.30pm at weekends. Green fees are £8 a day on weekdays and £10.50 a day at weekends and Bank Holidays. Bar meals and high teas are served every day except Monday.
Location
Goswick, Berwick-upon-Tweed TD15 2RW
The club is situated off the A1, 4 miles south of Berwick-upon-Tweed.

RAC recommended hotel
Kings Arms ★★★ (0289) 307454 A former Georgion coaching inn in traditional style, standing on a main street.

BLYTH
(0670) 367728
An 18-hole flat parkland course built over an old

colliery (6533 yards, SSS 71). There are some testing holes round a large lake. Visitors play only on weekdays before 3pm unless you are with a member. Green fees are £10 a day or £8 per round (£5 if you are with a member). There is a large practice area. Full catering facilities are available. Whitley Bay is within easy access and there are many castles in the area.
Location
New Delaval, Blyth, Northumberland
The club is 14 miles north of Newcastle. Take the A193 coastal road 6 miles north of Whitley Bay to Blyth.

DUNSTANBURGH CASTLE
(0665) 562
An 18-hole seaside links course with beautiful surroundings (Yellow, 6038 yards, White, 6298 yards, SSS 70). The castle is on one side of the course and a bird sanctuary on the other. Visitors are welcome at all times. Green fees on application. Meals are available by arrangement. Local attractions include Dunstanburgh Castle.
Location
Embleton, Alnwick, Northumberland NE66 3XU
The course is off the A1, 8 miles north east of Alnwick.

RAC recommended hotel
Dunstanburgh Castle ★★ (066 576) 203 A stone-built village inn retaining much original character.

HEXHAM
(0434) 603072
A particularly attractive 18-hole undulating parkland course with some fine views (6026 yards, SSS 68). Provided you have a handicap certificate, visitors are welcome at any time. Green fees are £9 per round or £12 a day, or half price if you are with a member. Lunches, high teas and dinners are served daily. Hadrian's Wall is within easy access.
Location
Spital Park, Hexham, Northumberland NE46 3RZ
The club is on the A69, 1 mile west of Hexham town centre.

RAC recommended hotels
Beaumont ★★★ (0434) 602331 A three storey brick-built traditional style hotel in the centre of town near the Abbey
Royal ★★ (0434) 602270 An extended stone-built coaching inn situated on the main street in the town centre near the Abbey.
County ★★ (0434) 602030 Privately-owned stone-built 15th century hotel on main street in town centre.

MAGDALENE FIELDS
(0289) 306384
A municipal 18-hole seaside course with parkland fairways and sea bays as natural hazards (6551 yards, SSS 71). Visitors are welcome and a handicap is not necessary except for competitions. There is a practice area. Green fees are £5.75 per round on weekdays and £6.25 per round at weekends. Meals are available during the summer and at other times by arrangement. Local attractions include the historic old walled town, Holy Island and the many castles in the vicinity.
Location
Berwick-upon-Tweed
The club is situated 5 minutes walk from the town centre. It is signposted from Marygate.

RAC recommended hotel see Berwick-upon-Tweed.

MORPETH
(0670) 519980
A pleasant 18-hole parkland course with views over the Cheviots (6215 yards, SSS 70). Visitors are welcome but, unless you are with a member, a handicap certificate is required. Green fees are £8 per round, £12 a day on weekdays and £10 per round, £18 a day at weekends and Bank Holidays. Fees are £5 with a member on weekdays and £6 at weekends. Meals are available in the clubhouse but booking is advisable. There are several castles in the area, good beaches, and Holy Island is within easy reach.
Location
The Common, Morpeth, NE61 2BT
The course is on the A197, 1 mile south of Morpeth.

NEWBIGGIN-BY-THE-SEA
(0670) 817344
An 18-hole seaside course (6423 yards, SSS 71). There is a particularly difficult hole called the Quarry, where the sea actually comes in. Visitors are welcome and a handicap certificate is not required. Green fees are £5.50 on weekdays and £7.50 at weekends and Bank Holidays. Lunches are served every day except on Tuesday. The are many castles in the area, and Holy Island is nearby.
Location
Newbiggin-by-the-Sea, Northumberland
The club is on the A197, 9 miles east of Morpeth.

PRUDHOE
(0661) 32466
A challenging 18-hole parkland course with natural hazards and easy walking (5812 yards, SSS 68). Visitors are welcome on weekdays. Green fees are £8 per round or day (£4 with a member) on weekdays and £10 per round or day (£5 with a member) at weekends. There is a restaurant and a bar where snacks are served. Local attractions include Prudhoe Castle and Hadrian's Wall, and the club is within easy reach of Corbridge, Hexham and Newcastle.
Location
Eastwood Park, Prudhoe, Northumberland NE42 5DX
The club is 12 miles west of Newcastle on the A695.

ROTHBURY
(0669) 20718
A flat 9-hole open meadowland course (5146 metres, SSS 67) with natural hazards, situated by a river. Visitors of all playing abilities are welcome on weekdays and most Sundays. Green fees on application. There is a bar which is open at weekends and onTuesday, Thursday and Friday. Local attractions include Cragside Hall and Gardens.
Location
Old Racecourse, Rothbury, Morpeth, Northumberland NE65 7UB
Leave the A697 15 miles north east of Morpeth for the B6344 to Rothbury.

SEAHOUSES
(0665) 720794
An 18-hole seaside links course with easy walking (5336 yards, SSS 66). Visitors are welcome at all times. Green fees on application. A practice net is available. There is a bar where snacks are available and lunch is served.
Location
Beadnell Road, Seahouses, Northumberland NE68 7XT
Leave the A1, 12 miles north of Alnwick, for the B1341 and turn south onto the B1340 at Bamburgh towards Seahouses.

RAC recommended hotels
Beach House ★★ (0665) 720337 A 2-storey detached villa with an extension overlooking the sea.
Olde Ship ★★ (0665) 720200 Two-storey stone-built inn, with modern extension, on street beyond harbour. Putting.

STOCKSFIELD
(0661) 843041
An 18-hole wooded parkland course (5594 yards, SSS 68). Visitors who are members of a bona fide golf club are welcome at any time on weekdays and after 4pm at weekends. Two practice nets are available. Green fees on application. Sandwiches are always available and meals can be arranged by booking beforehand. Local attractions include Hadrian's Wall and the Kielder Reservoir.
Location
New Ridley, Stocksfield, Northumberland NE43 7RE
The club is on the A695 between Corbridge and Prudhoe.

WARKWORTH
(0665) 711596
A 9-hole seaside course with some fine views (5856 yards, SSS 68). Visitors are welcome at all times except on competition days, which are held mostly on Saturday, and on Tuesday between midday and 5pm (Ladies Day). A handicap certificate is not necessary. Green fees are £5 on weekdays (£3 with a member) and £7 at weekends and Bank Holidays (£4 with a member). There are several castles including Warkworth Castle, a Norman Church, the Nature Reserve at Hauxley, and some lovely beaches, all within 2 miles.
Location
Warkworth, Northumberland
Leave the A1 15 miles north of Morpeth for the B6345 at Felton and then take the A1068 to Warkworth.

WOOLER
A 9-hole (18 tee) hilltop inland heathland course (6353 yards, SSS 70) with wonderful views of Glendale, over the Cheviots to the sea and into Scotland . The 7th fairway is a Neolithic Hill Fort with rare Cup and Ring markings. The club is a young one and visitors are particularly welcome. Green fees are £4 on weekdays and £5 at weekends. Juniors can play for 50p. There is a bar which is open on summer evenings and a guest house. Local attractions include Alnwick and Bamburgh castles, Flodden Field, Berwick, the local beaches and Lindisfarne Island.
Location
Dodd Law, Doddington, Wooler
Leave Alnwick by the B6346 and turn onto the A697 to Wooler. The club is 2 miles north east of the town on the Berwick road.

RAC recommended hotel
Tankerville Arms ★★ (0668) 81581 Stone-built 17th century former coaching inn. Privately owned.

NOTTINGHAMSHIRE

BEESTON FIELDS
(0602) 257062
An 18-hole parkland course with tree-lined fairways (6414 yards, SSS 71). Practice nets are available. Visitors of all playing abilities are welcome by arrangement. Green fees are £12 on weekdays and £15 at weekends and Bank Holidays. Meals are served daily. Local attractions include the National Water Sports Centre and Sherwood Forest visitors centre.
Location
Beeston Fields, Nottingham NG9 3DD
The club is situated of the A52 4 miles west of Nottingham. On the M1, junction 25.

RAC recommended hotels
Novotel ★★★ (0602) 720106 A large modern complex near the M1. Swimming pool.
Post House ★★★ (0602) 397800 Modern hotel strategically placed at M1/A52 junction.
Europa ★★ (0602) 728481 A privately-run hotel in an extensively refurbished Victorian building.

BULWELL FOREST
(0602) 278008
An 18-hole moorland course with lots of natural hazards (5572 yards, SSS 67). Visitors of all playing abilities are welcome, and green fees are £3.70 per round. Meals are available by arrangement.

Location
Hucknall Road, Bulwell, Nottingham NG5 9LQ
Take the A610 north from Nottingham and follow the signs for Bulwell or Hucknall. The course is 4 miles from the city centre, 3 miles from the M1 junction 26.

RAC recommended hotels see Nottingham City.

CHILWELL MANOR
(0602) 258958
A good, flat 18-hole parkland course (6379 yards, SSS 69). Visitors of all playing abilities are welcome on weekdays but are restricted to four playing in any one hour. Green fees are £10 (£5 with a member). Lunch is served on weekdays and evening meals by arrangement.
Location
Meadow Lane, Chilwell, Nottingham NG9 5AE
Leave Nottingham on the A6005 and the club is just past Beeston, 4 miles west of the city centre at Chilwell.

RAC recommended hotel see Beeston Fields.

COXMOOR
(0623) 557359
A fine 18-hole wooded heathland course with easy walking and some good views (6501 yards, SSS 72). There is also a practice area and nets. Provided you have a handicap certificate, visitors are welcome but you must book a tee-off time one week in advance. Green fees are £16 on weekdays and £20 at weekends. There is a restaurant which is open daily. Local attractions include Hardwick Hall, Chatsworth House and Newstead Abbey.
Location
Coxmoor, Sutton-in-Ashfield, Notts NG17 5LF
The club is situated on the A611, 2 miles south west of Mansfield, 5 miles from the M1, exit 27.

RAC recommended hotels in Mansfield
Midland ★★ (0623) 24668 Situated on fringe of the central area, a completely refurbished hotel.
Pine Lodge ★★ (0623) 22308 Two, stone-faced Victorian houses with a modern extension to the rear. Close to M1, junction 27.

EDWALTON MUNICIPAL
(0602) 234775
A 9-hole gently sloping parkland course (3336 yards, SSS 36). Three is also a Par 3 9-hole course (1592 yards, SSS 27) and a large practice ground. Players of all abilities are welcome, particularly beginners. Green fees are £2.30 on weekdays, £2.80 at weekends for the main course and £1.40 on weekdays, £1.80 at weekends for the Par 3 course. There are reduced rates after 5pm at weekends. The bar is open all day and lunch and evening meals are served.
Location
Edwalton Village, Nottingham
Follow the Nottingham ring road to the south of the city and the course is signposted from the ring road. Turn left at Edwalton Hall Hotel.

HOLLINWELL
(0623) 753225
A fine 18-hole undulating moorland course (7020 yards, SSS 72). It is a championship course and something of a formidable test of golf. Visitors are welcome but the course is reserved for members between 12.30pm and 2.30pm on Wednesday, and for ladies before 12.30pm on Friday. No visitors may play on Saturday. Green fees are £22 per round or £25 a day. Full catering facilities are available daily.
Location
Hollinwell, Derby Road, Kirkby in Ashfield, Notts NG17 7QR
Leave the M1 at junction 27 and continue north along the A611 for 2 miles.

RAC recommended hotels in Mansfield.

KILTON FOREST
(0909) 472488
An 18-hole sandy heathland course (6569 yards, SSS 72). It is a particularly good course in the winter. Visitors are welcome at all times. Green fees are £4 on weekdays and £5.50 at weekends. There is a restaurant and bar snacks are also served. The club is well situated for visits to Sherwood Forest, Clumber Park (NT), Chatsworth House and Thoresby Hall.
Location
Blyth Road, Worksop S81 0TL
The club is situated 1 mile north east of Worksop on the B6045.

LINDRICK
(0909) 475282
An 18-hole heathland course with lots of gorse (6615 yards, SSS 72). Visitors are welcome on weekdays but prior notice is required. Players of all abilities are welcome. Green fees are £15 per round or day between November and March, and £20 per round or day between April and October, and £25 a day at weekends. Lunch is served on most days and evening meals can be arranged for visiting parties.
Location
Lindrick, Worksop, Notts S81 8BH
Leave the M1 at junction 31 and take the A57 to Worksop. The club is 4 miles west of the town.

MAPPERLEY
(0602) 265611
An 18-hole hilly meadowland course with easy walking (6224 yards, SSS 70). Visitors are welcome but there are some restrictions at weekends, so it is best to check beforehand. Golfing dress is required. Green fees are £7.50 on weekdays and £9 at weekends. Lunches and evening meals are served daily except Wednesday, when snacks only are available. The course is within easy access of Nottingham and the Castle.
Location
Central Avenue, Mapperley Plains, Nottingham NG3 5RH
Central Avenue is about 4 miles north east of Nottingham. From Nottingham, take the B684 Woodborough Road and turn right at Speeds (Volvo) Garage.

NEWARK
(063684) 282
A reasonably flat 18-hole wooded parkland course in a quiet situation (6486 yards, SSS 71). Visitors of all playing abilities are welcome. Green fees are £11 per round, £13 a day on weekdays and £15 per round, £16 a day at weekends and Bank Holidays. Meals are available by arrangement with the Steward except on Friday, bar snacks are normally served. Local attractions include Newark Castle and Belvoir Castle.
Location
Coddington, Newark, Notts NG24 2QX
The club is situated 4 miles east of Newark on the A17 Sleaford road, 1 mile east of Coddington near the junction with the A1.

RAC recommended hotels
Grange ★★ (0636) 703399 Attractive stone building previously a large Victorian house.
Ram ★★ (0636) 702255 A stone building in town centre; opposite the Castle.

NOTTINGHAM CITY
(0602) 278021
A municipal 18-hole parkland course (6120 yards, SSS 70). There is a practice area. Visitors are welcome on weekdays and also at weekends if you book in advance. Green fees are £3.80 a day on weekdays. Meals are served. Nottingham Forest is nearby.
Location
Lawton Drive, Bulwell, Nottingham NG6 8BL
The club is 3 miles north west of the city centre.

RAC recommended hotels
Albany ★★★★ (0602) 470131 A modern high-rise building situated in centre of city.
Royal Moat House ★★★★ (0602) 414444 Large modern city centre hotel, attractively furnished. Winter garden. Squash, gymnasium.
Savoy ★★★★ (0602) 602621 A large modern hotel in the north of city centre.
Stakis Victoria ★★★★ (0602) 419561 A large Victorian style hotel ideally located in city centre.
Bestwood Lodge ★★★ (0602) 203011 Former Victorian hunting lodge set in a country park. Tennis.
Strathdon Thistle ★★★ (0602) 418501 A modern purpose-built city centre hotel with conference and function facilities.
Walton's ★★★ (0602) 475215 Stone-built former lodge to Park with modern extension.
Rufford ★★ (0602) 814202 Pleasant 1920s style resident conveniently near to test cricket ground.
Sherwood ★★ (0602) 603261 White-painted hotel on inner ring road. Facing large open park.
Westminster ★★ (0602) 623023 Two Edwardian houses, linked together, conveniently situated on main northern approach to the city.

OXTON
(0602) 653545
An attractive, wooded 27-hole meadowland course which is somewhat exposed (6041 yards, SSS 72). There is also a 30-bay floodlit driving range which is open between 8.30pm and 10.30pm. Visitors of all playing abilities are welcome but you should book in advance at weekends. Green fees are £7.50 per round on weekdays and £9 per round at weekends and Bank Holidays. There are reductions if you are under 16 or over 60. Local attractions include Centre Parcs in Nottingham Forest.
Location
Oaks Lane, Oxton, Southwell, Notts NG15 0RH
From the A60 5 miles north of Nottingham, turn onto A614; 4 miles north east turn off to Oxton. Club is between A614 and A6097.

RAC recommended hotel
Saracen's Head ★★★ (0636) 812701 A modernised historic hotel with Stuart associations. Near the Minster.

RADCLIFFE-ON-TRENT
(06073) 3000
A flat 18-hole wooded parkland course with a good finish (6381 yards, SSS 71). Provided you have a handicap certificate, visitors are welcome except on Tuesday and weekends. Green fees are £14 on weekdays. There is a bar and full catering facilities are available by arrangement. Nottingham and the Castle is only 6 miles away.
Location
Dewberry Lane, Cropwell Road, Radcliffe-on-Trent, Notts NG12 2JH
The club is situated off the A52 Nottingham-Grantham road, 7 miles east of Nottingham.

RETFORD
(0777) 703733
A 9-hole woodland course (5697 yards, SSS 70). Visitors of all playing abilities are welcome on weekdays and with members at weekends. Green fees on application. Full catering facilities are available daily. The course is in the heart of Robin Hood country.
Location
Brecks Road, Ordsall, Notts DN22 7UA
Take the A620 from Worksop to East Retford.

RAC recommended hotel
West Retford ★★★ (0777) 706333 An historic 18th century manor house set in extensive grounds with modern extensions.

RUDDINGTON GRANGE
(0602) 846141
An 18-hole meadowland course with natural hazards including lakes, streams and mature trees

(6500 yards, SSS 71). Visitors who have a handicap certificate are welcome but you should book at weekends. Green fees are £15 per round, £18 a day on weekdays and £20 per round, £24 a day at weekends. There is a restaurant and bar and other facilities include a swimming pool. Nottingham is only 3 miles away.
Location
Wilford Road, Ruddington, Nottingham NG11 6NB
Take the A52 from Nottingham to the Nottingham Knight island and turn right to Ruddington. The club is half a mile outside the town.

SHERWOOD FOREST
(0602) 26689
A traditional 18-hole wooded heathland course of championship standard (6701 yards, SSS 73). Visitors are welcome on any day provided you arrange it beforehand. The club prefers you to have a handicap certificate. Tuesday is Ladies Day. There are two practice grounds. Green fees are £15 per 18 holes, £20 a day on weekdays and £20 a day at weekends. There are two dining rooms, a bar and a lounge. Local attractions include Sherwood Forest and Centre Parcs.
Location
Eakring Road, Mansfield, Notts NG18 3EU
Leave the M1 at exit 27 and follow the signs for Mansfield. Proceed via Southwell Road and Oak Tree Lane.

RAC recommended hotel see Coxmoor.

STANTON-ON-THE-WOLDS
(06077) 2044
An 18-hole meadowland course (6437 yards, SSS 71). There is a practice ground. Visitors are welcome on weekdays if there are no competitions in progress. Green fees are £9 per round, £11 a day on weekdays and £12 at weekends and Bank Holidays. There is a bar and restaurant where meals are served by prior arrangement with the Steward.
Location
Stanton-on-the-Wolds, Keyworth, Notts NG12 5AH
Take the A606 south from Nottingham and turn off at the Blue Star Garage, 9 miles from the city.

WOODHOUSE
(0623) 23521
A 9-hole parkland course (2411 yards, SSS 65). Visitors of all playing abilities are welcome. Green fees are £2 per 9 holes and £3 per 18 holes. The Friar Tuck is next door to the course and serves bar snacks. Local attractions include Sherwood Forest, and the museum and theatre in Mansfield.
Location
Leeming Lane North, Mansfield Woodhouse NG19 9EN
The club is off the A60, 2 miles north of Mansfield.

WOOLLATON PARK
(0602) 787574
An attractive 18-hole tree-lined course (6494 yards, SSS 71) situated in the deer park of a stately home. Visitors are welcome on weekdays and at weekends by application. Green fees are £11 per round or £17 a day. Lunch is available daily except Monday and bar snacks are normally served. Nottingham Castle is within easy reach and the Robin Hood Centre is nearby.
Location
Woollaton Park, Nottingham NG8 1BT
Turn off the A52 ring road at Middleton Boulevard, 3 miles from the city centre.

WORKSOP
(0909) 477732
An 18-hole sandy heathland course (6651 yards, SSS 72). Provided you have a handicap certificate, visitors are welcome, but you should telephone in advance. Green fees are £14 per round or day on weekdays and £17 per round at weekends and Bank Holidays. Full catering facilities are available by arrangement. Local attractions include Clumber Park (NT).
Location
Windmill Lane, Worksop, Notts S80 2SQ
The club is on the south side of the town. From the town centre, approach the club via Lowtown Street and Netherton Road. The course is adjacent to Worksop College.

RAC recommended hotel
Charnwood ★★★ (0909) 591610 Modern purpose-built hotel in 3 acres of landscaped gardens with picturesque pond.

OXFORDSHIRE

BADGEMORE PARK
(0491) 572206
An 18-hole parkland course with numerous trees and easy walking (6112 yards, SSS 69). There is a practice ground. Visitors who are experienced players, and preferably with a handicap certificate, are welcome on weekdays and at weekends by arrangement. Buggies are for hire. Green fees are £14 per round on weekdays and £18 per round at weekends and Bank Holidays. Full catering facilities are available. Local attractions include Oxford, Blenheim Palace and Grays Court.
Location
Badgemore Park, Henley-on-Thames, Oxon RG9 4NR
Leave the M4 at junction 8/9 on the Henley and Oxford Spur. Cross over the river into Henley and carry on straight through the town. The club is about three quarters of a mile on the left.

RAC recommended hotel see Henley.

BURFORD
(099 382) 2583
A good 18-hole parkland course (6405 yards, SSS 71). Provided you have a handicap certificate, visitors are welcome on weekdays only. Green fees are £18 a day. Full catering facilities are available. Local attractions include the Cotswold Wildlife Park.
Location
Burford, Oxon OX8 4JG
The club is 19 miles west of Oxford at the junction of the A40 and A361, at the Burford roundabout.

CHERWELL EDGE
(0295) 711591
An 18-hole public parkland course (5322 yards, SSS 68). Visitors of all playing abilities are welcome at all times. Green fees are £3.80 on weekdays and £4.90 at weekends. A six-day mid-week ticket can be bought for £6.50. Lunches, snacks and evening meals are available. Places to visit include Sulgrave Manor, George Washington's birthplace, and the club is situated in the lovely Cotswold countryside.
Location
Chacombe, Banbury, Oxon
The course is 3 miles east of Banbury on the A442 towards Northampton.

RAC recommended hotels
Whateley Arms ★★★★ (0295) 263451 A 17th-century building of local stone with a modern extension. It is situated in some attractive gardens.
Banbury Moat House ★★★ (0295) 59361 Fine, well-modernised Georgian hotel in heart of town.
Cromwell Lodge ★8 (0295) 59781 Charming 17th century Cotswold stone building. Large walled private garden.
Lismore ★★ (0295) 67661 A three-storey red-brick Victorian building on main Oxford-Banbury road. Gardens to rear.
Wroxton House ★★ (029 573) 482 Attractive building of local stone, with part thatched roof.

CHESTERTON
(0869) 241204
A flattish 18-hole meadowland course (6224 yards, SSS 70) on an old farm with lots of bunkers and water hazards. There is also a practice ground and putting green. Visitors who have golfing experience are welcome during the week but must book to play at weekends and Bank Holidays. Green fees are £10 on weekdays and £15 at weekends and Bank Holidays. Bar food is served daily between midday and 3pm (last orders 2.30pm), and groups of between 20 and 170 can be catered for. Local attractions include Oxford, Blenheim Palace, Bladon and Woodstock.
Location
Chesterton, Nr Bicester, Oxon OX6 8TE
From Oxford, take the A421 Bicester road. Turn left at the Chesterton sign and left again at the Red Cow public house. It is about 1½ miles.

CHIPPING NORTON
(0608) 2383
An attractive 18-hole undulating downland course (6283 yards, SSS 70) with a large number of trees. There is also a practice ground and putting green. Visitors of all playing abilities are welcome only on weekdays unless you are with a member. Green fees are £14 or £7 with a member. Lunches and evening meals are served daily. Places to visit locally include Blenheim Palace, Stratford-upon-Avon and Stow-on-the-Wold.
Location
Southcombe, Chipping Norton, Oxon
The club is half a mile south of the town centre on the London road or, if you are driving north, turn left at the junction of the A34/A44.

RAC recommended hotel
Crown and Cushion ★★ (0608) 2533 A 15th-century building of local stone. Situated in the town centre.

FRILFORD HEATH
(0865) 390864
Two lovely 18-hole flat wooded heathland courses (Red, 6768 yards, SSS 73 and Green, 6006 yards, SSS 69) with large greens. Both courses feature an abundance of heather, pine, birch, and flowering gorse. There are two practice areas. Provided you have a handicap certificate, visitors are welcome but you must phone in advance. Green fees are £20 (£12 with a member) on weekdays and £27 (£12 with a member) at weekends. Cooked meals are available by prior arrangement and snacks at any time. Local attractions include Oxford, and Pusey House.
Location
Frilford Heath, Abingdon, Oxon OX13 5NW
The course is situated off the A338 Oxford-Wantage road, 3 miles west of Abingdon.

RAC recommended hotels
Abingdon Lodge ★★★ (0235) 553456 A modern purpose-built hotel close to A34 with an attractive and unusual hexagonal building.
Upper Reaches ★★★ (0235) 22311 An attractive ancient converted abbey cornmill situated close to the River Thames.
Crown and Thistle ★★ (0235) 22556 A 17th-century coaching inn with an attractive cobbled courtyard, situated near the River Thames.

HENLEY
(0491) 575742
An 18-hole undulating parkland course (6330 yards, SSS 70) with a steep hill. Provided you have a handicap certificate, visitors are welcome on weekdays and also at weekends if you are with a member. Green fees are £15 per round or day.

Catering arrangements may be made with the Steward.

Location

Harpsden, Henley-on-Thames, Oxon RG9 4HG
Take the M4 to Reading and then follow the A4155 to Caversham and Henley. Turn left to Harpsden village 1 mile before reaching Henley and the clubhouse is on the left.

RAC recommended hotel

Edwardian ★★ (0491) 578678 A flamboyant 1890 half-timbered building, with balconies and oriel windows, close to town centre and river.

HUNTERCOMBE
(0491) 641207

An attractive 18-hole wooded heathland course (6108 yards, SSS 70) overlooking the Oxfordshire plain. There is a practice ground. Provided you have a handicap certificate, visitors are welcome. Visitors with 3 or 4 ball games must play after 10am. Neckwear and a jacket is required in the clubhouse. Green fees are £19.50 on weekdays. Bar snacks are available at all times. Local attractions include Dorchester for antiques, the Regatta, and Stonor Park (NT).

Location

Nuffield, Henley-on-Thames, Oxon RG9 5SL
The club is off the A423, 6 miles from Henley towards Oxford.

NORTH OXFORD
(0865) 54924

An 18-hole parkland course (5805 yards, SSS 67) with easy walking. Visitors are welcome but the club prefers you to have a current handicap. Green fees are £15 on weekdays and £20 at weekends. Full catering facilities are available. Oxford and Blenheim Palace are both within easy reach.

Location

Banbury Road, Oxford OX2 8E2
The course is between Summertown and Kidlington on the Banbury road, 2½ miles north of Oxford city centre.

RAC recommended hotel

Oxford Moat House ★★★ (0865) 59933 A large modern hotel on the northern outskirts of the city. Facilities include an indoor swimming pool, putting, squash, sauna, solarium and gymnasium.

SOUTHFIELD
(0865) 242158

A challenging 18-hole undulating parkland course (6230 yards, SSS 70). The club is the home of both the City and University clubs. Visitors are welcome on weekdays but not on Bank Holidays. A handicap certificate is required for those playing after 3pm. Green fees on application. Full catering facilities are available except on Monday. Oxford city centre is within easy reach of the club.

Location

Hill Top Road, Oxford OX4 1PF
The course is situated between Headington and Cowley. Follow Cowley Road and then Southfield Road and turn right into Hill Top Road.

RAC recommended hotels

Randolph ★★★★ (0865) 247481 A large, Gothic-style, Victorian building with elegant furnishings, centrally situated.
Cotswold Lodge ★★★ (0865) 512121 Large and attractive stone-built Victorian house, with rear extensions; half a mile north of city centre.
Eastgate ★★★ (0865) 248244 Victorian stone building in keeping with surrounding colleges. In city centre.
Linton Lodge ★★★ (0865) 53461 Former private house with modern extension in Victorian residential area.
Foxcombe Lodge ★★ (0865) 730746 A gabled former private house set in attractive gardens on Boars Hill overlooking Oxford (3 miles away).
Royal Oxford ★★ (0865) 248432 Traditional stone building close to railway station.
Tree ★★ (0865) 775794 Red-brick Victorian house in village of Iffley. Attractive gardens.
Victoria ★★ (0865) 724536 Well-modernised converted private house with modern facilities. In residential area.
Westwood Country C/H ★★ (0865) 735408 Attractive country house set in lawns and woods, in rural setting near Oxford. Sauna, gymnasium.

TADMARTON HEATH
(0608) 737278

A fairly short 18-hole heathland course (5917 yards, SSS 69) with narrow fairways and lots of gorse which can make it difficult. Visitors who have a handicap certificate can play on weekdays only. Green fees on application. Full catering facilities are available. Local attractions include Broughton Castle.

Location

Wiggington, Banbury, Oxon OX15 5HL
Take the B4035 road 5 miles west of Banbury towards Shipston on Stour.

SHROPSHIRE

BRIDGNORTH
(074 62) 3315

An attractive 18-hole parkland course (6668 yards, SSS 72) situated on the banks of the River Severn. The course is one of the oldest and longest in the country. Visitors of all playing abilities are welcome daily. Green fees are £12.50 on weekdays and £20 at weekends and Bank Holidays, half price if you are with a member. Full catering facilities are available except on Monday. Local attractions include the Severn Valley Railway.

Location

Stanley Lane, Bridgnorth, Salop WV16 4SF
The club is situated 1 mile from the town centre. Go through the High Street, along Broseley Road for some 400 yards, and turn right into Stanley Lane.

RAC recommended hotels

Falcon ★★ (07462) 3134 A 17th century coaching inn in the Low Town area of Bridgnorth.
Old Vicarage C/H ★★ (074 64) 497 Attractive Edwardian vicarage in 2 acres of lovely grounds. Family-run.
Parlors Hall ★★ (0746) 767058 Red-brick building dating to the 12th century with a walled garden, in Low Town of Bridgnorth.
Whitburn Grange ★ (0746) 766786 A refurbished Victorian building in the centre of town.

CHURCH STRETTON
(0694) 722281

An 18-hole undulating moorland course with some fine turf and outstanding views (5008 yards, SSS 65). Visitors are welcome on weekdays and on Saturday and Sunday by arrangement. Green fees are £7 on weekdays and £11 at weekends and Bank Holidays. Catering facilities are available by prior arrangement with the Steward.

Location

Hunters Moon, Trevor Hill, Church Stretton, Salop SY6 7AA
The course is about half a mile off the A49 west of the town, adjacent to Carding Mill Valley.

RAC recommended hotels

Long Mynd ★★★ (0694) 722244 A large, purpose-built offering panoramic views from the hillside. Facilities include swimming pool, putting, sauna, solarium and gymnasium.
Stretton Hall ★★★ (0694) 723224 Attractive mellowed brick and stone mansion with secluded gardens.
Mynd House ★★ (0694) 270662 Red-brick Edwardian house with modern extensions in 4 acres of gardens. At foot of Long Mynd Hill.

HAWKSTONE PARK HOTEL
(093 924) 611

Two exceptionally beautiful parkland courses, both with natural hazards and fine views; The Hawkstone, 18 holes (6203 yards, SSS 66) and The Weston, 18 holes (5063 yards, SSS 66). Provided you have a handicap certificate, visitors are welcome but you should book in advance. Buggies are available for hire. Green fees on application. There is a hotel restaurant and a bar where snacks are served. Shrewsbury and Chester are within easy access.

Location

Weston under Redcastle, Shrewsbury SY4 5UY
Take the A49 from Shrewsbury towards Whitchurch and the club is 14 miles north.

RAC recommended hotel

Hawkstone Park C/H ★★★ Elegant Georgian country house, in large park. Swimming pool, golf, putting, tennis, fishing, gymnasium, billiards.

HILL VALLEY GOLF AND COUNTRY CLUB
(0948) 3584

An American-style 18 hole undulating parkland course with water hazards (6050 yards, SSS 69) and a 9-hole par 3 course (2553 yards, SSS 64). Visitors of all playing abilities are welcome but a handicap certificate is required for the 18 hole course, whereas beginners are welcome on the 9 hole course. Green fees are £11 on weekdays and £15 at weekends for 18 holes and £7 for 9 holes. Breakfasts, lunches and dinners are served daily and conferences and wedding receptions can be catered for. Other club facilities include squash, tennis, snooker and saunas. Specialised golf lessons are available through John Garner's school of golf. The club is within easy reach of Chester, Shrewsbury and Oswestry.

Location

Terrick Road, Whitchurch, Salop SY13 4JZ
The club is 1 mile north from the centre of Whitchurch, on the A41/A49 trunk road. It is signposted.

RAC recommended hotels

Dodington Lodge ★★★ (0948) 2539 An attractive Georgian house on southern approach to town.
Terrick Hall C/H ★★★ (0948) 3031 An attractive white-faced Victorian country house in secluded woodlands. Facilities include putting, tennis, squash, sauna, billiards.
Hollies ★★ (0948) 2184 Three-storey Victorian building with motel chalets. On main road.
Redbrook Hunting Lodge ★★ (0948 73) 204 An attractive former hunting lodge on Welsh borders. Set in 2½ acres.

LILLESHALL HALL
(0952) 604776

An 18-hole wooded parkland course (5906 yards, SSS 68). Visitors may play unaccompanied on weekdays but you must be with a member at weekends. A handicap certificate may be asked for. Green fees are £12.50 per day (£5 with a member) on weekdays and £8 (with a member only) at weekends and Bank Holidays. Christmas week is £18 (£8 with a member). Full catering facilities are available between 9am and 6.30pm. Local attractions include the Iron Bridge Gorge, Weston Park and Lilleshall Abbey Ruins.

Location

Lilleshall, Newport, Salop TF10 9AS
Take the A41 north and about 5 miles before Newport turn off into Sheriffhales Road. Two miles later turn right into Abbey Road, Lilleshall.

RAC recommended hotel

Royal Victoria ★★ (0952) 820331 A refurbished Victorian hotel conveniently situated in the centre of Newport.

LLANYMYNECH
(0691) 830542
An 18 hole upland course (6114 yards, SSS 69) situated on the site of an early British encampment, and with extensive views. At the 4th hole you stand in Wales and drive into England. There is a practice area. Visitors are welcome but there are restrictions on competition days. A handicap certificate is required. Green fees are £10 on weekdays and £15 at weekends and Bank Holidays. Lunches and evening meals are served daily except Monday. Local attractions include Offa's Dyke and Powys Castle.
Location
Pant, Oswestry, Salop SY10 8LB
The club is located 1 mile west of the A483 Welshpool-Oswestry road, 6 miles south of Oswestry. Turn by the Cross Guns Inn in the village of Pant, from where it is signposted.

RAC recommended hotels see Oswestry.

LUDLOW
(058477) 285
An interesting 18 hole flat parkland course (6239 yards, SSS 70) set in a racecourse. There is a practice ground. Provided you have a handicap certificate, visitors are welcome. Green fees on application. Full catering facilities and bar service are available. Interesting places to visit locally include Ludlow Castle and the Acton Scott Museum.
Location
Bromfield, Ludlow, Salop SY8 2BT
Take the A49 Ludlow-Shrewsbury road and 2 miles out of Ludlow turn right onto the Bridgnorth road. It is well signposted from there.

RAC recommended hotels
Dinham Hall ★★★ (0584) 6464 Sandstone building with attractive bow windows; in walled garden next to Ludlow Castle.
Feathers ★★★ (0584) 875261 A famous timbered hotel with a billiards room.
Overton Grange C/H ★★★ (0584) 873500 An Edwardian house with some pleasant grounds situated in the open country, 1½ miles from the town centre.
Angel ★★ (0584) 2581 Ancient coaching inn with Lord Nelson connections.

MARKET DRAYTON
(0630) 652266
A very pretty 18 hole undulating meadowland course (6214 yards, SSS 70) with wonderful views. Visitors of intermediate playing standard are welcome on weekdays only. Green fees are £10 on weekdays. There is a bar and high-class catering is available by arrangement with the Secretary. There is a bungalow which sleeps six and is available for golfing holidays.
Location
Sutton, Market Drayton, Salop
Leave Market Drayton south via Walkmill Road, the course is 1 mile past the swimming baths.

RAC recommended hotels
Goldstone Hall C/H ★★★ (063 086) 202 Early Victorian house incorporating building from previous centuries. Five acres of mature gardens. Billiards.
Corbet Arms ★★ (0630) 2037 An ivy-clad former coaching inn situated in the town centre.

MEOLE BRACE
(0743) 64050
A pleasant 12 hole parkland course (yards, SSS 68). The club is a municipal one and visitors of all playing abilities are welcome. It is necessary to book at weekends. Green fees are £2.10 per 12 holes, £2.95 per 18 holes on weekdays and £2.60 per 12 holes, £3.70 per 18 holes at weekends. There are no catering facilities, but The Brooklands public house is very close. Local attractions include the War Museum in Shrewsbury.
Location
Meole Brace, Shrewsbury SY2 6QQ
The course is just south of Shrewsbury very close to the junction of the A5 and A49.

RAC recommended hotels in Shrewsbury.

OSWESTRY
(069188) 221
An 18 hole parkland course (6046 yards, SSS 69). There is a practice ground available. Visitors are welcome but you must be a member of recognised golf club and hold a handicap certificate, or be playing with a member. Green fees are £10 on weekdays and £14 at weekends. There is a reduction if you are with a member. Full catering facilities are available daily.
Location
Aston Park, Oswestry, Salop SY11 4JJ
The course is just off the A5 approximately 2 miles south of Oswestry.

RAC recommended hotels
Wynnstay ★★★ (0691) 655261 A three-storey Georgian town centre hotel with an elegant porch and ancient bowling green.
Sweeney Hall C/H ★★ (0691) 652450 A gracious Georgian country house quietly situated in a 100 acres park. Facilities includes billiards.

SHIFNAL
(0952) 460330
An 18 hole wooded course (6422 yards, SSS 71) situated in glorious parkland with easy walking. Provided you have a handicap certificate, visitors are welcome on weekdays by prior arrangement and at weekends with a member. Green fees are £12 per round or £15 a day. A very attractive country mansion serves as the clubhouse and lunches and evenings meals are served daily. Local attractions include the Iron Bridge, Blists Hill Open Air Museum, RAF Cosford Museum and Weston Park.
Location
Decker Hill, Shifnal, Salop TF11 8QL
The club is on the B4379 just 1 mile north of Shifnal, 1 mile south of the A5.

RAC recommended hotel
Park House ★★★★ (0952) 460128 A well-appointed hotel in an elegantly furnished Georgian building situated in own grounds. Facilities include indoor swimming pool, sauna, solarium.

SHREWSBURY
(074372) 2976
An interesting 18 hole meadowland course (6212 yards, SSS 70) with a railway track running through the middle. There is a large practice ground. Visitors who have a handicap certificate are welcome. Green fees are £10 on weekdays and £16 at weekends and Bank Holidays. Full catering facilities are available daily. Church Stretton is close by and Iron Bridge Gorge is within easy reach.
Location
Condover, Salop SY5 7BL
Take the A49 4 miles south west of Shrewsbury and follow the signs for Condover and the golf club.

RAC recommended hotels
Lion ★★★ (0743) 53107 An ancient coaching inn with Dickensian connections.
Prince Rupert ★★★ (0743) 236000 Black and white 15th century building with oak beams and modern comforts.
Radbrook Hall ★★★ (0743) 236676 Former country house on outskirtes of town. Squash, sauna, solarium, gymnasium, billiards.
Beauchamp ★★ (0743) 3230 Large modernised and extended house overlooking the Severn. Sauna, solarium.
Shelton Hall C/H ★★ (0743) 3982 A red-brick Victorian country house in pleasant grounds.
Shrewsbury ★★ (0743) 231246 An 'Olde worlde' 19th century hotel, at the foot of the Welsh bridge.

TELFORD HOTEL GOLF & COUNTRY CLUB
(0952) 585642
An 18 hole undulating meadowland course (6274 yards, SSS 70) with easy walking . The course is an attractive one with three lakes, American-style bunkers and fine greens. Provided you have a handicap certificate, visitors are welcome. Green fees are £14 on weekdays and £18 at weekends and Bank Holidays. The club is part of a country club and meals are served daily. Other facilities include an indoor heated swimming pool, squash, snooker and sauna. Local attractions include Blists Hill Open Air Museum, the Iron Bridge and Coalport China Works.
Location
Great Hay, Telford, Salop TF7 4DT

Turn off the A442 to Sutton Hill, 4 miles south of Telford Centre and the A5/M54 junctions.

RAC recommended hotel
Telford Hotel Golf and Country Club ★★★ (0952) 587878 A modern hotel developed around 18th century red-brick country house. It overlooks the golf course and gorge. Facilities include indoor swimming pool, putting, squash, sauna and snooker.

WREKIN
(0952) 44032
An 18 hole undulating parkland course (5657 yards, SSS 67) with some hard walking. There is a small practice ground. Visitors are welcome on weekdays before 5pm. Green fees are £10 per day on weekdays and £12 at weekends and Bank Holidays. Catering facilities can be arranged if you book in advance with the Stewardess.
Location
Ercall Woods, Wellington, Telford TF6 5BX
Leave the M54 and turn back along Holyhead Road, following the signs to Golf Links Lane.

RAC recommended hotels
Buckatree C/H ★★★ (0952) 641821 A well-appointed former manor house in quiet grounds at the foot of Wrekin.
Charlton Arms ★★ (0952) 251351 Characteristic old coaching inn in the heart of the Shropshire countryside.
Falcon ★★ (0952) 255011 Off M54, a family-run hotel once an 18th century inn.

SOMERSET

BREAN
(027875) 467
A flat 18 hole moorland/meadowland course (5436 yards, SSS 66). Provided you have a handicap certificate, visitors are welcome on weekdays and at weekends after midday. Green fees are £5.50 on weekdays and £9 at weekends. Bar snacks are available at the clubhouse and meals and entertainment at the adjoining Leisure Centre.
Location
Coast Road, Brean, Burnham-on-Sea, Somerset TA8 2RF
Leave the M5 at junction 22 and follow the signs for Brean Leisure Centre on the right.

RAC recommended hotels see Burnham & Berrow.

BURNHAM & BERROW
(0278) 785760
An 18 hole championship links course with some large sandhills (6327 yards, SSS 72). Visitors who are members of a recognised club and have a handicap certificate are welcome except on Saturday mornings. Advance booking is necessary. Green fees are £18 on weekdays and £25 at weekends and Bank Holidays. Full catering facilities are available between 11am and 6pm and meals outside these hours by arrangement. Some dormitory accommodation is available at the club.
Location
St Christopher's Way, Burnham-on-Sea, Somerset TA8 2PE
Leave the M5 at exit 22 and the course is 1 mile north of Burnham-on-Sea.

RAC recommended hotels
Dunstan House ★★ (0278) 784343 Georgian period house with gardens. Few minutes walk from sea.
Royal Clarence ★★ (0278) 783138 Three-storey building, once a coaching inn. Fine sea views.

ENMORE PARK
(027 867) 481
An 18 hole undulating wooded parkland course (6443 yards, SSS 71) with some splendid views. Visitors who are members of a bona fide golf club and have a current handicap certificate are welcome on weekdays, but it best to telephone beforehand for weekend games. Green fees are £12 on weekdays and £15 at weekends. Lunch and evening meals are available.
Location
Enmore, Bridgwater, Somerset TA5 2AN
Leave the M5 at junction 23 for Bridgwater. Turn left at the traffic lights in the town and continue for 1 mile. The course is signposted 2 miles on the left.

RAC recommended hotel
Walnut Tree Inn ★★★ (0278) 662255 An attractive coaching inn in the village of North Petherton. There is some motel-type accommodation and facilities include a solarium.

MENDIP
(0749) 840570
An 18 hole undulating downland course (5982 yard, SSS 69) with extensive views. This course can provide quite a test of golf. Visitors of all playing abilities, except complete beginners, are welcome on weekdays, but at weekends you must be accompanied by a member unless you belong to an affiliated club. There is a practice ground and indoor net. Green fees are £12 on weekdays and £20 at weekends. Full catering facilities are available daily. Local attractions include Wells Cathedral.
Location
Gurney Slade, Bath, Somerset BA3 4UT
The club is situated 3 miles north of Shepton Mallet, just off the A37.

RAC recommended hotel
Charlton House ★★★ (0749) 2008 17th century manor house in extensive grounds, to east of town. Indoor swimming pool, tennis, sauna.

MINEHEAD & WEST SOMERSET
(0643) 2057
A flat 18 hole seaside links course (6130 yards, SSS 69) with good turf. Visitors are welcome. Green fees are £11 on weekdays and £13.50 at weekends and public holidays. Snacks are always available and other meals by arrangement with the Steward or Stewardess.
Location
The Warren, Minehead, Somerset TA24 5SJ
The course is situated beside the beach at the eastern end of the town, three quarters of a mile from the town centre.

RAC recommended hotels
Benares ★★★ (0643) 704911 Spacious hotel with attractive garden, in quiet residential area.
Northfield ★★★ (0643) 705155 A pleasant hotel with gardens, in a residential area. Facilities include indoor swimming pool, putting, sauna and gymnasium.
Beaconwood ★★ (0643) 702032 Villa style hotel with pleasant garden. Away from town on high ground with spectacular views. Swimming pool, putting, tennis.
Remuera ★★ (0643) 702611 A spacious residence with attractive garden and views of coast. Putting.
Winsor ★★ (0643) 702171 Spacious hotel, near to sea and shops. Privately-owned and run.

TAUNTON & PICKERIDGE
(082342) 240
An 18 hole undulating course (5927 yards, SSS 68) with panoramic views. Visitors are welcome on weekdays by arrangement but a handicap certificate is required. Green fees are £10 on weekdays and £13 at weekends and Bank Holidays. Lunches and evening meals are served at the club. Local attractions include the Wellington Monument, and Taunton is only 4 miles away.
Location
Corfe, Taunton, Somerset TA3 7BY
Take the B3170 4 miles south of Taunton, pass through Corfe village and then take the first left.

RAC recommended hotels
Castle ★★★★ (0823) 27262 Once part of a Norman fortress, this is an imposing hotel with an interesting garden.
County ★★★ (0823) 337651 A large Georgian hotel of character, set in the centre of town.
Crest ★★★ (0823) 332222 New purpose-built hotel just off junction 25 of M5 overlooking countryside. Sauna, gymnasium.
Rumwell Manor ★★★ (0823) 254861 Recently refurbished Georgian building, in 5 acres of grounds on the A38 west of town. Swimming pool.
Corner House ★★ (0823) 284683 Victorian brick-built house in Gothic style. West from town centre.
Falcon ★★ (0823) 442502 Privately-owned, spacious residence standing in its own grounds.
Heatherington Grange ★★ (0823) 461777 Modernised and extended 18th century coaching inn on the A38 between Taunton and Wellington.

VIVARY
(0823) 289274
An 18 hole undulating parkland course (4620 yards, SSS 63) with some pond hazards. This is a municipal course and visitors of all playing abilities are welcome. There is a practice ground and also a putting green. Green fees are £5.25. Places of interest locally include Taunton Museum.
Location
Taunton, Somerset
The course is situated in the centre of Taunton.

RAC recommended hotels in Taunton.

WELLS
(0749) 72868
A particularly beautiful 18 hole meadowland/parkland course (5354 yards, SSS 67) with superb views. Visitors of all levels of handicap are welcome. There is a practice area. Green fees are £10 on weekdays and £12 at weekends. There is a bar and lunches and evening meals are served daily. There are caravan facilities available adjacent to the course. Wells Cathedral is worth visiting and the town centre is within easy reach.
Location
East Horrington Road, Wells, Somerset BA5 3DS
The club is 1 mile east of the city centre opposite Mendip Hospital.

RAC recommended hotels
Swan ★★★ (0749) 77647 Attractive 15th century coaching inn with fine view of Cathedral. Squash.
White Hart ★★ (0749) 72056 Privately-owned 15th century attractive former coaching inn in main street.

WINDWHISTLE
(046030) 231
A flat 12 hole parkland course (6055 yards, SSS 69) with some wonderful views. Visitors of all playing levels are welcome but it is advisable to telephone first. There are also chipping and putting greens. Green fees are £8 on weekdays and £10 at weekends and Bank Holidays. There is a bar and catering facilities are available between Monday and Saturday. The club is opposite a Wildlife park.
Location
Cricket St Thomas, Chard, Somerset TA20 4DG
The club is situated on the A30, 5 miles from Crewkerne, 3 miles from Chard, opposite the Manor Born Wildlife park.

RAC recommended hotel
Shrubbery ★★ A substantial, stone-built hotel on $2^1/_2$ acres of gardens situated on the A303 near the centre of Ilminster. Facilities include swimming pool and tennis.

YEOVIL
(0935) 22965
An 18 hole undulating parkland course (6139 yards, SSS 69) situated beside the River Yeo. The 14th

and 15th holes are particularly testing. Visitors of all playing abilities are welcome on weekdays but only golfers with a handicap certificate may play at weekends. You must ring in advance to book a weekend game and it is also advisable to check availability during the week. There is also a practice ground and putting green. Green fees are £12 on weekdays and £14 at weekends. There is a bar and dining room with full facilities daily except Monday. Local attractions include Sherborne Castle and Montacute House (NT).

Location
Sherborne Road, Yeovil, Somerset BA21 5BW
The club is situated 1 mile east of Yeovil on the A30 towards Sherborne, on the right before you reach Babylon Hill.

RAC recommended hotels
Manor Crest ★★★ (0935) 23116 A large attractive 18th century hotel, in easy reach of the town centre.
Yeovil Court ★★★ (093586) 3746 A cream-painted hotel situated on the A30 on the outskirts of town but with a country aspect.
Mermaid ★★ (0935) 23151 A privately-owned inn of considerable character, situated in the centre of Yeovil.
Three Choughs ★★ (0935) 74886 Stone-built inn with character. Situated in centre of Yeovil.

STAFFORDSHIRE

ALSAGER GOLF AND COUNTRY CLUB
(0270) 875700
An 18 hole parkland course (6206 yards, SSS 70). Visitors who are members of another golf club are welcome on weekdays except Tuesday mornings, and at weekends if you are with a member. Green fees are £10 per round. There is a restaurant and bar. Stoke-on-Trent is within easy access and other attractions include Nantwich, a medieval village, and Alton Towers, only 40 miles away.

Location
Andley Road, Alsager, Stoke-on-Trent, Staffs ST7 2UR
Leave the M6 at junction 16 for the A500 east and turn onto the A5011 to Alsager, approximately 2 miles from the motorway.

BARLASTON
(078 139) 2795
A very picturesque 18 hole meadowland course (5800 yards, SSS 68) lying alongside the River Trent. Visitors are welcome every day but not before 10.30am at weekends. Green fees are £9 on weekdays and £12 at weekends. There is a bar. Local attractions include Wedgwood at Barlaston, and Stoke-on-Trent.

Location
Meaford Road, Barlaston, Stone ST15 8UX
The club is situated a quarter of a mile south of Barlaston, three quarters of a mile north of Stone off the A34.

RAC recommended hotels see Stone.

BEAU DESERT
(05438) 2626
An 18-hole heathland course (6300 yards, SSS 71) surrounded by fir and spruce trees. Provided you have a handicap certificate, visitors are welcome on weekdays but you should telephone the Pro if you wish to play at weekends. Green fees are £18 a day. Full catering and bar facilities are available. Local attractions include Cannock Chase.

Location
Hazelslade, Hednesford, Cannock, Staffs WS12 5PT
Take the A460 from Cannock through Hednesford and the club is signposted from here.

BRANSTON
(0283) 43207
An 18 hole undulating parkland course (6458 yards, SSS 71) with several lakes, lying adjacent to the River Trent. Provided you have a handicap certificate, visitors are welcome on weekdays. Green fees are £9 on weekdays and £12 at weekends (£5 with a member). Full catering facilities are available except on Monday.

Location
Burton Road, Branston, Burton-upon-Trent, Staffs DE14 3DP
Take the A5121 off the A38 towards Burton-upon-Trent, pass the church on the right, go over the railway bridge, pass the petrol station on your right and the entrance to the club is 200 yards further on the right.

RAC recommended hotels see Burton-upon-Trent

BROCTON HALL
(0785) 662627
An 18 hole parkland course (6095 yards, SSS 69) with easy walking. Visitors who have a handicap certificate are welcome. Green fees are £15 on weekdays and £17 at weekends and Bank Holidays. Catering facilities are available by arrangement. Local attractions include Stafford Castle and Shugborough Hall.

Location
Brocton, Staffs ST17 OTH
Take the A34 4 miles south of Stafford and turn left at the crossroads signposted Brocton. The club entrance is 300 yards on your left.

RAC recommended hotels see Stafford Castle.

BURSLEM
(0782) 837006
A 9 hole moorland course (5527 yards, SSS 67) with some hard walking. Visitors of all playing abilities are welcome on weekdays and on Saturday if you are with a member. Green fees are £7 a day (£3 with a member). Catering facilities are available by arrangement with the Steward. Alton Towers is within easy access.

Location
Wood Farm, High Lane, Tunstall, Stoke-on-Trent, Staffs ST6 7JT
Leave Burslem centre by Hamil Road and turn left at High Lane junction. The club is 2 miles on your right.

RAC recommended hotel
Hanchurch Manor C/H ★★★ 19th century Tudor-style manor house with tall chimneys and stone-mullioned windows, set on high ground overlooking a lake.

BURTON-UPON-TRENT
(0283) 44551
An 18 hole meadowland course (6555 yards, SSS 71). Visitors are welcome but a letter of introduction from a bona fide golf club is necessary together with a current handicap certificate. It is also advisable to book in advance. Green fees are £10 on weekdays and £15 at weekends and Bank Holidays. Full catering facilities are available at the club except on Monday. The Bass Brewery Museum is a place worth visiting in the vicinity.

Location
43 Ashby Road East, Burton-upon-Trent, Staffs DE15 0PS
The club is on the A50 Burton-Ashby road, 3 miles from Burton centre.

RAC recommended hotels
Riverside Inn ★★★ (0283) 511234 White-painted Georgian house with modern extension in quiet setting. Lawns run down to River Trent.
Stanhope Arms ★★★ (0283) 217954 A gabled, red-brick hotel situated beside the A50 a couple of miles east of the town.
Newton Park C/H ★★★ (0283) 703568 Stone-built country house hotel in Georgian manner. Pleasant gardens.
Needwood Manor C/H ★★ (028 371) 2932 Victorian manor house in 2 acres of grounds on edge of Needwood Forest.

CRAYTHORNE
(0283) 64329
An 18 hole parkland course (5230 yards, SSS 66). There is also a 9 hole pitch and putt course and a floodlit driving range. Provided you have a handicap certificate, visitors are welcome. Green fees are £7 on weekdays, £8 on Saturdays and £9 on Sundays and Bank Holidays. There are bars, and a restaurant which is open daily. There are several museums in Burton-upon-Trent which are worth visiting.

Location
Craythorne Road, Stretton DE13 0AZ
The club is $1^{1}/_{2}$ miles north of Burton-upon-Trent, off the A38 junction with the A5121. Follow the signposts for Stretton from here.

DRAYTON PARK
(0827) 251139
An 18 hole parkland course (6414 yards, SSS 71) with some wooded areas. Provided you have a handicap certificate, visitors are welcome by arrangement on weekdays. There is a practice area. Green fees are £14 per day or round. Full catering facilities are available from 10.30am. Local attractions include Tamworth Castle grounds and there is also a zoo adjacent to the course.

Location
Drayton Park, Tamworth, Staffs B78 3TN
Follow the A4091 for 2 miles south of Tamworth and the club is next to the Drayton Manor Leisure Park.

GOLDEN HILL
(0782) 784715
An 18 hole parkland course (5957 yards, SSS 68) where 5 holes are played over water. The course is a public one and visitors are welcome but you should book with the Secretary beforehand. Equipment can be hired. Green fees are £3.20 on weekdays and £3.50 at weekends. There is a bar and restaurant with full facilities. There is a Heritage Trail at Stoke-on-Trent and the Festival Leisure Park is within easy reach.

Location
Mobberley Road, Golden Hill, Stoke-on-Trent, Staffs ST6 5SS
The course is situated between Tunstall and Kidsgrove on the A50.

RAC recommended hotels in Newcastle-under-Lyme.

GREENAWAY HALL
(0782) 503158
An 18 hole meadowland course (5676 yards, SSS 67) with some splendid views of the Pennines. Visitors are welcome as guests of a member. Green fees on application. Catering facilities are available by prior arrangement with the Steward.

Location
Stockton Brook, Stoke-on-Trent, Staffs ST9 9LI
The course is situated off the A53 Stoke-Leek road, approximately 5 miles from Stoke.

INGESTRE PARK
(0889) 270061
An 18 hole undulating meadowland course (6376 yards, SSS 70) situated in the grounds of Ingestre Hall. Visitors of all playing abilities with a handicap certificate are welcome on weekdays and with a member at weekends. Green fees are £14. Full catering facilities are available. Local attractions include Ingestre Hall, a Christopher Wren church and Shugborough Hall.

Location
Ingestre, Stafford, Staffs ST18 0RE
The club is approximately 6 miles east of Stafford, off the A51, via Great or Little Haywood.

LAKESIDE RUGELEY
(0889) 583181
A 9 hole parkland course (4768 yards, SSS 63). Visitors are welcome as guests of a member.

Green fees are £2.50. There is a bar where snacks are served. Local attractions include Lichfield Cathedral and Shugborough Hall.
Location
Rugeley Power Station, Rugeley, Staffs WS15 1PR
The course is situated in the grounds of Rugeley Power Station, 2 miles south east of the town centre on the A513.

LEEK
(0538) 384779
A challenging 18 hole moorland course (6229 yards, SSS 70). Visitors are welcome on weekdays before 3pm, provided you have a handicap certificate. Green fees are £15 on weekdays and £20 at weekends. Lunch is served daily except Sunday and evening meals every day except Sunday and Monday. Local attractions include Alton Towers and the moors.
Location
Cheddleton Road, Leek, Staffs
The club is 1 mile from Leek on the A520 Stone road.

RAC recommended hotel
Peak Weavers ★ (0538) 383729 Red-brick mansion in garden 5 minutes walk from town centre.

NEWCASTLE MUNICIPAL
(0782) 627596
An open 18 hole parkland course (6256 yards, SSS 70) situated on the side of a hill. The course is a municipal one and visitors, particularly beginners, are welcome at all times. There is a private 26-bay floodlit driving range, a computerised Petron fitting centre and two Pro shops. Green fees are £3.55 on weekdays and £4.15 at weekends. Lunches and dinners are served by arrangement. Newcastle is within easy reach.
Location
Keele Road, Newcastle, Staffs ST5 2QB
Leave the M6 at junction 15 for the A525 and then continue along the road for 2 miles.

NEWCASTLE-UNDER-LYME
(0782) 618526
An 18 hole parkland course (6427 yards, SSS 71). Visitors are welcome on weekdays but you must have a current handicap certificate. Green fees are £15 (£5.50 with a member). Lunch and evening meals are served daily and there is a bar where snacks are available.
Location
Whitmore Road, Newcastle-under-Lyme, Staffs ST5 2QB
The club is 1½ miles south west from Newcastle-under-Lyme on the A53 Shrewsbury road.

RAC recommended hotels
Clayton Lodge ★★★ (0782) 613093 Early Victorian building with extensions and conference facilities.
Post House ★★★ (0782) 717171 A modern well-designed hotel set in landscaped gardens. It is situated close to the M6 and facilities include an indoor swimming pool.
Borough Arms ★★ (0782) 629421 A privately-run hotel in an 18th-century listed building.

STAFFORD CASTLE
(0785) 223821
A 9 hole meadowland course (6347 yards, SSS 70). Visitors of all playing abilities are welcome on weekdays. Green fees are £7. Catering facilities are available daily except Monday. Local attractions include Stafford Castle.
Location
Newport Road, Stafford
The course is situated half a mile from Stafford main street.

RAC recommended hotels
Tillington Hall C/H ★★★ (0785) 53531 A country house type hotel, in its own ground, situated near the motorway. Facilities include an indoor swimming pool, tennis, gymmnasium and billards.
Abbey ★★ (0785) 58531 Pleasant hotel close to town centre.
Albridge ★★ (0785) 54100 Two-storey late Victorian building set beside A449 in the suburbs.
Garth ★★ (0785) 56124 On outskirts of town, convenient for M6, hotel with modern bedrooms.
Swan ★★ (0785) 58142 An old coaching house with modernised bedrooms, in the centre of the town.
Vine ★★ (0785) 51071 An old inn of character situated in the centre of the town.

STONE
(0785) 813103
A challenging 9 hole meadowland course (6140 yards, SSS 69) which overlooks the sea. Visitors of all playing abilities (including children) are welcome on weekdays. Green fees are £10. Lunches and evening meals are served daily except Monday. Local attractions include the Wedgwood Potteries.
Location
Filley Brooks, Stone, Staffs ST15 0NB
The club is approximately half a mile north of Stone on the A34, adjacent to the Wayfarer Hotel.

RAC recommended hotels
Stone House C/H ★★★ (0785) 814764 A Regency country house hotel in a landscaped garden. Facilities include a swimming pool, putting, sauna, solarium and gymnasium.
Crown Osprey ★★★ (0785) 813535 An 18th century coaching inn with oak panelled restaurant and modern facilities.

TAMWORTH
(0827) 53850
An 18 hole undulating moorland course (6083 yards, SSS 72). Visitors of all playing abilities are welcome at all times. Green fees are £4.25 per round and £2.75 per 9 holes. There is a reduction for juniors. There is a bar where snacks are served and a licensed restaurant. Drayton Manor Park and Tamworth Castle are worth visiting.
Location
Eagle Drive, Tamworth, Staffs B77 4EG
The club is situated down Mercian Way, off the Tamworth -Polesworth road and adjoining the Amington Industrial Estate. It is signposted from Tamworth roundabout.

TRENTHAM
(0782) 658109
An 18 hole parkland course (6644 yards, SSS 72) with some testing holes. Provided you have a handicap certificate, visitors are welcome on weekdays and also at weekends if you have permission from the Secretary. There is a practice area. Green fees are £15 on weekdays and £18 at weekends. Lunches are served daily and bar snacks and evening meals by arrangement. The club also has squash courts and a snooker room. Local attractions include Alton Towers.
Location
14 Barlaston Road, Trentham, Stoke-on-Trent, Staffs ST4 8HB
Take the A34 3 miles south of Newcastle-under-Lyme and turn off at the Trentham roundabout onto the A5035 Uttoxeter road. Take the first turning on the right by the National Westminster Bank and the club is immediately on your right.

RAC recommended hotels see Newcastle-under-Lyme.

TRENTHAM PARK
(0782) 65880
A fine 18 hole parkland course (6644 yards, SSS 72). Provided you have a handicap certificate, visitors are welcome on weekdays. Green fees are £12. Full catering facilities are available daily except Monday. Trentham Gardens are nearby and the Wedgwood Potteries are worth a visit.
Location
Trentham Park, Trentham, Stoke-on-Trent, Staffs ST4 8AE
Take the A34 for 4 miles south of Newcastle-under-Lyme and the club adjoins Trentham Gardens near junction 15 of the M6.

RAC recommended hotels see Newcastle-under-Lyme.

UTTOXETER
(0889) 564884
An open 18 hole parkland course (5695 yards, SSS 69) with some scenic views . Visitors are welcome but you must book for a weekend game. There is a practice net and also a putting green. Green fees are £8 on weekdays and £12 at weekends, or £3 if you are with a member. There is a bar and snacks are normally served. Alton Towers is only 6 miles away.
Location
Wood Lane, Uttoxeter, Staffs ST14 8JR
The club is situated approximately half a mile from Uttoxeter racecourse.

RAC recommended hotels
White Hart ★★★ (08893) 2437 A 16th-century coaching inn modernised and extended but retaining many attractive original features.
Bank House ★★ (0889) 566922 A traditional red-brick Georgian town house situated opposite the church.

WESTWOOD
(0538) 383060
A 13 hole parkland/moorland course (5501 yards, SSS 67). The course is to be expanded to 18 holes (6100 yards). Visitors are welcome except on Sundays and Bank Holidays, and if you wish to play on Saturday you must be with a member. Green fees are £8 on weekdays (£4 with a member) and £5 on Saturday. There is a bar. The surrounding area is good for fishing, sailing and walking, and other local attractions include Alton Towers, the pottery museums in Stoke-on-Trent and the Peak District National Park.
Location
Newcastle Road, Walbridge, Leek, Staffs
The club is on the west boundary of Leek on A53.

RAC recommended hotel in Leek.

WHITTINGTON BARRACKS
(0543) 432317
An 18 hole moorland course (6457 yards, SSS 71). Visitors are welcome on weekdays but you must have a handicap certificate or a letter of introduction. Green fees are £15 per round or day. Snack lunches and evening meals are available except on Monday. Lichfield Cathedral and Shugborough Hall are nearby.
Location
Tamworth Road, Lichfield, Staffs WS14 9PW
The course is situated on the A51, 2½ miles from Lichfield station.

RAC recommended hotels
George ★★★ (0543) 415817 Modernised coaching inn in city centre near Cathedral.
Little Barrow ★★★ (0543) 414500 Modern purpose-built hotel in city centre convenient for Cathedral.
Angel Croft ★★ (0543) 258737 A brown brick 18th century residence situated near the Cathedral.

WOLSTANTON
(0782) 622413
An 18 hole meadowland/parkland course (5807 yards, SSS 68). Provided you have a handicap certificate, visitors are welcome on weekdays. Green fees on application. Lunch is served every day except Friday. Local attractions include Clenton Gardens and Alton Towers.
Location
Dimsdale Old Hall, Hassam Parade, Newcastle-under-Lyme, Staffs ST5 9DR

Take the A34 $1^1/_2$ miles north west of Newcastle-under-Lyme and turn off at the Lymelight Hotel into Dimsdale Parade. Take the first right into Hassam Parade and right again for the club entrance.

RAC recommended hotels see Newcastle-under-Lyme.

SUFFOLK

ALDEBURGH
(0728) 452890
A delightful 18-hole heathland seaside course which is ideal for those on holiday (6330 yards, SSS 71). There is also a 9-hole course (4228 yards, SSS 64). Visitors who have a handicap certificate are welcome on weekdays and also at the weekend by arrangement with the Secretary. Green fees on application. Lunch is served daily. Local attractions include The Maltings and the Aldeburgh Festival.
Location
Saxmundham Road, Aldeburgh, Suffolk IP15 5PE
The club is situated 1 mile from the town centre on the A1094.

RAC recommended hotel
Brudenell ★★★ (0728) 452071 A pleasant holiday hotel on the seafront. There are some good views of the sea from the restaurant.

BUNGAY AND WAVENEY VALLEY
(0986) 2337
An 18-hole links type course on heathland around some neolithic stone workings (6000 yards, SSS 68). Visitors are welcome on weekdays only, unless you are with a member when you are also welcome at the weekend. The club prefers you to have a handicap certificate. Green fees are £12 per round or day. Full catering facilities are available daily except on Monday when only snacks are served. Ersham Otter Trust is within easy reach and there is also a castle in Waveney valley.
Location
Outney Common, Bungay, Suffolk NR35 1DS
The course is on the A143 Bury St Edmunds to Great Yarmouth road, approximately a quarter of a mile from the town centre.

BURY ST EDMUNDS
(0284) 5979
An 18-hole undulating parkland course with easy walking (6615 yards, SSS 72). Provided they have a handicap certificate, visitors are welcome but not before 10am at weekends unless they are playing with a member. Green fees are £12.50 a day on weekdays and £16 a day at weekends. Full catering facilities are available every day. The club is close to the historic city of Bury St Edmunds.
Location
Tuthill, Bury St Edmunds, Suffolk IP28 6LG
The course is 2 miles from Bury St Edmunds on the A45 towards Newmarket. Leave the A45 at the roundabout and follow the A1106.

RAC recommended hotels
Angel ★★★ (0284) 753926 An elegant, historic creeper-covered Georgian hotel in a square near the Cathedral.
Butterfly ★★★ (0284) 760884 Modern purpose-built hotel with rustic decor in rural setting.
Suffolk ★★★ (0284) 753995 An old coaching inn of character in the town centre.

CRETINGHAM
(072882) 275
A 9-hole meadowland course (1955 yards, SSS 30). Visitors of all playing abilities are welcome daily from 8am until dusk. Green fees are £5 on weekdays and £6 at weekends and Bank Holidays. Light snacks are available daily. Other facilities at the club include tennis (hard court) and snooker.
Location
Cretingham, Woodbridge, Suffolk IP13 7BA
From A12 at Woodbridge, take B1079 and B1077 north. At Peats Corner turn right on A1120 to Earlsham, turn right again to Cretingham.

FELIXSTOWE FERRY
(0394) 286834
An 18-hole seaside links course with some fine views (6042 yards, SSS 70). Provided they have a handicap certificate visitors are welcome on weekdays and after 10.30am at weekends and Bank Holidays. There is a practice area. Green fees are £12 a day on weekdays and £14 at weekends and Bank Holidays. It is half price if you are playing with a member. Lunch is available daily and evenings meals by arrangement. Felixstowe and Woodbridge are within easy reach.
Location
Ferry Road, Felixstowe, Suffolk IP11 9PY
Take the A45 to Felixstowe and follow the signs to the Yachting Centre.

RAC recommended hotels
Orwell Moat House ★★★★ (0394) 285511 A spacious red-brick hotel in the grand tradition.
Marlborough ★★ (0394) 285621 A large four-storey hotel in a commanding position on the seafront.
Waverley ★★ (0394) 282811 Victorian building in high position overlooking sea. Solarium.

FLEMPTON
(02884) 291
A 9-hole breckland course (6074 yards, SSS 69). It is flat and sandy but very attractive and one of the best 9-hole courses in the county. Visitors are welcome on weekdays by arrangement and with a member at weekends and Bank Holidays. No handicap certificate is required but you must have some knowledge of the game. Green fees are £15 per 18 holes, £20 a day. Catering facilities are available by arrangement. The course is within easy access of Bury St Edmunds.
Location
Flempton, Bury St Edmonds, Suffolk IT28 6DQ
Follow the A1101 from Bury St Edmunds towards Mildenhall for about 4 miles and the course is on the right.

RAC recommended hotels in Bury St Edmunds.

FORNHAM PARK
(0284) 706777
An 18-hole flat parkland course with lots of water hazards (6212 yards, SSS 70). Visitors of all playing levels are welcome. Green fees on application. There is a restaurant and bars where snacks and meals are available. The club is attached to a country club and other facilities include sauna and snooker.
Location
Fornham St Genevive, Bury St Edmunds, Suffolk
The club is situated 2 miles from Bury St Edmunds. Leave the A45 for the A1101 to Mildenhall through the village of Fornham St Genevieve.

RAC recommended hotels in Bury St Edmunds.

HAVERHILL
(0440) 61951
A 9-hole parkland course with a river running through (5680 yards, SSS 68). Players of all levels are welcome and there is a video training centre linked to the golf course. Green fees are £10 on weekdays (£5 with a member) and £15 at weekends and Bank Holidays (£5 with a member). Local attractions include Audley End Mansion, Saffron Walden, Lavenham and Clubford Hall Vineyard.
Location
Coupals Road, Haverhill, Suffolk GB9 7UW
Take the A604 from Cambridge and half a mile south east of Haverhill turn into Chalkestone Way, near the railway viaduct, then right again in Coupals Road after passing the Snooker Club.

IPSWICH
(0473) 728941
A lovely 18-hole heathland course with well-maintained greens with lakes and some very attractive trees (6405 yards, SSS 71). It is a long established first-class course. There is also a 9-hole course (3860 yards, SSS 59). Provided they have a handicap certificate of at least 18, visitors are welcome on the 18-hole course on weekdays by advance arrangement. There are no restrictions for the 9-hole course. Green fees are £14 per round or day for 18 holes on weekdays, £16 at weekends and £5 on weekdays and £7.50 at weekends and Bank Holidays for the 9-hole course. Full catering facilities are available.
Location
Purdis Heath, Bucklesham Road, Ipswich, Suffolk IP3 8QU
The club is situated 3 miles east of Ipswich off the A45. Turn into Bucklesham Road at the roundabout by St Augustine's Church.

RAC recommended hotels
Hintlesham Hall C/H ★★★★ (047 387) 268 Fine Elizabethan manor with Georgian facade set in 18 acres of parkland, 6 miles west of town. Tennis, fishing, riding, billiards.
Belstead Brook C/H ★★★ (0473) 684241 Converted period farmhouse with modern residential wing. 7 acres of grounds.
Ipswich Moat House ★★★ (047 386) 444 Modern hotel with extensive function facilities outside town. Sauna, solarium, gymnasium.
Marlborough ★★★ (0473) 257677 A delightfully situated luxury hotel set in a residential area opposite a park.
Novotel ★★★ (0473) '£'$)) Well-kept modern hotel in city centre with attractive open-plan public areas.
Post House ★★★ (0473) 690313 A modern hotel with a swimming pool and coffee shop which is open all day.
Great White Horse ★★ (0473) 256558 Famous old coaching inn with covered courtyard. Dickensian associations.

LINKS
(0638) 663000
An 18-hole undulating parkland course (6162 yards, SSS 71). Provided they have a handicap certificate, visitors are welcome but not before 11.30 am on Sunday unless they are with a member. There are two practice grounds. Green fees are £15 on weekdays and £20 at weekends. Full catering facilities are available except on Monday. Local attractions include the Racecourse which is actually opposite the club and the Horse Racing Museum at Newmarket.
Location
Cambridge Road, Newmarket, Suffolk CB8 0TG
The club is located 1 mile south of Newmarket High Street, opposite the racecourse.

RAC recommended hotels
Newmarket Moat House ★★★ (0638) 667171 Well-adapted modern building, originally flats. Adjoins town and Heath.
Rutland Arms ★★★ (0638) 664251 A former coaching inn with modern residential wings. The hotel is situated in the town centre.
White Hart ★★★ (0638) 663051 An attractive gabled hotel situated in the town centre, with associations with horse racing.

NEWTON GREEN
(0787) 77501
A 9-hole moorland course (5488 yards, SSS 68). Visitors who have a handicap certificate are welcome on weekdays only. Green fees are £10 per round or day. Hot and cold snacks are served daily. The town of Lavenham is nearby.
Location
Newton Green, Sudbury, Suffolk

The club is on the A134, 3 miles east of Sudbury.

RAC recommended hotel
Mill ★★★ (0787) 75544 A beautifully converted water mill and granary with a modern extension overlooking the river.

ROOKERY PARK
(0502) 560380
An 18-hole parkland course (6649 yards, SSS 72). Visitors who have a handicap certificate are welcome throughout the year. There is a practice ground and a 9 hole par 3 course. Green fees are £12 a day on weekdays and £14 at weekends. There are two bars and full catering facilities are available.
Location
Beccles Road, Carlton Colville, Lowestoft NR33 8HJ
The course is on the A146 2 miles west of Lowestoft.

RAC recommended hotel
Victoria ★★★ (0502) 4433 A hotel in traditional grand style, occupying a commanding position overlooking the beach. Facilities include a swimming pool.

ROYAL WORLINGTON AND NEWMARKET
(0368) 71226
A particularly good 9-hole links course (3105 yards, SSS 70). Visitors of all playing abilities are welcome on weekdays but you must telephone in advance to book. Green fees are £15 (£7 with a member) on weekdays and £17.50 at weekends. Lunches and teas are served daily. The historic town of Bury St Edmunds provides many attractions include the Cathedral and Ely, with its Cathedral, is within easy reach.
Location
Worlington, Bury St Edmonds, Suffolk IP28 8SD
Take the A45 from Newmarket and then the A11 towards Mildenhall. Turn left to Royal Worlington.

RAC recommended hotels
Riverside ★★★ (0638) 717274 Large Georgian building with gardens down to the river. Fishing.
Smoke House Inn ★★★ (0638) 713223 16th century building with exposed beams. Bedrooms in new wings. Fishing, riding.
Bell ★★ (0638) 717272 A family-owned and managed, well-preserved old coaching inn in Mildenhall town centre.

RUSHMERE
(0473) 727109
An 18-hole undulating heathland course with lots of gorse (6287 yards, SSS 70). Visitors who have a handicap certificate are welcome on weekdays and also at weekends and Bank Holidays after 2.30pm. Green fees are £9 per round, £12 a day on weekdays and £12 at weekends. Full catering facilities are available.
Location
Rushmere Heath, Ipswich, IP4 5QQ
The club is off the A1214 just east of Ipswich. Turn into Glenavon Road and follow the signs.

RAC recommended hotels in Ipswich.

SOUTHWOLD
(0502) 723234
A 9-hole commonland course with fine sea views (60001 yards, SSS 69). Provided they have a handicap certificate, visitors are welcome except on competition days. There is also a 4 acre practice ground. Green fees are £9 on weekdays and £12 at weekends and Bank Holidays. Snacks and lunches are available by arrangement with the Steward. There are lots of lovely local walks around the quiet town of Southwold and the coastal bays.
Location
The Common, Southwold, Suffolk IP18 6TB
From the A12 follow the A1095 signposted Southwold. Once in Southwold turn right at the Kings Head Hotel and proceed across the Common. The golf club is about half a mile on the right hand side.

STOWMARKET
(04493) 473
An 18-hole parkland course (6101 yards, SSS 69). Visitors of all playing abilities are welcome on weekdays but you must have a handicap certificate to play at the weekend. Green fees are £10 on weekdays and £16.50 at weekends. Meals are usually available at all times.
Location
Lower Road, Onehouse, Stowmarket, Suffolk IP14 3DA
Take the B1115 from Stowmarket and 2½ miles south west turn right to Onehouse.

THORPENESS
(072 845) 2176
A varied 18-hole heathland course with natural hazards (6241 yards, SSS 71). Provided they have a handicap certificate, visitors are welcome on weekdays by arrangement. There is a large practice ground. Green fees are £15 per round on weekdays and £20 per round at weekends. There is an hotel on site and full catering facilities are available. Local attractions include Aldeburgh, The Maltings and the Music Festival, and the 16th century Moat Hall.
Location
Thorpeness, Suffolk IP16 4NH
Leave the A12 at Saxmundham and turn onto the B1119 and then the B1353 to Thorpeness.

WALDRINGFIELD HEATH
(0473) 36768
An 18-hole heathland course (5837 yards, SSS 68). Visitors of all playing abilities are welcome but there are some restrictions at weekends and Bank Holidays so it is best to telephone ahead. Green fees are £8 per round, £12 a day on weekdays and £10 per round, £14 a day at weekends. There is a bar and restaurant.
Location
Newbourne Road, Waldringfield, Woodbridge IP12 4PT
The club is situated 5 miles north of Ipswich east off the A12.

RAC recommended hotel
Seckford Hall ★★★ (0394) 385678 A beautifully preserved and enlarged Tudor mansion set in 34 acres south of Woodbridge. Facilities include an indoor swimming pool, fishing and a gymnasium.

WARREN HEATH
(0473) 726821
This is a driving range only and visitors are welcome between 8am and 7pm every day. Green fees are are £1.50 per 100 balls. The golf courses of Ipswich, Rushmere, Alesbourne and Woodbridge are all close by.
Location
Bucklesham Road, Ipswich IP3 8TZ
The course is situated between Bucklesham Road and Old Felixstowe Road.

WOODBRIDGE
(03943) 2038
A particularly lovely 18-hole heathland course situated on high ground (6314 yards, SSS 70). It is also one of the best in the county. There is also a 9-hole course (4486 yards, SSS 62). Provided they have a handicap certificate, visitors are welcome on weekdays. Green fees are £15 per round, £20 a day. Bar snacks and meals are available by arrangement. The course is 17 miles from Aldeburgh and the Snape Maltings.
Location
Bromeswell Heath, Woodbridge, Suffolk IP12 2PF
The club is 2 miles east of Woodbridge off the A12. Go through the village of Melton onto the B1084.

RAC recommended hotel
Seckford Hall ★★★ (0394) 385678 A beautifully preserved and enlarged Tudor mansion set in 34 acres south of Woodbridge. Facilities include an indoor swimming pool, fishing and a gymnasium.

WOOD VALLEY
(0502) 712244
A 9-hole heathland course with natural hazards (2781 yards, SSS 67). Visitors who have a handicap certificate are welcome on weekdays but if you wish to play at weekends or Bank Holidays you must be accompanied by a member. Green fees are £6 on weekdays and £7 on Saturdays. There is a bar and light refreshments are normally served, full meals by arrangement.
Location
The Common, Beccles, Suffolk
The club is 1 mile off the A146 approximately 9 miles west of Lowestoft.

RAC recommended hotels
Kings Head ★★ (0502) 712147 Traditional town centre in hotel in market place.
Waveney House ★★ (0502) 712270 Listed building, delightfully located on banks of river with gardens. Fishing.

SURREY

ADDINGTON COURT
081-657 0281
There are actually two challenging courses here, The Championship (5577 yards, SSS 67), and The Falconwood (5513 yards, SSS 67). There is also a 9-hole course for beginners and a pitch and putt course. The course is public and visitors are welcome. Non golfing members are also welcome. There is a full teaching practice ground. Green fees are £6 for the Championship course, but you need to apply to the club for the Falconwood fees. Full catering facilities are available daily.
Location
Featherbed Lane, Addington, Surrey CR0 9AA
The course is two miles east of Croydon. Turn off the A2022 at Addington Village.

RAC recommended hotels
Holiday Inn ★★★★ (081) 680 9200 A modern hotel in a central position. Facilities include an indoor swimming pool, squash, sauna, solarium and gymnasium
Selsdon Park ★★★★ (081) 657 8811 A greatly enlarged Tudor mansion situated in 200 acres. Facilities include indoor and outdoor swimming pools, golf, putting, tennis, squash, sauna, solarium, gymnasium and billiards.
Post House ★★★ 081-688 5185 Modernised hotel, reconstructed from former Airport reception building.
Briarley ★★ 081-654 1000 Three-storey hotel in quiet road; Victorian building with modern facilities.
Central ★★ 081-688 5644 Owner-run hotel, in former private residences in quiet street. Convenient for station.

ADDINGTON PALACE
081-654 3061
An 18-hole parkland course with hard walking and an interesting 12th hole called the 'Fountain' (6282 yards, SSS 71). Visitors are welcome on weekdays and with a member at the weekends and Bank Holidays. Green fees are £20 per round. Snacks and meals are available during the day except on Monday.
Location
Gravel Hill, Addington Park, Croydon, Surrey CR0 5BB
The course is situated 2 miles from East Croydon station on A12.

BANSTEAD DOWNS
081-642 2284
An 18-hole downland course with narrow fairways (6169 yards, SSS 69). Visitors of all playing abilities

are welcome but you need a letter of introduction to play between Monday and Friday and to be accompanied by a member at weekends and Bank Holidays. Green fees are £20 before 12 noon for 2 rounds and £15 after 12 noon for 1 round. Catering facilities are available between 11am and 6pm with dinner by arrangement.

Location

Burdon Lane, Belmont, Sutton, Surrey SM2 7DD
The club is 100 yards east of the junction between the A217 and B2230 or 10 minutes from Belmont Station.

RAC recommended hotel

Thatched House (Acclaimed) 081-642 3131

BARROW HILLS
(0932) 848717

An 18-hole parkland course with natural hazards (3090 yards, SSS 53). Visitors are welcome but only if accompanied by a member. Green fees on application.

Location

Longcross, Chertsey
The club is located 4 miles west of Chertsey.

BETCHWORTH PARK
(0306) 882052

An 18-hole parkland course with some hilly spots giving a fair test of golf (6266 yards, SSS 70). Visitors of all playing levels are welcome on weekdays except Tuesday and Wednesday morning, and at weekends except Sunday morning. Green fees are £20 on weekdays and £27 at weekends. Catering facilities are available including dinner by arrangement. Local attractions include Polesdon Lacey and Box Hill.

Location

Reigate Road, Dorking, Surrey RH4 1NZ
Take the A25 towards Reigate, 1 mile east of Dorking and the entrance is opposite the horticultural gardens.

RAC recommended hotels

Burford Bridge ★★★★ (0306) 884561 A large hotel set in some pleasant gardens situated at the bottom of Box Hill. Facilities include a swimming pool.

White Horse ★★★ (0306) 881138 Modernised coaching inn, with new block at rear. Swimming pool.

BRAMLEY
(0483) 892696

An 18-hole parkland course with some fine views (5910 yards, SSS 68). Visitors who have a handicap certificate are welcome on weekdays. There is also a practice area and a golf range. Green fees are £15 per round, £20 a day. Bar snacks and a grill menu are available daily.

Location

Bramley, Guilford, Surrey GU5 0AL
The club is situated 4 miles south of Guildford on the A281, Guildford to Horsham road, between the villages of Shalford and Bramley.

BURHILL
(0932) 227345

A delightful, fairly short 18-hole parkland course with some lovely trees (6224 yards, SSS 70). Visitors are welcome by arrangement but a handicap certificate is required. Green fees are £25 a day or £16 after 12 noon. Lunch and snack bar facilities are available except on Monday.

Location

Walton-on-Thames, Surrey KT12 4BL
Turn off the A3 onto the A245 towards Byfleet, and turn right into Seven Hills Road and again into Burwood Road and the entrance is second on the right, or from Walton Railway Bridge go through Burwood Park.

RAC recommended hotels

Oatlands Park ★★★ (0932) 847242 A large Victorian-Edwardian building in extensive grounds. It was once a Royal residence.

Ship Thistle ★★★ (0932) 848364 Modernised old coaching inn with extension at rear. In town centre.

CAMBERLEY HEATH
(0276) 23258

A superb wooded 18-hole undulating heathland course with some varied and difficult holes (6402 yards, SSS 71). Provided you have a handicap certificate visitors are welcome but by invitation only. Green fees on application. A buggy fleet is available and clubs can be hired. There is also a practice ground. Meals and snacks are served .

Location

Golf Drive, Camberley, Surrey GU15 1JG
Leave the M3 via exit 3 from the north or exit 4 from the south and turn onto the A325 Camberley to Portsmouth road. Follow the signs to Frimley and Bagshot. The club is approximately 1 mile south of Camberley.

RAC recommended hotel

Frimley Hall ★★★ (0276) 28321 A converted manor house with pleasant terraces and lawns.

COOMBE WOOD
081-942 2388

A flat 9-hole parkland course (1655 yards, SSS 70). There is also a covered floodlit driving range with 18 bays which is open between 9am and 10pm daily. Visitors are welcome at all times although it is advisable to book at the weekends. Green fees are £2.50 on weekdays and £3 (or £2 for OAPs and juniors) at weekends. There is a public bar and food is available.

Location

George Road, Kingston Hill, Surrey KT2 7NS
The club is situated off the A243, opposite Chessington South Station, 500 yards from Chessington World of Adventure.

RAC recommended hotel

Kingston Lodge ★★★ 081-541 4481 A two-storey white stucco hotel built around a pleasant central courtyard, There is an attractive conservatory-style restaurant.

CHIPSTEAD
(073 75) 55781

An 18-hole hilly parkland course (5454 yards, SSS 67). Visitors of all playing levels are welcome on weekdays. Green fees are £16 a day or £12 after 2pm(£7 with a member). Lunch is served daily except on Monday but you must book in advance.

Location

How Lane, Coulsdon, Surrey CR3 3PR
From the A217 follow the signs to Chipstead. The course is by Chipstead station (Tattenham Corner Line).

COOMBE HILL
081-942 2284

A magnificent 18-hole wooded parkland course (6286 yards, SSS 71). In spite of being so close to London, the course is particularly tranquil. Visitors are welcome on weekdays but a high level of play is expected. Green fees are £45 on weekdays. Lunches are served daily.

Location

Kingston Hill, Surrey, KT2 7DG
Leave the A3 for Coombe Lane west (A238) towards Kingston, and the club is about a quarter of a mile.

COMBE WOOD
081-942 0388

An 18-hole wooded parkland course (5210 yards, SSS 66). Provided they have a handicap certificate, visitors are welcome on weekdays. Green fees on application. Catering facilities are available except on Monday and Tuesday. Local attractions include Richmond Park and the River Thames which is close by.

Location

George Road, Kingston Hill, Surrey KT2 7NS
The course is 1 mile north of Kingston-on-Thames, off Kingston Hill.

COULSDON COURT
081-660 0468

A public 18-hole parkland course with some good views over the surrounding countryside (6030 yards, SSS 70). Visitors are welcome at any time but you should telephone first for confirmation. Green fees are £5.50 on weekdays and £7.75 at weekends. Snacks, breakfasts, lunches, barbecues and dinners. The club also has full conference and banquet facilities. Other facilities include tennis, squash, solarium and gymnasium.

Location

Coulsdon Road, Coulsdon, Surrey CR3 2LL
The club is just off the A23, 2 miles south of Croydon and 2 miles north of the M25 and M23.

RAC recommended hotels see Addington Court.

CRANDALL GOLF COURSE
(0252) 850 880

An 18-hole parkland course with some holes played over chalk pits (6278 yards, SSS 70). There is also a putting green and covered 14-bay driving range. The course is public and visitors of all playing abilities are welcome at any time. Green fees are £10 on weekdays and £15 at the weekend. There is a restaurant and also conference facilities for up to 20 people. Local attractions include the very pretty village of Crondall which dates back to 800.

Location

Oak Park, Hoatle Lane, Crondall, West Farnham, Surrey GU10 5PB

RAC recommended hotels

See Farnham.

CROHAM HURST
081-657 2075

A tree-lined 18-hole parkland course surrounded by hills (6274 yards, SSS 70). The course has a reputation of 'being difficult to score but easy to play', but nevertheless it is a relaxing course for all levels of play. Visitors are welcome on weekdays but it is advisable to telephone beforehand. Green fees are £18 a day on weekdays. Full catering facilities are available between 10am and 6pm daily.

Location

Croham Road, South Croydon, Surrey CR2 7HJ
The club is situated on the A2022, half a mile from South Croydon station, on the road to Selsdon. The entrance is on the right hand side.

RAC recommended hotel

Selsdon Park ★★★★ 081-657 8811 A greatly enlarged Tudor mansion situated in 200 acres. Facilities include indoor and outdoor swimming pools, golf, putting, tennis, squash, sauna, solarium, gymnasium and billiards.

CUDDINGTON
081-393 0952

An 18-hole parkland course with easy walking (6282 yards, SSS 70). Visitors who have a handicap certificate or a letter of introduction are welcome by appointment. Green fees are £20 a day. Full catering facilities are available by arrangement. There is a snooker room at the clubhouse.

Location

Banstead Road, Banstead, Surrey SM7 1RD
The course is 200 yards from Banstead Station.

DORKING
(0306) 886917

A 9-hole undulating parkland course with easy walking (5120 yards, SSS 65). Visitors are welcome on weekdays and also at the weekends and on Bank Holidays if you are with a member. Ladies Day is Wednesday morning. The course provides a good test of golf for all standards. Green fees are £12.50 a day or £9.50 per round. Snacks are available and meals by arrangement. The course is close to Box Hill.

Location
Chart Park, Dorking, Surrey RH5 4BX
The club is situated on the A24, half a mile south of the junction with the A25, 1 mile south of Dorking.

RAC recommended hotels
Burford Bridge ★★★★ (0306) 884561 A large hotel set in some pleasant gardens situated at the bottom of Box Hill. Facilities include a swimming pool.
White Horse ★★★ (0306) 881138 A modernised coaching inn, with a new block at the rear. There is a swimming pool.

DRIFT
(04865) 4641
An 18-hole wooded course with lots of ponds (6404 yards, SSS 71). Visitors of all playing abilities are welcome on weekdays. Green fees on application. Bar snacks and evening meals are available daily except Monday and lunches by arrangement.
Location
The Drift, East Horsley, Surrey KT24 5HD
Turn off the A3 onto the B2039 signposted East Horsley and the club is situated approximatiely 2 miles from here, just off the Drift Road which runs between Ockham Road and Forest Road, East Horsley.

RAC recommended hotel
Thatchers ★★★ (048 65) 4291 A half-timbered hotel with a modern extension in attractive grounds. There is a swimming pool.

EFFINGHAM
(0372) 52203
A long 18-hole downland course with tree-lined fairways (6488 yards, SSS 71). Visitors who have a handicap certificate are welcome on weekdays by arrangement. Green fees are £25 a day or £20 after 2pm. Lunch, teas, evenings meals and snacks are available daily. The club also has 4 tennis courts and 2 squash courts. Local attractions include The Royal Horticultural Society gardens at Wisley.
Location
Guildford Road, Effingham, Surrey KT24 5PZ
The club is situated on the A246, 4 miles from Leatherhead and 8 miles east of Guildford.

EPSOM
(037 27) 21666
An 18-hole downland course (5668 yards, SSS 67) close to the racecourse. Visitors of all playing levels are welcome on weekdays from 11am except on Tuesday when you can play after 12.30pm, however, it is advisable to telephone in advance. There is a practice ground and also a practice putting green. Green fees on application. Catering facilities are available by arrangement. The course is close to the town centre.
Location
Longdown Lane, Epsom, Surrey KT17 4JR
Leave the A240 for the B288 and the club is situated 200 yards northof Epsom Downs station.

RAC recommended hotel
Drift Bridge ★★ (073 73) 52163 A large detached public house convenient for Epsom race course.

FARNHAM
(025 18) 2109
An 18-hole course with a lovely mixture of heathland and pine with parkland (6313 yards, SSS 70). Visitors are welcome on weekdays and as guests of a member at the weekend, although players with a handicap of over 21 would find the course difficult. There is a putting green and a practice ground. Green fees are £21 a day or £18 per round. Full catering facilities are available by arrangement. Frensham Ponds, Waverley Abbey and Farnham town centre are all within easy access.
Location
The Sands, Farnham, Surrey GU10 1PX
The club is 1 mile east of Farnham off the A31 Crooksbury Road . You should turn off at the signposts to The Sands and the club is near the 'Jolly Farmer'.

RAC recommended hotels
Bush ★★★ (0252) 715237 A well-known 17th-18th century coaching inn with a modern block, set in pleasant gardens.
Frensham Pond ★★★ (025 125) 3175 Delightful detached house overlooking pond; in a rural setting. Indoor swimming pool, squash, sauna, solarium, gymnasium.
Bishop's Table ★★ (0252) 710222 An 18th-century terrace house, furnished to a very high standard. There is a large garden.
Pride of the Valley ★★ (042 873) 5799 Small detached country inn, beside lovely woods and common land.
Trevena House C/H ★★ (0252) 716908 Mock Tudor detached building in quiet grounds of main A31. Swimming pool, tennis.

FARNHAM PARK
(0252) 715216
A 9-hole par 3 parkland course situated in Farnham Park (1161 yards, SSS 54). The course is particularly suitable for beginners and visitors are welcome at all times, although normal golf rules apply. Clubs are available for hire. Green fees are £2 on weekdays for seniors and £1.50 for juniors, £2.50 and £1.50 respectively at weekends. Light snacks are normally served. There is a cricket ground in the Park and Farnham Castle is close by.
Location
Folly Hill, Farnham, Surrey
The club is about three quarters of a mile north of Farnham next to the Castle in Farnham Park.

FERNFELL
(0483) 276626
An 18-hole partly wooded parkland course situated at the foot of the Surrey hills. Visitors of all playing abilities are welcome on weekdays and also at weekends and Bank Holidays, although not in the mornings. Green fees are £9 on weekdays and £15 at weekends. It is £5 at all times if you are playing with a member. There is a bar and coffee shop. The clubhouse is a 400 year old barn and other facilities include tennis, swimming pool, snooker and sauna.
Location
Barhatch Lane, Cranleigh, GU6 7NG
The club is off the A281 1 mile from Cranleigh.

FOXHILLS
(093287) 2050
There are two heathland courses here finishing on the same green. The Chertsey, 18-holes, (6880 yards, SSS 73) with tree-lined fairways and The Longcross, 18-hole, Par 3 (6747 yards, SSS 72) with lakes and large bunkers. Visitors are welcome, as guests of a member, between Monday and Friday. Green fees are £16 per round or £23 a day. Buggies can be hired. There are two restaurants together with bars which provide a service daily. Other facilities include tennis, squash, swimming and a health club.
Location
Stonehill Road, Ottershaw, Surrey KT16 0EL
Leave the A320 Chertsey to Woking road at the Otter Public House and turn right and then right again into Foxhills Road. The club is behind St Peter's Hospital.

GATTON MANOR
(030 679) 555
A wooded 18-hole undulating parkland course with a particularly scenic layout running through woods and alongside lakes (6145-6902 yards, SSS 69-73). Visitors of all playing abilities are welcome except on Sunday morning. There are practice facilities and also a games room. Green fees on application. Meals and bar snacks are served daily. The club can provide a quiet country retreat weekend for non-golfing members.
Location
Ockley, Dorking, Surrey RH5 5PQ
The club is approximately 1½ miles south west of Ockley, off the A29, 9 miles south of Dorking.

GOAL FARM
(04867) 3183
A challenging very pretty 9-hole par 3 course with marvellous greens (1283 yards, SSS 54). The course is public but visitors can only play on weekdays as competitions are played at the weekend. There is a practice net and bunker and also a putting green. Green fees are £3.80 on weekdays, £4.20 at weekends for 18 holes and £2 on weekdays, £2.20 at weekends for 9 holes. Light refreshments are served.
Location
Pirbright GU24 OP2
The club on off the A322 between Woking and Guildford.

GUILDFORD
(0483) 63941
An 18-hole downland course with lots of trees (6080 yards, SSS 70). Visitors of all playing abilities are welcome on weekdays and also at the weekends if accompanied by a member. Green fees are £20 on weekdays and £25 at weekends. Bar snacks are normally served and there is a restaurant where meals can be booked in advance. Local attractions include Merrow Downs and Guildford Cathedral.
Location
High Path Road, Merrow, Guildford, Surrey GU1 2HI
From Guildford take the Epsom Road (A246) amd turn right at the third set of traffic lights.

RAC recommended hotels
Post House ★★★★ (0483) 574444 Newly built, long, low, red-brick building just off the A3. Indoor swimming pool, sauna, solarium, gymnasium.
Manor at Newlands C/H ★★★ (0483) 222624 Gabled stucco manor house in 9 acres of parkland and gardens just off A25 east of the city.
White Horse ★★★ (0483) 54511 A Georgian building with modern rooms situated near the town centre.
Clavadel ★★ (0483) 69066 Converted Edwardian gabled house, well furnished and decorated in style.

HANKLEY COMMON
(025125) 2493
An 18-hole heathland course with excellent greens and a spectacular 18th hole (6403 yards, SSS 71). It is a dry and sandy links-type course. Provided they have a handicap certificate, visitors are welcome on weekdays and by arrangement with the Secretary at weekends and Bank Holidays. There is a practice ground. Green fees are £18 per round, £25 a day on weekdays and £25 a round at weekends and Bank Holidays. There is a restaurant and two bars which provide full facilities.
Location
Tilford Road, Tilford, Farnham, Surrey GU10 2DD
Take the A3 to Hindhead, over the railway crossing and turn right at the lights at Hindhead, or, if you are on the A31(Farnham by-pass) turn left at the lights, 3 miles from the level crossing on the A287,

RAC recommended hotels see Farmham.

HOEBRIDGE
(048 62) 22611
There are three meadowland courses here. The Hoebridge, 18 holes (6536 yards, SSS 71), The Maybury, 18 holes (2230 yards, Par 3) and The Shey Copse, a 9-hole intermediate course (2900 yards). There is also a 25-bay covered floodlit driving range. Visitors of all levels are welcome at any time but you need to book 6 days in advance. Green fees are Hoebridge £7.50 per round, Maybury £4.90 per round and Shey Copse £3 per round. Breakfast is served between 8 and 10am,

lunch between 12 and 3pm and dinner between 5 and 9pm daily. The club also has 12 full sized snooker tables. Local attractions include Guildford Cathedral, the Royal Horticultural Gardens at Wisley and Blackmore Bird World.

Location
Old Woking Road, Old Woking, Surrey GU22 9JH
The course is on the B382 Old Woking road between Old Woking and West Byfleet.

RAC recommended hotels
Northfleet ★★ (048 62) 22971 A long, two-storey building of 1920s appearance conveniently situated just off the Woking-Guildford road.
Wheatsheaf ★★ (048 62) 73047 Completely refurbished hotel pleasantly situated close to town centre.

HINDHEAD
(042873) 4614
A particularly attractive 18-hole hilly heathland course with some hard walking (6349 yards, SSS 70). Visitors are welcome on weekdays and at weekends by arrangement. A good handicap is necessary as the course is not suitable for absolute beginners. Green fees are £15 on weekdays (£7 with a member) and £20 at weekends (£10 with a member). Lunches and teas are served daily.

Location
Churt Road, Hindhead, Surrey GU26 6HX
The club is on the A287, 1½ miles north of Hindhead.

RAC recommended hotel
Devil's Punchbowl ★★★ (042 873) 6565 A gabled, cream and black building with modern bedroom accommodation.

KINGSWOOD
(0737) 832188
An 18-hole flat parkland course with easy walking (6821 yards, SSS 73). Visitors are welcome when tees are available. Green fees are £35 a day on weekdays and £30 per round at the weekend. There is a large practice area. Full restaurant facilities, including an à la carte menu are available daily. Snooker and squash facilities are also available at the clubhouse.

Location
Sandy Lane, Kingswood
The club is situated 4 miles south of Sutton just off the A217.

RAC recommended hotel
Bridge House ★★★ (0737) 244821 A modern two-storey hotel built on top of Reigate Hill.

LALEHAM
(093 28) 564211
An 18-hole meadowland course with lots of bunkers (6203 yards, SSS 70). Visitors are welcome on weekdays only. Green fees are £13 a day. Full catering facilities are available. The course is situated opposite Thorpe Park.

Location
Laleham Reach, Chertsey, Surrey KT16 8RP
From the M25 follow the directions to Thorpe Park. The entrance is just opposite, through Penton Park.

RAC recommended hotel
Great Fosters ★★★★ (0784) 33822 Elizabethan manor house with antique furniture. Extensive gardens and parkland. Swimming pool, tennis, sauna.
Runnymede ★★★★ (0784) 33822 A modern hotel with fine views overlooking the Thames close to Runnymede.
Bridge ★ (0932) 564408 Pleasant riverside inn overlooking Thames. Easy access to Heathrow.

LEATHERHEAD
(037 284) 3966
An 18-hole parkland course with ditches but easy walking (6088 yards, SSS 69). Visitors of all playing abilities are welcome. Green fees are £27.50 on weekdays and £32.50 at weekends. Full restaurant facilities are available and there is a snooker room and sauna. Local attractions include Chessington World of Adventure and Polesden Lacey.

Location
Kingston Road, Leatherhead, Surrey KT22 0DP
Leave the M25 at the Leatherhead interchange, junction 9 and turn onto the A243 road to Kingston.

LIMPSFIELD CHART
(088 388) 2106
A 9-hole parkland course situated in National Trust land (5718 yards, SSS 68). Visitors are welcome on Monday, Tuesday, Wednesday and Friday. There is also a driving range. Green fees on application. Meals are served daily.

Location
Limpsfield, Oxted, Surrey RHB 0SL
The club is situated on the A25 between Oxted and Westerham. East of Oxted continue over the traffic lights to the club 300 yards on right.

RAC recommended hotel
King's Arms ★★★ (0959) 62990 An old coaching inn which has been modernised, situated in the centre of Westerham.

MALDEN
081-942 0654
An 18-hole parkland course with Beverley Brook passing through (6201 yards, SSS 70). Visitors of all playing abilities are welcome on weekdays but there are some restrictions at weekends so it is best to check beforehand. Green fees are £19 on weekdays and £25 at weekends. Catering facilities are available on Wednesday, Thursday, Friday and weekends.

Location
Traps Lane, New Malden, Surrey KT3 4RS
The club is situated half a mile from New Malden station, close to the A3 between Wimbledon and Kingston.

MITCHAM
081-648 1508
A wooded 18-hole meadowland course (5935 yards, SSS 68). Visitors are welcome on weekdays but players are expected to have a handicap of 18 or below. Green fees are £7. Meals and snacks are available daily.

Location
Carshalton Road, Mitcham Junction, Surrey CR4 4HN
The club is by Mitcham Junction station, on the A237 off the A23.

MOORE PLACE
(0372) 63533
A 9-hole undulating course in some very pretty parkland with lots of trees (3512 yards, SSS 58). The course is public and all visitors are welcome. Green fees are £3.50 on weekdays and £4.50 at weekends. There are two restaurants and a bar and lunches and evenings meals are normally available.

Location
Portsmouth Road, Esher, Surrey KT10 9LN
The course is on the A3 Portsmouth Road, half a mile from the centre of Esher towards Cobham.

NEW ZEALAND GOLF CLUB
(093 23) 45049
An 18-hole heathland course with lots of heather and trees (6012 yards, SSS 69). The course is very tight with narrow fairways and is a real test of golf. Visitors are welcome by arrangement on weekdays. Green fees are £22 per round, £26 a day on weekdays. There is a bar and restaurant where meals and bar snacks are available by arrangement. Local attractions include Thorpe Park and The Boating Centre.

Location
Woodham Lane, Woodham, Weybridge, Surrey KT15 3QD
Leave the A3 and join the A245 at Cobham. Follow the road past West Byfleet and the course is on the right at the junction with Woodham Lane and Sheerwater Road.

NORTH DOWNS
(088 385) 2057
An 18-hole undulating course situated on high ground with some lovely views (5787 yards, SSS 68). Provided they have a handicap certificate, visitors are welcome on weekdays. Green fees on application. Bar lunches are available daily except on Monday.

Location
Northdown Road, Woldingham, Caterham, Surrey CR3 7AA
At the Eastbourne Road (A22) roundabout at Caterham take the Woldingham road.

OAK SPORT CENTRE
081-643 8363
An 18-hole meadowland course (5975 yards, SSS 68). The course is public and visitors are welcome. Green fees are £5 on weekdays, £7 at weekends for the 18-hole course, and £3 on weekdays, £5 at weekends, for the 9-hole course. Fees are £1.30 for juniors and OAPS on weekdays for 18 holes and £1.30 for juniors and OAPS on weekday for 9 holes. There is a public bar which is open during normal pub hours and refreshments are served throughout the day.

Location
Woodmansterne Road, Carshalton, Surrey SM5 4AN
The club is situated on the B2032 1 mile south of Carshalton Beeches station. It is signposted north of the A2022, halfway between the A217 and A237.

PURLEY DOWNS
081-657 8347
An 18-hole downland course (6243 yards, SSS 70). Visitors are welcome between Monday and Friday by arrangement with the Secretary but you must be a member of a recognised golf club and have a current handicap. Green fees are £17.50. Bar snacks, lunches, teas and evening meals are available.

Location
106 Purley Downs Road, Purley, Surrey CR2 0RB
Take the A22 south from Purley then turn east on the A2022 at the Volkswagen Building. The course is on the left near Riddlesdown station.

PUTTENHAM
(0483) 810498
A very pretty 18-hole tree-lined heathland course (5367 yards, SSS 66). Provided they have a handicap certificate, visitors are welcome on weekdays. Green fees are £18 a day. Full catering facilities are available. Local attractions include Guildford Cathedral, Bird World at Farnham and Loseley House.

Location
Heath Road, Puttenham, Guilford, Surrey GU13 1AL
The club is halfway between Farnham and Guildford, just off the A31, 4 miles west of Guildford.

RAC COUNTRY CLUB
(037 22) 763111
Two 18-hole parkland courses, The Old Course (White tees, 6702 yards, yellow tees, 6147 yards, SSS 72) and The Coronation (White tees, 5474 yards, yellow tees, 5153 yards, SSS 67). Visitors are welcome only if they are the guest of a member. Green fees on application. A full catering service is available. The club is near Epsom Racecourse.

Location
Woodcote Park, Epsom, Surrey KT18 7EW
The club is 1 mile from Epsom station, just off the A24.

REDHILL & REIGATE
(0737) 240777
A wooded 18-hole moorland course (5238 yards, SSS 66). Visitors of all playing abilities are welcome

between Monday and Friday at any time, after 11am on Saturday and on Sunday after 11am between October and May. There is also a small practice area. Green fees are £9 on weekdays and £12 at weekends. Bar snacks are available everyday except Monday.
Location
Clarence Lodge, Pendleton Road, Redhill, Surrey RH1 6LB
The course is south of Reigate beside the A23. From Reigate, take A217 south for 1 mile, turn left at traffic lights on to A2044, then left again into Pendleton Road.

RAC recommended hotel
Nutfield Priory C/H ★★★ (0737) 822066 Vast neo-Gothic mansion, complete with a tower, stained glass and gargoyles, set in 40 acres of grounds. Indoor swimming pool, squash, sauna, solarium, gymnasium, billiards.

REIGATE HEATH
(0737) 242610
A 9-hole heathland course (5554 yards, SSS 67). Visitors are welcome on weekdays but you should telephone beforehand. The course is a good test of golfing skills and is not suitable for beginners. Green fees on application. There is a full à la carte restaurant, bars and a snack bar. Local attractions include Windmill Church which is adjacent to the clubhouse.
Location
Reigate Heath, Reigate RH2 8QR
The club is situated south of the A25 to the west of Reigate.

RAC recommended hotels
Bridge House ★★★ (0737) 244821 Modern two-storey hotel built on top of Reigate Hill.
Reigate Manor ★★★ (0737) 240125 A refurbished Georgian manor house, with modern additions, situated on Reigate Hill. Facilities include sauna, solarium and gymnasium.

RICHMOND
081-940 4351
A particularly lovely 18-hole parkland course (5965 yards, SSS 69). The course is situated on the edge of Richmond Park with some very old trees. Visitors of all playing abilities are welcome on weekdays by prior arrangement. Green fees on application. Bar snacks are available every day. Local attractions include Hampton Court, Kew Gardens and the clubhouse itself which is a small Georgian mansion.
Location
Sudbrook Park, Richmond, Surrey TW10 7AS
From the A307 1 mile south of Richmond, look for Sudbrook Lane on your left.

RAC recommended hotels
Petersham ★★★★ 081-940 7471 An impressive five-storey Victorian Gothic building with fine views of the River Thames.
Richmond Hill ★★★ 081-940 2247 A large Georgian hotel, situated at the top of Richmond Hill. Facilities include squash.

ROYAL MID-SURREY
081-940 1894
Two 18-hole parkland courses, The Inner (5544 yards, SSS 67) and The Outer (6052 yards, SSS 70). Both courses have bunkers and are exceptionally flat. Visitors are welcome on weekdays if they have a letter of introduction from their own club or are playing with a member. You can also play at weekends and Bank Holidays by prior arrangement. There is a practice ground, practice shed and shipping area. Green fees are £30 per round on weekdays. Lunch is served daily except Monday. The club is 10 minutes from Richmond Park and Kew Gardens is not far. The River Thames runs at the end of the course.
Location
Old Deer Park, Richmond, Surrey TW9 2SB
The club is 250 yards from Richmond roundabout on the A316. The entrance is by the Richmond Athletic Ground.

ST GEORGE'S HILL
(0932) 842406
A well-wooded 18-hole heathland course with some very hard walking (6492 yards, SSS 71). There are a number of rather difficult par 4s on this course. Visitors who have a handicap certificate are welcome but you must book a tee time in advance. Green fees on application. There is a full restaurant where lunch is served daily. Local attractions include Guildford Cathedral, The Royal Horticultural Society gardens at Wisley and Windsor.
Location
St George's Hill, Weybridge, Surrey KT13 0NL
From junction 10 of the M25, turn onto the A3 and then A245 to Woking. The club is about 1½ miles on the right.

SANDOWN PARK
(0372) 63340
A 9-hole parkland course (5656 yards, SSS 67). There is also a 9-hole par 3 course (1193 yards), a 9-hole pitch and putt course and a floodlit 33-bay driving range which is open until 10.30pm. The course is public and visitors of all playing abilities are welcome at any time. Green fees are £3.50 on weekdays and £5.70 on weekdays. Lunch is served daily and dinner by arrangement. The club is convenient for Hampton Court.
Location
Moor Lane, Esher, Surrey KT10 8AN
The course is about 1 mile from Esher station in the centre of Sandown Park racecourse, just off the Portsmouth road.

RAC recommended hotel
Hilton International ★★★ (0932) 68683 A modern hotel set in 27 acres of parkland. Facilities include swimming pool, tennis, squash, sauna and gymnasium.

SELSDON PARK HOTEL
081-657 8811
An 18-hole parkland course situated in magnificent grounds (6402 yards, SSS 71). Visitors are welcome although the course is not suitable for novice golfers. You should contact the Pro to arrange a tee time. Green fees are £15 on weekdays, £20 on Saturday and £25 on Sunday and Bank Holidays. You can play 36 holes on weekdays for £22.50.
Location
Sanderstead, South Croydon, Surrey CR2 8YA
The club is 3 miles south of Croydon on the A2022 Purley to West Wickham road, near the junction with the B275.

RAC recommended hotel
Selsdon Park ★★★★ 081-657 8811 A greatly enlarged Tudor mansion situated in 200 acres. Facilities include an indoor swimming pools and outdoor swimming pools, golf, putting, tennis, squash, sauna, solarium, gymnasium and billiards.

SHILLINGEE PARK
(0428) 53237
A 9-hole undulating parkland course (2500 yards, SSS 63), Visitors of all playing abilities are welcome but it is advisable to book either in person or by phone. Green fees are £6 for 9 holes, £10 for 18 holes and £12 a day on weekdays, and £6 for 9 holes, £12 for 18 holes and £14 a day at weekends. Juniors and OAPs can play for £4 per 9 holes, £6 per 18 holes and £8 a day on weekdays and £4 per 9 holes, £8 per 18 holes and £10 a day at weekends. Breakfast and lunch is served on Sunday and between Tuesday and Saturday a full à la carte menu or bar food is served at lunchtime and in the evening.
Location
Chiddingford, Goldalming, Surrey GU8 4TA
Leave the A3 at Milford and turn on the A283 to Chiddingfold. Once in Chiddingfold turn left at the Green and continue for 2 miles before turning right.

SHIRLEY PARK
081-654 1143
A pleasant 18-hole parkland course with some fine views over Shirley Hills (6210 yards, SSS 70). Visitors who have a handicap certificate are welcome at any time between Monday and Friday. There is a practice area. Green fees are £17.50 per round or day. Lunches, teas and dinners are available daily.
Location
194 Addiscombe Road, Croydon CR0 7LB
The course is 1½ miles from east Croydon station.

RAC recommended hotels see Croydon and Addington.

SILVERMERE
(0932) 67275
A tight 18-hole course with a combination of woodland, parkland and meadowland (6333 yards, SSS 71); 7 holes are played over heathland, 10 holes over open parkland and one hole, the 17th, is played over a lake. Visitors of all playing abilities are welcome but you must book a week in advance. Members only can play on Saturday and Sunday mornings. There is a 34-bay floodlit driving range which is open till 10pm daily. Green fees are £10 on weekdays and £14 at weekends. Full catering facilities are available from 8am daily. The Royal Horticultural Society gardens at Wisley are within easy reach and also Hampton Court.
Location
Redhill Road, Cobham, Surrey KT11 1EF
From junction 10 of the M25 take the B366 to Byfleet and Silvermere is half a mile on the right. If you are coming from London take the A3 to the Cobham turn-off and then the A245 to Byfleet, and the club is half a mile on the left in Redhill Road.

RAC recommended hotel
Hilton International ★★★ (0932) 68683 A modern hotel set in 27 acres of parkland. Facilities include swimming pool, tennis, squash, sauna and gymnasium.

SURBITON
081-398 3101
An 18-hole parkland course with easy walking (6211 yards, SSS 70). Provided they have a handicap certificate, visitors are welcome with some reservations so it is best to check beforehand. Green fees are £28 per person. Full catering facilities are available. Local attractions include Hampton Court, Kew Gardens, Sandown racecourse, Kempton Park racecourse and Thorpe park.
Location
Woodstock Lane, Chessington, Surrey KT9 1UG
The club is 2 miles east of Esher, off the A3 at the Ace of Spades roundabout.

RAC recommended hotel
Haven ★★ 081-398 0023 A privately run detached Edwardian house lying back on the main Surbiton-Esher Road.

TANDRIDGE
(0883) 712273
A hilly 18-hole parkland course with some fine views (6250 yards, SSS 70). Visitors are welcome on Monday, Wednesday and Thursday and at other times if you are with a member. Green fees are £16.50. Lunch is served daily except on Tuesday.
Location
Oxted, Surrey RH8 9NQ
The course is situated off the A25 by Oxted.

RAC recommended hotel
Hoskins ★★ (0883) 12338 A round modern public house with letting rooms.

THAMES DITTON AND ESHER
081-398 1551
A 9-hole parkland course (5606 yards, SSS 65). The 9 holes are played twice from different tees. Visitors of all playing abilities are welcome at all times except Sunday morning before 1pm. Green fees are £6 on weekdays and £8 at weekends and Bank Holidays. Cold lunches, hot snacks are served daily and a buffet can be provided for societies.
Location
Scilly Isles, Portsmouth Road, Esher, Surrey
The club is off the A3 by the Scilly Isles roundabout, approximately a quarter of a mile from Sandown Park racecourse.

TYRRELLS WOOD
(0372) 376025
A very hilly 18-hole wooded parkland course with easy walking (6219 yards, SSS 70). Visitors who have a handicap certificate are welcome by prior arrangement though there are some limitations at weekends. There is a small practice ground. Green fees are £22 on weekdays and £30 at weekends. Catering facilities are available.
Location
Tyrrells Wood, Leatherhead, Surrey KT22 8QP
Take the A24 Leatherhead by-pass and turn off on to B2033 towards Headley, and then after 200 yards, turn right into the Tyrrells Wood Estate. It is about 1 mile from junction 9 of the M25.

RAC recommended hotel
Burford Bridge ★★★★ (0306) 884561 A large hotel set in some pleasant gardens situated at the bottom of Box Hill. Facilities include a swimming pool.

WALTON HEATH
(073781) 2380
Two 18-hole heathland championship courses, The Old (6813 yards, SSS 72) and The New (6659 yards, SSS 72). Provided they have a handicap certificate and a letter of introduction, visitors are welcome on weekdays and also at the weekends if they are invited by a member. Green fees are £30 or £27 after 11.30am. Lunches and afternoon teas are served daily. The club is within easy reach of Epsom racecourse, Box Hill and Leith Hill.
Location
Tadworth, Surrey KY20 7TP
Leave the M25 at exit 8 and follow the A217 towards London. Turn off to your left onto the B2032 and the golf club is about 1 mile on your left.

WENTWORTH
(09904) 2201
There are four beautiful courses here, situated in the heart of the Surrey heathland belt, The West (6945 yards, SSS 74) and The East (6176 yards, SSS 70), both wooded 18-hole heathland courses and two new ones, The South, an 18- hole course (7000 yards, SSS 72) and The Executive a 9-hole course. The P.G.A. Championships are played here and also the World Match in October. Visitors who have a handicap certificate are welcome on weekdays but you must telephone in advance to book. Green fees are £69 for the West course and £46 for the East with fees for the two new courses on application. Breakfast, lunch and evening meals are served daily. There is also accommodation at the clubhouse. Local attractions include Virginia Water, Windsor and Ascot racecourse.
Location
Virginia Water, Surrey GU25 4LS
The club is just off the A30 at the junction with the A329 to Ascot. It is about 3 miles from the M25 and M3.

WEST BYFLEET
(09323) 45230
A pretty 18-hole heathland/parkland course with a famous 'pond' hole (6211 yards, SSS 70). Visitors can play on weekdays only but all abilities are welcome. Green fees on application. Snacks,

lunches and teas are served and evening meals by arrangement every day except Sunday when only lunch is served. The club is within easy reach of the Royal Horticultural Society gardens at Wisley.
Location
Sheerwater Road, West Byfleet, Surrey KT14 6AA
The club is on the A245, about three quarters of a mile west of West Byfleet.

WEST HILL
(04867) 4365
An interesting 18-hole heath and heather course (6368 yards, SSS 70). Visitors are welcome between Monday and Friday but you must have a current handicap. Green fees are £20 per round and £30 a day. Full catering facilities are available. Local attractions include Virginia Water, Windsor Great Park and the Royal Horticultural Society gardens at Wisley.
Location
Bagshot Road, Brookwood, Surrey GU24 0BH
The club is situated on the A322 which connects Guildford to Bagshot. The club entrance is next to the railway bridge at Brookwood.

WEST SURREY
(04868) 21275
An 18-hole wooded parkland course with some tight fairways (6247 yards, SSS 71). Provided they have a handicap certificate, visitors are welcome but the club prefers you to arrange it beforehand to avoid reservations or restrictions. Green fees are £16 per round, £25 a day on weekdays and £30 at weekends and Bank Holidays. Full restaurant facilities are available by arrangement but you are expected to wear a collar and tie in the dining room.
Location
Enton Green, Godalming GU8 5AG
The course is about 1½ miles from Milford traffic lights on the A3, half a mile from Milford station crossing.

WINDLEMERE
(09905) 8727
A 9-hole gently undulating parkland course. There is also a 12-bay floodlit driving range. The club is open to the public and players of all abilities are welcome. Green fees are £7 for 18 holes on weekdays, £8 for 9 holes at weekends and Bank Holidays and £4 on weekdays, £4.80 at weekends for juniors and OAPs. Bar snacks are always available. Local attractions include Virginia Water, Ascot racecourse and Thorpe Park.
Location
Windlesham Road, West End, Woking, Surrey GU24 9QL
Take the A322 from Bagshot towards Guildford and turn left onto the A319 towards Cobham. The course is on the left opposite the Gordon Boys' School.

WOKING
(048 62) 60053
A charming 18-hole heathland course which has the distinction of being the first course of its kind in Surrey (6322 yards, SSS 70). Visitors who are a member of a recognised golf club and have a current handicap certificate are welcome on weekdays but you must book in advance. Green fees are £20 per round and £30 a day. Lunches are available every day but you should order it in advance. The Royal Horticultural Society gardens at Wisley and Guildford Cathedral are within easy reach of the club.
Location
Pond Road, Hook Heath, Woking, Surrey GU22 0JZ
Just south of the first road bridge over the Woking/Brookwood railway, take Hollybank Road. Immediately turn right into Golf Club Road and right at the end to the clubhouse.

RAC recommended hotels
Northfleet ★★ (048 62) 22971 A long, two-storey building of 1920s appearance conveniently situated just off the Woking/Guildford Road.
Wheatsheaf ★★ (048 62) 73047 Completely refurbished hotel pleasantly situated close to town centre.

WOODCOTE PARK
081-668 2788
An 18-hole slightly undulating parkland course (6624 yards, SSS 71). Provided you have a handicap certificate visitors are welcome on weekdays. Green fees are £20. Bar snacks are served daily. There is a snooker room at the club. The club is situated at the far end of Meadow Hill, which is just off Smitham Bottom Lane, Purley. Turn off the A23 in Coulsdon.
Location
Meadow Hill, Bridle Way, Coulsdon, Surrey CR3 2QQ

WORPLESDON
(04867) 2277
An 18-hole heathland course with superb greens and a challenging finish (6422 yards, SSS 71). Visitors who have a handicap certificate are welcome on weekdays with an introduction from a Club Secretary. Green fees are £20 per round, £30 a day. Lunch is served daily except on Tuesday.
Location
Heath House Road, Woking, Surrey GU22 0RA
Take A322 from Guildford towards Bagshot and after 4 miles turn right into Heath House Road.

EAST SUSSEX

ASHDOWN FOREST HOTEL
(030282) 4866
An 18-hole heathland/woodland course (5510 yards, SSS 67). Visitors are welcome on any day but it is advisable to check first, particularly at weekends. Green fees are £10 per round, £15 a day during the week and £12.50 per round, £20 a day at weekends and Public Holidays. There is a restaurant with full service daily and bar snacks are always available.
Location
Chapel Lane, Forest Row, E Sussex RH18 5BB
The club is situated in the village of Forest Row, 3 miles south of East Grinstead on the A22. Turn left onto the B2110 and Chapel Lane is the fourth on the right.

RAC recommended hotels
Roebuck ★★★ (034 282) 3811 Detached red-brick Georgian building in pleasant gardens. Just off A22.
Brambletye ★★ (034 282) 4144 Pleasing late Victorian-Edwardian style residence with modern extension to rear.
Chequers Inn ★★ (034 282) 3333 An ancient tile-hung inn with modern bedroom accomadation.

BRIGHTON AND HOVE
(0273) 556482
A 9-hole downland course with views over the sea (5722 yards, SSS 68). Visitors of all playing abilities are welcome. Green fees are £10 for 18 holes, £5 for 9 holes on Monday to Saturday, and £15 for 18 holes and £6 for 9 holes on Sunday. Full catering facilities are available. Local attractions include the Dyke, the Lanes and Brighton sea front.
Location
Dyke Road, Brighton, E Sussex BN1 8YJ
The club is north of Brighton, about 2½ miles up Dyke Road on the left-hand side.

RAC recommended hotels
Old Ship ★★★ (0273) 29001 A well-known historic hotel overlooking the seafront.
Grand ★★★★★ (0273) 21188 Elegantly reconstructed luxury hotel superbly situated facing the sea. Swimming pool. sauna, solarium and gymnasium.
Hospitality Inn ★★★★★ (0273) 206700 Stylish hotel on seafront centred around the spacious four-storey high Atrium lounge/reception area, Ballroom. Indoor swimming pool, sauna, solarium and gymnasium.
Bedford ★★★★ (0273) 29744 Recently refurbished, tall modern hotel on the sea front. Guests may use leisure facilities of Metropole hotel.
Brighton Metropole ★★★★ (0273) 775432 Imposing Victorian red-brick sea front hotel with impressive decor. Car park adjacent. Indoor swimming pool, sauna, solarium and gymnasium
Granville ★★★ (0273) 26302 Small luxuriously furnished hotel on sea front. Near Brighton Centre. Solarium.
Norfolk Resort ★★★ (0273) 738201 Fine Regency hotel attractively modernised. Well situated on sea front. Indoor swimming pool, sauna, solarium and gymnasium.

COODEN BEACH
(04243) 2040
An established 18-hole seaside parkland course (6450 yards, SSS 71). Visitors of all playing abilities are welcome at any time. Green fees are £15 on weekdays and £18 at weekends and public holidays. Full catering facilities are available.
Location
Cooden Sea Road, Cooden, E Sussex TN39 4TR
Leave Eastbourne on the A259 Hastings road and follow the Cooden Beach sign at the Little Common roundabout.

RAC recommended hotel
Cooden Resort ★★★ (042 43) 2281 A modernised 1930s holiday hotel situated on the beach. Indoor and outdoor swimming pools, sauna and solarium.

CRANBROOK
(0580) 712833
A picturesque 18-hole parkland course set in a wooded area (6216 yards, SSS 70). Provided you have a handicap certificate, visitors are welcome, but there is a weekend booking system. Green fees are £17 on weekdays and £25 at weekends. Full restaurant facilities are available every day except Monday. Local attractions include Sissinghurst Castle, Scotney Castle and Lamberhurst Vineyard.
Location
Benenden Road, Cranbrook, Kent TN17 4AL
Take the A229 south of Maidstone for 14 miles. The club is 1½ miles from Sissinghurst on the Benenden road (B2086).

RAC recommended hotels
Kennel Holt ★★ (0580) 712032 A lovely Elizabethan manor house in 5 acres of landscaped gardens.
Willesley ★★ (0580) 713555 A typical historic Kentish red-brick building set in 4 acres of gardens.

CROWBOROUGH BEACON
(08926) 61511
A scenic 18-hole heathland course with some testing holes (6279 yards, SSS 70). Provided you have a handicap certificate or a letter of introduction, visitors are welcome on weekdays and after 3pm at weekends and Bank Holidays. Green fees are £20 per round or £30 a day during the week and £20 per round at weekends. Full catering facilities are available every day although breakfast is by prior arrangement. Local attractions include Buxted Park.
Location
Beacon Road, Crowborough, E Sussex TN6 1UJ
From Tunbridge Wells take the A26, and Crowborough Beacon is just off the road about 8 miles south.

RAC recommended hotel

Winston Manor ★★★ (0892) 652772 Small detached hotel on A26 at Southern edge of town. Privately-owned.

DALE HILL
(0580) 200112
An 18-hole parkland/meadowland course (6055 yards, SSS 69). Visitors are welcome on weekdays but it necessary to telephone first to obtain a tee time. You can also play after 10am at weekends by prior arrangement. Green fees are £15 a day on weekdays and £16.50 at weekends. Full catering facilities are available daily, and breakfast can be provided if it is ordered in advance. Interesting places to visit locally include Bewl Bridge Reservoir, Rudyard Kipling's house at Batemans (NT), Scotney Castle and Leeds Castle.
Location
Ticehurst, Wadhurst, E Sussex TN5 7DQ
From London, turn off the A21 onto the B2087 at Flimwell towards Ticehurst.

EAST BRIGHTON
(0273) 604838
An 18-hole downland course with wonderful panoramic views over the sea (6304 yards, SSS 70). There are some ancient cattle sheds and pits on the course which provide for some hazardous playing. Visitors are welcome on weekdays and at weekends, but you must book first. There are competitions on most weekends. Lunch is served daily except Monday. The club is close to Brighton and the Marina.
Location
Roedean Road, Brighton, E Sussex BN2 5RA
Follow the A259 from Brighton town centre and turn left opposite the Brighton Marina.

RAC recommended hotels
See Brighton.

EASTBOURNE DOWNS
(0323) 20827
An 18-hole downland seaside course (6635 yards, SSS 72). Visitors of all playing abilities are welcome at any time. Green fees are £10 for 18 holes. The club is close to the centre of Eastbourne.
Location
East Dean Road, Eastbourne, E Sussex BN20 8ES
The club is situated on the A259 west of Eastbourne.

RAC recommended hotels
Grand ★★★★★ (0323) 412345 Luxury hotel overlooking sea. Indoor/outdoor swimming pool, putting, sauna, solarium, gymnasium and billiards.
Cavendish ★★★★ (0323) 410222 Elegant and impressive hotel, opposite the Bandstand on the sea front. Billiards.
Queen's ★★★★ (0323) 22822 An elegant Victorian hotel well-situated on the seafront overlooking the pier. Billiards.
Chatsworth ★★★ (0323) 411016 Pleasant four-storey family-run hotel on sea front. Sun terrace.
Cumberland ★★★ (0323) 30342 Large pleasant, family-run hotel on sea front opposite bandstand.
Princes ★★★ (0323) 22056 A family-run Victorian terrace hotel in a quiet area just off the sea front.
Lansdowne ★★★ (0323) 25174 A large family hotel set in an attractive terrace on the seafront. Billiards.
Wish Tower ★★★ (0323) 22676 A family hotel near the Winter Gardens and Devonshire Theatre.

DYKE
(079156) 296
A fine 18-hole downland course considered to be one of the most difficult courses in Sussex (6212 yards, SSS 71). Situated on the Downs, it provides some wonderful views both over the sea and the countryside. Provided you have a handicap certificate, visitors are welcome, but you must telephone the Secretary first to check availability. Green fees are £14 per round, £16 a day on weekdays and £20 per round at weekends. Full catering facilities are available daily. Brighton itself provides many other attractions.
Location
Dyke Road, Brighton, E Sussex BN1 8YJ
Take the Dyke Road from Brighton and the club is about $4^1/_2$ miles north of the town.

RAC recommended hotels
See Brighton.

GATWICK MANOR HOTEL
(0293) 24470
An interesting 9-hole course (1109 yards, SSS 27). Visitors are welcome at any time. Green fees on application. The course is owned by the hotel which provides full catering facilities. Gatwick Airport is 1 mile away.
Location
Crawley
The club is on the A23 to Crawley, 1 mile south of Gatwick Airport towards Crawley.

HASTINGS
(0424) 52981
An 18-hole undulating parkland course (6248 yards, SSS 70). It is a municipal golf course so visitors are welcome at all times, but it is necessary to book if you wish to play on a weekend morning. Green fees are £6.50 on weekdays and £8 at weekends and Bank Holidays. There are also reductions for OAPs, juniors and students. Full catering facilities are available. Local attractions include Battle and Hastings itself.
Location
Battle Road, St Leonards-on-Sea, E Sussex TN37 7AB
Take the A2100 Hastings-Battle road and the club is 3 miles north west of Hastings.

RAC recommended hotel
Beauport Park C/H ★★★ (0424) 65122 An attractive converted Georgian manor house set in gardens and parkland. Swimming pool, golf, putting, tennis, squash and riding.

HIGHWOODS
(0424) 212625
A well-established 18-hole undulating course (6218 yards, SSS 70). Provided they have a handicap certificate, visitors are welcome, but no visitors can play before midday on Sunday unless they are accompanied by a member. Green fees are £16 per round or day on weekdays and £20 at weekends and Bank Holidays. Lunch can be provided by arrangement on weekdays, and snacks and tea are always available. The course is close to Battle, Hastings and the Hurstman Zoo.
Location
Ellerslie Lane, Bexhill-on-Sea, E Sussex TN39 4LJ
From Eastbourne or Hastings, take the A259 and the club is 2 miles west of Bexhill. If you are coming from Battle, take the A269 via Ninfield and turn right at Lunsford Cross.

HOLLINGBURY PARK
(0273) 552010
An 18-hole undulating downland course overlooking the sea (6502 yards, SSS 71). Visitors are welcome at any time. Green fees are £8 per round or £12 a day. There is a restaurant which is open all week. Local attractions include Brighton and the Pavilion.
Location
Ditchling Road, Brighton, E Sussex BN1 7HS
Take the A23 from Brighton town centre, turn left at the one-way system and go up the hill to the top. Turn left and the club is 200 yards on the right.

RAC recommended hotels
See Brighton.

HORAM PARK
(04353) 3477
A 9-hole undulating parkland/woodland course (2844 yards, SSS 66). Visitors of all playing abilities are welcome at any time except on Saturday morning. Green fees are £6 for 9 holes, £10 for 18 holes on weekdays and £6.50 and £12 respectively at weekends. There is a carvery which is open daily except Monday, and bar meals are also available. Local attractions include Mickleham Priory.
Location
Chiddingly Road, Horam, Nr Heathfield, E Sussex TN21 0JJ
From Eastbourne, take the A22 to Lower Horsebridge and then turn onto the A167 towards Horam. The club is $^1/_2$ mile south of Horam on the Chiddingly road (13 miles north of Eastbourne).

LEWES
(0273) 473245
An interesting 18-hole downland course with some panoramic views (5951 yards, SSS 69). Visitors of all playing abilities are welcome on weekdays, subject to society meetings, but you can only play on Saturday after 3pm and on Sunday after 10.30am. Green fees are £10 on weekdays and £13 at weekends and Bank Holidays. The full-time Steward can provide a la carte meals or simple bar snacks. Local attractions include Lewes town centre, Bentley Wildfowl Trust at Iffield, and Glyndebourne.
Location
Chapel Hill, Lewes, E Sussex
The club is situated on the A27 Lewes-Eastbourne road opposite Mawling Street and Cliffe High Street.

RAC recommended hotels
Shelleys ★★★ (0273) 472361 A modernised Georgian building situated in the High Street.
White Hart ★★ (0273) 476694 A Georgian coaching inn which has been modernised, situated in the High Street.

PEACEHAVEN
(0273) 514049
An undulating 9-hole downland course which can be prone to winds (5007 yards, SSS 65). Provided you have a handicap certificate, visitors of all playing levels are welcome on weekdays and after 11.30am at weekends and Bank Holidays. Green fees on application. Lunch and bar snacks are available daily except on Monday and Tuesday. The club is convenient for both Brighton and Lewis.
Location
Brighton Road, Newhaven, E Sussex BN9 9UH
You will find the course on the A259 from Brighton, 1 mile west of Newhaven.

RAC recommended hotels
Olde Place ★★ (0273) 31051 Detached Georgian building with modern motel block at rear.
White Horse ★★ (0273) 300301 A detached building overlooking the sea in pleasant cliff top site.

PILTDOWN
(082572) 2033
An attractive 18-hole undulating moorland course with easy walking (6059 yards, SSS 69). Visitors who have a letter of introduction or a handicap certificate are welcome, but not before 9.30am, and not on Tuesday, Thursday or Sunday mornings unless you are the guest of a member. Green fees are £20 per round or day. Lunch can be provided by arrangement and bar snacks are always available.
Location
Piltdown, Uckfield, E Sussex TN22 3XB
The club is $2^1/_2$ miles west of Uckfield, between the A272 and the B2102.

RAC recommended hotel
Ye Maidens Head ★★ (0825) 762019 A pleasant old coaching inn conveniently situated in Uckfield High Street.

ROYAL ASHDOWN FOREST
(034282) 2018
An extremely scenic undulating moorland course with some splendid views over the Forest. An 18-hole course (6439 yards, SSS 71) it can be extremely difficult with plenty of gorse and heather as well as a stream running through. Provided you have a handicap certificate visitors are welcome although there are some restrictions at weekends and Bank Holidays. It is advisable to telephone first to make a booking. Green fees are £20 on weekdays and £25 at weekends. A four-course lunch can be arranged for social events and casual 'golfers' soup and sandwiches' is always available.
Location
Chapel Lane, Forest Row, East Grinstead, E Sussex RH18 5LR
Follow the A22 East Grinstead-Eastbourne road, and 4½ miles south of East Grinstead turn left into Forest Row. Opposite the church, turn onto the B2110 and after ½ mile turn right into Chapel Lane. At the top of the hill turn left and you will see the club house over the heath.

RAC recommended hotels
See Forest Row

ROYAL EASTBOURNE
(0323) 29738
A famous course which celebrated its centenary in 1987. It is a fine 18-hole undulating downland course with some challenging holes (6109 yards, SSS 69). Visitors are welcome by arrangement. Green fees are £15 on weekdays and £20 at weekends. Full catering facilities are available every day except Monday.
Location
Paradise Drive, Eastbourne, E Sussex BN20 8BP
The club is ½ mile from Eastbourne Town Hall on the west side of town.

RAC recommended hotels
See Eastbourne

RYE
(0797) 225241
One of the best 18-hole links courses in Britain (6301 yards, SSS 71). Visitors can play only if they are introduced by a member, and the maximum handicap is 18. Green fees are £19.50 per round. Lunch is served every day except Tuesday. The club is situated 2½ miles from Rye.
Location
Camber, Rye, E Sussex TN3 6QS
Take the A259 to Rye and then take the Camber road to Lydd.

RAC recommended hotels
George ★★★ (0797) 2221144 A modernised coaching in with oak beams, in the centre of the town.
Mermaid ★★★ (0797) 223065 One of the oldest inns in England, with antique furniture and linenfold panelling. Tucked away among the cobbled streets of Rye.
Hope Anchor (0797) 222216 ★★ A small, 18th century hotel in a quiet backwater commanding fine views.
Flackley Ash ★★★ (0797) 721651 Georgian mansion in own grounds. Indoor swimming pool, sauna, solarium and gymnasium.
Ship In ★★ (0797) 222233 Historic small inn set between warehouses on Strand Quay.

SEAFORD
(0323) 892442
Another course which celebrated its centenary in 1987, this is an interesting 18-hole downland course (6233 yards, SSS 70). Visitors of all playing abilities are welcome on weekdays after 9.30am but it is advisable to telephone in advance. Green fees on application. Breakfast, lunch, tea and dinner are always available. Places to visit nearby include Brighton and Eastbourne.
Location
East Blatchington, Seaford, E Sussex BN25 2JD
The club is off the A259 to the north of Seaford.

SEAFORD HEAD
(0323) 894843
An 18-hole undulating seaside course (5348 metres, SSS 68). Visitors of all playing abilities are welcome. Green fees are £6 on weekdays and £7 at weekends and Bank Holidays. There are bar facilities and light snacks are available. The club is close to the seaside resorts of Brighton and Eastbourne.
Location
Southdown Road, Seaford, E Sussex BN25 4JS
The club is situated S of the A259 at Seaford, 12 miles from Brighton or 8 miles from Eastbourne.

WATERHALL
(0273) 508658
An 18-hole hilly downland course with some hard walking (5692 yards, SSS 68). Visitors are always welcome. Green fees are £5.50 per round, £8 a day on weekdays, and £7 per round at weekends and Bank Holidays. Full catering facilities are available during the summer, but are limited during the winter months.
Location
Mill Road, Brighton, E Sussex BN1 8YN
Take the road north west out of Brighton to the downs and the club is 5 miles from the centre towards Saddlescombe and Devils Dyke.

WEST HOVE
(0273) 419738
An 18-hole downland course (6130 yards, SSS 69). Visitors who are handicap players are welcome all day on weekdays, and in the afternoon at weekend. Green fees are £10 on weekdays and £20 at weekend. Full catering facilities are available. The club is convenient for visiting Brighton.
Location
369 Old Shoreham Road, Hove, E Sussex
The club is north of Portslade station at the junction with the A272.

RAC recommended hotels
See Brighton

WILLINGDON
(0323) 410983
A fine 18-hole downland course although somewhat hilly and very tough (6049 yards, SSS 69). Visitors are always welcome on weekdays but it is advisable to telephone ahead. Green fees are £9 or £12 for 36 holes on weekdays and £12 or £15 for 36 holes at weekends and Bank Holidays. Catering facilities can be provided by arrangement.
Location
Southdown Road, Eastbourne, E Sussex BN20 9BU
Take the A22 north of Eastbourne and the club is about half a mile along the road.

RAC recommended hotels
See Eastbourne

WEST SUSSEX

BOGNOR REGIS
(0243) 821929
A varied 18-hole flat parkland course (6238 yards, SSS 70). Provided they have a handicap certificate, visitors are welcome on weekdays but with a member only at weekends between April and October. There is a practice area. Green fees are £16 on weekdays and £20 at weekends. Bar snacks are normally available and meals are served by arrangement.
Location
Downview Road, Felpham, Bognor Regis, W Sussex PO22 8JD
Take the A259 Littlehampton to Bognor road and turn right at the traffic lights at Felpham village 2 miles from Bognor Regis.

RAC recommended hotel
Royal Norfolk ★★★ (0243) 826222 A distinctive Regency building set in pleasant gardens enjoying good sea views. Facilities include an indoor swimming pool, putting and tennis.

COPTHORNE
(0342) 712508
An 18-hole wooded heathland course with easy walking (6550 yards, SSS 71). Visitors are welcome on weekdays and afternoons at the weekend. Green fees are £15 per round, £20 a day on weekdays and £30 at weekends. Lunches are served every day and evening meals can be arranged. Local attractions include Standen (NT) and Wakehurst Place Gardens.
Location
Bovers Arms Road, Copthorne, Crawley, W Sussex
Leave the M23 at exit 10 and take the A264 1 mile towards East Grinstead.

RAC recommended hotel
Copthorne ★★★★ (0342) 714971 An attractive hotel built around a farmhouse set in extensive grounds. Facilities include putting, squash, sauna, solarium and gymnasium.
Effingham Park ★★★★ (0342) 714994 Superb new hotel of Spanish appearance on 40 acres of parkland. Conference and leisure centre. Indoor swimming pool, 9-hole golf, putting, sauna, solarium, gymnasium.

COTTESMORE
(0293) 28256
There are two undulating meadowland courses here with lakes, silver birches and rhododendrons. The Old, 18 holes (6100 yards, SSS 70) and The New, 18 holes (5400 yards, SSS 68). Visitors are welcome on weekdays and after 11am at weekends. A current handicap is required for the Old Course. Green fees are £14 on weekdays and £18 at weekends for both courses. There is a restaurant and a lounge bar which serve hot and cold snacks.
Location
Buchan Hill, Pease Pottage, Crawley, W Sussex
Leave the M23 at the last exit through Pease Pottage, and the club is 1 mile on the right down the Horsham Road.

COWDRAY PARK
(073 081) 3599
An 18-hole undulating parkland course with some hard walking (5972 yards, SSS 70). Visitors of all playing abilities are welcome on weekdays and also at weekends by arrangement. There are two practice grounds. Green fees are £14 before noon, £10 after noon on weekdays and £20 at weekends. Bar snacks are served daily and evening meals by arrangement. Local attractions include Petworth (NT) and Goodwood House.
Location
Midhurst, W Sussex GU29 0BB
The club is situated 1 mile east of Midhurst on the A272.

RAC recommended hotels
Spread Eagle ★★★ (073 081) 6911 A fine historic 15th-century building of great character, with individually styled bedrooms.
Angel ★★ (073 081) 2421 A former 16th-century white-fronted coaching inn situated in the centre of town.

EFFINGHAM PARK
(0342) 716528
A 9-hole parkland course (1749 yards, SSS 30). Visitors of all playing abilities are welcome except on Saturday and Sunday morning and Bank Holidays. Green fees are £4 on weekdays and £6 for 9 holes, £8.50 for 18 holes and £7 for 9 holes, £10 for 18 holes at weekends and Bank Holidays. Snacks, lunches and suppers are served daily. The club is attached to an RAC recommended hotel

complex where facilities include swimming, sauna, solarium and gymnasium.
Location
West Park Road, Copthorne, W Sussex
Leave the M23 at exit 10 marked Copthorne and the club is on the Copthorne to Lingfield road.

GOODWOOD
(0243) 774968
An 18-hole downland/parkland course situated in an idylic spot with sloping fairways and some splendid views of the Downs and the coast (6318 yards, SSS 70). Visitors are welcome on weekdays but only at weekends and Bank Holidays if you hold a handicap certificate, and then not before 10am. There are limited practice facilities. Green fees are £16 on weekdays and £25 at weekends. Light snacks are available and lunches and dinners by arrangement except on Monday. Local attractions include Goodwood House, Arundel Castle, Fishbourne Roman Palace and Chichester Cathedral.
Location
Goodwood, Chichester, West Sussex PO18 0PN
Take the A286 5 miles north of Chichester to Goodwood racecourse.

RAC recommended hotel
Goodwood Park ★★★ (0243) 775537 An ancient inn, refurbished and expanded, standing on the Goodwood estate. Indoor swimming pool, golf, tennis, squash, sauna, solarium, gymnasium, billiards.

HAM MANOR
(0903) 783288
A gently undulating 18-hole parkland course (6243 yards, SSS 70). The course has the distinction of having an 1837 Derby winner buried on the green. Visitors who have a handicap certificate are welcome with some reservations so it is advisable to telephone ahead. Green fees are £20 on weekdays and £25 at weekends. Lunch is served daily except on Monday. Arundel Castle is nearby and the sea and downs within easy reach.
Location
Angmering, W Sussex BN16 4JE
The course is situated on the A259 between Worthing and Littlehampton.

RAC recommended hotels see Littlehampton.

HAYWARDS HEATH
(0444) 414457
An 18-hole parkland course (6206 yards, SSS 70). Provided they have a handicap certificate, visitors are welcome, except on competition days, subject to tee reservations. There is a practice area. Green fees are £15 per round, £20 a day on weekdays and £20 per round, £30 a day at weekends and Bank Holidays. Lunch is available daily and evening meals by arrangement.
Location
High Beech Lane, Haywards Heath, W Sussex RG16 1SL
The club is situated 2 miles north of Haywards Heath near Lindfield.

HILL BARN
(0903) 37301
An 18-hole open downland course (6224 yards, SSS 70) with some trees and views as far as the Isle of Wight. The course is public and visitors of all playing abilities are welcome on weekdays and in the afternoon at weekends. There is a putting green and also a practice area although balls are not provided. Green fees are £7 on weekdays and £8 at weekends. Breakfasts, snacks and hot meals are available throughout the day.
Location
Hill Barn Lane, Worthing, West Sussex BN14 9QE
The club is situated north of Worthing off the Upper Brighton Road. It is signposted at the Excess roundabout.

RAC recommended hotels see Worthing.

IFIELD GOLF AND COUNTRY CLUB
(0293) 20222
An 18-hole hilly parkland course with a winding river (6289 yards, SSS 70). Visitors are welcome on weekdays and also at the weekend if they are accompanied by a member. Green fees are £20 per round or day on weekdays and £15 with a member at weekends. Full catering facilities are available daily.
Location
Rusper Road, Ifield, Crawley, West Sussex RH11 0LW
Leave the M23 at Crawley junction and follow the signs to Brighton and the A23. After 3 roundabouts take the right turning and then left into Ifield Drive. Then take the second right after the shops and the first left into Rusper Road. The club is then signposted.

LITTLEHAMPTON
(0903) 717170
A very pretty 18-hole links and meadowland course with good views (6244 yards, SSS 70). Visitors are welcome at all times. Green fees are £16 on weekdays and £22 at weekends. Full catering facilities are available daily. The course overlooks the Yacht Club and West Beach is close by.
Location
170 Rope Walk, Riverside, Littlehampton, W.Sussex BN17 5DL
From Littlehampton take the A259 to Bognor Regis. After crossing the bridge over the river take the first turn signposted.

RAC recommended hotel
The Beach ★★ (0903) 717277 A large hotel in pleasant grounds situated on the seafront. Facilities include a swimming pool and snooker.

MANNINGS HEATH
(0403) 210228
An 18-hole undulating parkland course with streams running through 11 of the holes (6404 yards, SSS 71). Two famous holes are the 12th, the 'Waterfall' and the 13th, the 'Valley'. There is a family of squirrels living at the 9th and 10th holes! Visitors with a handicap certificate are welcome on weekdays although preferably by prior arrangement. Green fees are £14 per round and £18 a day on weekdays. Lunch and dinner is served by arrangement. Local attractions include Leonards Lee Gardens and Nyman's Gardens.
Location
Goldings Lane, Mannings Heath, West Sussex RH13 6JU
The club is situated 3 miles south east of Horsham off the A281.

RAC recommended hotel
Ye Olde King's Head ★★ (0403) 53126 Attractive 15th-century former coaching inn in the town centre.

PYECOMBE
(07918) 53272
An 18-hole downland course situated on the South Downs (6234 yards, SSS 70). Visitors of all playing abilities are welcome after 9.15am on weekdays, after 2pm on Saturday and after 3pm on Sundays. There are two practice areas. Green fees are £12.50 on weekdays and £25 at weekends. There is a club dining room and a bar which is open daily.
Location
Clayton Hill, Pyecombe, W Sussex BN45 7FF
The course is on the A273, half a mile from the junction with the A23 at Pyecome, 5 miles north of Brighton.

SELSEY
(0243) 602203
A testing 9-hole seaside course with natural ditches (5402 yards, SSS 68). Visitors who have a handicap certificate are welcome on weekdays and also at weekends if you are with a member. Green fees are £9 per 18 holes on weekdays and £14 per 18 holes at weekends and Bank Holidays. Snacks and lunches are served daily.
Location
Golf Links Lane, Selsey, Chichester, West Sussex PO22 9DR
The club is situated on the B2145, 7 miles south of Chichester.

TILGATE FOREST
(0293) 30103
A championship 18-hole parkland course with an interesting 17th hole (6359 yards, SSS 70). The course is possibly the best public golf course in Britain and visitors of all levels are welcome. Green fees are £6.50 per round, £12.50 a day on weekdays and £9.30 per round or day on Friday and at weekends. There is a restaurant and bar where snacks are available.
Location
Titmus Drive, Tilgate, Crawley, West Sussex
Leave the M23 at Pease Pottage and follow the A23 north towards Crawley. When you come to the first roundabout turn right and follow the signs.

WEST CHILTINGTON
(079 83) 3574
An 18-hole gently undulating course with spectacular views (5969 yards, SSS 69). Visitors of all playing abilities are welcome at all times. There is also a 13-bay driving range. Green fees are £8.50, £5 after 6pm on weekdays and £12, £6 after 6pm, at weekends. Bar snacks are available daily.
Location
Broadford Bridge Road, West Chiltington, Sussex RH20 2YA
The club is situated 2 miles east of Pulborough, just off A283.

RAC recommended hotel
Chequers ★★ (0798) 872486 Small period house -a two-storey listed building now a family-run hotel.

WEST SUSSEX
(079 82) 2563
An 18-hole heathland course (6156 yards, SSS 70). There is a large practice ground. Visitors who hold a current handicap certificate and a letter of introduction are welcome except on Tuesday and at weekends when you must be invited by a member. Lunches and teas are served daily. The many local attractions include Arundel Castle, the Chalk Pits at Amberbey, and Parham House.
Location
Pulborough, West Sussex RH20 2EN
The club is situated 1½ miles east of Pulborough between Storrington and Pulborough on the A283.

WORTHING
(0903) 60801
There are two 18-hole downland courses here, The Lower, considered to be one of the best in the country, (6477 yards, SSS 72) and The Upper, a shorter but tricky course (5243 yards, SSS 66). Visitors who have a handicap certificate are welcome on weekdays. Green fees are £18 on weekdays and £22 at weekends and Bank Holidays. Lunch is served daily except on Monday when only snacks are available.
Location
Links Road, Worthing, W Sussex BN14 9QZ
The club is located on the A27 at the top of the hill near the Offington roundabout at the junction with the A24 London road.

RAC recommended hotels
Burlington ★★★ (0903) 211222 Splendid Victorian hotel on the seafront, well equipped and tastefully furnished.
Chatsworth ★★★ (0903) 36103 A fine four-storey Georgian building beside a garden square near the seafront. Facilities include sauna, solarium and gymnasium and billiards.

TYNE & WEAR

BOLDON
(0783) 364182
A fairly flat 18-hole meadowland course with easy walking (6348 yards, SSS 70). On a good day, the sea is visible from the tee. Visitors of all handicaps are welcome on weekdays but there are restrictions at weekends. Green fees on application. There is a bar where snacks are served and meals are available by arrangement.
Location
Dipe Lane, East Boldon, Tyne & Wear NE36 0PQ
Take the A1018, and then the A184 3 miles north west of Sunderland, towards Boldon, and the club is approximately 1 mile from the roundabout at the junction of ther A19 and A1.

CITY OF NEWCASTLE
091-285 1775
A flat 18-hole parkland course which can be windy (6508 yards, SSS 71). Visitors are welcome at any time. Green fees are £9/(£4 with a member) on weekdays and £13/(£5 with a member) at weekends and Bank Holidays. Bar snacks, sandwiches and lunches are served every day except Monday. The new Metro Centre is worth visiting.
Location
Three Mile Bridge, Gosforth, Newcastle upon Tyne NE3 2DR
The course is 3 miles north of Newcastle city centre, on the left-hand side of the main A1 heading north, opposite the Three Mile Inn.

RAC recommended hotels
Gosforth Park Thistle ★★★★ 091-236 4111 A modern hotel in grounds adjacent to the Racecourse. Facilities include an indoor swimming pool, golf, tennis, squash, sauna, solarium and gymnasium.
Holiday Inn ★★★★ 091-236 5432 Modern purpose-built two-storey hotel, near A1. Indoor swimming pool, sauna solarium, gymnasium.
County Thistle ★★★ 091-232 2471 In city centre opposite the station, a modernised Victorian hotel.
Crest ★★★ 091-232 6191 Modern brick-built eight-storey hotel in city centre.
Hospitality Inn ★★★ 091-281 7881 Attractive modernised hotel 1 mile from city centre.
Imperial Swallow ★★★ 091-281 5511 Traditional building efficiently modernised; includes leisure centre and choice of restaurants. Indoor swimming pool, sauna, solarium, gymnasium.
Northumbria ★★★ 091-281 4961 Modernised hotel 1 mile north-east of city centre. Sauna.
Stakis Airport ★★★ (0661) 24911 Three-storey brick-built modern hotel within airport area. Many function facilities.
Swallow ★★★ 091-232 5025 Modern city-centre hotel near to Newcastle central station. Indoor swimming pool, sauna, solarium, gymnasium.
Cairn ★★ 091-281 1358 Converted from a terrace of houses; situated 1 mile from city centre on main road north.
Morrach ★★ 091-281 3361 Three-storey brick-built hotel conveniently placed by main suburban road.

GARESFIELD
(0207) 561278
An 18-hole undulating parkland course in a particularly attractive woodland setting (6603 yards, SSS 70). Visitors are welcome on weekdays and at weekends between 10.30am and 2.30pm. Green fees are £6 a day, £5 per round on weekdays and £8 a day at weekends and Bank Holidays. There is a practice area and practice nets. Full catering and bar facilities are available. Local attractions include Beamish Open Air Museum, Chopwell Woods and Tantobie Railway.
Location
Chopwell, Tyne & Wear NE7 7AP
Take the A694 Newcastle–Consett road to Rowland's Gill and then follow the B6315 to High Spen. From there take the Chopwell road, and the club is 1 mile on your left.

GEORGE WASHINGTON
091-417 2626
An 18-hole championship parkland course (6000 yards, SSS 72). There is also a 9-hole course, putting green and a 21-bay floodlit driving range. The course is a public one and visitors are welcome at all times. Green fees of £3.10 per person apply during the week. Full catering facilities are available at the Moat House Hotel, which also has a gymnasium complex, indoor swimming pool, squash, snooker, sauna and solarium. Local attractions include the Beamish Open Air Museum.
Stone Cellar Road, High Usworth, District 12, Washington, Tyne & Wear NE37 1PH.
The club is near the Washington Moat House Hotel and is well signposted from the A1(M).

RAC recommended hotel
Washington Moat House ★★★ 091-417 2626 A modern purpose-built hoted in red brick, swimming-pool, golf, putting, squash, sauna, solarium, gymnasium and billiards.

GOSFORTH
091-285 3495
An 18-hole meadowland course (6043 yards, SSS 69). Provided they have a handicap certificate, visitors are welcome on weekdays. Green fees are £8.50/(£5 with a member) on weekdays and £12/(£6 with a member) at weekends and Bank Holidays. Full catering facilities are available daily except Monday.
Location
Broadway East, Gosforth, Newcastle upon Tyne NE3 5ER
Take the A6127 for 3 miles north of Newcastle city centre and turn right at the first main roundabout after the Regent Centre Metro station.

RAC recommended hotel
Gosforth Park Thistle ★★★★ 091-236 411 A modern hotel in grounds adjacent to the Racecourse. Facilities include an indoor swimming pool, golf, tennis, squash, sauna, solarium and gymnasium.

NEWCASTLE UNITED
091-286 4693
An 18-hole moorland course with natural hazards (6498 yards, SSS 71). Visitors are welcome on weekdays and no handicap certificate is required. There is a practice area. Green fees are £6 on weekdays and £8 at weekends. The fee is £5 with a member. The course is close to Newcastle.
Location
Ponteland Road, Cowgate, Newcastle upon Tyne NE5 3GW.
The club is situated 1 mile west of the city centre in the direction of the airport.

RAC recommended hotels
See City of Newcastle.

PONTELAND
(0661) 22689
An open 18-hole meadowland course with some fine views (6512 yards, SSS 71). Visitors are welcome between Monday and Friday and a handicap certificate is not required. Green fees are £12 a day, £10 per round/(£4 with a member). Visitors may also play at weekends if they are the guest of a member. Full catering facilities are available during normal bar opening hours, and by arrangement at other times.
Location
53 Bell Villas, Ponteland, Newcastle upon Tyne NE20 9BD
The course is on the A696 road to Jedburgh, 2 miles north of Newcastle Airport.

RAVENSWORTH
091-487 2843
An 18-hole moorland/parkland course with some fine sea views (5872 yards, SSS 68). Provided you have a handicap certificate, visitors are welcome on weekdays. Green fees are £8/(£5 with a member) on weekdays and £12/(£8 with a member) at weekends and Bank Holidays. Full catering facilities are available daily except Monday. Local attractions include the Beamish Open Air Museum.
Location
Moss Heaps, Wrekenton, Gateshead, Tyne & Wear NE9 7UU
Two miles south east of Gateshead.

RAC recommended hotels
Riverside Lodge ★★★ 091-495 0282 The riverside location makes a quiet setting for this modern hotel which is conveniently close to town centre and A1(M).
Swallow ★★★ 091-477 1105 Modern hotel located off A1(M), 2 miles from Newcastle city centre. Indoor swimming pool, sauna, solarium, gymnasium.
Springfield ★★★ 091-477 4121 A 1930s building with modern bedrooms, there is a car park on the A1.

RYTON
091-413 3737
An 18-hole moorland/parkland course (6034 yards, SSS 69). Visitors are welcome on weekdays and by arrangement at weekends. Green fees are £5 on weekdays and £7 at weekends and Bank Holidays. Full catering facilities are available by arrangement.
Location
Stanners Dr, Clara Vale, Ryton, Tyne & Wear NE4Q 3TD
The club is situated off the A695, 8 miles west of Newcastle. You should follow the signs from Ryton to Wylam, and then to Clara Vale.

SOUTH SHIELDS
091-456 0475
An 18-hole seaside course with some good views of the coastline (6264 yards, SSS 70). Visitors are welcome at all times. Green fees are £10 on weekdays and £15 at weekends and Bank Holidays. There is a bar and meals are available at any time. Local attractions include Marsden Grotto, the Leisure Complex and Amusement Park, and the local beaches.
Location
Cleadon Hills, South Shields, Tyne & Wear NE34 8EG
Take the A1018 north from Sunderland and turn off at Quarry Lane, near the Cleadon Chimney, a prominent landmark.

RAC recommended hotels
Sea ★★★ 091-427 0999 A 1930s style, 3-storey red-brick purpose-built hotel on the seafrong. Situated near the town centre.
New Crown ★★ 091-455 3472 A stone-built hotel located on the seafront with some lovely views of the harbour and beaches.

TYNEMOUTH
091-257 4578
An 18-hole parkland course with easy walking (6403 yards, SSS 71). Visitors who are bona fide members of a golf club are welcome on weekdays. Green fees are £10 per round/(£5 with a member) on weekdays and £12 per round/(£6 with a member at weekends. Lunches, teas and snacks are served daily except Monday. The local beaches are very good and within easy access.
Location
Spital Dene, Tynemouth, North Shields, Tyne & Wear NE30 2ER
Take the A1058 or A193 from Tynemouth to course in west of town.

RAC recommended hotel
Park ★★★ 091-257 1406 A 1930s style brick-built hotel in the residential area on the seafront. Facilities include solarium and gymnasium.

TYNESIDE
091-413 2742
An open 18-hole parkland course, hilly with some water hazards (6055 yards, SSS 69). Visitors who have a handicap certificate are welcome at all times, with or without a member. There is a practice field. Green fees are £9 per round, £11 a day on weekdays and £15 per round at weekends. There is a bar which serves snacks, tea and coffee, and lunches, high teas and dinners are avilable between 8am and 10pm. Local attractions include the Metro Centre, Beamish Open Air Museum and Hadrian's Wall.
Location
Westfield Lane, Ryton, Tyne & Wear NE40 3QE
Take the A695 from the south side of the Tyne for 7 miles west of Newcastle, and turn north at Ryton. Go down to Old Ryton village, then left past the Cross Inn, and then take the next right at the end of a row of old houses on the right-hand side.

WALLSEND
091-262 4231
A municipal 18-hole parkland course (6459 yards, SSS 72) where visitors are welcome at all times. Green fees are £3.30 on weekdays and £4.20 at weekends. Hot and cold snacks are served throughout the day.
Location
Bigges Main, Wallsend on Tyne NE28 8SX
From Newcastle, take the A1058 North Shields road and turn off at the sign to Wallsend Sports Centre.

WEARSIDE
091-534 2518
An 18-hole meadowland/parkland course with a stream and ravine crossing some of the holes (6323 yards, SSS 70). Visitors who are bona fide members of a golf club and have a handicap certificate are welcome. There is also a 4-hole Par 3 course, and separate practice tees. Green fees are £9 a day/(£7 with a member) on weekdays and £15 a day/(£10 with a member) at weekends. There is a restaurant and bar facilities which are normally open during the summer months. Between the end of October and the end of March, snacks only are available on Monday. The course lies beneath the famous Penshaw Monument and is flanked by the Washington Wild Fowl Park and the River Wear.
Location
Coxgreen, Sunderland SR4 9JT
The club is situated on the south bank of the River Wear. Take the A183 Chester-le-Street road off the A19 and, after 400 yards, turn right at the Offerton/Coxgreen sign. Turn left at the small T-junction and follow the road down the hill to the clubhouse.

WESTERHOPE
091-286 9125
A pretty 18-hole parkland course with tree-lined fairways (6407 yards, SSS 71). There are some good views across to the airport. Visitors are welcome on weekdays only. Green fees are £9, or £6 if you are with a member. Lunches and high teas are available every day except Monday.
Location
Whorlton Grange, Westerhope, Newcastle upon Tyne NE5 1PP
From the A69, west of Newcastgle, take the A696 north east. At roundabout, take B6324 west to Whorlton Grange. The Club is by the Jingling Gate pub.

RAC recommended hotels
See City of Newcastle.

WHICKHAM
091-488 7309
An 18-hole undulating parkland course with some uphill walking (6129 yards, SSS 69). Visitors may play at any time during the week but reservations are necessary at weekends. A handicap certificate is preferred. Green fees are £8/(£4 with a member) on weekdays and £12/(£6 with a member) at weekends. Snacks are available and meals by arrangement. Local attractions include Gibside Estate (Bowes Lyons) and the Metro Centre in Newcastle.
Location
Hollinside Park, Whickham, Newcastle upon Tyne NE16 5BA
The club is situated 5 miles west of Newcastle towards Whickham.

WHITBURN
091-529 2144
An 18-hole parkland course (6035 yards, SSS 69). Visitors are welcome on weekdays, but for weekend play you are asked to telephone the Pro beforehand to check if a competition is being played. Green fees are £7.50 a day on weekdays/(£5 with a member) and £7.50 per round, £12 a day at weekends/(£8 with a member). Full catering facilities are available. The course is close to the seaside.
Location
Lizard Lane, South Shields, Tyne & Wear NE34 7AH
The course is half-way between Sunderland and South Shields off the A183 coast road.

RAC recommended hotels
Seaburn ★★★ 091-529 2041 On the seafront this recently refurbished 1930s hotel has a modern extension. Facilities include an indoor swimming pool, sauna, solarium and a gymnasium.
Roker ★★ 091-567 1786 A white-painted terraced hotel overlooking the sea front.
Puffin Billy ★★★ 091-529 2020 Unusual hotel on a railway theme – the restaurant and bar are in two genuine Pullman railway carriages! Separate accommodation block.
Howbray Park ★★★ 091-567 8221 Four-story brick-built town centre hotel, with public park at rear.

WHITLEY BAY
091-252 0180
An 18-hole undulating seaside course with a stream running through (6617 yards, SSS 72). The course actually runs close to the sea. Visitors are welcome on weekdays, and at weekends with a member. Green fees are £10, or £5 with a member. Full catering facilities are available daily except Monday. Local attractions include St Mary's Island Nature Reserve, and Spanish City Amusement Park.
Location
Claremont Road, Whitley Bay, Tyne & Wear NE26 30P
The club is on the A183, 10 miles north east of Newcastle, on the north side of Whitley Bay.

WARWICKSHIRE

ATHERSTONE
(0827) 13110
An 11 hole undulating parkland course (6239 yards, SSS 70). Provided they have a handicap certificate, visitors are welcome on weekdays. There is a practice ground. Green fees are £19 (£5 with a member). Full catering facilities are available daily except Tuesday. Local attractions include Bosworth Fields.
Location
The Outwoods, Atherstone, Warwicks CV9 2RL
Take the Coleshill road out of Atherstone and the club is about half a mile on your left.

RAC recommended hotels
Old Red Lion (082 77) 3156 A historic inn conveniently situated in the main street of town.

KENILWORTH
(0926) 58517
An 18 hole undulating parkland course (6408 yards, SSS 71). Visitors are welcome at any time but it is advisable to telephone the Pro beforehand. A handicap certificate is preferred. There is a practice ground and a 9 hole Par 3 course. Green fees on application. Full catering facilities are available every day but you should make arrangements with the Stewardess. Local attractions include Warwick Castle, Kenilworth Castle, Coventry Cathedral and Stoneleigh Abbey.
Location
Crew Lane, Kenilworth, Warwickshire CV8 2EA
Follow the A429 north east from Kenilworth towards Coventry. Turn right into Common Lane to course on Crew Lane.

RAC recommended hotels
De Montfort ★★★★ (0926) 55944 A modern hotel close to the historical Kenilworth Castle. Facilities include a snooker room.
Chesford Grange ★★★ (0926) 59321 An attractive rambling Victorian house with landscaped gardens, in a rural setting.
Clarendon House ★★★ (0926) 57668 Ancient inn with restaurant. Located in older part of town.

LEAMINGTON AND COUNTY
(0926) 425961
An 18 hole undulating parkland course with panoramic views (6425 yards, SSS 71). Visitors of all playing abilities are welcome. Green fees on application. Lunches and evening meals are served daily except Monday. The Royal Pump Room, Jephson Gardens and the Museum and Art Gallery in the town are worth visiting, and Warwick Castle and Stratford-upon-Avon are within easy reach.
Location
Golf Lane, Whitnash, Leamington Spa, Warwickshire CV31 2QA
The club is 2 miles south of the town centre off the A452.

RAC recommended hotel
Falstaff ★★★ (0926) 312044 In residential area, a hotel converted from fine Regency residences.
Manor House ★★★ (0926) 423251 Attractive former manor house. The first lawn tennis club was founded here.
Regent ★★★ (0926) 427231 Named by permission of the Prince Regent, this is an elegant Regency hotel.
Abbacourt ★★ (0926) 311188 Former private residence, now a hotel situated on town outskirts.
Adams ★★ (0926) 450742 Privately-owned early 19th-century hotel, refurbished but retaining it's period charm. Solarium.
Angel ★★ (0926) 881296 Attractive three-strey Georgian building painted white. Conveniently sited for shops.
Beech Lodge ★★ (0926) 422227 Former private house converted to hotel in residential area.
Berni Royal ★★ (0926) 883561 Refurbished, cream-painted, four-storey. Georgian building in town centre.

NEWBOLD COMYN
(0926) 421157
A varied 18 hole parkland course with some hard walking (6259 yards, SSS 70). The first 9 holes are hilly, and the last 9 flat. The course is a municipal one and visitors are welcome at all times. Green fees are £2.50 on weekdays and £3.90 at weekends and Bank Holidays. There is a bar and restaurant. Local attractions include The Royal Pump Room, Jephson Gardens, and Warwick Castle.
Location
Newbold Terrace East, Leamington Spa, Warwicks
The club is situated off the B4099 Willes Road.

NUNEATON
(0203) 347810
An 18 hole undulating meadowland course (6412 yards, SSS 71). Provided you have a handicap certificate, visitors are welcome on weekdays, but only with a member at weekends. Green fees are £17 (with a member) on weekdays and £6 at weekends. Full catering facilities are available every day except Monday. The course is 8 miles from Coventry.
Location
Golf Drive, Whitestone, Nuneaton, Warwicks CV11 6QF
Leave the M6 at junction 3 for the A444 and, 2 miles south of Nuneaton, turn onto the B4114 to the south of the town.

RAC recommended hotel
Long Shoot ★★ (0203) 329711 A modern hotel with an attractive, distinctive roof.

PURLEY CHASE
(0203) 395348
An 18 hole meadowland course with some difficult water hazards (6604 yards, SSS 71). The course is situated on the highest point in the area. Visitors who have a handicap certificate are welcome at any time on weekdays and at weekends in the afternoons. There is a floodlit driving range. Green fees on application. Full catering facilities are available daily.
Location
Ridge Lane, Atherstone, Nuneaton, Warwicks CV10 0RB
Take the A5 $1^1/_2$ miles south to Mancetter Island, and turn right at Pipers Lane. There are tourist signs on all approaches.

RUGBY
(0788) 542306
An 18 hole parkland course with a stream running through, and a viaduct crossing it (5457 yards, SSS 67). Visitors of all playing abilities are welcome on weekdays and at weekends and Bank Holidays with a member. Green fees are £9.50 per round or day. Lunch and dinner served everyday except Tuesday. The club is close to Rugby School, and the interesting canal system.
Location
Clifton Road, Rugby CV21 3RD
Take the Rugby-Market Harborough road and turn right just past the railway bridge as you leave the town.

RAC recommended hotel
Post House ★★★★ (0788) 822101 A modern hotel in gardens adjacent to the junction 18 of the M1. Facilities include a gymnasium and billiards.

STRATFORD-UPON-AVON
(0789) 205749
A splendid 18 hole parkland course with some testing holes (6309 yards, SSS 70). Visitors are welcome on weekdays by arrangement, but the club does prefer players with a handicap certificate. Green fees on application. Snacks and meals are available at all times. Local attractions include Stratford-upon-Avon and Warwick Castle.
Location
Tiddlington Road, Stratford-upon-Avon, Warwicks CV37 7BA
The course is half a mile from the river bridge on the B4089.

RAC recommended hotels
Moat House International ★★★★ (0789) 414411 Overlooking the river Avon, a modern hotel situated in centre of town. Indoor swimming pool, fishing, sauna, solarium, gymnasium, billiards.
Shakespeare ★★★★ (0789) 294771 Ancient timbered building convenient for theatre. Open fires in winter.
Welcombe C/H ★★★★ (0789) 295252 Fine large country mansion in extensive grounds. Two golf courses. Putting, tennis, billiards.
Alveston Manor ★★★ (0789) 204581 Well-furnished manor house with modern extensions, pleasant grounds.
Arden ★★★ (0789) 294949 A hotel, partly Regency, with modern extensions. Opposite the theatre.
Falcon ★★★ (0789) 205777 An ancient black and white inn with modern extensions.
Grosvenor House ★★★ (0789) 269213 A hotel in two-storey white Georgian buildings. Sauna, solarium, gymnasium.
Swan's Nest ★★★ (0789) 66761 Located by riverside, an ancient inn with modern extensions.
White Swan ★★★ (0789(297022 Ancient timbered building near American fountain. Interesting public rooms.
Coach House ★★ (0789) 204109 Two substantial early Victorian houses on edge of town.
Swan House ★★ (0789) 67030 Attractive building (Georgian and 19th-century) adjacent to Mary Arden's House.

WARWICK
(0926) 494316
A 9-hole meadowland course with easy walking (2682 yards, SSS 66). There is also a floodlit driving range. Visitors may play at any time except on Sunday mornings, and players of all abilities including beginners are welcome. Green fees are £1.80 per 9 holes on weekdays and £2.10 per 9 holes at weekends and Bank Holidays. There is a bar which opens during normal licensing hours. Warwick and the Castle are nearby.
Location
The Racecourse, Warwick CV34 6HW
From the junction of the A41 and A46, continue for half a mile towards Warwick and turn right into the racecourse.

RAC recommended hotel
Hilton National ★★★★ (0926) 499555 Spacious odern brick-built hotel. Indoor swimming pool.
Glebe ★★★ (0926) 624218 Attractive former vicarage converted to hotel with restaurant.
Lord Leycester ★★ (0926) 491481 Modernised Georgian coaching inn; located close to town centre.
Warwick Arms ★★ (0926) 492759 A 18th century former coaching inn, now modernised, located near the Castle.

WELCOMBE HOTEL
(0789) 295252
A wooded 18 hole undulating parkland course (yards, SSS) with some spectacular views of the River Avon, Stratford and the Cotswolds. Provided you have a handicap certificate, visitors are welcome but a telephone booking is essential, and no visitors may play on Saturday or Sunday mornings. Green fees are £15 on weekdays and £17.50 at weekends and Bank Holidays. There is a Golfers Bar which is open daily, and a restaurant in the hotel. Other facilities include putting, tennis and billiards. Stratford-upon-Avon and Warwick Castle are both within easy reach.
Location
Warwick Road, Stratford-upon-Avon, Warwickshire CV37 0NR
The club is $1^1/_2$ miles from Stratford on the A46 to Warwick.

RAC recommended hotel
Welcombe ★★★★ (0789) 295252 A fine large country mansion in extensive grounds.

WEST MIDLANDS

BELFRY
(0675) 70301
There are two 18 hole parkland courses here, situated in a 370-acre park; The Brabazon, a challenging championship course withstreams and lakes providing water hazards (6975 yards, SSS 72), and The Derby (6077 yards, SSS 70). Visitors are welcome at all times but you must book 14 days in advance unless there is a party of 16 or more golfers. A handicap certificate of 24 or better is required for the Brabazon course. Full practice facilities are available and there is a 17-bay floodlit driving range. Buggies can be hired for £15 per round or £20 a day, but you must book in advance. Green fees are £23 on weekdays and £25 at weekends for the Brabazon course, and £9 on weekdays and £11 at weekends for the Derby course. All prices are per round. There are two bars where snacks are served and full meals are available in the hotel.
Location
Lichfield Road, North Wishaw, Sutton Coldfield, West Midlands B76 9PR
Leave the M6 at junction 4 and follow the signs to Lichfield along the A446. The club is sited at the junction of the A4091 to Tamworth and the A446 to Lichfield.

RAC recommended hotel
Belfry ★★★★ (0675) 70301 A lovely Victorian house with extensions. Outstanding leisure facilities include an indoor swimming pool, putting, tennis, squash, sauna, solarium, gymnasium and billiards.

BLOXWICH
(0922) 405724
An 18 hole undulating parkland course with natural hazards (6286 yards, SSS 70). Provided you have a handicap certificate, visitors are welcome on weekdays and with a member at weekends. Green fees are £14 (£5 with a member). There is a bar where lunches and teas are served, and evening meals by arrangement every day except Monday. Local attractions include Chase Water for watersports.
Location
Stafford Road, Bloxwich, Walsall, W Midlands WS3 3PQ
The club is situated off the A34 Walsall-Cannock road, 4 miles north of Walsall centre.

RAC recommended hotels in Walsall.

BOLDMERE
021-354 3379
An 18 hole parkland course (4463 yards, SSS 62). Visitors of all playing abilities are welcome at any time. Green fees are £3.90 on weekdays and £4.60 at weekends. Full catering facilities are available throughout the day. Sutton Park is nearby.
Location
Monmouth Drive, Sutton Coldfield, W Midlands
The course is on the A452 Chester road, 6 miles north east of Birmingham city centre.

RAC recommended hotels in Sutton Coldfield.

BRAND HALL
021-552 7475
An 18 hole wooded parkland course with easy walking (5813 yards, SSS 68). There are some good hazards including streams, and a dog-leg 10th hole which is particularly testing. The course is municipal and visitors are welcome at any time. There is a practice area. Green fees are £3 a day. There is a bar and cafeteria which are open daily. Dudley, which holds the Black Country Museum, a castle and a zoo, is only 3 miles away.
Location
Heran Road, Oldbury, Warley, W Midlands
Leave the M5 at junction 2 and turn onto the A4123. Turn right at the traffic lights and the course is signposted from here.

CALDERFIELDS
(0922) 640540
An 18 hole parkland course with a lake which crosses some tees (6700 yards, SSS 72). There is

also a putting green and a practice area. Visitors of all playing levels are welcome at any time. Green fees are £8 on weekdays and £10 at weekends. There is a restaurant which is open every day, and a bar which serves snacks.

Location

Aldridge Road, Walsall, W Midlands WS4 2JS
Leave the M6 at junction 7 for the A454 Aldridge road.

RAC recommended hotels in Walsall.

CITY OF COVENTRY (BRANDON WOOD)
(0203) 543133

An 18 hole parkland course with easy walking (6530 yards, SSS 71). The River Avon runs through the course. Visitors of all playing abilities are welcome. There is an 11 bay floodlit driving range. Green fees on application. There is a licensed restaurant where meals are served every day, and a bar. Local attractions include Coventry Cathedral, and Stratford-upon-Avon is within easy access.

Location

Brandon Lane, Brandon, Coventry
The course is situated on the banks of the River Avon, on the A45, 6 miles south of Coventry, about 120 yards south of the London Road roundabout.

RAC recommended hotel

Brandon Hall ★★★ (0203) 54257 A former country residence located in peaceful surroundings. Facilities include putting and squash.

COCKS MOOR WOODS
021-444 3584

An 18 hole tree-lined parkland course (5742 yards, SSS 68). Visitors of all playing abilities are welcome. Green fees are £2.80 per 9 holes, £3.90 per 18 holes on weekdays and £3.10 per 9 holes, £4.60 per 18 holes at weekends. Snacks are served daily.

Location

Alcester Road South, King's Heath, Birmingham B14 6ER
The course is situated on the A435 near the city boundary.

COPT HEATH
(0564) 772650

A flat 18 hole parkland course (6504 yards, SSS 71). Visitors who are bona fide members of a golf club and with an official club handicap are welcome on weekdays, and with a member at weekends. The club also has full practice facilities. Green fees are £20 per round, £22.50 a day on weekdays. Lunches and evening meals are served daily except Monday. The course is convenient for the National Exhibition Centre, and within easy reach of both Stratford-upon-Avon and Warwick.

Location

Warwick Road, Knowle, Solihull, W Midlands B93 9LN
Leave the M42 at junction 5 for the A41, and the club is about a quarter of a mile from here.

RAC recommended hotels

Arden ★★★ (067 55) 3221 A modern hotel, well situated for the airport, station and the NEC. Facilities include swimming pool, sauna, solarium and gymnasium and snooker.
George ★★★ 021-711 2121 A former coaching inn with a modern extension, situated near the town centre.
St John's Swallow ★★★ 021-711 3000 Large modern red-brick hotel with conference facilities. Indoor swimming pool, sauna, solarium, gymnasium.
Flemings ★★ 021-706 0371 Four large linked Victorian houses in a part residential, part business area. Billiards.

COVENTRY
(0203) 414152

An undulating parkland course (6613 yards, SSS 72). Visitors are welcome on weekdays, but the club prefers you to hold a current handicap certificate. Green fees are £17.50. Full catering facilities are available. Stratford-upon-Avon and Warwick Castle are both within easy reach.

Location

Finham Park, Coventry CV3 6PJ
The club is 2 miles south of Coventry city centre on the A444 Stoneleigh-Leamington Spa road.

RAC recommended hotels

De Vere ★★★★ (0203) 633733 Impressive large modern city centre hotel adjacent ot the Cathedral. Billiards.
Ansty Hall C/H ★★★ (0203) 612222 A mellow, red-brick, 17th-century house in 8 acres of grounds on edge of village only half a mile from M6, junction 2.
Chace Crest ★★★ (0203) 303398 Former Victorian residence extended and developed; in suburbs.
Crest ★★★ (0203) 613261 Large modern hotel situated in own grounds. Convenient to motorway. Indoor swimming pool, sauna, solarium, gymnasium.
Novotel ★★★ (0203) 365000 Motel-type modern hotel in pleasant garden. Swimming pool, sauna, solarium, gymnasium, squash, snooker.
Old Mill ★★★ (0203) 303588 Converted mill house set in 5 acres of garden beside River Sowe.
Post House ★★★ (0203) 402151 A modern hotel located on the Western outskirts of the city.
Allesley ★★ (0203) 403272 Light, modern, purpose-built hotel on west side of city.
Beechwood ★★ (0203) 338662 Charming former farmhouse set in pleasant grounds 3 miles north of the city.

DARTMOUTH
021-588 2131

A 9 hole undulating meadowland course with a testing first hole, and two brooks running through (6060 yards, SSS 69). Visitors of all playing abilities are welcome on weekdays, and at weekends with a member, but not on medal days. Green fees are £12.50 on weekdays (£4.50 with a member) and £12 at weekends. There is a dining room with a full menu, but you are advised to book in advance.

Location
West Bromwich, W Midlands B71 4DW
Take the West Bromwich-Walsall road and turn right at Churchfield. The course is located behind Churchfield High School.

RAC recommended hotel
West Bromwich Moat House ★★★ 021-553 6111 This modern motorway hotel is alongside the M5 overlooking Sandwell Valley.

DRUIDS HEATH
(0922) 55595
A challenging 18 hole undulating course (6914 yards, SSS 73). Provided you have a handicap certificate, visitors are welcome on weekdays. Green fees are £12 on weekdays (£5 with a member) and £17 (£8.50 with a member) after 2pm at weekends. Local attractions include Sutton Park, Tamworth Castle and Cannock Chase.

Location
Stonnall Road, Aldridge, W Midlands WS9 8JZ
The course is between Sutton Coldfield and Walsall, off the A452.

DUDLEY
(0384) 537719
An 18 hole very hilly parkland course (5715 yards, SSS 67). Visitors of all playing abilities are welcome on weekdays, but there are restrictions at weekends. Green fees are £8.50. Meals are served daily. Local attractions include Dudley, the castle ruins, Chima Priory ruins, the Black Country Museum, the Geological Museum, and the zoo.

Location
Turners Hill, Rowley Regis, Warley, W Midlands B65 9DP
One mile south of the town centre.

RAC recommended hotels
Ward Arms ★★★ (0384) 52723 A extended and rebfurbished two-storey hotel beside the main road to Birmingham.
Station ★★ (0384) 53418 A Victorian town centre hotel near the castle.

EDGBASTON
021-454 1736
An 18 hole parkland course situated in some very pretty countryside (6118 yards, SSS 69). Visitors are welcome at all times, but the club prefers you to hold a current handicap certificate. Green fees are £16 on weekdays and £22 at weekends and Bank Holidays. Lunch is served daily and other meals by arrangement. Other facilities at the club include snooker. Local attractions include the Botanical Gardens and the Edgbaston Priory Tennis Club.

Location
Church Road, Edgbaston, Birmingham B15 3TB
From the city centre, take the A38 Bristol road and after 1 mile, at the second set of traffic lights, turn right into Priory Road. At the end turn left into Church Road and the club entrance is 200 yards on the left.

RAC recommended hotels
Copthorne ★★★★ 021-200 2727 Ultra-modern city centre hotel. Indoor swimming pool.
Holiday Inn ★★★★ 021-631 2000 Large modern hotel in city centre. Indoor swimming pool.
Midland ★★★★ 021-643 2601 Modernised 19th century hotel.
Plough & Harrow ★★★★ 021-454 4111 Well-appointed, superbly furnished hotel in Victorian building. Sauna.
Strathallen Thistle ★★★★ 021-455 9777 Modern hotel of circular design with covered parking facilities.
Grand ★★★ 021-236 7951 Modernised Victorian hotel opposite Cathedral.

ENVILLE
(0384) 872074
There are two fairly flat moorland courses here; The Highgate, 18 holes (6541 yards, SSS 72) and The Lodge, 18 holes (6207 yards, SSS 70). Provided you have a handicap certificate, visitors are welcome on weekdays and also at weekends with a member. Green fees are £20 a day (£5 with a member). Full catering facilities are available daily except Monday. Places worth visiting include Kimver Edge.

Location
Highgate Common, Enville, Stourbridge, W Midlands DY7 5BN
Take the A458 Bridgnorth road and continue past the Fox Inn. Turn right to the Halfpenny Green aerodrome.

RAC recommended hotel
Talbot ★★ (0384) 394350 Attractive former coaching inn situated in the town centre.

FOREST OF ARDEN HOTEL GOLF & COUNTRY CLUB
(0676) 22118
There are two courses here, a championship 18 hole parkland and moorland course (6962 yards, SSS 72) and a 9 hole beginners course. Provided you have a handicap certificate, visitors are welcome. Green fees are £12 on weekdays and £15 at weekends. There is a restaurant and a members bar where snacks are served. Other facilities include tennis, swimming pool, squash, fishing, snooker, sauna, solarium and gymnasium. There is another bar by the poolside.

Location
Maxstoke Lane, Meriden, Coventry, Warwickshire CV7 7HR
The club is close to the M6 junction 4 or M42 junction 6, off the A45, 10 miles north west of Coventry and 2½ miles east of Birmingham International Airport.

RAC recommended hotel
Forest of Arden ★★★ (0676) 22118
See above.

FULFORD HEATH
(0564) 822806
An 18 hole meadowland course situated on two sides of the River Cole (6216 yards, SSS 70). Provided you have a handicap certificate, visitors are welcome on weekdays. Green fees are £12 per round or £15 a day. Lunches and evening meals are served daily except Monday. Local attractions include Stratford-upon-Avon and Warwick Castle, and the club is convenient for the National Exhibition Centre.

Location
Tanners Green Lane, Wythall, Birmingham B47 6BH
The club is situated 1 mile from the main Alcester road.

GAY HILL
021-430 6523
An 18 hole meadowland course (6522 yards, SSS 71). Visitors who have a handicap certificate are welcome on weekdays but only with a member at weekends, and not before 12.30pm on Sunday. Green fees are £18 a day. Meals are available daily. The course is very convenient for the National Exhibition Centre.

Location
Alcester Road, Hollywood, Birmingham B47 5PP
The club is on the A435, 7 miles from the city centre.

RAC recommended hotel
Westmead ★★★ 021-445 1202 Modern hotel developed from a pre-war building in a rural area on the busy A441 8 miles from Birmingham.

GRANGE
(0203) 451465
A 9 hole well-bunkered meadowland course with a river affecting 5 holes (3001 yards, SSS 69). Visitors of any reasonable ability are accepted to play on weekdays before 2pm and on Sunday after midday. Green fees are £7 per round, £10 a day on weekdays and £10 a round on Sunday. Coventry and Stratford-upon-Avon are both within easy reach.

Location
Copsewood, Coventry, W Midlands CV3 1HS
The club is situated 2½ miles from Coventry city centre, on the A428 Binley Road.

RAC recommended hotels in Coventry.

GREAT BARR
021-357 1232
An 18 hole meadowland course with easy walking (6545 yards, SSS 72). Visitors of all playing abilities are welcome on weekdays, but they must have a handicap certificate to play at weekends. Green fees are £12 on weekdays. Catering facilities are available by arrangement. The club also has a

snooker room. There are some fine views from the course of Barr Beacon National Park and the club is convenient for the city centre.
Location
Chapel Lane, Great Barr, Birmingham B43 7BA
The course is adjacent to exit 7 of the M6, 6 miles north west of Birmingham.

RAC recommended hotels
Great Barr ★★★ 021-357 1141 A mainly modern hotel in a quiet leafy suburb, 6 miles from the city centre.
Post House ★★★ 021-357 7444 A modern hotel, adjacent to the motorway. Facilities include a swimming pool.

HAGLEY
(0562) 883701
A very scenic 18 hole meadowland course situated beneath the Clent Hills and with some spectacular views (6353 yards, SSS 72). There is also a new lake being excavated. Visitors are welcome on weekdays and also at weekends with a member, but only after 1pm. Green fees are £13 per round, £15 a day on weekdays and £7 at weekends. There is a bar which serves snacks, and an à la carte restaurant. Local attractions include the wonderful countryside, the Glass Museum at Stourbridge, and the Black Country Museum and Zoo at Dudley.
Location
Wassel Grove, Hagley, Stourbridge DY9 9JW
The club is off the A456 Kidderminster-Birmingham road. If you are travelling from the M5, leave it at junction 3.

RAC recommended hotel
Talbot ★★ (0384) 394350 An attractive former coaching inn situated in the town centre.

HALESOWEN
021-550 1041
An 18 hole parkland course (5754 yards, SSS 68). Visitors of all playing abilities are welcome on weekdays and Bank Holidays by arrangement, but not at weekends. Green fees are £9 per round or £12 a day. Full catering facilities are available daily except Monday.
Location
The Leasowes, Halesowen, W Midlands B62 8QF

HANDSWORTH
021-5540599
An 18 hole parkland course which has some tight fairways (6312 yards, SSS 70). Provided you have a handicap certificate, visitors are welcome on weekdays. Green fees are £15 (£5 with a member). Lunches and dinners are served daily except Monday. There is a large practice area and putting green, and the club also has squash and snooker facilities. Birmingham city centre and the 14th-century Aston Hall are within easy reach.
Location
11 Sunningdale Close, Handsworth Wood, Handsworth, Birmingham B20 1NP
The club is 3 miles north west of the city centre off the A41, 1 mile from the M6. Leave the motorway at junction 7 and continue via the A34 Birmingham road, Old Walsall Road, Vernon Avenue, Westover Road, and Craythorn Avenue.

RAC recommended hotels
Great Barr ★★★ 021-357 1141 A mainly modern hotel in a quiet leafy suburb, 6 miles from the city centre.
Post House ★★★ 021-357 7444 A modern hotel, adjacent to the motorway. Facilities include a swimming pool.
West Bromwich Moat House ★★★ 021-553 6111 This modern motorway hotel is alongside the M5 overlooking Sandwell Valley.

HARBORNE
021-427 1728
An 18 hole undulating parkland/moorland course with some tight fairways (6240 yards, SSS 70). Visitors who have a handicap certificate are welcome on weekdays, and at weekends and Bank Holidays with a member. Green fees are £15 (£5 with a member). There is a bar and dining room which is open every day except Monday. Local attractions include the Black Country Museum.
Location
40 Tennal Road, Birmingham B32 2JE
The club is 3 miles west of Birmingham city centre, off the A4040 through Harborne village and War Lane.

HARBORNE CHURCH FARM
021-427 1204
A 9 hole municipal parkland course with easy walking (4514 yards, SSS 62). Visitors of all playing abilities are welcome at any time. Green fees on application. There is a café which serves snacks and meals.
Location
Vicarage Road, Harborne, Birmingham B17 0SN
From Birmingham, continue down Broad Street, Harborne Road and War Lane to Vicarage Lane.

HATCHFORD BROOK
021-743 9821
A flattish 18 hole parkland course (6164 yards, SSS 69). The course is a municipal one and visitors of all playing abilities are welcome. Green fees on application. There are catering facilities available when the course is open. The course is actually next to Birmingham Airport, and is also convenient for the National Exhibition Centre.
Location
Coventry Road, Sheldon, Birmingham B26 3PY
The club is almost on the city boundary, adjacent to the Airport, on the main A45 road to Coventry.

HEARSALL
(0203) 713470
A wooded 18 hole tree-lined parkland course with easy walking (5963 yards, SSS 69). The 4th hole has a stream running through. Provided you have a handicap certificate, visitors are welcome on weekdays from 7.30am, and with a member on Sunday. Green fees are £14 on weekdays, £16 on Saturday and £8 on Sunday. There is a restaurant and bar where sandwiches and lunches are available daily, and evening meals by arrangement. Local attractions include Coventry Cathedral, Kenilworth Castle, Stratford and Warwick.
Location
Beechwood Avenue, Coventry CV5 6DF
The club is located off the A45 $1^1/_2$ miles south of the city centre.

RAC recommended hotels in Coventry.

HILL TOP
021-554 4463
A challenging 18 hole parkland course with gently sloping fairways and fine greens (6114 yards, SSS 69). Visitors of all playing abilities are welcome. Green fees are £4.60 on weekdays and £3.90 at weekends. Hot and cold meals are served whilst the course is open.
Location
Park Lane, Handsworth, Birmingham B21 8LJ
From the West Bromwich exit on the M5, take the Birmingham road and turn first left past West Bromwich Albion football club.

RAC recommended hotels in Handsworth.

HIMLEY HALL
(0902) 895207
A 9 hole parkland course with some lovely views (3090 yards, Par 3). The course is public and visitors are welcome at all times. Green fees are £2.20 for 9 holes, £3.50 for 18 holes on weekdays, and £2.70 for 9 holes, £4 for 18 holes at weekends.
Location
Log Cabin, Himley Hall Park, Dudley, W Midlands
Take the A449 Wolverhampton-Kidderminster road and turn at the traffic lights, signposted Dudley, onto the B4176. From there turn into Himley Hall Park which is on your left.

RAC recommended hotel
Himley House ★★ (0902) 892468 An elegant Georgian building set in pleasant grounds.

KINGS NORTON
(0564) 826789
A championship 27 hole undulating parkland course in three loops of 9, and with some water hazards (Blue, 9 holes, 3567 yards; Red, 9 holes, 3497 yards, SSS 72; and Yellow, 9 holes, 3294 yards). Provided you have a handicap certificate, visitors are welcome on weekdays, and with a member at weekdends after midday. No visitors are allowed on Bank Holiday weekends or on Easter Tuesday. Green fees are £15 a day or £12 per round. Full catering facilities are available daily. Stratford-upon-Avon is within easy reach.
Location
Brockhill Lane, Weatheroak, Alvechurch, Birmingham B48 7ED
Leave the M42 at junction 3, towards Weatheroak, and the club is about 2 miles away.

RAC recommended hotel
Perry Hall ★★★ (0527) 579976 Renovated 17th-century house, one-time home of A. E. Houseman..

LADBROOK PARK
(05644) 2264
An undulating parkland course with tree-lined fairways (6407 yards, SSS 71). Provided you have a handicap certificate, visitors are welcome by prior arrangement. Green fees are £13. Full catering facilities are available by arrangement every day except Monday. The course is within easy reach of Stratford-upon-Avon and Henley-in-Arden.
Location
Poolhead Lane, Tanworth in Arden, Solihull B94 5ED
Leave the M40/M42 at the interchange and continue along the M42 to junction 4. Turn off onto the A34 south until you come to Hockley Heath. The course is 4 miles from here on the A4023.

RAC recommended hotels see Copt Heath.

LICKEY HILLS
021-453 3159
A very scenic 18 hole hilly parkland course (6010 yards, SSS 69). The course is public and visitors are welcome at all times. Green fees are £2.80 per 9 holes, £3.90 per 18 holes on weekdays, and £3.10, £4.60 at weekends. There is a cafeteria which is open daily. Local attractions include Lickey Hills Country Park and Monument Hill View Point
Location
Rose Hill, Old Birmingham Road, Rednal, Birmingham B45 8RR
Leave the M5 at junction 4, and the course is 10 miles south east of Birmingham city centre.

LITTLE ASTON
021-353 2066
An 18 hole parkland course, often regarded as one of Britain's finest inland courses, which has staged several major events (6724 yards, SSS 73). Visitors of all playing abilities are welcome on weekdays. Green fees are £20 during the summer and £15 in winter. Lunch is served by arrangement every day except Monday.
Location
Streetly, Sutton Coldfield B74 3AN
The club is situated 3 miles north of Sutton Coldfield, in Little Aston Park.

RAC recommended hotels in Sutton Coldfield.

MAXSTOKE PARK
(0675) 64915
An 18 hole parkland course with trees and a lake (6437 yards, SSS 71). Visitors of all playing abilities are welcome on weekdays and at weekends with a

member. There are two practice areas. Green fees are £12 per round or £16 a day. Lunch is served daily.

Location

Castle Lane, Coleshill, Birmingham B46 2RD
Leave the M6 at junction 4 and take the A446 to Coleshill. From there, turn onto the B4147 to Nuneaton, and the club is 3 miles further on the right.

RAC recommended hotels

Coleshill ★★★ (0675) 65527 A modern hotel in red-brick but with timbered buildings dating to the 16th-century.
Grimstock Country ★★★ (0675) 62121 Former private house with modern bedroom wing added. Set in attractive gardens in rural situation.

MOOR HALL
021-308 6130

An 18 hole parkland course (6219 yards, SSS 70). Visitors of all playing abilities are welcome on weekdays only. There is a practice area. Green fees are £17 per round, £23 a day (£5 with a member). Full catering facilities are available daily except Monday. Local attractions include Sutton Park.

Location

Moor Hall Drive, Four Oaks, Sutton Coldfield B75 6LN
The course is situated 2 miles from Sutton Coldfield on the A453 Tamworth road.

RAC recommended hotel

Moor Hall ★★★ 021-308 3751 An attractive former residence greatly extended and situated adjacent to the golf course. Facilities include a sauna, solarium and gymnasium.

MOSELEY
021-444 4957

An 18 hole parkland course with a lake, a pond and a stream, allproviding natural hazards (6227 yards, SSS 70). Provided you have a handicap certificate and a letter of introduction, visitors are welcome on weekdays. Green fees are £20 (£5 with a member). Dining facilities are available in the club house by arrangement with the Steward. Local attractions include Sarehole Mill.

Location

Springfield Road, King's Heath, Birmingham B14 7DX
The club is located on the Birmingham ring road, approximately half a mile east of Alcester Road.

NORTH WARWICKSHIRE
(0676) 22259

A 9 hole parkland course with easy walking (3186 yards, SSS 70). Visitors of all playing abilities are welcome on weekdays except Thursday (Ladies Day) before 1pm, and also at weekends if you are with a member. Green fees are £18 on weekdays. There is a bar where snacks are served. The club is situated in the heart of England.

Location

Hampton Lane, Meriden, W Midlands CV7 7LL
Take the A45 for 6 miles north of Coventry, and the club is on the B4102 about 1 mile from Stourbridge, approximately midway between Birmingham and Coventry.

RAC recommended hotel

Manor ★★★ (0676) 22735 A picturesque Georgian residence set in the countryside. Facilities include a swimming pool.

NORTH WORCESTERSHIRE
021-475 1047

An 18 hole meadowland course (5919 yards, SSS 69). Visitors are welcome on weekdays, and with a member at weekends and Bank Holidays. Green fees are £10. Full catering facilities are available in the clubhouse.

Location

Frankley Beeches Road, Northfield, Birmingham B31 5LP
From the city centre, take the main A38 road to Northfield and turn right at Frankley Beeches Road by the Black Horse public house. Then take the third road on the left, which brings you straight to the club.

OLTON
021-705 1083

An 18 hole parkland course (6229 yards, SSS 71). Visitors are welcome on weekdays except Wednesday, but the club prefers you to hold a current handicap certificate. Green fees are £14 (£5.50 with a member) on weekdays and (£5 with a member) at weekends and Bank Holidays. Catering facilities are available by arrangement. Stratford-upon-Avon and Warwick are within easy reach.

Location

Mirfield Road, Solihull, W Midlands B91 1JH
The club is situated 7 miles south of Birmingham off the A41.

RAC recommended hotels **see Copt Heath.**

OXLEY PARK
(0902) 25445

An undulating 18 hole parkland course (6168 yards, SSS 69). Visitors of all playing abilities are welcome, but booking is advisable at weekends. Green fees are £5 on weekdays and £12 at weekends. There is a bar, and lunch is served every day except Monday, and other meals by arrangement. Local attractions include Iron Bridge Gorge, the Black Country Museum and Dudley Zoo.

Location

Bushbury, Wolverhampton WV10 6DE
The club is situated 1½ miles from the M54/A449 junction, 1½ miles from Wolverhampton town centre, just off the A449.

RAC recommended hotels

Connaught ★★★ (0902) 24433 Light and pleasant modern hotel conveniently situated on the A41. Sauna, solarium.
Goldthorn ★★★ (0902) 29216 Pleasantly extended 19th-century former private residence.
Mount ★★★ (0902) 752055 A former residence now much extended and set in some lovely gardens.
Park Hall ★★★ (0902) 331121 A Georgian style hotel set on a hill, overlooking the countryside.
Castlecroft ★★ (0902) 764040 Attractive two-storey late Victorian building overlooking cricket ground. Solarium.
Fox ★★ (0902) 21680 Town-centre hotel, popular with business people. Attractive bedrooms.
York ★★ (0902) 758211 Small hotel conveniently situated near town centre. Owner-run.

PENN
(0902) 341142

An 18 hole heathland course (6465 yards, SSS 71). Visitors of all levels are welcome on weekdays, although the course is a tough one. Green fees are £12 (£4 with a member). Lunch is served on weekdays except Monday, and dinner on weekdays except Monday and Wednesday. Local attractions include Baggeridge Country Park where horse riding facilities are available.

Location

Penn Common, Penn, Wolverhampton, W Midlands WN4 5JN
The club is situated 2 miles south west of Wolverhampton off the A449.

RAC recommended hotels **see Oxley Park.**

PATSHULL PARK
(0902) 700100

A very pretty 18 hole parkland course landscaped by Capability Brown (6460 yards, SSS 71). Visitors are welcome, but you should telephone first to make a tee reservation. Green fees are £14 per round, £20 a day on weekdays and £18 per round, £24 a day at weekends and Bank Holidays. Buggies can be hired for £14 per round or £24 a day but you need to book in advance. There is a hotel on site with full facilities. Telford is within easy reach and local places of interest include Iron Bridge Gorge, the Black Country Museum and Dudley Zoo.

Location

Burnhill Green, Pallingham, Wolverhampton, W Midlands WV6 7HR
Leave the M54 at exit 3 towards Albrighton and from here follow the signposts to Patshull.

RAC recommended hotel

Patshull Park Hotel ★★★ (0902) 700100 A modern hotel overlooking some trout lakes in peaceful surroundings. Other facilities include putting, fishing, sauna, solarium, gymnasium and billiards.

PYPE HAYES
021-351 1014

A pretty 18 hole parkland course (5811 yards, SSS 68). Visitors of an intermediate standard are welcome. There is also a practice net. Green fees are £3.90 per 18 holes, £2.80 per 9 holes on weekdays and £4.60 per 18 holes, £3 per 9 holes at weekends. Full catering facilities are available daily.

Location

Eaglehurst Road, Walmley, Sutton Coldfield, W Midlands B76 8EP
Leave the M6 at junction 6 and turn onto the Tyburn Road. From there it is 1 mile to Eaglehurst Road.

RAC recommended hotels

New Hall C/H ★★★★ 021-378 2442 Crenellated medieval manor house, reputed to be the oldest inhabited moated house in England, with extension in keeping, all lavishly refurbished. In 26 acres of grounds.
Penns Hall ★★★★ 021-351 3111 Considerably extended 17th-century residence in spacious grounds with lake. Indoor swimming pool, fishing, squash, sauna, solarium, gymnasium, billiards.

ROBIN HOOD
021-706 0061

An 18 hole parkland course (6609 yards, SSS 72). Provided you have a handicap certificate, visitors are welcome on weekdays, except on Tuesday mornings and Bank Holidays. Green fees on application. Bar snacks are available between Tuesday and Friday and evening meals by arrangement. Local attractions include Baddesley Clinton House (NT), Packwood House (NT) and the local shopping centre.

Location

St Bernards Road, Solihull, W Midlands B92 7DJ
The club is situated 6 miles south of Birmingham on the A41. From Olton station, travel north east up St Bernards Road for 1 mile and the club house is on the right-hand side.

RAC recommended hotels **see Copt Heath.**

ROSE HILL
021-453 3159

An 18 hole parkland course (6006 yards, SSS 69). Visitors of all playing abilities are welcome. Green fees are £3.90 per 18 holes, £2.80 per 9 holes on weekdays and £4.60 per 18 holes, £5.10 per 9 holes at weekends. Snacks are served daily.

Location

Lickey Hills, Rednal, Birmingham
From junction 4 on the M5, turn towards Lydiate Ash and Lickey Hills is 1 mile.

SHIRLEY
021-744 6001

A flattish 18 hole parkland course (6445 yards, SSS 71). Visitors of all playing abilities are welcome on weekdays but not atweekends. Green fees are £15 on week days. Meals are served everyday except Monday. Local attractions include Packwood House (NT) and Baddesley Clinton House (NT).

Location
Stratford Road, Solihull, W Midlands B90 4EW
Leave the M42 at junction 4 and, 500 yards north, turn onto the A34, about 7 miles south of Birmingham.

RAC recommended hotels see Copt Heath.

SPHINX
(0203) 458890
A 9 hole parkland course (4104 yards, SSS 60). Visitors are welcome on all days except Sunday. Green fees are £3.50 per day. There is a bar where snacks are served during the evening. The golf course is part of a sports complex, and other facilities include squash, crown green bowling, cricket and football. The complex is near the city of Coventry.
Location
Siddeley Avenue, Coventry
The club is situated near the city centre. If you are travelling on the M6, leave it at the Walsgrave exit, junction 5.

RAC recommended hotels in Coventry.

SOUTH STAFFORDSHIRE
(0902) 751065
An 18 hole parkland course (6621 yards, SSS 72). Visitors are welcome every weekday, (except on Tuesday morning, which is Ladies Day) and at weekends if accompanied by a member. There are two practice grounds. Green fees are £4 per round, £18 a day. There is a bar, and snacks, lunches and dinners are served daily.
Location
Danescourt Road, Tettenhall, Wolverhampton WV6 9BQ
The club is 3 miles west of Wolverhampton town centre, on the A41 to Telford.

RAC recommended hotels see Oxley Park.

SANDWELL PARK
021-553 4637
A championship 18 hole parkland links course (6422 yards, SSS 72). Visitors are welcome at any time during the week, and at weekends if accompanied by a member. A handicap of at least 24 is preferred. Green fees are £14 per round, £20 a day. There are full catering facilities every day except Monday. There is a shopping centre within a mile, and Drayton Park is also within easy reach.
Location
Birmingham Road, West Bromwich, W Midlands B71 4JJ
Leave the M5 at junction 1, and the club is very close, approximately a quarter of a mile from West Bromwich Albion football ground.

RAC recommended hotel
West Bromwich Moat House ★★★ 021-553 6111 This modern motorway hotel is alongside the M5 overlooking Sandwell Valley.

STOURBRIDGE
(0384) 395566
An 18 hole parkland course (6178 yards, SSS 69). Visitors are welcome on weekdays and with a member at weekends. A handicap certificate is required. Green fees are £15. Full catering facilities are available daily except Monday. Local attractions include Royal Brierley and Stourbridge Stewart Glass.
Location
Worcester Lane, Pedmore, Stourbridge DY8 2RB
The club is situated 2 miles from Stourbridge town centre on the Worcester road.

RAC recommended hotel
Talbot ★★ (0384) 394350 An attractive former coaching inn situated in the town centre.

SUTTON COLDFIELD
021-353 9633
An excellent 18 hole parkland course (6541 yards, SSS 71). Visitors are welcome on weekdays except on Tuesday mornings, however, the club does prefer you to hold a handicap certificate. Green fees are £14 per day (£4 with a member) on weekdays and £18 per day (£4 with a member)) at weekends and Bank Holidays. Lunches and snacks are available daily except Monday. The club is very convenient for the National Exhibition Centre and Cannock Chase.
Location
110 Thornhill Road, Streetly, Sutton Coldfield B74 3ER
The club is situated in Sutton Park on the B4138, which is 1 mile off the A452, 9 miles north east of Birmingham centre. The nearest motorway access is junction 6 of the M6.

RAC recommended hotels
New Hall C/H ★★★★ 021-378 2442 Crenellated medieval manor house, reputed to be the oldest inhabited moated house in England, with extension in keeping, all lavishly refurbished. In 26 acres of grounds.
Penns Hall ★★★★ 021-351 3111 Considerably extended 17th-century residence in spacious grounds with lake. Indoor swimming pool, sauna, solarium, gymnasium, billiards.
Moor Hall ★★★ 021-308 3751 Attractive former residence greatly extended. Adjacent to golf course. Sauna, solarium, gymnasium.
Sutton Court Hotel ★★★ 021-355 6071 A charming red-brick turreted Victorian building, managed by the owner.
Berni Royal ★★ 021-355 8222 Refurbished, red-brick Georgian building in town centre.

WALMLEY
021-373 0029
An attractive 18 hole parkland course with an abundance of trees (6537 yards, SSS 72). Visitors are welcome on weekdays, but a handicap certificate is preferred. There is a practice ground. Green fees are £15 per round or day (£3.50 with a member). Full catering facilities are available except on Monday. The club is close to Sutton Park and the centre of Birmingham.
Location
Brooks Road, Wylde Green, Sutton Coldfield, W Midlands B72 1HR
Six miles N of Birmingham on the main Sutton Coldfield road, and about a quarter of a mile north of Chester Road, by the Yenton public house, turn right at Greenhill Road. Brooks Road continues from this.

RAC recommended hotels see Pype Hayes.

WARLEY
021-429 2440
A municipal 9 hole parkland course (2606 yards, SSS 64). Visitors of all playing abilities are welcome at all times. Green fees are £1.70 per 9 holes, £3.20 per 18 holes on weekdays and £2.10 per 9 holes, £4 per 18 holes at weekends. Juniors can play for £1.60 during the week and £2 at weekends. Full catering facilities are available. Local attractions include Dudley Zoo and Hagley Hall.
Location
Lightwoods Hill, Warley, W Midlands B67 5ED
Three miles from Birmingham city centre, turn right off the A456 at Beechwood Road, then left and first right. The course is behind the Dog public house.

WALSALL
(0922) 6135
A wooded 18 hole parkland/meadowland course (6232 yards, SSS 70). Visitors who have a handicap certificate are welcome on weekdays, but you must be with a member at weekends. Green fees are £18 per round, £22 a day. Full catering facilities are available at all times. Local attractions include the Black Country Museum, Cannock Chase and Afton Hall (NT).
Location
The Broadway, Walsall, W Midlands WS1 3EY
The club is situated 1 mile south of Walsall centre, 400 yards from the Crest Motel.

RAC recommended hotels
Barons Court ★★★ (0543) 452020 Mock tudor-style hotel with well-appointed bedrooms. Indoor swimming pool, sauna, solarium, gymnasium.
Friendly Lodge ★★★ (0922) 724444 Newly built, long low hotel with large picture windows, conveniently placed by M6, junction 10. Indoor swimming pool, sauna, gymnasium.
Post House ★★★ 021-357 7444 A modern hotel, adjacent to the motorway. Facilities include a swimming pool.
Crest ★★★ (0922) 33555 A large modern purpose-built hotel with three bars.
Abberley ★★ (0922) 27413 Detached white two-storey building adjacent to the ring road.
Bescot ★★ (0922) 22447 Converted red-brick 1930s house in garden. Close to M6, junction 9.
County ★★ (0922) 32323 A small traditional hotel quietly set in a residential area.
Royal ★★ (0922) 24555 Bright modern hotel with five-storey extension. Continental style café and restaurant.

WILTSHIRE

BRINKWORTH
(066 641) 277
A 9 hole course (6086 yards, SSS 69). Visitors are welcome at all times. Green fees are £3 on weekdays and £3.50 at weekends. Catering facilities are available by arrangement. Lacock, a National Trust village, is nearby.
Location
Longmans Farm, Brinkworth, Chippenham SN15 5DG
The club is situated 2 miles north of Chippenham on the A429 Malmesbury road.

RAC recommended hotel
Bell House ★★★ (0249) 720401 Two-storey white stone building (15th-century origin) set in attractive garden.

BREMHILL PARK
(0793) 782946
An 18 hole parkland course with easy walking, but with some testing dog-leg holes (5880 yards, SSS 71). Visitors are welcome at any time although advance booking is necessary on Sunday. Green fees are £2 a day (£4 with a member) abd £10 at weekends (£6 with a member). Lunches and light snacks are served daily. Local attractions include Bowood House and Chalk White Horse.
Location
Shrivenham, Swindon, Wilts SN6 8HH
Take the A420 Swindon-Oxford road 6 miles from Swindon, and turn off the by-pass into Shrivenham. The club is on the east boundary of the village.

RAC recommended hotels in Swindon.

BROOME MANOR
(0793) 32403
There are two public courses here; one 18 hole wooded parkland course with water hazards (6359 yards, SSS 70) and one 9 hole parkland course (2745 yards, SSS 67). There is also an excellent floodlit covered driving range. Visitors of all playing abilities are welcome. Green fees are £4.75 per 18 holes on weekdays, £5.25 at weekends, and £2.85 per 9 holes on weekdays, £3.15 at weekends. The club room is run separately and full catering facilities are available daily.
Location
Pipers Way, Swindon, Wilts SN3 1RG
The club is located 2 miles from junction 15 of the M4, 1 mile from Swindon Old Town.

RAC recommended hotels in Swindon.

CHIPPENHAM
(0249) 652040
An 18 hole meadowland course with some testing holes (5540 yards, SSS 67). Visitors who are bona fide members of a golf club are welcome, but they should also hold a current handicap certificate. Green fees are £15 on weekdays and £18 at weekends. Lunch is served every day except Monday, when there are limited catering facilities.
Location
Malmesbury Road, Chippenham, Wilts SN15 5LT
Leave the M4 at junction 17 and turn onto the A429. The club is 1 mile from the town centre.

RAC recommended hotel
Angel ★★ (0249) 652615 Attractive 17th-century coaching inn with modern motel complex to the rear.

HIGH POST
(0722273) 356
A challenging and imaginative 18 hole downland course with lots of blackthorn, and some lovely views over Salisbury Plain (6267 yards, SSS 70). Visitors are welcome, but the club requires you to hold a handicap certificate to play at weekends. There is a large practice ground. Green fees are £16 on weekdays, £14 per round, £20 a day at weekends. There is a bar, and full catering facilities are available daily. Local attractions include Salisbury, Old Sarum and Stonehenge.
Location
Great Dunford, Salisbury, Wilts
The course is situated halfway between Salisbury and Amesbury on the A345.

KINGSDOWN
(0225) 742530
An 18 hole downland course (6254 yards, SSS 71). Provided you have a handicap certificate, visitors are welcome at all times except on competition days. Green fees are £12.50 on weekdays and £15 at weekends. There is a dining room where meals are served, and a bar where snacks are available. The course is within easy reach of Bath.
Location
Kingsdown, Corsham, Wilts SN14 9BS
From the A4 between Chippenham and Bath, turn onto the A365 at Box. A quarter of a mile on, turn right uphill. Course is 2 miles further on.

RAC recommended hotels
Rudloe Park ★★★ (0225) 810555 Portland stone mansion in attractive grounds. Views down valley to Bath.
Methuen Arms ★★ (0249) 714867 Privately-owned 17th-century Cotswold stone building. Near town centre.

MARLBOROUGH
(0672) 52147
A pleasant, if somewhat breezy 18 hole downland course with some wonderful views (6440 yards, SSS 71). Visitors are welcome on weekdays and also at weekends if you hold a handicap certificate, except when there are competitions being held. Green fees are £12 per round, £15 a day (£7.50 with a member) on weekdays and £15 per round, £20 a day (£10 with a member) at weekends. There is also a practice ground and putting green. A restaurant, which serves both snacks and full meals, is open most of the day. Local attractions include Bowood House and Gardens, and Littlecote Park which has a miniature railway.
Location
The Common, Marlborough, Wilts SN8 1DU
The club is situated approximately three quarters of a mile from the town centre on the A345 to Swindon.

RAC recommended hotels
Castle and Ball ★★★ (0672) 515201 A 17th-century hotel of considerable character, carefully modernised over the years.
Ivy House ★★★ (0672) 515333 Three-storey Georgian former coaching inn, with attractive walled garden.

NORTH WILTS
(038086) 627
An 18 hole downland course situated on high ground (6450 yards, SSS 71). Visitors, preferably with a handicap certificate, are welcome at all times. Green fees on application. Full catering facilities are available. Both Avebury and Castle Combe are close by.
Location
Bishops Cannings, Devizes, Wilts SN10 2LP
The course is 1 mile from the A4 at Quemerford, Calne, 4 miles from Devizes.

RAC recommended hotels
Bear ★★ (0380) 2450 A 16th-century former coaching inn overlooking the attractive marketing square.
Lansdowne Strand ★★ (0249) 812488 White two-storey building. Former 16th-century coaching with cobbled courtyard.

RAF UPAVON
(0980) 630787
A 9 hole undulating downland course (5116 yards, SSS 67). Visitors are welcome on weekdays, but there are some restrictions at weekends. So it is advisable to telephone ahead. Green fees are £8 on weekdays and £10 at weekends. Catering facilities are available by arrangement. Local attractions include Salisbury, the Cathedral, and Stonehenge.
Location
RAF Upavon, York Road, Upavon, Pewsey, Wilts SN9 6BQ
The club is situated 2 miles south east of Upavon village on the A342.

SALISBURY AND SOUTH WILTSHIRE
(0722) 742645
A challenging 18 hole parkland course (6146 yards, SSS 70) situated in some most attractive countryside, and considered to be the leading course in the county. There are some spectacular views of Salisbury Cathedral from the green. There is a practice ground. Visitors are welcome, but the club requires you to have a handicap certificate to play at weekends. Green fees are £13 on weekdays and £20 at weekends. There is a bar, and a full catering service is available. Salisbury, with its beautiful cathedral is nearby, also Wilton House.
Location
Netherhampton, Salisbury, Wilts SP2 8PR
The course is on the A3094, 2 miles from Salisbury and 1 mile from Wilton, opposite Netherhampton village.

RAC recommended hotel
Rose and Crown ★★★ (0772) 27908 A charming 2-storey timber framed building dating from the 14th-century and situated by the river.

SWINDON
(067 284) 327
An 18 hole undulating downland course with some fine greens and extensive views (6226 yards, SSS 70). Visitors of all playing abilities are welcome on weekdays. Green fees are £17.50 a day, £11.50 per round on weekdays and £21 a day, £13 per round at weekends. Fees are £11.50 after 4pm at weekends. There is a bar where snacks are served, and also a restaurant. Local attractions include Littlecote House with its steam railway and falconry.
Location
Ogbourne St George, Marlborough, Wilts SN8 1TB
Leave the M4 at junction 15 and take the A345 towards Marlborough for approximately 4 miles.

RAC recommended hotels
Blunsdon House ★★★★ (0793) 721701 In attractive gardens, this hotel has been greatly modernised and extended. Indoor swimming pool, putting, tennis, squash, sauna, solarium, gymnasium, billiards.
Crest ★★★ (0793) 831333 Spacious modern purpose-built in own grounds in the outskirts.
Goddard Arms ★★★ (0793) 692313 Attractive old established inn set in the older part of town.
Peartree at Purton ★★★ Cotswold-stone former vicarage tactfully extended and set in attractive gardens.
Post House ★★★ (0793) 24601 Conveniently situated away from the centre of the town, a modern hotel with conference facilities. There is also an indoor swimming pool, sauna, solarium and gymnasium.
South Marston ★★★ (0793) 827777 On outskirts of Swindon, modern purpose-built hotel. Indoor/outdoor swimming pool, squash, sauna, solarium, gymnasium, billiards.
Wiltshire ★★★ (0793) 28282 In town centre, a modern tall purpose-built hotel.
Kings Arms ★★ (0793) 22156 Modernised period coaching inn situated in the Old Town.
School House ★★ (0793) 851198 Stone-built, listed Victorian school in village on outskirts of Swindon.

WEST WILTS
(0985) 212702
An 18 hole downland course situated on a hilltop, but with fine turf and some testing holes (5701 yards, SSS 68). Visitors all levels of handicap are welcome. Green fees are £12.50 on weekdays and £20 at weekends. Full meals and snacks are available at all times. Longleat Safari Park is within 1 mile.
Location
Elm Hill, Warminster, Wilts BA12 0AU
The club is situated on the A350, approximately half a mile out of Warminster, on the Westbury Road.

RAC recommended hotel
Old Bell ★★ (0985) 217111 An old-established former coaching inn with a colonnaded arcade in the town centre.

WORCESTERSHIRE

ABBEY PARK
(0527) 63918
A pleasant 18 hole parkland course (5857 metres, SSS 71). Visitors of all playing abilities are welcome. There is also a driving range. Green fees are £5 on weekdays, £5.50 at weekends for 18 holes and £3 on weekdays, £3.50 at weekends for 9 holes. There are 3 bars where snacks are available and 2 restaurants where meals are served. The course includes 2 fly-fishing lakes and also a health and leisure centre. Stratford-upon-Avon and Warwick are within easy reach.
Location
Abbey Park, Dagnell End Road, Redditch, Worcs B98 7BD
The club is north of Redditch on the B4101, off the A441 Redditch road to Birmingham.

RAC recommended hotel in Redditch.

BLACKWELL
021-445 1994
An 18 hole parkland course (6202 yards, SSS 71). Visitors may play unrestricted on weekdays but only with a member at weekends and Bank Holidays. The club prefers you to hold a current handicap certificate. Green fees are £20. Full catering facilities are available but you must book in advance.
Location
Blackwell, Bromsgrove, Worcs B60 1PY
The club is 10 miles south of Birmingham and 3 miles east of Bromsgrove. South from Blackwell village centre, take Station Road go under the railway bridge and the club entrance is on the left.

RAC recommended hotel
Perry Hall ★★★ (0527) 579976 A renovated 17th-century house, one-time the home of A.E. Houseman.

BROADWAY
(0386) 853683
An 18 hole undulating parkland course (6122 yards, SSS 70) situated on the edge of the Cotswolds with some spectacular views. Provided you have a handicap certificate, visitors are welcome but not on Saturday and prior notification is advised. Green fees are £16 on weekdays and £19 at weekends. Lunches and evening meals are available every day except Monday. Local attractions include the lovely Cotswold countryside, Snowshill Manor (NT), Broadway village and Hidcote Manor (NT).
Location
Willersey Hill, Broadway, Worcs WR12 7LG
The club is situated 2½ miles east of Broadway off the A44.

RAC recommended hotels
Lygon Arms ★★★★ (0386) 852255 World famous luxury 15th-century inn of Cotswold stone with pleasant gardens. Tennis.
Dormy House ★★★ (0386) 852711 A fine 17th-century Cotswold stone country house overlooking Broadway.
Broadway ★★★ (0386) 852401 An old timber-framed building (mainly 16th-century) with recent extensions. Facilities include putting.

CHURCHILL AND BLACKDOWN
(0562) 700200
A pretty 9-hole somewhat hilly meadowland course (5399 yards, SSS 67) with some good views. Visitors are welcome on weekdays but only with a member at weekends and Bank Holidays. Green fees are £7.50 a day (£3 with a member). Lunches and evening meals are served daily except Monday.
Location
Churchill Lane, Blakedown, Kidderminster, Worcs DY10 3NB
The club is situated 3 miles north east of Kidderminster. Turn off A456 by a railway viaduct in the village of Blakedown.

RAC recommended hotel in Kidderminster.

DROITWICH
(0905) 774344
An 18 hole undulating meadowland course (6040 yards, SSS 69). Visitors who have a handicap certificate are welcome on weekdays and with a member at weekends. Green fees are £10. There is a restaurant where full meals are served and also a bar where snacks are available. Local attractions include Brine Barn and the Malvern Hills.
Location
Westford House, Ford Lane, Droitwich WR9 0BQ
Leave the M5 at junction 5 and take the A38 towards Droitwich. Take the first turning right, in approximately 1 mile, to golf course in half a mile. The club is approximately 1 mile north of the town.

EVESHAM
(0386) 860395
A 9 hole parkland course (6415 yards, SSS 71) situated on the banks of the River Avon with some fine views of the Cotswolds. There is a small practice area. Visitors who hold a current handicap are welcome on weekdays and with a member at weekends. Green fees are £9. There is a bar where snacks are also available. Worcester with its lovely Cathedral is only 8 miles away and Sudeley is worth visiting.
Location
Cray Combe Links, Fladbury, Pershore, Worcs WR10 2QS
From A435 north of Evesham, take the B4084 west for 4 miles to Fladbury.

RAC recommended hotels
Evesham ★★★ (0386) 765566 A Tudor and Georgian mansion set in quiet, pleasant 2½ acre garden. Facilities include indoor swimming pool and putting.
Northwick Arms ★★★ (0386) 40322 A refurbished 3-storey Victorian building overlooking the River Avon.

HABBERLEY
(0562) 745756
A 9 hole hilly parkland course (5104 yards, SSS 69). Visitors, with any level of handicap, who are members of a recognised club are welcome on weekdays. There is a practice area. Green fees are £9. There is a bar, and catering facilities are available by prior arrangement. Local attractions include West Midland Safari Park, the Severn Valley Railway and Telford Bridge at Bewdley.
Location
Habberley, Kidderminster, Worcs DY11 5RG
The course is situated 3 miles north west of Kidderminster on the road to Trimpley.

RAC recommended hotel in Kidderminster.

KIDDERMINSTER
(0562) 822303
An 18 hole parkland course (5659 yards, SSS 70) with natural hazards. Visitors who are members of a recognised club are welcome on weekdays. Green fees are £14. Full catering facilities are available every day except Monday. Local attractions include Harvington Hall, West Midland Safari Park, Kingsford Country Park and Kimber Edge (NT).
Location
Russel Road, Kidderminster, Worcs DY10 3HT
The course is signposted off the A449 and is 1 mile south of the town centre.

RAC recommended hotel
Gainsborough House ★★★ (0562) 820041 Modern two-storey hotel, personally managed by the proprietor.

LITTLE LAKES
(0299) 266385
A challenging 9 hole undulating parkland course (6247 yards, SSS 72). Visitors of all playing levels are welcome on weekdays. Green fees are £7.50. Lunch is served daily. Other club facilities include a swimming pool and tennis courts. West Midlands Safari Park and the Severn Valley Steam Railway are both close by.
Location
Lye Head, Rock, Bewdley, Worcs DY12 2UZ
Take the A456 for 2 miles west of Bewdley and turn left at the Greenhouse and Garden Centre. The course is about half a mile from here.

RAC recommended hotels
Black Boy ★★ (0299) 402199 A 17th-century inn of character adjacent to the River Severn.
George ★★ (0299) 402117 Situated in the town centre, a coaching inn with attractive bow windows and a rear courtyard. Facilities include fishing.

PITCHEROAK
(0527) 41054
A wooded 9 hole undulating parkland course (4724 yards, SSS 63). The course is a municipal one and visitors are welcome at any time. Green fees are £2 per 9 holes, £3 per 18 holes on weekdays and £3.50 per 9 holes, £3.50 per 18 holes at weekends. There is a restaurant and bar. A sports centre is close by.
Location
Plymouth Road, Redditch, Worcs B97 4NP
The club is situated near the town centre, close to the bus and railway station.

RAC recommended hotel in Redditch.

REDDITCH
(0527) 43309
An 18 hole course (6671 yards, SSS 72) where the first 9 holes are parkland and the second 9 holes are wooded. There are many natural hazards including large ponds and ditches. There are also two practice areas. Visitors who are members of a bona fide golf club are welcome on weekdays and with a member at weekends. There is a bar and a restaurant which provides meals everyday except Monday.
Location
Lower Grinsty, Green Lane, Callow Hill, Redditch, Worcs B97 5JP
The course is 3 miles west of Redditch town centre, between the A448 Redditch-Bromsgrove road and the A441 Astwood Bank to Redditch road. Follow the signs to Callow Hill.

RAC recommended hotel
Southcrest ★★★ (0527) 41511 A modernised 19th-century residence in parklands.

TOLLADINE
(0905) 21074
A 9-hole meadowland course with some spectacular views of Worcester city (5134 yards, SSS 67). Visitors are welcome on weekdays and at weekends and Bank Holidays with members. Green fees are £6 (£3 with a member) on weekdays and £3.70 at weekends. Snacks are available every day except Monday.
Location
Tolladine Road, Worcester WR4 9BA
The club is about 1 mile east of the city centre. Take the road to Warndon from junction 6 of the M5.

RAC recommended hotels in Worcester.

WORCESTER
(0905) 422555
An 18 hole parkland course (5946 yards, SSS 68) with lots of trees. Provided you have a handicap certificate visitors, are welcome on weekdays and with a member at the weekends. Green fees are £18. Full catering facilities are available daily except Monday. Local attractions include Tewksbury Abbey, Malvern Wells and Worcester with its Cathedral, porcelain factory and Greyfriars.
Location
Boughton Park, Worcester WR2 4EZ
Take the A4103 west towards Hereford; the club is on the edge of the city.

RAC recommended hotels
Fownes ★★★ (0905) 613151 An elegant town centre hotel converted from a large Victorian building, once a glove factory. Fishing, sauna, gymnasium.
Gifford ★★★ (0905) 726262 Modern city centre hotel opposite Cathedral. Billiards.
Star ★★ (0905) 24308 A former coaching inn of character. Near railway station.
Ye Olde Talbot ★★ (0905) 23573 Near Cathedral, a modernised inn with well-appointed bedrooms.

WORCESTERSHIRE
(0684) 575992
A lovely 18 hole meadowland/parkland course (6449 yards, SSS 71) with some splendid views of the Malvern Hills. The course has lots of natural hazards including ditches and trees and one hole is approached over a small lake. Visitors who are a member of another golf club and hold a current handicap certificate are welcome but not before 10am on weekdays. Green fees are £12 on weekdays and £15 at weekends. Lunches, teas, snacks and dinners are available but you should order in advance. There is also a snooker room at the club house. Local attractions include Malvern, Elgar's birthplace and Lower Brockhampton Tudor House.
Location
Wood Farm, Malvern Wells, Worcs WR14 4PP
Two miles south of Great Malvern, turn off the A449 onto the B4009 and follow the signs for the club.

RAC recommended hotels
Abbey ★★★ (0684) 892332 A splendid ivy clad country hotel adjoining an old Benedictine Priory.
Colwall Park ★★★ (0684) 40206 An Edwardian hotel, with modernised well-appointed bedrooms.
Foley Arms ★★★ (0684) 573397 An early 19th-century fomer coaching inn, situated near the town centre. This hotel is family-run.
Broomhill ★★ (06845) 64367 Family-run modernised Victorian hotel, high in hills with panoramic views.
Essington ★★ (0684) 561177 Family-run Victorian hotel in 2 acres of terraced garden.
Holdfast Cottage C/H ★★ (0684) 310288 Small 17th-century country house in 2 acres of beautiful gardens.
Malvern Hills ★★ (0684) 40237 Attractive country hotel with panoramic views; close to British Camp. Solarium.
Mount Pleasant ★★ (0684) 561837 A Georgian building in the centre of town, overlooking the Abbey.
Royal Malvern ★★ (0684) 563411 A large Victorian building right in the centre of Great Malvern.
Thornbury House ★★ (0684) 572278 Former Victorian house in quiet residential area. Convenient for trains.

NORTH YORKSHIRE

ALDWARK MANOR
(03473) 353
A 9-hole parkland course situated in the park which surrounds Aldwark Manor Hotel (2551, 2569 yards, SSS 66). There is a practice ground. Visitors are welcome at all times. Green fees are £6 on weekdays, £12 at weekends. Full catering facilities are available in the Golf Club Bar and also at the Aldwark Manor Hotel. The club is only 11½ miles from the York.
Location
Aldwark Manor, Aldwark Alne, York YO6 2NF
Aldwark Alne is situated 5 miles south east of Boroughbridge off the A1 and 11½ miles north west of York via the A19.

AMPLEFORTH COLLEGE
(0439) 70678
A 10-hole course (4018 yards, SSS 63).
Location
56 High Street, Helmsley, York YO6 5AE
The course is situated off the driveway to Gilling Castle in the centre of Gilling East Village, 18 miles north of York on the B1363.

RAC recommended hotels in Helmsley
Black Swan ★★★ (0439) 70466 Attractive old building, partly Tudor, situated in market place.
Feversham Arms ★★★ (0439) 70766 Attractive stone building on corner by church and market place. Swimming pool and tennis.
Crown ★★ (0439) 70297 Charming ivy-covered old building of character, at the head of the market place.
Feathers ★★ (0439) 70275 Lovely stone-built hotel with Georgian facade but dating from the 15th century.

BEDALE
(0677) 22568
A quiet 18-hole parkland course with a wonderful collection of trees (5599 yards, SSS 66). Visitors of all levels are welcome on weekdays and also at the weekend. Green fees are £10 on weekdays and £15 at weekends. Full catering facilities are available daily except on Monday. The course is situated in the heart of James Herriot Country in the Yorkshire Dales and Fountains Abbey is nearby.
Location
Leyburn Road, Bedale, N Yorks DL8 1EZ
The course is close to the northern boundary of the town, on the A684.

CATTERICK GARRISON
(0748) 833268
An 18-hole undulating moorland/parkland course with some fine views of the Pennines and the Cleveland Hills (6291 yards, SSS 70). Visitors are welcome at all times. Green fees are £9 on weekdays and £12 at weekends and Bank Holidays. There is a restaurant and snacks are also served everyday except Monday. The course is in the centre of James Herriot Country and Richmond is within easy access.
Location
Leyburn Road, Catterick Garrison, N Yorks DL9 3QE
Approximately 6 miles south of Scotch Corner, turn off the A1 at Catterick Bridge and from here it is 2½ miles to Catterick Garrison.

RAC recommended hotel
Bridge House ★★ (0748) 818331 A 15th-century coaching inn attractively set on the banks of the River Swale opposite the race course. Facilities include fishing.

CRIMPLE VALLEY
(0423) 883485
A 9-hole meadowland course with gently sloping fairways (2500 yards, SSS 33). Visitors are welcome between 6.30am and dusk. Green fees are £3 per 9 holes, £5.50 per 18 holes or £7 a day. Breakfast is served on Saturday and Sunday and lunches everyday except Sunday. The course is close to Harrogate.
Location
Hookstone Wood Road, Harrogate
The course is 1 mile south of the town centre. Turn off the A61 at Appleyards garage onto Hookstone Road. The club is signposted to the right.

RAC recommended hotels in Harrogate see Oakdale.

EASINGWOLD
(0347) 21486
An 18-hole wooded parkland course with easy walking (6262 yards, SSS 70), Visitors of all playing abilities are welcome. Green fees are £12 a day on weekdays and £15 a day at weekends and Bank Holidays. There is a bar and lunches and dinners are served daily except Monday. There are numerous historic places nearby.
Location
Stillington Road, Easingwold YO6 3ET
About 12 miles north of York turn off the A19 and as you come into Easingwold turn right immediately past the garage. The course is about half a mile along Stillington Road.

RAC recommended hotel
George ★★ (0347) 21698 A stone-built hotel with Georgian style windows, a focal point in Easingwold. Facilities include a solarium.

FILEY
(0723) 513293
An 18-hole seaside course with a stream running through and some fine sea views (6030 yards, SSS 69). Visitors can play unaccompanied if they are a member of another golf club. There is a large practice area. Green fees are £9 on weekdays and £12 at weekends. Full catering facilities are available at all times.
Location
West Avenue, Filey, N Yorks YO14 9BQ
The course is about 1 mile south of the town centre in a private road off the end of West Avenue.

RAC recommended hotel
White Lodge ★★★ (0723) 514771 An elegant white building enjoying some fine sea views.

FULFORD
(0904) 413579
A championship 18-hole parkland course with some wonderful greens (6779 yards, SSS 72). Provided you have a handicap certificate, visitors are welcome by prior arrangement. Green fees are £18 on weekdays. Morning coffee, lunches and evening meals are served daily. Local attractions include National Railway Museum and the Jorvik Centre with its historic Viking exhibition.
Location
Heslington Lane, Heslington, York YO1 5DY
Leave York by the A19 and follow the signs to the University, turning left towards Heslington.

RAC recommended hotels in York.

GANTON
(0944) 70329
A championship 18-hole heathland course in a beautiful, peaceful setting with plenty of bunkers and a fine spread of gorse. The course can be difficult when the winds sweep across (6693 yards, SSS 73). Visitors are welcome by prior arrangement but a minimum handicap of 18 for men and 24 for ladies is required. Green fees on application. Catering facilities are available. Local attractions include York, Castle Howard, Flamingo Land and the scenic North Yorkshire moors.
Location
Ganton, Scarborough, N Yorks YO12 4PA
The course is situated about 11 miles west of Scarborough on the A64.

GHYLL
(0282) 842466
A 9-hole parkland course with some spectacular views (5708 yards, SSS 69). Visitors are welcome except on Sunday when there are usually competitions. Green fees are £5 on weekdays and £6 at weekends. (£4 at any time with a member). There is a bar where snacks are served on Friday evening and Saturday lunchtime. Parties can be catered for.
Location
Thornton-in-Craven, N Yorks
The course is situated 1 mile from Barnoldswick off the A56.

HARROGATE
(0423) 863158
A fine and well established parkland course with varied but challenging greens, 18-holes (6204 yards, SSS 69). Visitors are welcome but the club prefers you to be a member of a recognised golf club. Parties over 12 can play but by prior arrangement with the Secretary. Green fees are £15 on weekdays and £22 at weekends and Bank Holidays. Full catering facilities are available. The course is near to Knaresborough, the River Nidd, castle and Mother Shipton's Cave and also Harrogate itself.
Location
Forest Lane Head, Starbeck, Harrogate, N Yorks HG2 7TF
The club is about 1 mile from Knaresborough on the A59 Harrogate to Knaresborough road.

RAC recommended hotels in Harrogate
Crown ★★★★ (0423) 567755 Large, traditional stone-built hotel in pleasant surroundings in town centre.
Majestic ★★★★ (0423) 56872 Elegant domed six-storey Victorian hotel set amidst extensive gardens. Indoor swimming pool, tennis, squash, sauna, solarium, gymnasium and billiards.
Old Swan ★★★★ (0423) 500055 Elegant stone-built hotel, circa 1770, in 4 acre garden. Near conference centre. Putting, tennis.
Cairn ★★★ (0423) 504005 Modernised late Victorian hotel close to conference centre.
Fern ★★★ (0423) 523866 Stone-built hotel in elegant corner of town. Easy access to shops.
Grants ★★★ (0423) 560666 Proprietor-run hotel in stone building of charm near town centre.

Hospitality Inn ★★★ (0423) 64601 Splendid Victorian stone buildings overlooking West Stray and gardens.
Hotel St George ★★★ (0423) 561431 Fine 19th century building with spacious public rooms. Indoor swimming pools, sauna, solarium and gymnasium.
Russell ★★★ (0423) 509866 Imposing hotel overlooking Valley Gardens. Distinctive turreted Victorian building.
Ascot House ★★ (0423) 531005 Attractive Victorian house, recently refurbished, near conference centres.
Caesars ★★ (0423) 565818 Stone Victorian building with spacious ground floor rooms. Terraced garden.
Gables ★★ (0423) 505625 Turreted stone-built hotel; easy access to conference centre and exhibition halls.
Green Park ★★ (0423) 504681 Late Victorian stone building with fine views over public gardens.
White House ★★ (0423) 501388 A 'mock Victorian' villa, built in 1836, overlooking the famous Stray.

HEWORTH
(0904) 424618
An 11-hole meadowland/parkland course with easy walking (6078 yards, SSS 69). Visitors are welcome on weekdays but are restricted at the weekends depending on the availability of tee reservations. Green fees are £6 on weekdays and £7 at weekends and Bank Holidays(£4 with a member). Lunches are served daily except on Monday.
Location
Muncaster House, Muncastergate, York YO3 9JX
The club is situated $1^1/_2$ miles from the city centre on the A1036/A64 York to Scarborough road.

RAC recommended hotels in York.

KIRBYMOORSIDE
(0751) 31525
A wooded 18-hole undulating moorland course (5958 yards, SSS 68). Visitors of all playing levels are welcome at all times. Green fees are £9(£5 with a member) on weekdays and £12(£6 with a member) at weekends. Meals and snacks are available daily. Local attractions include Flamingo Land, the nearby coastal resorts, the North Yorkshire moors and Rydale Folk Museum
Location
Manor Vale, Kirbymoorside, N Yorkshire YO6 6EQ
You will find the club on the A170 Thirsk to Scarborough road.

RAC recommended hotel
George and Dragon ★★ (0751) 31637 A stone building overlooking the market place. There is a pleasant, well-tended garden.

KNARESBOROUGH
(0423) 862690
An 18-hole wooded parkland course (6083 yards, SSS 70). Provided you have a handicap certificate, visitors are welcome at all times. Green fees are £10 per round, £12 a day on weekdays and £16 at weekends and Bank Holidays. Full catering facilities are available daily except Monday and Tuesday when snacks only are served. Knaresborough town and castle and the River Nidd are all worth visiting and Ripon is not far.
Location
Butterhills, Boroughbridge Road, Knaresborough HG5 0QQ
The course is $1^1/_2$ miles from the town centre off the main Boroughbridge road.

RAC recommended hotel
Dower House ★★★ (0423) 863302 A fine modern building overlooking private gardens. Facilities include indoor swimming pool, sauna, solarium and gymnasium.

MALTON AND NORTON
(0653) 697912
Two 18-hole parkland courses (White, 6411 yards, SSS 71 and Yellow, 6141 yards, SSS 69). The course is fairly testing with a hidden pond at the 8th hole but with some fine views. Visitors are welcome but are restricted on club competition days. A handicap certificate is preferred. Full catering facilities are available daily with breakfast by arrangement. Local attractions include Castle Howard, Flamingo Land, the East Coast resorts and York.
Location
Welham Park, Malton, N Yorks YO17 9QE
From the A64 York to Scarborough road, turn off into Malton and towards. Turn right at the Norton level crossing; the club is approximately three-quarters of a mile from here.

RAC recommended hotels
Green Man ★★ (0653) 692662 A traditional style market town hotel situated in a central position.
Leat House ★★ (0653) 692027 A friendly hotel in a modernised 18th-century manor house, part brick, part stone, with attractive conservatory.
Talbot ★★ (0653) 694031 A fine old stone inn situated in the centre of the market town.

MASHAM
(0765) 89379
A 9-hole parkland course with the River Burn meandering through the course (5244 yards, SSS 66). Visitors are welcome on weekdays and also at weekends if you are accompanied by a member. Green fees are £10 a day. Catering is available by arrangement.
Location
Swinton Road, Masham, Ripon, Yorks
The club is 8 miles north west of Ripon on the A6108.

OAKDALE
(0423) 502806
A testing 18-hole undulating parkland course with a stream running through and some panoramic views over the Vale of York. There is a practice ground.

Visitors who are members of a bona fide golf club are welcome. Green fees are £15 a day on weekdays and £20 at weekends and Bank Holidays. There is a dining room which is open every lunchtime except Monday and which serves dinner by arrangement. Local attractions include Knaresborough, Fountains Abbey, Ripon, York and the Dales.

Location
Oakdale, Harrogate HG1 2LN
The club is three quarters of a mile from the town centre. Leave the Ripon(A61) road at Kent Road and the course is situated about a quarter of a mile from the Royal Hall.

RAC recommended hotels in Harrogate.

PANNAL
(0423) 871641
A championship 18-hole heavily wooded moorland course (6659 yards, SSS 72). Visitors are welcome on weekdays but you must be a member of a bona fida golf club with an official handicap. Green fees are £17 per round, £22 a day on weekdays and £22 per round at weekends and Bank Holidays. Meals are served daily. The course is near to Harrogate, Knaresborough and York, and the Yorkshire Dales and North York Moors are within easy reach.

Location
Follifoot Road, Pannal, Harrogate HG3 1ES
The club is just off the A61 Leeds to Harrogate road at Pannal.

RAC recommended hotels in Harrogate.

PIKE HILLS
(0904) 706566
An 18-hole parkland course (6048 yards, SSS 69). Visitors are welcome on weekdays before 4.30pm and also at Bank Holidays and weekends if you are accompanied by a member. Green fees are £10 per round or day in summer and £8 per round or day in winter(between October and March). Full catering facilities are available daily except on Monday. The course is surrounded by a nature reserve.

Location
Tadcaster Road, Copmanthorpe, York YO2 3UW
The club is 4 miles from York on the Tadcaster Road, on the right hand side of the road going west.

RICHMOND
(0748) 2457
An 18-hole parkland course (5704 yards, SSS 68). Visitors are welcome at all times. Green fees are £8 per round or day on weekdays and £12 at weekends and Bank Holidays. Full catering facilities are available everyday except Monday. Local attractions include Richmond Castle and the River Swale.

Location
Bend Hagg, Richmond, N Yorkshire DL10 5EX
Take the A6108 from Scotch Corner and turn right at the traffic lights after 4 miles.

RAC recommended hotel
Frenchgate ★★ (0748) 2087 A small hotel in a quaint cobbled street near the town centre.

RIPON CITY
(0765) 3640
A 9-hole undulating parkland course with some testing holes and hard walking (5645 yards, SSS 67). Visitors are welcome at any time except on Wednesday between 12 noon and 1pm but you must be a member of a recognised golf club. Catering arrangements can only be made for parties and by prior arrangement. Local attractions include Lightwater Valley, Fountains Abbey, Jervaulx Abbey, the Yorkshire Dales and Ripon.

Location
Palace Road, Ripon, N Yorkshire HG4 3HH
The course is 1 mile west on the A6108 towards Leyburn.

RAC recommended hotels
Ripon Spa ★★★ (0765) 2172 A traditional Edwardian style hotel with its own grounds and pleasant gardens.
Bridge ★★
Unicorn ★★ (0765) 2202 A historic posting house with white-painted Georgian facade.

SCARBOROUGH NORTH CLIFF
(0723) 360786
An 18-hole seaside parkland course with some fine views (6425 yards, SSS 71). There are no restrictions for visitors except before 10am on Sunday but you must be a recognised golfer. There is a practice area. Green fees are £12 a day on weekdays and £16 a day at weekends and Bank Holidays. Scarborough is a seaside town with all the usual amenities and there is a castle. The North York Moors are within easy reach.

Location
North Cliff Avenue, Burniston Road, Scarborough YO12 6PP
The course is 2 miles north of the town centre on the coast road (Burniston Road). You should turn right along North Cliff Av.

RAC recommended hotels
Holbeck Hall ★★★★ (0723) 374374 Fine brick building, in commanding position on South Cliff.
Royal ★★★★ (0723) 364333 A beautiful example of the best of Regency architecture and luxury. Indoor swimming pool, sauna, solarium, gymnasium and billiards.
Esplanade ★★★ (0723) 360382 Traditional resort hotel with four-storeys. Fine views over South Bay.
Palm Court ★★★ (0723) 368161 Pleasantly modernised town centre hotel. Swimming pool, sauna and gymnasium.
Brooklands ★★ (0723) 376576 Family-run hotel in four-storey Victorian building overlooking gardens on South Cliff.
Central ★★ (0723) 365766 A stately Georgian

building overlooking gardens in the centre of Scarborough.
Crescent ★★ (0723) 360929 A late Victorian stone building overlooking gardens in the town centre.
Red Lea ★★ (0723) 362431 Large established hotel in terrace of elegant Victorian houses overlooking South Bay. Indoor swimming pool, sauna, solarium and gymnasium.
Southlands ★★ (0723) 361461 Large, mainly brick building, situated in South Cliff residential area. Solarium.

SCARBOROUGH SOUTH CLIFF (0723) 374737

An 18-hole seaside parkland course situated on a cliff top with some panoramic sea views. (6085 yards, SSS 69). Visitors are welcome but you must hold a current handicap certificate. Green fees are £11.50 on weekdays and £15 at weekends and Bank Holidays. Full catering facilities are available. Local attractions include Scarborough Castle, the beaches, some beautiful coastal villages and Peasolm Park.

Location
Deepdale Avenue, Scarborough YO11 2UE
This course is 1 mile south of Scarborough on the main Filey road.

SELBY (075782) 622

An 18-hole flat part links, part parkland course (6246 yards, SSS 70). Visitors are welcome on weekdays but you must be a member of a recognised golf club and the club also prefers you to hold a current handicap certificate. There is a practice ground. Green fees are £13 per round, £16 a day on weekdays. There are full catering facilities every day. The York is nearby and Selby Abbey and Flamingo Land are worth visiting.

Location
Mill Lane, Brayton Bariff, Selby, N Yorks YO8 9LD
Turn south off the A63 Leeds roadat the Wheatsheaf in Hambleton, then turn left at the cemetery and right again. You will find the course is the next on the left.

RAC recommended hotel
Londesborough Arms ★★ (0757) 707355 A refurbished traditional inn, situated in the centre of the town next to the Abbey church.

SETTLE (07292) 3912

A pretty 9-hole parkland/moorland course (4600 yards, SSS 62). Visitors are welcome on weekdays and Saturday but there are restrictions on Sunday. Green fees are £3 a day on weekdays and £5 at weekends. There is a bar which is open on Sunday.

Location
Buckhaw Brow, Settle, N Yorkshire BD24
The club is 1 mile north of Settle on the main A65 Settle-Kendal road, opposite the Giggleswick Quarry.

RAC recommended hotel
Falcon Manor ★★★ (07292) 3814 A large stone-built manor situated on the outskirts of the town.

SKIPTON (0756) 3922

A fine 18-hole fell-land course situated on high ground with magnificent views and a mountain stream running through adding to the challenges (6191 yards, SSS 70). Visitors who are members of a bona fide golf club are welcome every day except Monday but it is advisable to telephone beforehand. Green fees are £7.50 on weekdays and £10 at weekends and Bank Holidays. Full catering facilities are available every day except Monday. Skipton is the 'Gateway to the Dales' and there is also a castle.

Location
Skipton, N Yorkshire BD23 1LL
The course is 1 mile from the town centre on the Skipton northern bypass.

RAC recommended hotel
Town House ★★ (0756) 4891 Victorian Gothic manor house in 2 acres of gardens. Good views.

THIRSK & NORTHALLERTON (0845) 22170

A 9-hole meadowland course (6257 yards, SSS 70). Visitors are welcome although the club does prefer it if you hold a current handicap certificate and are a member of a recognised golf club. Parties are also welcome by arrangement. There is a small practice area. Green fees on application. Full catering facilities are available everyday except Tuesday. The 'James Herriot' stories are based in Thirsk and other attractions include the White Horse Gliding Club, the 'Mousy' Thompson craftsmen at Kilburn and the beautiful surrounding countryside.

Location
Thornton-Le-Street, Thirsk, N Yorkshire YO7 4AB
Leave Thirsk on the A168 and take the Northallerton spur about half a mile from the dual carriageway on the A19. The club is 2 miles north of Thirsk.

RAC recommended hotels
Golden Fleece ★★ (0845) 23108 A creeper-cald town centre inn, furnished in early 19th-century tradition.
Sheppard's ★★ (0845) 23655 18th century Georgian building in picturesque village on the outskirts of Thirsk.

WHITBY (0947) 602768

An 18-hole seaside course situated on a cliff top with some good coastal views (5706 yards, SSS 69). Visitors in parties of over 12, who are experienced golfers, are welcome and prices are £14.50 on weekdays and £17.50 at weekends and Bank Holidays. This fee includes coffee on arrival, soup and sandwiches for lunch and full evening meals and a day of golf. Normal green fees for individuals are £9 on weekdays and £12 at weekends and Bank Holidays. A weekly ticket can be bought for £42. There are catering facilities every day except Monday. Local attractions include Whitby Abbey, harbour and sands and the North York Moors.

Location
Low Straggleton, Whitby, N Yorkshire YO21 3SR
The club is on the main coastal road between Whitby and Sandsend(A174).

RAC recommended hotels
Royal ★★ (0947) 602234 An impressive large white-faced hotel overlooking the sea and Esk estury.
Saxonville ★★ (0947) 602631 A 3-storey family-run hotel, situated in the quiet area near the sea on West Cliff.
Sneaton Hall C/H ★★ (0947) 605929 A stone-built hotel in village. Fine views over the countryside.

YORK (0904) 490304

An attractive championship 18-hole wooded heathland course with some pond hazards (6275 yards, SSS 70). Visitors are welcome but the course is popular and so you should ring beforehand to check tee availability. There is a practice ground. Green fees are £14(£7 with a member) on weekdays and £17(£8.50 with a member) at weekends. Local attractions include the York with its Minster, museums, etc, and Castle Howard, the moors and the coastal resorts.

Location
Lords Moor Lane, Strensall, York YO3 5XF
The club is situated 6 miles north of York, near Strensall Barracks and Village.

RAC recommended hotels in York
Crest ★★★★ (0904) 648111 Built of charming rustic brick, a dignified modern building in centre.
Middlethorpe Hall ★★★★ (0904) 641241 Handsome Queen Anne mansion beautifully furnished. Set in large park.
Royal York ★★★★ (0904) 653681 A gracious Victorian building set in pleasant gardens. Fine views. Putting.
Viking ★★★★ (0904) 659822 A modern hotel situated in the centre of the city overlooking the River Ouse. Sauna, solarium and gymnasium.
Ambassador ★★★ (0904) 641316 A stately listed building in spacious gardens on main road on south side of the city.
Dean Court ★★★ (0904) 625082 Large mellow brick building, with new wing beneath West Tower of the Minster.
Disraelis ★★★ (0904) 781181 Hotel in own grounds conveniently situated for the City of York.
Fairfield Manor ★★★ (0904) 625621 Large building of Yorkshire brick in own grounds; 4 miles north of York. Putting.
Hudson's ★★★ (0904) 621267 Hotel complex of a converted Victorian house with an attractive new wing.
Kilima ★★★ (0904) 625787 Detached brick hotel on fringe of city. Pleasant views at rear.
Novotel ★★★ (0904) 611660 Purpose-built four-storeyed hotel on riverside at edge of walled city. Boat landing and riverside terrace. Indoor swimming pool.
Pavilion ★★★ (0904) 622099 Charming Georgian house with well proportioned rooms; on main A19 to south of city.
Penguin Abbey Park ★★★ (0904) 658301 Modern hotel behind mellow brick Georgian facade. Fringe of city centre.
Post House ★★★ (0904) 707921 Modern stone building outside city walls and adjacent to York Racecourse. Putting.
Swallow Chase ★★★ (0904) 701000 Hotel in traditional style with modern extensions, overlooking York Racecourse. Indoor swimming pool, putting, sauna, solarium and gymnasium.
Abbots Mews ★★ (0904) 634866 Converted and enlarged Victorian cottage and coach house, now an attractive hotel in a central position.
Alhambra Court ★★ (0904) 628474 Close to the old walled city, a family-run hotel in a substantial three-storeyed brick building.
Ashcroft ★★ (0904) 659286 Medium sized hotel with annexe. In the country near the Racecourse.
Beechwood Close ★★ (0904) 658378 Brick-built hotel situated in attractive area on northern edge of city. Family-owned. Putting.
Cottage ★★ (0904) 643711 Two connected stone-built Victorian houses overlooking village green, 15 minutes from city centre.
Elmbank ★★ (0904) 610653 Refurbished, stone-built hotel with some fine original art nouveau decor. Sauna, solarium.
Heworth Court ★★ (0904) 425156 Pleasantly set in a suburb with some rooms charmingly designed around a courtyard.
Hilbra Court ★★ (0904) 768335 A small modern hotel 4 miles north of the city.
Knavesmire Manor ★★ (0904) 702941 Sympathetically converted early 19th century mansion, once home of Rowntree family, overlooking the Racecourse. Indoor swimming pool, sauna.
Newington ★★ (0904) 625173 Pleasant medium sized hotel on the fringe of the city. Indoor swimming pool, sauna, solarium.
Savages ★★ (0904) 610818 Attractive Victorian double storeyed building in residential area on the fringe of the city. Solarium, gymnasium.
Sheppard ★★ (0904) 620500 Small hotel in early 19th century building near city centre.
Town House ★★ (0904) 636171 Attractive listed Victorian brick building with modern amenities.

SOUTH YORKSHIRE

ABBEYDALE
(0742) 360763
A fine wooded parkland course (6419 yards, SSS 71). Visitors are welcome at any time by prior arrangement. Green fees are £15 on weekdays and £20 at weekends.. There is a restaurant and also a bar where snacks are served. Local attractions include Abbeydale Industrial Hamlet, an historic museum.
Location
Twentywell Lane, Dore, Sheffield, S Yorkshire S17 4QA
The club is situated 5 miles south of Sheffield off the A621 Sheffield to Baslow road, near the Dore and Totley station.

RAC recommended hotels
St George ★★ (0742) 583811 A country club hotel set in 11 acres of grounds. Indoor swimming pool, fishing, sauna, solarium, gymnasium.
Beauchief ★★★ (0742) 620500 A 3-storey stone-building with a modern bedroom wing, situated om the south-west edge of the city. Facilities include sauna, solarium and gymnasium.
Sheffield Moat House ★★★ (0742) 378140 Modern, purpose-built hotel on ring road to the south of the city. Indoor swimming pool, solarium and gymnasium.

AUSTERFIELD PARK
(0302) 710841
An 18-hole moorland course with some testing holes (6828 yards, SSS 73). Visitors of all playing levels are welcome both weekdays and weekends. There is a practice area and also a driving range. Green fees are £10 a day. There are full restaurant facilities and also a bar where snacks are served. The club is near Doncaster Leisure Centre.
Location
Cross Lane, Austerfield, N Bawtry, Doncaster, S Yorkshire
The club is off the A614, 4 miles north of Bawtry.

RAC recommended hotels
Mount Pleasant ★★★ (0302) 868219 An interesting period hotel situated in open country, with lawns and country gardens
Crown ★★★ (0302) 710341 An 18th-century posting inn with some fine antiques and modern amenities.

BARNSLEY
(0226) 382856
An 18-hole undulating meadowland course with mostly easy walking (6048 yards, SSS 69). Visitors of all playing abilities are welcome. Green fees are £3.25 on weekdays and £4.25 at weekends. There is a bar where meals are served.
Location
Wakefield Road, Staincross, N Barnsley, S Yorkshire S75 6JZ
You will find the club on the A61, 3 miles north of Barnsley, 5 miles south of Wakefield.

RAC recommended hotels
Queens ★★★ (0226) 731010 A gracious Victorian Building, situated in the town centre.
Ardley Moat House ★★★★ (0226) 289401 An attractive 18th-century stone building with modern wings and some lovely views. Facilities include billards.
Royal ★ (0226) 203658 A handsome, modernised 18th-century building, situated in the town centre.

BEAUCHIEF
(0742) 620040
An 18-hole sloping meadowland course with natural water hazards and surrounded by woods (5423 yards, SSS 66). The course is a public one and visitors of all playing abilities are welcome by arrangement. Green fees on application. There is a cafe and bar where meals are served daily except on Tuesdays. The Abbeydale Sports Club, Leisure Centre and Dry Ski Slope is in the area.
Location
Abbey Lane, Sheffield S8 0DB
Situated south of Sheffield. Take the A621 Baslow road to Abbey Lane.

RAC recommended hotels south of Sheffield see Abbeydale.

BIRLEY WOOD
(0742) 648213
A 9-hole hilly parkland course without many trees (5200 yards, SSS 70). The course is part of a leisure centre and 18 holes are planned by 1990. It is a municipal course and visitors are welcome at all times. Green fees are £2.20 and £1.10 for children. Full catering facilities are available locally.
Location
Birley Lane, Sheffield SI2 3BP
Turn off the M1 at junction 30 and follow the A616 road to Mosborough. The club is 4 miles south of Sheffield.

CONCORD PARK
(0742) 613605
A hilly 18-hole wooded parkland course with some good views (4302 yards, SS 62). The course is a municipal one and visitors of all playing abilities are welcome. Green fees are £4.20.
Location
Shiregreen Lane, Sheffield S5
The club is off the A6135, 3½ miles north of Sheffield next to the Concord Sports Centre, Shiregreen. You should leave the M1 at junction 34.

CROOKHILL PARK
(0709) 862979
An 18-hole parkland course (5846 yards, SSS 68). Visitors are welcome but you should book in advance. If you are a novice, equipment can be hired. Green fees are £4 with juniors and OAPs playing for £2. There is a bar where snacks are available. Local attractions include Conisborough Castle.
Location
Carr Lane, Conisborough, Nr Doncaster
Leave the A1(M) at the Doncaster by-pass for the A630 to Sheffield. Two miles along the road turn left in Conisborough onto the B60694.

DONCASTER
(0302) 868316
An attractive 18-hole undulating heathland course surrounded by trees (6220 yards, SSS 70). Visitors who are members of a bona fide golf club are welcome with or without a member during the week but there are some reservations at weekends so it best to check beforehand. Green fees are £12 on weekdays and £15 at weekends. Main meals are available by prior arrangement every day except Wednesday. Local attractions include Conisborough Castle.
Location
278 Bawtry Road, Bessacarr, Doncaster, S Yorkshire DN4 7PD
The course is easy to locate between Doncaster and Bawtry on the A638.

RAC recommended hotel
Mount Pleasant ★★★ (0302) 868219 An interesting period hotel situated in open country, with lawns and country gardens.

DONCASTER TOWN MOOR
(0302) 535286
A flat 18-hole wooded parkland course (5923 yards, SSS 68). Visitors of all playing abilities are welcome every day except Sunday before 11.30am. Green fees are £9 on weekdays and £11 at weekends. Lunches are served daily. There is a new leisure complex nearby with a great variety of sport.
Location
Neatherds House, Belle Vue, Doncaster, S Yorkshire DN4 5HU
The clubhouse is near racecourse roundabout. It has the same entrance as Doncaster Rovers Football Club.

RAC recommended hotels
Danum Swallow ★★★ (0302) 342261 An impressive town centre hotel, 5 minutes from the station.
Doncaster Moat House ★★★ (0302) 310197 Modern hotel in the grounds of the 17th century Warmsworth Hall which contains the hotel's conference suites. Convenient for A1(M).
Mount Pleasant ★★★ (0302) 868219 Interesting period hotel in open country, with lawns and country garden.
Beverley Court ★★ (0302) 882724 Modern, family-run hotel in village, 2 miles from Racecourse.
Regent ★★ (0302) 364180 Modernised fine Regency building in central square of stone Victorian houses. Sauna.

DORE AND TOTLEY
(0742) 360492
An 18-hole flat parkland course (6301 yards, SSS 70). Visitors who have a handicap certificate are welcome by prior arrangement. Green fees are £10 per round, £12 a day. Full catering facilities are available daily except Monday. Local attractions include Chatsworth House and Park.
Location
Broadway Road, Sheffield S17 4QR
The course is south of Sheffield off the A61 Sheffield to Chesterfield road on Holmesfield road.

RAC recommended hotels south of Sheffield see Abbeydale.

GRANGE PARK
(0709) 558884
A municipal 18-hole testing parkland course with some spectacular views (6461 yards, SSS 71). Visitors of all playing abilities are welcome at any time. There is a practice ground. Green fees are £2.50 on weekdays and £3.20 at weekends. Catering facilities are available on request. The surrounding countryside is particularly attractive.
Location
Upper Wortley Road, Rotherham S61 2SJ
The course is 2 miles west of the town on the A629. There is easy access from the M1.

RAC recommended hotels in Rotherham.

HALLAMSHIRE
(0742) 302153
An 18-hole moorland course situated on high ground with some lovely views (6396 yards, SSS 71). Visitors who are members of a bona fide golf club are welcome on weekdays but there are some limitations at weekends. Green fees are £15 on weekdays and £20 at weekends and Bank Holidays. There are full dining facilities available except on Tuesday. There is a snooker room at the club, Local attractions include Chatsworth House.
Location
Sandygate, Sheffield S10 4LA
Take the A57 from the centre of Sheffield and turn off at the left fork at Crosspool, 3 miles from the town centre. From there is it approximately 1 mile to the course.

RAC recommended hotels
Hallam Tower Post House ★★★★ (0742) 670067 A modern high-rise hotel in a residential area. Facilities include indoor swimming pool, sauna, solarium and gymnasium.
Rutland ★★★ (0742) 664411 A substantial series of buildings, forming a large hotel.

HALLOWES
(0246) 413734
A pleasant 18-hole undulating moorland course (6134 yards, SSS 71). Visitors of all playing abilities are welcome but you should check with the

Professional beforehand. There is a large practice area. Green fees on application. Catering facilities are available by arrangement with the Stewardess.

Location

Hallowes Lane, Dronfield, Sheffield S18 6UA
Take the A61 Sheffield to Chesterfield road into Dronfield, not the by-pass, and turn sharp right under the railway bridge. The club is signposted.

RAC recommended hotels

Grosvenor House ★★★★ (0742) 720041 A modern, city centre hotel with attractive decor and furnishings.
Charnwood ★★★ (0742) 589411 Attractive converted Georgian house in city centre. Privately owned and managed.
Sheffield Moat House ★★★ (0742) 378140 Modern, purpose-built hotel on ring road to south of city. Indoor swimming pool, sauna, solarium and gymnasium.

HICKLETON
(0709) 892496

An 18-hole undulating meadowland course with a stream running through (6361 yards, SSS 70). Visitors of all playing abilities are welcome but you should be a member of a recognised golf club. There are practice facilities. Green fees on application. Full catering facilities are available by arrangement everyday except Monday. Local attractions include Barnborough Church.

Location

Hickleton, Doncaster, S Yorkshire
The course is 7 miles from Doncaster on the A635 to Barnsley. Once in Hickleton village turn right to Thurmscoe and the club is 500 yards on the right.

HILLSBOROUGH
(0742) 349151

A lovely 18-hole undulating moorland/parkland course (5518 metres, SSS 69) Visitors who are members of a bona fide golf club are welcome on weekdays. Green fees are £14 on weekdays and £20 at weekends. Soup and sandwiches are available at lunchtime except on Friday and full meals can be arranged. There are lots of interesting nature walks near Rivelin.

Location

Worrall Road, Sheffield S6 4BE
The club is situated 3 miles from the city centre via Middlewood Road and Dykes Hall Road.

LEES HALL
(0742) 552900

An 18-hole parkland/meadowland course with some splendid views over Sheffield (6137 yards, SSS 69). Visitors are welcome at all times. Green fees are £10 plus VAT between Monday and Friday and £15 plus VAT at weekends and Bank Holidays. Full catering facilities are available daily except Tuesday. Local attractions include Graves Park and the Rother Valley Water Park.

Location

Hemsworth Road, Norton, Sheffield S8 8LL
The club is situated 3 miles south of Sheffield. Take the A61 and then the B6054 towards Gleadless, taking the first exit at the roundabout. Follow the road to the next roundabout passing the water tower on your left. From there take the first exit and the course is 300 yards on your right.

RAC recommended hotels south of Sheffield see Abbeydale.

PHOENIX
(0709) 382624

An 18-hole undulating meadowland course which can be windy at times (6145 yards, SSS 69). Visitors who are members of a bona fide golf club are welcome. There is also a new driving range which is open to the public and an extensive Pro shop. Green fees are £9 a day(£3 with a member) on weekdays and £11 a day(£4 with a member) at weekends and Bank Holidays. Full catering facilities are available by arrangement. The Meadow Hall Shopping Centre is only 1 mile away and Wentworth House is near by.

Location

Pavilion Lane, Brinsworth, Rotherham
The club is situated 1 mile along Bawtry Lane turning from the Rinsley roundabout on the M1. Pavilion Lane is 1 mile on your left.

RAC recommended hotels in Rotherham.

RENISHAW PARK
(0246) 432044

An 18-hole parkland course with easy walking (6253 yards, SSS 70). Provided you have a handicap certificate and are a member of an affiliated club, visitors are welcome on weekdays but you should ring the club beforehand to check about dress code. Green fees are £11.50 per round, £13.50 a day on weekdays and £13 per round, £15 a day at weekends and Bank Holidays. Full catering facilities are available but you should give 24 hours notice. There is also a snooker room at the club. The course is part of the Sitwell Estate.

Location

Station Road, Renshaw, Sheffield S31 9UZ
Leave the M1 at junction 30 and follow the sign for Eckington. The club is approximately 1½ miles on the right.

RAC recommended hotels

Park Hall C/H ★★★ (0246) 434897 A 16th century manor house in rural surroundings.
Sitwell Arms Osprey ★★★ (0246) 435226 A stone-built hotel situated in the historic village of Renishaw.

ROTHERHAM
(0709) 850812

An 18-hole wooded parkland course with easy walking (6323 yards, SSS 70). Visitors who are members of a bona fide golf club are welcome by arrangement with the Professional. Societies must be booked through the Secretary. Green fees are £15 a day on weekdays and £18 at weekends and Bank Holidays. Full catering facilities are available daily. Local attractions include Conisborough Castle.

Location

Thrybergh Park, Thrybergh, Rotherham S65 4NU
If you are coming from the A1(M) the club is situated on the main road from Doncaster, the A631 to Rotherham, 3 miles from the M18 at Bramley or 7 miles from M1 junction 35.

RAC recommended hotels

Rotherham Moat House ★★★★ (0709) 364902 Situated in a residential area, an attractive modern hotel with two restaurants.
Facilities include sauna, solarium and gymnasium.
Brentwood ★★ (0709) 382772 A well established privately-owned hotel in residential area. Close to town.
Brecon ★★ (0709) 828811 Situated in a quiet residential area, a pleasant origional hotel building with a modern annexe.
Elton ★★ (0709) 545681 Modernised farmhouse built in traditional stone. Near M18.

ROUNDWOOD
(0709) 523471

A 9-hole meadowland course (5646 yards, SSS 67). The course is part of a sports complex and there are also three crown bowling greens, football, hockey and cricket. The course should also be extending to 18 holes within the two years or so. Visitors are welcome but you should book to play at the weekends and no visitors are allowed before 2.30pm on Saturday. Green fees are £6 on weekdays (£4 with a member) and £7 at weekends(£5 with a member). Juniors can play on weekdays for £2. There is a bar and a restaurant which is open Wednesday, Thursday, Friday and Saturday. Local attractions include Wentworth Wood House, a Country Club and park, and Conisborough Castle(the setting for 'Ivanhoe' by Sir Walter Scott).

Location

off Green lane, Rawmarsh, Rotherham S62 6LA
The club is 2 miles north of Rotherham on the A633.

SHEFFIELD TRANSPORT DEPT
(0742) 373216

An 18-hole mixed parkland course (3966 yards, SSS 62). Visitors are welcome but you should hold a current handicap certificate. Green fees are 50p at all times. There is a bar which is open in the evenings. The club is within 5 minutes of some lovely countryside and Abbeydale Industrial Hamlet is one mile away.

Location

Green Hill Main Road, Meadow Head, Sheffield SH7 RE
The course is on the outer ring road, the A57. If you are coming on the M1 leave it at junction 34.

RAC recommended hotel south of Sheffield see Abbeydale.

SICKLEHOLME
(0433) 51306
An 18-hole hillside meadowland course situated in the beautiful Peak District (6064 yards, SSS 69). Visitors are welcome but not on Wednesday morning. Green fees are £12.50 on weekdays and £15 at weekends and Bank Holidays. Catering facilities are available by arrangement. The Pennine Way is close by and also Chatsworth House.
Location
Saltergate Lane, Bamford, Sheffield S30 2BH
You will find the course on the A625, 14 miles west of Sheffield, near the Marquis of Granby.

SILKSTONE
(0226) 790328
An 18-hole undulating meadowland course with some splendid views of the Pennines (6045 yards, SSS 70). Visitors who hold a recognised handicap certificate are welcome on weekdays. Green fees are £10 per round or day with parties of more than twelve at £16 a day including coffee, lunch and supper. Full catering facilities are available daily except Monday. Local attractions include Cannon Hall and Cawthorne Park.
Location
Field Head, Silkstone, Barnsley, S Yorks S75 4OD
Leave the M1 at junction 37 and then drive 1 mile on the A628 towards Manchester. The club is just beyond Dodworth village.

RAC recommended hotels in Barnsley.

SITWELL PARK
(0709) 541046
An 18-hole undulating parkland course with easy walking (6203 yards, SSS 70). Visitors who are members of a bona fide golf club are welcome. Green fees are £12 per round or day on weekdays and £14 at weekends. Meals are served everyday except on Tuesday. Local attractions include Conisborough Castle and Wentworth Wood House and Gardens.
Location
Shrogswood Road, Rotherham, S Yorks S60 4BY
Leave the M1 at exit 33 or the M18 at the Bramley turn off and take the A631. The club is 2 miles south east of Rotherham.

RAC recommended hotels in Rotherham.

STOCKSBRIDGE AND DISTRICT
(0742) 882003
A 15-hole moorland course (5055 yards, SSS 65). Provided you have a handicap certificate visitors are welcome at any time. Green fees are £8 a day on weekdays and £12 a day at weekends. Catering facilities are available by request on any day except Monday. The club is very close to the beautiful Peak District.
Location
30 Royd Lane, Townend, Deepcar, Sheffield S30 5RZ
The course is 9 miles from Sheffield on the A616 heading towards Manchester.

TANKERSLEY PARK
(0742) 468247
A hilly 18-hole parkland course which can be prone to winds (3204 yards, SSS 79). Visitors of all playing abilities are welcome on weekdays and also after 3pm on Saturday and Sunday. Green fees are £10 per round, £12 a day or £6 with a member. There is a bar which serves snacks and full dinners can be arranged. Local attractions include Wortly Top Forge Steam Museum.
Location
High Green, Sheffield S30 4LG
Leave the M1 at junction 35 towards Chapletown and the course is 1 mile off the A6135 north of Chapletown.

THORNE
(0405) 815173
An 18-hole parkland course (5522 yards, SSS 67). The course is developing with bunkers and a watering system. Many new trees have been planted. There is also a practice ground. Visitors are welcome at all times. Green fees are £4 per round on weekdays and £5 at weekends. Local attractions include the Canal Marina which is a short walk from the club and where boats can be hired, Doncaster with its racecourse, museum and leisure centre and the old market town of Thorne.
Location
Kirton Lane, Thorne, Doncaster DN8 5RJ
Leave the M18 at junction 5/6 and take the A18. The club is 10 miles from Doncaster, 15 from Scunthorpe.

RAC recommended hotel
Belmont ★★ (0302) 812320 A small modern hotel and restaurant situated in the centre of a quiet market town.

TINSLEY PARK
(0742) 560237
A wooded 18-hole parkland course (6045 yards, SSS 69). The club is a municipal one and visitors of all playing abilities are welcome at any time. Green fees are £4.50. There is a cafe which is open daily except Tuesday.
Location
High Hazel Park, Darnall, Sheffield S9
Take the A57 off the M1 at junction 33 and when you reach the traffic lights, turn right into Greenland Road and then right again by the bus depot.

RAC recommended hotels south of Sheffield see Abbeydale.

WATH
(0709) 878677
An 18-hole parkland course which can prove to be quite challenging (5776 yards, SSS 68). Visitors of all playing abilities are welcome on weekdays and also at the weekends if you are accompanied by a member. Green fees are £10 a day, (£5 with a member). There is a bar where snacks are served. Thryber Leisure Park is within easy reach of the club.
Location
Abdy, Blackamoor, Rotherham, S Yorks S62 7SJ
Take the A633 from Rotherham through Rawmarsh and then the B6090 towards Wentworth. Turn right along the B6089 taking the signed road to the clubhouse which is 300 yards on your right.

WHEATLEY
(0302) 831655
A fairly flat 18-hole parkland course with lots of bunkers and some water hazards (6345 yards, SSS 70). Visitors who are members of a bona fide golf club are welcome. There is also a practice ground and a putting green. Green fees are £9 per round, £11.50 a day on weekdays and £12 per round, £14.50 a day at weekends and Bank Holidays. There is a restaurant which is open daily.
Location
Armthorpe Road, Doncaster, S Yorks DN2 5QB
Follow the southern ring road out of Doncaster on the A18 then east along the edga of the Racecourse until you reach the next crossroads. The clubhouse is on your right opposite a large water tower.

RAC recommended hotels in Doncaster.

WORTLEY
(0742) 885294
An 18-hole undulating wooded parkland course which is quite sheltered from the wind (5983 yards, SSS 69). Visitors who are members of a bona fide golf club are welcome and parties can play on Wednesday and Friday. Green fees are £12 on weekdays and £18 at weekends. Catering facilities are available if you order in advance.
Location
Hermit Hill Lane, Wortley, Sheffield S30 4DF
Leave the M1 at junction 35 and take the A629 through Wortley village, then first right.

WEST YORKSHIRE

ALWOODLEY
(0532) 681680
A championship 18-hole heathland course in a superb setting (6301 yards, SSS 70). Visitors who are members of a bona fide golf club are welcome on weekdays subject to prior notice. Green fees on application. Full catering facilities are available by arrangement.
Location
Wigton Lane, Alwoodley, Leeds, W Yorkshire
The club is 5 miles north of Leeds via the A61.

RAC recommended hotel
Harewood Arms ★★ (0532) 886566 A traditional stone-built inn with sympathetic new extensions, situated opposite the entrance to Harewood House.

BAILDON
(0274) 584266
A hilly 18-hole moorland course with lots of bracken (6178 yards, SSS 70). Visitors of all playing abilities are welcome on weekdays and at weekends by arrangement. Green fees on application. There is a bar and also a restaurant where lunches are served everyday except Monday.
Location
Moorgate, Baildon, Shipley, W Yorks BD17 5PP
The course is situated 5 miles north of Bradford. Take the A6037 to Shipley and the club is approximately three quarters of a mile north east on the A6038. Turn left at the Junction Hotel.

RAC recommended hotels see Bingley.

BEN RHYDDING
(0943) 608759
A 9-hole moorland course with some wonderful views over the Wharfe valley (4711 yards, SSS 64). Visitors of all playing abilities are welcome at most times except Saturday and Sunday mornings. Green fees are £5 on weekdays and £7.50 at weekends. The lovely Yorkshire Dales and moors are within easy reach of the club.
Location
High Wood, Ben Rhydding, Ilkley, W Yorkshire LS29 8SB
The course is situated on the south east side of the town. Keep left after passing Wheatley Hotel and continue to the top of the hill.

RAC recommended hotels see Ilkley.

BINGLEY ST IVES
(0274) 562436
An 18-hole wooded parkland/moorland course (6480 yards, SSS 70). Visitors of all playing abilities are welcome on weekdays. There is a practice ground and also a snooker room at the clubhouse. Green fees are £3.95 per round, £6.20 a day on weekdays and £7.25 per round, £11.20 a day at weekends. Meals are available everday except Monday. Local attractions include Haworth, the home of the Brontes, and its environs.
Location
The Mansion, St Ives Estate, Bingley, W Yorkshire BD16 1AT
Take the A650 and turn off for Bingley town centre on the Harden to Cullingworth Road. Continue for about half a mile; turn right into the Estate.

RAC recommended hotel
Bankfield ★★★ (0274) 567123 A much extended early Victorian building set in 5½ acres of grounds.

BRADFORD
(0943) 75570
An 18-hole moorland/parkland course (6259 yards, SSS 70). Visitors of all playing abilities are welcome on weekdays and also at weekends, although not

before noon. Green fees are £15 on weekdays and £18 at weekends. Full catering facilities are available daily but advance booking is preferred.
Location
Hawksworth Lane, Guisele, Leeds, W Yorkshire LS20 8NP
Take the Ilkley road from Shipley and after approximately 3½ miles turn left at the top of Hollins Lane and continue 1 mile up Hawksworth for the club.

RAC recommended hotels
Stakis Norfolk Gardens ★★★★ (0274) 734734 A modern city centre hotel commanding views over town and gardens.
Baron ★★★ (0274) 611111 Modern hotel in residential area on northern outskirts of city. Indoor swimming pool, sauna, solarium, billiards.
Novotel ★★★ (0274) 683683 Modern multi-storey French-operated hotel. On M606. Swimming pool.
Victoria ★★★ (0274) 728706 Formerly a station hotel situated in the city centre. Elegant public rooms.

BRADFORD MOOR
(0274) 5638313
A 9-hole undulating meadowland course with some hard walking (SSS 68). Visitors of all playing abilities are welcome. Green fees on application. Meals are served daily. The course is in the heart of Bronte and Emmerdale Farm country.
Location
Scarr Hall, Pollard Lane, Bradford BD2 4RW
The course is situated off the A658, 2 miles north east of the city centre and 2 miles from the M62.

BRADLEY PARK
(0484) 539988
A challenging hilly 18-hole parkland course with panoramic views (6202 yards, SSS 70). Visitors of all playing abilities are welcome at anytime during the week and also at weekends. There are two practice grounds, a covered floodlit driving range and also a new pitch and putt course. Green fees are £4.25 on weekdays and £5.50 at weekends. Juniors and OAPs can play for half price on weekdays. There is a bar and a dining room which provides full facilities.
Location
Bradley Road, Huddersfield, W Yorkshire HD2 1DZ
Leave the M62 at exit 25 and follow the signs for Brighouse and then Huddersfield and turn right at the first roundabout. The entrance to the course is signposted midway along Bradley Road.

RAC recommended hotels see Huddersfield.

BRANSHAW
(0535) 43235
A very pretty 18-hole moorland course with extensive views (5121 yards, SSS 65). Visitors of all playing abilities are welcome on weekdays. Green fees are £6 on weekdays and £8 at weekends. Meals and bar snacks are served everyday except Monday but prior notice is required for large parties. Local attractions include the Bronte Museum.
Location
Branshaw Moor, Keighley, W Yorkshire
The club is situated on the B6143, 2 miles south west of Keighley.

RAC recommended hotel
Dalesgate ★★ (0535) 664930 Stone-built Victorian house, once a manse, with a modern extension.

CALVERLEY
(0532) 569244
An 18-hole parkland course (5516 yards, SSS 66) and also a 9-hole course. A driving range is planned for 1990. Visitors are welcome at any time on the 9-hole course and on weekdays and after 1pm at weekends on the 18-hole course. Green fees are £3 on weekdays, £4 at weekends for the 9-hole course and £7 on weekdays, £10 at weekends for the 18-hole course. There is a restaurant. Bradford and Leeds are within easy reach and the course is close to the lovely Yorkshire Moors. Kirkstall Abbey is only 5 miles away.
Location
Woodhall Lane, Pudsey LS28 5QY
The club is situated 4 miles north east of Bradford.

CASTLE FIELDS
A 6-hole course (2406, SSS 50 yards). **Location** Rastrick Common, Brighouse, Bradford 1 mile south of Brighouse.

CITY OF WAKEFIELD
(0924) 360282
A wooded 18-hole undulating parkland course (6405 yards, SSS 71). Visitors of all levels are welcome. Green fees are £3.60 on weekdays and £5.60 at weekends. Meals and snacks can be served for groups by arrangement with the Steward. Local attractions include Sandal Castle.
Location
Lupset Park, Horbury Road, Wakefield, W Yorkshire WF2 8QS
The club is approximately 1 mile from the city centre and 2 miles from M1 junctions 39 or 40. The course is on the A642 Huddersfield Road; turn off at the Empire Mail Order Stores.

RAC recommended hotels
Cedar Court ★★★★ (0924) 276310 A large modern hotel with bedrooms on the ground and first floor.
Stoneleigh ★★★ (0924) 369461 Several stone-built large attractive houses converted into hotel and restaurant.
Swallow ★★★ (0924) 372111 A modern brick-built hotel of distinctive design situated in the city centre.

CLAYTON
(0274) 880047
A 9-hole moorland course which can be very windy (5518 yards, SSS 67). Visitors of all playing abilities are welcome on weekdays and also on Saturday but not before 4pm on Sunday. Green fees are £5 on weekdays with or without a member and £7 at weekends. There is a bar where snacks are served and which is open every day except Monday. Other catering is by arrangement. Local attractions include National Museum of Photography, Cartwright Hall and Grounds and the Industrial Museum.
Location
Thornton View Road, Clayton, Bradford, W Yorkshire BD14 6JX
The club is 2 miles south west of Bradford. Take the A647 from Bradford and turn right and follow the signs to Clayton.

RAC recommended hotels in Bradford.

CLECKHEATON & DISTRICT
(0274) 874118
An 18-hole parkland course with some gentle hills (5847 yards, SSS 69). Visitors of all playing abilities are welcome. There is a practice ground. Green fees are £11(£4 with a member) on weekdays and £14(£5 with a member) at weekends. Morning coffee, lunch, afternoon tea and dinner is served every day except Monday.
Location
Bradford Road, Cleckheaton, W Yorks BD19 6BU
The club is 4 miles south of Bradford on the A638. Leave the M62 at exit 26.

RAC recommended hotel
Novotel ★★★ (0274) 683683 A modern multi-storey French-operated hotel. situated on the M606. Facilities include a swimming pool.

CROSLAND HEATH
(0484) 653216
An 18-hole moorland course with some good views (5962 yards, SSS 70). Visitors who have a handicap certificate are welcome by arrangement. Green fees are £9.50(£4 with a member) on weekdays and £12(£6 with a member) at weekends. Full catering facilities are available daily except Mondays. The Derbyshire National Park is near by and also the Victoria Monument at Castle Hill.
Location
Felk Stile Road, Crosland Heath, Huddersfield HD4 7AF
Take the A62 Huddersfield to Oldham road for 3 miles and then follow the signs for Goodalls Caravans.

RAC recommended hotels in Huddersfield.

DEWSBURY DISTRICT
(0924) 492399
An 18-hole undulating meadowland/moorland course (6256 yards, SSS 71). Visitors who have a handicap certificate are welcome on weekdays by prior arrangement and also on certain weekends. Green fees by application. Full catering facilities are available except Monday. The club is situated in the heart of Haworth Country.
Location
The Pinnacle, Sands Lane, Mirfield, W Yorks WF14 8HJ
The club is 2½ miles from Dewsbury. Turn off the A644 opposite the Swan Inn and then turn left into Steannard Lane. The club is signposted at Sands Lane.

EAST BIERLEY
(0274) 681023
An undulating 9-hole semi-moorland course with some tight fairways but easy walking (4692 yards, SSS 62). Visitors of all playing abilities are welcome on any day except Sunday. Green fees are £6 per round on weekdays and £8 per round at weekends. Catering facilities are available by prior arrangement.
Location
South View Road, Bierley, Bradford, W Yorks
The course is 3 miles south east of Bradford city centre on the Wakefield to Heckmondwike road. Turn off at Bierley Bar and down into South View Road.

ELLAND
(0422) 72505
A 9-hole parkland/meadowland course (5526 yards, SSS 66). Visitors of all playing abilities are welcome on weekdays but not when there are competitions being held so it is advisable to check beforehand. Green fees on application. There is a bar where snacks are served every day except Monday. The course is very close to the Pennine Way.
Location
Hammerstones, Leach Lane, Elland, W Yorks HX5 0QP
Leave the M62 at junction 24 between Huddersfield and Halifax and head for Blackley. The club is 1 mile on the left.

FERRYBRIDGE 'C'
(0977) 84188
A 9-hole course landscaped around a power station on an industrial site (5138 yards, SSS 65). Visitors are welcome but you must be accompanied by a member. Green fees are £2 on weekdays and £ at weekends and Bank Holidays. Local attractions include Pontefract Castle and Racecourse which is 3 miles away.
Location
P.O Box 39, Stranglands Lane, Knottingley WF11 85Q
The course is half a mile off the A1 on the B6136. Look for the Ferrybridge 'C' power station.

RAC recommended hotel
Darrington ★★ (0977) 791458 1930's brick-built hotel with easy access to nearby trunk road. Sauna, solarium.

FULNECK
(0532) 565191
A pretty 9-hole hilly parkland course (5564 yards, SSS 67). Visitors are welcome on most weekdays although there are some restrictions on Wednesday. Green fees are £4 on weekdays(£2 with a member).
Location
Fulneck, Pudsey
The course is located on the south side of the town which is approximately 5 miles west of Leeds towards Bradford.

GARFORTH
(0532) 863308
An 18-hole parkland course with some fine views and easy walking (6296 yards, SSS 70). Visitors who are members of a bona fide golf club are welcome on weekdays. Green fees are £12 on weekdays and £15 at weekends. Full catering facilities are available daily.
Location
Long Lane, Garforth, Leeds LS25 2DS
Take A63 six miles east of Leeds and then turn left on to the A642.

RAC recommended hotels in Leeds.

GOTT'S PARK
(0532) 638232
A rather tight 18-hole hilly parkland course (4449 yards, SSS 62). The course is a municipal one and visitors of all playing abilities are welcome. There is also a practice ground. Green fees are £3.75 on weekdays and £4.10 at weekends. Juniors, OAPs and the unemployed can play for £1.15 on weekdays and £1.29 at weekends. There is a cafe which serves both hot and cold meals and also a bar which is open in the evenings. Local attractions include Kirkstall Abbey and Museum and Armsley Mills Industrial Museum.
Location
Armley Bridge Road, Leeds LS12 2QX
The course is situated 3 miles west of the city centre on the main Leeds-Stanningly-Bradford road.

RAC recommended hotels in Leeds.

HALIFAX
(0422) 244171
An 18-hole moorland course with several stream hazards and some lovely views (6030 yards, SSS 70). Visitors of all playing abilities are welcome on weekdays and by prior arrangement at weekends. Green fees are £10 a day on weekdays and £15 a day at weekends and Bank Holidays (£5.50 with a member). There is a restaurant where lunches and dinners are served every day except Monday. The club is close to Haworth and the Bronte Museum and of course the historic town of Halifax.
Location
Union Lane, Ogden, Halifax HX2 8XR
The club is situated 4 miles from the town centre on the A629 to Keighley.

RAC recommended hotel
Holdsworth House ★★★ (0422) 240024 An attractive Jacobean stone-built hotel in 2 acres of landscaped gardens.
Wool Merchant ★★★ (0422) 368783 Converted from a restored woollen warehouse close to the centre of town.

HALIFAX BRADLEY HALL
(0422) 74108
An 18-hole moorland course (6213 yards, SSS 70). Visitors of all playing abilities are welcome. Green fees on application. Full catering facilities are available everyday except Tuesday. Local attractions include the historic town of Halifax and Calderdale.
Location
Stainland Road, Holywell Green, Halifax, W Yorks
The club is about halfway between Halifax and Huddersfield on the B6112.

RAC recommended hotels in Huddersfield.

HALIFAX WEST END
(0422) 363293
An 18-hole part moorland part parkland course (6003 yards, SSS 69). The course is actually a converted Racecourse and there are some good views of the Pennines. Visitors are welcome at most times and Tuesday is Ladies Day. Green fees are £8 on weekdays(£3.50 with a member) and £10 at weekends(£4 with a member). There is a bar where snacks are served and a full a la carte menu is available on request. Local attractions include 'Piece Hall' in Halifax, a Cloth Trade Museum, the Working Horse Museum, an Industrial Museum and Shibden Hall, an Elizabethan Manor house.
Location
Highroad Well, Halifax HX2 0NT
The course is 2 miles north west of Halifax off the A646.

RAC recommended hotels in Halifax.

HANGING HEATON
(0924) 461606
A 9-hole parkland course with easy walking and some lovely views (5874 yards, SSS 67). Visitors of all playing abilities who are members of a bona fide golf club are welcome on weekdays. Green fees on application. Lunch is served everyday except Monday. Market Day on Wednesday and Saturday.
Location
White Cross Road, Bennett Lane, Dewsbury, W Yorks WF12 7HJ
The club is situated 1 mile from the town centre on the main A653 Dewsbury to Leeds road.

HEADINGLEY
(0532) 679573
An 18-hole undulating moorland course situated on high ground (6238 yards, SSS 70). It is Leed's oldest course and offers some fine views of the surrounding countryside. Visitors are largely unrestricted although it is probably advisable to check beforehand. Green fees are £11 per round or day on weekdays and £13 per round, £15 a day at weekends and Bank Holidays. Full catering facilities are available daily although there are some restrictions on Friday.
Location
Back Church Lane, Adel, Leeds LS16 8DW
From the Leeds ring road take the A660 towards Otley. Turn right at the traffic lights and the course is just past Adel Church, about 5 miles from the city centre.

RAC recommended hotels
Parkway ★★★ (0532) 672551 A large 1930s building set in 2 acres of grounds overlooking a country park. Facilities include swimming pool, tennis, sauna, solarium, gymnasium and billards.
Chevin Lodge Country Park ★★★ (0943) 467818 Scandinavian style hotel with residents cabins in 50 acres of Birchwood near Otley. Facilities include fishing, sauna and solarium.

HEADLEY
(0274) 833481
A hilly 9-hole moorland course which although short can be rather challenging with some prevailing winds.(2457 yards, SSS 64). Visitors of all playing abilities are welcome on any weekday but not on Saturday or Sunday. Green fees are £5 on weekdays and also at weekends. Full catering facilities are available by arrangement. Haworth is about 5 miles away from the club.
Location
Headley Lane, Thornton, Bradford, W Yorks BD13 3AJ
The club is situated in the village of Thornton, 4 miles west of Bradford on the B6145.

RAC recommended hotels in Bradford.

HORSFORTH
(0532) 586819
An 18-hole undulating moorland course overlooking the airport (6243 yards, SSS 70). Visitors of all playing abilities are welcome between Monday and Friday. Green fees are £14 a day on weekdays and £18 at weekends. Full catering facilities are available although you should order dinner in advance. There are some restrictions on Monday.
Location
Layton Road, Horsforth, Leeds, W Yorks LS18 5EX
Take the A65 Leeds to Ilkley road and Layton Road is on the right after you have crossed the A6120 Leeds ring road. You will reach. The course is just after Rawdon.

RAC recommended hotels in Leeds.

HOWLEY HALL
(0924) 472432
A fine 18-hole parkland course with easy walking and some lovely views (6420 yards, SSS 71). Visitors of all playing abilities are welcome on any day except Saturday. Green fees are £10 per round, £13 a day on weekdays and £15 per round or day at weekends. Full catering facilities are available daily except Monday.
Location
Scotchman Lane, Morley, Leeds LS27 0NX
Turn off the A650 main Bradford to Wakefield road at the Halfway House Public House and take the B6123 to Morley.

RAC recommended hotels in Leeds.

HUDDERSFIELD
(0484) 26203
A challenging 18-hole parkland course (6424 yards, SSS 71) Visitors are welcome but times are restricted on Sundays. Reservation is advised but not essential. Green fees are £12.50 on weekdays and £15 at weekends and £5 with a member. Lunches and a la carte dinners are served everyday.
Location
Fixby Hall, Fixby, Huddersfield HD2 2EP
Leave the M62 at exit 24 and follow the A643 to Clough House Inn. From there take the first right down Lightridge and the clubhouse gates are on the right.

RAC recommended hotel
Briar Court ★★★ (0484) 519902 A modern stone-fronted building set back from the A629 some 2 miles from the M62.
George ★★★ (0484) 515444 A 5-storey stone-built hotel of character, situated in the town centre. Facilities include billards.
Old Golf House ★★★ (0422) 79311 Three-storey, stone-built hotel with modern extensions, once the clubhouse of a golf course. Situated next to M62 junction 23. Sauna, solarium, gymnasium.
Pennine Hilton International ★★★ (0422) 75431 Modern hotel of striking design adjacent to M62. Fine Pennine views.
Huddersfield ★★ (0484) 512111 Pleasant modern conversion of a Georgian building in town centre. Sauna, solarium.

ILKLEY
(0943) 600214
A particularly lovely 18-hole parkland course situated in the heart of Wharfedale. The River Wharfe winds itself through most of the course and is a major natural hazard on several occasions (6256 yards, SSS 70). Visitors who are a member of a bona fide club are welcome by arrangement. Green fees are £17 on weekdays and £25 at weekends and Bank Holidays. Full catering facilities are available. The club has a snooker room and fishing is also available. Other local attractions include Skipton Castle, Fountains Abbey and Bolton Abbey.

Location
Myddleton, Ilkley, W Yorks LS29 0BE
The course is on the west side of the town centre, off the A65, 18 miles north west of Leeds.

RAC recommended hotels
Cow and Calf ★★★ (0943) 607335 Fine example of a Yorkshire stone-built hotel. On Ilkley Moor.
Rombalds ★★★ (0943) 603201 Attractive early Victorian building situated on the fringe of Ilkley Moor.
Greystones ★★ (0943) 607408 Large stone house of quality, now a family-run hotel.

KEIGHLEY
(0535) 604778
A good 18-hole parkland course (6139 yards, SSS 70). Provided they have a handicap certificate visitors are welcome on weekdays, but not Saturday and with some reservation on Sunday. Green fees are £12 on weekdays and £16 at weekends and Bank Holidays. Full catering facilities are available everyday except Monday.
Location
Howden Park, Utley, Keighley, W Yorks BD20 6DA
The club is situated 1 mile north of Keighley on the A650 Skipton road, between the River Aire and the canal.

RAC recommended hotel
Dalesgate ★ (0535) 664930 A stone-bult Victorian house, once a manse, with a modern extension.

LEEDS
(0532) 659203
An 18-hole parkland course with some fine views (6097 yards, SSS 69). Visitors who are members of a bona fide golf club are welcome on weekdays and also at the weekend if you are accompanied by a member. Green fees are £11 per round, £14 a day. Catering facilities are available by arrangement. Local attractions include Harewood House.
Location
Elmete Lane, Leeds LS8 2LJ
Take the Leeds ring road to the A58 and turn left if you are coming from the east or right if coming from the west. Fork right at the next roundabout and turn right after 250 yards.

RAC recommended hotels
Hilton International ★★★★ (0532) 442000 A large modern high-rise city hotel with conference facilities. Near station.
Queens ★★★★ (0532) 431323 An imposing listed building in a neoclassic style.
Golden Lion ★★★ (0532) 436454 Modernised hotel close to shopping centre and motorway links.
Hilton National ★★★ (0532) 866556 Large modern hotel with spacious grounds. Swimming pool, sauna, gymnasium.
Merrion ★★★ (0532) 439191 High-rise city centre hotel with access from multi-storey car park.
Parkway ★★★ (0532) 672551 Large 1930's building set in 2 acres of grounds and overlooking country park. Swimming pool, tennis, sauna, solarium, gymnasium, billiards.
Stakis Windmill ★★★ (0532) 732323 A modern hotel with an original windmill an integral feature of the building.
Wellesley ★★ (0532) 430431 Elegant Victorian city centre hotel close to main railway station.

LIGHTCLIFFE
(0422) 202459
A 9-hole parkland course (5388 yards, SSS 68). Visitors who are members of a bona fide golf club are welcome every day except Wednesday and Saturday. Green fees are £6 on weekdays(£3 with a member) and £8 at weekends(£4 with a member). Lunches and evening meals are served daily except Thursday.
Location
Knowle Top Road, Lightcliffe, Halifax
The club is situated on the A58 Leeds to Halifax road in Lightcliffe/Hipperholme village.

LONGLEY PARK
(0484) 4522304
A 9-hole parkland course (5269 yards, SSS 66). Visitors of all playing abilities are welcome on weekdays but not Thursday and there are some restrictiions at weekends. Green fees are £5 on weekdays(£3.50 with a member) and £6.50 at weekends. (£4.50 with a member).
Location
Maple Street, off Somerset Road, Huddersfield HD5 9AX
The club is situated half a mile from the town centre on the Wakefield side.

RAC recommended hotels in Huddersfield.

LOW LAITHES
(0924) 273275
A challenging 18-hole undulating course with short holes (6448 yards, SSS 71). There is also a practice area. Visitors, including parties, of all playing abilities are welcome on weekdays but only individual visitors can play at weekends. There are some restrictions on dress so it is advisable to check beforehand. Green fees are £9 on weekdays and £12 at weekends and Bank Holidays, £6 and £8 if playing with a member. There is a bar and full catering facilities are available by advance arrangement.
Location
Parkmill, Flushdyke, Ossett, W Yorks.
Leave the M1 at exit 40 and follow the signs to Low Laithes and Flushdyke which is about 1 mile away.

RAC recommended hotel
Post House ★★★ (0924) 276388 A modern hotel with well designed accommodation.

MARSDEN
(0484) 844253
A 9-hole moorland course with natural hazards and some good views(5702 yards, SSS 68). Visitors of all playing abilities are welcome on weekdays. Green fees are £5 on weekdays(£3 with a member) and £10 at weekends and Bank Holidays(£5 with a member). Lunch is served everyday except Tuesday and evening meals by arrangement. The Tunnell End picnic area is close by.
Location
Mount Road, Hemplow, Marsden, Huddersfield HD7 6NN
The club is situated off the A62, 8 miles out of Huddersfield going towards Manchester.

RAC recommended hotel in Meltham.

MELTHAM
(0484) 850227
A gently sloping 18-hole moorland/parkland course situated in a wooded valley with some good views (6145 yards, SSS 70). There is also a restricted practice area. Visitors of all playing abilities are welcome on any day except Wednesday and Saturday. Green fees are £12 on weekdays and £15 on Sunday and Bank Holidays. Full catering facilities are available everyday except Tuesday. There is a snooker room at the clubhouse. Local attractions include Holmfirth and the Pennine National Park.
Location
Thick Hollins, Meltham, Huddersfield HD7 3DQ
The club is about half a mile east of Meltham, 6 miles south west of Huddersfield on the B6108. In Meltham take the B6107.

RAC recommended hotel
Durker Roods ★★★ (0484) 851413 A spacious Victorian hotel set in its own pleasant grounds.

MIDDLETON PARK
(0532) 700449
An 18-hole parkland course (5233 yards, SSS 67). The course is a municipal one and visitors of all playing abilities are welcome. Green fees are £3.75 per round, juniors £1.50, on weekdays and £4.10 per round, juniors £1.90, at weekends. Local attractions include Temple Newsam House, a local historic building.
Location
Middleton Park, Leeds
The course is 3 miles south of the city centre.

MOOR ALLERTON
(0532) 661154
A magnificent 27-hole undulating parkland course with some splendid views across the Vale of York. The course, which is of championship standard, is split into three, holes 1-18 The Lakes (6045 yards, SSS 71), 10-27 Blackmoor (6222 yards, SSS 72), and 1-9/19-27 The High Course (6930 yards, SSS 75). It also has a large practice ground, driving range and tennis courts. Provided they have a handicap certificate, visitors are welcome on weekdays. Green fees are £18.50 a day. Lunch is served every day and dinner on Tuesday, Wednesday and Thursday when unlimited numbers can be catered for, and Monday and Friday for parties of over 40. The club also has a snooker room and a sauna. Harewood House is nearby and Harrogate and York within easy reach.
Location
Coal Road, Wike, Leeds LS17 9NH
Take the A61 Harrogate Road for about 1 mile past the intersection with the A6120 ring road. Turn right in to Wigton Lane and when you reach the T-junction take the first left. From there take the first right and the club is then signposted.

RAC recommended hotels
Post House ★★★ (0924) 276388 A modern hotel with well designed accommodation. Situated in Bramhope.
Harewood Arms ★★ (0532) 886566 A traditional stone-built inn with sympathetic new extensions, opposite the entrance to Harewood House.

MOORTOWN
(0532) 686521
An 18-hole moorland course with easy walking situated within minutes of both the centre of Leeds and the Pennines and lovely Yorkshire Moors (6503 yards, SSS 72). Visitors of all playing abilities are welcome on weekdays and at weekends by prior arrangement with the Secretary and Professional. There is a large practice ground. Green fees on application. Lunch is served everyday except Monday and other meals by arrangement.
Location
Harrogate Road, Leeds LS17 7DB
The club is about 8 miles north of the city centre on the A61 road to Harrogate.

RAC recommended hotels in Moor Allerton.

MOUNT SKIP
(0422) 842896
A 9-hole moorland course with some magnficient views (5114 yards, SSS 66). Visitors of all playing abilities are welcome. Green fees are £5(half price with a member with further discounts for juniors). There is a restaurant which is open everyday except Monday. Local attractions include Hebden Bridge and the club is also near Haworth.
Location
Wadsworth, Hebden Bridge, W Yorks HX7 8PH
The club is 1 mile east of Hebden Bridge on the Birchcliffe Road, just past the Birchcliffe Centre.

RAC recommended hotel
Carlton ★★★ (0422) 844400 A restored Victorian sandstone building with hotel situated above shops in the centre of the town.

NORMANTON
(0924) 892943
A pleasant 9-hole flat meadowland course with some tight fairways (5184 yards, SSS 66). Visitors of all playing abilities are welcome on weekdays and

Saturday. Green fees are £4.50(£3.50 with a member) on weekdays and £8(£7 with a member) on Saturday. Full catering facilities are available. Local attractions include Pontefract Castle and racecourse.
Location
Snydale Road, Normanton, Wakefield, W Yorks WF6 1PA
Leave the M62 at junction 31 and the course is about half a mile from the centre of Normanton on the B6133.

NORTHCLIFFE
(0274) 596731
An 18-hole undulating wooded parkland course with some spectacular views over the moors (6065 yards, SSS 69). Visitors who have a handicap certificate are welcome at all times except Saturday. Tuesday is Ladies Day when no visiting parties can play. Green fees are £10 on weekdays and £15 at weekends and Bank Holidays. There is a bar where coffee and snacks are served everyday except Monday and dinners are available by arrangement with the Steward. The club also has a snooker room. The course is in the heart of Bronte country being near both Haworth and Thornton.
Location
High Bank Lane, Shipley, W Yorkshire BD18 4LJ
Take the A650 Bradford to Keighley road until you come to the Saltaire roundabout. From here turn up Moorhead Lane which leads into the High Bank Lane and the club is half a mile on your left.

RAC recommended hotel see Bingley.

OTLEY
(0943) 465329
A beautiful 18-hole wooded meadowland course with streams situated in the Wharfe valley with some splendid views of Wharfedale (6225 yards, SSS 70). Visitors of all playing abilities are welcome, however the course is quite busy and it is best to check beforehand for availability. Green fees are £13 on weekdays and £17 at weekends. Full catering facilities are available daily except Monday.
Location
West Busk Lane, Otley, W Yorkshire LS21 3NG
The course is off the A6038 Otley to Bradford road, 1½ miles from Otley centre.

RAC recommended hotel
Chevin Lodge Country Park ★★★ (0943) 467818 Scandinavian-style hotel withresidents' cabins in 50 acres of birchwood. Fishing, sauna, solarium.

OUTLANE
(0422) 74762
An 18-hole moorland course (5590 yards, SSS 67). Visitors of all playing abilities are welcome. Green fees are £8(£4 with a member) on weekdays and £12(£6 with a member) at weekends. Meals are served daily except Monday. There is a sports centre in Huddersfield.
Location
Slack Lane, Outlane, Huddersfield, W Yorkshire
Take the A640 Huddersfield-Rochdale road 4 miles out of Huddersfield and continue through Outlane village. Turn left under the motorway and the entrance is on the left just after the bus terminus.

PAINTHORPE HOUSE
(0924) 255083
An 9-hole undulating meadowland course with easy walking (4100, yards, SSS 60). Visitors of all playing abilities are welcome except on Sunday. There is also a bowling green. Green fees are £2 a day. The course is part of a Country Club and meals are served daily. There are two ballrooms with regular Saturday dinner dances and private functions can be catered for up to 400 people.
Location
Painthorpe Lane, Crigglestone, Wakefield, W Yorkshire
Leave the M1 at junction 39 and the club is off the A636, 2 miles south of Wakefield.

RAC recommended hotels in Wakefield.

PHOENIX PARK
(0274) 667178
An undulating 9-hole parkland course which can be testing (4774 yards, SSS 63). Visitors of all playing abilities are welcome on weekdays. Green fees on application. Catering facilities are available by arrangement with the Steward prior to your visit.
Location
Phoenix Park, Dick Lane, Thornbury, Bradford, W Yorkshire
Take the Leeds road from Bradford(A647) for 2½ miles until you reach the Thornbury roundabout. The course is situated at the side of the roundabout.

PONTEFRACT & DISTRICT
(0977) 792241
An 18-hole parkland course (6227 yards, SSS 70). Visitors of all playing abilities are welcome on weekdays. Green fees are £8.50 on weekdays and £9 at weekends. Full catering facilities are available daily except Monday. There is a bird sanctuary nearby.
Location
Park Lane, Pontefract, W Yorkshire WF8 4QS
Leave the M62 at exit 32 or take the A645 off the A1 and the club is situated on the B6134.

PONTEFRACT PARK
(0977) 702799
A municipal 9-hole undulating course (4068 yards, SSS 62). Visitors are welcome at all times. Green fees are £2.50, juniors £1.25 on weekdays and £3.60, juniors £2.50 at weekends. Local attractions include Pontefract Castle and the speciality of the local confectionary industry 'Pontefract cakes'.
Location
Park Road, Pontefract
The course is situated between the town and the M62 roundabout.

QUEENSBURY
(0274) 882155
A 9-hole undulating parkland course (5102 yards, SSS 65). Visitors of all playing abilities who are members of a bona fide golf club are welcome. Green fees are £6 on weekdays and £10 at weekends. It is £3 at all times if you are playing with a member. There is a bar which is open during normal licensing hours. There is a snooker room in the clubhouse. The course is situated in the heart of Bronte Country and Haworth is only 6 miles away.
Location
Brighouse Road, Queensbury, Bradford, W Yorkshire BD13 1QF
The club is situated 4 miles from Bradford on the A647.

RAC recommended hotels in Bradford.

RAWDON
(0532) 506040
A 9-hole undulating parkland course (5964 yards, SSS 69). Visitors are welcome on weekdays. Green fees are £7.50 a day. Lunch is served daily except on Monday. There are both hard and grass tennis courts. Local attractions include Kirkstall Abbey and Museum.
Location
Buckstone Drive, Rawdon, Leeds LS19 6BD
The club is on the A65, 6 miles from Leeds.

RIDDLESDEN
(0535) 602148
An 18-hole moorland course with quarry hazards and some lovely views (4185 yards, SSS 61). Visitors of all playing abilities are welcome at any time except before 10am on Sunday. Green fees are £4(£3 if you are introduced by a member) on weekdays and £7(£5 with a member) at weekends. Catering facilities are available by prior arrangement during the week and during normal bar opening hours at the weekend. Local attractions include Skipton Castle and Haworth.
Location
Howden Rough, Elam Wood Road, Riddlesden, Keighley, W Yorkshire
Take the A650 Keighley to Bradford road and turn left into Bar Lane then left again into Scott Lane which leads onto Scott Lane West and Elam Wood Road, approximately 2 miles.

RAC recommended hotel in Keighley.

ROUNDHAY
(0532) 662695
A pleasant 9-hole wooded parkland course with natural hazards and easy walking (5166 yards, SSS 65). There is also a practice ground. The course is a municipal one and visitors of all levels are welcome to play at any time. Green fees are £3.75 on weekdays and £4.10 at weekends. There is a restaurant which is open between Tuesday and Sunday in the evening and snacks are also available on Saturday and Sunday. The ground borders on Roundhay Park and the Canal Gardens.
Location
Park Lane, Leeds LS8 2EJ
The course is located 4 miles north of Leeds city centre. Take the A58 to Oakwood Clock and then turn into Princes Avenue and then Street Lane, finally turn right at Park Lane.

RAC recommended hotels in Leeds.

RYBURN
(0422) 831355
A particularly demanding 9-hole course situated on the top of a hill (5002 yards, SSS 65). The course can be windy. Visitors who have a handicap certificate are welcome at any time except when there are competitions being played. Green fees are £5 on weekdays(£4 with a member) and £7 at weekends(£6 with a member). There is a bar which is open during the evenings and also during the day at weekends. There are many local attractions including the Gibbet in Gibbet Street, Piece Hall-the cloth trade museum, Working Horse Museum, Industrial Museum, Shebden Hall, Sowerby Bridge and Wainshouse, a folly visible from the golf course.
Location
Norland, Sowerby Bridge, Halifax HX6 3QT
Take Station Road from Halifax to Sowerby Bridge and turn right up the hill and right again towards the Hobbit Inn. The club is signposted left just after the cottages.

RAC recommended hotel
Hobbit ★★ (0422) 832202 Sympathetically extended stone-built inn set high up with panoramic views of the Calder Valley and moors.

SAND MOOR
(0532) 685180
A picturesque 18-hole undulating parkland/moorland course overlooking Wharfedale (6429 yards, SSS 71). The course has plenty of trees and some holes are adjacent to water. Visitors who are members of a bona fide golf club are welcome on weekdays but times reserved for members are between 12 noon and 1.30pm every day, between 9.30am and 10.30 on Tuesday and between 8.30am and 12 noon on Thursday. Green fees are £15 per round, £18 a day on weekdays and £22 at weekends. Full catering facilities are available everday except Monday when lunch and snacks only are served. There is a snooker room at the clubhouse. The course also overlooks Lord Hardwood's estate and the Eccup Reservoir.
Location
Alwoodley Lane, Leeds LS17 7DJ
Take the A61 from Leeds city centre for 6 miles and turn left into Alwoodley Lane. The course is approximately half a mile on your right.

RAC recommended hotels in Leeds.

SCARCROFT
(0532) 892263
An 18-hole parkland course with easy walking (6426 yards, SSS 71). Provided you have a handicap certificate, visitors are welcome on weekdays and also at the weekends if you have arranged it beforehand. Green fees are £16 per round or day on weekdays and £22 per round or day at weekends. It is £6 at all times if you are accompanied by a member. Meals are served everyday except Monday.
Location
Syke Lane, Leeds LS14 3BQ
Take the A58 north east of Leeds towards Wetherby and turn left at the New Inn into Syke Lane.

SHIPLEY
(0274) 568652
A fine, slightly undulating 18-hole parkland course with easy walking and some fine views(6203 yards, SSS 70). There is also a practice area and net putting green. Visitors are welcome at all times except on Tuesday before 2pm and Saturday before 4pm. Green fees are £10.50 a day and £13 at weekends and Bank Holidays. You can play for £5 at any time if you are with a member. Bar snacks are normally available and evening meals served by arrangement with the Steward, everyday except Monday.
Location
Beckfoot Lane, Cottingley Bridge, Bingley, W Yorkshire BD16 1LX
The club is situated on the A650 Bradford to Keighly road at Cottingley Bridge, Bingley.

RAC recommended hotel in Bingley.

SILSDEN
(0535) 52998
An undulating 14-hole moorland/meadowland course (4870 yards, SSS 64). There are some fine views of the Aire Valley. Visitors of all playing abilities are welcome on weekdays and at weekends. with some restrictions of Saturday afternoon and Sunday morning. Green fees are £5 on weekdays(£3 with a member) and £10 at weekends.(£5 with a member). Local attractions include East Riddlesden Hall(NT) and the course is also close to Bronte country.
Location
High Brunthwaite, Silsden, Keighley BD20 0NH
Take the A629 4 miles from Keighley and turn onto the A6034 to Silsden town centre. Turn right at the canal for the course.

SOUTH BRADFORD
(0274) 679195
A challenging 9-hole undulating meadowland course with lots of trees and ditches (6004 yards, SSS 69). Visitors of all playing abilities are welcome on weekdays but you should check with the club beforehand on dress rules. Green fees are £8 on weekdays(£3.50 with a member) and £12 at weekends.(£6 with a member). Lunches and evening meals are served everyday except Monday. There is also a snooker room.
Location
Pearson Road, Odsal, Bradford BD6 1BJ
Leave the M606 along Rooley Avenue to the Odsal roundabout and turn into Cleckheaton Road. From there turn left in to Stadium Road and then Pearson Road to the club.

RAC recommended hotel
Novotel ★★★ (0274) 683683 A modern multi-storey French-operated hotel, situated on the M606. Facilities include swimming pool.

SOUTH LEEDS
(0532) 700479
An 18-hole parkland course with undulating fairways, hard walking and fine views (5890 yards, SSS 68). There is also a practice fairway. Visitors who are members of a bona fide golf club are welcome at any time if you are accompanied by a member or by previous arrangement. Green fees are £10 on weekdays and £13 at weekends.. Full catering facilities are available daily except Monday. There is a leisure centre at Rothwell.
Location
Gipsy Lane, Beeston Ring Road, Leeds LS11 5TU
Take the Leeds to Dewsbury road to the traffic lights at the Tommy Wass Hotel and then follow the ring road for 100 yards. You should then turn left into Gipsy Lane which leads to the clubhouse.

RAC recommended hotels in Leeds.

TEMPLE NEWSAM
(0532) 645624
There are two undulating parkland courses here, both 18 holes, (6448 yards, SSS 70) and (6029 yards, SSS 71). Visitors of all playing abilities are welcome. Green fees on application. Meals are served at the weekend. Local attractions include Temple Newsam House, Museum and Farm.
Location
Temple Newsam Road, Leeds LS15
The club is situated on the A63 Selby road, 5 miles from Leeds city centre. You should follow the signs for Temple Newsam House. The course is also easily reached by public transport.

WAKEFIELD
(0924) 258778
A sheltered 18-hole parkland course with easy walking (6626 yards, SSS 72). Visitors of all playing abilities are welcome by arrangement. Green fees are £13 on weekdays and £16 at weekends. Full catering facilities are available everyday except Monday. Local attractions include Nostell Priory and Pugneys Country Park.
Location
Woodthorpe Lane, Sandal, Wakefield WF2 6JH
The course is 3 miles south of Wakefield on the A61. If you are coming from the M1 leave it at exit 39.

RAC recommended hotels
Cedar Court ★★★★ (0924) 276310 A large modern hotel with bedrooms on the first and ground floor.
Stoneleigh ★★★ (0924) 369461 Several stone-built large attractive houses converted into hotel and restaurant.
Swallow ★★★ (0924) 372111 A modern brick-built hotel of distinctive design

WEST BOWLING
(0274) 724449
An 18-hole parkland/meadowland course (5770 yards, SSS 68). Visitors of all playing levels are welcome on weekdays. Green fees are £10 on weekdays(£5 with a member) and £16 at weekends(£8 with a member). Lunches and evening meals are served everyday except Monday. The course is situated in the heart of Bronte Country.
Location
Newall Hall, Rooley Lane, Bradford, W Yorkshire BD5 8LB
The course is on the Bradford inner ring road, 2 miles from the town centre, adjacent to the M606 and M62.

RAC recommended hotel
Novotel ★★★ (0274) 683683 A modern multi-storey French-operated hotel, situated on the M606. Facilities include swimming pool.

WEST BRADFORD
(0274) 542767
A windy 18-hole undulating meadowland course (5752 yards, SSS 68). Visitors of all playing abilities are welcome on weekdays. Green fees are £9 on weekdays(£5 with a member) and £12 at weekends and Bank Holidays(£8 with a member). Meals are served daily except on Monday. The club offers golf package deals. There is also a snooker room. Local attractions include Black Hill Trust(NT).
Location
Chellow Grange, Bradford, W Yorkshire BD9 6NP
The club is situated on the B6144, 3 miles from Bradford on the Haworth road.

RAC recommended hotels in Bradford.

WEST END
(0422) 53608
An 18-hole moorland course (6003 yards, SSS 69). Visitors of all playing abilities are welcome. Green fees are £8 on weekdays(£3.50 with a member) and £10 at weekends(£4 with a member). Full catering facilities are available daily except on Monday.
Location
The Racecourse, Paddock Lane, Highroad Well, Halifax,
Take the A61 Burnley road from the town centre and when you reach the traffic lights complex at King Cross, 1 mile from town, turn a sharp right at the sign to Warley. Ascend Warley road until you come to the T-junction, about three-quarters of a mile away, and then turn left to Highroad Well village. From here continue through the village and turn right at the end, up Court Lane. The club is then signposted.

RAC recommended hotels in Halifax.

WETHERBY
(0937) 63375
An 18-hole parkland course with some good views (6235 yards, SSS 70). There is a 12.15am to 1.15pm reservation time for members but otherwise visitors of all playing abilities are welcome at all times. There are two practice grounds. Green fees are £10.50 per round, £14 a day on weekdays and £19 per round or day at weekends. Lunches is served everyday except Monday.
Location
Linton Lane, Wetherby, LS22 4JF
The club is situated off the A1 at Wetherby.

RAC recommended hotels
Wood Hall C/H ★★★★ (0937) 67271 Stately Georgian mansion in 100 acres of parkland and woods running down to the River Wharfe. Lovely views. Fishing, billiards.
Penguin ★★★ (0937) 63881 Modern hotel with attractive flagstone-floored public area. At junction A1/A58.

WHITWOOD GOLF & COUNTRY CLUB
(0977) 512835
A 9-hole parkland course (6282 yards, SSS 70). Visitors are welcome but you will need to book if you wish to play at the weekend. Green fees are £2.50 on weekdays and £3.60 at weekends. There is a bar.
Location
Altofts Lane, Whitwood, Castleford WP10 5PZ
Leave the M62 at junction 31 and the club is 1 mile along the A655.

WOODHALL HILLS
(0532) 554594
A 18-hole undulating parkland course with some hard walking (6102 yards, SSS 69). Visitors of all playing levels are welcome on most days although there are restrictions on Saturday. It is advisable to telephone the club beforehand. Green fees are £12 a day, £9 per round, on weekdays and £14 a day, £11 per round at weekends and Bank Holidays. Full catering facilities are available daily except Monday.
Location
Woodhall Road, Calverley, Pudsey, W Yorkshire
The club is 1 mile from the Pudsey roundabout on the main Leeds to Bradford road,(A647), 6 miles from Leeds. It is signposted from Calverley.

WOODSOME HALL
(0484) 602971
An 18-hole parkland course with an historic clubhouse (6068 yards, SSS 69). Visitors are welcome on weekdays although not until after 4pm on Tuesday. There are limitations at weekends so it it best to telephone beforehand. Green fees are £12 on weekdays(£5.50 with a member) and £15 at weekends and Public Holidays(£6.50 with a member). Full catering facilities are available daily except Monday.
Location
Fenay Bridge, Huddersfield, W Yorkshire HD8 0LQ
The club is situated 5 miles south east of Huddersfield on the A629 Sheffield to Penistone road.
RAC recommended hotels in Huddersfield.

CHANNEL ISLANDS

ALDERNEY
048 182 2835
An undulating 9-hole seaside course (2528 yards, SSS33). Visitors are welcome at all times. Green fees are £8 weekdays and £10 at weekends. Bar snacks are available and lunch on Sunday. Situated on the small northernmost Channel Island.
Location
Routes des Carriers, Alderney, Channel Islands
The course is 1 mile east of St Annes, the main town on the island.

LA MOYT
0534 43401
A demanding 18-hole links course (6512 yards, SSS72). Visitors are welcome by arrangement and with a handicap certificate. Green fees are £22 weekdays and £25 at weekends. Situated on the Island of Jersey with numerous places of interest.
Location
La Moyt, Jersey
Drive from the airport south along the main road, turning right at the traffic lights. The course is signposted further along this road on the right.
RAC recommended hotels
Atlantic ★★★★ (0534) 44101 Light modern 3 storey modern hotel in gardens.
L'Horizon ★★★★ (0534) 43101 Elegant modern hotel overlooking a sandy beach.
St Brelade's Bay ★★★★ (0534) 46141 Family owned and managed, a white-painted luxury holiday hotel in lovely gardens right beside the beach.
Chateau de la Valeuse ★★★ (0534) 46281 Four-storey white-painted hotel with fine views of long sandy beach. Swimming pool.
Beau Rivage ★★ (0534) 45983 White-painted, four-storey building with sun terrace and verandahs overlooking the picturesque bay.

ISLE OF MAN

CASTLETOWN
(0625) 822201
An interesting seaside course with 18 holes (6804 yards, SSS 73). Visitors are all welcome though check for starting times. Green fees are £12 per day. Full meals are served every day in the hotel on the course. The course shares the leisure facilities of the hotel and is situated in the historic town of Castletown with many local places of interest including Derby Fort and Derby Round Tower at either end of the course.
Location
Fort Island, Castletown, Isle of Man.
Drive east out of Castletown towards the airport and round to the course on Dreswick Point overlooking the bay.

RAC recommended hotel
Castletown Golf Links ★★★ (0624) 822201. Magnificently situated hotel on the south coastline. Indoor swimming pool, sauna, solarium, golf, putting, billiards.

DOUGLAS
(0624) 75952
A municipal parkland course with 18 holes (6080 yards, SSS 69). Visitors of all levels are welcome. Green fees available on application. Snacks and meals are available from May to September. Situated in Douglas with all its seaside amenities.
Location
Pulrose Road, Douglas, Isle of Man.
1 mile south of Douglas on the A5 near the power station.

RAC recommended hotels
Empress ★★★ (0624) 27211. In premier position on the promenade. Indoor swimming pool, sauna, solarium, gymnasium, snooker.
Palace ★★★ (0624) 74521. Modern purpose-built hotel with casino. Indoor swimming pool, sauna, solarium, gymnasium, snooker.
Rutland ★★ (0624) 21218. Modernised family-run hotel on the promenade.
Sefton ★★★ (0624) 26011 Impressive five storey Victorian building in central position on Harris Promenade. Indoor swimming pool, sauna, solarium, gymnasium.
Ascot ★★★ (0624) 75081 Four-storey red-brick building close tothe promenade.
Edelweiss ★★ (0624) 75115 Four-storey white-painted building set back from the promenade.

HOWSTRAKE
(0624) 20430
A moorland and seaside course with 18 holes (5367 yards, SSS 66). Visitors of all levels are welcome on weekdays, and at weekends by arrangement. Green fees are £5 on weekdays and £7 at weekends. Snacks and meals are available everyday. Situated north of Douglas with all its seaside amenities.
Location
Groudle Road, Onchan, Isle of Man.
Take A11 from Douglas to Onchan Head and the course which overlooks the sea.

RAC recommended hotels see Douglas.

RAMSEY
(0624) 812244
A parkland course with 18 holes (6019 yards, SSS 69). Visitors are welcome with a handicap certificate. Green fees are £8 on weekdays and £10 at weekends. Lunch daily and full meals by request. Places of interest locally are 'The Island' and the rural life museum. Part of the TT Motorbike circuit.
Location
Brookfield, Ramsey.
Take A2 north from Douglas through Laxey to Ramsey. The course is a 5 minute walk inland from the town centre.

RAC recommended hotel
Grand Island ★★★★ (0624) 812455. Large Victorian hotel overlooking the sea. Indoor swimming pool, sauna, solarium, riding, putting, gymnasium, snooker.

ROWANY
(0624) 834108
A seaside course with 18 holes (5840 yards, SSS 69). Visitors of all levels are welcome. Green fees are £7 on weekdays and £8 at weekends. Restaurant facilities with lunch, evening meals and snacks available. Local places of interest include a maritime museum, Milner's Tower, and just south is the Manx village of Creignesh.
Location
Rowany Drive, Port Erin, Isle of Man.
The course is off the promenade.

RAC recommended hotel
Cherry Orchard ★★★ (0624) 833811.. Modern hotel in the town, 5 minutes from the beach. Indoor swimming pool, sauna, solarium.

PEEL
(0624) 843 456
A moorland course with 18 holes (5914 yards, SSS 65). Visitors are welcome on weekdays and by arrangement at weekends. Green fees are £6 on weekdays and £8 at weekends. Snacks and light meals are available by arrangement. Situated in a delightful fishing port with a castle and many facilities.
Location
Rheast Lane, Peel, Isle of Man.
On the outskirts of Peel, inland on the A1 towards Douglas.

PORT ST MARY
(0624) 834932
A municipal seaside links course with 9 holes (2711 yards, SSS 66). All visitors are welcome. Green fees are £3. Snacks and meals are available. Local

places of interest include the traditional Manx village of Creignesh and the seaside towns of Port Erin and Port St Mary.

Location

Callow Road, Port St Mary, Isle of Man.
Drive south from Castletown on the A7; the course is on the coast overlooking the sea.

SCILLY ISLES

ISLES OF SCILLY
(0720) 22692

A 9-hole moorland course with a sea view from every tee (5974 yards, SSS69). All visitors are welcome weekdays and Saturday. Green fees are £7.75 per day. Meals are available. The only course in the islands with their beautiful scenery and many places of interest.

Location

St Mary's, Isles of Scilly
1 mile from Hugh Town in St Mary's.

RAC recommended hotels in St Mary's

Atlantic ★★ (0720) 22417 Family hotel right by the beach. Sun lounge enjoys harbour views.
Godolphin ★★ (0720) 22316 Large stone-built hotel in quiet situation yet central to Hughtown. Sauna.
Tregarthen's ★★ (0720) 22540 Historic building enjoying magnificent views of harbour and other islands.

SCOTLAND

BORDERS

DUNS
(0361) 83327
A varied 9 hole undulating meadowland course with natural hazards including water and slopes (5754 yards, SSS 68). Visitors are welcome. Green fees are £4 per day on weekdays and £5 at weekends. Fees are half price from the 1 November until 15 March.
Location
Hardens Road, Duns, Berwickshire
The club is about 1 mile west of Duns on the A6105

EYEMOUTH
(08907) 50551
A 9 hole seaside course (5446 yards, SSS 66). Visitors are welcome without restrictions. Green fees are £3 on weekdays and £4 at weekends. Catering facilities are available by arrangement.
Location
Gunsgreen House, Eyemouth RD14 4DW
The course is 2½ miles north of Burnmouth. 6 miles north of Berwick-on-Tweed, towards the coast. It is signposted on the A1107 off the A1.

GALASHIELS
(0896) 3724
An 18 hole hillside course (5309 yards, SSS 67) with splendid views and a very steep 10th hole. It is a municipal course and there are no restrictions on visitors. There is also a practice ground. Green fees are £4 per round Monday to Saturday and £4.50 on Sunday. Catering facilities are available at weekends.
Location
Ladhope Recreation Ground, Galashiels, Selkirkshire
The course is situated at the north east side of the town, a quarter of a mile from the A7.

RAC recommended hotels
Kingsknowes C/H ★★★ (0896) 58375 A red-sandstone Victorian style mansion. Facilities include putting, tennis.
Abbotsford Arms ★★ (0896) 2517 19th-century stone-built inn in residential area of town. Fishing.

GATEHOUSE
(055 74) 654
A 9 hole undulating course (4796 yards, SSS 63) situated amongst the hills with lovely views of the Solway Firth and Fleet Bay. Visitors are welcome. Green fees are £4.50 per day. Other facilities at the club include tennis.
Location
Laurieston Road, Gatehouse-of-Fleet
The course is a quarter of a mile off the main A75 road.

RAC recommended hotels
Bank O' Fleet (05574) 302
Cally Palace C/H ★★★★ (055 74) 341 Former stately home with imposing classical portico; set in fine scenery. Swimming pool, putting, tennis, fishing, sauna, solarium.
Murray Arms ★★★ (055 74) 207 One-time coaching house set at side of quiet main street of small town. Tennis.

HAWICK
(0450) 72293
An 18 hole undulating wooded parkland course with fine views (5929 yards, SSS 69). Visitors of all playing abilities are welcome without restriction as long as there are no competitions being held. Green fees are £5 per round, £8 per day on weekdays and £8 at weekends. Full catering facilities are available. Local attractions include Teviot Dale Leisure Centre, Kielder Forest and Hawick Museum.
Location
Vertish Hill, Hawick, Roxburghshire
The course is south of Hawick on the A7. It is 40 miles north of Carlisle and 50 miles south of Edinburgh.

RAC recommended hotels
Elm House ★★ (0450) 2866 A late Victorian house near the town centre, now a family-run hotel.
Kirklands ★★ (0450) 72263 A hillside Victorian villa in its own small grounds overlooking the town.
Mansfield House ★★ (0450) 73988 A stone-built former mansion (1878) in ten acres of grounds, family-owned. Facilities include billiards.

HIRSEL
(0890) 2678
A sheltered 9 hole parkland course with trees and hard walking (2828 yards, SSS 67). Visitors are welcome at any time. Green fees are £3.50 per day on weekdays and £4.50 per day at weekends. Catering facilities are available between April and September and at other times by arrangement.
Location
Kelso Road, Coldstream, Berwickshire TS12 4LG
The course is at the west end of Coldstream on the A697, Edinburgh to Newcastle road.

RAC recommended hotels
Tillmouth Park C/H ★★★ (0890) 2255 Imposing stone-built Victorian mansion of four stories in parkland. Fishing.
Collingwood Arms ★★ (0890) 2424 A friendly hotel in attracive stone-built Georgian coaching inn on the A697. Billiards.

JEDBURGH
(0835) 63587
A 9 hole undulating parkland course (5522 yards, SSS 67) with easy walking but which can be windy. Visitors of all playing abilities are welcome except on competition days. Green fees on application. Bar meals are available at the weekend between June and September and at other times by arrangement. Jedburgh Abbey and Castle Jail are nearby.
Location
Dunion Road, Jedburgh, Roxburghshire
Leave the town by way of Castlegate and the club house is about half a mile on the right.

RAC recommended hotel
Ferniehurst Mill Lodge (Acclaimed) Hotel. Riding.

KELSO
(0573) 23009
A flat 18 hole parkland course with easy walking (6066 yards, SSS 69). The course is actually within the race course and there is also a practice ground. Visitors of all playing abilities are welcome. Green fees on application. Catering facilities are available during opening hours except on Monday and Tuesday. Local attractions include Floors Castle.
Location
Racecourse Road, Kelso, Roxburghshire TD5 7SL
The course is 1 mile north of the town centre within the National Hunt Racecourse.

RAC recommended hotels
Cross Keys ★★★ (0573) 23303 Completely modernised four-storey hotel with Georgian facade. Dominates town square. Sauna, solarium, gymnasium.
Ednam House ★★★ (0573) 24168 Fine Georgian house in town centre with rear facing River Tweed.

LAUDER
(057) 82409
A 9 hole undulating course (6002 yards, SSS 70). Visitors are welcome without reservation. Green fees on application. There are no catering facilities but there are good hotels in Lauder.
Location
Galashiels Road, Lauder
The course is off the A68, half a mile from Lauder.

MELROSE
(089682) 2855
A 9 hole parkland course with tree-lined fairways situated on a hillside (5464 yards, SSS 69). Visitors are welcome on weekdays and Sunday by arrangement with the Secretary. Green fees on application. Snacks are available.
Location
Dingleton, Melrose, Roxburghshire
The course is half a mile south of Melrose town centre at the base of Eildon Hills.

RAC recommended hotels
Burt's ★★ (089 682) 2870 Traditional family-run hotel set amidst beautiful countryside. Billiards.
George & Abbotsford ★★ (089 682) 2308 Stone-built three-storey coaching inn set in middle of town.

MINTO
(0450) 87220
An 18 hole parkland course situated in wooded surroundings with easy walking (5460 yards, SSS 68). Visitors are welcome at all times. Green fees are £5 on weekdays and £6 at weekends. There are bar and catering facilities available.
Location
Minto Village, by Denholme, Hawick, Roxburghshire
The course is 5 miles north east of Hawick off the A698. Turn left in Denholm for Minto.

RAC recommended hotels in Hawick.

PEEBLES
(0721) 20197
An undulating 18 hole parkland course with some good views (6137 yards, SSS 69). The course is a municipal one and visitors of all levels, particularly beginners, are welcome. Green fees are £5.50 per round, £9 a day on weekdays and £9 per round, £12 a day at weekends and Bank Holidays. Snacks and meals are served every day. Edinburgh is within easy reach.
Location
Kirkland Street, Peebles EH45 8EU
The course is north west of the town, off the A72.

RAC recommended hotels
Hydro ★★★ (0721) 20602 A very large hotel in the grand style set in 30 acres of ground on the hill above town. Facilities include an indoor swimming pool, putting, tennis, squash, riding, sauna, solarium, gymnasium and billiards.
Park ★★★ (0721) 20451 A traditional Scottish-style private house which has been extended. Facilities include putting.
Tontine ★★★ (0721) 20892 19th-century inn with later extensions and elegant public rooms.
Cringletie House C/H ★★ Large Victorian mansion in quiet location with magnificent views from all rooms. Putting, tennis.

ST BOSWELLS
(0835) 22359
An attractive 9 hole meadowland course (2625 yards, SSS 65) with easy walking situated along the banks of the River Tweed. Visitors of all playing abilities are welcome at any time except during club competitions. Green fees are £4 per round or day on weekdays and £5 per round or day at weekends. Catering facilities are available by arrangement. Local attractions include Dryburgh Abbey, with memorials to Sir Walter Scott and Field-Marshal Earl Haig's burial place, and the River Tweed.
Location
St Boswells, Roxburghshire TD6 0AT
The club is about half a mile off the A68 Newcastle-Edinburgh road at the junction with the B6404.

SELKIRK
(0750) 20621
A 9 hole undulating moorland course (5640 yards, SSS 67). Visitors are welcome at all times. Green fees are £6 at weekends and £4 on weekdays. There are no catering facilities.
Location
The Hill, Selkirk
The course is 1 mile south of Selkirk on the A7 to Hawick.

RAC recommended hotel
Ettrickshaws Country House C/H ★★★ (0750) 52229 Large three-storey Edwardian house in own grounds above river. In rural area. Fishing.

TORWOODLEE
(0896) 2260
A 9 hole parkland course with natural hazards (5800 yards, SSS 68). Visitors of all playing abilities are welcome but there are restrictions on Saturday. No denims may be worn. Green fees on application. Full catering facilities are available every day except Tuesday.
Location
Edinburgh Road, Galashiels, Selkirkshire
Leave Galashiels on the A7 to Edinburgh and the entrance to the course is 1 mile on the left.

RAC recommended hotels in Galashiels.

WEST LINTON
(0968) 60463
An 18 hole moorland course with splendid views of the Pentland Hills (6024 yards, SSS 69). Visitors of all playing abilities are welcome on weekdays. There are two practice areas. Green fees are £7 per round and £9 a day. There is a dining room and lunches, high teas, morning coffee and afternoon teas are served everyday except Tuesday. There are also bar facilities. Local attractions include Neidpath Castle.
Location
West Linton, Peebleshire
The club is situated on the A702, 17 miles south west of Edinburgh.

CENTRAL

ABERFOYLE
(08772) 441
A particularly scenic 18 hole hillside course with wooded areas (5205 yards, SSS 66). Visitors of all playing abilities are welcome. Green fees are £10 per day. There is a bar and light meals are available at weekends. Local places of interest include Lake of Montieth, Queen Mary's Prison, and Rob Roy's birthplace.
Location
Braeval, Aberfoyle, Stirlingshire FK8 3RL
The club is situated 1 mile from Aberfoyle on the A81 Stirling road, 18 miles west of Stirling, near the Trossachs.

ALLOA
(0259) 722745
An 18 hole parkland course (6230 yards, SSS 70). Visitors of all playing abilities are welcome. Green fees are £7 per round, £12 per day. There are two practice grounds and a snooker room at the club house. Full catering facilities are available. Local attractions include Stirling Castle.
Location
Shawpark, Sauchie, Clackmannanshire FK10 3AX
The course is on the A908 between Alloa and Tillicoultry.

ALVA
(0259) 60431
A 9 hole undulating course (2407 yards, SSS 64). Visitors of all playing abilities are welcome. Green fees on application. There are no catering facilities. Nearby are some lovely walks around Alva Glen.
Location
Beauclerc Street, Alva, Clackmannanshire FK12 5LE
The course is on the A91, 3 miles north of Alloa.

BONNYBRIDGE
(0324) 812645
A testing 9 hole undulating moorland course with tight greens and easy walking (6060 yards, SSS 69). Visitors of all playing abilities are welcome if accompanied by a member. Green fees on application. There is a bar and meals are served although this is limited during the winter. Stirling Castle and Falkirk are both within easy reach.
Location
Larbert Road, Bonnybridge, Stirlingshire
The club is 3 miles west of Falkirk on the B816.

RAC recommended hotel in Falkirk.

BRAEHEAD
(0259) 722078
An 18 hole part parkland, part meadowland course (6013 yards, SSS 69). Visitors who have a handicap certificate are welcome at all times but you should telephone ahead for a starting time. Green fees are £6 flat rate on weekdays and £6 per round, £10 a day at weekends. There are catering facilities at the weekend. Local attractions include Wallace Monument, Stirling Castle and Alva Glen.
Location
Cambus, By Alloa, Clackmannanshire
The club is 1 mile west of Alloa on the A907 Stirling to Alloa road.

BRIDGE OF ALLAN
(0786) 832332
A 9 hole hilly parkland course with good views (4932 yards, SSS 65). Visitors of all playing abilities are welcome on weekdays and Sunday. Green fees are £5 on weekdays and £7 on Sunday. Bar snacks are served at weekends and after 7.30pm on weekdays. Local attractions include Stirling Castle and the Wallace Monument.
Location
Sunlaw, Bridge of Allan, Stirling
Take the road from Stirling and when you reach the bridge over the River Allan, turn up the hill. The golf course is 1 mile from here.

RAC recommended hotel
Royal ★★★ (0786) 832284 A completely modernised, traditional style stone-built hotel situated in the town centre.

DOLLAR
(02594) 2400
A tight 18 hole hillside course (5144 yards, SSS 66). Visitors are welcome on weekdays but only if accompanied by a member at weekends. Green fees on application. Meals are served by arrangement, although there is a bar menu at lunchtime and in the evening. Local places of interest include Castle Campbell.
Location
Brewlands House, Dollar, Clackmannanshire

FALKIRK
(0324) 611061
An 18 hole parkland course (6202 yards, SSS 70) with wooded areas, lots of gorse and a stream running through. There is an old Roman Baths on site. Visitors are welcome on weekdays, before 4pm only, if they are unaccompanied, but at any time if accompanied by a member. There is a large practice area. Green fees are £7 per round, £12 per day. Lunch, bar snacks and high tea served daily. Local attractions include Roman remains.
Location
Stirling Road, Cumlins, Falkirk
The club is 1½ miles west of Falkirk town centre on the A9.

RAC recommended hotel
Stakis Park ★★★ (0324) 28331 A modern purpose-built hotel in the outskirts of the town.

GLENBERVIE
(0324) 562605
An 18 hole parkland course with fine views (6469 yards, SSS 71). Visitors are welcome by introduction only. Green fees are £15 per round or £20 per day. Lunches, high teas and dinners are served. There are two practice areas.
Location
Stirling road, Larbert, Stirlingshire FK5 4SJ
The course is 1 mile north of Larbert on the A9 Falkirk to Stirling Road.

RAC recommended hotel in Falkirk.

GRANGEMOUTH MUNICIPAL
(0324) 714355
A municipal 18 hole parkland course (6314 yards, SSS 71). Visitors who have a handicap certificate are welcome but golf shoes must be worn. Green fees on application. Meals are served with 24 hours notice.
Location
Polmont Hill, Polmont, Falkirk, Stirlingshire
Leave the M9 at junction 4 and follow the signpost at the roundabout to Polmont Hill.

RAC recommended hotel in Polmont.

MUCKHART
(025 981) 423
An 18 hole undulating moorland course (6115 yards, SSS 70). Visitors of all playing abilities are welcome but a telephone call to check availability is advisable at the weekends. Green fees are £6 per round, £10 a day on weekdays and £10 per round, £15 a day at weekends. Lunches are served every day and evening meals by arrangement. Local attractions include Rambling Bridge Gorge.
Location
Drumburn Road, Muckhart, Dollar, Clackmannanshire FK14 7JH
The club lies between the A91 and A823 south of Muckhart, 14 miles east of Stirling. It is signposted off the above roads.

POLMONT
(0324) 711277
A 9 hole hilly parkland course (3044 yards, SSS 69) with views of the River Forth and Ochil Hills. Visitors of all playing abilities are welcome at any time on weekdays and after 4pm on Saturday. Green fees are £3 on weekdays, £4 on Saturday and £5 on Sunday. With a member a round ticket costs £1.50. Full catering facilities are available by

arrangement with the Secretary. Local places of interest include Falkirk, Bathgate and Becraigs Country Park.
Location
Manuelrigg Maddiston, by Falkirk, Stirlingshire
The course is 4 miles south of Falkirk. Take the first right after the Central Region Fire Brigade Headquarters.

RAC recommended hotel
Inchyra Grange ★★★ (0324) 711911 Situated in its own grounds, a sandstone former private mansion with modern extensions. Facilities include indoor swimming pool, sauna, solarium, gymnasium and billiards.

STIRLING
(0786) 64098
An 18 hole hilly parkland course with splendid views (5976 yards, SSS 69). Visitors of all playing abilities are welcome on weekdays. Green fees are £8.50 per round and £12 per day on weekdays. Lunches and high teas are available by arrangement. Local attractions include Stirling Castle, Wallace Monument and the Field of Banockburn.
Location
Queens Road, Stirling FK8 2QY
The course is half a mile west of the town centre on the A811, on the left hand side, 1 mile from the railway and bus stations. .

RAC recommended hotel
Golden Lion ★★★ (0786) 75351 A stone-built hotel of 16th-century origins, situated in the town centre.

TILLICOULTRY
(0259) 50124
A 9 hole undulating meadowland course nestling at the foot of the Ochil Hills (2528 yards, SSS 66). Visitors of all playing abilities are welcome on weekdays and also at the weekend by arrangement. Green fees are £5 on weekdays and £5.50 at weekends. Bar meals are available between April and September and catering for parties by prior arrangement. Stirling Castle and the Wallace Monument are within easy reach.
Location
Alva Road, Tillicoultry FK13 6BL

TULLIALLAN
(0259) 30396
A rather hilly 18 hole parkland course (5982 yards, SSS 69). Visitors of all playing abilities are welcome by arrangement with the Professional. Green fees on application. Meals and snacks are served.
Location
Alloa Road, Kincardine on Forth, By Alloa
The course is $1^1/_2$ miles north of Kincardine Bridge on Alloa Road, next to the Police College.

DUMFRIES

CASTLE DOUGLAS
(0556) 2801
A 9 hole parkland course (5400 yards, SSS 66). Visitors are welcome without reservation except on Thursday after 4pm and on competition days. Green fees on application. There are bar facilities in the evening.
Location
Abercromby Road, Castle Douglas, Kirkcudbrightshire
The course is in the centre of town, 400 yards from the town clock on the Ayr road.

RAC recommended hotels
Douglas Arms ★★ (0556) 2231 Large 200-year-old coaching house in town centre.
Urr Valley C/H ★★ (0556) 2188 Red sandstone country house set amongst rolling hills half a mile off A75.
Imperial ★★ (0556) 2086 Two-storey stone-built hotel in the Scottish style. On main street.

COLVEND
(055663) 398
A particularly attractive undulating 9 hole meadowland course on the Solway coast (2322 yards, SSS 63). Visitors of all abilities, particularly beginners, are welcome. Between April and September the course closes at 4.40pm on Tuesday and 5pm on Thursday. Full lunch and dinner facilities are available between April and October but during the winter months this is restricted to weekends. Local attractions include Sandyhills beach and Sweetheart Abbey.
Location
Sandyhills, By Dalbeattie, Kirkcudbrightshire DG5 4PY
The course is 6 miles from Dalbeattie on the A710 Solway coast road.

DUMFRIES & COUNTY
(0387) 53585
An 18 hole parkland course (5928 yards, SSS 68). There are limited practice facilities. Visitors of all playing abilities are welcome any day except Saturday. Green fees are £11.50 on weekdays and £10 at weekends. There is a restaurant and also a bar where snacks are available. The course is in the heart of Burns Country and other attractions include Caerlaverock Castle, Drumlenorig Castle and Dumfries.
Location
Edinburgh Road, Dumfries DG1 1JX
The club is 1 mile north of Dumfries town centre on the A701 Edinburgh road.

RAC recommended hotel
Cairndale ★★★ (0387) 54111 Red brick Victorian building conveniently situated near town centre.
Hetland Hall ★★★ (0387) 84201 Impressive country house set in fine grounds to south east of Dumfries. Putting, fishing, sauna, solarium, gymnasium, billiards.
Station ★★★ (0387) 54316 A large handsome Victorian stone building of character.
Skyline ★★ (0387) 62416 Small hotel, well situated in town centre.

DUMFRIES & GALLOWAY
(0387) 63582
An 18 hole parkland course (5782 yards, SSS 68). Visitors are welcome without reservation. Green fees are £6.50 on weekdays and £9 at weekends. Full catering facilities are available except on Monday.
Location
Laurieston Av, Dumfries DG2 7NY
The course is on the A75 west of Dumfries.

RAC recommended hotels in Dumfries see Dumfries and County.

KIRKCUDBRIGHT
(0567) 30542
An 18 hole hilly parkland course with hard walking (5598 yards, SSS 67). Visitors are welcome except on competition days. Green fees on application.
Location
Stirling Crescent, Kirkcudbright
Turn left off the A711 onto the B727 in Kirkcudbright and the course is signposted near the centre of town.

RAC recommended hotel
Selkirk Arms ★★ (0557) 30402 A hotel of 18th-century origins. There is a sheltered garden with a spacious lawn.

LANGHOLM
(0541) 80559
A 9 hole hillside course with hard walking (5246 yards, SSS 66). Visitors are welcome on both weekdays and weekends without any reservation. Green fees are £3 per round or day or £1.50 if you are with a member. Catering facilities can be arranged.
Location
Whitaside, Langholm, Dumfrieshire DG13 0JR
The course is between Carlisle and Hawick on the A7. Turn off at the Market Place in the centre of town and the club is about 400 yards from here.

RAC recommended hotel
Eskdale ★★ (038 73) 80357 A three-storey stone-built coaching house set in the town centre.

LOCHMABEN
(0387) 810552
An undulating 9 hole parkland course situated between two lochs (5304 yards, SSS 66). Visitors of all playing abilities are welcome, except on competition days, but players must complete the course by 5pm. Green fees on application. Lunches and snacks are served between noon and 2.30pm and arrangements for meetings can be made. Local attractions include Lochmaben town and Castle.
Location
Castlehill Gate, Lochmaben, Dumfrieshire DG11 1NT

Leave the A74 at Lockerbie for the A709 for Dumfries.

RAC recommended hotel
Balcastle ★★ (0387) 810239 A red sandstone building well-situated in the outskirts of the small town

LOCKERBIE
(05762) 3363
A 9 hole parkland course with some good views (2614 yards, SSS 66). Visitors are welcome on weekdays and also on Sunday between 12 noon and 3pm. Green fees on application. A limited catering service is available by arrangement.
Location
Currie Road, Lockerbie, Dumfrieshire DG11 2ND
Take the A74 to Lockerbie and then turn on to the road to Langholm. Turn left at the T-junction towards Corrie and the club is about half a mile on your right.

RAC recommended hotels
Dryfesdale ★★★ (057 62) 2427 Carefully converted 18th century country house with splendid panoramic views.
Lockerbie House ★★★ (05762) 2610 A beautiful Georgian country house in 78 acres of park and woodland.
Queen's ★★★ (057 62) 2415 Small Victorian mansion in local stone in own pleasant grounds. Indoor swimming pool, putting, fishing, sauna, solarium, gymnasium, billiards.
Somerton House ★★ (057 62) 2583 Red sandstone building at southern edge of town. Close to A74.

MOFFAT
(0683) 20020
A picturesque 18 hole hillside course (5218 yards, SSS 66). Visitors are welcome without introduction although there is restricted play on Wednesday when visitors can only play before 12 noon. Green fees are £5 per round, £7 a day on weekdays and £9 a day at weekends. There is also a small practice area and a putting green. Coffee and lunches are served each day except Thursday.
Location
Coatshill, Moffat DG10 9SB
Leave the A74 at Beattock on the A701 and the club sign is 1 mile on your left.

RAC recommended hotel
Moffat House ★★★ (0683) 20039 A stone-built Georgian manor house in landscaped gardens. The hotel is situated close to the town.
Annandale Arms ★★ (0683) 20013 Family-managed hotel in fine four-storey building in town centre.
Balmoral ★★ (0683) 20288 Distinguished three-storey building of traditional style. Facing wide main street.
Star ★★ (0683) 20156 Interesting listed building-reputedly 'narrowest hotel in Scotland'.

NEW GALLOWAY
(06442) 239
A scenic 9 hole hilly course with fine turf (5058 yards, SSS 65). Visitors are welcome except when there are open competitions. Green fees are £5 a day. Catering facilities are available in the village. The course is beautifully situated on the edge of the Galloway Hills overlooking Loch Ken.
Location
Castle Douglas, Kirkcudbrightshire DG7 3RP
The course is easily located on the way out of the village on the A762.

RAC recommended hotels
Ken Bridge ★ (064 42) 211 An attractive two-storey building on the banks of the river Ken. Facilities include fishing.
Kenmure Arms ★ (064 42) 240 A modernised family-managed hotel in a three-storey stone building with distinctive gables.

NEWTON STEWART
(0671) 2172
A 9 hole parkland course (5500 yards, SSS 67) situated in very pretty countryside in the Galloway hills and with a forest backdrop. Visitors of all playing abilities are welcome at all times. Green fees are £5 on weekdays and £6 at weekends. There are lounge facilities and meals and bar lunches are served all week. Local attractions include the beaches and forest walks.
Location
Kirroughtree Avenue, Minnigaff, Newton, Stewart, Dumfries and Galloway DG8
If you are coming from the South leave the A75 at the sign to Minnigaff village.

RAC recommended hotel
Kirroughtree ★★★★ (0671) 2141 An early 18th-century country house with a distinctive tower. Facilities include putting and tennis.

PORTPATRICK (DUNSKEY)
(077681) 273
A very pretty undulating 18 hole meadowland/seaside course (5644 yards, SSS 67) with natural hazards and situated on a cliff top. Visitors who hold a current handicap certificate are welcome but it is best to book beforehand. No visitors can play on competition days. There is a practice ground. Green fees are £10 per day weekdays, £10 per round at weekends, £45 for a fortnightly ticket and £35 for a weekly ticket. Juniors who are playing with an adult can play for half price. There is also a short 9 hole course which is half the stated prices. Meals are served everyday except Monday. Portpatrick itself is worth visiting.
Location
Portpatrick, Stranraer, Wigtownshire DG9 8TB
Take the A75 or A77 to Stranraer and then the A77 to Portpatrick. Fork right at the War Memorial and 300 yards on the club is signposted.

RAC recommended hotels
Fernhill ★★★ (077 681) 220 Attractive 19th-century building on hill with pleasant sea views.
Mount Stewart ★★ (077 681) 291 Pleasing two-storey building with good view over the harbour.
Portpatrick ★★ (077 681) 333 Large turreted cliff-top hotel dominating north side of harbour. Swimming pool, golf, tennis, billiards.

POWFOOT
(04612) 2866
An 18 hole semi-links course (6266 yards, SSS 70). Visitors of all playing abilities are welcome on weekdays. Green fees on application. Lunches and teas are served by arrangement except on Friday. Local attractions include the 8th century Ruthwell Cross in a local church, and Gretna Green.
Location
Cummertrees, Annan, Dumfrieshire
Take the B724 Annan to Dumfries road and the club is signposted approximately 3 miles from Annan.

RAC recommended hotels in Annan
Queensberry Arms ★★★ (046 12) 2024 Attractive white-painted two-storey hotel set in town centre.
Corner House ★ (046 12) 2754 Town centre hotel with two-storeys over shops. Ornate exterior.

ST MEDAN
(098 87) 358
A 9 hole seaside course with fine views (4454 yards, SSS 62). Visitors are welcome at all times. Green fees are £5 per round per 18 holes, £8 per day. Weekly tickets can be bought for £25. There is a full licence and catering facilities are available between 11am and 11pm daily except Tuesday. Local attractions include Whithorn archaelogical dig, the beaches and Galloway with its hills.
Location
Monreith, Port William, Wigtownshire DG8 8NJ
The course is 3 miles south of Port William on the A747.

RAC recommended hotels
Corsemalzie House ★★★ (098 886) 254 A 19th-century stone-built country mansion set in some magnificent wooded grounds.
Monreith Arms ★★ (098 87) 232 A pleasant stone-built family managed hotel overlooking the harbour.

SANQUHAR
(0659) 50577
A 9 hole parkland course with some good views (2572 yards, SSS 68). Visitors are welcome. Green fees on application. There is a snooker room at the club. Local attractions include the oldest Post Office in Britain, and there is also a salmon river by the course.
Location
Old Barr Road, Sanquhar, Dumfrieshire DG4 6JZ

The course is situated off the A76 Dumfries to Kilmarnock road, a quarter of a mile from Sanquhar.

RAC recommended hotel
Nithsdale ★ (0659) 50506 A small and pleasant family-managed hotel situated on a main street.

SOUTHERNESS
(038 788) 677
A flat 18 hole seaside links course with fine views (6554 yards, SSS 72). The club is the scene of many championship games. A large practice area is available. There are no restrictions on visitors and players of all levels are welcome. Green fees are £10 a day or £40 for a weekly ticket. Full bar and catering facilities are available.
Location
Southerness, Dumfries DG2 8AZ
The club is 16 miles south west of Dumfries off the A710.

RAC recommended hotels
Hetland Hall C/H ★★★ (0387) 84201
Impressive country house set in fine grounds.
Abbey Arms ★ (038 785) 215 A three-storey stone-built hotel in New Abbey. Popular with fishermen.

STRANRAER
(0776) 3539
An 18 hole parkland course (6300 yards, SSS 71). Visitors are welcome. Green fees are £8 per round on weekdays and £10 at weekends; £19 per day on weekdays, £14.50 at weekends. A weekly ticket can be bought for £37.50. There is also a practice ground. There are no catering facilities on Monday. Local attractions include Loch Ryan, Portpatrick and the local beaches.
Location
Crechmore, Stranraer DG9 0LF
Take the A718 from Stranraer towards Leswalt and the golf club is well signposted on the right.

RAC recommended hotels
North West Castle ★★★★ (0776) 4413 A large white Regency building with a sheltered garden. Facilities include an indoor swimming pool, sauna, solarium, billiards and a curling rink.

THORNHILL
(0848) 30546
An 18 hole moorland/parkland course with fine views (6011 yards, SSS 69). Visitors of all playing abilities are welcome. There is a practice ground. Green fees are £8 on weekdays, £10 at weekends and £32 for a week. Full catering facilities are available.
Location
Blacknest, Thornhill, Dumfries
The club is 14 miles north of Dumfries on the A76 to Thornhill village. Once in the village you should turn right at the cross roads and the course is 1 mile on the right.

RAC recommended hotel
Buccleuch & Queensberry ★★ (0848) 30215 An attractive 3-storey Victorian stone-built hotel in the centre of a small town.
Trigony House C/H ★★ (0848) 31211 A two-storey typically Scottish country house in its own secluded grounds. Fishing.
George ★★ (0848) 30326 Refurbished family-run hotel, once a coaching inn, on A76 in the centre of town.

WIGTOWN AND BLADNOCH
(098 84) 3354
A slightly hilly 9 hole parkland course (2732 yards, SSS 67) with splendid views over Wigtown Bay to the Galloway Hills. Visitors of all playing abilities can play at any time and beginners are particularly welcome. Green fees are £4.50 on weekdays and £6.50 on Sunday and Bank Holidays. Juniors can play for half price. Catering facilities are available by arrangement although the bar is open in the evening. Local attractions include the Whithorn Excavations.
Lightlands Avenue, Wigtown, Wigtownshire
Turn right at the town square and then left at Agnew Crescent, 400 yards on the right.

WIGTOWNSHIRE COUNTY
(05813) 420
An 18 hole seaside links course with easy walking (5715 yards, SSS 68). Visitors of all playing abilities are welcome. Green fees are £6 a day on weekdays and £7 at weekends. Catering facilities are available between April and September. There are many local attractions including Glenluce Abbey and lots of Forestry Commission picnic areas.
Location
Mains of Park, Glenluce, Newton Stewart, Wigtownshire DG8 0QN
The course is 8 miles east of Stranraer on the A75, 2 miles west of Glenluce.

RAC recommended hotel in Stranraer.

FIFE

ABERDOUR
(0383) 860256
An 18 hole parkland links course (5469 yards, SSS 67) situated by the Firth of Forth with some lovely views. Visitors of all playing abilities are welcome on weekdays but you should telephone the Professional for a tee reservation. Green fees are £8 per round or £10 per day on weekdays. Full catering facilities are available by arrangement with the Clubmaster except Tuesday.
Location
Seaside Place, Aberdour, Fife KY3 0TX
Travelling from Inverkeithing, turn off the A92 in Aberdour village. The course is by the coastal route to Burntisland.

RAC recommended hotel
Woodside ★★★ (0383) 860328 Traditional style stone-built hotel with unique 'Orient Line' cocktail bar. Sauna.

ANSTRUTHER
(0333) 312055
A 9 hole seaside links course (4120 yards, SSS 63). Visitors of all playing levels are welcome except on competition days. Green fees are £4.50 per day on weekdays and £6 per day at weekends. Juniors can play for £2.50 at all times. There is a lounge bar where snacks are available and also a dining room where lunches are served. Local attractions include the Fishery Museum and Kellie Castle.
Location
Marsfield, Shore Road, Anstruther, Fife KY10 3DZ
Anstruther is 4 miles south of St. Andrews. Turn south of the A917 at the Craw's Nest Hotel.

RAC recommended hotels
Craws Nest ★★★ (0333) 31069 A large pleasant white-painted two storey building on the edge of the town. Facilities include sauna and solarium.
Smugglers Inn ★★ (0333) 310506 A long attractive stone-built former inn with 14th-century origins.

AUCHTERDERRAN
(0592) 721 579
A 9 hole undulating moorland/parkland course (5400 yards, SSS 66). Visitors are welcome at all times. Green fees on application. There are bar facilities.
Location
Woodend Road, Cardenden, Fife KY5 0NH
The course is situated north of Auchterderran High School on the Glenrothes-Cardenden Road.

BURNTISLAND
(0592) 874093
An 18 hole moorland course (yards, SSS 68) with some splendid views over the sea and also of the Forth Bridge from the 10th hole. Visitors with a handicap certificate are welcome but should contact the Professional for a starting time. Green fees on application. Snacks and meals are served.
Location
Dodhead, Burntisland, Fife
The course is on the B923, 1 mile north east of the town centre.

CANMORE
(0383) 724969
An 18 hole undulating parkland course with a stream (5474 yards, SSS 66). Visitors are welcome on weekdays and on Saturday after 4pm. Green fees are £16 per round, £19.50 per day on weekdays and £12 per round at weekends. There is a bar and full catering facilities are available. Local attractions include Pitten Park.
Location
Venturefair Ave, Dunfermline, Fife
The club is 1 mile north of Dunfermline on A823.

RAC recommended hotels in Dunfermline.

CRAIL
(0333) 50278
An 18 hole seaside links/parkland course (5720 yards, SSS 68). Provided you have a handicap certificate, visitors are welcome and there are only restrictions on competition days and members priority times. Green fees are £8 per round, £12 a day on weekdays and £10 per round, £15 a day at weekends. A full catering service is available. Local attractions include Crail Museum, Cambo Adventure Park and some lovely coastal walks.
Location
Balcomie Clubhouse, Fifeness, Crail KY10 3XN
The club is 2 miles east of Crail.

RAC recommended hotel
Craw's Nest ★★★ (0333) 310691 A large pleasant white painted hotel on the edge of town. Facilities include a sauna and solarium.

CUPAR
(0334) 53549
A 9 hole course (5300 yards, SSS 65) situated on the side of a hill with some fine views. Visitors with a handicap certificate are welcome every day except Saturday. Green fees are £5 on weekdays and £6 on Sunday. Juniors can play for £2 on weekdays. There is a bar, and lunch and high tea is served by arrangement. Local attractions include Hilltarvit House.
Location
Hilltarvit, Cupar
The course is three-quarters of a mile south of Cupar, 10 miles from St Andrews, off the A91.

DUNFERMLINE
(0383) 723534
An 18 hole parkland course (6244 yards. SSS 70). Visitors are welcome between Monday and Friday. Green fees are £14 per day or £8.50 per round. Morning coffee, lunches and high teas are served in the historic club house.
Location
Pitfirrane, Crossford, Dunfermline KY12 8QV
Leave the M90 at junction 3 and take the A907 to Dunfermline and then west by the A94 to Crossford. The club is situated 4 miles west of Dunfermline on the road to Kincardine Bridge.

RAC recommended hotels
Keavil House ★★★ (0383) 736258 A mansion house with modern extensions in own grounds.
King Malcolm Thistle ★★★ (0383) 722611 Light two-storey modern purpose-built hotel in outskirts of town.
Pitbauchlie House ★★★ (0383) 722282 Early 20th-century two/three-storey stone-built residence in own grounds. Solarium.
Pitfirrane Arms ★★★ (0383) 736132 A modernised and extended stone-built former coaching inn in the centre of the village.

DUNNIKIER PARK
(0592) 261599
An 18 hole parkland course (6601 yards, SSS 72) with few bunkers and some fine views of the Firth of Forth. Provided you have a handicap certificate, visitors are welcome at any time, although it is advisable to book at weekends. Green fees are £3 per round on weekdays and £4.75 at weekends. Full catering facilities are available.
Location
Dunnikier Way, Kirkcaldy, Fife KY1 3LP

RAC recommended hotels in Kirkcaldy.

ELIE
(0333) 330301
A lovely, reasonably straight, 18 hole seaside links course (6241 yards, SSS 70) with holes reaching as far as the rocky coast and some spectacular views over the Firth of Forth. The course is also famed for its unique periscope by the first tee and is particularly popular with visitors. Visitors are welcome throughout the year. Green fees are £9 per round, £14 per day on weekdays and £12 per round, £18 per day at weekends. Lunches, soups, sandwiches are always available and high teas by arrangement with the Steward. The course is close to the Elie Sports Centre with its leisure facilities and cafeteria. Elie has the added distinction of being the birthplace of James Braid. Local attractions include Falkland Palace (NT), Hill of Tarint, Kellie Castle and East Nuk fishing village.
Location
Golf Club House, Elie, Leven, Fife KY9 1AS
The course is 12 miles from St Andrews on the A915, 6 miles from Leven on the A917.

GLENROTHES
(0592) 754561
A hilly 18 hole wooded parkland course (6449 yards, SSS 71) offering superb views and some interestingly named holes, 'Satan's Gateway' and 'Hell's End'. There are no restrictions on visitors but parties of more than 12 should book in advance through the Secretary. One month's notice is required. Green fees are £8 per round on weekdays and £4.15 at weekends. All types of catering facilities are available. The course is close to Loch Leven Nature Reserve and Falkland Palace.
Location
Golf Course Road, Glenrothes, Fife KY6 2LA
The course is situated at the west end of the town, 8 miles from the M90.

RAC recommended hotels
Albany ★★ (0592) 752292 A purpose-built hotel situated in the town centre.
Balgeddie House C/H ★★★ (0592) 742511 Former mansion on hillside above New Town. Own small grounds. Billiards.

KINGHORN
(0592) 890345
An 18 hole undulating links course (5246 yards, SSS 67) which can be quite testing. The course is situated on high ground with magnificent views over the Firth of Forth and the North Sea. It is a municipal course and visitors are welcome at all times, with parties by arrangement. Green fees are £2.80 on weekdays and £3.75 at weekends. Catering facilities are available by arrangement.
Location
Macduff Crescent, Kinghorn, Fife
The course is off the A92, 3 miles west of Kirkcaldy. There is a bus stop at the course and the railway station is only 3 miles away.

KIRKCALDY
(0592) 260370
An 18 hole wooded parkland course with a stream running through (6004 yards, SSS 70). There is a practice ground. Visitors are welcome at any time except Saturday. Green fees are £6.50 per round or £11 per day on weekdays and £7.50 per round, £15 per day at weekends. Full catering facilities are available daily.
Location
Balwearie Road, Kirkcaldy, Fife KY2 5LT
The course is on the A907 at the west end of the town.

RAC recommended hotels
Dean Park ★★★ (0592) 261635 Stone-built former private mansion with modern extensions; edge of town. Billiards.
Parkway ★★★ (0592) 262143 A modern, purpose-built hotel standing at the road junction in the town.

LADYBANK
(0337) 30814
A very beautiful 18 hole moorland course (6617 yards, SSS 72) with lots of pine and heather. Visitors are welcome at any time except on competition days. Green fees are £15 per round, £22 per day on weekdays and £17 per round, £25 per day at weekends. A full catering service is available. Local places of interest include Falkland Palace.
Location
Annsmuir, Ladybank, Fife KY7 7RA
The club is 6 miles south of Cupar on the main Edinburgh-Dundee road, on the north side of the village.

LESLIE
(0592) 741 449
A testing 9 hole parkland course (4940 yards, SSS 64). Visitors of all playing abilities are welcome at any time. Green fees are £4 on weekdays and £5 at weekends. There are bar facilities. Places of local interest include Falkland Palace.
Location
Balsillie, Leslie, Fife
The course is situated on the A911, west of Glenrothes.

RAC recommended hotel
Rescobie ★★ (0592) 742143 A secluded country

house in 2 acres of gardens.

LEVEN THISTLE
(0333) 26397
An 18 hole seaside links course (6434 yards, SSS 71). This top championship links course has been used for national and international events including the British Open qualifying competition. Visitors are welcome at all times but courtesy times are limited at weekends. Parties should telephone in advance. Green fees are £9.50 per round, £14 per day on weekdays and £12 per round, £16 per day at weekends. Breakfast, lunch, dinner, high tea and bar snacks are served daily. There are also two bars.
Location
Balfourst, Leven, Fife KY8 4HS
You should travel east along the promenade and turn left into Church Road. From there turn right into Links Road and the club house is at the end of the road on the left hand side.

LOCHGELLY
(0592) 80174
A rather windy 18 hole parkland course with easy walking (5491 yards, SSS 67). Visitors are welcome at any times. Green fees on application. Good catering facilities are available.
Location
Cartmore Road, Lochgelly, Fife
The course is on the west side of the town, off the A910.

LUNDIN
(0333) 320202
One of Fife's famous five, this 18 hole seaside links course (6377 yards, SSS 71) lies on a lovely stretch of coastline. It is a fairly short course with Roman stones on one of the fairways and some good coastal views. Visitors with a handicap certificate are welcome any day between Monday and Friday and also on Saturday afternoon after 2.30pm. Catering facilities are available daily except Monday.
Location
Golf Road, Lundin Links, Fife KY8 6BA
The course is 3 miles east of Leven on the A915 Leven-St Andrews road.

RAC recommended hotel
Lundin Links ★★ (0333) 320207 An early 20th-century hotel built in the Tudor style and situated in its own small grounds.

PITREAVIE (DUNFERMLINE)
(0383) 722591
A pretty undulating parkland course (6086 yards, SSS 69) providing a good test of golf and some splendid views of the River Forth Valley. Visitors of all playing abilities are welcome every day but parties should reserve tees through the Professional beforehand. Green fees are £8 per round, £10.50 per day on weekdays and £16 a day at weekends. Full catering facilities are available but again, parties should book in advance. Local attractions include Dunfermline Abbey.
Location
Queensferry Road, Dunfermline, Fife KY11 5PR
From the A90(M) you should turn off for Dunfermline to join the A823. The course is halfway between Rosyth and Dunfermline on the east side of the dual carriageway.

RAC recommended hotels in Dunfermline.

ST ANDREWS
(0334) 75757
There are five courses at this famous club which dates back as early as the mid 1400s. Not only are the courses public but, under a licence drawn up by the Archbishop of St Andrews in 1552, the proprietor of the course was bound 'not to plough up any part of said golf links in all time coming'.
Balgrove Course
A 9 hole seaside course (1754 yards, SSS). This is a beginners course and all visitors are welcome.
St Andrews Eden Course
An 18 hole seaside course (5971 yards, SSS 69). Visitors of all playing abilities are welcome.
St Andrews Jubilee Course
A championship 18 hole seaside course (6284 yards, SSS 70). Visitors of all playing levels are welcome.
St Andrews New Course
An 18 hole seaside course (6604 yards, SSS 72). Visitors are welcome.
St Andrews Old Course
The original 18 hole seaside course with its famous holes such as Hell's Bunker, the Beardies and the Principal's Nose and even more difficult ones like the Road Hole with its difficult drive and the great expanse of fairway as you approach the Valley of Sin (6566 yards, SSS 72). There is also an extensive practice area. Visitors who hold a current handicap certificate and have a letter of introduction are welcome except on Sunday. Bookings should be made well in advance.
There are no catering facilities but plenty of good restaurants and hotels in the vicinity. Green fees for all courses are available on application
Location
St Andrews, Fife KY16 9JA
The club is situated on the A91 to St Andrews.

RAC recommended hotels
Rusack's ★★★★ (0334) 74321 Imposing five-storey stone-built traditional Victorian style hotel in formal gardens. Sauna, solarium.
Rufflets ★★★ (0334) 72594 Two-storey 1920s house in 10 acres of secluded grounds. Putting.
Scores ★★★ (0334) 72451 Seafront hotel conveniently located near to golf course.
St Andrews Golf ★★★ (0334) 72611 Seafront hotel with five views of the beach. Sauna, solarium.
Ardgowan ★★ (0334) 72970 Small family-run hotel conveniently located for golf course.
Parkland ★★ (0334) 73620 Hotel in a late Victorian 'castle' in its own grounds in residential area of town.

ST MICHAELS
(033 483) 365
A particularly attractive 9 hole undulating parkland course (5510 yards, SSS 67) situated in beautiful countryside with plantation surroundings and some lovely views over Fife and Tayside. Players of all levels are welcome at any time except Sunday before 1pm. Green fees are £6 per day on weekdays and £4 per round at weekends. Juniors under 16 may play for half price. There are both bar and lounge facilities where meals are available. Other facilities include changing rooms and showers.
Location
Leuchars, St Andrews, Fife
Turn off the A91 St Andrews-Cupar road on to the A919 to Leuchars. The course is 200 yards out of the village, past the railway bridge to the west.

SALINE
(0383) 852591
A 9 hole undulating moorland course (5302 yards, SSS 66) situated on a hillside with panoramic views of the Forth Valley. Visitors are welcome without any restrictions except on competition days which are held on Saturday. Green fees are £3 on weekdays and £4 on Sunday. There is a bar where snacks are served and full catering facilities are available by arrangement. The historic village of Culross is nearby and Dunfermline town within easy reach.
Location
Kinneddar Hill, Saline, Fife KY12 9UN
The course is approximately $4^1/_2$ miles north west of Dunfermline and is signposted off the A907 Dunfermline-Stirling road.

SCOONIE
(033) 27057
An interesting 18 hole parkland course (4503 yards, SSS 66) which is ideal for 36 hole events. There is also a practice ground. The course is a municipal one and visitors, particularly beginners, are welcome at any time. Green fees on application. Full catering facilities are available. Local attractions include St Andrews, and the 13th-century village of Culross.
Location
North Links, Leven, Fife
The course is about 10 miles south west of St Andrews, about 5 minutes drive from the centre of town.

SCOTSCRAIG
(0382) 552515
A rather tight seaside links course with lots of gorse (6496 yards, SSS 71). Visitors are welcome on weekdays and at weekends by arrangement, although the club prefers you to be a member of a recognised golf club. Green fees on application. Meals are served every day except Tuesday. St Andrews and the Tay Bridge are both attractive nearby places to visit.
Location
Golf Road, Tayport, Fife DD6 9DZ
From the B946 3 miles east of the south end of the Tay road bridge, turn left into the third street past the petrol station.

THORNTON
(0592) 771111
A difficult 18 hole flat parkland course (6177 yards, SSS 69) with the River Ore presenting some challenging holes. Visitors of all playing abilities are welcome at any time. Green fees on application. Lunch, snacks and high tea are served every day. There are some lovely picnic areas in Glenrothes.
Location
Station Road, Thornton, Fife KY1 4DW
The course is in the centre of the village of Thornton, about 1 mile east of the A92.

RAC recommended hotels in Glenrothes.

GRAMPIAN

ABOYNE
(03398) 86328
An 18 hole undulating parkland course with some lovely views (5330 yards, SSS 66). Visitors of all playing abilities are welcome. There is a practice ground. Green fees on application. Full catering facilities are available between April and October.
Location
Formaston Park, Aboyne, Aberdeenshire AB3 5HD
Travelling west on the A93 from Aberdeen, take the first turning on your right after entering the village. The club is signposted on the A93.

AUCHENBLAE
(056 12) 407
A 9 hole parkland course (2174 yards, SSS 30). Visitors are welcome but there are some restrictions on Wednesday and Friday, competition nights for members. Green fees are £2.50 a day on weekdays and £3 at weekends. There is a local shop which sells snacks.
Location
Auchenblae, Laurencekirk, Kincardineshire AB3 1JT
The course is 5 miles north of Laurencekirk, 2 miles west of Fordoun.

AUCHMILL
(0224) 714577
A 9 hole course (2538 metres, SSS 35). The course is a municipal one and visitors are welcome at all times. Green fees are £2.30 during the summer and £1.55 during the winter.
Location
Auchmill, Aberdeen

RAC recommended hotels
Bucksburn Moat House ★★★★ (0224) 713911

Based on a converted 17th-century grain mill 2 miles from airport. Indoor swimming pool.
Caledonian Thistle ★★★★ (0224) 640233 A traditional city-centre hotel refurbished to high standard. Sauna, solarium.
Copthorne ★★★★ (0224) 630404 Traditional stone building, completely redesigned internally into a smart modern hotel, in business part of city.
Skean Dhu ★★★★ (0224) 877000 Purpose-built, five-storey hotel just outside city. Swimming pool.
Ardoe House C/H ★★★ (0224) 867355 Scottish Baronial mansion set in wooded grounds in the lovely Dee Valley, 4 miles west of Aberdeen on B9077. Putting.
Dyce Skean Dhu ★★★ (0224) 723101 Modern, purpose-built hotel conveniently situated for city centre. Squash, sauna, solarium, gymnasium.
Stakis Tree Tops ★★★ (0224) 313377 Long modern villa-type building in attractive wooded grounds. Indoor swimming pool, tennis, sauna, solarium, gymnasium.
Westhill ★★★ (0224) 740388 Purpose-built hotel beside a shopping centre close to main A944 about 7 miles west of city. Sauna, solarium.
Ferryhill House ★★ (0224) 590867 In residential area of city, stone-built, two-storey villa with small grounds.
Imperial ★★ (0224) 589101 Traditional city-centre hotel 100 yards from station.

BALLATER
(03397) 55567
A flat 18 hole inland course with some spectacular scenery (5704 yards, SSS 67). Visitors of all playing abilities are welcome. Green fees are £10 a day on weekdays and £12 a day at weekends. Full catering facilities are available between 1 April and 15 October. Balmoral Castle is close by.
Location
Ballater, Aberdeenshire AB3 5QX
The club is situated 40 miles west of Aberdeen on the A93 on Deeside.

RAC recommended hotels
Craigendarroch ★★★★ (033 97) 55858 A Victorian house with modern extension situated in 29 acres of woodlands, overlooking the river Dee. Facilities include an indoor swimming pool, tennis, fishing, squash, sauna, solarium and gymnasium and billiards.
Darroch Learg ★★★ (033 97) 55443 Scottish style granite-built hotel on hillside enjoying fine views.
Glen Lui ★★★ (033 97) 55402 Much extended house quietly situated and with lovely views over golf course to the hills beyond.
Invercauld Arms ★★ (033 97) 55417 This hotel which stands on the edge of a village is a pleasant three-storey stone building.

BANCHORY
(03302) 2365
An 18 hole parkland course situated in a sheltered position surrounded by woodland (5305 yards, SSS 66). Visitors of all playing abilities are welcome. Green fees on application. There is a lounge bar and a full catering service. Local attractions include Balmoral, Crathes Castle and Drum Castle.
Location
Kinneskie, Banchory, Kincardineshire AB3 3TA
The course is 18 miles west of Aberdeen on N Deeside. 100 yards southwest of Banchory town centre.

RAC recommended hotels
Invery House ★★★★ (03302) 4782 An attractive well-modernised mansion, set in wooded grounds. Facilities include putting, tennis, fishing and billiards
Banchory Lodge ★★★ (03302) 2625 A lovely riverside mansion. Facilities include fishing, sauna and billiards.
Raemoir C/H ★★★ (033 02) 4884 Elegant Georgian stone-built mansion in quiet attractive grounds. Tennis, golf, sauna, solarium, gymnasium.
Tor-na-Coille ★★ (033 02) 2242 Fine granite-built Victorian residence on hillside on edge of town. Squash.
Burnett Arms ★★ (033 02) 4944 Traditional stone-built hotel standing on main street in town centre.

BALNAGASK
(0224) 876407
An undulating 18 hole seaside links course (5468 yards, SSS 70). The course is a municipal one and visitors are welcome. The Nigg Bay Club plays here. Green fees are £4.60 during the summer months and £3.10 in winter.
Location
St Fitticks Road, Aberdeen
The course is 2 miles south east of the city centre.

RAC recommended hotels in Aberdeen see Auchmill.

BON-ACCORD
(0224) 633464
An 18 hole coastal links course (6384 yards, SSS 70). The course is a municipal one and visitors of all levels are welcome. Green fees are £4.20 per round during the summer, Juniors can play before 5pm for £2.35 and £2.80 per round, Juniors before 5pm £1.70 during the winter. Catering facilities are available by arrangement with the Steward. The course is near the beach and there is an open carnival.
Location
19 Golf Road, Aberdeen AB2 1QB
The course is beside Pittodrie Stadium near the beach.

RAC recommended hotels in Aberdeen see Auchmill.

BRAEMAR
(03397) 41618
An 18 hole parkland/moorland course situated in beautiful countryside in Royal Deeside (4916

yards, SSS 64). Visitors of all playing abilities are welcome. Green fees are £6 a day, £5 a round on weekdays and £8 a day, £6 a round at weekends. Full catering facilities are available every day except Tuesday and Wednesday. Local attractions include the Royal Lochmagar Distillery and Braemar Castle.
Location
Cluniebank, Braemar, Aberdeenshire AB3 5XX
The course is signposted within easy walking distance of the village, approximately half a mile from the village centre.

BUCKPOOL
(0542) 32236
A rather windy 18-hole seaside links course overlooking the Moray Firth (6259 yards, SSS 70). Visitors are welcome and parties by arrangement. Green fees are £4 a day on weekdays and £6 a day at weekends. Catering facilities are available at weekends and also at other times by arrangement.
Location
Barhill Road, Buckie, Banffshire AB5 1DU
Leave the A98 towards Buckpool. The course is at the end of the road.

RAC recommended hotel
Cluny ★★ (0542) 32922 A three-storey stone-built town centre hotel in town square.

CALEDONIAN
(0224) 632443
An 18 hole municipal course situated on land which was given to the people by Robert Bruce (6384 yards, SSS 70). Visitors of all playing abilities are welcome. Green fees on application. Snacks are available on request.
Location
20 Golf Road, Aberdeen
The course is adjacent to Pittodrie Stadium.

RAC recommended hotels in Aberdeen see Auchmill.

CRUDEN BAY
(0779) 812285
A good 9 hole seaside links course (4710 yards, SSS 62) and an 18 hole course (6370 yards, SSS 71). Visitors are welcome but not on competition days before 3.30pm. There are also some restrictions at weekends so it is best to check beforehand. Green fees are £12 a day on weekdays and £15 a day at weekends. There is a bar and full restaurant facilities. Local attractions include Slains and Buller Buchan.
Location
Aulton Road, Cruden Bay, Peterhead, Aberdeenshire AB4 7NN
The course is 7 miles S of Peterhead, 23 miles north of Aberdeen on the coastal route.

RAC recommended hotel in Peterhead.

CULLEN
(0542) 40585
An 18 hole seaside course laid out on two levels with lots of rocks and ravines (4610 yards, SSS 62). Visitors of all playing abilities are welcome. Green fees are £4.50 on weekdays and £5 at weekends. Lunches are served between May and September.
Location
The Links, Cullen, Buckie, Banffshire
The course is 200 yards from the A98 on the west side of Cullen.

RAC recommended hotels
Seafield Arms ★★★ (0542) 40791 An early 19th-century stone-built former coaching inn on the main street.
Cullen Bay ★★ (0542) 40472 Long, two-storey hillside building over main road, fine sea views.

DEESIDE
(0224) 867697
An 18 hole parkland course (5972 yards, SSS 69). There is also a new 9 hole course (6632 yards, SSS 72). Visitors are welcome with a handicap certificate, or if a member of a recognised golf club, with a letter of introduciton from the Secretary. Green fees are £12 a day on weekdays and £15 a day at weekends and Bank Holidays. Full catering facilities are available. Local attractions include lots of castles and Aberdeen itself.
Location
Bieldside, Aberdeen
The course is 3 miles west of Aberdeen on the A93 North Deeside road.

RAC recommended hotels in Aberdeen see Auchmill.

DUFF HOUSE ROYAL
(02612) 2062
A flat 18 hole parkland course with two tiers bordered by woodlands and the River Deveron (6161 yards, SSS 69). Visitors are welcome without introduction at all times, although a handicap certificate is preferred. Tee times are restricted at weekends and during July and August. Green fees are £6.50 per round, £9 per day on weekdays and £9 per round, £11 per day at weekends. There is a lounge and full catering facilities are available between March and October. There are lots of fishing villages close by .
Location
Barnyards, Banff, Banffshire AB4 3SX
The course is two minutes from the town centre off the A97 and A98.

RAC recommended hotel
Banff Springs ★★★ (02612) 2126 A modern two-storey hotel on a hillside on the edge of town.

ELGIN
(0343) 54238
An 18 hole undulating moorland/parkland course laid out on sandy subsoil (6401 yards, SSS 71). The course is one of the best inland courses in the north of Scotland and accuracy is demanded on its fine greens. Visitors of all playing abilities are welcome after 9.30am on weekdays and 10am at weekends. Green fees are £7 per round, £12 a day on weekdays and £9 per round, £14 a day at weekends. Full catering facilities are available every day except Tuesday and Thursday afternoon. Full bar facilities are available daily. Local attractions include Brodie Castle (NT), Spinney Castle (NT) and Elgin Cathedral.
Location
Hardhillock, Elgin, Morayshire IV30 3SX
From the centre of Elgin take the A941 Rothes road to the south side of New Elgin, and then turn left on to Birnie road for 1 mile to the clubhouse. Turn off the A941 where it is indicated to the golf course.

RAC recommended hotel
Eight Acres ★★★ (0343) 543077 A modern purpose-built hotel on the outskirts of town. Facilities include an indoor swimming pool, squash, sauna, solarium, gymnasium and billiards.
St Leonards ★★ (0343) 543077 Modern purpose-built hotel on outskirts of town.

FORRES
(0309) 72949
An 18 hole undulating parkland course (9615 yards, SSS 69) surrounded by wooded countryside. There are some testing holes, including the 16th which plays over a pond but the walking is relatively easy. There is also a practice ground and a putting green. Visitors who have a handicap certificate are welcome. Green fees are £8 a day or £6 per round. Bar snacks are normally available and meals by arrangement.
Location
Muiryshade, Forres IV36 0RD
The club is 1 mile south from the clock tower in the town centre, by St Leonards Road and Edgehill Road.

RAC recommended hotels
Park ★★ (0309) 72328 A Victorian-style stone-built former mansion in small grounds.
Ramnee ★★ (0309) 72410 A former private villa in small grounds in the outskirts of Forres.

FRASERBURGH
(0346) 28287
A challenging 18 hole undulating seaside links course (6217 yards, SSS 70). Visitors of all playing abilities are welcome without any restrictions. There is also a practice area. Green fees are £7 on weekdays and £10 at weekends. Bar lunches are available daily and evening meals can be arranged. Local attractions include Aden Park.
Location
Philorth, Fraserburgh, Abderdeenshire AB4 5TL
The course is 1 mile south east of Fraserburgh on the A92 Fraserburgh to Abderdeen road. You should turn right off the road to Cairnbulg.

RAC recommended hotel
Alexandra ★★ (0346) 28249 A traditional style

late Victorian granite-built hotel, situated in the town centre. Facilities include sauna.

GARMOUTH AND KINGSTON
(034 387) 388
An 18 hole seaside course (5649 yards, SSS 67). Visitors of all playing abilities are welcome. Green fees are £4 per round, £6 a day. Catering facilities are available by arrangement with the Secretary. Other club facilities include snooker and fishing. There are some lovely forest walks and Elgin Cathedral is nearby.
Location
Garmouth, Fochabers, Moray IV32 7LU

RAC recommended hotel
Gorden Arms ★★ (0343) 820508 A stone-built former coaching inn, fronting on to the main street.

HAZELHEAD
(0224) 321830
There are two 18 hole treelined moorland courses here (5303 yards, SSS 68 and 5673 yards, SSS 70). The course is municipal and all visitors are welcome. Green fees are £4.20 per 18 holes, £2.10 per 9 holes. Winter and Junior rates are available on application.
Location
Hazelhead Park, Aberdeen
The club is 4 miles west of the city centre.

RAC recommended hotels in Aberdeen see Auchmill.

HOPEMAN
(0343) 830578
An 18 hole seaside links course with a spectacular 12th hole (5439 yards, SSS 66). Visitors of all playing abilities are welcome at all times. Green fees are £5 on weekdays and £7 at weekends. Snacks and bar facilities are available. Moray is a seaside resort and ideal for a holiday.
Location
Hopeman, Moray IV30 2SS

HUNTLY
(0466) 2643
An 18 hole parkland course situated between the River Bogie and River Deveron (5399 yards, SSS 66). Provided you have a handicap certificate visitors are welcome every day except Wednesday and Thursday. Green fees are £6 a day on weekdays and £8 per day at weekends. You can buy a weekly ticket for £20. Full catering facilities are available by arrangement. Aberdeen is 38 miles away.
Location
Cooper Park, Huntly, Aberdeenshire
The course is on the A96, half a mile from the town centre,

RAC recommended hotel
Castle ★★ (0466) 2696 A stone-built mansion, sitauted in 5 acres of hillside, there are some fine views. Facilities include putting and fishing.

INVERALLOCHY
(03465) 2324
A windy 18 hole seaside links course with some splendid views of the North Sea from the tee (5137 yards, SSS 65). Visitors are welcome at all times. Green fees are £3 a day. There are limited catering facilities available.
Location
Inverallochy, Nr Fraserburgh, Aberdeenshire
The course is 3 miles south of Fraserburgh, on the east side of the village, on the B9033.

RAC recommended hotels in Fraserburgh.

INVERURIE
(0467) 24080
A wooded 18 hole parkland course (5096 yards, SSS 65). Visitors of all playing abilities are welcome but booking prior to arrival is advisable (0467) 20193. Green fees are £6 a day on weekdays and £8 at weekends. Full catering facilities are available daily. Local attractions include Fyfe Castle, Craigiebar Castle and Benahay.
Location
Blackhall Road, Inverurie, Aberdeenshire
The club is on the A96 Aberdeen to Inverness road.

RAC recommended hotels
Strathburn ★★★ (0467) 24422 Modern purpose-built hotel overlooking park at west end of town.
Gordon Arms ★★ (0467) 20314 A three-storey stone-built hotel in traditional market-town style, situated in the town centre.

KEITH
(05422) 2469
An undulating 18 hole parkland course with natural hazards (5811 yards, SSS 68). Visitors are welcome. Green fees on application. Catering facilities are available by arrangement.
Location
Fife Park, Keith, Banffshire
The course is situated half a mile off the A96 Keith to Dufftown road.

KINTORE
(0467) 32631
A 9 hole undulating moorland course (2650 yards, SSS 66). The course is open to visitors daily except Monday, Wednesday and Friday after 4pm and players of all abilities are welcome. Green fees are £5 a day on weekdays and £6 at weekends. Catering facilities are available by booking in advance. There is salmon and trout fishing available very near to the course.
Location
Balbithan Road, Kintore, Inverurie, Aberdeenshire
Leave the A96 as you reach the centre of Kintore, 12 miles north west of Abderdeen.

MACDONALD
(0358) 20576
A flat 18 hole parkland course with trees, stream and pond (5986 yards, SSS 69). There is also a practice putting green and two practice nets. Visitors are welcome. Green fees are £3 on weekdays and at weekends. Full catering facilities are available daily.
Location
Hospital Road, Ellon, Aberdeenshire AB4 9AW
Leave Ellon by the A948 Auchnagatt road and take the first turning on your left.

RAC recommended hotel
New Inn ★ (0358) 20425 An historic small inn set in the market place.

MORAY
(034 381) 2081
There are actually two fine links courses here, the Old Course (6643 yards, SSS 72) and the New Course (6005 yards, SSS 69) situated on the Moray Firth where the weather is normally quite mild. Provided they have a handicap certificate, visitors are welcome at all times. Green fees are £7 per round, £10 a day for the Old Course and £6 per round, £8 a day for the New Course. Full catering facilities are available during the summer months and also at weekends from October to March. Local attractions include the Whisky Trail.
Location
Stotfield Road, Lossiemouth, Moray IV31 6QS
From Elgin take the A96 Aberdeen to Inverness road and then continue onto the A941 Elgin to Lossiemouth road. The course is 6 miles north of Elgin.

MURCAR
(0224) 704354
An 18 hole seaside course with some hard walking (6240 yards, SSS 70). Visitors are welcome on weekdays. Green fees are £7 per round before 11.30am and £12 a day on weekdays. Snacks, lunches and dinners are served.
Location
Bridge of Don, Aberdeen AB2 8BD
The course is 3 miles north east of Aberdeen on the A92.

NEWBURGH-ON-YTHAN
A 9 hole seaside links course (6404 yards, SSS 71). Visitors are welcome everyday except Tuesday after 4pm, between May and September. Green fees on application. There are no catering facilities. There is a bird sanctuary adjacent to the course.
Location
Newburgh, Aberdeenshire AB4 0AW
The club is 14 miles north of Aberdeen on the Peterhead road. As you enter the village of Newburgh turn right at Ythan Hotel.

RAC recommended hotel
Udny Arms ★★ (035 86) 89444 Situated at the roadside in the centre of the village, a three-storey stone-built 19th-century hotel. Facilities include golf and fishing.

NIGG BAY
(0224) 871286
An 18 hole seaside course with hard walking (5984 yards, SSS 69). Visitors are welcome at all times. Green fees are £4.80 per round. There is a leisure centre in Abderdeen.
Location
St Fitticks Road, Balnagask, Aberdeen
The course is south east of the city centre.

RAC recommended hotels in Aberdeen see Auchmill.

NORTHERN
(0224) 632269
An 18 hole seaside course with hard walking (5838 metres, SSS 71). As the course is a municipal one, visitors are welcome at all times. Green fees on application. Catering facilities are available at weekends and by arrangement during the week.
Location
Golf Road, Kings Links, Aberdeen
The course is east of the city centre, off Beach Esplanade, near Pittodrie Stadium.

RAC recommended hotels in Aberdeen see Auchmill.

PETERHEAD
(0779) 72149
An 18 hole seaside links course (6182 yards, SSS 70) and also a children's 9 hole course (2950 yards, SSS 60). Visitors are welcome at any time. Green fees are £6.50 on weekdays and £10.50 at weekends. Catering facilities are available by prior arrangement with the Steward. There is a fishing trail close to the club.
Location
Craigewan Links, Peterhead, Aberdeenshire AB4 6LT
The course is between the A92 and A975, 30 miles north of Aberdeen.

RAC recommended hotel
Waterside Inn ★★★ (0779) 71121 A modern two-storey building with an unusual slate roof, situated on the main road on the northside of the town. Facilities include indoor swimming pool, sauna, solarium, gymnasium and snooker.

ROYAL ABERDEEN
(0224) 702571
Two championship 18 hole links courses with easy walking (4033 yards, SSS 60, and 6372 yards, SSS 71). Provided they have a handicap certificate, visitors are welcome. Green fees are £20 per day, £16 per round on weekdays. Full catering facilities are available daily. Aberdeen is within easy reach.
Location
Balgownie, Bridge of Don, Aberdeen AB2 8AT
Take the A92 2 miles north of Aberdeen and cross the River Don. Turn right at the first set of traffic lights and continue along Links Road to the course.

RAC recommended hotels in Aberdeen see Auchmill

ROYAL TARLAIR
(0261) 32897
An 18 hole undulating seaside course (5866 yards, SSS 68). Visitors are welcome at any time. Green fees are £7 a day on weekdays and £8 a day at weekends. Catering facilities are available every day and at weekends. Local attractions include Pennancrove, an old fishing village, Old Duff House and there are also some splendid beaches nearby.
Location
Buchan St, Macduff AB4 1TA
The course is on the A98, 48 miles from Aberdeen.

RAC recommended hotel
Highland Haven ★★ (0261) 32408 A four-storey stone-built hotel with first-floor sun lounge, overlooking the harbour and the sea. Facilities include sauna, solarium, gymnasium and billiards.

SPEY BAY
(0343) 820424
An 18 hole seaside links course with fine views (6059 yards, SSS 68). Visitors who have a handicap certificate are welcome at all times. Green fees on application. Meals are served at the club. A further attraction is the local castle trail.
Location
Spey Bay, Fochabers, Moray
Turn off the A96 Fochabers road near Fochabers Bridge and continue to follow the B9104 Spey Bay road as far as the coast.

RAC recommended hotels
Gordon Arms ★★ (0343) 820508 Stone-built former coaching inn in main street.

STONEHAVEN
(0569) 62124
A testing 18 hole seaside/parkland course with three gullies (5103 yards, SSS 65). Provided they have a handicap certificate, visitors are welcome except on Saturday and Sunday morning. Green fees are £7 on weekdays and £8.50 at weekends. Full catering facilities are available including bar lunches. The course overlooks the sea and has wonderful views. There is a leisure centre at Stonehaven.
Location
Cowie, Stonehaven AB3 2RH
Take the A92 1 mile north of the town to the new roundabout at the Commodore Hotel. From there take the second exit on your left and pass the Leisure Centre on your right.

RAC recommended hotel
Commodore ★★★ (0569) 62936 A modern purpose-built hotel standing at the roadside on the edge of town.

STRATHLENE
(0542) 31798
A rather windy undulating 18 hole moorland/ seaside course with lovely views (6180 yards, SSS 69). Visitors are welcome. Green fees are £5 on weekdays and £6 at weekends. Catering facilities are available by arrangement. Local attractions include Spey Walk.
Location
Portessie, Buckie, Banffshire AB5 2DJ
Take the A942 from the main Banff to Inverness Road to Buckie and take the signposted turning to Strathlene.

RAC recommended hotel in Buckie.

TARLAN
(033981) 81413
A difficult 9 hole undulating wooded parkland course with easy walking (5812 yards, SSS 68). There are no restrictions on visitors but telephone first to check whether there are club competitions being held. There is a small practice ground. Green fees are £4 on weekdays and £6 at weekends. Catering facilities are available by arrangement.
Location
Tarlan, Aboyne, Aberdeenshire AB3 4YL
The club is on the A93, 31 miles west of Aberdeen and 11 miles north east of Ballater.

TORPHINS
(033982) 493
A 9 hole undulating heathland course situated on a hill top with views of the Grampians and Cairngorms (2330 yards, SSS 63). Visitors can play at any time except during competitions. Green fees are £4 a day on weekdays and £5 at weekends. Snacks are served daily.
Location
Golf Road, Torphins, Banchory, Abderdeenshire AB3 4JT
The club is 6 miles west from Banchory on the A980.

TURRIFF
(0888) 62745
A picturesque 18 hole meadowland/parkland course (6105 yards, SSS 69). Visitors are welcome and societies by arrangement with the Secretary. Green fees are £6 per round, £9 per day on weekdays and £9 per round, £11 per day at weekends. Catering facilities are available by arrangement. Local attractions include Den Park and local boating.
Location
Rosehall, Turriff, Aberdeenshire AB5 7H
The course is on the Aberdeen side of the town, about 1 mile up Huntly Road on the B9024. It is signposted.

WESTHILL
(0224) 740159
An 18 hole undulating parkland/moorland course (5866 yards. SSS 69). Visitors who have a handicap certificate are welcome except between 4.30pm and 7pm on Sunday, and Saturday after 3.30pm. Green fees are £6 per round, £8 per day on weekdays and £7 per round, £9 per day at weekends and Bank Holidays. Full catering facilities are available by arrangement. Aberdeen is within easy access.
Location
Westhill Heights, Westhill, Skene, Aberdeenshire AB3 6TY
The club is 6 miles from Aberdeen on the A944 Aberdeen to Alford road. The course is on the north side overlooking the town.

HIGHLAND

ABERNETHY
(0479 82) 305
A particularly attractive 9 hole undulating course (2484 yards, SSS 66). Visitors of all playing levels are welcome. Green fees on application. Meals are served every day. Families with children are particularly welcome. Local attractions include the osprey hide at Loch Garten.
Location
Nethybridge, Inverness-shire
The course is on the B970 Grantown on Spey–Coylumbridge road, a quarter of a mile north of Nethybridge.

RAC recommended hotel
Nethybridge ★★★ (047982) 203 A large traditional Victorian hotel situated in the heart of Spey valley. Facilities include billiards.

ALNESS
(0349) 883877
A short but challenging 9 holes with splendid views over the Moray Firth (4718 yards, SSS 63). Visitors of all playing abilities, including beginners, are welcome at any time. Green fees are £3 on weekdays and £4 at weekends. OAPs can play for £2 and Juniors for £1.25 on weekdays and OAPs £3 and Juniors £1.50 at weekends. There is a licensed bar where snacks are served. Local attractions include the Monument at the top of Fireish and pony trekking. Inverness is within easy access.
Location
Ardross Road, Alness, Ross-Shire
The course is situated on the A9, ten miles north east of Dingwall.

ASKERNISH
A 9 hole course (5114 yards, SSS 67) close to the Atlantic. Visitors are welcome at all times. Green fees on application.
Location
Askernish, Lochboisdale, South Uist, Western Isles
Take the ferry from Oban to South Uist. The course is 5 miles north west of Lochboisdale.

RAC recommended hotel
Lochboisdale ★★ (08784) 332 A traditional highland hotel overlooking a harbour, a popular area for fishing and ornithology. Facilities include fishing and billiards.

BOAT OF GARTEN
(0479 83) 282
An 18 hole undulating woodland course (5720 yards, SSS 68). Visitors of all playing levels are welcome, although the course is not really suitable for complete beginners. Green fees are £8 on weekdays and £10 at weekends when booking is necessary. Full catering facilities are available all day. Local attractions include an Osprey hide near Loch Garten, Strathspey private railway and River Spey salmon fishing.
Location
Boat to Garten, Inverness-shire Ph24 3BQ
Take the old A9 road 5 miles north of Aviemore and turn right on to the B970.

RAC recommended hotel
The Boat ★★★ (047983) 258 A substantial stone-built fully modernised hotel. Facilities include fishing.

BRORA
(0408) 21417
An 18 hole seaside links course with fine views (6110 yards, SSS 69). Visitors are welcome at any time but there may be restrictions on tournament days. Green fees are £6 per round, £25 per week, £35 per fortnight, £40 per 3 weeks and £45 per month. Catering facilities are available during June, July and August and by request for parties.
Location
Golf Road, Brora, Sutherland KW9 6QS
The course is approximately 65 miles north of Inverness on the A9. There is a signpost in the middle of the village giving directions.

RAC recommended hotels
Links ★★★ (0408) 21225 A modernised hotel overlooking the sandy beach, with some particularly attractive rooms.
Royal Marine ★★★ (04080) 21252 A former stately house situated in its own grounds close to the golf course. Facilities include indoor swimming pool, putting, fishing, sauna and billiards.

CARRBRIDGE
(047984) 674
A 9 hole parkland/moorland course (2623 yards, SSS 66). Visitors are welcome except when there is a tournament (usually in September). Green fees on application.
Location
Carrbridge, Inverness-shire PH23 3AU
The course is about 200 yards from the village on the A938.

RAC recommmended hotel
Fairwinds (Acclaimed) (047 984) 240.

FORT AUGUSTUS
(0320) 6460
A 9 hole moorland course with narrow fairways and lovely views (5454 yards, SSS 68). Visitors are welcome and tickets are available at the clubhouse. There are minimum restrictions. Green fees are £4

on weekdays and £6 at weekends. A weekly ticket can be bought for £15. Self-catering facilities are available.
Location
Markethill, Fort Augustus, Inverness-shire
The entrance to the course is off the A82, just beyond the 30mph restriction south of the village.

RAC recommended hotels
Lovat Arms ★★★ (0320) 6206 A family-run traditional hotel with large rooms. Facilities include putting.
Inchnacardoch Lodge ★★ (0320) 6258 19th-century hunting lodge charmingly set in elevated position.

FORTROSE AND ROSEMARKIE
(0381) 20529
An 18 hole seaside course (5973 yards, SSS 69) with sea on three sides. It is a good links course suitable as a holiday course with easy walking and a testing 4th hole. Visitors of all playing abilities, including beginners, are welcome. Green fees are £7.50 a day on weekdays and £8 per round, £12 a day at weekends. Bar snacks are available all year round. Local attractions include Groam House Museum, Inverness and Dingwall.
Location
Ness Road East, Fortrose, Ross-Shire IV10 8SE
Fortrose is about 16 miles north of Inverness on the Black Isle. Take the A9 north from Inverness, across Kessock Bridge, through Munlochy and follow the signs to Fortrose.

FORT WILLIAM
(0397) 4464
An 18 hole moorland course (5686 metres, SSS 71). Visitors are welcome at any time. Green fees are under review. The club has a full licence and bar snacks are served.
Location
North Road, Torlundy, Fort William PH33 6RD
The club is situated off the A82 Fort William to Inverness road, 2 miles north of Fort William.

RAC recommended hotels
Inverlochy Castle ★★★★ (0397) 2177 Impressive Victorian building now a luxury hotel. In 500 acres of grounds stretching down to River Lochy. Tennis, billiards.
Mercury Motor Inn ★★★ (0397) 3117 Modern custom-built motel overlooking Loch to south of the town. Sauna, billiards.
Croit Anna ★★ (0397) 2268 Large family-owned tourist hotel, built on an original Highland Croft.
Grand ★★ (0397) 2928 Fully modernised three-storey 20th-century building conveniently set in the town centre.
Nevis Bank ★★ (0397) 5721 White-painted hotel close to Ben Nevis foothills. Sauna, solarium, gymnasium.

GAIRLOCH
(0445) 2407
A fine 9 hole seaside links course situated alongside Gairloch Sands with extensive views to Skye (2093 yards, SSS 63). Visitors are welcome from Monday to Saturday but there is no golf on Sunday. Green fees are £5 per day, £3 per round or £20 for a weekly ticket. Gairloch Museum is worth visiting.
Location
Gairloch, Ross-Shire IV21 2BE
The course is on the A832, south of the town.

RAC recommended hotels
Creag Mor ★★★ (0445) 2068 Modern two-storey hotel, recently extended, in elevated position with views over harbour.
Old Inn ★★ (0445) 2006 Modernised 19th-century hotel situated in own grounds beside harbour.

GOLSPIE
(04083) 3266
An 18 hole links/heathland/seaside/meadowland course (5900 yards, SSS 68) with natural hazards including beach heather. Visitors of all playing abilities can play at any time. Green fees are £8 per day, £40 per week and £55 per fortnight. A practice area is available. There is a licensed restaurant and bar snacks are available between May and September. Local attractions include Dunrobin Castle.
Location
Ferry Road, Golspie, Sutherland
Take the first right in Golspie off the A9 from Inverness.

RAC recommended hotel
Golf Links ★★ (04083) 3408 A small stone-built hotel, convenient for the beach and the golf course. Facilities include putting.
Sutherland Arms ★★ (040 83) 3234 Reputedly oldest inn in Sutherland, pleasantly modernised.

GRANTOWN-ON-SPEY
(0479) 2079
An 18 hole moorland, parkland and woodland course with easy walking (5745 yards, SSS 67). The location is an ideal holiday spot and visitors are welcome at anytime. Green fees are £6 on weekdays and £7 at weekends. Morning coffee, lunches and high teas are served daily. Local attractions include a Whisky Trail
Location
Golf Course Road, Grantown-on-Spey
Leave the A9 at Aviemore and continue along the A939 to Grantown. The course is situated at the north end of the town.

RAC recommended hotel
Garth ★★★ (0479) 2836 A privately owned stone-built house with modern extensions.
Seafield Lodge ★★ (0479) 2152 In quiet street, two-storey stone-built Edwardian former private house.

INVERGORDON
(0349) 852116
An easy 9 hole parkland course with good greens but which can be windy (6028 yards, SSS 69). There are some good views. Visitors are welcome at any time, but Ladies competitions are held on Monday and Wednesday evenings and Men's competitions on Tuesday and Thursday evenings and all day Saturday. Green fees are £3 on weekdays, £3.50 at weekends. Under 18's can play for 50p on weekdays and £1.50 at weekends. The club house is situated 1 mile from the course, close to the centre of town. Bar lunches are served on Saturday.
Location
Cromlet Drive, Invergordon, Ross and Cromarty IV18 0EU
The club house is in King George Street and the course at Invergordon.

INVERNESS
(0463) 239882
A flat 18 hole parkland course with a stream crossing (6226 yards, SSS 70). Visitors who have a handicap certificate are welcome although there are restrictions on Saturday. There are two practice grounds. Green fees are £9 per round, £12 a day on weekdays and £10 per round, £15 a day at weekends. Sandwiches, lunches, high teas and dinners are served all week except Thursday between May and September. Inverness Castle is nearby.
Location
Culcabock Road, Inverness IV2 3XQ
The course is situated 1 mile from the town centre on the south side of the River Ness.

RAC recommended hotels
Bunchrew House C/H ★★★ (0436) 234917 Restored 17th-century house with turrets and gables set in 15 acres of grounds on shores of Beauly Forth, west of town.
Caledonian ★★★ (0463) 235181 A large modern town centre hotel catering for tourists and businessmen alike. Facilities include a swimming pool, sauna, solarium, gymnasium and billiards.
Kingsmills ★★★ (0463) 237166 A modernised hotel beside the golf course on the south side of town. Facilities include an indoor swimming pool, putting, sauna, solarium and gymnasium.
Mercury ★★★ (0463) 239666 Large modern custom-built hotel, conveniently situated to east of town.
Palace ★★★ (0463) 223243 Modernised hotel in terraced property on riverside near town centre.
Station ★★★ (0463) 231926 Large Victorian building with ornate stairway. Centrally situated near station.
Cumming's ★★ (0463) 232531 Stone-built terrace building conveniently situated for rail and coach terminals.
Drumossie ★★ (0463) 236451 Busy tourist hotel in elevated position overlooking Moray Firth.
Glen Mhor ★★ (0463) 234308 19th-century mansion on banks of River Ness; convenient for town centre.
Lochardil ★★ (0463) 235995 Castellated Victorian building with impressive staircase set in 5

acres of grounds on south side of town.
Loch Ness House ★★ (0463) 231248 19th-century mansion alongside A82.
Muirtown ★★ (0463) 234860 Small purpose-built chalet motel situated in the outskirts of town.

KINGUSSIE
(054 02) 600
An 18 hole hill type course (5504 yards, SSS 67). Visitors can play unrestricted at all times. Green fees are £6.50 per round, £8.50 a day on weekdays and weekends. Catering facilities can be arranged. Local attractions include Spey Valley.
Location
Gynack Road, Kingussie, Inverness-shire PH21 1LR
Leave the A9 at the north end of the village and drive into the village. Turn right at the Duke of Gordon Hotel and continue to the end of the road. The club is signposted.

LYBSTER
An attractive 9 hole moorland course with easy walking (1898 yards, SSS 62). The course is one of the smallest in Scotland. Visitors are welcome on a 'pay before play in the money box provided' basis. Green fees on application. There are no catering facilities but plenty in the village.
Location
Main Street, Lybster, Caithness KW1 6BL
The club is 13 miles south of Wick on the A9. Turn down the village main street and the golf course entrance is opposite the football pitch.

MUIR OF ORD
(0463) 870825
A well-established 18 hole moorland/parkland course (5129 yards, SSS 65) with tight fairways and easy walking. There are some testing holes. Visitors are welcome without restrictions. Green fees are £7 on weekdays, £8 at weekends, Juniors £2, and £26 for a weekly ticket. Snacks and bar lunches are available every day and full meals at the weekend. Inverness is within easy reach.
Location
Great Northern Road, Muir of Ord, Ross and Cromarty IV6 7SX
The club is situated 12 miles north of Inverness on the A862.

RAC recommended hotel
Ord Arms ★★ Red sandstone mansion, much extended over the years, beside the A862. Billiards.

NAIRN
(0667) 53208
A championship 18-hole seaside links course (6556 yards, SSS 71). Visitors who have a handicap certificate are welcome. Green fees on application. Catering facilities can be arranged. Local attractions include Brodie Castle and Cawder Castle.
Location
Seabank Road, Nairn IV12 4HB
The course is situated 1 mile north of the A96. When you are just west of Nairn, turn off onto Seabank Road at the church.

RAC recommended hotels
Carnach House ★★ (0667) 52094 Attractive mansion in 8 acres of wooded grounds overlooking Moray Firth, 2 miles west of town.
Windsor ★★★ (0667) 53108 A stone-built hotel which was formerly three houses which have now been modernised and linked together. Facilities include riding.
Alton Burn ★★ (0667) 52051 A stone-built hotel with extensions situated on the edge of town. Facilities include a swimming pool, putting, tennis and riding.
Newton ★★★ (0667) 53144 A splendid stone-built mansion in extensive grounds. Facilities include sauna, solarium, tennis and putting

NAIRN DUNBAR
(0667) 52741
An 18 hole seaside links course with good sea views but which can be breezy particularly at the 6th, 7th and 8th holes (6431 yards, SSS 71). Visitors are welcome at all times. Green fees are £9 on weekdays and £11 at weekends. Catering facilities are available. Interesting places to visit include Fort George.
Location
Lochloy Road, Nairn IV12 5AE
The course is situated on the southern shore of the Moray Firth, on the A96, about half a mile east of the town. It is 15 miles east of Inverness and 5 miles from Inverness Airport.

NEWTONMORE
(05403) 328
A lovely 18 hole moorland/parkland course with easy walking (5890 yards, SSS 68) situated close to the River Spey. There are some fine views. Visitors are welcome at all times. Green fees are £7 on weekdays and £28 for a weekly ticket. Meals and snacks are served daily. The club is close to the Wild Life Park.
Location
Golf Course Road, Newtonmore, Inverness-shire PH20 1AP
Leave the A9 when you are 2 miles south of Newtonmore and the road to the golf course is in the centre of the village, 150 yards away.

RAC recommended hotels
Mains ★★ (05403) 206 A substantial stone-built hotel in the main street of the town. The hotel is family-owned.
Weigh Inn ★★ (054 03) 203 Two-storey stone-built hotel in centre of village. Billiards.

REAY
(084 781) 288
A pretty 18-hole undulating seaside course with natural hazards and which has the distinction of being the farthest north mainland seaside course (5865 yards, SSS 68). Visitors can play at any time provided there are no competitions being held. Green fees are £5 a day or £18 for a weekly ticket. Juniors can play for half price.
Location
By Thurso, Caithness KE14 7RE
The course is 11 miles west of Thurso towards Bettyhill.

ROYAL DORNOCH
(0862) 810219
A challenging 18 hole seaside course (6577 yards, SSS 72). Visitors who have a handicap certificate are welcome on weekdays and at weekends, although tee reservations should be made in advance. Green fees are £20 per day, £15 per round on weekdays and £20 per day at weekends. A weekly ticket can be bought for £70. Full catering facilities are available every day except Monday when they are limited. Other club facilities include tennis, fishing and riding. Local attractions include Dornoch Castle and Dunrobin Castle.
Location
Golf Road, Dornoch, Sutherland IV25 3LW
Take the A9 from Inverness and then the A949 for Dornoch. The club is signposted in the town.

RAC recommended hotels
Royal Golf ★★★ (0862) 810283 A stone-built tourist hotel situated beside the golf course. Facilities include golf, putting, solarium.
Burghfield House ★★ (0862) 810212 A traditional Victorian turreted mansion house in a peaceful situation. Facilities include putting, fishing.
Dornoch Castle ★★ (0862) 810216 A fine 450-year-old castle in the centre of a tourist and golfing town.

SCONSER
(0478) 2277
A 9 hole links course (4796 yards, SSS 63). Visitors are welcome at all times. Green fees are £4 per round, £6 per day on weekdays and £12 for a weekly ticket.
Location
Sconser, Isle of Skye, Inverness-shire
The club is situated between Broadford and Portree on the main road.

STORNOWAY
(0851) 2240
A scenic 18 hole parkland/moorland course with tree-lined fairways (5119 yards, SSS 66). The 11th hole, the 'Dardanelles', is the most difficult par 5 in Europe. Visitors with a handicap certificate are welcome Monday to Saturday; there is no golf on Sunday. Green fees are £10 per day or £5 per round. A weekly ticket can be bought for £25 and a fortnightly ticket for £30. Catering facilities are available by arrangement. Local attractions include the Callanish Stones, the lovely local beaches and the Isle of Lewis itself.
Location
Castle Grounds, Stornoway, Isle of Lewis PA87 0XP
The course is 5 minutes walk from the town centre, just within the main entrance to the castle grounds.

RAC recommended hotel
Royal ★ (0851) 2109 Terrace building on main street near town centre and busy harbour.

STRATHPEFFER SPA
(0997) 21219
An 18 hole undulating upland course (4792 yards, SSS 65) with hard walking and panoramic views of the moorland and mountains. There are no bunkers but plenty of natural hazards including a testing hole across a loch. There is a small practice area. Visitors of all playing abilities are welcome without reservation. Green fees are £5 per round and £7 per day. A weekly ticket can be bought for £20. The club is licensed and meals and snacks are available every day except Monday. Local attractions include the Victorian Spa.
Location
Strathpeffer, Ross-Shire IV14 9AS
The club is about 5 miles west of Dingwall on the A834 and a quarter of a mile north of the village.

RAC recommended hotels
Highland ★★ (0997) 21457 A large modernised, tourist-orientated hotel.
Holly Lodge ★★ (0997) 21254 A small family run Victorian hotel situated in its own pleasant grounds.
Mackay's ★★ (0997) 21542 Substantial three-storey hotel set back from main street in town centre.

TAIN
(0862) 2314
An 18-hole parkland links course (6222 yards, SSS 70/68) with a river running through which affects 3 holes, easy walking and some good views. Visitors of all playing abilities are welcome. Green fees on application. Catering facilities are available by arrangement with the Club Steward. Tain Museum and the Glen Morangie Distillery are both worth visiting.
Location
Tain, Ross-Shire IV19 1PA
Take the A9 north and turn right in the middle of the High Street. The club is approximately half a mile from the town centre.

RAC recommended hotels
Mansfield ★★★ (0862) 2052 A turreted building situated in its own well kept grounds.
Morangie House ★★★ (0862) 2281 A sympathetically modernised Victorian mansion in spacious grounds on the north side of town.

Royal ★★★ (0862) 2013 A large privately owned hotel on a corner site in the centre of town.

TARBAT
(086287) 236
An easy 9 hole seaside links course with splendid views (2329 yards, SSS 63). Visitors are welcome every day except Sunday. Green fees are £2. There are no catering facilities.
Location
Portmahomack, Ross-Shire IV20 1YQ
The course is situated on the B9165 off the A9, about 7 miles east of Tain.

THURSO
(0847) 63807
A flat 18 hole parkland course with wonderful views of Pentland Firth and the Orkneys (5818 yards, SSS 69). The course is a municipal one and there are no restrictions on visitors. Green fees are £4 per day. Catering facilities are available on Tuesday and Thursday evening and lunch is served on Saturday and Sunday during the summer season.
Location
Newlands of Geise, Thurso, Caithness
The club is 2 miles south west of Thurso station on the B870.

RAC recommended hotels
Pentland ★★ (0847) 63202 A family-owned modernised stone and tile faced building on a corner site.
Royal ★★ (0847) 63191 Large privately owned hotel, within a terrace building, in town centre. Billiards.
St Clair ★★ (0847) 66481 A family-owned substantial stone built hotel in the main street of the town centre.

TORVEAN
(0463) 237543
An 18 hole flat parkland course (4308 yards, SSS 62). The club is a municipal one and visitors are always welcome although prior booking is preferred. There is a practice area and putting green. Green fees on application. There are limited catering facilities.
Location
Glenurquhart Road, Inverness, Inverness-shire
The club is on the A82 towards Fort William, 1 mile west of the city centre, on the west side of the Caledonian Canal.

RAC recommended hotels in Inverness.

WICK
(0955) 2726
A windy 18-hole seaside links course with easy walking (5976 yards, SSS 69). Visitors are welcome, subject to club and open competitions. Green fees are £8 a day.
Location
Reiss, Wick, Caithness KW1 4RW
The course is 2½ miles north of Wick on the A9. You should turn right at the signpost and from there it is three quarters of a mile to the clubhouse.

RAC recommended hotel
Mackays ★★ (0955) 2323 A purpose-built substantial Victorian hotel conveniently situated near the town centre.

ORKNEY
(0856) 2457
An easy 18 hole parkland course (5406 yards, SSS 68) with some hazards. There are fine views over Kirkwall and the islands. Visitors of all playing abilities are welcome at all times. Green fees are £4 per day and £15 per week. There are no catering facilities but there is a bar which is open in the evenings during the summer months.
Location
Grainbank, St Ola, by Kirkwall, Orkney
The club is situated half a mile west of Kirkwall.

SHETLAND
(059584) 369
A challenging 18 hole undulating moorland course (5776 yards, SSS 70) with hard walking. This is the most northerly course in Britain. A burn runs through the course providing a natural hazard and the greens are excellent. Visitors, including Juniors, are welcome at all times. Green fees on application. Bar snacks are available.
Location
Dale, P.O Box 18, Lerwick, Shetland
The course is 3 miles north of Lerwick on the main road.

RAC recommended hotels
Shetland ★★★ (0595) 5515 Modern three-storey building with stone-faced buttresses. Overlooks harbour and bay. Indoor swimming pool, sauna, solarium, gymnasium.
Grand ★★ (0595) 2826 A prominent building on a main street in the centre of town. There is hotel accommodation on the first and second floors.
Queens ★★ (0595) 2826 A substantial stone-built hotel on the waters edge by the harbour.

STROMNESS
(0856) 850772
A testing 18 hole seaside links course (4600 yards, SSS 64) with easy walking. This is a beautiful holiday course with wonderful views of Scapa Flow. Visitors with a handicap certificate are welcome on any day. Green fees are £4 per day. There are no catering facilities but there is a bar. Local attractions include Skara Brae.
Location
Ness, Stromness, Orkney K16 3DU
The course is adjacent to the Point of Ness in the southern extremity of Stromness.

RAC recommended hotel
Stromness ★★ (0856) 850298 A large stone-built privately owned hotel in the town centre overlooking the harbour.

LOTHIAN

BABERTON
031-453 4911
An 18 hole parkland course (6098 yards, SSS 69). Visitors of all playing abilities are welcome on introduction by a member. Green fees on application. Full catering facilities are available.
Location
Baberton Avenue, Juniper Green, Edinburgh EH14 3DU
The club is situated on the Lanark road, 5 miles west of Edinburgh.

BATHGATE
(0506) 630505
An 18 hole parkland course with easy walking (6328 yards, SSS 70). Visitors of all playing abilities are welcome except on competition days. Green fees are £9 on weekdays and £12 at weekends. Coffee, lunch and high tea are served. The city of Edinburgh provides many attractions.
Location
Edinburgh Road, Bathgate, West Lothian EH48 1BA
The course is 400 yards east of George Square, towards Edinburgh town centre.

RAC recommended hotel
Golden Circle ★★★ (0506) 53771 A modern purpose-built hotel, situated near Edinburgh, on the Glasgow road.

BRAIDHILLS NO 1
031-447 6666
A flattish 18 hole municipal heathland course with fine views of Edinburgh and the Firth of Forth (1st 9 holes, 2490 metres, 2nd 9 holes, 2749 metres, SSS 70).
Braidhills No 2 A municipal 2 x 8 hole course (1st 9 holes, 1998 metres, 2nd 9 holes 2422 metres, SSS 65). Visitors are welcome at all times during the winter and between 7pm and 10pm in the summer. Green fees are £3.50 for adults and £1 for Juniors, OAPs and UB40s before 5pm, and £2 at weekends and after 5pm on weekdays.
Location
The course is at Braid Hills on the south side of Edinburgh

RAC recommended hotel
Braid Hills ★★★ 031-447 8888 A Victorian hotel on hillside in the residential outskirts of the city, with some fine views.

BRAIDS UNITED
031-447 3327
Two 18 hole hillside courses, (5731 yards, SSS 68) and (4832 yards, SSS 64). Visitors can play unrestricted. Green fees are £3 per round. There are no catering facilities.
Location
22 Braids Hill Approach, Edinburgh EH10
The course is at Braid Hills, on the south side of Edinburgh.

BROOMIEKNOWE
031-663 9317
A gently undulating 18 hole parkland course with easy walking (6046 yards, SSS 69). The course is laid out on high ground with magnificent views. Visitors are welcome on weekdays. Green fees on application. Bar lunches are always available and evening meals by arrangement with the Steward.
Location
36 Golf Course Road, Bonnyrigg, Midlothian EH19 2HZ
The club is situated on the south side of Edinburgh on the A6094 from Dalkeith. Take the Bonnyrigg road at Eskbank (Dalkeith) roundabout and the club is about 1 mile from here.

BRUNTSFIELD LINKS
031-336 1479
An 18 hole parkland course (6407 yards, SSS 71) with some testing holes and fine views of the Forth Estuary. Visitors who have a handicap certificate are welcome on weekdays by appointment. Green fees on application. Lunches are served every day and evening meals during the playing season. The course is close to the centre of Edinburgh with all its amenities.
Location
32 Barton Avenue, Davidsons Main's, Edinburgh EH4 6JH
Take the A90 to Davidson's Mains, about 2-3 miles west of Edinburgh city centre.

RAC recommended hotel
Barnton Thistle ★★★ 031-339 1144 A Victorian hotel with modern bedrooms, situated at the crossroads on the outskirts of the city. Facilities include sauna.

CARRICKVALE
031-337 1932
A flat 18 hole meadowvale course particularly suitable for beginners (6299 yards, SSS 70). Visitors who hold a current handicap certificate are welcome. Green fees on application. Catering facilities are available by arrangement.
Location
Glendevon Park, Edinburgh EH12 5VZ
The course is situated opposite the Post House Hotel, down Balgreen Road.

CRAIGMILLAR PARK
031-667 2837
An 18 hole parkland course with fine views (5846 yards, SSS 68). Visitors are welcome but unless introduced by a member they must produce a current handicap certificate, a letter of introduction or proof of a club membership. Visitors must be off the first tee by 3.30pm on weekdays and cannot play at weekends or Bank Holidays. Green fees are £8 per round, £12 per day. Bar lunch and high tea

are served on request. The club is within easy reach of Edinburgh's amenities.

Location

1 Observatory Road, Edinburgh EH9 3HG
The club is approximately 3 miles from the city centre, close to the Royal Observatory at Blackford Hill.

RAC recommended hotel

Iona ★★ 031-447 5050 A stone-built Georgian-style former private residence with modern extensions.

DALMAHOY
031-333 1845

There are two upland courses here, one a championship course, The East, 18 holes (6664 yards, SSS 72) and The West, 18 holes (5121 yards, SSS 66). There is also an extensive practice area. Visitors are welcome every day. Green fees on application. Full catering facilities are available

Location

Dalmahoy, Kirknewton, Midlothian EH27 8EB
The course is on the A71, 7 miles west of Edinburgh, 3 miles from the ring road.

DUDDINGSTON
031-661 7688 4301

An undulating 18 hole semi-seaside parkland course with a burn, some testing holes and easy walking (6647 yards, SSS 72). The course can be windy. Visitors who have a handicap certificate are welcome on weekdays. Green fees are £10.50 per round, £17.50 per day. There is a bar and a restaurant where lunch and high tea are served.

Location

Duddingston Road, Edinburgh EH15 3QD
The course is situated adjacent to the A1, Willowbrae Road. east of the city centre.

RAC recommended hotels in Edinburgh.

Caledonian ★★★★★ 031-225 2433 Large, elegant, luxury hotel of six-storeys in prime position at west end of Princes Street.
Edinburgh Sheraton ★★★★★ 031-229 9131 Opposite the Usher Hall, a custom-built modern seven-storey luxury hotel. Indoor swimming pool, sauna, solarium, gymnasium.
Carlton Highland ★★★★ 031-556 7277 Large and impressive hotel conveniently near station. Indoor swimming pool, squash, sauna, solarium, gymnasium, billiards.
George ★★★★ 031-225 1251 Modernised, impressive city centre hotel with Georgian facade. Spacious public areas.
Hilton International ★★★★ 031-332 2545 Modern, purpose-built luxury hotel on a beautiful woodland riverbank.
Royal Scot ★★★★ 031-334 9191 Large, modern, luxurious hotel on outskirts of city. Indoor swimming pool, putting, sauna, solarium, gymnasium.
Scandic Crown ★★★★ Stone-built hotel designed to blend with the historic buildings of the old town.
Sheraton ★★★★ 031-229 9131 Modern hotel designed to blend with its historic surroundings.
Albany ★★★ 031-556 0397 Handsome terraced houses converted to hotel on fringe of elegant New Town area.
Barnton Thistle ★★★ 031-339 1144 Victorian hotel with modern bedrooms. At crossroads in outskirts. Sauna.
Braid Hills ★★★ 9310447 8888 Victorian hotel on hillside in residential outskirts of city.
Capital ★★★ 031-334 3391 Modern hotel on outskirts of city, towards airport. Leisure complex.
Crest ★★★ 031-332 2442 Large, light, modern purpose-built hotel on main road into city.
Ellersly House ★★★ 031-337 6888 Early 20th-century house in own small grounds in residential suburbs.
King James Thistle ★★★ 031-556 0111 Modern, city centre hotel. Convenient for sightseeing and shopping.
Mount Royal ★★★ 031-225 7161 Large, Victorian hotel, greatly modernised. Fine aspect on Princes Street.
Old Waverley ★★★ 031-556 4648 A large, five-storey stone-built hotel above shops in Princes Street.
Post House ★★★ 031-334 0390 Pleasing five-storey concrete modern hotel with good views to countryside.
Roxburghe ★★★ 031-225 3921 Handsome, four-storey, stone-built hotel in an Adam square.
Clarndon ★★ 031-337 7033 Attractive, converted terraced houses in row of similar buildings.
Hailes ★★ 031-442 3382 Modern two-storey hotel adjoining high rise suburban shopping complex.
Harp ★★ 031-334 8235 Modernised and extended village inn on main road in city suburb.
Iona ★★ 031-447 5050 Three-storey, stone-built Georgian-style former private residence with modern extensions.
Lady Nairne ★★ 931-661 3396 Two-storey, grey stone building set back from road in pleasant gardens.

Murrayfield ★★ 031-337 1844 Stone-built Edwardian-style former private residence with later extension.
Royal Ettrick ★★ 031-228 6413 Two-storey sandstone villa in quiet residential area.

DUNBAR
(0368) 62317
One of Scotland's oldest 18 hole links course with a burn and strong sea wind (6426 yards, SSS 71). Visitors of all abilities are welcome. Green fees are £12 per day on weekdays, and £20 at weekends and Bank Holidays. Full catering facilities are available. Local attractions include John Muir Country Park, some lovely cliff top walks and the harbour.
Location
East Links, Dunbar EH42 1LT
The course is half a mile from Dunbar centre on the sea side of the town.

RAC recommended hotels
Bayswell ★★ (0368) 62225 Victorian resort hotel on cliff-top on town outskirts. Fine sea views.
Redheugh ★★ (03698) 62793 Victorian building in red sandstone situated in a quiet area of the town.

GIFFORD
(062 081) 267
A 9 hole meadowland/woodland course (5613 metres, SSS 69). Visitors of all playing abilities are welcome except on Tuesday and Wednesday from 4pm or Saturday and Sunday from midday. The club is closed on the first Sunday of every month. Green fees are £5 daily. There are no catering facilities.
Location
c/o Sec Calroust, Tweeddale Avenue, Gifford EH41 42N
The course is 4½ miles south of Haddington off the A6137.

GLEN
(0620) 2221
An 18 hole seaside parkland course with superb views (6098 yards, SSS 69). There is a practice area on course and a practice putting green at the club house. Visitors of all playing abilities are welcome at any time. Green fees are £6.25 per round on weekdays and £9 per round at weekends. There is a bar where lunch is served and also high tea and coffee. Local attractions include Tantallon Castle and Dorleton Castle.
Location
Tantallon Terrace, North Berwick, East Lothian EH39 4LE
The course is approximately 22 miles north east of Edinburgh on the A198. Follow the road along East Beach and the club house is the last building on the right. It is opposite Bass Rock and only 1 mile from the station.

RAC recommended hotels in North Berwick.

GLENCORSE
(0968) 77189
A very attractive 18 hole parkland course with a burn affecting 10 holes (5205 yards, SSS 66). Provided they have a handicap certificate, visitors are welcome. Green fees are £8 per round, £12 per day on weekdays, and £12 per round at weekends. There is a bar and lunch and high tea are served. Local attractions include the Chapel in Rosaline and the crystal factory in Penicuik.
Location
Milton Bridge, Penicuik, Midlothian EH26 0RD
The club is on the A701, 9 miles south of Edinburgh on Peebles road.

GREENBURN
(0501) 70292
An 18 hole moorland course (6210 yards, SSS 70). Provided they have a handicap certificate, visitors are welcome weekdays but booking is necessary at weekends. Green fees are £6 per round, £9 per day on weekdays, and £7 per round, £10.50 per day at weekends. Local attractions include Fauldhouse and Edinburgh.
Location
Fauldhouse, West Lothian EH47 9HG
The course is midway between Glasgow and Edinburgh. Turn off the M8 at Whitburn and continue for 3 miles.

GULLANE
(0620) 842255
Three lovely links courses situated in a delightful village (No 1 (6466 yards, SSS 71); No 2 (6127 yards, SSS 70); and No 3 (5128 yards, SSS 65). No 1 is a championship course and is unusual in that it is quite a hilly downland course. The first tee is actually in the village and the views from the course are quite wonderful. Visitors have a handicap certificate are welcome on all courses between Monday and Friday and on course Nos 2 and 3 at all times. Lunch is served every day except Monday and other meals are provided by arrangement. Local attractions include North Berwick and Edinburgh.
Location
Gullane, East Lothian EH31 2BB
The course is situated off the A1 on the A198 to Gullane.

RAC recommended hotels
Greywalls ★★★ (0620) 842114 Situated beside the Muirfield Golf Course, Lutyens house in a lovely Jekyll garden. Facilities include putting, tennis.
Queen's ★★ (0620) 842275 A large 18th-century stone-built mansion situated in the centre of the village. Facilities include putting.

HADDINGTON
(062 082) 3627
An 18 hole parkland course with bush and tree-lined fairways (6280 yards, SSS 70). Visitors of all playing abilities are welcome between Monday and Friday at any time and between 10am and midday, and 2pm and 4pm on Saturday and Sunday. Green fees are £6.65 per round, £9.90 per day on weekdays and £8 per round, £11.50 per day at weekends. There is a bar where snacks and meals are served and full lunch and high tea are also available. The course is 12 miles from the River Forth and there are many lovely walks in the vicinity.
Location
Amisfield Park, Haddington, East Lothian
The course is 17 miles east of Edinburgh on the A1. Cross Victoria Bridge on the east edge of the town and the golf course is 500 yards on the left.

HARBURN
(0506) 871256
A reasonably flat 18 hole parkland course (5843 yards, SSS 68). There is also a practice net and ground. Visitors are welcome at all times without prior notice. Green fees are £6 per round, £8.50 per day on weekdays, and £7.50 per round, £10 per day at weekends. Bar snacks are normally available and full catering facilities by arrangement.
Location
West Calder, West Lothian EH55 8RS
The course is 2 miles south of West Calder. Turn south off the A70 Lanark to Edinburgh road to West Calder.

HONOURABLE COMPANY OF EDINBURGH GOLFERS
(0620) 842123
A difficult 18 hole championship links course situated on the coast (6601 yards, SSS 73). Visitors with a handicap of 18 or better (gentleman), or 24 (ladies), who are members of a recognised golf club, are welcome to play on Tuesday, Thursday and Friday morning but book in advance. Green fees are £35 per round or £50 per day. There is a self service dining room where morning coffee, lunch and afternoon tea are available. The area is particularly good for golf and Berwick is within easy reach.
Location
Muirfield, Gullane, East Lothian EH31 2EG
Leave Gullane for North Berwick on the A198, turn down the last road on your left.

RAC recommended hotels in Gullane.

KILSPINDIE
(087 57) 358
A short, tight 18 hole seaside course with plenty of bunkers (5410 yards, SSS 66). Subject to members' demands, visitors are welcome but it is advisable to enquire in advance. Green fees on application. Full catering facilities are available.
Location
Aberlady, East Lothian EH32 0QD
The course is situated on the south bank of the Forth estuary. Immediately east of Aberlady village, take the private road to the left. This leads to the club.

RAC recommended hotel
Kilspindie House ★★ (087 57) 682 A two-storey stone-built hotel in a picturesque village. An interesting 'golf addicts' bar.

KINGSKNOWE
031-441 4030
A hilly 18 hole parkland course (5979 yards, SSS 69). There is also a practice area. Visitors are welcome on weekdays although the club does prefer you to hold a current handicap certificate. Green fees are £7.50 per round, £10 per day on weekdays and £10 per round at weekends. Lunch and high tea are served every day except Monday. Other club facilities include snooker. The club is very convenient for Edinburgh city centre.
Location
326 Lanark Road, Edinburgh EH14 2JD
The course is west of Edinburgh on the A71 and the No 44 bus goes straight there from Edinburgh city centre.

RAC recommended hotels see Duddingston.

LIBERTON
031-664 8580
An undulating 18 hole wooded parkland course (5299 yards, SSS 66). Provided they have a handicap certificate, visitors are welcome at any time except after 5pm on Monday, Wednesday and Friday. Green fees on application. Full catering facilities are available. The course is close to Edinburgh city centre.
Location
297 Gilmerton Road, Edinburgh EH16 5JU
The club is south of Edinburgh on the A7. There is a visitor's car park and Nos 3 and 8 buses go to the Lodge Gate from Edinburgh.

LINLITHGOW
(0506) 842585
An 18 hole undulating parkland course (5858 yards, SSS 68) with wooded areas. It is set in lovely surroundings with panoramic views. There is also a small practice ground and net. Visitors of all playing abilities are welcome except on Wednesday and Saturday. Green fees are £6 per round, £8.50 per day on weekdays, and £7.50 per round, £10 per day on Sunday. Full catering facilities are available. Local attractions include Linlithgow Palace, Mary Queen of Scot's birthplace, Edinburgh and Stirling.
Location
Braehead, Linlithgow, West Lothian EH49 6QF
Take the M9 from Edinburgh and the course is south west of Linlithgow, about 20 miles from Edinburgh. Take the left fork at the west end of Linlithgow.

LIVINGSTON
(0506) 38843
An 18 hole meadowland course (6636 yards, SSS 72). Visitors are welcome at any time. Green fees are £7 per round, £10 per day on weekdays, and

£12 per round, £16 per day at weekends. Meals are served. The course is part of the Country Club and other facilities include swimming pool, sauna, steam room, jacuzzi, 10-pin bowling, snooker, multi-gym and squash courts.

Location

Carmondean, Livingston, West Lothian EH54 8PG
Leave the M8 at Livingston interchange and follow the signposts to Knightsridge. The club is signposted from here.

LONGNIDDRY
(0875) 52141

A fairly testing 18 hole parkland/seaside course (6210 yards, SSS 70). Visitors of all playing abilities are welcome except on competition days and Bank Holidays. It is, however, advisable to telephone in advance. Green fees on application. There is a dining room which is open daily except on Friday, and a bar which serves soup and sandwiches. Local attractions include North Berwick, Tantallon Castle and Dirleton Castle.

Location

Links Road, Longniddry, East Lothian EH32 0NL

RAC recommended hotels

Kilspindie House ★★ (08757) 682 A stone-built hotel with an interesting 'golf addicts' bar, situated in a picturesque village.

Marine ★★★ (0620) 2406 A large sandstone-built Victorian style hotel with extensions overlooking the sea. Facilities include swimming pool, putting, tennis, squash, sauna solarium and billiards.

LOTHIANBURN
031-445 2206

A hilly 18 hole course with 'T'-shaped wooded areas situated at the foot of the Pentland Hills. Sheep provide natural hazards on the course. There are two practice areas. Visitors of all playing abilities are welcome on weekdays. Green fees are £6 per round, £8 per day on weekdays and £7.50 per round, £10 per day at weekends and Bank Holidays. There is a bar where meals are served and lunch and high tea are also available. The course is very convenient for Edinburgh city centre.

Location

106 Bigger Road, Edinburgh EH10 7DU
The course is on the A702 just off the ring road at the south ring road.

LUFFNESS NEW
(0620) 843114

An undulating 18 hole links course (6122 yards, SSS 69). Visitors with a current handicap certificate are welcome on introduction by a member or by arrangement. Green fees on application. Lunch, high tea and dinner are served every day except Mondays. The course is close to Edinburgh city centre.

Location

Aberlady, East Lothian EH32 0QA
The course is just east of Edinburgh. Follow the A198 trunk road along the coast. The club lies between Aberlady and Gullane.

RAC recommended hotels in Gullane.

MERCHANTS OF EDINBURGH
031-447 219

A challenging 18 hole hilly parkland course (4889 yards, SSS 65). Visitors must be introduced by a member, but parties may apply in writing to the Secretary for a reservation. Green fees are £4.50 per round on weekdays and £6.50 per round at weekends. Other club facilities include snooker. Meals are available most days if ordered in advance. Local attractions include Edinburgh Castle, Holyrood House and Edinburgh itself with its famous festival.

Location

10 Craighill Gardens, Edinburgh EH10 5PY
The course is on the south side of Edinburgh off the A701.

RAC recommended hotels see Duddingston.

MORTONHALL
031-447 6974

An 18 hole moorland course with fine views of Edinburgh (6557 yards, SSS 71). Visitors who are members of a bona fide golf club are welcome. Green fees on application. Snacks and lunch are served. There is a dry ski slope close by and other attractions include the city of Edinburgh itself with its famous castle and festival.

Location

231 Braid Road, Edinburgh EH10 6PB
The course is 2 miles south of the city centre, on the south side of the Braid Hills. Take the A702 south from the City to the Morningside traffic lights and continue up Braid Road for 1 mile. The course is on the left.

RAC recommended hotel in Braid Hills

MURRAYFIELD
031-337 3478

An 18 hole parkland course with some good views; situated on the side of Corstorphine Hill (5727 yards, SSS 68). Provided they have a handicap certificate and a letter of introduction, visitors are welcome. There is also a practice area and putting ground. Green fees are £2 per round for both visitors and members. Visiting clubs pay £18 per day or £12 per round. Meals are served every day except Sunday. Local attractions include Edinburgh Castle, Zoo and Festival as well as the city centre.

Location

43 Murrayfield Road, Edinburgh EH12 6EU
The course is 2 miles west of the city centre.

RAC recommended hotels

Ellersly House ★★★ 031-337 6888 An early 20th-century house in own small grounds in the residential suburbs.

Post House ★★★ 031-334 0390 A pleasing modern hotel with some good views of the countryside.

Murrayfield ★★ 031-337 1844 A stone-built former private residence with a later extension.

MUSSELBURGH
031-665 2005

An 18 hole wooded parkland course with rivers (6623 yards, SSS 72). Visitors with a handicap certificate are welcome by prior arrangement. Green fees on application. There are full dining room facilities except on Tuesday. Local attractions include Edinburgh city centre and East Lothian with its lovely beaches.

Location

Monktonhall, Musselburgh, Midlothian
The club is situated 1 mile south of Musselburgh off the A1.

NEWBATTLE
031-663 2123

An 18 hole undulating parkland course laid out on three levels (6012 yards, SSS 69). Visitors are welcome between Monday and Friday but not before 4pm on Bank Holidays. Jeans or trainers not permitted either on the course or in the club house. There is also a small practice area. Green fees are £7.50 per round, £12 per day. Full catering facilities are available by arrangement.

Location

Abbey Road, Dalkeith, Midlothian
The course is 7 miles south west of Edinburgh on the A7. Take the Newbattle exit at Eskbank roundabout, continue uphill opposite the police station, and the club is 300 yards on the right.

RAC recommended hotel

Eskbank Motel ★★ 031-663 3234 Stone-built Victorian house with modern motel accommodation behind.

PORTOBELLO
031-669 4361

A 9 hole public parkland course with easy walking (2400 yards, SSS 32). Visitors of all playing abilities are welcome. Green fees are £1.75 and Juniors, OAPs and UB40s play for £1.75 up to 5 pm. There are no catering facilities. Portobello Beach is only 10 miles from the club.

Location

Stanley Road, Portobello, Edinburgh EH15

PRESTONFIELD
031-667 1273

An 18 hole parkland course with magnificent views (6216 yards, SSS 70). Visitors of all playing abilities are welcome on weekdays but not between midday and 1.30pm on Saturday or before 11.30am on Sunday. There is a practice area. Green fees are £9 per round, £10 per day. Full catering facilities are available daily except Monday when snacks only are served. Local attractions include Edinburgh city centre, Edinburgh Castle and Holyrood House.

Location

6 Prestonfield Road North, Edinburgh EH16 5SH
The course is just off Dalkeith Road, close to the Commonwealth Pool.

PUMPHERSTON
(0506) 32869

A 9 hole undulating parkland course with plenty of bunkers, testing holes and fine views of the Pentland Hills (5154 yards, SSS 65). Visitors are welcome but must be accompanied by a member. Green fees on application. Bar snacks are served.

Location

Drumshoreland Road, Pumpherston, Livingston EH53 0LF
The course is 1 mile south of Uphall, off the A89.

RAC recommended hotel in Uphall.

RATHO PARK
031-333 1752

A flat 18 hole parkland course with easy walking (6028 yards, SSS 69). Visitors of all playing abilities are welcome at any time. Green fees are £10 per round, £15 per day and £17.50 at weekends. Morning coffee, snacks, lunch, high tea and dinner are served every day except Monday. The course is close to Edinburgh airport.

Location

Ratho, Newbridge, Midlothian EH28 8NX
The course is situated 8 miles west of Edinburgh with access from the A71 or A8.

RAVELSTON
031-315 2486

A 9 hole parkland course (5200 yards, SSS 66). Visitors with a current handicap certificate are welcome if accompanied by a member or recommended by the local hotel. Green fees on application. Light snacks are available. The club is close to Edinburgh city centre.

Location

24 Ravelston Dykes Road, Blackhall, Edinburgh EH4 5NZ
Take the A90 Queensferry Road, leading to the Forth Bridge Road, and turn left at the pedestrian crossing at Blackhall. From here turn into Craigcrook Road and the club is the second left.

RAC recommended hotel

Crest ★★★ 031-332 2442 A large, light, modern purpose-built hotel on the main road into the city.

ROYAL BURGESS
031-339 2075

A pleasant 18 hole parkland course with plenty of variety (6604 yards, SSS 72). The club has the distinction of being the oldest golf club in the world. Visitors are welcome on weekdays only, and should note that there are no changing facilities for women. Green fees on application. Lunch and bar snacks are served. The club is within easy reach of Edinburgh city centre.

Location

181 Whitehouse Road, Edinburgh EH4 6BY
Take the A90 to Queensferry and the course is situated behind the Barnton Thistle Hotel.

RAC recommended hotel
Barnton Thistle ★★★ 031-339 1144 A Victorian hotel with modern bedrooms. The hotel is situated on the outskirts of the city. Facilities include a sauna.

ROYAL MUSSELBURGH
(0875) 810276
An 18 hole parkland course (6237 yards, SSS 70). Visitors are welcome but the club prefers them to have a handicap certificate. Green fees are £10 per round, £16 per day on weekdays and £15 per round at weekends. Coffee, lunch and high tea are served, together with snacks, every day except Tuesday. The club house is a 12th-century building and there is a mining museum close by.
Location
Preston Grange House, Prestonpans, East Lothian

SILVERKNOWES
031-336 5359
An 18 hole links course (6210 yards, SSS 70) with a particularly long 18th hole. The course is situated on the coast overlooking the Firth of Forth. There is also a practice area. The course is a public one and visitors of all playing abilities are welcome at any time. There are no catering facilities. Local attractions include Edinburgh and Lauriston Castle.
Location
Silverknowes, Parkway, Edinburgh EH4 5ET

SWANSTON
031-445 2239
An 18 hole hillside course with a steep climb at two of the holes (5024 yards, SSS 65). Visitors are welcome on weekdays and with some restrictions at the weekends. Green fees on application. Meals are served every day except Tuesday. Other club facilities include a children's TV room.
Location
111 Swanston Road, Edinburgh EH10
The course is located 5 miles from the centre of Edinburgh on the lower slopes of the Pentland Hills.

TORPHIN HILL
031-441 1100
A particularly lovely 18 hole hillside course (5030 yards, SSS 66). There are no restrictions on visitors except on competition days. Green fees are £4 on weekdays and £7 at weekends. There is a dining room which is open every day except Tuesday and a bar where snacks are served.
Location
Torphin Road, Colinton, Edinburgh EH13 0PG
The club is situated on the south west side of Colinton village at the terminus of the No 9 and No 10 bus.

RAC recommended hotel in Braid Hills.

TURNHOUSE
031-339 1014
An 18 hole parkland/heathland course (6171 yards, SSS 69) with some fine views. Visitors are welcome on weekdays only. Green fees are £8 per round and £12 per day. Lunch and high tea are served every day except Monday. Local attractions include Edinburgh city and Castle and the Festival.
Location
154 Turnhouse Road, Edinburgh EH12 0AD

RAC recommended hotels
Barnton Thistle ★★★ 031-339 1144 A Victorian hotel with modern bedrooms. The hotel is situated on the outskirts of the city. Facilities include a sauna.
Royal Scot ★★★★ 031-334 9191 A large modern luxurious hotel on the outskirts of the city. Facilities include an indoor swimming pool, putting, sauna, solarium and gymnasium.

UPHALL
(0506) 856404
A windy meadowland course with easy walking (6250 yards, SSS 68). Visitors of all abilities, including beginners, are welcome. Green fees are £8 on weekdays and £10 at weekends. There is a bar where snacks are served and meals by arrangement. Local attractions include Linlithgow Loch and Castle, Edinburgh and Stirling.
Location
Uphall, West Lothian
The club is on the outskirts of Uphall adjacent to the A8 Edinburgh to Glasgow road.

RAC recommended hotel
Houstoun House ★★★ (0506) 853831 A 16th-century laird's fortified house with modern extension linking to converted ancilliary buildings set in parkland off the A89.

WEST LOTHIAN
(0506) 826030
An 18 hole undulating meadowland course with lovely views of the River Forth (6578 yards, SSS 71). There is also a practice area. Visitors of all playing levels are welcome during the week and by arrangement at the weekend. Green fees are £5 per round, £7 per day on weekdays and £6 per round, £9 per day at weekends. Meals are available by request. Local attractions include the Bo'ness Steam Railway.
Location
Airngarth Hill, Linlithgow, West Lothian
The course is situated on a hill separating Bo'ness and Linlithgow, marked by the Hope Monument.

WINTERFIELD
(0368) 62280
An 18 hole seaside course with spectacular views (5035 yards, SSS 65). Visitors of all playing abilities are welcome particularly beginners. Green fees on application. Meals are served every day except Thursday. Local attractions include Dunbar Castle, the local beaches and John Muir Park.
Location
North Road, Dunbar, East Lothian
The course is on the west side of Dunbar.

RAC recommended hotels in Dunbar.

STRATHCLYDE

AIRDRIE
(0236) 62195
A very pretty 18 hole parkland course (6004 yards, SSS 69). Visitors are welcome with an introduction from the Secretary of their own club. Green fees on application. Meals and snacks are served everyday.
Location
Rochsoles, Airdrie ML6 5DZ
From Airdrie Cross, situated in the centre of town, continue north on the Glenmavis Road. The club is approximately 1 mile from the Cross.

RAC recommended hotel
Tudor ★★ (0236) 64144 Town centre hotel conveniently situated–pleasant white-washed appearance.

ALEXANDRA
041-556 3711
A wooded 9 hole parkland course (1968 yards, SSS 30). The course is a public one and visitors are welcome at all times. Green fees on application. Catering facilities are available.
Location
Sannox Gardens, Alexandra Parade, Glasgow G31 8SE
The course is situated half a mile east of the city centre.

RAC recommended hotels in Glasgow.

ANNANHILL
(0563) 21644
An 18-hole parkland course (6270 yards, SSS 70). Visitors are welcome at all times except Saturday. Green fees on application. Snacks are served throughout the weekend and breakfasts, lunches, dinners or high teas are available by arrangement.
Location
Irvine Road, Kilmarnock KA3 1DW
The course is on the main Kilmarnock to Irvine road.

RAC recommended hotel
Howard Park ★★★ (0563) 31211 A modern 4-storey building situated in the outskirts of town.

ARDEER
(0294) 64542
An 18-hole parkland course with natural hazards (6630 yards, SSS 72). Visitors are welcome on any day except Saturday but you should hold a current handicap certificate. Green fees are £6 per round Monday to Friday, £10 a day and £8 per round, £14 a day on Sunday. Full catering facilities are available.
Location
Greenhead, Stevenston, Ayrshire
Follow the A78 on the High Road by passing Stevenston (signs for Largs and Greenock) and turn right into Kerelaw Road. Continue for 1 mile. The course is adjacent to the water works.

RAC recommended hotels in Irvine.

AYR BELLEISLE
(0292) 41258
An 18 hole parkland course with tree-lined fairways and wonderful views of the sea (6550 yards, SSS 72). The course is a municipal one and visitors are welcome at all times. Green fees on application. Meals and snacks are available in the hotel. Local attractions include Ayr, Burns Cottage, the Burns Centre and Brigadoon.
Location
Belleisle Park, Doonfoot Road, Ayr,
The course is 1½ miles south west of the town centre on the A719.

RAC recommended hotels
Fairfield House ★★★★ (0292) 267461 Victorian Glasgow merchant's house on the seafront, recently restored to its original elegance. Indoor swimming pool, sauna, solarium, gymnasium.
Belleisle House ★★★ (0292) 42331 A country house in public park area. Facilities include golf and putting.
Caledonian ★★★ (0292) 269331 Purpose-built modern hotel, close to shops, harbour and sea. Indoor swimming pool, sauna, solarium, gymnasium, billiards.
Kylestrome ★★★ (0292) 262474 Recently refurbished, two-storey hotel, conveniently situated between town centre and the seafront.
Pickwick ★★★ (0292) 260111 Well furnished stone-built Victorian hotel, close to sea. Putting, fishing.
Savoy Park ★★★ (0292) 266112 An interesting turreted residence with a pleasant garden.
Station ★★★ (0292) 263268 Three-storey hotel in the traditional Scottish style; beside station.
Ayrshire and Galloway ★★ (0292) 262626 Centrally situated traditional hotel which overlooks town centre square.
Burns Monument ★★ (0292) 42466 Historic (1829) riverside hotel set amongst own magnificent gardens. Fishing.
Chestnuts ★★ (0292) 264393 Family-run hotel with small garden; on coast road.
Gartferry ★★ (0292) 262768 Substantial 19th century building set in attractive award-winning garden.
Old Racecourse ★★ (0292) 262873 A large Victorian house in its own grounds. The hotel is convenient for the beach and the town centre.

AYR DALMILLING
(0292) 263893
An 18 hole meadowland course with easy walking (5401 yards, SSS 68). There is also a practice area. Visitors are welcome and beginners are particularly

welcome. Green fees are £4.40 per round, £7 per day between Monday and Friday and £8.85 per day, £5.60 a round at weekends. Tea, coffee, lunch and high tea are served every day except Tuesday and catering for parties can be arranged.
Location
Westwood Ave, Whitletts, Ayr
The course is $1^1/_2$ miles from the town centre on the north east boundary, off the A77.

RAC recommended hotels in Ayr see Belleisle.

AYR SEAFIELD
(0292) 41258
A public self-starting 18 hole parkland/seaside course (5244 or 4889 yards, SSS 66). Visitors with a handicap certificate are welcome, and can play between 7.30am and 10pm during the summer. Green fees on application. A weekly ticket covering 8 local courses can be bought for £32.90. This covers Seafield, Belleisle, Dormilling, Girvan, Maybole, Loch Green, Fullarton and Darley. The course is close to Ayr, Burns Cottage, the Burns Centre and Brigadoon.
Location
Ayr, Ayrshire
The course is on the south boundary of Ayr, $1^1/_2$ miles from the town centre in Belleisle Park on the A719.

RAC recommended hotels in Ayr see Belleisle.

BALLOCHMYLE
(0290) 50469)
An 18 hole parkland course (5952 yards, SSS 69). Provided they have a handicap certificate, visitors are welcome on weekdays. Green fees are £12 per day on weekdays and £18 at weekends. Morning coffee, lunch and high tea is served every day. The course is 9 miles from the coast.
Location
Ballochmyle, Mauchline, Ayrshire KA5 6RR
The course adjoins the A76(T) Kilmarnock to Dumfries road, 1 mile south of Mauchline village.

BALMORE
(0360) 2120240
An 18 hole parkland course with the River Fletcher running through (5736 yards, SSS 67). There are some fine views from the course. Visitors are welcome between 8am and sunset. Green fees on application. There is a restaurant which is open daily.
Location
The course is 2 miles north of Glasgow, 7 miles from the city centre.

BARSHAW
041-889 2908
A municipal 18 hole meadowland course (5673 yards, SSS 67). Visitors are welcome without being introduced by a member during the week and beginners are encouraged. Green fees are £2.70 per round. OAPs, UB40 holders and those under 16 can play for £1.35. The course is situated in the heart of the historic Paisley countryside.
Location
Barshaw park, Glasgow Road, Paisley, Renfrewshire
Leave the M8 at the Arkleston interchange and continue on the A737 from Glasgow west to Paisley and the course is situated about 1 mile before Paisley Cross.

BEARSDEN
041-942 2351
A 9 hole parkland course (5569 yards, SSS 68) with easy walking. There are some fine views of the city. Visitors are welcome if introduced by a member or by a letter of introduction. Green fees are £2 on weekdays and £4 at weekends. Meals and snacks are available at all times. Local attractions include the Trossachs parkland area.
Location
Thorn Road, Bearsden, Glasgow
The club is situated 1 mile from Bearsden Cross on Thorn Road, 7 miles north west of Glasgow.

RAC recommended hotel in Milngavie.

BEITH
(05055) 3166
A 9-hole hilly course with wonderful views of the Old Kilpatrick Hills and views of seven counties from the 6th hole. (5600 yards, SSS 67). Provided they have a handicap certificate, visitors are welcome between Monday and Friday and also on Sunday morning. Green fees are £4 and juniors under 18 £2. Snacks are served everyday. The course is actually situated on very historical ground and St Inans Chair is close by.
Location
Threepwood Road, Bigholm Road, Beith
The course is situated about 1 mile east of Beith.

BELLSHILL
(0698) 745124
A flattish 18 hole parkland course with a pond at the 3rd hole (6605 yards, SSS 72). Visitors are welcome throughout the year between 9.30am and dusk but not before 8.30am. The course can prove quite difficult and a handicap certificate is recommended. Green fees are £9 on weekdays and £12 at weekends. Full catering facilities are available. The club is close to Strathclyde Park and Loch for windsurfing and water skiing and also nature walking. There is also a caravan park.
Location
Orbiston, Bellshill MH4 2RZ
The club is about 10 miles south of Glasgow on the Bellshill -Motherwell road.

BIGGAR
(0899) 20618
An 18 hole wooded parkland course (5416 yards, SSS 66) with some fine views. The course is public and visitors are not restricted although booking by telephone (0899) 20319 is recommended. Green fees are £5.50 on weekdays and £7.50 at weekends. There is a licence and catering facilities are available every day except Monday. The club facilities include tennis and another local attraction is the Puppet Theatre.
Location
The Park, Broughton Road, Biggar, Lanarkshire
Take the A702 from Edinburgh, the A74 from Glasgow or the M8 and turn off at Newhouse. The course is 1 mile east of Biggar on the Broughton Road, opposite the police station.

RAC recommended hotel
Shieldhill C/H ★★★★ (0899) 20035 Based on a 12th-century keep, a historic mansion, elegantly furnished.

BISHOPBRIGGS
041-772 1810
An 18 hole parkland course (6041 yards, SSS 69). Provided they have a handicap certificate visitors are welcome if accompanied by a member or by prior application to the committee. Green fees are £2 if introduced by a member, otherwise £12. Meals and snacks are served every day. There is a snooker room at the club house.
Location
Brackanbrae Road, Bishopbriggs, Glasgow G64 2DN
Leave Glasgow north by the A803 and continue for 4 miles. Approximately 200 yards short of Bishopbriggs Cross you should turn left for the club.

BLAIRBETH
041-634 3855
An 18 hole parkland course (5448 yards, SSS 67). Visitors are welcome if accompanied by a member. Green fees on application. Catering facilities are available by arrangement.
Location
Burnside, Rutherglen, Glasgow
The course is 1 miles south of Rutherglen via Stonelaw Road, off the A749.

RAC recommended hotel
Burnside ★★ 041-634 1276 Purpose-built, long, low hotel in quiet residential area, near station on Glasgow suburban railway.

BLAIRMORE & STRONE
(036984) 217
A scenic 9 hole hilly parkland/moorland course with plenty of trees (2112 yards, SSS 62). Visitors are welcome at all times. Green fees are £4 per round or day but visitors should note that there are often delays on Saturday afternoon and Monday evening. There is a bar.
Location
Strone, By Dunoon, Argyll PA23 8TJ
The club is situated on the high road above Strone village, 9 miles north of Dunoon on the A880.

RAC recommended hotels
Abbeyhill ★★ (0369) 2204 Family-run hotel in a pleasant garden overlooking Firth of Clyde.
Argyll ★★ (0369) 2059 A traditional hotel in the town centre with a view of the pier.
Esplanade ★★ (0369) 4070 Prominent white-painted building pleasantly situated overlooking lawns down to West Bay. Putting, sauna.

BONNYTON
(035 53) 2781
An 18 hole moorland course (6252 yards, SSS 71). Visitors are welcome on weekdays. Green fees are £2.50. Lunch and high tea are served on weekdays and Sunday, and lunch and dinner on Saturday. Bar lunch served every day.
Location
Eaglesham, Glasgow G76 0QA

BOTHWELL CASTLE
(0698) 853177
An 18 hole flat meadowland course particularly suitable for older players (6426 yards, SSS 71). Provided they have a handicap certificate, visitors are welcome on weekdays between 8am and 3.30pm but it is advisable to book with the Professional beforehand. Golf clubs and caddy cars are available for hire. Green fees are £8.50 per round, £12 per day. Snacks, lunch, high tea and dinner are served daily. Local attractions include The Duke of Hamilton's Lodge and Bothwell Castle.
Location
Blantyre Road, Bothwell, Glasgow
The course is adjacent to the M74, 3 miles north of Hamilton.

RAC recommended hotels
Bothwell Bridge ★★★ (0698) 852246 A red sandstone building close to the centre of Bothwell and only $1^1/_2$ miles from the M74.
Silvertrees ★★ (0698) 852311 An attractive 19th-century building with modern annexes, situated in a quiet residential area.

BRODICK
(0770) 2349
An 18 hole seaside course (4404 yards, SSS 62). Visitors can play throughout the week. Green fees are £5 per round, restricted after 3.30pm and £7 per day. OAPs can play unrestricted for £5 and Juniors under 16 may play for £3 per day or £2 per round after 3.30pm. All players of intermediate standard and above are welcome. Light lunches can be arranged by contacting the Steward beforehand. Local attractions include Brodick Castle and the adjoining adventure playground.
Location
Brodick, Isle of Arran
The course is reached by ferry from Ardrossan and is about half a mile from Brodick pier.

RAC recommended hotels
Auchrannie Country House C/H ★★★ (0770) 2234 A 19th-century stone-built mansion set in

wooded grounds. Putting.
Douglas ★★ (0770) 2155 19th-century red sandstone building in wooded grounds overlooking bay.

CALDERBRAES
(0698) 813425
A 9 hole parkland course overlooking the Clyde Valley (5046 yards, SSS 67). Visitors introduced by a member are welcome. Green fees on application. Snacks, lunch and dinner are served every day.
Location
57 Roundknowe Road, Uddingston, Lanarkshire G71 7TS
The course is situated at the start of the M74, 4 miles from Glasgow.

CALDWELL
(050585) 329
An 18 hole moorland course with a burn (6102 yards, SSS 69). This course is particularly pleasant to play on. Visitors are welcome on weekdays but it is advisable to book in advance. Green fees are £9 per round or £14 per day. Full catering facilities are available on weekdays.
Location
Uplawmoor, Renfrewshire
The course is 15 miles from Glasgow, off the A736, 5 miles south west of Barrhead and 12 miles north east of Irvine.

RAC recommended hotel
Dalmeny Park ★★ 041-881 9211 An extended, modernised, 19th- century house situated in its own grounds.

CAMBUSLANG
041-641 3130
A 9 hole parkland course (6072 yards, SSS 69). Visitors of all playing abilities are welcome if introduced by a member. Green fees are £7.50. Full catering facilities are available. The course is close to Glasgow city centre and places worth visiting include Chatelherault House.
Location
30 Westburn Drive, Cambuslang, Glasgow G65 7HX
You will find the course 1 mile from the station in Cambuslang, off the main Glasgow-Hamilton road.

CAMPSIE
(0360) 310244
A pretty 18 hole hillside course (5517 yards, SSS 67). Visitors are welcome on weekdays and by prior arrangement at weekends. Green fees are £6 per round on weekdays and £7 at weekends. Bar snacks are always available and meals by prior arrangement during the week and at all times at the weekend. There is some good hill walking nearby.
Location
Crow Road, Lennoxtown, Glasgow G65 7HX
The course is just north of Lennoxtown on the B822.

RAC recommended hotel
Glazertbank (0360) 310790

CAPRINGTON
(0563) 21915
An 18 hole parkland course (5718 yards, SSS 68). The course is a municipal one and visitors are welcome at all times. Green fees on application.
Location
Ayr Road, Kilmarnock KA1 4UW
The course is south of Kilmarnock on the Ayr Road.

RAC recommended hotels see Annanhill.

CARDROSS
(0389) 841754
A testing 18 hole parkland course (6466 yards, SSS 71). There is a practice ground. Visitors are welcome on weekdays and also at weekends if they are accompanied by a member. Green fees are £10 per round, £15 per day. There is a bar where snacks are served and tea is available every day except Monday. Local attractions include Dumbarton Castle and Loch Lomond.
Location
Main Road, Cardross, Dumbarton G82 5LB
The course is between Dumbarton and Helensburgh on the A814, west of Dumbarton.

CARLUKE
(0555) 71070
An 18 hole undulating parkland course with a challenging 11th hole (5805 yards, SSS 68). Visitors with a handicap certificate are welcome on weekdays until 4.30pm, except Tuesday. Green fees are £9 per day or £1 if you are playing with a member. Full catering facilities are available daily except Tuesday. Local attractions include Strathclyde Pleasure Park.
Location
Hallcraig, Mauldslie Road, Carluke ML8 5HG
The club is about $1^1/_2$ miles from the the traffic lights in the town centre, on the road to Hamilton and Larkhall.

CARNWATH
(0555) 840251
An attractive 18 hole undulating course (5855 yards, SSS 69). Provided they have a handicap certificate, visitors are welcome on Monday, Wednesday, Friday and Sunday. Green fees are £10 on weekdays and £12 at weekends. Meals are served in the club house although it is limited on Tuesday and Thursday. The city centre of Glasgow is within easy reach.
Location
1 Main Street, Carnwath
The club is 5 miles north east of Lanark.

CARRADALE
(05833) 387
A pretty 9 hole undulating course with natural hazards (2387 yards, SSS 63). Carradale is a seaside holiday town and there are far-reaching views of the sea from the course. Provided they have a handicap certificate, visitors are welcome at all times and no introduction is necessary. Green fees are £4 per round, £5 per day. Weekly terms are available on application. Catering facilities are available at local hotels. Nearby attractions include Campbeltown, Somerled and Saddell Abbey.
Location
Carradale, Campbeltown, Argyll, PA28 6QX
The course is off the B842 from Campbeltown to Carradale, on the south side of the village.

CATHCART CASTLE
041-638 9449
An 18 hole undulating parkland course (5832 yards, SSS 68). Visitors with a handicap certificate are welcome, if introduced by a member. Green fees on application. Snacks and meals are served.
Location
Mearns Road, Clarkston, Glasgow G76 7YL
The club is on the A77, 7 miles from Glasgow.

CATHKIN BRAES
041-634 6605
An 18 hole moorland course (6266 yards, SSS 71). Visitors who hold a current handicap certificate are welcome on weekdays by prior arrangement. There is also a practice ground. Green fees are £10 per round, £15 per day. Full catering facilities are available daily except Monday. The centre of Glasgow is within easy reach.
Location
Cathkin Road, Rutherglen, Glasgow G73 4SE
The course is south east of Glasgow off the road to East Kilbride.

RAC recommended hotel in Blairbeth.

CAWDER
041-772 5167
There are two 18 hole parkland courses here. The first, The Cawdor is a hilly course with some testing holes (6229 yards, SSS 71). The Keir is a flat course (5877 yards, SSS 69). Visitors who have a handicap certificate are welcome on weekdays by arrangement with the Secretary. Green fees on application. Lunches are served in the club house. The club is 15 minutes from Glasgow.
Location
Cadder Road, Bishopbriggs, Glasgow G64 3QD
The course is about half a mile east of Bishopbriggs off the A803.

CLOBER
041-956 1685
An 18 hole parkland course with a testing 5th hole (5068 yards, SSS 65). Visitors are welcome on weekdays before 4.30pm Monday to Thursday, and 4pm on Friday. Green fees are £5 per round. Full catering facilities are available on Tuesday, Wednesday, Friday and at weekends. Snacks are served on Monday and Thursday.
Location
Craigton Road, Milngavie G62 7HP
The course is 7 miles north west of Glasgow.

RAC recommended hotel in Milngavie
Black Bull Thistle ★★★ 041-956 2291 A traditional hotel in the town centre catering for both tourists and business people.

CLYDEBANK & DISTRICT
(0389) 73289
An 18 hole parkland course (5825 yards, SSS 68). Provided they have a handicap certificate, visitors of all levels are welcome on weekdays and at weekends if accompanied by a member. Green fees are £12 per day. Meals are served daily.
Location
Hardgate, Clydebank, Dunbartonshire G81 5QY
The course is off Great Western Road, 8 miles north west of Glasgow.

CLYDEBANK OVERTOWN
041-952 6372
An interesting 18 hole undulating parkland course (5643 yards, SSS 66). The course is a municipal one and visitors are welcome at all times. Green fees are £2.60 Monday to Saturday and £23 on Sunday and Bank Holidays. There is a cafe attached to the Pro Shop. The course is only 20 minutes drive from Loch Lomond.
Location
Overtown Road, Clydebank, Dunbartonshire
From Partick continue along Dumbarton Road and turn right at Dalmuir Station. It is 5 minutes from here.

COCHRAN CASTLE
(0505) 20146
A wooded 18 hole undulating moorland course with two small streams running through (6226 yards, SSS 70). Provided they have a handicap certificate, visitors are welcome on weekdays and at weekends if accompanied by a member. There is a practice ground. Green fees are £12 per day or £8 per round. Full catering facilities and bar snacks are available every day except Monday.
Location
Craigston, Scott Avenue, Johnstone PA5 0HF
The course is situated approximately a quarter of a mile off the Johnstone-Beith road to the south of the town. Look for the Bird in the Hand Hotel as a good landmark near the turning to the club.

COLVILLE PARK
(0698) 63017
An 18 hole parkland course with some testing holes (6208 yards, SSS 70). Visitors are welcome but parties can only play midweek by prior arrangement. Green fees for parties are £10 per day. Full catering facilities are available. Local attractions include Chatelerault Country Park where there are some good walks.
Location
Jerviston Estate, Motherwell, Strathclyde ML1 4UG
The course is on the A723, 1 mile north of Motherwell town centre.

RAC recommended hotel
Garrion ★★★ (0698) 64561 A purpose-built hotel, situated in the town centre. Sauna.

CORRIE
(077081) 223
A lovely undulating 9 hole heathland course (3896 yards, SSS 61) with views of the mountains and the coast. Visitors who have a handicap certificate are welcome at all times. Green fees are £3 per day and £1.50 for Juniors. Meals and snacks are always available. An added attraction is the Isle of Arran itself which is good walking country.
Location
Sannox, Isle of Arran
Take the ferry to Brodick and the course is 7 miles north on the A84 coastal road.

COWAL
(0369) 5673
An 18 hole moorland course with some spectacular views of the Clyde estuary and the surrounding hills (6250 yards, SSS 70). Visitors are always welcome. Green fees are £6.50 per round, £8.50 per day on weekdays and £11 per round, £13.50 a day at weekends. A weekly ticket can be bought for £33. Full catering facilities are available during the season. The Ben More Gardens are worth visiting.
Location
Ardenslate Road, Kirn, Dunoon, Argyll PA23 8LT
The club is a quarter of a mile from the A815 at Kirn on the north east boundary of Dunoon.

RAC recommended hotel
Rosscairn (Acclaimed) (0369) 4344

COWGLEN
041-632 0556
An 18 hole undulating parkland course (6006 yards, SSS 69). Visitors who hold a current handicap certificate are welcome if introduced by a member or by a letter to the Secretary. Green fees are £7 per round and £10 per day. Lunch and dinner are served and bar snacks are also available. Local attractions include The Burrell Collection and Glasgow city centre.
Location
301 Barrhead Road, Glasgow G43
The club is on the south side of Glasgow. Follow the signs to the Burrell Collection which is opposite the Pollock Golf Club.

CROW WOOD
041-779 1943
An 18 hole parkland course (6209 yards, SSS 70). Provided they have a handicap certificate, visitors are welcome when accompanied by a member. Green fees are £8 per round and £12 per day. Meals are served all week.
Location
Garnkirk Estate, Muirhead, Chryston, Glasgow G69 9JF
The course is 1 mile north of Stepps on the A80.

RAC recommended hotel
Garfield House ★★★ 041-779 2111 Converted house close to Glasgow-Stirling road. Conference facilities.

CUMBERNAULD
(0236) 734969
A fairly difficult 18 hole flat course with a few burns and ponds (6800 yards, SSS 71). Visitors are welcome between 8am and dusk on weekdays. Green fees are £3.50 on weekdays and £4.50 at weekends. There are two bars, a dining room and lounge, and lunch and high tea are served every day except Monday and Tuesday. Local attractions include the Country Park and Sports Centre.
Location
Palacerigg Country Park, Cumbernauld G67 3HU
Take the A80 to Cumbernauld and follow the signs to the Country Park.

DOUGLAS PARK
041-942 2220
An 18 hole course (5957 yards, SSS 68). Visitors are welcome when accompanied by a member. Green fees on application. Meals are served by arrangement.
Location
Hillfoot, Bearsden, Glasgow
The course is situated next to Hillfoot station, 20 yards past the traffic lights at the Milngavie Road-Boclair road junction, on the east side of the town.

RAC recommended hotel in Milngavie.

DOUGLAS WATER
(0555) 2295
A 9 hole undulating parkland course (2947 yards, SSS 69). Visitors of all playing abilities are welcome. Green fees are £2.50 per day on weekdays and £3.50 at weekends and Bank Holidays. Catering facilities are available by arrangement.
Location
Ayr Road, Rigside, Lanark
The course is situated 7 miles south west of Lanark on A70, 2 miles east of the A74. It is signposted Rigside.

DOUGLASTON
041-956 5750
An 18 hole parkland course (6683 yards, SSS 72). The course is open to the public and visitors are welcome at any time. Green fees are £5 on weekdays and £6 at weekends and Bank Holidays. There are full catering facilities. Loch Lomond is only a half hour drive away.
Location
Strathblane Road, Milngavie, Glasgow G62
Leave Glasgow city centre and take the A879 and A81 7 miles north of the city.

RAC recommended hotel in Milngavie.

DRUMPELLIER
(0236) 24139
An 18 hole parkland course (6227 yards, SSS 70). Visitors are welcome on weekdays except Bank Holidays. Green fees are £10 per round or £15 per day. Full catering facilities are available except on Thursday. Local attractions include the Heritage Park and Glasgow city centre.
Location
Drumpellier Ave, Coatbridge ML5 1RX
The course is 1 mile from Coatbridge off the A89, 8 miles east of Glasgow.

RAC recommended hotel
Coatbridge ★★★ (0236) 24392 A purpose built hotel in the west of the town, with easy access to the A74 and Glasgow.

DULLATUR
(023 67) 23230
An 18 hole undulating moorland course with natural hazards (6195 yards, SSS 70). Visitors of all playing abilities are welcome on weekdays by arrangement. Green fees are £10 per day or £6 per round. Full catering facilities are available. Glasgow city centre is only 15 miles away.
Location
Dullatur, Glasgow
The course is 12 miles east of Glasgow, north of Cumbernauld on the Kilsyth road via Dullatur. It is about 1½ miles from Cumbernauld village.

DUMBARTON
(0389) 32830
A flat 18 hole meadowland course (5654 yards, SSS 69). Visitors are welcome on weekdays. Green fees are £10 a day. Lunch and snacks are available daily except Tuesday. Local attractions include Dumbarton Castle.
Location
Broadmeadows, Dumbarton, Dunbartonshire G82 2BQ
The course is off the A814 a quarter of a mile north of Dumbarton, 15 miles north west of Glasgow.

RAC recommended hotel
Dumbuck ★★ (0389) 34336 A family-run stone-built hotel in a quiet position on the east of town. Facilities include billiards.

DUNAVERTY
An 18 hole undulating seaside course (4597 yards, SSS 63). Visitors are welcome at all times. Green fees are available on application to the Campbeltown Courier office. Snacks are available at the club.
Location
Southend, Campbeltown, Argyll PA28 6RF
The club is situated about 10 miles south of Campbeltown on the B842.

RAC recommended hotels
Royal ★★ (0586) 52017 Fine red sandstone building prominently situated at pierhead. Views over loch.
Seafield ★★ (0586) 54385 Small traditional hotel looking out over the loch across the road.

EASTER MOFFAT
(0236) 842289
An 18 hole moorland/parkland course (6221 yards, SSS 70). Provided they have a handicap certificate, visitors are welcome. Green fees are £6 per round, £8 per day on weekdays and £15, which includes food, on Sunday. Full catering facilities are available during the playing season, May to September or otherwise by arrangement.
Location
Mansion House, Plains, By Airdrie, Lanarkshire

EAST KILBRIDE
(035 52) 20913
A rather windy 18 hole undulating meadowland course (6419 yards, SSS 71) with some hard walking. Visitors are welcome accompanied by a member. Green fees are £5 per round, £8 per day. Full catering facilities are available except on Monday and Friday.
Location
Chapelside Road, Nerston, East Kilbride G74 4PF
Leave Glasgow on the A7 East Kibride road and turn off at Nerston village by Borlands Cars.

RAC recommended hotels
Bruce ★★★ (03552) 29771 A modern hotel situated in the town.
Crutherland C/H ★★★ (035 52) 37633 Country house in quiet rural situation, convenient for New Town and Glasgow. Putting, fishing.
Stuart ★★★ (03552) 21161 Conveniently situated in the town centre, a modern, purpose-built hotel.

EAST RENFREWSHIRE
(035 55) 206
An 18 hole moorland course with a loch (6100 yards, SSS 70). Visitors are welcome at all times. Green fees are £12 per round, £18 per day on weekdays. There is full dining room service with meals served every day.
Location
Loganswell, Pilmuir, Newton Mearns, Glasgow
The course is off the A77, 1 mile from Mearns Cross.

RAC recommended hotel
MacDonald Thistle ★★★ 041-638 2225 A large modern hotel conveniently situated for Glasgow city centre and airport. Facilities include sauna, solarium and gymnasium.
Redhurst ★★ 041-638 6465 Two-storey, purpose-built hotel in residential area.

EASTWOOD
(035 55) 261
An 18 hole moorland course (5886 yards, SSS 68). Visitors are welcome and also parties by prior appointment with the Secretary. Green fees are £9 per round or £14 per day. Snacks, lunch and dinner are served daily. The club is only 15 minutes from Glasgow City Centre.

Location
Muirshield, Loganswell, Newton Mearns, Glasgow G77 6RX
Take the A77 from Glasgow and the club is 3 miles south of Newton Mearns Cross at the junction with Old Mearns Road.

RAC recommended hotels in East Renfrewshire.

ELDERSLIE
(0505) 22835
An 18 hole undulating parkland course with some fine views (6004 yards, SSS 69). There is a putting green and also practice areas. Visitors are welcome but full facilities are only available between Monday and Friday and booking is advisable. Green fees are £9 per round or £13 per day. There is a restaurant and bar which is open daily except Thursday. Facilities include a snooker room and many local attractions.
Location
63 Main Road, Elderslie, Renfrewshire PA5 9AZ
Leave the M8 at the Linwood turn-off, and turn left at the roundabout. Continue along Linwood Road to the main traffic lights and turn right for the club.

RAC recommended hotel
Excelsior ★★★★ 041-887 1212 A modern sound-proofed hotel situated next to the airport terminal. Facilities include a solarium.

ERSKINE
(0505) 863327
An 18 hole parkland course (6287 yards, SSS 70). Visitors of all playing abilities are welcome if introduced by, or playing with, a member. There is also a putting green and practice area. Green fees on application. There is a restaurant and bar where lunch, tea and dinner are served to members and guests only, or by special arrangement. Glasgow is 12 miles away and the Ayrshire coast and Trossachs are within easy reach.
Location
Bishopton, Renfrewshire PA7 5PH
Leave the M8 north at the Bridge Toll barrier and turn left along the B815 for approximately 1 mile.

GIRVAN
(0465) 4346
A municipal seaside and meadowland course with sea views (5078 yards, SSS 65). Visitors are welcome at all times. Green fees are £4.40 per round, £7 a day on weekdays and £5.80 per round, £8.85 per day at weekends. Meals are served by arrangement. Local attractions include Culzean Castle and the lovely local bays.
Location
Girvan, Ayrshire KA26 9HW
The course is off the A77 from Glasgow to Ayr, on the coast road to Stranraer.

RAC recommended hotels
Kings Arms ★★ (0465) 3322 An attractive four-storey former coaching inn, close to the beach.
Westcliffe ★★ (0465) 2128 Part of a seafront terrace, close to shops and harbour. Solarium.

GLASGOW (AYR)
(0294) 311347
A beautiful 18 hole links parkland course with splendid turf (6500 yards, SSS 71). The course is used as a qualifying course for the Open Championship. Visitors who have a handicap certificate by application. Green fees are £20 per round. Lunch is served daily except on Monday. The course is in the heart of Burns country.
Location
Gailes, By Irvine, Ayrshire
The course is 2 miles south of Irvine on the road to Troon. Follow the signs for Gailes.

RAC recommended hotels in Irvine.

GLASGOW
041-942 2340
A fine 18 hole tree-lined parkland course (5968 yards, SSS 69) situated on the River Kelvin with extensive views. The course is one of the best in Scotland amd there is also a practice area and putting green. Visitors with a handicap certificate are welcome but they must apply to the club beforehand. Green fees are £16 per round. Lunch and high tea are served but smart dress is obligatory. Local attractions include the Burrell Collection in Glasgow which is only 5 miles away.
Location
Killermont, Bearsden, Glasgow G61 2TW
The course is 6 miles north west of Glasgow just off the A81, near the Killermont Bridge.

RAC recommended hotels
Albany ★★★★ 041-248 2656 Large, city centre hotel. Spacious and luxurious. Billiards. Indoor swimming pool planned.
Holiday Inn ★★★★ 041-226 5577 Luxurious modern central hotel with spacious bedrooms and leisure facilities. Indoor swimming pool, squash, sauna, solarium, gymnasium.
Hospitality Inn ★★★★ 041-332 3311 Modern nine-storey building on a corner site in the city centre.
Stakis Grosvenor ★★★★ 041-339 8811 A traditional Victorian style luxurious city hotel overlooking the famous Botanic Gardens.
Crest ★★★ 041-248 2355 Large custom-built modern hotel in city centre; close to station.
Ewington ★★★ 041-423 1152 Family-run traditional hotel in terrace building overlooking Queen's Park. Billiards.
Swallow ★★★ 041-427 3146 Modern hotel, minutes from the M8. Glasgow airport 5 miles. Indoor swimming pool, sauna, solarium, gymnasium.
Tinto Firs ★★★ 041-637 2353 Attractive refurbished hotel in residential area, close to the city centre.
Newlands ★★ 041-632 9171 Stone-built modernised small hotel situated in south of city.
Sherbrooke ★★ 041-427 4227 Privately-owned small red sandstone 'castle' building in quiet residential area.

GLEDDOCH
(047554) 304
A flat 18 hole parkland and moorland course with fine views over the Firth of Clyde (6333 yards, SSS 71). Visitors of all playing abilities are welcome by arrangement with the Professional. There is a practice area, indoor driving bay and a putting green. Other sporting facilities include the riding school, squash and sauna which are available to temporary members. Green fees are £15. There is a bar, lounge and restaurant which remains open all day.
Location
Langbank, Renfrewshire PA14 6YE
Take the M8 west of Glasgow and continue past the airport to Langbank. Both Langbank and Gleddoch House are signposted.

RAC recommended hotel
Gleddoch House ★★★ (047554) 711 An elegant country house set in a 250 acre estate which includes the golf course. Facilities include an indoor swimming pool, golf, squash, riding, sauna and billiards.

GLENCRUITTEN
(0631) 62868
A varied 18 hole hilly parkland/moorland course set in a lovely quiet situation (4452 yards, SSS 63). Visitors are welcome on weekdays with some restrictions on Thursday and Saturday. However, the club does prefer some proof of membership of a recognised club. There is also a practice area. Green fees on application. Meals and snacks are available. Local attractions include a Rare Breeds Park and a Sea Life Centre.
Location
Glencruitten Road, Oban
The course is 1 mile from the town centre off the A816

RAC recommended hotels in Oban
Alexandra ★★★ (0631) 62381 Traditional holiday hotel overlooking harbour.
Caledonian ★★★ (0631) 63133 An extensive Victorian style building with good sea views.
Columba ★★★ (0631) 62183 Stone-built hotel dominating the North Pier with fine sea, mountain and island views.
Lancaster ★★ (0631) 62587 Family-run stone-built hotel overlooking Oban Bay at the north end of the town. Indoor swimming pool, sauna, solarium.
Manor House ★★ (0631) 62087 Georgian manor house, built of local stone, with gardens down to the shore. Views over bay.
Rowan Tree ★★ (0631) 62954 Modern town-centre hotel convenient for ferries to the islands.

GOUROCK
(0475) 31001
An 18 hole moorland course with a testing 8th hole. There are some splendid views over the Firth of Clyde and Holy Loch (6492 yards, SSS 71). Visitors are welcome on weekdays and also at weekends if accompanied by a member. A handicap certificate is preferred. Green fees are £7 per round or £12 per day. There is a restaurant where lunch, tea and dinner are served by arrangement and bar snacks are normally available. Local attractions include the River Clyde, the local bays and the Highland Games, held in August.
Location
Cowal View, Gourock, Renfrewshire PA19 6HD
The course is 2 miles west of Gourock Station via Victoria Road, Golf Road and Cowal View. It is just above the Yacht Club.

GREENOCK
(0475) 20793
A testing 27 hole moorland course with spectacular views of the Clyde estuary (5346 yards, SSS 68). Provided they have a handicap certificate, visitors are welcome at any time except Saturday. There is also a 9 hole course where children are welcome. Green fees on application. Full catering facilities available except on Thursday. The River Clyde is nearby and it is only 20 minutes to the Highlands and 40 minutes to Glasgow from the club.
Location
Forsyth Street, Greenock, Renfrewshire PA16 8RE
The club is situated 1 mile south west of the town centre on the main road to Gourock, away from the River Clyde.

RAC recommended hotel
Tontine ★★★ (0475) 23316 A modernised 19th-century hotel in a quiet square in the town centre.

HAGGS CASTLE
041-427 1157
A wooded 18 hole parkland course which can be quite difficult (6464 yards, SSS 71). Both the Scottish National Championships and the Glasgow and Scottish Open have been held at the club. There is a practice area and putting green. Visitors are welcome but you should contact the Professional beforehand. Green fees are £14 per round or £21 per day. Full catering facilities are available. Local attractions include the Burrell Collection and Glasgow city centre which is only 5 minutes away.
Location
70 Dumbreck Road, Glasgow G41 4SN
At the end of the M77 from Glasgow continue straight ahead at the roundabout and the course is situated south west of Glasgow near Ibrox Stadium and Bellahouston Park.

RAC recommended hotels in Glasgow.

HAMILTON
(0698) 282872
A particularly lovely 18 hole parkland course (6264 yards, SSS 70). There is also a practice area and a putting green. Visitors are welcome if they are with a member or otherwise by arrangement. Green fees are available by request. Snacks are served daily and meals by arrangement. Local attractions include Chatelherault House.
Location
Riccarton, Ferniegair, Hamilton, Lanarkshire
Leave the M74 at the Hamilton turn-off and continue for 1½ miles up Larkhall Road.

HAYSTON
041-776 1244
An 18 hole undulating course with tree-lined fairways (6042 yards, SSS 69). Visitors can play on weekdays before 4.30pm unless introduced by a member, and beginners are particularly welcome. There is a practice area. Green fees are £9 per round or £15 per day. A full catering service is available from 9am until closing. Bar snacks and lunch are available every day and high tea and dinner are served if ordered in advance. Local attractions include Stirling Castle and the club is 20 minutes from Glasgow.
Location
Campsie Road, Kirkintilloch, Glasgow G66 1RN
The club is 10 miles north east of Glasgow off the A803 via Bishopbriggs and Kirkintilloch, 1 mile north of Kirkintilloch.

HELENSBURGH
(0436) 74173
An 18 hole hilly moorland course with spectacular views of Loch Lomond and the River Clyde (6053 yards, SSS 69). Visitors with a handicap certificate are welcome on weekdays. Green fees are £8 per round, £12 per day. There is a bar and lunches are served daily.
Location
15 Abercromby Street, Helensburgh, Dunbartonshire G84 9JD
Abercromby Street is just off Sinclair Street on the north east side of town.

RAC recommended hotel
Commodore ★★★ (0436) 6924 A modern hotel overlooking the sea at the west end of town.

HILTON PARK
041-956 4657
There are two 18 hole moorland courses here, both with panoramic views. The Allander, (5361 yards, SSS 69) and The Hilton, (5489 yards, SSS 70). There is a practice area. Provided they have a handicap certificate, visitors are welcome on weekdays by prior arrangement. Green fees are £10 per round or £15 per two rounds. There is a bar and full catering facilities are available. Local attractions include Loch Lomond.
Location
Aulmarroch Estate, Stockiemuir Road, Milngavie, Glasgow G62 9HB
The course is 8 miles north of Glasgow on the A809.

RAC recommended hotel in Milngavie.

HOLLANDBUSH
(0555) 893484
A challenging 18 hole parkland and moorland course with tree-lined fairways (6100 yards, SSS 70). There is also a practice area. Visitors are welcome at all times. Green fees are £6 on weekdays and £8 at weekends. Meals are served in the club house.
Location
Acretophead, Lesmahagow
Leave the M74 or A74 between Lesmahagow and Coalburn.

INNELLAN
(0369) 3546
A wooded 9 hole undulating parkland course (4878 yards, SSS 63). Visitors are welcome at any time except Monday evening. Green fees are £4 per day on weekdays and £5 at weekends. Catering facilities can be arranged for parties. The views from the course are spectacular and there are many forest walks. Knockamallie Castle ruins are close by.
Location
Knockamillie Road, Innellan, Argyll
The course is 4 miles from Dunoon by road, situated on a hill behind the village. There are directions at Innellan Pier.

RAC recommended hotel
Osborne (Acclaimed) (036 983) 445 Private hotel. Billiards.

IRVINE
(0294) 75626
A challenging 18 hole fairly flat links course (6434 yards, SSS 71). Visitors are welcome on weekdays except Saturday. There is a practice ground. Green fees on application. Meals and snacks are served every day except Monday.
Location
Bogside, Irvine KA12 8SN
Continue through Irvine towards Kilwinning and turn left after Ravenspark Academy. Carry on straight for about half a mile over the railway bridge.

RAC recommended hotels
Hospitality Inn ★★★★ (0294) 74272 A modern purpose-built hotel on the edge of New Town. Facilities include an indoor swimming pool and fishing.
Montgreenan Mansion House ★★★ (0294) 57733 Attractive country house set in extensive grounds situated 4 miles north of Irvine off A736. Tennis, billiards.
Redburn ★★ (0294) 76792 A modern purpose-built hotel on the outskirts of town.

IRVINE RAVENSPARK
(0294) 76983
An 18 hole meadowland course (6429 yards, SSS 71). Visitors are welcome every day. Green fees are £6 on weekdays and £9 at weekends. Lunch and high tea are served daily. There is also a bar but no jeans or training shoes are allowed. Local attractions include Eglington Castle.
Location
Kidsneuk, Irvine, Ayrshire
The course is on the A78 between Irvine and Kilwinning at Ravenspark Academy.

RAC recommended hotel
Hospitality Inn ★★★★ (0294) 74272 A modern purpose-built hotel on the edge of New Town. Facilities include an indoor swimming pool and fishing.

KILBIRNIE PLACE
(0505) 683398
An 18 hole parkland course with easy walking (5411 yards, SSS 67). Visitors are welcome on weekdays and Sunday. Green fees on application. Meals are served at weekends.
Location
Largs Road, Kilbirnie, Ayrshire
The course is on the outskirts of Kilbirnie.

KILMALCOM
(050587) 2139
An 18 hole moorland course with easy walking and fine views. There are some testing holes (5890 yards, SSS 68). Visitors are welcome on weekdays but must be accompanied by a member at weekends. Green fees are £10 per round and £15 per day. Full catering facilities are available.
Location
Porterfield Road, Kilmalcom, Renfrewshire PA13 3PD
Take the A740 to Linwood and then the A761 to the Bridge of Weir.

KILMARNOCK
(0292) 311077
An 18 hole seaside course (6473 yards, SSS 71). Visitors are welcome on Monday, Tuesday, Thursday and Friday. Green fees are £21 on weekdays. Coffee, lunch, snacks and high tea are served. The course is in the heart of Burns Country.
Location
29 Hillhouse Road, Barassie, Troon, Ayrshire KA10 6SY

RAC recommended hotels in Troon.

KILSYTH LENNOX
(0236) 822190
An undulating 9 hole moorland and parkland course (5944 yards, SSS 69) with some hard walking but splendid views across central Scotland. A second 9 hole course is currently under construction. Visitors with a handicap certificate are welcome without introduction before 5pm on weekdays and after 4pm on Saturday and 2pm on Sunday. Green

fees are £5 per day on weekdays and £5 per round at weekends. There is a bar and lounge and snacks are normally available. Both Glasgow and Edinburgh are within easy reach.
Location
Tak-Ma-Doon Road, Kilsyth, Glasgow G65 0HX
The course is 12 miles north east of Glasgow on the A80.

KIRKHILL
041-641 3083
An 18 hole meadowland course (5862 yards, SSS 69). Visitors of all playing abilities are welcome by arrangement with the Secretary. Green fees on application. Full meals are served by arrangement with the Clubmistress and bar snacks are normally available. Local attractions include the zoo in Glasgow and Strathclyde Park.
Location
Greenless Road, Cambuslang, Glasgow G72 8YN
Follow the East Kilbride road from Burnside and take the first turning on the left, just past the Cathkin by-pass roundabout.

KIRKINTILLOCH
041-776 1256
An attractive 18 hole meadowland course (5269 yards, SSS 66) with views of the Campsie Hills. Visitors with a handicap certificate are welcome, but must be accompanied by a member. Green fees on application. Full catering facilities are available every day except Monday and Tuesday. There is some lovely countryside surrounding the club.
Location
Todhill, Campsie Road, Kirkintilloach, Glasgow G66 1RN
The course is 1 mile from Kirkintilloch on the road from Kirkintilloch to Lennoxtown.

KNIGHTSWOOD
041-959 2131
A 9 hole parkland course (2717 yards, SSS 66). The course is a public one and visitors of all playing abilities are welcome. Green fees are £1.30 per 9 holes on weekdays and £1.60 at weekends. Juniors, OAPs and UB40 holders can play for £1 at weekends and Juniors for 30p, OAPs for 50p on weekdays. Glasgow city centre is within easy reach and there are plenty of parks.
Location
Lincoln Ave, Knightswood, Glasgow
The club is off Dumbarton Road coming from the city centre.

KYLES OF BUTE
(0700) 811355
A 9 hole undulating moorland course exposed to the wind but with magnificent views (2389 yards, SSS 32). Visitors are welcome at any time except Sunday morning. Green fees are £4 a day or £2 if you are under 18. Tea, coffee and snacks are available.
Location
Tighnabruaich, Argyll
Take the A885 from Dunoon then the B836 to Tighnabruaich and continue through the village to Kames Cross. From there take the B8000 to Millhouse and the club entrance is at the top of the first rise.

LAMLASH
(07706) 296
An 18 hole undulating moorland course (4681 yards, SSS 63) with spectacular views of the sea and mountains. Visitors of all playing abilities are welcome. Green fees on application. There is a licensed bar and a tea room. Brodick Castle is 10 minutes away.
Location
Lamlash, Brodick, Isle of Arran KA27 8JU
The club is situated on the A841 Lamlash-Whiting Bay road, just three miles south of Brodick ferry terminal.

RAC recommended hotels in Brodick.

LANARK
(0555) 3219
A championship 18 hole moorland course (6423 yards, SSS 71). Provided they have a handicap certificate, visitors are welcome on weekdays. Green fees on application. There is a resident chef and full catering facilities are available including a bar. Local attractions include New Lanark Hill and Lanark Country Park.
Location
The Moor, Whitelees Road, Lanark ML11 7RX
Leave the A73 or A72 at Lanark, turn left into Whitelees Road and continue for about half a mile. The club is approximately three-quarters of a mile from the railway station.

RAC recommended hotel
Popinjay ★★★ (055 586) 441 On the banks of the Clyde, in Rosebank, a fine Tudor revival style (1900) building. Facilities include fishing.

LARGS
(0475) 673594
An 18 hole parkland and seaside course with views to the Isle of Arran (6220 yards, SSS 70). Visitors with a handicap certificate are welcome. Green fees are £16 per day or £10 per round. Full catering facilities are available. The course is situated in the heart of Burns Country and Ayr and Glasgow are both within easy reach.
Location
Irvine Road, Largs, Ayrshire KA30 8EU
The course is 1 mile south of Largs on the A78, 28 miles from Glasgow.

RAC recommended hotels
Elderslie ★★ (0475) 686460 A Victorian building on the seafront. It has commanding views of Firth of Clyde.
Glen Eldon ★★ (0475) 673381 A two-storey building with a pleasant garden.
Queen's ★★ (0475) 675311 Small family-run hotel fronted by well-kept lawns. Good sea views. Putting.
Springfield ★★ (0475) 673119 Overlooking sea front, a three-storey building with pleasant views of Firth of Clyde. Putting.

LARKHALL
(0698) 881113
A 9 hole municipal inland course (6236 yards, SSS 70). Visitors of all playing abilities are welcome. Green fees on application. There is a bar and meals are served at weekends.
Location
Burnhead Road, Larkhall, Lanarkshire
Leave the M74/A74 and the course is on the east side of the town, on the B7019.

LEADHILLS
(0659) 74222
A short but challenging 9 hole moorland course (2400 yards, SSS 62) which has the distinction of being the highest golf course in Great Britain, and which can be very windy. Visitors of all playing abilities are welcome at any time. Green fees are £2.50 on weekdays and £3.50 at weekends. Local attractions include the Lead Mining Museum and New Lanark.
Location
Leadhills, Biggar, Lanarkshire ML12 6XR
You will find the course within the village at the rear of the hotel, 6 miles from the A74 at Abington.

LENZIE
041-776 1535
An 18 hole moorland course (5982 yards, SSS 69) which is 100 years old in 1990. Visitors are welcome if accompanied by a member. Green fees on application. Meals and snacks are available every day except Monday. Glasgow city centre is within easy reach.
Location
19 Crosshill Road, Lenzie, Glasgow G66 3DA
Take the A80 to Stepps and turn left at the traffic lights into Lenzie road.

LETHAMHILL
041-770 6220
An 18 hole municipal parkland course (6073 yards, SSS 69). Visitors of all playing abilities are welcome. Green fees are £2.50 for adults, £1.50 for Juniors on weekdays and £3 at weekends and Bank Holidays. There is a tea room at the club which is open between April and September and there is a restaurant close by. Glasgow city centre is within easy reach.
Location
Cumbernauld Road, Glasgow G33 1AH
The course is situated on the A80 adjacent to Hogganfield Loch, 3 miles north east of the city centre.

LINN PARK
041-637 5871
An 18 hole parkland course (4848 yards, SSS 65). Provided they have a handicap certificate, visitors are welcome. There are practice nets and also a putting green. Green fees on application. Teas and snacks are normally available. The course is only 4 miles from the city centre.
Location
Simshill Road, Glasgow G44
The club is situated off the B766, 5 miles south of Glasgow, on the road to Carmunnock.

RAC recommended hotel
Busby ★★ 041-644 2661 Small hotel located in an attractive setting.

LITTLEHILL
041-772 1916
An 18 hole parkland course (6228 yards, SSS 69). There are no restrictions on visitors and beginners are particularly welcome. Green fees on application. There is a restaurant within the club house. Glasgow is within reasonable distance.
Location
Auchinairn Road, Bishopbriggs, Glasgow
The course is located 3 miles north of the city centre, close to Stobhill General Hospital.

LOCHRANZA
(077 083) 273
A 9 hole course (1815 yards, SSS 29). Visitors are welcome at all times and the club particularly encourages Juniors and OAPs. Green fees are £2 per round or £15 for a weekly ticket. Juniors can play for £1.25. Cold snacks are available. The Isle of Arran is particularly beautiful for a holiday visit.
Location
Lochranza, Isle of Arran GA27 8HJ

LOCHWINNOCH
(0505) 842153
An extremely attractive 18-hole parkland course providing testing golf and some hard walking (6202 yards, SSS 70). It is situated in a quiet scenic country village and overlooks a bird santuary and a boating loch. Provided you have a handicap certificate visitors are welcome on weekdays until 4pm and at weekends by arrangement. Green fees are £8 a day. There is a bar and full catering facilities are available everyday except Monday. Local attractions include Lochwinnock Nature Reserve and the Indoor Bowling Club.
Location
Burnfoot Road, Lochwinnoch, Renfrewshire
The club is situated on the A760 about 10 miles south west of Paisley. Take the first on the right after Struthers garage and the course is 400 yards along Burnfoot Road.

LOUDOUN
(0563) 821993
An attractive 18 hole parkland course (5854 yards, SSS 68). Visitors are welcome on weekdays. Green fees on application. Catering facilities are available.
Location
Galston, Ayrshire KA4 8PA

From Kilmarnock, take the Edinburgh road, the A71, east towards Galston. The club lies on the main road between Galston and Newmills.

MACHRIE
(0496) 2310
A 18 hole seaside links course (6226 yards, SSS 71). Visitors with a handicap certificate are welcome at all times. Green fees are £12.50 per round. The is the only course on this beautiful island. Other facilities include tennis.
Location
Machrie Hotel, Port Ellen, Isle of Islay, Argyll PA42 7AN
The course is situated on the A846 adjacent to the airport, 4 miles from Port Ellen. Take the plane from Glasgow or the ferry from Mennacraig.

MACHRIE BAY
(077084) 267
A fairly flat 9 hole seaside course (2123 yards, SSS 32) with extensive views of the coast. Visitors of all playing abilities are welcome at any time and family foursomes are played on Tuesday and Friday during July and August. Green fees on application. Snacks are available during the months of June, July and August. Local attractions include Brodick Castle.
Location
c/o Sec, Camus Ban, Machrie, by Brodick, Isle of Arran KA27 8DZ
The course is 3½ miles north from Blackwaterfoot. Take the ferry to Brodick and continue via String Road to Machrie.

RAC recommended hotel
Kinloch ★★★ (077 086) 444 Small modern hotel in own grounds overlooking sea. Indoor swimming pool, squash, sauna, solarium, gymnasium, billiards.

MACHRIHANISH
(058 681) 213
A splendid 18 hole seaside links course of championship standard (6228 yards, SSS 70). There is also a 9 hole course (2395 yards) and a practice area. Visitors who have a handicap certificate are welcome at all times but the club is popular and it is advisable to book in advance. Green fees are £8.50 per round, £10.50 per day on weekdays and £10 a day at weekends. There are full catering and bar facilities. A special flight/golf package is also available. Campbeltown is very close.
Location
Machrihanish, Campbeltown, Argyll
The club is situated 5 miles west of Campbeltown on the B843.

MILLPORT
(0475) 530311
An 18 hole seaside/moorland course (5831 yards, SSS 68) situated on a hill overlooking the Firth of Clyde and some splendid views over Bute to the Mull of Kintyre. There is also a large practice area. Visitors with a handicap certificate are welcome at all times. Green fees on application. Meals are served daily. Other facilities include bowling and cycling.
Location
Golf Road, Millport, Isle of Cumbrae KA28 0BA
Take the McBrayne car ferry from Largs slip to Cumbrae slip. This takes seven minutes.

MILNGAVIE
041-956 1619
A fairly testing 18 hole moorland course (5818 yards, SSS 68) with some hard walking, and which can be quite windy at times. There are some good views. Visitors are welcome at any time provided they are accompanied by a member. Green fees are £10 per day on weekdays and £10 per round, £16 per day at weekends. Catering for parties is available by arrangement. The course is situated near Glasgow.
Location
Laighpark, Milngavie, Glasgow G62 8EP
The course is off the A809, Glasgow-Drymen road, north west of Glasgow. Approximately 1 mile past Stockiemuir Service Station turn right at the signpost. The course is about 1½ miles from Milngavie.

RAC recommended hotel
Black Bull Thistle ★★★ 041-956 2291 A traditional hotel in the town centre, catering for both tourists and business people.

MOUNT ELLAN
(0236) 872277
An 18 hole undulating meadowland course with lots of bunkers (5526 yards, SSS 68). Visitors are welcome by arrangement. Green fees are £8 on weekdays and £9 at weekends. Full catering facilities are available.
Location
Johnston House, Johnston Road, Gartcosh, Glasgow
The club is situated 1 mile south of the A80 Glasgow-Stirling road, three quarters of a mile north of Gartcosh.

OLD RANFURLY
(0505) 613612
An interesting 18 hole moorland course (6266 yards. SSS 70). Visitors with a handicap certificate are welcome on weekdays by introduction and at weekends if accompanied by a member. Green fees are £1.50 per round on weekdays and £2 per round at weekends if introduced by a member. Snack lunch and high tea are available.
Location
Ranfurly Place, Bridge of Weir, Renfrewshire PA11 3DE
The club is situated 7 miles west of Paisley.

PAISLEY
041-884 3903
An 18 hole moorland course which can be windy but has some fine views (6424 yards, SSS 71). Visitors are welcome mid week before 4pm provided they have a letter of introduction or made prior arrangements with the secretary. There is also a practice area. Green fees are £8 per round, £12 per day. Both meals and bar snacks are available. Local attractions include the Burrell Museum in Glasgow which is only 8 miles away.
Location
Braehead, Paisley PA2 8TZ
From Glasgow take the A737 to Paisley and about 3 miles south of Paisley centre, go up Causeyside Street into Neilston Road. Turn right into Glenburn and then left at the roundabout for the club.

RAC recommended hotel
Excelsior ★★★★ 041-887 1212 A modern sound-proofed hotel situated next to the airport terminal. Facilities include a solarium.

POLLOK
041-632 1080
A wooded 18 hole parkland course (6257 yards, SSS 70) with a river running through. Male visitors with a handicap certificate are welcome Monday to Friday. Green fees are £15 per round and £20 per day. There is a dining room which serves lunch, tea and dinner, and snacks are served in the lounge. Local attractions include the Burrell Collection in Glasgow.
Location
90 Barrhead Road, Glasgow G43 1BG
The club is on the A762, 4 miles south of Glasgow city centre.

RAC recommended hotels in Glasgow.

PORT BANNATYNE
(0700) 2009
A 13 hole hilly seaside course (4654 yards, SSS 63) with magnificent views over the Clyde estuary. There is a particularly difficult 4th hole. Visitors are not restricted and parties are welcome. Green fees are £5 on weekdays, £5 at weekends or a weekly ticket for £20. Juniors can play for £3 on weekdays and weekends or a weekly ticket for £12. Catering is available by arrangement and there are also eating facilities in the village about a quarter of a mile away. Local attractions include Rothesey Castle and the lovely local bays and beaches.
Location
Bannatyne Mains Road, Port Bannatyne, Isle of Bute
The course is 2 miles north of Rothesay ferry terminal on the A845.

PORT GLASGOW
(0475) 704181
An 18 hole undulating course situated on a hill overlooking the Clyde (5712 yards, SSS 68). There are some spectacular views from Dumbarton to Cowal Hills. Visitors are welcome on weekdays until 3.55pm if not introduced by a member and at any time if so introduced. Green fees are £6 per round or £10 per day. Meals are served by arrangement. Local attractions include Newark Castle and Port Glasgow.
Location
Devol Farm Industrial Estate, Port Glasgow, Renfrewshire PA14 5XE

PRESTWICK
(0292) 77404
An 18 hole seaside links course with natural hazards (6544 yards, SSS 72). Visitors are welcome by arrangement and advance booking is essential. You must also be a member of a recognised golf club. Green fees on application. There is a dining room for men only, and the Cardinal room for mixed company where casual dress is allowed and light lunches are served.
Location
2 Links Road, Prestwick, Ayrshire KA9 1QG
The course is 1 mile from Preswick airport, adjacent to Prestwick station. It is 40 minutes by car from Turnberry Hotel, 10 minutes from Troon, 15 minutes from Ayr.

RAC recommended hotels
Carlton Toby ★★★ (0292) 76811 Purpose-built hotel convenient for Ayr and Prestwick.
North Beach ★★ (0292) 79069 Small hotel convenient for golf course, station and beach. Billiards.
St Nicholas ★★ (0292) 79568 Family-managed hotel in three-storey Victorian building. Convenient for beach and town.

PRESTWICK ST CUTHBERT
(0292) 77101
A flat 18 hole parkland course with some trees and natural hazards but which can be windy at times (6470 yards, SSS 71). There are limited practice facilities. Visitors of all playing abilities are welcome on weekdays and at weekends, if playing with a member. Green fees are £7 per round, £12 per day. Bar snacks, lunch and dinner are served daily. Local attractions include Culzean Castle (NT) and Ayr.
Location
East Road, Prestwick, Ayrshire KA9 2SX
The course is off the main Ayr-Prestwick road, A77, at Bellevue Road, near Prestwick airport.

PRESTWICK ST NICHOLAS
(0292) 77608
An 18 hole links course with lots of heather and easy walking. There are good views of the Firth of Clyde (5926 yards, SSS 68). Provided they have a handicap certificate, visitors are welcome on weekdays. Green fees are £15 per day or £10 per round. Lunch and high tea are served every day. The course is in the heart of Burns Country.
Location
Grangemuir Road, Prestwick, Ayrshire KA9 1SN
The course is situated on the seafront, off the A79. From Main Street turn into Grangemuir Road

which runs down to the sea.

RALSTON
041-882 1349
An 18 hole parkland course (6100 yards, SSS 69). Visitors are only welcome if you are part of an organised party. Green fees by arrangement. Meals are served at the club.
Location
Strathmore Avenue, Ralston, Paisley, Renfrewshire PE1 3EP
The course is situated to the east of Paisley, off the main Paisley to Glasgow road.

RANFURLY CASTLE
(0505) 612609
An 18 hole undulating moorland course (6284 yards, SSS 70). Visitors with a handicap certificate and an introduction from a member are welcome on weekdays . There is also a practice ground. Green fees on application. Snacks, lunch and high tea are served. The course is only 30 minutes from the coast.
Location
Golf Road, Bridge of Weir, Renfrewshire PA11 3HN
Take the M8 from Glasgow and leave it at junction 29. From there take the A240 and A761 to the Bridge of Weir.

RENFREW
041-886 6692
A tree-lined 18 hole parkland course with featured rivers (6818 yards, SSS 73). There is also a practice ground. Visitors are welcome with a handicap certificate and an introduction by a member. Green fees are £9 per round or £12 per day. There are restaurant facilities and a bar.
Location
Blythswood Estate, Inchinnan Road, Renfrew
Take the A8 to Renfrew and turn in at the Stakis Normandy Hotel.

RAC recommended hotels
Excelsior ★★★★ 041-887 1212 A modern sound-proofed high rise building nexr to the airport terminal. Facilities include a solarium.
Stakis Normandy ★★★ 041-886 4100 A modern hotel convenient for the airport. There is a Bayeux tapestry feature in the foyer.

ROTHESAY
(0700) 2244
An 18 hole undulating course (5440 yards, SSS 67). Visitors with a handicap certificate are welcome. Green fees are £6.50 per day or £8.50 at weekends. A fornightly ticket is available for £30. Full catering facilities every day. Local attractions include the fishing and Rothesay Castle and bays.
Location
Canada Hill, Rothesay, Isle of Bute PA20 7HN
Access to the Island is by steamer from Wemyss Bay which runs every hour during the day from May to October.

RAC recommended hotels
St Ebba (Highly Acclaimed) (0700) 542683
Ardyne (Highly Acclaimed) (0700) 542052

ROUTENBURN
(0475) 673230
An 18 hole seaside hill course with splendid views over the Firth of Clyde (5650 yards, SSS 67). Visitors with a handicap certificate are welcome on weekdays. Green fees are £3.50 per round, £6.70 per day or £25 for a weekly ticket. It is £19 at weekends. Full catering facilities are available every day except Thursday. Local attractions include Kelburn Country Park and Largs Marina.
Location
Largs, Ayrshire KA30 8SQ
Take turning inland from A78 1 mile north of Largs.

RAC recommended hotels in Largs.

ROYAL TROON & PORTLAND
(0292) 311555
There are two seaside links courses here. The Championship, 18 holes (6641 yards, SSS 71) and the Portland, 18 holes (6274 yards, SSS 71). Provided they have a handicap certificate, visitors are welcome between Monday and Thursday but there are starting time restrictions so it is advisable to telephone ahead. The maximum handicap is 18. No ladies are allowed on the old course (Championship). Green fees are £40 on the Championship course and £25 on the Portland course. There is a bar where snacks are available and there is also a full restaurant service.
Location
Craigend Road, Troon, Ayrshire KA10 6EP
The course is 3 miles from Prestwick Airport on the B749.

RAC recommended hotels in Troon.

SANDYHILLS
041-778 1179
An 18 hole parkland course (6253 yards, SSS 70). Visitors holding a current handicap certificate are welcome by arrangement. Green fees are £7 per round or £10 per day. Full catering facilities are available except Monday. Glasgow city centre is within easy reach.
Location
223 Sandyhills Road, Glasgow G32 9NA
From Tollcross Road, on the east side of Glasgow, turn left at Killin Street and then right into Sandyhills Road.

SHISKINE
(077086) 293
A 12 hole seaside course (3000 yards, SSS 42) with some wonderful sea views. Visitors are welcome at all times. Green fees are £5. There is a club house and snacks are available June to September. Other facilities are tennis and bowling. Local attractions include Brodick Castle.
Location
Blackwaterfoot, Isle of Arran KA27 8HA

RAC recommended hotel in Machrie Bay.

SHOTTS
(0501) 20431
A semi-flat 18 hole wooded moorland course (6125 yards, SSS 70) with the distinction of the 4th hole being the most difficult in Scotland. There is also a practice area. There are no restrictions on visitors during the week. Green fees are £8 per day on weekdays and £10 at weekends. Full catering facilities are available between April and October.
Location
Blairhead, Shotts ML7 5BJ
The course is midway between Edinburgh and Glasgow, 2 miles from the M8, off Benhar Road.

SKELMORLIE
(0475) 520152
A pretty 13 hole parkland/moorland course with splendid views over the Firth of Clyde (5104 yards, SSS 65). Provided they have a handicap certificate, visitors are welcome on any day except Saturday between March and October. Green fees are £8 per day on weekdays and £11 at weekends. Lunch, dinner and tea are served on Wednesday and at weekends. Glasgow is within easy access.
Location
Skelmorlie, Ayrshire PA17 5ES
The course is 1 mile from Wemyss Bay station, 5 miles north of Largs, 8 miles south of Gounock.

RAC recommended hotel
Manor Park ★★★ (0475) 520832 A country house with extensive grounds and fine views of Firth Of Clyde.

STRATHAVEN
(0357) 20421
An 18 hole parkland course (6226 yards, SSS 70) with magnificent views over the town and valley. Visitors are welcome on weekdays and parties on Monday and Thursday. Green fees are available by request. There is a bar and full catering facilities are available throughout the day. Local attractions include Strathaven Castle.
Location
Overton Ave, Glasgow Road, Strathaven ML10 6NF
The course is situated on the ouskirts of the town on the A726.

RAC recommended hotel
Strathaven ★★★ (0357) 21778 A three-storey Adam-designed house on the outskirts of the town, conveniently situated for the M74.

TARBERT
(088 02) 565
A lovely 9 hole, hilly, seaside course (2230 yards, SSS 64). Visitors are welcome without restrictions. Green fees are £3 per 9 holes, £4 per 18 holes. There is a licenced bar in the club house. Local attractions include Tarbert Castle.
Location
Kilberry Road, Tarbert, Argyll
Take the A83 road to Campbeltown from Tarbert for 1 mile and then turn right onto the B8024 for approximately a quarter of a mile to the club house.

RAC recommended hotel
Stonefield Castle ★★★ (088 02) 836 A Baronial building, situated in a wooded garden overlooking the loch. Facilities include swimming pool, putting, tennis, sauna, solarium and billiards.
Anchor ★★ (088 02) 577 White-painted hotel, close to harbour, with good views.

TORRANCE HOUSE
(035 52) 33451
A windy 18 hole parkland course with several testing holes and some hard walking (6640 yards, SSS 71). Provided they have a handicap certificate, visitors are welcome although there are some reservations. Green fees on application. Meals are served.
Location
Strathaven Road, East Kilbride, Glasgow G75 0QZ

RAC recommended hotels
Bruce ★★★ (035 52) 29771 A modern hotel centrally situated in the town.
Stuart ★★★ (035 52) 21162 Conveniently situated, a modern purpose-built hotel in the town centre.
Crutherland ★★★ (035 52) 37633 A country house in a quiet rural situation, convenient for New Town and Glasgow. Facilities include putting, fishing.

TROON MUNICIPAL
(0292) 312464
A municipal club with three courses. The Lochgreen, 18 holes (6687 yards, SSS 72), The Darley, 18 holes (6327 yards, SSS 70) and The Fullerton, 18 holes (4784 yards, SSS 63). The course is particularly good for Juniors and beginners. There is also a practice ground. Visitors are welcome. Green fees are £5.60 per round, £8.80 per day on weekdays, £6.70 per round, £10.70 a day at weekends for the Lochgreen and Darley courses, and £4.75 per round, £6.25 per day on weekdays, £4 per round, £7.45 per day at weekends for the Fullerton course. Full catering facilities are available.
Location
Harling Drive, Troon, Ayrshire KA10 6NE
Take the A77 from Glasgow and follow the directions for Troon. The course is 100 yards from the station.

RAC recommended hotels
Marine Highland ★★★★ (0292) 314 444 Dignified Victorian sandstone building with views of sea and links. Indoor swimming pool, squash, sauna, solarium, gymnasium, billiards, putting.
Piersland House ★★★ (0292) 314747 Privately-

owned hotel close to two golf courses and the beach. Putting.
Sun Court ★★★ (0292) 312727 Large elegant extended Edwardian residence. Own real tennis court. Squash.
Ardneil ★★ (0292) 311611 A Victorian house with modern extensions. The hotel is family run and convenient for the sea. Facilities include billiards.
Craiglea ★★ (0292) 311366 A Victorian building with fine views of Firth of Clyde.
South Beach ★★ (0292) 312033 A white Victorian building of character with a sun lounge facing the sea. Facilities include putting, sauna, solarium and billiards.

TURNBERRY HOTEL
(0655) 31000
There are two seaside courses here both with magnificent views over Turnberry Bay to Arran and Ailsa Craig. Both are championship courses. The Ailsa, 18 holes (6950 yards, SSS 70) and The Arran, 18 holes (6276 yards, SSS 69). Visitors with a current handicap certificate are welcome by prior arrangement, as are day visitors. Green fees for hotel residents are £18.50 for the Ailsa course, £11 for the Arran course and day visitors can play for £27.50 per day between Monday and Friday, and £32.50 at weekends for the Ailsa course and £17 for the Arran course. There is a club house restaurant and bar which are open between 8am and 10pm and day visitors are welcome in the Hotel.
Location
Turnberry Hotel, Turnberry, Ayrshire KA26 9LT
The course is situated off the A77 from Glasgow just before you reach Girvan.

RAC recommended hotel
Turnberry ★★★★★ (0655) 31000 An elegant Edwardian hotel with magnificent sea views. Facilities include an indoor swimming pool, golf, putting, tennis, riding, sauna, solarium, gymnasium and billiards.

VALE OF LEVEN
(0389) 52351
An 18 hole moorland course overlooking Loch Lomond with splendid views (5156 yards, SSS 66). The course can be quite difficult with its natural hazards including burns, trees and gorse. Visitors are welcome on weekdays only between April and October, unless introduced by a member, but at any time during the winter months. Green fees are £5 per day on weekdays and £10 at weekends.
Location
Northfield Course, Bonfield, Alexandria, Dunbartonshire
Leave the A82 at Bonhill for the club.

RAC recommended hotel in Balloch
Balloch ★★ (0389) 52579 An old-established traditional stone-built tourist hotel near the end of Loch Lomond.

VAUL
(087 92) 566
A 9 hole seaside course (6246 yards, SSS 70). Visitors of all playing abilities are welcome but there is no golf on Sunday. Green fees are £3 per day, £10 for one week. The surrounding area is good for country walks, wind surfing and there are some lovely beaches.
Location
Scarinish, Isle of Tiree, Argyll

WESTERN GAILES
(0294) 311649
A splendid 18 hole links course with excellent turf (6664 yards, SSS 72). There are magnificant views across the Firth of Clyde. Visitors with a handicap certificate are welcome on weekdays except Thursday and Saturday, and no ladies can play on Tuesday. It is advisable to book in advance. Green fees on application. Lunch, snacks and high tea are always available and dinner by arrangement. Local attractions include the Burns Museum in Irvine and Culzean Castle.
Location
Gailes, By Irvine, Ayrshire KA11 5AE
The course is 5 miles north of Troon on the A78.

RAC recommended hotels in Irvine.

WEST KILBRIDE
(0294) 823911
A fine links course with views of the Isle of Arran (6247 yards, SSS 70). Provided they have a handicap certificate and a letter of introduction, visitors are welcome on weekdays but not at weekends or Bank Holidays. Green fees on application. Lunch, high tea and dinner are served daily. Local attractions include Isle of Arran and Burns Country.
Location
33-35 Fullerton, Drive, Seamill, West Kilbride, Ayrshire KA23 9HT
Take the A78 Greenock-Ayr road and leave it at Seamill.

WHITECRAIGS
041-639 4530
A particularly lovely 18 hole parkland course (6230 yards, SSS 70). Visitors of all playing abilities are welcome but only by introduction. Green fees are £16 per round or £1 if you are playing a member. Lunch is served every day except Monday. Local attractions include the Burrell Collection.
Location
72 Ayr Road, Giffnock, Glasgow G46 6SW
The course is 7 miles south of Glasgow on the A77, 1½ miles north east of Newton Mearns.

RAC recommended hotel see East Renfrewshire.

WILLIAMWOOD
041-637 1783
A hilly 18 hole wooded parkland course (5808 yards, SSS 68) with a small lake and a pond. The course can be quite tricky. There is a practice area and a putting green. Visitors holding a current handicap certificate are welcome by introduction only unless they live more than 40 miles away. Green fees on application. Lunch and evening meals are served every day although they should be ordered in advance. Glasgow city centre is within easy reach.
Location
Clarkston Road, Netherlee, Glasgow G44
The club is 5 miles south of the city centre on the B767, beside the Clarkston Toll on Clarkston Road.

RAC recommended hotels see East Renfrewshire.

WINDYHILL
041-942 7157
An 18 hole undulating moorland/parkland course (6254 yards, SSS 70). Visitors of all playing abilities are welcome on weekdays. There is a practice area and caddy cars are available. Green fees on application. Bar and full catering facilities are available. The course is within easy reach of Loch Lomond as well as Glasgow city centre.
Location
Bal Jaffray Road, Bearsden, Glasgow G61 4QQ
Take the A739 from Glasgow for 8 miles then turn right onto the A809. After 1 mile turn left onto the A810 and the club is 1 mile on the right.

RAC recommended hotel in Milngavie.

WISHAW
(0698) 372869
An 18 hole parkland course (6160 yards, SSS 69). Visitors are welcome on weekdays and Sunday but not Saturday. Green fees are £6 per round or £9 per day on weekdays and £13 on Sunday. Lunch, high tea are served and dinner if ordered before 6pm. The course is within easy reach of Hamilton.
Location
55 Clieland Road, Wishaw, Lanarkshire ML2 7PL
Take the M74 south east of Glasgow. The course is in the centre of town, 3 miles south of Motherwell.

TAYSIDE

ABERFELDY
(0887) 20535
A 9 hole parkland course (2733 yards, SSS 67) with easy walking situated by the River Tay near the Wade Bridge and Black Watch Monument. Visitors of all playing abilities are welcome. Green fees on application. There is a bar and snacks are normally available.
Location
Taybridge Road, Aberfeldy, Perthshire PH15 2BH
Leave the A9 at Ballinluig and the course is about 10 miles from here, off the A827.

RAC recommended hotels
Weem ★★ (0887) 20381 A stone-built 17th-century coaching inn of character.
Moness House C/H ★★★ Attractive, white-painted, 18th-century house in 35 acres of grounds. Indoor swimming pool, putting, sauna, solarium, gymnasium, billiards.

ALYTH
(08283) 2268
A windy 18 hole moorland course with easy walking (6226 yards, SSS 70). Visitors of all playing abilities are welcome. Green fees on application. Full catering facilities are available.
Location
Pitcrocknie, Alyth, Perthshire
Take the A926 to Alyth and about half a mile from the major roundabout take the B954 Glenisla road.

ARBROATH
(0241) 72272
An 18 hole seaside course (6078 yards, SSS 69). The course is a municipal one and visitors are welcome at all times. Green fees on application. Snacks are normally served and meals by arrangement.
Location
Elliot, Arbroath, Angus
The course is on the A92, 2 miles south of Arbroath.

RAC recommended hotel
Seaforth ★★ (0241) 72232 Red sandstone 1930's-style building with later extension. In outskirts.

AUCHTERARDER
(0764) 62804
A flat 18 hole parkland course, partly wooded, with easy walking (5737 yards, SSS 68). Visitors of all playing abilities are welcome weekdays and also at weekends unless Open Competitions are being held. Green fees are under review. There is a bar where snacks are served and lunch and dinner is also available.
Location
Orchil Road, Auchterarder, Perthshire PH3 1L
The course is off the A9 to the south west of the town, near Gleneagles.

RAC recommended hotel
Gleneagles ★★★★★ (0764) 62231 A famous luxury hotel set in magnificent countryside. Facilities include an indoor swimming pool, golf, putting, tennis, fishing, squash, riding, sauna, solarium and gymnasium and billiards.

BLAIR ATHOLL
(079681) 274
A flat 9 hole parkland course with easy walking situated alongside a river (5710 yards, SSS 69). Visitors of all playing abilities are welcome. Green fees are £5 per round or day on weekdays and £7 at weekends. There is a bar where snacks are served and meals are available. Local attractions include Blevi Castle and the Old Mill.
Location
Blair Atholl, Perthshire
The course is situated on the A9, 6 miles north of Pitlochry.

BLAIRGOWRIE
(0250) 2594
Two flat 18 hole wooded moorland courses, the Rosemount, (6588 yard, SSS 72). and the Lansdowne (6895 yards, SSS 73). There are also three practice grounds and a 'Wee' course. Visitors with current handicap certificate are welcome, although booking in advance is necessary on Monday, Tuesday and Thursday, and through starting on Wednesday, Saturday and Sunday. Green fees are £15 per round, £20 a day on weekdays and £20 per round at weekends. Green fees for the 'Wee' course are £6 for the day. Full catering facilities are available.
Location
Rosemount, Blairgowrie, Perthshire PH10 6LG
Take the A923 out of Perth and turn right at the 'Rosemount' sign.

RAC recommended hotels
Altamount House ★★ (0250) 3512 A stone-built former private house situated in its own small grounds in the outskirts of the town.
Rosemount Golf ★★ (0250) 2912 A three-storey former private house with modern extensions in pleasant gardens.

BRECHIN
(03562) 2383
An 18 hole rolling parkland/meadowland course (5267 yards, SSS 66). Players of all levels are welcome at any time, particularly beginners. Parties are welcome by prior arrangement. There are some restrictions on Wednesday which is Ladies Day. Green fees are £10.50 a day on weekdays and £11.50 on Saturday and Sunday. There is a bar and excellent catering facilities. Local attractions include Montrose seaside, Brechin Cathedral, Brechin Round Tower, Edzell Castle and Brechin Castle.
Location
Trinity, by Brechin, Angus DD9 7PD
The course is in Trinity Village, 1 mile north of Brechin by the B966.

RAC recommended hotels in Edzell.

CAIRD PARK
(0382) 453606
An 18 hole wooded parkland course (6303 yards, SSS 70). Mains Castle is in the centre of the course. There is a practice range. Visitors are welcome but booking in advance is recommended. Green fees on application. Catering facilities by arrangement. Local attractions include *HMS Discovery*, Scott's ship, and St Andrews.
Location
Mains Loan, Dundee, Tayside DD4 9BX
The course is situated on the northern edge of the city, just off Kingsway.

RAC recommended hotels in Dundee
Stakis Earl Grey ★★★★ (0382) 29271 Recently opened five-storey hotel on northern side of River Tay with landscaped gardens to river. Indoor swimming pool, sauna, solarium, gymnnasium.
Angus Thistle ★★★ (0382) 26874 Large modern purpose-built hotel in city centre.
Invercarse ★★★ (0382) 69231 Victorian house , with extensive modern additions, in pleasant grounds. River views.
Queen's ★★★ (0382) 22515 A five-storey stone-built traditional Victorian style hotel in city centre.
Swallow ★★★ (0382) 641122 Historic 'colonial' mansion extended to include indoor swimming pool, putting, sauna, solarium, gymnasium.

CALLANDER
(0877) 30090
A partly wooded 18 hole parkland course with panoramic views (5125 yards, SSS 66). There is also a small lake. Visitors are welcome at any time. Green fees are £8 per round, £10 a day on weekdays and £12 per round, £12 a day at weekends. Full catering facilities are available and the bar is open all day. Local attractions include the Woollen Mills and Deanstor Distilleries.
Location
Aveland Road, Callander, Perthshire FK17 8EN
Take the A84 from Stirling and turn right at the Roman Camp Hotel about half a mile from the town centre car park. The club house is signposted.

RAC recommended hotels
Roman Camp ★★★ (0877) 30003 A 17th-century stone-built former hunting lodge set in some beautiful gardens. Facilities include fishing.
Dalgair House ★★ (0877) 30283 A small hotel, recently opened, above a popular resturant in the town.
Glenorchy ★★ (0877) 30329 Stone-built villa with an extension in own grounds beside main road to west of town. Putting.

CAMPERDOWN
(0382) 623398
A flat 18 hole championship wooded parkland course (6561 yards, SSS 72). The course is a municipal one and visitors are welcome but all enquiries should be made to the General Manager of Parks, 353 Clepington Road, Dundee. Green fees are £6.50. Catering facilities are by arrangement, telephone 621993. Other sporting facilities are also available.
Location
Camperdown Park, Dundee
The course is situated in Coupar Angus Road, close to the Kingsway junction.

RAC recommended hotels in Dundee see Caird Park.

CARNOUSTIE
(0241) 53249
There are actually three championship seaside links courses here. The Burnside, 18 holes (6020 yards, SSS 69), Buddon Links, 18 holes (5732 yards, SSS 68) and Championship, 18 holes, 6931 yards, SSS 74). Visitors are welcome but are restricted to their handicap for the Championship course and there are some limitations on the others so it is advisable to check beforehand. Golf trolleys are permitted only between May and October. Green fees are £19 per round, £28 a day. Catering facilities can be arranged with other local clubs. Local attractions include Glamis Castle, Arbroath Abbey and Dundee.
Location
Links Parade, Carnoustie, Angus DD7 5JE
The course is off the A630, 12 miles east of Dundee.

RAC recommended hotel
Glencoe ★★ (0241) 53273 Overlooking the golf course and the sea, a former villa with modern extensions.

COMRIE
(0764) 70544
An attractive 9 hole highland course (5962 yards, SSS 69). Visitors are welcome at all times. Green fees are £5 on weekdays and £6 at weekends. Coffee and light snacks are available during the summer season.
Location
c/o Sec, Donald C McGlashan, 10 Polinard, Comrie, Perthshire
The course is on the A85, 6 miles west of Crieff, at the east end of Comrie village.

RAC recommended hotel
Comrie ★★ (0764) 70239 A detached villa with some later extensions, situated at the end of the main village street.

CRAIGIE HILL
(0738) 22644
An 18 hole hilly course (5739 yards, SSS 66). Visitors are welcome on weekdays but you must make a telephone booking if you wish to play at the weekend. Green fees are £6 per round or £2.50 with a member, £8 a day on weekdays and £10 per day at weekends or £5.75 after 4pm. Full catering facilities are available. Local attractions include Scone Palace.
Location
Cherrybank, Perth PH2 0NE
The course is about 1 mile west of Perth with easy access from the Stirling to Perth Road.

RAC recommended hotels
Huntingtower ★★★ (0738) 83771 A late Victorian house, ½ mile from the A85, set in 3½

acres of gardens. Facilities include putting, fishing.
Isle of Skye Osprey ★★★ (0738) 24471 Formerly four separate Victorian buildings, now linked, extended and modernised.
Lovat ★★★ (0738) 36555 Two-storey stone-built former private houses with linking extension.
Queen's ★★★ (0738) 25471 Traditional style six-storey stone and brick-built hotel. Indoor swimming pool, sauna, solarium, gymnasium.
Royal George ★★★ (0738) 24455 Large Georgian stone-built hotel with fine river views.
Salutation ★★★ (0738) 30066 Four-storey traditional hotel on main street; dating from 16th-century.
Stakis City Mills ★★★ (0738) 28281 Original old mill buildings converted to modern hotel.

CRIEFF
(0764) 2397
There are actually two parkland courses here, The Ferntower, an 18 hole course (6402 yards, SSS 71) and The Dornock, a 9 hole course (4772 yards, SSS 63). There are also two practice areas. Visitors of all levels of handicap are welcome except between midday and 2pm on weekdays. It is necessary to book at weekends. Green fees on application. There are full restaurant facilities although it is advisable to book. Bar meals are also available.
Location
Perth Road, Crieff, Perthshire PH7 3LR
Take the A85 Perth to Crieff road for 17½ miles and the course is situated at the 40 mph limit as you enter Crieff.
Creiff ★★ (0764) 2632 An attractive-looking hotel well situated near the town centre. Facilities include sauna, solarium, gymnasium.
Cultoquey House C/H ★★ (0764) 3253 Fine stone-built late Georgian house set in 6 acres of grounds. Putting, tennis, fishing, riding, billiards.
Lock's Acre ★★ (0764) 2526 Small hotel set in its own grounds with magnificent views.
Murray Park ★★ (0764) 3731 Former private villa, built of stone, set in own grounds.

DALMUNZIE
(025085) 226
An attractive 9 hole undulating course with hard walking (2035 yard, SSS 62). The course is the highest in Britain. Visitors welcome at any time. Green fees are £3 a day or £2.75 per round. Full catering facilities available in the hotel.
Location
Spittal of Glenshee, Blairgowrie, Perthshire PH10 7QE
The course is on the A93 Blairgowrie to Braemar road, 22 miles north of Blairgowrie.

DOWNFIELD
(0382) 825595
A fine 18 hole undulating parkland course situated in a wooded area (6804 yards, SSS 73). The Gelly burn is a natural hazard for several holes. There are extensive practice grounds. Visitors are welcome on weekdays between 9.30am and 11.48am and between 2.18pm and 3.48pm. Green fees are £12 per round, £18 per day. Catering facilities are available but book in advance.
Location
Tunberry Avenue, Dundee DD2 3QP
From the centre of Dundee, turn off Kingsway into the A923 and 100 yards from the roundabout turn right into Harrison road. After 50 yards from here turn left and it is about half a mile to the club house.

DUNBLANE NEW
(0786) 823711
An 18 hole undulating parkland course with fountains and some spectacular views (6876 yards, SSS 68). Visitors are welcome between Monday and Friday although it is advisable to pre-book by telephone. Green fees are £11 per round or £16 a day. There are full catering facilities.
Location
Perth Road, Dunblane, Perthshire FK15
The course is on the A9, 6 miles north of Stirling.

DUNKELD AND BIRNAM
(035 02) 524
An interesting 9 hole moorland course (5264 yards, SSS 66) with panoramic views of the surrounding countryside and a testing 9th hole. Visitors are welcome at all times. Green fees are £5 a day on weekdays and £6 at weekends. Full catering facilities are available.
Location
Fungarth, Dunkeld, Perthshire
To reach the course, turn right 1 mile north of Dunkeld on the A9.

RAC recommended hotels
Stakis Dunkeld House ★★★★ (035 02) 771 A large hotel in a 280 acre estate situated on the banks of the River Tay. Fishing, tennis.
Atholl Arms ★★ (035 02) 219 Traditional 16th-century inn extended to three-storeys.

DUNNING
(076484) 398
A 9 hole parkland course (4836 yards, SSS 64). Visitors who hold a current handicap certificate are welcome at all times. Green fees on application. Catering facilities are available at the Dunning Hotel.
Location
Rollo Park, Dunning, Perth
The course is situated off the A9, 9 miles south west of Perth.

EDZELL
(03564) 7283
A lovely 18-hole undulating moorland course set in peaceful surroundings (6299 yards, SSS 70). Visitors are welcome and there is a practice ground and a putting green. Green fees on application. There is a lounge and bar and also a dining room where full meals are served.
Location
High Street, Edzell, By Brechin, Angus DD9 7TF
Take the A94 Forfar to Aberdeen road and turn onto the B966 at the end of the Brechin by-pass. The golf course is on the left.

RAC recommended hotels
Panmure Arms ★★ (035 64) 420 A stone-built hotel, with the appearance of a village inn. Facilities include indoor swimming pool, fishing, squash, sauna, solarium and billards.
Glenesk ★★★ (035 64) 391 A red-sandstone Victorian style hotel adjacent to the golf course. Facilities include indoor swimming pool, sauna, solarium, gymnasium, and billards.

FORFAR
(0307) 62120
An 18 hole undulating wooded moorland course (6255 yards, SSS 69). Visitors are welcome. Green fees are £19.50 on weekdays and £15 at weekends. Meals are served daily.
Location
Cunninghill, Arbroath Road, By Forfar, Angus DD8 2RL
The course is 1 mile from the town on the road to Arbroath.

GLENEAGLES HOTEL
(07646) 3543
There are two undulating moorland courses at this famous club. The King's, 18 holes (6471 yards, SSS 71) and Queen's 18 holes (5964 yards, SSS 69). Visitors who have applied in writing are welcome. Green fees on application to the golf office.
Location
Auchterarder, Perthshire PH3 1NF
Take the A9 from Perth south west for 16 miles.

RAC recommended hotel
Gleneagles ★★★★★ (0764) 62231 A famous luxury hotel set in magnificent countryside. Facilities include an indoor swimming pool, golf, putting, tennis, fishing, squash, riding, sauna, solarium and gymnasium and billiards.

KILLIN
(056 72) 312
A 9 hole parkland course with some fine views (2508 yards, SSS 65). Provided they have a handicap certificate visitors are welcome on weekdays and weekends. Green fees are £6 per day. Light meals are available.
Location
Killin, Perthshire FK21
The club is situated on the outskirts of the village on the Aberfeldy road going east.

RAC recommended hotels
Bridge of Lochay ★★ (056 72) 272 An old coaching inn on the river bank on the edge of the village. Facilities include fishing.
Killin ★★ (056 72) 296 A stone-built hotel with some out buildings in the grounds by the riverside.

KING JAMES VI
(0738) 32460
An 18 hole inland parkland course with easy walking (6026 yards, SSS 68). The course is situated on an island in the middle of the River Tay in the centre of Perth. Visitors are welcome everyday except Saturday. green fees are £6 per round, £9.50 a day on weekdays and £12.50 on Sunday.
Location
Moncreiffe Island, Perth PH2 8NR
Access to the club is by footbridge over the River Tay.

GREEN HOTEL
(0577) 63467
A pleasant flat 18 hole parkland course with easy walking (6111 yards, SSS 70). Visitors are welcome at all times. Green fees are £9 per round on weekdays or £12 for a day ticket and £12 per round at weekends, £16 a day.
Location
Beeches Park, Kinross, Perthshire
The club is 17 miles south of Perth.

RAC recommended hotel
Green ★★★ (0577) 63467 A 16th-century coaching inn with a later extension. Facilities include an indoor swimming pool, putting, sauna, solarium, gymnasium and billiards.

KIRRIEMUIR
(0575) 72729
An 18 hole moorland/parkland course with good views (5591 yards, Yellow tees, SSS 67, White tees, SSS 66). Visitors are welcome during the week, and at weekends if accompanied by a member. Green fees are £9.50 per day or £27 for a weekly ticket. Juniors are half price. Full catering facilities are available at the club house.
Location
Kirriemuir, Angus DD8 4LN
The club is 1 mile north of the town centre.

LETHAM GRANGE
(024 189) 373
An 18 hole undulating wooded parkland course with water holes (6789 yards, SSS 72). Provided they have a handicap certificate, visitors are welcome. Green fees are £12 on weekdays and £15 at weekends. There is a 50% reduction for residents and members. There is also a putting green and practice area. A la carte lunch and dinner are served in the hotel (★★★), and snacks are available throughout the day. Arbroath is very close.
Location
Letham Grange, Colliston, By Arbroath, Angus
From Arbroath take the A933, Brechin/Forfar road and approximately 4 miles from here turn right at the end of Colliston for the club.

MILNATHORT
(0577) 64069
A 9 hole parkland course (5411 yards, SSS 68). Visitors of all playing abilities are welcome except on competition days. Green fees are £5 on weekdays and £6 for a weekend ticket. Meals and snacks are available.
Location
South Street, Milnathort KY13 7AW
The course is off the M90, 1½ miles north of Kinross.

RAC recommended hotels
Windlestrae ★★★ (0577) 64733 Small country residence of two-storeys set in own grounds. Indoor swimming pool, putting, sauna, solarium, gymnasium, billiards.
Bridgend ★★ (0577) 63413 Recently modernised former private house, much extended over the years.
Kirklands ★★ (0577) 63313 Refurbished 18th-century coaching inn. Family run.

MONIFIETH
(0382) 532767
Two 18 hole seaside courses, the Medal (6657 yards, SSS 72) and the Ashludie (5123 yards, SSS 66). Visitors are welcome by arrangement with the Starter except on Saturday. A handicap certificate is preferred. Green fees are £9 per round, £14 per day for the Medal and £7 per round, £10 per day for the Ashludie on weekdays and £10 per round, £15 per day for the Medal, £8 per round, £12 per day for the Ashludie on Sunday. Meals are available at one of four clubs in the vicinity.
Location
Dundee, Angus DD5 4NG
The club is situated just outside Monifieth, on the A930, 6 miles east of Dundee between Broughty Ferry and Carnoustie.

MONTROSE LINKS TRUST
(0674) 72932
Two seaside links courses, the Medal, 18 holes, (6451 yards, SSS 71) and the Broomfield, 18 holes, (4815 yards, SSS 66). Provided you have a handicap certificate, visitors are welcome. Green fees are £10 per day, £7 per round on weekdays; £9.50 per day, £8.50 per round at weekends for the Medal course; £5.50 per day, £4.50 per round on weekdays, £6 per round, £7 per day at weekends for the Broomfield course. Catering facilities can be arranged in one of the member Golf Clubs.
Location
Trail Drive, Montrose, Angus DD10 8SW
The club is off the A92 Dundee to Aberdeen road, 1 mile from the town centre.

MURRAYSHALL
(0738) 52784
An undulating 18 hole course with tree-lined fairways situated in a beautiful parkland estate. (6416 yards, SSS 71). Visitors who are of reasonable playing standard are welcome at any time. Green fees are £10 per day, £6 per round on weekdays and £10 per round, £20 per day at weekends. Full club house facilities are available.

Location
Murrayshall, by Scone, Perthshire PH2 7PH
The course is situated on the A94. From Perth, turn right before New Scone.

RAC recommended hotel
Murrayshall House C/H ★★★ (0738) 51171 A country house in 400 acres of parkland.

MUTHILL
A 9 hole parkland course with some fine views (2371 yards, SSS 63). Visitors of all playing levels, including beginners, are welcome although there are restrictions in the evening and on days when club matches are taking place. Green fees are £4 per day on weekdays and £4.40 at weekends.
Location
Peat Road, Muthill, Crieff PH5 2AD
The course is 500 yards off the Stirling to Crieff road on the A822. It is signposted at the turning.

NORTH INCH
A municipal 18 hole course laid out on level terrain in an open tree-lined riverside park (4736 yards, SSS 65). All visitors are welcome 7.30am until dusk on weekdays and 8.00am until dusk on Sunday. Green fees are £2.65 on weekdays, £4.50 at weekends and £1.70 after 2pm, concessions £1.15.
Location
The course is near centre of Perth off the A9. Follow the signs to the Bell's sports centre.

PANMURE
(0241) 53120
A challenging 18 hole links course set in sandhills (6317 yards, SSS 70). The course has been used as a qualifying course for the Open Championship. Visitors who have a handicap certificate are welcome on any day except Saturday. Green fees are £12 per round, £18 per day Sunday to Friday. There is a bar and dining room. Snacks are served daily and meals every day except Monday.
Location
Barry, Angus, DD7 7RT
Take the A930 for 2 miles from Carnoustie and turn south in the centre of Barry. After 200 yards turn right for the club.

PITLOCHRY
(0796) 2796
An interesting 18 hole hill course with plenty of variety (5811 yards, SSS 68). Provided they have a handicap certificate, visitors are welcome at any time. Caddy cars are available for hire. Green fees on application. Meals and snacks are served all day with breakfast and dinner by arrangement.
Location
Golf Course Road, Pitlochry
The course is half a mile from the centre of Pitlochry on the A9.

RAC recommended hotels
Atholl Palace ★★★ (0796) 2400 Vast Victorian hotel in grand style–spacious, beautiful grounds. Swimming pool, putting, tennis, sauna, solarium, billiards.
Pitlochry Hydro ★★★ (0796) 2666 Substantial granite-built Victorian hotel in attractive grounds on hillside. Indoor swimming pool, putting, tennis, sauna, solarium, gymnasium.
Scotland's ★★★ (0796) 2292 Refurbished, four-storey stone-fronted hotel with extensions to rear.
Acarsaid ★★ (0796) 2266 Converted large private house with modern extensions overlooking main road. Putting.
Airdaniar ★★ (0796) 2266 Converted two-storey private house with modern extensions. On main road through town.
Birchwood ★★ (0796) 2477 Victorian house with later additions set in own small grounds.
Castlebeigh ★★ (0796) 2925 On hill overlooking town, stone-built house in small grounds.
Claymore ★★ (0796) 2888 Detached two-storey house, extended and modernised.
Craigrrack ★★ (0796) 2399 Stone and brick villa (with extensions) standing above road in outskirts.
Dundaroch ★★ (0796) 2862 Large Victorian stone-built two-storey hotel located on outskirts.

ST FILLANS
(0764) 85312
A beautiful 9 hole flat parkland course (5268 yards, SSS 66). Visitors are welcome at any time. Green fees are £5 a day on weekdays and £6 a day at weekends. The club is unlicensed, but snacks and light meals are available.
Location
St Fillans, Perthshire PH6 2NG
The course is on the A85 between Crieff and Lochearnhead at the east end of Loch Earn.

RAC recommended hotel
Drummond Arms ★★ (076485) 212 A stone-built traditional style hotel situated at the roadside overlooking Loch Earn.

STRATHTAY
A 9 hole hilly course with a Spin Kop high long hole (4980 yards, SSS 63). Visitors are welcome at any time although parties should give 10 days notice. Green fees are £4 between Monday and Saturday and £5 on Sunday. There are catering facilities just down the road at the hotel.
Location
Tighanoisinn, Grandtully, Perthshire PH15 2QT
The course is 4 miles west of Ballinkrig.

TAYMOUTH CASTLE
(088 73) 228
A fairly flat 18 hole parkland course (6066 yards, SSS 69). Visitors who have a reasonable standard of golf and knowledge of etiquette are welcome at any time although it is necessary to book in advance. Green fees are £10 per round, £15 a day on weekdays and £10 per round, £10 a day at weekends. Full catering facilities are available.
Location
Kenmore, by Aberfeldy, Tayside PH15 2NT
The club is situated 6 miles west of Aberfeldy.

RAC recommended hotel
Kenmore ★★★ (088 73) 205 A charming stone-built former inn on the banks of the Tay.

WALES

ANGLESEY

ANGLESEY
(0407) 810219
An 18-hole seaside course with a river (5713 yards, SSS 68). Visitors of all levels are welcome. Green fees are £6 on weekdays and £8 at weekends. Meals are available. Situated on the Island of Anglesey with good beaches.
Location
Station Road, Rhosneigr, Gwynedd LL64 5QT
Drive from Menai Bridge on the A5, and take the A4080 to the coast at Rhosneigr. The course is to the west of the town.

BARON HILL
(0248) 810231
An undulating seaside course with 9 holes (5564 yards, SSS 67). Visitors are welcome. Green fees are available on application. Sandwiches are available. Situated on the Island of Anglesey with castle, historic house and museum.
Location
Beaumaris, Gwynedd LL58 8YN.
Drive from Menai Bridge on the A545 along the coast, the course is before the town.

RAC recommended hotels
Bulkeley Arms ★★★ (0248) 810415. Built in traditional Welsh stone with panoramic views of Snowdon.
Bishopsgate ★★ (0248) 810302. Georgian town house with chinese Chippendale staircase.
Henllys Hall ★★ (0248) 811511 Set in 50 acres of woodland, an imposing 19th century mansion with distinctive clock tower. Swimming pool, tennis, sauna, solarium, gymnasium, billiards.

BULL BAY
(0407) 830960
An undulating seaside course with 18 holes (6160 yards, SSS 70). Visitors with a handicap certificate preferred on weekdays. Green fees are £7.50 on weekdays and £10 at weekends. Meals are available by arrangement. Situated on the Island of Anglesey with good watersports, walking and local sports centre.
Location
Bull Bay Road, Amlwch, Anglesey LL68 9RY.
Drive across the Menai Bridge, take the A5025 round the north coast to Amlwch. The course is through the town on Bull Bay.

RAC recommended hotel
Trecastell ★★ (0407) 830651. Edwardian hotel overlooking the bay.

HOLYHEAD
(0407) 3279
An undulating 18-hole course (6058 yards, SSS 70). Visitors are welcome with a handicap certificate. Green fees on application. Lunch and bar snacks are available, dinners by arrangement. Situated on the Island of Anglesey with the Stack lighthouse, nature reserve and good beaches.
Location
Trearddur Bay, Holyhead, Gwynedd LL65 2YG.
Drive over the Menai Bridge on the A5 to the coast at Holyhead.

RAC recommended hotels
Beach Hotel ★★★ (0407) 860332. Attractive modern hotel. Facilities include swimming pool, squash, sauna, solarium, billiards.
Trearddur Bay ★★★ (0407) 860301 Attractive and extensively-modernised white-faced hotel. Indoor swimming pool.
Seacroft ★★ (0407) 860348 Small intimate hotel.

LLANGEFNI
(0248) 722193
A 9-hole municipal course (1467 yards, SSS 28). All visitors welcome. Green fees are £1.40 on weekdays and £2.10 at weekends. Situated on the Island of Anglesey with good watersports facilities. Beaumaris Castle and several nature reserves are near by. The 'Tunnicliffe' Gallery is on the course.
Location
Llangefni, Anglesey LL777 D1
Drive west from the Menai Bridge on the A5 then turn right on the A5114 to Llangefni.

RAC recommended hotel
Nant yr Odyn ★★ (0248) 723354. Converted eighteenth century buildings.

CLWYD

ABERGELE AND PENSARN
(0745) 824034
A parkland course with 18 holes (6086 yards, SSS 69). Visitors are welcome preferably with a handicap certificate. Green fees are £12 on weekdays and £14 at weekends. Restaurant providing full meals except on Monday. Situated on the north coast near Colwyn Bay.
Location
Tan-y-Goppa Road, Abergele, Clwyd LL22 8DS
Take the A55 west to Abergele. The course is through the town, turn left on A547 in the Llanddulas direction.

RAC recommended hotels
Kinmel Manor ★★ (0745) 832014. Modernised Georgian style country house. Indoor swimming pool, sauna, solarium, gymnasium.

BRYN MORFYDD
(074 578) 280
A 9-hole parkland course (1190 yards). Visitors of all levels are welcome. Green fees are £4 per day. Bar snacks are available.
Location
The Princess Course, Bryn Morfydd Hotel, Llanrhaedr, Clwyd LL16 4NP
From the A55 take the A525 to St Asaph south past Denbigh to Llanrhaedr.

RAC recommended hotels in Denbigh

DENBIGH
(074 581) 4159
An undulating parkland course with 18 holes (5650 yards, SSS 67). Visitors are welcome, a handicap certificate is prefered. Green fees are £7 on weekdays and £9 at weekends. Restaurant on site with full meals, booking is advisable. Situated inland with its own castle, and not far from Rhuddlan Castle.
Location
Henllan Road, Denbigh, Clwyd.
From the A55 at St Asaphs, take the A525 to Denbigh. The course is on the B5382 road to Henllan.

RAC recommended hotel
Bull ★★ (074 571) 2582. A 16th-century listed building with a 17th-century panelled dining room.

FLINT
(03526) 2327
A 9-hole parkland course. Visitors are welcome on weekdays. Green fees are £4 per day. Meals are available by arrangemant. On the mouth of the River Dee with its own castle, not far from Holyhead and a military musem as well as St Winefride's Well.
Location
Cornist Park, Flint, Clwyd CH6 5HJ.
Take the A548 coast road to Flint. The course is a mile inland, turn off at the town hall, and follow signs.

HARWARDEN
(0244) 531447
A 9-hole parkland course (5620 yards, SSS 68). Visitors are welcome with a member only. Green fees are £5. Full catering facilities available. Places of interest include Harwarden castle and all the facilities of Chester are nearby.
Location
Groomsdale Lane, Harwarden, Deeside, Clwyd CH5 3EH.
From A55 take B5125 or A550 to Harwarden; turn off to course just west of Harwarden station.

HOLYWELL
(0352) 710040
A moorland course with 9 holes (6484 yards, SSS 71). Visitors of all levels are welcome. Green fees are available on application. Lunch and dinner are available if booked. Places of local interest include the Grange Cavern, military museum and St Winefride's Well.
Location
Brynford, Holywell, Clwyd CH8
Turn left at the traffic lights on the A55 from Chester at Holywell, 1 mile to the crossroads then turn right signposted Pantasaph.

RAC recommended hotel
Stamford Gate ★★ (0352) 712942. Modern hotel on the A55.

MOLD
(0352) 740318
An undulating parkland course with 18 holes (5545 yards, SSS 67). Visitors of all levels are welcome. Green fees are £7.50 on weekdays and £10 at weekends. Bar snacks and full meals are available. Situated in a mountainous region with a good tourist centre at Loggerheads.
Location
Clicain Road, Pantymwyn, Mold, Clwyd CH7 1TW
From the A55 take the A494 inland at Ewloe to Mold. The course is off the Denbigh road, turning left at the Clegg Arms, and right at the T junction, and the clubhouse is further on.

RAC recommended hotel
Arches ★★★ Modern hotel, featuring an arched brick facade, 1½miles north east of Mold, just off A494.
Bryn Awel ★★ (0352) 58622 Former private house with purpose-built annexe and spacious public rooms.

OLD COLWYN
(0492) 515581
An undulating meadowland course of 9 holes (5800 yards, SSS 66). Visitors are welcome except on Tuesday, Wednesday and Saturday afternoons. Green fees are £5 on weekdays and £6 at weekends and Bank Holidays. Dinner is available on weekdays and lunch as well at weekends by arrangement. Situated in Colwyn with the Welsh Mountain Zoo and Conway Castle nearby.
Location
Woodland Avenue, Old Colwyn, Clwyd LL29 9NL.
From the A55 in Old Colwyn, turn up Boddelwyddan Avenue between the chapel and the garage.

RAC recommended hotel
Lyndale ★★ (0492) 515429. Attractive Edwardian building off the A55.

OLD PADESWOOD
(0244) 547401
A meadowland course with 18 holes (6639 yards, SSS 72). Visitors of all levels are welcome. Green fees are £8 on weekdays and £10 at weekends. Bar snacks are available. Situated outside Mold with its tourist centre.
Location
Station Road, Padeswood, Mold, Clwyd CH7 4JL.
Take the A541 east from Mold for 1 mile; bear left on A5118. Course on right hand side.

RAC recommended hotel in Mold

PADESWOOD AND BUCKLEY
(0244) 550537
A parkland and meadowland course with 18 holes (5775 yards, SSS 68). Visitors, preferably with a handicap certificate, are welcome on weekdays and at weekends by arrangement. Green fees are £9 on weekdays and £11 at weekends and on Bank Holidays. Snacks and lunch available, evening meals by arrangement. Local places of interest include the Moelfannau sports area and there is a tourist centre in nearby Mold.
Location
The Cala, Station Lane, Padeswood, Mold, Clwyd LH7 4JD.
Take A541 east from Mold for 1 mile; bear left on A5118. Course on left hand side.

RAC recommended hotel in Mold.

PRESTATYN
(0745) 888353
A seaside course with 18 holes (6764 yards, SSS 72). Visitors are welcome, preferably with a handicap certificate, except on Saturday and Tuesday morning. Green fees are £8 on weekdays and £10 at weekends and Bank Holidays. Full catering facilities are available. Prestatyn is a seaside resort and there are numerous facilities.
Location
Marine Road East, Prestatyn, Clwyd LL19 7HS
Take the A548 to Prestatyn turn right over the railway line to Prestatyn Sands, and the course.

RHUDDLAN
(0745)590217
A parkland course of 18 holes (6045 yards, SSS 69). Visitors are welcome with a handicap certificate except on Sunday. Green fees are available on application. Lunch and dinner are served throughout the summer season except on Monday. Places of local interest include the famous castle.
Location
Meliden Road, Rhuddlan, Clwyd LL18 6LB
Take the A525 inland from Rhyl, the course is close to the historic house Bodrhyddan Hall on A5151.

RHYL
(0745) 35317
A seaside course with 9 holes (6185 yards, SSS 70). Visitors are welcome with a handicap certificate. Green fees are £7 on weekdays and £8 at weekends and on Bank Holidays. Bar snacks and meals are available except on Monday. Situated on the coast with sailing and Rhuddlan Castle nearby.
Location
Coast Road, Rhyl, Clwyd LL18.
On the A548 east of Rhyl. The course is 1 mile from the railway station towards Prestatyn.

RAC recommended hotel
Grange ★★ (0745) 353174. Attractive black and white gabled building on the East Promenade.

RUTHIN PWLLGLAS
(082 42) 2296
A parkland course with 9 holes (5418 yards, SSS 66). Visitors with a handicap certificate are welcome on weekdays and at weekends by arrangement. Green fees are £6 on weekdays and £8 at weekends. Places of local interest include the castle and St Peters church.
Location
Ruthin Pwllglas, Ruthin, Clwyd.
The course is just off the A494 south of the town taking the right fork before Pwllglas village.

RAC recommended hotels
Ruthin Castle ★★★ (082 42) 2664. A 13th-century building with modern comforts and medieval banquets.
Castle ★★ (082 42) 2479. Elizabethan and 18th-century building.

ST MELYD
(07456) 4405
An undulating meadowland course with 9 holes (5805 yards, SSS 68). Visitors are welcome. Green fees are £6 on weekdays and £8 at weekends and Bank Holidays. Restaurant facilities except on Tuesday. Situated outside the seaside resort of Prestatyn with a wildlife park and Bodrhyddan Hall close by.

Location
The Paddock, Prestatyn, Clwyd Ll19 9NB.
On the A547 road south from Prestatyn to Meliden.

VALE OF LLANGOLLEN
(0978) 860040
A parkland course with 18 holes (6461 yards, SSS 72). Visitors are welcome with a handicap certificate on weekdays and at weekends by arrangement. Green fees are £10 on weekdays and £12 at weekends. Full meals and snacks are available except on Tuesday. Situated in an area of outstanding natural beauty with a castle, Valle Crucis Abbey, Plas Newydd house and numerous other places of interest.
Location
Llangollen, Clwyd LL20 7PR.
Take the A5 to Llangollen.. The course is 1 mile east of the town.

RAC recommended hotels
Bryn Howel C/H ★★★ (0978) 860331. Late Victorian building with superb views.
Hand ★★★ (0978) 860303 Modernised 18th-century coaching inn overlooking River Dee. Fishing.
Royal ★★★ (0978) 860202. 17th-century building in riverside setting.
Tyn-y-Wern ★★ (0978) 860252 Pleasantly modernised hotel on A5. In own grounds amidst beautiful scenery. Fishing.

WREXHAM
(0978) 364268
An undulating sandy course with 18 holes (6078 yards, SSS 69). Visitors are welcome preferably with a handicap certificate. Green fees are available on application. Full meals and snacks are provided. Places of local interest include Erddig Hall and an industrial museum.
Location
Holt Road, Wrexham, Clwyd LL13 9SB.
Take the A483 south from Chester to Wrexham. The course is to the east of the town off the A534.

RAC recommended hotels
Llwyn Onn Hall C/H ★★★ (0978) 261225. Georgian building in secluded gardens.
Wynnstay Arms ★★★ (0978) 291010 Georgian hotel in the town centre.
Cross Lanes ★★ (0978) 780555. Nineteenth century buildings in grounds. Indoor swimming pool, putting, fishing, sauna, billiards.

DYFED

ABERYSTWYTH
(0970) 615104
An undulating meadowland course with 18 holes (5735 yards, SSS 68). Visitors are welcome at all times but should preferably be a member of a bona fide club. Green fees are £8 on weekdays and £10 at weekends. Bar snacks and meals are available. Places of interest include Rheidol narrow gauge railway, castle ruins and Nanteds Mansion.
Location
Brynymor, Aberystwyth, Dyfed SY23 2HY
The course is at the north end of the promenade immediately behind the seafront hotels.

RAC recommended hotels
Conrah C/H ★★★ (0970) 617941. Georgian country mansion. Indoor swimming pool, sauna.
Bay ★★ (0970) 617356. Four storey Georgian hotel on the promenade.
Belle Vue Royal ★★ (0970) 617558. Large Victorian building overlooking the bay.
Cambrian ★★ (0970) 612446 Pleasant 'mock Tudor' building close to town centre and opposite railway station.
Court Royale ★★ (0970) 611722 In town centre, three-storey Georgian former coaching inn.
Four Seasons ★★ (0970) 612120 Situated near centre of town, three-storey hotel with patio garden.
Groves ★★ (0970) 617623 Small hotel pleasantly situated near to town centre and beach.
Queensbridge ★★ (0970) 612343 White-painted, Victorian building with panoramic views of Cardigan Bay.

ASHBURNHAM
(05546) 2269
A championship links course with 18 holes (6916 yards, SSS 72). Visitors are welcome on weekdays if members of a bona fide club. Green fees are £12 per round on weekdays and £16 per round at weekends. Full meals and snacks are available except on Monday. Places of local interest include Pembray Leisure Park and Parc Howard Mansion.
Location
Cliffe Terrace, Burry Port, Dyfed SA16 0HN.
Off the M4 at junction 48 to Llanelli on the A4138. The course is through the town on the coast side at Burry Port off the A484.

RAC recommended hotels
Diplomat ★★★ (0554) 756156. Early 19th-century building. Indoor swimming pool, sauna, solarium, gymnasium.
Stradey Park ★★★ (0554) 758171. Elegant house high over the town.

BORTH AND YNYSLAS
(097 081)202
A seaside links course with 18 holes (6094 yards, SSS 70). Visitors are welcome at most times. Green fees are available on application. Snacks, lunches and dinners are available. Situated north of Aberystwyth with all its amenities.
Location
Borth, Dyfed SY24 5JS.
Take the B4572 off the A487 north of Aberystwyth, then B4353 to Borth.

RAC recommended hotels in Aberystwyth

CARDIGAN
(0293) 612035
A seaside meadowland course with 18 holes (6207 yards, SSS 70). Visitors are welcome at all times. Green fees are available on application. Snacks, lunches and dinners are available. Places of interest include the castle ruins and St Mary's church.
Location
Gwbert on Sea, Cardigan, Dyfed SA43 1PR.
From A487 in north part of Cardigan, take B4548 north west towards Gwbert. Course on right.

RAC recommended hotel
Cliff ★★★ (0239) 613241. Hotel on headland with panoramic views of Cardigan Bay. Swimming pool, golf, putting, fishing, squash, billiards.

CARMARTHEN
(0267) 87214
An undulating course of 18 holes (6212 yards, SSS 71). Visitors are welcome. Green fees are available on application. Full meals and snacks are available except on Wednesday. Places of interest include the county museum, castle and roman site and 14th-century gatehouse.
Location
Blaen-y-coed Road, Carmarthen, Dyfed SA33 6EH.
From A40 just east of Carmarthen, turn north on A485, then left on A484. At Bronwydd Arms and Gwili railway station, turn left on road to Blaen-y Coed for 2 miles to course on right.

RAC recommended hotel
Ivy Bush Royal ★★★ (0267) 235111. Pleasant hotel close to the town centre. Sauna.

CILGWYN
(0570) 45286
A parkland course with 9 holes (5318 yards, SSS 67). Visitors of all levels are welcome. Green fees are available on application. Restaurant and bar snacks available except on Monday. Situated in the heart of a scenic landscape with an old goldmine at Pumpfaint and close to the beaches and fishing areas.
Location
Llangybi, Lampeter, Dyfed SA48 8NN.
From Lampeter, take A485 north east for 4 miles to Llangybi, where turn left to course.

RAC recommended hotels
Falcondale ★★★ (0570) 422910. A substantial listed building in grounds. Tennis, fishing.
Black Lion Royal ★★ (0570) 422172. Georgian coaching house in the main shopping centre.

GLYNHIR
(0269) 850472
An undulating parkland and meadowland course with 18 holes (6090 yards, SSS 70). Visitors are welcome on weekdays. Green fees are £7 on weekdays and £9 at weekends. Restaurant and bar snacks available except on Monday.
Location
Glynhir Road, Llandybie, Ammanford, Dyfed SA18 2TF.
From A48/M4 junction 49 roundabout, take A483 through Ammanford towards Llandybie. Two miles beyond Ammanford turn right to course near Glynhir.

RAC recommended hotel
The Mill at Glynhir ★★ (0269) 850672. Converted mill with spacious garden. INndoor swimming pool, fishing.

HAVERFORDWEST
(0437) 3565
An undulating meadowland course with 18 holes (5908 yards, SSS 70). Visitors are welcome Green fees are £8 on weekdays and £10 at weekends. Bar snacks and meals are available. Situated near beautiful coastal areas with good walks, Norman castle, St Martin's church and priory ruins.
Location
Arnolds Down, Narberth Road, Haverfordwest, Dyfed SA61 2XQ.
The course is north of the A40 1 mile east of the town.

RAC recommended hotels
Mariners ★★ (0437) 763353. Modernised two-storey stone buildings close to the town centre.
Pembroke House ★★ (0437) 763652. Virginia-creeper-covered Georgian terraced house.

MILFORD HAVEN
(0646) 692368
A meadowland course with 18 holes (6071 yards, SSS 71). Visitors of all levels are welcome. Green fees are £7 on weekdays and £8 at weekends. Full meals and snacks are available. Situated in an interesting area with fishing and boating, bird sanctuaries and historic Pembroke with castle and museum.
Location
Woodbine House, Hubberston, Milford Haven, Dyfed SA73 3RX
The course is to the west of town at Hubberston, near the oil refinery.

RAC recommended hotels
Lord Nelson ★★ (0646) 695341. Overlooking the waterfront, a fine three-storey Georgian hotel.

NEWPORT (PEMBS)
(0239) 820244
A seaside course of 9 holes (6179 yards, SSS 69). Visitors of all levels are welcome. Green fees are £6.50 per day. Snacks are available. Situated within the Pembrokeshire National Park with sailing on Newport Bay.
Location
Newport, Dyfed SA42 0NR.
From A487 on east side of Newport, turn north. The course is out on the bayside, follow the Newport Sands signs.

ST DAVID'S CITY
(0437) 720392 (Tourist Office)
An undulating seaside course with 9 holes (5693 yards, SSS 70). Visitors are welcome. Green fees are £7. Places of interest include Bishops Palace, Cathedral and butterfly farm.
Location
Whitesands Bay, St David's, Dyfed SA62 6QY
From Haverfordwest take the A487 out to St David's. The course is out on the point near St David's head.

RAC recommended hotels
Warpool Court C/H ★★★ (0437) 720300. Three-storey grey stone building in extensive grounds. Swimming pool, tennis, sauna, gymnasium.
Old Cross ★★ (0437) 720387. In the square, a fine Georgian building.
St Nons ★★ (0437) 720239. Charming two-storey building in Welsh style.
Whitesands Bay ★★ (0437) 720403. Modern hotel by a lovely beach. Swimming pool, sauna, solarium.

SOUTH PEMBROKESHIRE
(0646) 683817
A seaside parkland course with 9 holes (5804 yards, SSS 69). Visitors of all levels are welcome. Green fees are £6 per day. Bar snacks are available and meals by arrangement. Situated in the historic town of Pembroke with its castle, docks and museum. Nearby is the Pembrokeshire coastal path.
Location
Defensible Barracks, Pembroke Dock, Dyfed SA72 6NT
Take the A477 to Pembroke. The course is out towards Pembroke Docks.

RAC recommended hotels
Court C/H ★★★ (0646) 672273. Modernised country mansion with elegant portico.
Hollyland Country House ★★ (0646) 681444. Georgian manor house in gardens.
Coach House Inn ★★ (0646) 684602 Attractive black and white building situated on main road through town. Large gardens. Solarium.
Lamphey House ★★ (0646) 672394 Cream-painted period building with an attractive garden, 1½ miles west of town on road to Tenby.
Milton Manor ★★ (0646) 651398 Three-storey Georgian manor house situated in 2½ acres of secluded grounds. Putting.
Underdown Country House ★★ (0646) 683350 Stone building in quiet seclusion of 4½ acres of trees and gardens.
Wheeler's Old King's Arms ★★ (0646) 683611 Three-storey late Georgian coaching inn situated in town centre.

TENBY
(0834)2978
An 18-hole links course (6232 yards, SSS 71). Visitors of all levels are welcome. Green fees are £11 on weekdays and £12.50 at weekends. Full meals and bar snacks are available. Situated on Carmarthen Bay with a castle, museum and historic house.
Location
The Burrows, Tenby, Dyfed SA70 7NP.
Take the A478 from Kilgetty to Tenby. The course is through the town on the A4139 out near Penally.

RAC recommended hotels
Imperial ★★ (0834) 3737. Traditional seaside hotel.
Atlantic ★★ (0834) 2881. Above south beach with cliff gardens.
Esplanade ★★ (0834) 3333 Four-storey cream-painted hotel high above South beach with superb views across the bay to Caldey Island.
Fourcroft ★★ (0834) 2886 Cliff top hotel in Georgian terrace with gardens down to beach. Swimming pool, sauna, solarium.
Royal Gate House ★★ (0834) 2255 Substantial five-storey hotel high above harbour. Indoor swimming pool, squash, sauna, solarium, gymnasium, billiards.
Royal Lion ★★ (0834) 2127 White-painted four-storey former coaching inn set in the High Street.

GLAMORGAN

ABERDARE
(0685) 871188
This 18-hole woodland course (5874 yards, SSS69) with its extensive views over the beautiful Cynn Valley welcomes visitors on weekdays. Green fees are £9 per day weekdays (£6 with a member) and £11 weekends (£7 with a member). Meals and bar snacks available every day except Monday. The club also has a snooker room and ladies lounge. Local interests include Aberdare Park with its three lakes, Brecon Beacon and the Vale of Neath.
Location
Abernant, Aberdare, Mid Glamorgan CF44 ORY
Situated off the A4059 half a mile north east of Aberdare town centre.

RAC recommended hotels see Merthyr Tydfil.

BARGOED
(0443) 830143
An 18-hole mountain course (6213 yards, SSS70). Visitors are welcome on weekdays and at

weekends with a member. Green fees are £12 (£7.50 with a member). Parties of ten or more by appointment. Cae Castle and Brecon Beacons are well worth a visit when you are not on 'The Green'.

Location

Heolddu, Bargoed, Mid Glamorgan CF8 8UP

Situated 17 miles north of Cardiff on the A469.

RAC recommended hotels

Maes Manor ★★★ (0495) 224551 Blackwood, Gwent NP2 OAG

This is a stunning manor house surrounded by nine acres of gardens with magnificent views.

BRYN MEADOWS C & C HOTEL
(0495) 225590

An 18-hole parkland course. Visitors are welcome on weekdays and with a member at weekends. Green fees are £10.50 weekdays (£8.50 with a member) and £13.50 (£10.50 with a member) at weekends. Excellent food available daily except Sunday.

Location

The Bryn, Hengoed, Mid Glamorgan CF8 7SM

Situated 15 miles north of Cardiff on lane turning nearly opposite The Crown Hotel on the A469.

BRYNHILL
(0446) 720277

An undulating 18-hole meadowland course (6000 yards, SSS69) where visitors can play on weekdays and on Saturday. Green fees are £15 (£8 with a member). Lunches and dinners are available daily except Monday. Places to visit nearby include Barry Island and the very fine Knap pebble beach.

Location

Port Road, Barry, S Glamorgan CF6 7PN

From Cardiff take the A48 to Culverhouse Cross, continue to Wenvoe. The club is on the right hand side of Port Road before a large roundabout.

RAC recommended hotels

The Mount Sorrel ★★★ (0446) 740069 Hotel with fine view over the Bristol Channel.

CAERPHILLY
(0222) 883481

A 14-hole undulating course (5819 yards, SSS71). Visitors are welcome on weekdays and with a member at the weekend and Bank Holidays. Green fees are £8 per round or £9.50 per day (with a member £5.50), and £22 per week Monday to Friday. Meals and snacks are available and nearby Castell Coch is well worth a visit.

Location

Pencapel, Mountain Road, Caerphilly, Mid Glamorgan CF8 1HJ

Situated 7 miles north of Cardiff on the A469.

CARDIFF
(0222) 753320

An 18-hole undulating parkland course (6016 yards, SSS70). Visitors are welcome on weekdays and with a member at weekends. Green fees are £20 (£7.50 with a member) and meals, snacks and bar facilities are available daily. Places to visit include Cardiff Castle and St Madons Garden Centre.

Location

Sherborne Avenue, Cyncold, Cardiff, S Glamorgan CF2 6SJ

Situated 2 miles north of Cardiff city centre, or take the M4, A48 or A48M to Pentwyn, exit on the Eastern Avenue, then take Pentwyn Industrial Road to Cyoncoed Village and into Sherborne Avenue at the Spar shop.

RAC recommended hotels

Angel ★★★★ (0222) 232633 An impressive Victorian hotel, recently restored with care, situated between the Castle and Cardiff Arms Park. Sauna, solarium, gymnasium, billiards.

Holiday Inn ★★★★ (0222) 388335 Tall Red-brickhotel in the city centre. Indoor swimming pool, squash, sauna, solarium, gymnasium.

Park ★★★★ (0222) 383471 Luxury city centre hotel, a substantial Victorian building.

Stakis Inn on the Avenue ★★★★ (0222) 732520 Luxury modern hotel of distinctive design. Set in own grounds. Indoor swimming pool, sauna, solarium, gymnasium.

Crest ★★★ (0222) 388681 Modern purpose-built hotel with extensive conference facilities. Near the castle.

Post House ★★★ (0222) 731212 Modern purpose-built hotel situated in outskirts near Pentwyn interchange on A48. Indoor swimming pool, sauna, solarium, gymnasium.

Royal ★★★ (0222) 383321 City centre hotel dating from Victorian times, now totally renovated. Billiards.

St Mellons ★★★ (0633) 680355 Modernised Victorian hotel between Cardiff and Newport. Indoor swimming pool, tennis, squash, sauna, solarium, gymnasium, billiards.

Wentloog Castle ★★★ (0633) 680591 An old house with a modern extension set in beautiful gardens. Sauna, solarium.

Campanile ★★ (0222) 549044 Large hotel, part of international budget hotel chain. Informal restaurant with English and Continental Cuisine.

Phoenix ★★ (0222) 764615 Three-storied brick-built hotel with black and white gables; modern extension to rear. In residential suburb on northern side of city.

Riverside ★★ (0222) 378866 Gabled stone-built hotel, pleasantly set in residential area on banks of River Taff.

Sandringham ★★ (0222) 32161 Four-storey hotel conveniently situated in the city centre.

CASTELL HEIGHTS
(0222) 861128

The visitor has a choice of two parkland courses here. For the 18-hole Mountain Lake course (7000 yards, SSS73) a handicap certificate is required. Alternatively, there is the 9-hole course (2670 yards, SSS66). Green fees for the Mountain Lake course are £12 on weekdays and £15 at weekends, and the 9-hole course is £3.50 on weekdays and £4 at weekends. Restaurant and bar facilities.

Location

Blaengwynlais, Caerphilly, Mid Glamorgan CF8 1NG

Situated 4 miles north of Cardiff and 2 miles south of Caerphilly on the Tongwynlais-Caerphilly Road. Take exit 32 on M4.

RAC recommended hotels see Cardiff.

CLYNE
(0792) 401989
An 18-hole moorland course (6312 yards, SSS71). Visitors are welcome if they are members of a bona fide club and have a handicap certificate. Green fees are £11 per day, £13 at weekends. Bar snacks and full meals are available except on Monday. Situated on the Gower peninsula west of Swansea. There are several castles, prehistoric monuments and good local beaches!
Location
120 Owls Lodge Lane, Mayals, Black Pill, Swansea SA3 5DP
Drive out of Swansea on the A4067 coast road turning inland from Black Pill on Mayal Road.

Recommended hotels see Swansea Bay.

CREIGIAU
(0222) 890263 5955
An 18-hole parkland course (5786 yards, SSS69). Visitors are welcome on weekdays. Green fees are £12 per day. Lunch and dinner are available except on Monday. Situated off the motorway outside Cardiff with its many attractions.
Location
Creigiau, Cardiff, S Glamorgan CF4 8NN
Drive north west out of Cardiff towards Llantrisant on the M4 taking the A4119 turn off, junction 34. The course is to the west of Llantrisant.

RAC recommended hotels see Cardiff.

DINAS POWIS
(0222) 512727
An 18-hole parkland course (5377 yards, SSS66). Visitors of all levels are welcome. Green fees are £12 weekdays, £15 at weekends. Snack and full meals are available. Situated just outside Cardiff with its castle and museums, there is a medieval village at Costmaston, near the course.
Location
Old Highwalls, Dinas Powis, S Glamorgan CF6 4AJ
Drive out of Cardiff on the A4055 Barny Road to Dinas Powis.

RAC recommended hotels see Cardiff.

FAIRWOOD PARK
(0792) 203648
An 18-hole parkland course (6606 yards, SSS72). Visitors are welcome. Green fees are available on request. Snacks and full catering facilities are available. Swansea with the good beaches of the Gower peninsula close by.
Location
Upper Killay, Swansea.
Drive out of Swansea on the A4118 towards the airport and Upper Killay.

RAC recommended hotels see Swansea Bay.

GLAMORGANSHIRE
(0222) 701185
An 18-hole parkland course (6150 yards, SSS70). Visitors are welcome if they have a handicap certificate, except on competition days and Bank Holidays. Green fees are £13 weekdays, £15 weekends. First class restaurant facilities available and bar snacks. Situated outside Cardiff with all its facilities near to Cosmeston Park medieval village.
Location
Lavernock Road, Penarth, S Glamorgan CF6 2UP
Drive out of Cardiff taking the A4160 towards Penarth Head, then on the B4267 towards Lavernock. The road passes the golf course.

RAC recommended hotel
Walton ★ (0222) 707782 Edwardian mock Tudor house in quiet residential area.

GLYNNEATH
(0639) 720452
An 18-hole hillside course (5499 yards, SSS68). Visitors are welcome. Green fees available on application. Places of interest include the Vale of Neath and Aberdulais Falls.
Location
Penycraig, Pontneathvaughan, Neath, W Glamorgan SA11 5UG
Driving eastwards from Swansea on the A483, A48 on to the A465 at Neath. The course is north of the town.

RAC recommended hotel see Neath.

INCO
(0792) 844216
A 12-hole course (6230 yards, SSS70). Visitors are welcome. Green fees are £8 on weekdays and £9 at weekends. Situated in the suburbs of Swansea with all the amenities of this city.
Location
Clydach, Swansea, W Glamorgan SA6 5EU
Situated in the Swansea Valley

RAC recommended hotels see Swansea Bay.

LANGLAND BAY
(0792) 366023
A seaside parkland course, 18 holes, (5812 yards, SSS69). Visitors with a handicap certificate are welcome. Green fees are £13 weekdays, £14.50 at weekends. Bar snacks and meals are available at all times. Situated in the heart of the Gower Region with splendid beaches and places of historic interest.
Location
Llangland Bay, Swansea, W Glamorgan SA3 4QR
Drive west from Swansea on the A4067 coast road out towards Mumbles Head and Langland Bay.

Recommended hotels
Osborne ★★★ (0792) 366274 Large modern hotel on clifftop.
Langland Court ★★ (0792) 361545 Mock Tudor building near to bay.

LLANISHEN
(0222) 755078
An 18-hole parkland course (5296 yards, SSS66). Visitors are welcome with a handicap certificate. Green fees are £15. Snacks and full meals are available except on Mondays. North of the city centre of Cardiff with the Welsh. Folk Museum very near.
Location
Cwm, Lisvane, Cardiff CF4 5UD
5 miles north of Cardiff through Llanishen via Heol Hir.

RAC recommended hotels see Cardiff.

LLANTRISANT AND PONTY CLUN
(0443) 22148
A 12-hole course (5712 yards, SSS68). Visitors are welcome with a handicap certificate on weekdays. Green fees are £12 weekdays. Bar meals are available on request. On the outskirts of Cardiff near the Welsh National Museum.
Location
Lanelay Road, Talbot Green, Ponty Clun, Mid Glamorgan CF7 8HZ
Drive north from Cardiff on the A4119 across the M4 to Llantrisant.

RAC recommended hotels see Cardiff.

MAESTEG
(0656) 732037
An 18-hole moorland course (5845 yards, SSS69). Visitors are welcome at all levels. Green fees are £9 on weekdays and £12 at weekends. Snacks and meals are available.
Location
Mount Pleasant, Neath Road, Maesteg, Mid Glamorgan CF34 9PR
Drive inland from Port Talbot on the A4107 taking the B4282 to Maesteg which passes the golf course.

MERTHYR TYDFIL
(0685) 3308
A 9-hole mountainous course (5794 yards, SSS68). Visitors are welcome. Green fees available on application. Snacks and bar meals are available. Places of interest include the local museum and the nearby Brecon Beacons National Park.
Location
Cilsanws Mt, Cefn Coed, Nr Merthyr Tydfil, Mid Glamorgan CF48 ?HW
Drive north off the Heads of the Valley Road, A465 at Cefn Coed.

RAC recommended hotels
Baverstock ★★★ (0685) 6221 Modern purpose built hotel overlooking the Beacons.
Castle ★★ (0685) 722327 Modern five-storey hotel in town centre.

MORLAIS CASTLE
(0685) 2822
A 9-hole moorland course (6255 yards, SSS71). Visitors are welcome except on Saturday afternoon. Green fees available on application. Lunch and dinner available. Situated just north of Merthyr Tydfil near the steam railway and on the edge of Brecon Beacons.
Location
Pant, Dowlais, Merthyr Tydfil, Mid Glamorgan CF48 2UY
Drive north of Methyr Tydfil towards the Brecon Mountain railway.

RAC recommended hotels see Merthyr Tydfil

MORRISTON
(0792) 771079
A parkland course of 18 holes, (5734 yards, SSS68). Visitors of all levels are welcome at all times. Green fees are £10 on weekdays and £16 at weekends. Lunch is served except on Monday. Just north of Swansea with all its facilities, the Dan'yr' Ogof Caves are particularly close.
Location
160 Clasemont Road, Morriston, Swansea, W Glamorgan SA6 6AJ
Drive 3 miles north from Swansea on the A4067 taking the A48 turn off west to Morriston.

RAC recommended hotels see Swansea Bay.

MOUNTAIN ASH
(0443) 472265
A mountain course of 18 holes (5485 yards, SSS68). Visitors of all levels are welcome. Green fees are £10 on weekdays, £12 at weekends. Meals and snacks are available except on Monday. Close to the Aberdare Country Park and on the borders of the beautiful Brecon Beacons National Park.
Location
Cefnpennar, Mountain Ash, Mid Glamorgan CF45 4ES
Take the A470 from Cardiff towards Abercynon, then take the A4059 Valley Road to Mountain Ash.

MT LAKES
(0222) 861128
An 18-hole park and heathland course (6851 yards, SSS72). Visitors with a handicap certificate are welcome. Green fees are £10 on weekdays, £12.50 at weekends. Full catering facilities. Places of interest locally include Caerphilly Castle and Castell Coch on the outskirts of Cardiff.
Location
Blaengwynlais, Caerphilly, CF8 1NG
Drive north 4 miles from the M4 junction 32 outside Cardiff on the Tongwynlais to Caerphilly Road. The course is next to the Castell Heights Golf Course.

NEATH
(0639) 643615
A mountain course of 18 holes (6465 yards, SSS72). Visitors of all levels are welcome. Green fees are £8 on weekdays, £12 at weekends. Meals and snacks are available except on Monday. Situated in the Vale of Neath with its nature reserve and Aberdulais Falls.
Location
Cadoxton, Neath, W Glamorgan SA10 7AH
Drive east from Swansea on the A483, onto the A48 to Neath, continuing east through the town to Cadoxton. The course is opposite the church.

Recommended hotels
Castle ★★ (0639) 643581 17th century coaching inn in town centre.
Cimla Court ★★ (0639) 65656 Mid-Victorian house with modern hotel block.

PALLEG
(0639) 842193
An undulating meadow and moorland course 9 holes, (3260 yards, SSS72). Visitors are welcome except on competition days. Green fees are available on application. Meals can be provided by arrangement except on Monday. Places of interest in the locality include Craig 'y' Nos Country Park and the Dan'yr' Ogof Caves.
Location
Palleg Road, Lower Cwmtwrch, Swansea.
Drive north from Swansea on the A4067 Brecon road for about 15 miles and turn left at the Aubrey Arms roundabout. The course is approximately 1 mile further on.

PENNARD
(0441) 283131
An 18-hole seaside course (6266 yards, SSS71). Visitors with a handicap certificate are welcome. Green fees are available on application. Bar snacks are served and meals can be provided by arrangement. Situated west of Swansea on the Gower peninsula with Langland Bay Beach and Pennard Castle ruins on the course.
Location
2 Southgate Road, Southgate, Swansea, W Glamorgan SA3 2BT

Recommended hotels
Osborne ★★★ (0792) 366274 Large modern hotel overlooking Langland Bay.
Norton House ★★★ (0792) 404891 Extended Georgian House with views of Swansea Bay.

PONTARDAWE
(0792) 863118
An 18-hole meadowland course (6061 yards, SSS69). Visitors are welcome if members of a bona fide golf club. Lunch is available every day. Green fees are £7 on weekdays and £10 at weekends. Places of local interest include a wildlife park and the Vale of Neath.
Location
Cefn Llan, Pontardawe, Swansea SA8 4NA
Drive north from Swansea on the A4067 under the M4 to Pontardawe.

PONTYPRIDD
(0443) 402359
An undulating mountain course, 18 holes (5650 yards, SSS68). Visitors are welcome. Green fees are £8 on weekdays and £10 at weekends. Special offer on weekdays of £12 includes a meal. Snacks are available and meals by arrangement. Places of local interest include the Pontypridd historic and heritage centre.
Location
Ty Gwyn, The Common, Pontypridd, Mid Glamorgan CS37 4DJ
Drive north from Cardiff on the A470 to Pontypridd.

PYLE AND KENFIG
(065 671) 3093
A seaside links course, 18 holes (6640 yards, SSS73). Visitors with a handicap certificate are welcome on weekdays. Green fees are £16. Full catering facilities are available. Places of local interest include Margawn Park with Abbey ruins. There are two castles in Bridgend.
Location
Waun-y-Mer, Kenfig, Mid Glamorgan, CF33 4PU
Drive from Cardiff west on the M4 taking junction 37 off to Porthcawl.

RAC recommended hotels see Porthcawl.

RAF ST ATHAN
(0446) 751043
A meadowland course 9 holes (5957 yards, SSS69). Visitors of all levels are welcome except on Sunday morning. Green fees £8 on weekdays and £10 at weekends. Bar snacks and full meals available. Places of interest nearby include a castle at St Donats and Barry Island and its amusement centre.
Location
Barry CF6 9WA
Take the A48 to Cowbridge, turn left on the B4270 to Llantwit Major. St Athan is 2 miles east of Llanwit Major on the B4265.

Recommended hotel
West House ★★ (044 65) 2406 Well maintained stone-built house, close to castle ruins.

RADYR
(0222) 842408
An 18-hole parkland course, in summer (6031 yards, SSS70; in winter 5616 yards, SSS68). Visitors with a handicap certificate are welcome on weekdays. Green fees are £16 per day. Full dining facilities except on Thursday. Close to Castle Coon, Cardiff and the city centre.
Location
Drysgolf Road, Radyr, Cardiff CF4 8BS
Drive north on the A470 taking the turn-off at Taffs Well.
Rac recommended hotels see Cardiff.

RHONDDA
(0443) 433204
A mountain top course with wonderful views, 18 holes (6428 yards, SSS70). Visitors are welcome on weekdays if members of a bona fide golf club. Green fees are available on application. Meals can be provided, preferably by arrangement, except on Monday. Part of the Rhondda Valley with the Ystard Rhondda Leisure Centre close by.
Location
Pontygwaith, Ferndale, Rhondda, Mid Glamorgan CF43 3PW
Drive out of Cardiff to Rhondda on the A470 taking the A4058 at Pontypridd to Porth. The course is 3 miles further on.

THE ROLLS OF MONMOUTH
(0600) 5353
An 18-hole undulating parkland course (6723 yards, SSS72). Visitors are welcome. Green fees are £16 weekdays, £18 at weekends. Meals and full facilities available 7 days. There are numerous historic castles in the area.
Location
The Hendre, Monmouth, Gwent MP5 4HG
Drive east from Abergavenny on the B4233 to Monmouth. The course is near the border.

Recommended hotels
Kings Head ★★★ (0600) 2177 17th century gabled house in town centre.

ROYAL PORTHCAWL
(065) 671 2251
A championship links course 18 holes (6605 yards, SSS74). Visitors are welcome by introduction. Green fees are available on application. Lunch and tea are served and evening meal by arrangement. Fine sandy beaches close by.
Location
Porthcawl, Mid Glamorgan CF36 3UW
Take A4229 to Porthcawl from junction 37 of M4.
RAC recommended hotels
Seabank ★★★ (065) 671 2261. Substantial building in prime position with fine sea views.
Glenaub ★★ (065) 671 8242 Privately owned hotel near seafront.
Seaways ★★ **(065 671) 3510 Two-storey white stone building pleasantly situated off main promenade. Family owned.**

SOUTHERDOWN
(0656) 880476
A downland course 18 holes (6613 yards, SSS73). Visitors with a handicap certificate are welcome weekdays. Green fees are £16 weekdays, £25 at weekends. Meals are served daily. Places of interest locally include the seaside resort of Porthcawl, Ogmore Castle and Coney Beach Funfair.
Location
Ewenny, Bridgend, Mid Glamorgan CF35 5BT
Leave M4 at junction 36 on A4061 to Bridgend. The course is on the B4524 towards Ogmore.

RAC recommended hotel.
Coed-y-Mwstwr C/H ★★★ (0656) 860621 Red-brick Victorian mansion in wooded gardens overlooking the Vale of Glamorgan.

SWANSEA BAY
(0792) 814153
An 18-hole links course (6302 yards, SSS70). Visitors are welcome. Green fees available on application. Meals are available all week. Places of local interest include the Pensyovir wildlife park.
Location
Jersey Marine, Neath, W Glamorgan SA10 6JP
Just off the A48 between Neath and Seansea

RAC recommended hotels
Dragon ★★★★ (0792) 651074 Imposing modern hotel adjacent to shopping area. Indoor swimming pool, sauna, solarium, gymnasium.
Dolphin ★★★ (0792) 650011 A modern three-storey stone building set in city centre.
Fforest ★★★ (0792) 588711 Modern red-brick hotel conveniently situated close to A483. Sauna, solarium.
Hilton National ★★★ (0792) 310330 Beside lake in enterprise park, a modern hotel with charming garden. Indoor swimming pool, sauna, gymnasium.
Beaumont ★★ (0792) 643956 Four-storey white painted hotel in main thoroughfare.
Oaktree Parc ★★ (0792) 817781 Close to the M4, a red-brick building set in a large garden.
Windsor Lodge ★★ (0792) 642158 An 18th-century stone building situated close to town centre. Sauna.

TREDEGAR AND RHYMNEY
(0685) 840743
An undulating mountain course 9 holes (2788 yards, SSS67). Visitors are welcome. Green fees are £5 on weekdays and £7.50 at weekends. Evening meals can be provided by arrangement. Places of local interest include Morlais Castle steam railway and museum.
Location
Cwmtysswg, Rhymney, Gwent NP2 3BQ
Drive north from Cardiff on A470 to Methyr Tydfil turning east on the A4040 to Rhymney. The course is on the B4256 about 1½ miles from the town.

WENVOE CASTLE
(0222) 594371
A parkland course 18 holes (6411 yards, SSS71). Visitors with a handicap certificate are welcome. Green fees are available on application. Lunch and dinner are available. Nearby is the St Fagans Welsh Folk Museum.
Location
Wenvoe, Cardiff CF5 6BE
Take the A48 west out of Cardiff and turn left on the A4050 towards Wenvoe; the course is about 2 miles on the right.

WHITCHURCH
(0222) 620125
An 18-hole parkland course (6245 yards, SSS70). Visitors with handicap certificate are welcome on weekdays. Green fees are £15 on weekdays and £20 at weekends. Meals served every day. Places of local interest include Coch Castle, Cardiff Castle, St Fagan's Folk Museum.
Location
Pontmawr Road, Whitchurch, Cardiff, S Glamorgan CF4 6XD
From junction 32 of M4, travel south 500 yards on A470, turn left at lights to club entrance.

WHITEHALL
(0443) 740245
A mountain course, 9 holes (5750 yards, SSS68). Visitors are welcome on weekdays. Green fees available on application. Meals can be provided by arrangement. Situated on the borders of the Brecon Beacon National Park.
Location
Nelson, Treharris, Mid Glamorgan CF46 6FT
Drive north of Cardiff on A470 to Methyr Tydfil, take the Treharis and Nelson exit at roundabout, turn right and drive south for a quarter of a mile, first left up Mountain Road.

RAC recommended hotels see Merthyr Tydfil.

GWENT

BLACKWOOD
(0495) 223152
A meadowland course with 9 holes (5304 yards, SSS 66). Visitors are welcome at all times. Green fees are available on application. Situated between the Brecon Beacons National Park and the city amenities of Cardiff.
Location
Cwmgelli, Blackwood, Gwent.
Drive north out of Cardiff on the A469 through Caerphilly to the junction with the A472. Turn right towards Pontllanfraith and Blackwood. The course is north of the town on the A4048.

RAC recommended hotel
Maes Manor ★★★ (0495) 224551. Beautiful manor house set in wooded grounds.

CAERLEON
(0633) 420342
A 9-hole meadowland course (3092 yards, SSS 68). Visitors are welcome at all times. Green fees are £2 on weekdays and £2.60 at weekends. Bar snacks are available. Situated on the outskirts of Newport with a priory, and Roman site and museum close by.
Location
Broadway, Caerleon, Gwent.
From junction 25 of M4 turn off to Caerleon; course is about 3 miles.

RAC recommended hotels in Newport

GREENMEADOW
(06333) 62626
A 14-hole course (5587 yards, SSS 77). Visitors of all levels are welcome. Green fees are £7 on weekdays and £9 at weekends. Meals and snacks are available. Situated inland from Newport with the Cwmbran leisure centre and nature reserve close by.
Location
Treherbert Road, Croesyceiliog, Cwmbran, Gwent NP44 2BZ.
From junction 26 of M4, take A4042 north on Cwmbran by-pass for about 4 miles to course.

RAC recommended hotel
Commodore ★★★ (06333) 4091. Modern hotel set in gardens.

LLANWERN
(0633) 412029
Two meadowland courses, an 18-hole course and a 9-hole course (6206 yards SSS 69 and 5674 yards). Visitors are welcome on weekdays if a member of a bona fide club. Green fees are available on application. Full meals and snacks are available. Jacket and tie to be worn in the evenings. Situated on the outskirts of Newport near Caerleon and the Roman site and museum.
Location
Golf House, Tennyson Avenue, Llanwern, Gwent NP6 2DY.
From junction 24 of M4, take A455 towards Llanwern and the coast.

RAC recommended hotels in Newport.

MONMOUTH
(0600) 2212
A 9-hole meadowland course (5454 yards, SSS 66). Visitors are all welcome. Green fees are £10 on weekdays and £15 at weekends. Snacks and meals are available except on Monday. Places of local interest include the castle ruins, the birthplace of Henry V and the Nelson museum.
Location
Leesebrook Lane, Monmouth, Gwent.
Take the A40 to Monmouth. The course is north of the town.

RAC recommended hotel
King's Head ★★★ (0600) 2177. Fine gabled building in town square.

MONMOUTHSHIRE
(0873) 2606
A meadowland course, 18 holes (6054 yards, SSS 69). Visitors are welcome with a handicap certificate. Green fees are £15 on weekdays and £20 at weekends. Full meals and snacks are available except on Tuesday. Part of the Welsh National Park with the Sugar Loaf mountain and several others within walking distance.
Location
Llanfoist, Abergavenny, Gwent NP7 9HE.
From junction 26 of M4 take the A4042 to Abergavenny. The course is on the B4269 road between Llanfoist and Llanellen just south of Abergavenny.

RAC recommended hotels
Angel ★★ (0873) 7121 Renamed former coaching inn which is situated in the twn centre.
Llanwenarth Arms ★★ (0873) 810550 16th-century building with modern annexe. On A40 enjoying superb views.

NEWPORT
(0633) 892683
An undulating parkland course with 18 holes (6370 yards SSS 71). Visitors are welcome on weekdays if a member of a recognised club. Green fees are £12 on weekdays. Meals and snacks are available except on Tuesday. Places of interest include a Norman castle, St Woolas Cathedral and the Roman site and museum at Caerleon.
Location
Great Oak, Rogerstone, Newport, Gwent NR1 6FX.
From M4 junction 27 take the B4591 signposted Highcross. The course is 1½ miles; turn right at the Vixen garage.

RAC recommended hotels
Celtic Manor ★★★★ (0633) 413000. Nineteenth century building surrounded by gardens. Sauna, solarium, gymnasium.
Hilton National ★★★ (0633) 41277. Modern hotel in wooded setting.
Kings ★★★ (0633) 842020 Opposite railway station, substantial five-storey building with a well-furnished and spacious lounge.
Newport Lodge ★★ (0633) 821818. Three storey modern hotel overlooking the M4 west of the town.

PONTNEWYDD
(06333) 2170
A meadowland course of 10 holes (5340 yards, SSS 67). Visitors of all levels are welcome on weekdays. Green fees are £8 on weekdays. Meals are available except on Monday. Situated close to the river with good fishing and a boating lake.
Location
West Pontnewydd, Upper Cwmbran, Gwent NP4 4AR.
From junction 26 of M4, take A4042 then A4057 through Cwmbran to Upper Cwmbran.

RAC recommended hotels in Cwmbran see Greenmeadow

PONTYPOOL
(0495) 5763655
An undulating mixed parkland and moorland course with 18 holes (6058 yards, SSS 69). Visitors are welcome with a handicap certificate. Green fees are £10 on weekdays and £15 at weekends. Situated on the outskirts of Pontypool with its leisure centre and coal museum.
Location
Trevethin, Pontypool, Gwent NP4 8DJ.

From junction 26 on the M4, take the A4042 to Pontypool. The course is north of the town, off the A4043 to Blaenavon

ST MELLONS
(0633) 680408
An 18-hole parkland course (6275 yards, SSS 70). Visitors are welcome on weekdays with a handicap certificate. Green fees are £14 on weekdays. Meals and snacks are available. Places of local interest include Tredegar House and Gardens as well as the amenities of Cardiff.
Location
St Mellons, Cardiff, Gwent CF3 8XS.
The course is on the A48 between Newport and Cardiff.

RAC recommended hotels
St Mellons ★★★ (0633) 680355. Modernised Victorian hotel. Indoor swimming pool, tennis, squash, sauna, solarium, gymnasim, billiards.
Wentloog Castle ★★★ (0633) 680591. An old house with modern extension set in gardens. Sauna, solarium.
Post House ★★★ (0222) 731212. Purpose-built hotel situated on the A48. Indoor swimming pool, sauna, solarium, gymnasium.

ST PIERRE
(0291) 625261
An old established parkland course and a new meadowland course, both have 18 holes (old course 6700 yards, SSS 73; new course 5762 yards, SSS 68). Visitors are welcome with a handicap certificate, but booking is advisable. Green fees are available on application. A restaurant and coffee shop provide meals and snacks. Part of a country club complex between Chepstow with its castle and museum and Caldicot with its castle, museum and country park.
Location
St Pierre Park, Chepstow, Gwent NP6 6YA.
On the borders by the Severn Bridge. The course is off the A48 on the Caldicot Road, 1 mile from the Chepstow roundabout.

RAC recommended hotel
St Pierre ★★★ (0291) 625261. A 14th-century manor house in 400 acres with country club. Indoor swimming pool, golf, putting, tennis, squash, sauna, solarium, gymnasium, billiards.

TREDEGAR PARK
(0633) 894433
An 18-hole parkland course (5575 metres, SSS 70). Visitors are welcome with a handicap certificate. Green fees are £11 on weekdays and £15 at weekends. Tredegar House is within the park and there are castles at Caerphilly, Caldicot and Chepstow.
Location
Bassaleg Road, Newport, Gwent NP9 3PX.
Take M4 junction 28 to A48 roundabout. Take A4072 north to golf course.

RAC recommended hotels in Newport

WEST MONMOUTHSHIRE
(0495) 310233
A mountain course with 18 holes (6097 yards, SSS 69). Visitors of all levels are welcome. A sturdy walking course–the highest in Wales! Green fees are available on application. Meals and snacks are available. Places of interest include Blaenavon Big Pit Mining Museum and Ebbw Vale.
Location
Pond Road, Nantyglo, Gwent NP3 4JX.
From junction 28 on M4, take A467 through Newbridge and Abertillery to Nantyglo. The course is signposted at the Dunlop Semtex roundabout.

GWYNEDD

ABERDOVEY
(0654) 72493
A championship links course of 18 holes (6445 yards, SSS 71). Visitors are welcome with a handicap certificate. Green fees are £12 per round weekdays and £14 per round at weekends with reductions after 2pm. Bar meals available, lunch and dinner by arrangement except on Monday. Situated on the estuary of the River Dovey with sailing and RSPB bird reserve.
Location
Aberdovey, Gwynedd LL35 0RT.
From Machynlleth, take the A493 through Aberdovey to course beside sea.

RAC recommended hotel
Trefeddian ★★★ (065 472) 213 Large seaside holiday hotel in gardens overlooking links and Bay. Indoor swimming pool, putting, tennis, solarium.

ABERSOCH
(075 881) 2622
Links course of 9 holes (5910 yards, SSS 68). Visitors of all levels are welcome. Green fees are available on application. Meals and snacks are served. Situated on the Lleyn peninsular with good beaches.
Location
Abersoch, Gwynedd LL53 7EY.
Take the A499 from Pwllheli out to Abersoch. The course is beyond the village.

RAC recommended hotels
Harbour ★★★ (075 881) 2406. Proprietor-run hotel enjoying fine views.
Porth Tocyn C/H ★★★ (075 881) 2966. Attractive white-faced hotel on it's own headland. Swimming pool, tennis.
Riverside ★★★ Overlooking harbour, a cream-painted hotel with modern purpose-built extension. Indoor swimming pool.
Deucoch C/H ★★ (075 881) 2680 Former farmhouse in grounds overlooking town. Well-equipped bedrooms.
Neigwl ★★ (075 881) 2363 Attractive small white-faced hotel overlooking bay. Family-owned and run.

BALA
(0678) 520359
A mountainous course of 19 holes (4970 yards, SSS 64). Visitors of all levels are welcome. Green fees are available on application. Meals are available on booking. Situated near Bala Lake with farm park nearby.
Location
Penlan, Bala, Gwynedd LL23 7SR.
Drive from Llangollen on the A5 takingthe A494 south at Druid to Bala.

RAC recommended hotels
Bala Lake ★★ (0678) 520344. Modern hotel overlooking lake and golf course.
Plas Coch ★★ (0678) 520309. Hotel on main, wide, tree lined street.
White Lion Royal ★★ (0678) 520314 Famous old coaching inn located in the high street.

BETWS-Y-COED
(069 02) 556
A parkland course of 18 holes (4996 yards, SSS 64). Visitors are welcome. Green fees are available on application. Meals and snacks are available except on Monday. Situated in famous scenic landscape with Gwydr Uchaf Chapel and castle nearby.
Location
Betws-y-Coed, Gwynedd LL24.
Drive south from Llandudno on the A470 inland to Betws-y-Coed.

RAC recommended hotels
Plas Hall C/H ★★★ (069 06) 206. Attractive Victorian building with river in wooded grounds. Fishing.
Royal Oak ★★★ (069 02) 219. Former coaching inn in picturesque riverside setting.
Waterloo ★★★ (069 62) 411 Purpose-built well-equipped modern complex surrounded by breathtaking scenery. Indoor swiming pool, sauna, solarium, gymnasium, billiards.
Gwydyr ★★ (069 02) 777 Family-run hotel in Victorian building in delightful suroundings.
Park Hill ★★ (069 02) 540 Converted Victorian house with modern well-equipped bedrooms. Own grounds. Indoor swiming pool, sauna.
Ty Gwyn ★★ (06902) 383. Coaching inn overlooking River Conwy.
Fairy Glen ★ (06902) 269. Stonewhite hotel.

CAERNARFON
(0286) 3783
A parkland course of 18 holes (5860 yards, SSS 69). Visitors of all levels are welcome. Green fees are £8 per day. Full meals and snacks available. Places of interest include a Roman site and Caernarfon Castle.
Location
Llanfaglan, Caernarfon, Gwynedd LL54 5RR
Caernarfon is on the A487. The course is 1/2 mile south of the town along the side of the Menai Strait.

RAC recommended hotels
Menai Bank ★ (0286) 673297. Three-storey residence overlooking the Menai Strait.
Muraill Park ★ (0286) 674647. Fine views of Snowdon.

CONWY
(0492) 593400
A championship links course of 18 holes (6901 yards, SSS 73). Visitors with a handicap certificate are welcome on weekdays, restricted at weekends. Meals and snacks are available except on Monday evening. Situated in the historic walled city of Conwy with its castle, historic house and Felin Isaf watermill museum.
Location
Morfa, Conwy, Gwynedd LL32 8ER
Take the A55 out of Conwy towards Bangor, turn off down Morfa Drive over the cattle grid, to the clubhouse on the left.

RAC recommended hotels
Sychnant Pass C/H ★★★ (0492) 596868. Edwardian country house. Sauna, solarum.
Berthlwyd Hall ★★ (0492) 592409. Victorian manor house in walled garden. Swimming pool.
Caerlyr Hall C/H ★★ (0492) 623518 Black and white gabled Victorian house, set in 2 1/2 acres, with panoramic views. Next to golf course.
Castle ★★ (0492) 592324 17th-century former coaching inn situated in the town centre.
Castle Bank ★★ (0492) 593888 Attractive building in peaceful grounds overlooking Conwy Estuary. Next to castle.
Lodge ★★ (049 269) 766 Modern purpose-built hotel set in an attractive garden.

CRICCIETH
(0766) 522154
An undulating hilltop course of 18 holes (5787 yards, SSS 68). Visitors of all levels are welcome. Green fees available on application. Meals and snacks served by arrangement. Places of local interest include Criccieth Castle and the Lloyd George museum.
Location
Ednyfed Hill, Criccieth, Gwynedd.
From the A487 turn off on B4411 or A497 to Criccieth. The course lies north of the town, up the hill.

RAC recommended hotels
Bron Eiflon C/H ★★★ (0766) 522385. Large country house in gardens. Fishing

George IV ★★ (0766) 522168. Imposing central hotel.
Parciau Mawr C/H88 (0766) 522368 Small privately-owned country house in gardens with wonderful views.
Plasgwyn ★★ (0766) 512559 Privately-owned converted house with modern extension.
Plas Isa ★★ (0766) 522443 Former private residence extensively modernised; overlooking Tremadog Bay.

DOLGELLAU
(0341) 422603
A parkland course of 9 holes (4512 yards, SSS 63). Visitors are welcome. Green fees are £6 per weekday and £7.50 at weekends. Meals and snacks are available. Situated near the Cader Idris climbing area, seaside closeby.
Location
Pencefn, Golfdown, Dolgellau, Gwynedd LL40 1SL.
Driving from Llangollen west on the A5 take the left fork A494 at Druid through Bala to Dolgellau. Turn off the town bypass onto the old A494, then turn right past the main bridge.

RAC recommended hotels
Dolserau Hall ★★ (0341) 422522. Well-appointed Victorian mansion in 5 acres of grounds. Fishing
George III ★★ (0341) 422525. Fine 17th-century building.
Royal Ship ★★ (0341) 422209 Four-storey stone-built town centre hotel dating from the 18th-century.

FFESTINIOG
(0766) 831829
A mountain course of 9 holes (5032 yards, SSS 66). Visitors are welcome. Green fees are £3 per day. Places of local interest include the slate quarries and the railway.
Location
Ffestiniog, Gwynedd.
Inland from Porthmadog on the A487 turn off the A470 to Ffestiniog. The course is before the village on the Bala road.

LLANDUDNO
(0492) 76450
A championship parklands links course of 18 holes (6513 yards, SSS 72). Visitors with a handicap certificate are welcome. Green fees are £12 weekdays, £16 at weekends. Situated near the Snowdonia National Park and the Conwy estuary with its wildlife park and a working watermill.
Location
Hospital Road, Llandudno, Gwynedd LL30 1HU.
On the north coast of Wales. The course is 1 mile from the town centre alongside the Llandudno hospital.

RAC recommended hotels
Bodysgallen Hall C/H ★★★ (0492) 84466 17th-century mansion with antique furniture. Superb views from spacious grounds. Tennis.
Empire ★★★ (0492) 860555 Modern family-run hotel in central position with roof garden. Indoor and outdoor swimming pools, sauna, solarium, billiards.
Gogarth Abbey ★★★ (0492)76211 Impressive building in sunny position on West Shore. Fine views. Indoor swimmng pool, putting, sauna, solarium.
Imperial ★★★ (0492) 77466. Classic Victorian building with sea views.
Risboro ★★★ (0492) 76343 Large elegant family-run hotel at foot of Great Orme. Sea front nearby. Indoor swimming pool, sauna, solarium, gymnasium, billiards.
St Tudno ★★★ (0492) 74411 Beautifully refurbished, distinctive small luxury hotel with views of bay. Indoor swimming pool.
Bedford ★★ (0492) 76647. Edwardian style building on the promenade.
Belle Vue ★★ (0492) 79547 Attractive building with painted stucco. Sun terrace overlooks the bay. Billiards.
Tudno Castle ★★ (0492) 77694 Attractive four-storey, cream-rendered. Near shops and promenade. Snooker.

NEFYN AND DISTRICT
(07580 720218
A seaside course of 18 holes (6335 yards, SSS 71) with a pub on the course. Visitors are welcome by arrangement. Green fees are £10 per day and £12 at weekends. Full meals and snacks are available.
Location
Morfa Nefyn, Pwllheli, Gwynedd LL53 6DA.
From Bangor on the A487, take the A499 at Llandwlog onto Llanaelhaearn where the B4417 goes onto Nefyn and Morfa Nefyn.

RAC recommended hotel
Woodlands Hall ★★ (0758) 720425. A Georgian house in beautiful grounds.

NORTH WALES
(0492) 75325
A seaside links course of 18 holes (6132 yards, SSS 69). Visitors with handicap certificates are welcome. Green fees are £12.50 on weekdays, £16 at weekends. Bar snacks and full meals available.
Location
72 Brymau Road, West Shore, Llandudno, Gwynedd LL30 2DZ.
From the A55, take the B5115 out to the West Shore.

RAC recommended hotels in Llandudno.

PENMAENMAWR
(0492) 623330
An undulating parkland course with 9 holes (5031 yards, SSS 65). Visitors of all levels are welcome. Green fees are £6 per day. On the coast between Conwy and Bangor.
Location
Conwy Old Road, Penmaenmawr, Gwynedd LL34 6RD.
Drive west from Conwy on the A55, turn left at Mountain View Hotel along the Conway Old Road.

RAC recommended hotels in Conwy

PORTMADOG
(0766) 512037
A seaside course with 18 holes (5838 yards, SSS 68). Visitors with a handicap certificate are welcome. Green fees on application. Meals and snacks are available.
Location
Morfa Bychau, Portmadog, Gwynedd LL49 9UU.
Take the A487 to Portmadog. The course is through the town on the Morfa Bychau road.

RAC recommended hotels
Madoc ★★ (0766) 512021 Attractive period hotel dating back to 1770, situated on side of square.
Tyddyn Llwyn ★★ (0766) 3903 Modern purpose-built, well equipped hotel enjoying good views. Riding.

PWLLHELI
(0758) 612520
A mixed parkland and links course with 18 holes (6110 yards, SSS 69). Visitors are all welcome. Green fees are £9 weekdays and £10 at weekends. Meals are available by arrangement.
Location
Golf Road, Pwllheli, Gwynedd LL53 5PS.
From Portmadog take the A497 to the centre of Pwllheli, then take Cardiff Road and bear right at the first fork.

RHOS-ON-SEA
(0492)49641
An undulating seaside course with 18 holes (6064 yards, SSS 69). Visitors of all levels are welcome. Green fees are £8.50. Snacks and lunches are available, dinner by arrangement.
Location
Penrhyn Bay, Llandudno, Gwynedd LL30 3PU.
From A55 take the B5115 outside Colwyn Bay towards Rhos-on-Sea. The course is on the promenade.

RAC recommended hotels in Llandudno.

ROYAL ST DAVIDS
(0766) 780361
A seaside course with 18 holes (6427 yards, SSS 71). Visitors with a handicap certificate are welcome. Green fees are £12 on weekdays, £14 at weekends. Full meals and snacks are available.
Location
Harlech, Gwynedd LL46 2UB.
Drive down from Portmadog on the A496 coast road towards Barmouth.

RAC recommended hotels
Castle Cottage (Acclaimed) (0766) 780479.
St David's (Acclaimed) (0766) 780366.

ST DENIOL
(0248) 353098
An undulating parkland course with 18 holes (5500 yards, SSS 67). Visitors of all levels are welcome. Green fees are £5. Meals can be supplied by arrangement.
Location
Penybryn, Bangor, Gwynedd LL57 2LX.
Driving along the A55 west to Bangor, the course is east of the town at the top of Beach Road overlooking Penrhyn harbour.

RAC recommended hotels
MenaiCourt ★★★ (0248) 354200 Renovated Victorian house, overlooking Menai Straits.
Telford ★★ (0248)352543. Converted dwelling house overlooking Menai Bridge.
Ty Uchaf ★★ (0248) 352219 Completely modernised and extended former coaching inn.

POWYS

BRECON
(0874) 2004
A meadowland course with 9 holes (5218 yards, SSS 66). Visitors are welcome. Green fees are £4 on weekdays and £5 at weekends.
Location
Newton Park, Llanfaes, Brecon, Powys
Take the A40 from Abergavenny. The course is 300 yards from the bypass south of town.

RAC recommended hotels
Aberclydach House ★★ (087 487) 361. Victorian mansion standing in well-kept gardens.
Castle of Brecon ★★ (0874) 4611. Stone-built hotel attached to castle ruins.
Wellington ★★ (0874) 5225 In town centre, a three-storey white-painted Georgian hotel

BUILTH WELLS
(0982) 553296
A parkland course with 18 holes (5760 yards, SSS 67). Visitors are welcome at any time. Green fees are £8 on weekdays and £9 at weekends. Meals are available by arrangement.
Location
Builth Wells, Powys LD2 3NF.
The course is on the west of the town, reached from the A483.

RAC recommended hotel
Pencerrig Country House C/H ★★(0982) 553226. Extended country house in 3 acres of grounds.
Lion ★★ (0982) 553670 Former coaching inn in a commanding position beside the River Wye.

CRADOC
(0874) 3658
An 18-hole parkland course (6318 yards, SSS 71). Visitors of any level are welcome. Green fees are

£8 on weekdays and £11 at weekends. Snacks and full meals are available except on Monday.
Location
Penoyre Park, Cradoc, Brecon, Powys Ld3 9LP. Drive from Abergavenny on the A40 through Brecon and north on B4520. Turn left to Cradoc.

KNIGHTON
(0547) 528646
An undulating course with 9 holes (5320 yards, SSS 66). Visitors are welcome. Green fees are £4 on weekdays and £6 at weekends. Snacks are available at weekends.
Location
The Ffrydd, Knighton, Powys LD7 1EF.
Drive from Ludlow west on the A49 taking the A4113 into Wales; Knighton is right on the border.

RAC recommended hotel
Knighton ★★★ (0547) 520530 Recently refurbished town-centre hotel.

LLANDRINDOD WELLS
(0597) 823873
A mountain course with 18 holes (5749 yards, SSS 68). Visitors of all levels are welcome and the green fees are available on application. Snacks are available by arrangement.
Location
Llandrindod Wells, Powys LD1 5NU
Take the A483 from Brecon to Llandrindod Wells. The course is east of the town just above the lake.

RAC recommended hotels
Metropole ★★★ (0597) 822881. Spacious Edwardian hotel. Indoor swimming pool, sauna, solarium, gymnasium.
Glen Usk ★★ (0597) 822085. Elegant Victorian hotel.

MACHYNLLETH
(0654) 2000
An undulating course with 9 holes (5726 yards, SSS 67). Visitors are welcome except on competition days. Green fees are £7 on weekdays. Meals only by arrangement.
Location
Newtown Road, Machynlleth, Powys SY20 8UH
Take the A487 from Aberystwyth along the Dovey estuary to Machynlleth. The course is on the A489.

RAC recommended hotel
Dolguog Hall ★★ (0654) 2244. Seventeenth century building in beautiful grounds.

OLD RECTORY
(0873) 810373
A 9-hole course (1409 yards, SSS 54). Visitors are welcome. Green fees are £6 per day. Full restaurant facilities provided by the hotel on the course, except on Monday.
Location
Llangattock, Crickhowell, Powys NP8 1PH.
Take A40 west from Abergavenny to Crickhowell. Turn left in the town centre to Llangattock.

RAC recommended hotel
Gliffaes C/H ★★ (0874) 730371. Victorian mansion with Italianate campaniles overlooking the River Usk. Putting, tennis, fishing, snooker.

ST GILES
(0686) 625844
An undulating parkland course with 9 holes (5864 yards, SSS 68). Visitors are welcome on weekdays and some weekends. Green fees are £5.50 on weekdays and £6.50 at weekends. Meals are available by arrangement with the Steward, except on Monday.
Location
Pool Road, Newtown, Powys SY16 3AJ.
Take the A483 south from Shrewsbury to Newtown. The course is 1 mile east of the town.

RAC recommended hotel
Elephant and Castle ★★ (0686) 626271. Town hotel adjacent to the River Severn. Fishing.

ST IDLOES
(05512) 2559
A slightly undulating hillside course with 9 holes (5320 yards, SSS 66). Visitors are welcome. Green fees are available on application. Meals can be supplied by arrangement.
Location
Pen-Rhallt, Llanidloes, Powys.
Take A44 inland from Aberystwyth to Llangurig and A470 on to Llanidloes. The course is off the B4569 north of the town.

WELSHPOOL
(0938) 83249
A mountain course with 18 holes (5708 yards, SSS 69). Visitors of all levels are welcome but the course is not suitable for beginners. Green fees are £6 on weekdays and £8 at weekends. Snacks and meals are available.
Location
Golfa Hill, Welshpool, Powys SY21
Take A458 west from Shrewsbury to Welshpool. The course is on the west of the town on the A458.

RAC recommended hotels
Edderton Hall C/H ★★ (093 876) 339. Georgian country house in $2^1/_2$ acres of grounds. Fishing.
Royal Oak ★★ (0938) 552217. Substantial 18th-century red brick hotel.

NORTHERN IRELAND

Co ANTRIM

BALLYCASTLE
(02657) 62536
An 18 hole links and parkland course (5882 yards, SSS 69), overlooking the harbour. Visitors with a handicap certificate are welcome. Green fees are £8 on weekdays and £10 at weekends and Bank Holidays. Snacks are available and full catering facilities by arrangement. There are beautiful coastal walks near the course which is situated in a small bay.
Location
Cushendall Road, Ballycastle, Co Antrim BT54 6QP
Ballycastle is on the A2 coast road 40 miles west of Larne or 26 miles from Ballymena on the A44.

BALLYCLARE
(09603) 22696
An 18 hole parkland course with lakes and a river (5840 metres, SSS 71). Visitors with a handicap certificate are welcome except on Thursday and at weekends. Green fees are £6 on weekdays and £10 at weekends. Meals are served by prior arrangement.
Location
25 Springvale Road, Ballyclare, Co Antrim.
Travel north from Belfast, through Mossley on to the A8 for Ballyclare then take the B94 for 2 miles to the course.

BALLYMENA
(0266) 861207
A parkland course of 18 holes (5168 yards, SSS 67). Visitors are welcome on weekdays and at weekends. Green fees are £8 on weekdays (£6 with a member), £10 at weekends, (£7 with a member). A restaurant provides a full service and snacks are available at the bar.
Location
128 Raceview Road, Broughshane, Ballymena.
Situated 2 miles east of the town on the A42 towards Carnlough.

BALMORAL
(0232) 381514
An 18 hole parkland course (5679 metres, SSS 70). Visitors are welcome every day except Saturday. Green fees are £10 per round, £15 per day. Catering facilities are available. Local attractions include the Ulster Museum and botanical gardens.
Location
518 Lisburn Road, Belfast BT9 6GX
Take the Lisburn Road south west out of the city centre. The club house is on the right, opposite the Balmoral Halt station.

RAC recommended hotels
Europa ★★★★ (0232) 327000 A luxury high-rise hotel in the centre of Belfast.
Stormont ★★★ (0232) 658621 Formerly a mansion house, near Stormont Castle and grounds.

BALVOIR PARK
(0232) 491693
An established parkland course, 18 holes with splendid views (6276 yards, SSS 70). Visitors with a handicap certificate are welcome but telephone first. Green fees are £12 for weekdays except Wednesday, £15 at weekends, Wednesday and Bank Holidays. There are very good dining facilities.
Location
73 Church Road, Newtonbreda, Belfast BT8 4AN
Travel south from Belfast on the A24 Ormeau Road, for 4 miles towards Carryduff.

BUSHFOOT
(02657) 31317
A 9 hole course (5572 yards, SSS 67) established in the 19th-century . Visitors with a handicap certificate are welcome. Green fees are £6 on weekdays and £70 at weekends and Bank Holidays. Bar snacks and meals are available in the new club house. There are good walks along the magnificent cliffs leading to the Giant's Causeway.
Location
50 Bushfoot Road, Portballintrae, Bushmills, Co Antrim BT57 8RR
Take the A2 coast road east out of Portrush past Dunluce Castle to Bushmills, then travel 1 mile north to Ballintrae.

RAC recommended hotels
Bushmills Inn ★★★ (02657) 32339 A listed coaching inn restored and extended in keeping. Now an attractive hotel.
Bayview ★★ (02657) 31453 Standing at the roadside; an interesting mixture of buildings.

CAIRNDHU
(0574) 83324
An 18 hole parkland course (6112 yards, SSS 69) with spectacular sea views. All visitors are welcome except on Saturday. Green fees are £8 on weekdays, £11 at weekends. Half price for ladies! Snacks are available and evening meals on weekdays. A more comprehensive service is available at weekends or by request. Places of interest include the port of Larne and Olderlfeet Castle.
Location
192 Coast Road, Ballygally, Larne BT40 2QC
Approximately 3½ miles north of Larne on the A7.

RAC recommended hotels
Ballygally Castle ★★★ (0574) 83212
17th-century castle, greatly extended and modernised, facing sandy beach. Tennis, fishing.
Halfway ★★ (0574) 83265 Modern hotel in an attractive location on Antrim coast road.

CARRICKFERGUS
(09603) 62203
An 18 hole park and meadowland course (5752 yards, SSS 68) with the first hole played over water. Visitors are welcome except on Saturday but must have a handicap certificate. Green fees are £7 on weekdays and £10 at weekends and Bank Holidays. Snacks are available and meals, if requested in advance. Local places of interest include the castle in Carrickfergus.
Location
North Road, Carrickfergus BT38 8LP
About 9 miles north of Belfast on the A2 coast road..

RAC recommended hotels
Dobbin's Inn ★ (09603) 51905 A charming historic building of three-storeys on the shores of the Belfast Lough.

CLIFTONVILLE
(0232) 744158
A meadowland course (3120 yards, SSS 70) of 9 holes, bisected by rivers. Visitors of all levels are welcome on weekdays and Sunday afternoon. The green fees are £7.50 for weekdays and £10 at weekends. A restaurant provides full catering facilities and bar snacks are available.
Location
44 Westland Road, Belfast BT14 6NH
Take the Antrim Road out of the centre of Belfast, turning right down Cavehill Road to the course.

RAC recommended hotels in Balmoral.

CUSHENDALL
(02667) 71318
A 9 hole seaside course (4678 yards, SSS 63) with a river around most holes. Visitors are welcome on weekdays and at weekends, though a timesheet operates on Sunday. Green fees are £7 per day and £9 at weekends and Bank Holidays. Snacks are available at the bar. There are lovely coastal walks and Glenarff Forest park and nature reserve are also in the area.
Location
Shore Road, Cushendall, Ballymena, Co Antrim BT44 OQQ.
25 miles north of Larne on the A2 coast road turn right at the Curfew Tower in the Cushendall village.

RAC recommended hotels
Thornlea ★★ (02667) 71223 An attractive, small, white modern building adjacent to the golf course.

DUNMURRY
(0232) 610834
An 18 hole parkland course (5832 yards SSS 68). Visitors are welcome on weekdays but only after 5pm on Tuesday and Thursday. Ladies are required to have a handicap certificate. Green fees are £9 on weekdays and £12 at weekends and Bank Holidays. Meals are available every day.
Location
91 Dunmurry Lane, Dunmurry, Belfast BT17 9JS
Drive south west out of Belfast city through Dunmurry village on the Upper Malone Road.

RAC recommended hotel
Conway ★★★★ (0232) 626546 An elegant former residence in 14 acres of woodland. Offers modern accommodation.

FORTWILLIAM
(0232) 370770
An 18 hole meadowland course (5769 yards, SSS 67). Visitors with a handicap certificate are welcome most days except Saturday. Green fees are £9 on weekdays and £12 at weekends. Lunch and evening meals are available. Places of interest include Belfast Castle.
Location
Downview Avenue, Belfast B15 4EZ
3 miles north of Belfast on the A2 opposite the Castle.

RAC recommended hotels in Belfast.

GREENISLAND
(0232) 862236
A 9 hole meadowland course (5887 yards, SSS 68). Visitors are welcome; except on Saturday. Green fees are £7 on weekdays and £10 on Sunday. Meals

and bar snacks are available. Situated between Belfast and Carrickfergus with plenty of interesting places locally.
Location
156 Upper Road, Greenisland, Carrickfergus, Belfast BT38 8RW
9 miles north of Belfast on the A2 coast road towards Carrickfergus. The course is opposite the station.

RAC recommended hotels in Carrickfergus.

THE KNOCK
(02318) 3251
A well-established 18 hole parkland course (5845 metres, SSS 71). Visitors are welcome except on Saturday and Wednesday afternoon. The green fees are £12 on weekdays, (£6 with a member), £16 on Sunday and Bank Holidays, (£8 with a member). Bar snacks and meals are available, though on Sunday afternoon there is a limited facility. Situated on the east side of Belfast near the Stormont (Houses of Parliament) and the Ulster Folk and Transport Museum.
Location
Summerfield, Upper Newtonards Road, Dundonald, Belfast BT16 OQX
Cross the Queens or Albert Bridge eastwards on the A2 and continue for approximately 4 miles; the course is just past Stormont.

LARNE
(09603) 82228
A seaside links course of 9 holes (6082 yards, SSS 69) within sight of the lighthouse. Visitors with a handicap certificate are welcome but not on Saturday. Green fees £4 on weekdays and £8 on Sunday. Catering is available. The course is situated on the Island of Magee off Larne with coastal walks and a nature reserve.
Location
54 Ferris Bay Road, Islandmagee, Larne, BT40 3RT
From the A2 coast road, cross to the Island of Magee at Whitehaven; the course is on the northern-most tip of the island.

LISBURN
(0846) 677216
An 18 hole park and meadowland course (5708 metres, SSS 72). Visitors are welcome but telephone beforehand. Green fees are £10 on weekdays and £15 at weekends. Meals are available seven days a week.
Location
68 Eglantine Road, Lisburn, Co Antrim BT27 5RQ
Situated south of Belfast on the A1, the course is on the right, 3 miles south of Lisburn.

MALONE
(0232) 612758
Two mature parkland courses, an 18 hole (6499 yards, SSS 71) and a 9 hole (2895 yards, SSS 34). Visitors with a handicap certificate are welcome except on Wednesday and after 5pm on Saturday. Green fees are available on application. Meals and snacks are available all week but there is restricted service on Sunday after 2pm.
Location
240 Upper Malone Road, Dunmurry, Belfast BT17 9LB
Drive south out of Belfast for 5 miles on the Upper Malone Road.

RAC recommended hotels in Dunmurry.

MASSEREENE
(08494) 62096
An 18 hole parkland course (6614 yards, SSS 72) on the side of Loch Neagh . Visitors are welcome except on Saturday, the club's competition day. Green fees on application. Bar snacks, lunch and dinner are available. Local places of interest include a steam locomotive centre and the historic town of Antrim.
Location
51 Lough Road, Antrim BT41 4DQ
Just 1 mile south of Antrim towards the Aldergrave airport.

ORMEAU
(0232) 641069
A 9 hole parkland course, (5308 yards, SSS 65) part of a leisure park complex. Visitors of all levels are welcome on weekdays. Green fees are £4 on weekdays. There are no catering facilities. The course is set in Ormeau Park, and close to many of Belfast's amenities.
Location
2 miles south of the city centre on the Ormeau Road.

RAC recommended hotels in Belfast.

ROYAL PORTRUSH
(0265) 822314
A well-established group of seaside courses on the tournament circuit. The Valley course 18 holes (6273 yards, SSS 71). The Dunluce course 18 holes (6784 yards, SSS 72)
Skerries course 9 holes (1187 yards, SSS).
Visitors with a handicap certificate are welcome but must book in advance. Green fees are as follows:
Valley course £9 weekdays and £12 at weekends.
Dunluce course £14 weekdays and £25 at weekends.
Skerries 75p weekdays and at weekends.
Catering facilities are excellent, and include an à la carte menu and high tea. This course is on the tip of Ireland with magnificent coastal walks, and Dunluce Castle and the Giant's Causeway both within easy reach.
Location
Bushmills Road, Portrush BT56 8JQ
1 mile on the A2 coast road east of Portrush

RAC recommended hotel
Bushmills Inn ★★★ (02657) 32339 A listed 19th-century coaching inn restored and extended in keeping, and now an attractive hotel.

SHANDON PARK
(0232) 793730
An 18 hole parkland course (6252 yards, SSS 69). Visitors are welcome on weekdays and Sunday. Green fees are £9 on weekdays, and £12 at weekends. Bar snacks and meals are available. Situated 3 miles from Belfast city centre near Stormont (Houses of Parliament) and Park.
Location
73 Shandon Park, Belfast BT5 6NY
Take the Knock dual carriageway south of the city towards Stormont.

RAC recommended hotels in Belfast.

WHITEHEAD
(09603) 53631
An undulating 18 hole parkland course (6426 yards, SSS 71). Visitors are welcome except on Saturday. Green fees are £6 on weekdays, £8.50 at weekends, with reductions for parties over 20. Meals can be arranged with the steward. On the Island of Magee there are several places of interest including another golf course!
Location
McCrae's Brae, Whitehead, Co Antrim BT38 9NZ
Travel north out of Belfast on the A2 coast road through Carrickfergus to Whitehead, crossing onto the island where the course is signposted.

RAC recommended hotels
Magheramorne ★★★ (0574) 79444 Carefully restored Victorian mansion, informal gardens and natural grounds.

Co ARMAGH

COUNTY ARMAGH
(0861) 522501
A parkland course of 18 holes (6147 yards, SSS 69). Visitors with a handicap certificate are welcome on weekdays. Telephone first at weekends. Green fees are £6 on weekdays, and £9.50 at weekends. Lunch and dinner are available in the restaurant as well as bar snacks. Locally the Palace of Armagh is worth a visit.
Location
Demesne, Newry Road, Armagh, Co Armagh.
On the A28, a quarter of a mile towards Newry.

LURGAN
(0762) 322087
An established 18 hole course in parkland (5836 metres, SSS 70). Visitors of all levels are welcome, though not on Saturday. Green fees are £9 on weekdays, and £11 at weekends with a reduction when playing with a member. There is a restaurant service except on Monday but snacks are available in the lounge bar. Places of local interest include the Lough Neagh and Lurgan Park, one of the largest in Ireland.
Location
The Demesne, Lurgan, Co Armagh
From the centre of Lurgan, take Windsor Avenue, and the course is past the castle gates.

PORTADOWN
(0762) 355356
An 18 hole parkland course (5621 metres, SSS 70). Visitors are welcome except on Saturday and ladies day on Tuesday. Green fees are £5 on weekdays and, £7 at weekends. Meals served by arrangement.
Location
192 Gilford Road, Carrickblacker, Portadown, Co Armagh BT63 5LF
Take the A50 south east for 2 miles. The course is situated just beyond the Metal Box factory.

RAC recommended hotels
Seagoe ★★★ (0762) 333076 Extensively modernised hotel with lovely landscaped garden.

TANDRAGEE
(0762) 841272
An 18 hole parkland course (6084 yards, SSS 69). Visitors are welcome, but must be accompanied by a member in the evening and at weekends. Green fees are available on application. Meals are served from 12.30pm onwards.
Location
Markethill Road, Tandragee, Craigavon BT62 2ER
Take A27 for 5 miles south of Portadown to Tandragee. The course is west of the town on the B3.

Co DOWN

ARDGLASS
(0396) 841219
An 18 hole seaside links course on a peninsula (5462 mteres, SSS 69). Visitors with a handicap certificate are welcome at all times. Green fees are £7 on weekdays, and £10 at weekends. Reductions are available when playing with a member. There is a large bar for snacks and full meals are available. Several interesting historic sites in the area including Inch Abbey.
Location
Castle Place, Ardglass, Co Down
Travel south east out of Belfast on the A7 through Downpatrick taking the B1 towards the coast. The course is on Ringford point behind the coastguard station.

RAC recommended hotels
Abbey Lodge ★★★ (0396) 4511 A two-storey building of modern design in its own grounds beside the A7.

BANBRIDGE
(08206) 25211
An unusual 12 hole parkland course (5724 yards, SSS 68). Visitors with a handicap certificate are welcome. Ladies have preference on Tuesday, and

Saturday is competition day for men. Green fees are £5 on weekdays, and £7 at weekends. Fees are reduced when playing with a member. Bar snacks are available but meals can be provided by arrangement.
Location
Huntley Road, Banbridge, Co Down
South west of Belfast on the A1. The course is half a mile outside Banbridge beside the river.

CARNALEA
(0247) 270368
An 18 hole seaside course with meadowland (5548 yards, SSS 67). All visitors are welcome. Green fees are £6 weekdays, and £9.25 at weekends and Bank Holidays. Fees are reduced when playing with a member. Full catering facilities with a restaurant and two bars. Places of interest include the Ulster Folk and Transport Museum.
Location
Station Road, Bangor, Co Down BT19 1EZ
Take the A2 east out of Belfast to Carnalea station, 1 mile west of Bangor.

CLANDEBOYNE
(0247) 271767
Two 18 hole courses with mixed cover. Ava is a moorland and parkland course (5172 metres, SSS 67). Dufferin is a park and woodland course (5915 metres, SSS 72). Visitors with handicap certificates are welcome but there are restrictions at weekends. Green fees are £9 and £10 on weedays, and £12 and £15 at weekends. Full meals and bar snacks are available. Situated between Bangor and Newtownards, both towns offer places of interest.
Location
Tower Road, Conlig, Newtownards BT23 3PN
Take the A2 coast road east from Belfast towards Bangorand turn south on the A21. The course is in the village of Conlig before you reach Newtownards.

BANGOR
(0247) 270922
An undulating parkland course of 18 holes (6450 yards, SSS 71). Visitors with a handicap certificate are welcome onMonday, Wednesday, Friday and Sunday. Green fees are £10.50 per day and £15 at weekends, with a reduction for playing with a member. A dining room provides lunch and evening meals. The Ulster Folk and Transport Museum is of local interest.
Location
Broadway, Bangor, Co Down BT20 4RH
Travel east out of Belfast on the A2 coast road. The course is three quarters of a mile out of town.

DONAGHADEE
(0247) 883624
A mixed meadowland and seaside course of 18 holes (5576 metres, SSS 69). Visitors of all standards are welcome but at weekends and Bank Holidays they must be accompanied with a member. Green fees are £8 per day, and £10.50 at weekends and Bank Holidays. Meals are available with two lounge bars-a restricted service is available on Monday.
Location
84 Warren Road, Donaghadee, Co Down BT21 OPQ
From Belfast, travel east on the A2, about 18 miles round the coast through Bangor. The course is just outside Donaghadee on the B21.

DOWNPATRICK
(0396) 612152
An 18 hole parkland course (5823 yards, SSS 68). All visitors are welcome both on weekdays and weekends. Green fees are £8 for weekdays and £10 at weekends; with reductions when playing with a member. Meals are available but there is a limited service in the evening. Places of local interest include the cathedral; Inch Abbey and Castleward.
Location
Saul Road, Downpatrick, Co Down BT30 6PA
Take the A24 south from Belfast to Carryduff, turn on to the A7 to the coast and Downpatrick. The course is on the east side of the town.

RAC recommended hotels
Abbey Lodge ★★★ (0396) 4511 A two-storey modern building set in its own gardens on the north side of town.

HELEN'S BAY
(0247) 852601
A long-established 9 hole course (5154 metres, SSS 67). Visitors are but must be accompanied by a member on Saturday. Green fees are £7 on weekdays and £10 at weekends and Bank Holidays. Fees are reduced when playing with a member. Meals and snacks are available. The Ulster Folk and Transport Museum is within easy distance.
Location
Golf Road, Helen's Bay, Bangor, Co Down
East of Belfast on the A2 coast road, just before you reach Bangor.

HOLYWOOD
(02317) 2138
An undulating parkland course of 18 holes (5885 yards, SSS 68). Visitors with a handicap certificate are welcome on weekdays but play may be restricted at weekends. A restaurant service is available every day except on Monday and there are bar snacks. Apart from nearby Belfast, include the Ulster Folk and Transport Museum.
Location
Nun's Walk, Demesne Road, Holywood, Co Down BT18 9DX
Approximately 6 miles east of Belfast on the A2 coast road.

RAC recommended hotel
Culloden ★★★★ (02317) 5223 Fine 19th-century Scottish baronial style mansion in 12 acres of garden.

KILKEEL
(06937) 62296
A 9 hole public parkland course (5623 metres, SSS 69). Visitors are welcome, though ladies must have a handicap certificate. Green fees are £6.50 per round on weekdays and £7 at weekends and Bank Holidays. Meals and snacks are available. Situated in a delightful fishing village.
Location
Mourne Park, Ballyardle, Co Down BT34 4LB
Take the A2 coast road either south from Newcastle or drive south east from Newry.

RAC recommended hotels
Kilmorney Arms ★★ (06937) 62220 A three-storey family hotel on a corner site.

KIRKISTOWN CASTLE
(02477) 71233
A links course of 18 holes (6151 yards, SSS 70). Visitors are required to have a handicap certificate. Green fees are available on application. Meals and snacks are both available. Situated on a peninsula between Strangford Lough and the Irish Sea, there are plenty of beautiful coastal walks and also a motor racing circuit at Portavogie.
Location
142 Main Road, Cloghy, Newtownards, Co Down BT22 1HZ
Take the A20 south from Newtownards towards Portaferry and turn off on the B173 for Cloghy.

MAHEE ISLAND
(0238) 5412234
An unusual 9 hole course (5588 yards, SSS 67) on a small island. Visitors with a handicap certificate are welcome. Restrictions operate on Saturday before 4.30pm and on Monday. Green fees are £5 on weekdays and £10 at weekends and Bank Holidays. Meals are available by arrangement. There are various historic sites and the Ulster Way follows the side of the Lough near the island.
Location
Comber, Newtownards, Co Down
Take the A20 and A22 east from Belfast to Comber, continue on to Killinchey where Mahee Island is signposted.

ROYAL BELFAST
(0232) 428165
A long established 18 hole parkland course (6205 yards, SSS 69). Visitors must be introduced by a member or by a letter from their club secretary. Green fees are £14 on weekdays and £16 at weekends and Bank Holidays. Full catering facilities available. Situated just east of Belfast with all its attractions, the Ulster Folk Museum being particularly close.
Location
Station Road, Craigavad, Holywood BT18 OBP
Take the A2 east out of Belfast, towards Holywood; the course is on the right.

RAC recommended hotels
Culloden ★★★★ (02317) 5223 A fine 19th-century Scottish baronial mansion in 12 acres of garden.

ROYAL COUNTY DOWN
(03967) 23314
Two 18 hole links courses. Course No 1, the Championship course (6968 yards, SSS 73) and No 2 (4083 yards, SSS 65). Visitors are welcome but with a handicap certificate and by prior arrangement. Green fees are £18 per weekday and £20 at weekends. Meals provided by arrangement. The surrounding area is of great beauty with the Mountains of Mourne and there are also several nature reserves and historic sites nearby.
Location
Newcastle BT33 OAN
Take the A2 south from Belfast to Newcastle. The course is on the north side of town approaching from the town centre.

RAC recommended hotel
Sieve Donard ★★★ (03967) 24830 A glorious mansion in 6 acres with a frontage on a private beach.

SCRABO
(0247) 812355
A testing course of 18 holes (5699 metres, SSS 71). Visitors are welcome on weekdays but must book in advance for weekends. Green fees are £7 weekdays and £9 weekends and Bank Holidays. Places of local interest are the Abbey in Newtownards and Mount Stewart house.
Location
233 Scrabo Road, Newtownards, Co Down BT23 4SL
Take the A20 east from Belfast; Scrabo Hill is signposted just outside Newtownards.

SPA
(0238) 562365
A recently extended 18 hole course of mixed wood and parkland (5938 metres, SSS 72). Visitors of all levels are welcome on weekdays. Green fees are £5 on weekdays and £10 at weekends. Snacks are available and parties catered for by arrangement.
Location
20 Grove Road, Ballynahinch, Co Down BT24 8PN
Take the A24 south east from Belfast to Ballynahinch; the course is 1 mile out of town on the B175.

WARRENPOINT
(06937) 72219
A testing 18 hole parkland course (5640 metres, SSS 70) on the border between Northern Ireland and Eire. Visitors are welcome on Sundays Monday, Thursday and Friday. Green fees are £10 on weekdays and £12 at weekends. Full meals and bar snacks are available. There are squash and snooker facilities. The surroundings of the Mountains of Mourne and the Carlingford Lough

are of great scenic beauty and provide plenty of walks.
Location
Lower Dromore Road, Warrenpoint, Co Down BT34 3LN
Travel south from Belfast on the A24 and then east on the A2 coastal road, or take the inland route via the A1 and Newry. Warrenpoint is on Carlingford Lough and the golf course overlooks Eire across the Lough.

Co FERMANAGH

BLACKLION
(017) 53024
A 9 hole course right on the border (5544 metres, SSS 69). Visitors are welcome at any time. Green fees are IR£3 at weekdays and IR£4 at weekends.
Location
Toam, Blacklion, Fermanagh
On the border where the A4 road west from Enniskillen turns into the N16 to Sligo.

ENNISKILLEN
(0365) 25250
A recently extended 18 hole parkland course (5574 metres, SSS 70) amidst a lakeland area. All visitors are welcome with no restrictions. Green fees are available on application. Bar snacks are available. Situated beside the Castle Coole estate and on the Lower Lough Erne there are numerous historic sites and places of interest nearby.
Location
Castle Coole, Enniskillen, Co Fermanagh
About 1 mile east of the town on the B80.

RAC recommended hotels
Killyhevlin ★★★ (0365) 23481 Charmingly irregular, white painted building in well kept grounds near the A4, east of the town. Fine views over Lough Erne. Fishing.

Co LONDONDERRY

CASTLEROCK
(0265) 848215
An 18 hole and a 9 hole course, both located by the sea (6121 yards, SSS 72) and (2457 metres, SSS 34). The 9 hole has a lot of water. Visitors must have a handicap certificate and are welcome on weekdays and Sunday, but only after 2.30pm on Saturday. Green fees are as follows: 18 hole course £10 weekdays, (£6 with a member), £15 weekends, (£8 with a member). 9 hole course £3 weekdays, £5 weekends. A restaurant and two bars provide full catering facilities. There is also a large practice area. Situated on the north coast of Ireland with its magnificent coastline and other outstanding golf courses.
Location
65 Circular Road, Castlerock, Co Londonderry BT51 4TJ
On the A2 coast road, East of Londonderry and 6 miles west of Coleraine. The course is right on the coast on the west bank of the river inlet.

CITY OF DERRY
(0504) 311369
Two parkland courses. Dunhugh 9 holes (4708 yards, SSS 63) and Prehen 18 holes (6362 yards, SSS 71). Visitors are welcome with a handicap certificate at any time on the Dunhugh course but are restricted to before 4.30pm on weekdays and only by arrangement at weekends on the Prehen course. Green fees are available on application. Snacks and full catering facilities are available. Situated just outside the historic walled city of Londonderry which has many places of interest.
Location
49 Victoria Road, Londonderry BT47 2PU
Alongside the main road to Strabane, 3 miles from the Craigavon bridge and the city centre.

RAC recommended hotel
Everglades ★★★★ (0504) 49200 Long, low built modern hotel beside the busy A5 on the south side of the city. Gymnasium

MOYOLA PARK
(0648) 68392
An 18 hole parkland course (6517 yards, SSS 71) with the 8th hole played over water. Visitors are welcome. Green fees are available on application. Meals are available at weekends and on weekdays by arrangement.
Location
Shanemullagh, Castledawson, Magherafelt, Co Londonderry BT45 8DG
Turn left off the A6 on to the A31 to Castledawson. The course is along the Curran Road to the left of the village.

PORTSTEWART
(026583) 2015
Another pair of excellent seaside courses on the north coast; Strand 18 holes (6784 yards, SSS 72). Town 18 holes (4733 yards, SSS 62). Visitors are welcome with a handicap certificate, but must book in advance. Green fees are as follows: Strand £10 weekdays, £15 weekends and Bank Holidays. Town £3 weekdays and £5 Bank holidays. Meals are available on request. On the coast, with Dunluce Castle and and the Giants Causeway nearby.
Location
117 Strand Road, Portstewart, Co Londonderry BT55 7PG
Right on the coast, 4 miles west of Portrush on the A2.

RAC recommended hotels
Windsor ★ (026583) 2523 Four-storey family hotel opposite the picturesque harbour.

Co TYRONE

DUNGANNON
(086 87) 22101
An 18 hole parkland course (5818 yards, SSS 68). Visitors of any level are welcome at any time. Green fees are £6 weekdays, and £8 at weekends. Meals are available only by prior arrangement. Places of interest locally are the Castle at Castlecaufield and Altmore House.
Location
Springfield Lane, Dungannon, Co Tyrone
On the south west side of Lough Neath at the end of the M1 motorway from Belfast. The course is on the north west side of Dungannon out on the B43 road to Donaghmore.

RAC recommended hotels
Inn on the Park ★★★ (086 87) 24953 In $7^1/_2$ acres of secluded grounds, an attractive two-storey white building. Tennis and snooker.

FINTONA
(0662) 841480
A 9 hole parkland course with the river Quiggery passing through (6251 yards, SSS 70). Visitors are welcome on weekdays but telephone first for weekends. Green fees are available on application. Bar snacks are available. Close to the Ulster American Folk Park and Museum.
Location
Ecclesville, Demesne, Fintona, Co Tyrone
Travel west on the A505 from Cookstown. On reaching Omagh take the B83/B122 to Fintona about 9 miles south west.

KILLYMOON
(06487) 62254
An 18 hole parkland course (5513 metres, SSS 69). Visitors with a handicap certificate are welcome except on Saturday, club competition day. Green fees are £7 weekdays and £10 at weekends. Fees are reduced when playing with a member. Meals are available if ordered in advance. Just outside Cookstown, with several early historic sites around; Drum Manor Forest Park and Mountjoy Castle.
Location
200 Killymoon Road, Cookstown, Co Tyrone BT80 8TW
Travel south on the A29 from Dungannon to Cookstown; the course is signposted opposite Drum Road down a private road.

NEWTOWNSTEWART
(06626) 61466
A hilly 18 hole parkland course (5468 metres, SSS 69). Visitors are welcome but please book in advance to avoid competition days. Green fees are £5 weekdays and £7 at weekends. There is a practice ground available. Meals available by arrangement. Places of interest locally include Harry Avery's Castle and the Ulster American Folk Park.
Location
38 Golf Course Road, Newtownstewart, Co Tyrone BT78 4HU
North of Omagh on the A5 through the town, head south west on the B84 towards Drumquin.

OMAGH
(0662) 3160
An undulating 18 hole parkland course (5051 metres, SSS 67). Visitors are welcome except on Tuesday and Saturday. Green fees are £5 on weekdays and £7 at weekends. Bar snacks are available but full catering can be arranged for parties by arrangement.
Location
Dublin Road, Omagh, Co Tyrone BT78 1HX
One mile south of the town on the main Dublin road, A5.

RAC recommended hotel
Royal Arms ★★ (0662) 3262 Fine 18th-century building with pleasant garden at rear. Billiards.

STRABANE
(0504) 382271
An 18 hole parkland course (5865 yards, SSS 69). Visitors with a handicap certificate are welcome at any time. Green fees are £5 per day and £7 at weekends. Meals can be provided by arrangement.
Location
Ballycolman, Strabane, Co Tyrone BT82 9PH
Travel south from Londonderry to Strabane on the A5, continue 1 mile through town on the Dublin road with the river on the left. The course is beside a church and three schools.

RAC recommended hotels
Fir Trees ★★★ (0504) 885932 Two-storey, L-shaped hotel pleasantly situated on the south side of the town beside the A5.

REPUBLIC OF IRELAND

Co CARLOW

BORRIS
(0503) 73143
A 9 hole parkland course (6026 yards, SSS 69). Visitors are welcome on weekdays, and with a member, on Sunday. Green fees are IR£5 weekdays, and IR£6 at weekends. Meals by arrangement and for society meetings only. Places of interest around are Duiske Abbey, Ullard Church on High Cross and Jerpoint Abbey.
Location
Deer Park, Borris, Co Carlow
Take N9 south out of Carlow, turn off onto the R705 at Leighhimbridge passing through Muine Bheag (Bagenalstown) to the village of Borris.

CARLOW
(0503) 42599
A testing parkland course of 18 holes (6347 yards, SSS 70). The venue of the Irish pro/am championships. Visitors are welcome on weekdays. Green fees are IR£8 weekdays, IR£11 at weekends. Full catering facilities. Situated east of this historic town with several interesting buildings; Irelands largest Dolmen at Brownes Hill and the site of the first engagement of the 1798 rebellion.
Location
Deerpark, Dublin Road, Carlow, Co Carlow
The course is 1 mile from the station on Naas Road (N9).

Recommended hotels
Royal B ★ (0503) 31621 Town centre hotel in walled garden.
Seven Oaks B ★ (0503) 31308 Modern hotel in landscaped grounds; 2 minutes walk from town centre.

Co CAVAN

BELTURBET
(049) 22287
A 9 hole parkland course (5180 yards, SSS 64). Visitors are welcome at any time. Green fees are IR£5 weekdays and weekends. Meals can be provided by arrangement. Bar snacks available. Situated in picturesque area of numerous lakes and rivers.
Location
Erne Hill, Belturbet, Co Cavan
Belturbet is just over 5 miles north of the city of Cavan on the N3.

COUNTY CAVAN
(049) 31283
A parkland course of 18 holes (5119 metres, SSS 69). Visitors are welcome on weekdays and Saturday. Green fees are IR£6 per day. Meals and bar snacks are available. Situated in a historic city within site of the first engagement of the 1798 rebellion; cathedral and Ireland's largest Dolmen at Browne's Hill.
Location
Arnmore House, Drumelis, Cavan
One mile from of Cavan on the N198

Recommended hotel
Kilmore B ★ (049) 32288 Long, low hotel in landscaped gardens 2km out of Cavan.

VIRGINIA
(049) 44103
A 9 hole course (4520 yards, SSS 62) within the Park Hotel grounds. Visitors are welcome at any time. Green fees on application. Meals and snacks are available in the hotel. Situated on the Lough Ramor with good course fishing. Local sights include a monalithic cemetery with over 30 graves.
Location
Virginia, Co Cavan.
Fifty miles north of Dublin on the N3 to Cavan on the northern shore of Lough Ramor.

Recommended hotel
Park Hotel B ★ (049) 47235

Co CLARE

DROMOLAND
(061) 71144 ext 618
An undulating parkland 18 hole course (6098 yards, SSS 71) in the grounds of Dromoland Castle Hotel. Visitors are welcome. Green fees are IR£15 per day. The hotel provides meals and snacks. Situated on the Fergus estuary not far from the delightful town of Ennis with its Fransiscan friary and twisting streets. Brown trout fishing for the angler.
Location
Newmarket on Fergus, Co Clare
Travel east of Ennis on the N18 towards Shannon airport. The town is at the R470 turn-off.

ENNIS
(0654) 21070
A parkland course of 18 holes (5890 yards, SSS 68). Visitors are welcome on weekdays and Saturday; restricted on Sunday. Green fees are IR£16. Meals and bar snacks are available. Just outside the delightful town of Ennis, with its narrow, twisting streets, Franciscan friary and cathedral, 15 miles north of Shannon airport.
Location
Dumbiggie, Ennis, Co Clare
The course is 1 mile west of Ennis.

Recommended hotels
Old Ground A (065) 28127 Well-modernised part 18th-century building in town.
Queens B ★ (065) 28963. Refurbished traditional hotel in town centre.

KILKEE
(048) 341
A 9 hole meadowland course in Moore Bay (6185 yards, SSS 69). Visitors are welcome any time. Green fees are £5.50 per day, and £22 per week. Snacks are available and meals for societies can be provided by arrangement. Situated in an area of renowned beauty with coastal walks and views across to the Aran Islands.
Location
East End, Kilkee, Co Clare
Travel west from Kilrush on the N67 coast road to the Atlantic coast and Kilkee. The course is just out of town on George's Head.

KILRUSH
(065) 51138
A 9 hole parkland course (2739 yards, SSS 67). Visitors are welcome any time. Green fees are £5 per day. Bar snacks are available. Located on the Shannon estuary, attractions including Scattery Island and a 122ft round tower.
Location
Parknamoney, Kilrush, Co Clare
The main town is in the south west of County Clare on the Shannon estuary; the course is to the north east of town on the R483.

Recommended hotel
Inis Cathaigh B (065) 51036

LAHINCH
(065) 81003
Two 18 hole seaside courses; famous for its championships. Old course (6702 yards, SSS 73); Castle (5265 yards, SSS 67). Visitors are welcome on weekdays but are restricted at weekends. Green fees are as follows:
Old IR£19 weekdays, and IR£18 at weekends;
Castle IR£10 weekdays, and IR£18 at weekends.
Meals and snacks are available. A seaside resort on the Liscannor Bay with several interesting historic sites, Kilmacreehy Church and O'Connor Castle.
Location
Lahinch, Co Clare
From the N18 Galway-Limerick road take the R460 at Gort to Corofin then turn right on the R476 past Leamanch Castle and Kilfenora to Lahinch. From Ennis take the R85.

Recommended hotel
Vaughans Aberdeen Arms A (065) 81100

SHANNON
(06) 61020
An interesting 18 hole parkland course (6854 yards, SSS73) which runs between the airport and the Shannon estuary. Visitors are welcome on weekdays. Green fees are IR£12 per day. Lunch, dinner and bar snacks are available. Places of interest locally include Bunratty Castle.
Location
Shannon Airport, Shannon, Co Clare
North of Limerick on the N18, follow the signs out to the airport.

Recommended hotels
Shannon International A (061) 61122 Long, low, modern hotel close to the airport.
Dromoland A ★ (061) 71144

SPANISH POINT
(65) 84198
A links course of 9 holes (6171 metres, SSS 54) set in a small bay. Visitors with a handicap certificate are welcome. Green fees are £5 on weekdays. There are no catering facilities. Situated 7 miles along the coast from Lahinch golf course at the foot of the spectacular Spanish Point Cliffs.
Location
Spanish Point, Miltown Malbay, Co Clare
Drive round on the N67 coast road, north from Kilrush or travel out of Ennis on the R474. The course is 2 miles from Miltown Malbay near the power station.

Recommended hotel
Bay View B (065) 84006

Co CORK

BANDON
(023) 4111
A parkland course of 18 holes (5496 yards, SSS 69). Visitors are welcome every day. Green fees are IR£7 on weekdays, and IR£9 at weekends. Bar snacks and lunch are available. Situated 1½ miles west of Bandon which has one of the earliest Irish Protestant churches and original town stocks. There is good fishing in the Bandon river.
Location
Castlebernard, Bandon, Co. Cork
Take the N71 south from Cork. The course is through Bandon on the river side.

Recommended hotel
Munster Arms B ★ (023) 41562

BANTRY
(027) 50579
A 9 hole course in one of the most beautiful Irish bays. Visitors are welcome and green fees are IR£6. The setting is marvellous, a sheltered bay with numerous inlets and islands. Bantry House is almost a palace with suitably magnificent contents.
Location
Donemark, Bantry, Co Cork
Take the wriggling coast road, the N71, from Killarney or travel from Cork via the N71/R586. The course is just outside Bantry near the Reenydonagan lake.

Recommended hotel
Westlodge B ★ (021) 50360 Modern hotel in grounds of 25 acres.

CORK
(021) 353451
An exciting parkland championship course of 18 holes (6635 yards, SSS 72) built round a quarry. It has hosted most of the major golfing events in Eire including the RTV Rentals Championships and Carrolls International. Visitors are welcome on weekdays except Thursday. Green fees are IR£12 weekdays, and IR£15 at weekends. Full catering facilities are available. The course is just outside the city with its Gothic cathedral and many interesting buildings. The 'Blarney Stone', 15th-century castle is only 6 miles away.
Location
Little Island, Co Cork
Travel east from Cork on the N25, and take the R623 loop road to Little Island and the golf course.

Recommended hotels
Jurys A ★ (021) 276622 Luxurious modern hotel in spacious grounds on River Lee.
Fitzpatrick Silver Springs A (021) 507533 Ultra-modern hotel on main Dublin-Waterford road.
Imperial A (021) 274040 Recently renovated, old worlde historic hotel in city centre.
Arbutus Lodge B ★ (021) 501237 Elegant town house in lovely gardens.
Country Club B ★ (021) 502922 Modern hotel overlooking River Lee.
Moores B ★ (021) 271291 Traditional hotel in quiet area near city centre.

CHARLEVILLE (RATH LUIRC)
(063) 81257
An 18 hole parkland course (6380 yards, SSS 69). Visitors are welcome on weekdays but may be restricted at weekends. Green fees are IR£6 on weekdays, and IR£7 at weekends. Soup and sandwiches are available. There are several early historic sites in the area, Slievereagh, Cush and Duntryleague megalithic tombs.
Location
Ardmore, Charleville, Co Cork
On the N20, 25 miles south of Limerick at the crossroads with the R515 at Rath Luirc/Charleville.

COPH
(021) 812399
A 9 hole course (4338 metres, SSS 63). Visitors are welcome on weekdays, and after midday at weekends. The green fees are IR£4 and IR£5 respectively. Situated at the mouth of Cork harbour; the town has a maritime museum featuring the Lusitania disaster, as hundreds of victims were buried here; the Titanic also called here on her only voyage.
Location
Ballywilliam, Cobh.
Fifteen miles from Cork, via the N25, and the R625 to Cobh. The course is 1 mile north of the town.

DONERAILE
(022) 24137
A 9 hole parkland course (5528 yards, SSS 67). Visitors are welcome weekdays and weekends. Green fees are IR£3. Lunch and dinner are served. Situated near the Butteant Castle and 13th-century friary, 9 miles out of the spa town of Mallow with its Elizabethan clockhouse and lovely 18th-century buildings.
Location
Doneraile, Co Cork
North out of Cork on the N20 past Mourne Abbey through Mallow to the crossroads at Butteant, take the V R522 to Doneraile. The course is by the Awbeg River behind the town.

DOUGLAS
(021) 891085
A beautifully landscaped 18 hole parkland course, (6179 yards, SSS 67) 'not a killer'. Visitors are welcome on weekdays but reservations are necessary at weekends. Green fees are IR£11 weekdays, and IR£12 at weekends. Snacks and meals are available. On the outskirts of the city of Cork with all its amenities, are historic buildings, museums etc.
Location
Maryborough Hill, Douglas, Co Cork
Travel south east out of the city centre on the R609, over the bridge at Douglas. The course is half a mile further on.

Recommended hotels in Cork.

DUNMORE
(023) 33352
A 9 hole course (4464 yards, SSS 61) overlooking Clonakilty Bay. Visitors are welcome at any time. Green fees are IR£4.
Location
Clonakilty, Co Cork
Take the N71 coast road from Cork to Clonakilty. The course is south of the town out on the headland of Duneen Bay.

EAST CORK
(021) 631687
A parkland course 18 holes (5207 yards, SSS 67). Visitors are welcome with a handicap certificate on weekdays. Green fees are IR£7. Lunches are available every day except Sunday. Situated 10 miles outside the historic city of Cork. The Fota wildlife park is particularly close. Midleton itself is far more famous for its distillery of 'Paddy Whiskey'.
Location
Goatacrue, Midleton, Co Cork
Travel east out of Cork on the main Waterford Road, N25. At the Midleton roundabout turn left, the course is signposted and is half a mile further along the road.

Recommended hotels
Ballymaloe House A (021) 652531 Gracious country house on the owner's farm, 1½ miles from the sea.

FERMOY
(025) 31472
An indulating course, 18 holes (5550 yards, SSS 68). Visitors are welcome on weekdays, except Monday and Wednesday afternoon. Green fees are IR£6. Bar snacks are available and lunch and dinner by arrangement. Situated on one of Ireland's best salmon and trout rivers. Places of historic interest are Labbacalle hill with its huge dolmen and megalithic tomb and, right next to the course, Can Tigherhagh Hill Fort.
Location
The course is off the N8 Cork road, 2 miles south of the town, behind the hil fort.

GLENGARRIFF
A 9 hole links course (4328 yards, SSS 61) in the beautiful Bantry Bay area. Visitors are welcome. Green fees are IR£4. A famous scenic area with numerous walks and viewpoints. There are also sailing facilities in Glengarriff Harbour.
Location
Glengarriff, Co Cork
Take the N71 south from Killarney straight into the harbour area.

Recommended hotels
Cassey's B (027) 63010
Eccles B (027 63319 Holiday hotel on the shores of Bantry Bay.

KANTURK
(029) 50534
A 9 hole golf course, (5527 yards, SSS 69) inland from Mallow. Visitors are welcome at any time. Green fees are IR£4. Kanturk is at a crossroads of six roads known forMacDonagh's Folly, a huge Norman-type castle started in 1609 and never finished!
Location
Fairy Hill, Kanturk, Co Cork
The R579 from Cork winds inland in a north west direction and passes the golf course just after it crosses the N72 and River Blackwater. The course is on the R579 Cork-Kanturk road, just north of the River Blackwater and the N72 crossing.

KINSALE
(021) 772197
A parkland course of 9 holes (5332 yards, SSS68) on a coastal inlet. Visitors are welcome on weekdays but not weekends. Green fees are IR£6 per day. Lunch and dinner are available. Kinsale is a fishing and yachting centre with several interesting buildings-Mulrose Church, Desmond Castle and Charles's Fort in nearby Sumer Cove.
Location
Ringenane, Belgooly, Co Corke
Travel south of Cork on the R600 for about 8 miles. The course is before the town, turn left after passing Belgooly village.

Recommended hotels
Acton's A (021) 772135 Modernised hotel overlooking the picturesque harbour.
Blue Haven B ★ (021) 772209 Small, cosy, owner-run hotel in the centre of town.

MALLOW
(022) 21145
A testing parkland 18 hole course extended from a long 9 hole course (6559 yards, SSS 71). Visitors are welcome on weekdays except Tuesday. Green fees are available on application. Lunch and dinner are served, also bar snacks. Known as 'The Bath of Ireland', Mallow has some lovely 18th-century buildings and an Elizabethan clockhouse and spa well. Excellent fishing nearby and the town is also now known for its racecourse.
Location
Ballyellis, Mallow, Co Cork
The course is east of the town at Mallow Bridge.

Recommended hotel
Longueville House A (022) 47156 A Georgian mansion set in a wooded estate.

MACROOM
(026) 41072
A parkland course of 9 holes (5439 metres, SSS 68). Visitors are welcome at any time. Green fees

are IR£5. Full meals are provided if required. On the edge of the Gaelic speaking area. A huge castle dominates the town and another, Carrigaphonca Castle, nearby, in a picturesque river valley.
Location
Lackaduve, Macroom, Co Cork
West from Cork on the N22 or on the R618, a more scenic route, the two converge just outside Macroom. The course is in the south west of the town.

Recommended hotel
Castle B ★ (026) 41074 Family-owned and managed traditional hotel in town centre.

MAHON
(021) 362480
The municipal 18 hole course in Cork (4818 yards, SSS 66). Visitors are welcome at any time. Green fees are IR£5 on weekdays, and IR£6 at weekends. Bar snacks available. Lunch and dinner by prior arrangement. In the southern suburbs of Cork with all the amenities this town offers including the 'Lion of Cork' and St Ann's Church, where visitors are allowed to play tunes on its eight bells. Blarney Castle is not far away either.
Location
Cloverhill, Blackrock, Co Cork
Take the main Douglas Road R609, turn left on the Old Blackrock road, at the junction of the R600 and R609.

Recommended hotels in Cork.

MITCHELSTOWN
(025) 24072
A parkland course of 9 holes (5057 metres, SSS 67). Visitors are welcome and green fees are IR£6. Meals can be provided for societies by arrangement. The town is famed for its cheese, Ronald Reagan's ancestral home at Ballyporeen and the limestone caves which include the biggest in the British Isles.
Location
Mitchelstown, Co Cork
Travel north from Cork on the main Dublin road, N8. Mitchelstown is at the junction of the N8 and the N73.

MONKSTOWN
(021) 841225
An 18 hole parkland course, (6170 yards, SSS 68) looking across to Cobh in Cork harbour. Visitors are welcome on weekdays, except on Tuesday and Wednesday. Green fees are IR£10 on weekdays, and IR£11 at weekends. Lunch and dinner are served. Local attractions are Cork and its historic buildings and museums-Blarney Castle to the west of the city and the ancient port of Cobh on the opposite bank with its 'Lusitania' connections.
Location
Parkgariffe, Monkstown, Co Cork
South of Cork on the R610, follow the bank of Lake Mahon through Passage West on to Monkstown and the course.

Recommended hotels in Cork.

MUSKERRY
(021) 385104
An 18 hole parkland course, (5786 meters, SSS 70) with the River Shournagh running through. Visitors are welcome on weekdays, except Wednesday afternoon and Thursday morning. Green fees are IR£12 on weekdays. Snacks are available and meals if ordered in advance. Situated 7 miles west of Cork through the village of Blarney, with its castle and famous stone.
Location
Carrigrohane, Co Cork
Travel west out of Cork on the R617 through Blarney or take the N22 west, then on the R579 towards Blarney village.

Recommended hotel
Blarney Park A (021) 385281

SKIBBEREEN
(028) 21227
A 9 hole moorland course (5774 yards, SSS 68). Visitors are welcome. Green fees are IR£6 per round, and IR£42 for a week. The town has a cathedral and the ruins of a 14th- century abbey where hundreds of victims of the 1846/7 Famine lie buried. Beautiful views from the headlands over the Carbery coast and its numerous islands.
Location
Skibbereen, Co Cork
Take the coastal road, N71, from Cork via Bandon and Clonakilty. The course is out of town on the R595 towards Baltimore.

YOUGHAL
(024) 92787
An excellent 18 hole meadowland course with unusual crossed fairways (6223 yards, SSS 69). Visitors are welcome on weekdays. Green fees are IR£7 for men, and IR£5 for ladies. The new club house provides full catering facilities. Apart from fishing and boating, this historic town has many interesting places including Walter Raleigh's house, the Collegiate Church of St Mary's, Ireland's largest medieval parish church and the remains of a 13th-century priory.
Location
Knockaverry, Youghal, Co Cork
Take the N25 Cork-Waterford road to Youghal. The course is on the headland, overlooking the town and Youghal Bay.

Co DONEGAL

NORTHWEST
(074) 61027
A traditional, gently undulating seaside course, 18 holes (6203 yards, SSS 69). Visitors are welcome on weekdays except Wednesday, and at weekends on application. Green fees are IR£5 on weekdays, and IR£6 at weekends. Lunch and dinner are served and bar snacks are available. Close to the seaside resort of Buncrana with sandy bays for 3 miles. The town boasts two castles.
Location
Lisfannon, Fahan, Lifford, Co Donegal
The course is 2 miles south of Buncrana on the R238.

Recommended hotels in Buncrana.

OTWAY
(074) 58319
A 9 hole links course (4134 yards, SSS 60) on the shore of Lough Swilly. Visitors are welcome at any time. Green fees on application. Lough Swilly offers good salmon fishing and brown trout in local lakes.
Location
Rathmullen, Co Donegal
From Letterkenny, take the R245 north to Rathmullan. The course is outside the town, beside the lough.

Recommended hotels
Rathmullan House A (074) 58188 A gracious country house by Lough Swilly. Tennis, fishing.
Fort Royal B ★ A delightful country house on Lough Swilly. Tennis, squash, golf.

PORTSALON
(074) 59102
An 18 hole seaside course (5844 yards, SSS 68) on the shores of Lough Swilly. Visitors are welcome on weekdays. Green fees are IR£5. On the Fanad peninsula, opposite Dunree Head Lighthouse, with spectacular views. The Lough offers salmon fishing and brown trout in local lakes.
Location
Portsalon, Co Donegal
From Letterkenny, take the R245 north through Rathmullan to Millford. Turn right on the R246 to Portsalon.

ROSAPENNA
(074) 55301
A championship 18 hole seaside course with ocean views (6254 yards, SSS 70). Visitors are welcome at all times. Green fees are IR£7 on weekdays, and IR£8 at weekends. Meals are available by arrangement with the Rosapenna Hotel. The 'Atlantic drive' possibly the best scenic drive in Co Donegal, encompasses the golf course; there are some interesting prehistoric buildings at nearby Carrickart.
Location
Downies, Co Donegal
From Londonderry west to Letterkenny on the N13. On to Millford on the R245 and round to Carrickart on Mulroy Bay. The course is on the R248 which branches off to Rosapenna and Downies.

Recommended hotel
Rosapenna Golf A (074) 55301

BALLYBOFEY & STRANORLAR
(0704) 31093
A 18 hole parkland course (5913 yards, SSS 68). Visitors are welcome but preferably not on Wednesday, Thursday and Friday. Green fees are IR£5. Snacks are available and meals by prior arrangement. Just across the border is Strabane, with its American associations, and various interesting buildings including Gray's print shop.
Location
Ballybofey, Co Donegal
The club is signposted on the Donegal-Strabane road about a quarter of a mile outside Stranorlar.

Recommended hotels
Jacksons B ★ (074) 31021 Large, family-run hotel on banks of River Finn overlooking woods of Drumboe.
Kee's B ★ (074) 31018 Recently modernised, family-run hotel with a cosy atmosphere.

BUNCRANA
A municipal 9 hole course (2020 yards, SSS 59). Visitors are welcome. Situated in Buncrana, with 3 miles of fine golden sand, a bronze age burial chamber and Dolmen, and an 18th-century castle.
Location
Buncrana, Co Donegal
Take the R238 north from the N13, the Letterkenny-Londonderry road, at Bridgend and travel alongside Lough Swilly.

Recommended hotels
Lake of Shadows B ★ (077) 61005
White Strand B ★ (077) 61059

BUNDORRAN
A 'beautiful but crafty' 18 hole seaside and parkland course (6328 yards, SSS 69) running along the hilltop and venue for many internationals. One of Ireland's top golf courses. Visitors are welcome at all times though a timesheet operates at weekends. Bar snacks are available but meals can be provided at the hotel on the course, the Great Northern. A popular seaside resort with a wide beach, lots of interesting cliff walks with curious rock shapes caused by sea erosion.
Location
Bundoran, Co Donegal
Take the N15 Sligo-Donegal road along the coast of Donegal Bay to Bundorran.

Recommended hotels
Great Northern A (072) 41204 On the golf course
Holyrood B ★ (072) 41232 Family-run in the centre of town
Bayview B ★ (072) 41296

DONEGAL
(073) 34054
A championship seaside links course of great length (7271 yards, SSS 73). Visitors are welcome at all

times. Green fees are IR£5 weekdays, and IR£6 weekends. Bar snacks are available. Station Island with Patrick's Purgatory is near the course and there is a Jacobean castle.
Location
Murvagh, Ballintra, Co Donegal
The course is south of Donegal, off the N15 road to Sligo.

Recommended hotels
Hyland Centra A (073) 21027
Abbey B ★ (073) 21014
Ernam Park B ★ (073) 21065 Period hotel on its own island joined to the mainland by a causeway.

DUNFANAGHY
(074) 36208
An 18 hole seaside course (5066 metres, SSS 66). Visitors welcome at all times. Green fees are IR£4 weekdays, and IR£5 at weekends. On the coast near Horn Head and magnificent cliffs.
Location
Dunfanaghy, Co Donegal
Take the N56 from Letterkenny; the course is a quarter of a mile off the main road, east of the village.

Recommended hotels
Arnolds B ★ (074) 36208
Carrig-Rua B ★ (074) 36133 Recently renovated old coaching inn with sea views.

GREENCASTLE
(077) 81013
A 9 hole seaside course (5386 yards, SSS 65). Visitors are welcome on weekdays; but playing may be restricted at weekends. Green fees are IR£5 weekdays, and IR£7 at weekends. Bar snacks and meals are available at all times. On the side of Lough Foyle opposite Magilligan Point. The coast is rugged, beautiful and dotted with lighthouses.
Location
Greencastle, via Lifford, Co Donegal
Travel north east on the R238 from Londonderry following the coast of Lough Foyle towards Inoshowen Head. The course is just out of Greencastle, behind the lighthouse.

GWEEDORE
(075) 31140
An 18 hole seaside course (6230 yards, SSS 69). Visitors are welcome at all times. Green fees are IR£5 weekdays, and IR£6 at weekends. Lunch is served at weekends. Out on the west coast of Donegal not far from the Rosses, an area of little lakes and streams, ideal for fishermen.
Location
Derrybeg, Gweedore, Co Donegal
Turn off the N56 coast road on to the R257 to Bunbeg and Derrybeg and the course.

LETTERKENNY
(074) 21150
An 18 hole seaside course (6299 yards, SSS 71), at the head of Lough Swilly inlet. Visitors are welcome, except on Tuesday and Wednesday. Green fees are IR£5. Snacks are available and meals by arrangement. A centre for salmon fishermen, the town has a fine modern cathedral; nearby are the ruins of a friary and Cowal cemetary with many interesting tombstones. Glenveagh National Park and castle are worth a visit.
Location
Barnhill, Letterkenny, Co Donegal
The course is on the R245 outside of town on the Lough.

Recommended hotels
Mount Errigal A (074) 22700
Gallagher's B ★ (074) 22066

NARAN AND PORTNOO
(075) 45107
An 18 hole seaside course (5950 yards, SSS 68). Visitors are welcome all week except Sunday. Green fees are IR£6 on weekdays. Bar snacks are available. Situated on Dunmore head with a stone fort and views across Gweebarra Bay. Good salmon and trout fishing and Essarauka waterfall. Near Ardara, is the centre of Donegal's homespun tweeds and associated crafts.
Location
Portnoo, Co Donegal
From Donegal take the N56 along the coast to Killybegs then north to Ardara where the R261 goes out to Naran and the Portnoo course.

Co DUBLIN

BALBRIGGAN
(01) 412173
An 18 hole meadowland course (5717 metres, SSS 70). Visitors are welcome on weekdays except Tuesday. Green fees are IR£7. Bar snacks are available and lunch and dinner can be provided by arrangement. The Skerries is nearby and St Patrick Island. There is a farm machinery museum inland at Man O'War.
Location
Blackhall, Balbriggan, Co Dublin
Drive north from Dublin on the N1 straight to Balbriggan about (17 miles). The golf course is outside town.

BALLINASCORNEY
(01) 512516
A 9 hole course (5322 yards, SSS 66). Visitors are welcome at all times; green fees are aavailable on application. On the outskirts of Dublin with all that this elegant, historic town can offer.
Location
Ballinascorney, Tallaght, Co Dublin
Drive west out of Dublin on the N81.

Recommended Hotels
Berkeley Court A ★ (01) 601711 Elegant, modern hotel with a mixture of up-to-date and antique furnishings.
Jurys A ★ (01) 60500 Deluxe, modern hotel close to main shopping area. Conference facilities. Indoor/outdoor swimming pool.
Shelbourne A ★ (01) 766471/616006 Luxury hotel in elegant period building in Dublin's most fashionable area.
Buswells A (01) 764013 Lansdowne B (01) 684079 Family-run hotel in heart of Georgian Dublin.
Orwell Lodge C (01) 977 256 Refurbished period house in quiet area.

BEAVERSTOWN
(01) 436439
An 18 hole inland course (yards, SSS 72). Visitors are welcome. Green fees are IR£8. Bar snacks available. Situated in the northern suburbs of Dublin, 4 miles from the airport, with all the amenities of this elegant Georgian city.
Location
Beaverstown, Donabate, Co Dublin
15 miles north of Dublin city towards the airport.

Recommended hotels in Ballinasorney
Berkeley Court A ★ (01) 601711 Elegant, modern hotel with a mixture of up-to-date and antique furnishings.
Shellbourne A ★ (01) 766471 (01) 616006 Luxury hotel in elegant period building in Dublin's most fashionable area.
Buswells A (01) 764013
Lansdowne B (01) 684079 Family-run hotel in heart of Georgian Dublin.
Orwell Lodge C (01) 977 256 Refurbished period house in quiet area.

BEECH PARK
(01) 580522
An 18 hole inland course (yards, SSS 67). Visitors are welcome at all times. Green fees are IR£9. To the west of Dublin with all its amenities.
Location
Johnstown, Rathcoole, Co Dublin
Take the N7 west from Dublin to Rathcoole. The course is 7 miles from Rathcoole on the Kitteel road.

CASTLE
(01) 904207
An 18 hole parkland course (6240 yards, SSS 69). Visitors are welcome on Monday, Wednesday, Thursday morning and Friday. Green fees are IR£11 on weekdays. Lunch and dinner available. Situated in the elegant city of Dublin with all its amenities.
Location
Woodside Drive, Rathfarnham, Dublin 14
Drive south from the city on the N81, turn left after Terenure, then second right.

Recommended hotels in Dublin

CARRICKMINES
(01) 895676
An 18 hole course (6044 yards, SSS 69). Visitors are welcome on weekdays and with a member at weekends. Green fees are on application. 7 miles from Dublin and all its amenities.
Location
Carrickmines, Dublin
Drive south out of Dublin on the R117.

Recommended hotels in Dun Laoghaire.

CLONTARF
(01) 311305
A 18 hole parkland course (5447 metres, SSS 68). Visitors are welcome on Tuesday, Thursday and Friday. Green fees are IR£11. Lunch and dinner are available as well as bar snacks. Situated near the city centre with all the amenities of this historic city.
Location
Donnycarney House, Malahide Road, Dublin 3
North east of Dublin on the Malahide Road.

Recommended hotels in Dublin.

CORBALLIS
(01) 450583
An 18 hole seaside course (4971 yards, SSS 64). Visitors are welcome on weekdays but play may be restricted at weekends. Green fees are available on application. Catering available by arrangement. Situated north of Dublin with its historic sites and museums. There are sailing facilities off Malahide.
Location
Donabate, Co Dublin
Travel north out of Dublin on the N1 through Swords, then turn right on the R126 towards Donabate.

DEERPARK HOTEL
(01) 322624
A testing 18 hole course (6647 yards, SSS 73) and a pitch and put course. Visitors are welcome on weekdays but by arrangement only at weekends. Green fees are IR£4.80 weekdays and IR£6.40 weekends. Full meals and snacks are available from the hotel situated on the course, 8 miles north of Dublin with its attractions. More locally, the Hill of Howth and peninsula are a known beauty spot with Castle Howth and Aideen's Grave worth visiting.
Location
Howth, Co Dublin
Travel north out of Dublin on the Howth road which curves round the peninsula overlooking Dublin Bay. The course is on the lighthouse side.

Recommended hotel
Deerpark Hotel B (01) 322624 Modern hotel with golf complex overlooking the sea.

DONABATE
(01) 436346
An 18 hole parkland course (6187 yards, SSS 69). Visitors are welcome on weekdays except Wednesday. Green fees are IR£9 weekdays and

IR£13 weekends. Full facilities with restaurant, bar and snack bar. Close to Dublin with several other golf courses along this coastline, sailing at Malahide and a castle and round tower at Swords for more local interest.

Location

Donabate, Co Dublin
Driving from Dublin out on the N1 about 16 miles past Dublin Airport, through Swords, take the R126 turn right to Donabate.

Recommended hotels in Dublin.

DUN LAOGHAIRE
(01) 803916

A popular suburban 18 hole parkland course (5463 metres, SSS 69). Visitors are welcome on weekdays except Thursday and Wednesday afternoon. There are no facilities available on Saturday. Green fees are IR£13 weekdays and IR£15 on Sunday. Lunch, dinner and bar snacks are available during the season. Situated 7 miles out of Dublin near the car ferry terminal. Dalkey Castle and Ballybrack megalithic tomb are close by.

Location

Eglinton Park, Dun Laoghaire, Co Dublin
Follow the railway along the coast road south east towards the car ferry terminal. Turn right before the station, up York Road to the golf course.

Recommended Hotels

Royal Marine A (01) 801911 Large, grey-stone hotel close to ferry terminal overlooking the sea.
Victor B ★ (01) 853555

EDMONDSTOWN
(01) 932461

Another 18 hole parkland course in the suburbs of Dublin (5663 metres, SSS 69). Visitors are welcome on weekdays. Green fees are IR£10 weekdays and IR£12 at weekends. Full catering facilities on the course. Apart from Dublin's obvious attractions there are several other golf courses in the vicinity.

Location

Edmondstown, Rathfarnham, Dublin 16
From the city centre, drive south past St Patrick's cathedral and take the N81 through Terenure to Rathfarnham.

Recommended hotels in Dublin.

ELM PARK
(01) 693438

Another of Dublin's 18 hole courses, (5485 metres, SSS 68) this one with sports club facilities on site. Visitors are welcome on weekdays but telephone first. Green fees are IR£13 on weekdays, IR£18 at weekends. There are full facilities for meals and snacks.

Location

Nutley House, Dannybrook, Dublin 4
Travel south east out towards Donnybrook for 2 miles. The course is close to the University College and next to Vincents Hospital.

Recommended hotels in Dublin.

FOREST LITTLE
(01) 401183

An 18 hole parkland course (5852 metres, SSS 70) adjacent to Dublin airport. Visitors are welcome on weekdays except Tuesday and Friday morning. Green fees are IR£12 per day. Snacks are available and an à la carte menu after 5pm. Situated on the outskirts of Dublin with all its amenities. Donsoghly Castle and St Doulagh's Church are nearby.

Location

Forest Little, Cloghran, Co Dublin
North of Dublin on the N1, half a mile after the airport.

FOXROCK
(01) 895668

An 9 hole parkland course (5699 metres, SSS 69). Visitors are welcome on Monday, Wednesday morning, Thursday, Friday and with a member on Sunday. Green fees are available on application. Snacks are available. Near the coast with Dalkey Island, two castles and Ballybrack megalithic tomb in the immediate vicinity.

Location

Take the coast road south to Dun Laoghaire and the car ferry terminal, continue past the castles on the Dalkey point. The course is on the right.

Recommended hotels in Dun Laoghaire.

GRANGE
(01) 932832

An 18 hole parkland course (5517 metres, SSS 69). Visitors are welcome on weekdays except Tuesday and Wednesday afternoon. Green fees are IR£14 on weekdays and IR£17 at weekends. Lunch, dinner and bar snacks available. Situated south of Dublin with all its amenities.

Location

Grange Road, Rathfarnham, Dublin 16
Drive south out of the city centre past St Patrick's Cathedral, take the N81 to Rathfarnham. The course is off Dodder Park Road.

HERMITAGE
(01) 268491

A championship 18 hole course (6034 metres, SSS 71). Visitors are welcome on Monday, Thursday and Friday. Green fees are IR£15 on weekdays, IR£20 at weekends. Lunch, dinner and snacks are available. Situated west of Dublin and its attractions; also near Phoenix Park, with its botanical gardens and zoo.

Location

Lucan, Co Dublin
Take the N4 road west through Palmerston. The course is 2 miles short of the village of Lucan on the right, next to the river.

HOWTH
(01) 323055

An 18 hole heathland course (5573 metres, SSS 69). Visitors are welcome on weekdays, preferably on Monday, Tuesday or Friday. Green fees are IR£10 on weekdays. Snacks are available. Located on the peninsula of Howth, with St Mary's Abbey and another golf course sharing this small area.

Location

Follow the coast road round to Howth, about 9½ miles from Dublin.

Recommended hotels

Deerpark Hotel B (01) 322624 Modern hotel with golf complex.
Howth Lodge B ★ (01) 390288
Family run hotel with direct access to the beach.

ISLAND
(01) 436462

An 18 hole seaside course (6320 yards, SSS 71). Visitors are welcome on weekdays except Wednesday and Thursday. Green fees are IR£10 weekdays and IR£15 at weekends. Snacks and lunch are available and dinner by arrangement. Local interest includes a castle and round tower at Swords, two more golf courses and sailing off Malahide.

Location

Corbaths, Donabate, Co Dublin
Drive north out of Dublin on the N1 through Swords turning right on the R126 to Donabate.

KILLINEY
(01) 851983

A 9 hole parkland course (6201 yards, SSS 69). Visitors are welcome most days. Green fees are IR£10. Snacks are available. Near the ferry terminal at Dun Laoghaire, two castles and Ballybrack megalithic tombs.

Location

Killiney, Co Dublin
Travel out of Dublin on the N11 towards Bray. Killiney is on the left side, 3 miles past Dun Laoghaire.

Recommended hotels

Fitzpatrick Castle A ★ (01) 851533 Luxury hotel in castle with modern extension in keeping. Spacious grounds.
The Court A (01) 851622

KILTERNAN HOTEL
(01) 955559

An 18 hole course, part of a hotel complex (5413 yards, SSS 66). Visitors are welcome but must be accompanied by a member. Green fees are IR£5 weekdays and IR£7 at weekends. Full catering service provided by the hotel.

Location

Drive south east out of Dublin on the Enniskerry Road. The hotel and course are just past Golden Ball.

MALAHIDE

One of several courses on this section of coast. 9 holes (5568 yards, SSS 67). Visitors are welcome except on Sunday and Wednesday. Green fees on application. Simple meals are available. Sailing off Malahide and all the attractions of Dublin's city centre are only 8 miles away.

Location

Coast Road, Malahide, Co Dublin
Drive north out of Dublin on the N1 and turn right on the R106 out of Swords to Malahide. The course is the other side of the town.

MILLTOWN
(01) 976090

An 18 hole parkland course in the southern suburbs of Dublin (5669 metres, SSS 69). Visitors are welcome except on Tuesday and Wednesday afternoon. Green fees are IR£14 on weekdays. Lunch, dinner and bar snacks are available. Within easy reach of most of the major attractions of Dublin.

Location

Lower Churchtown Road, Dublin 14
3 miles south of the city centre over the south ring road through Ranelagh.

Recommended hotels in Dublin.

LUCAN
(01) 282106

A 9 hole parkland course (6281 yards, SSS 70). Visitors are welcome on weekdays until 3pm. Green fees are IR£8. Lunch, dinner and snacks are available. The course is situated out past Phoenix Park with its zoo and botanical gardens.

Location

Celbridge Road, Lucan, Co Dublin
Drive west on the N4 through Lucan, turn left on the R403; the course is on the left.

NEWLANDS
(01) 592903

An 18 hole parkland course (6184 yards, SSS 69). Visitors are welcome on Monday, Thursday and Friday. Green fees are IR£14. Full catering facilities are available. There is a round tower in Clondalkin close by and all the amenities of Dublin about 6 miles away.

Location

Clondalkin, Co Dublin 22
Take the N7 south west out of Dublin towards Casement Aerodrome. The course is on the left just past the junction with the R113.

PORTMARNOCK
(01) 323082

Twenty seven holes, with 3 courses, available. 'A' (7079 yards, SSS 75); 'B' (7047 yards, SSS 75); 'C' (6596 yards, SSS 74). Ireland's premier tournament venue. Visitors are welcome by arrangement. Green fees on application. Full catering facilities available. Situated on the coast with sailing nearby.

Location

Portmarnock, Co Dublin
Drive north east out of Dublin along the R107 coast road, turning right towrds the coast and on to

Portmarnock. Turn right at the Jet Garage onto a private road to the course.

RATHFARNHAM
(01) 931201
A 9 hole parkland course (5787 metres, SSS 70). Visitors are welcome on weekdays except Tuesday. Green fees are IR£9. Lunch and dinner available by arrangement. Situated in the southern suburbs of Dublin.
Location
Newtown, Rathfarnham, Dublin 16
Drive out of the city centre past St Patrick's Cathedral; take the N81 through Terenure to Rathfarnham. The course is 2 miles further south on the right hand side.

RUSH
(01) 437548
A 9 hole seaside links course (5598 metres, SSS 69). Visitors are welcome but with restrictions on Wednesday, Thursday and at weekends. Green fees are IR£7. Full catering facilities available. Local interest includes St Patrick's Island and the Skerries; and a farm machinery museum at Lusk.
Location
Rush, Co Dublin
Travel north on the N1 through Swords; turn right on the R127, and right again to Rush.

Recommended hotel in Skerries.

ROYAL DUBLIN
(01) 336346
An 18 hole seaside links course (6929 yards, SSS 73). Venue for many championships, a fine test of golf. Visitors are welcome on weekdays except Wednesday and at weekends by arrangement. A handicap certificate is required. Green fees are IR£18 on weekdays and IR£20 at weekends. Lunch, dinner and snacks are available. Situated on an island in the centre of Dublin Bay.
Location
Bull island, Dollymount, Dublin 3
Drive north east out of the city centre towards Howth on the coast road, turn right onto Bull Island which is parallel to the coast.

Recommended hotels in Dublin.

ST ANNES
(01) 332979
A 9 hole seaside course sharing Bull Island with the Royal Dublin Club (5813 metres, SSS 68). Visitors are welcome by appointment on Thursday only. Green fees are IR£12. Meals are available by arrangement. Dublin with all its facilities is 4 miles away.
Location
Bull Island, Clontarf, Dublin 5
Drive north east out of Dublin towards Howth on the coast road, turning right on to Bull Island.

SKERRIES
(01) 491567
An 18 hole parkland course (5852 yards, SSS 70). Visitors are welcome on Monday, Thursday and Friday. Green fees are IR£10 on weekdays and IR£12 at weekends. Lunch, dinner and snacks available. Situated on Skerries with its islands, including St Patrick's and Red Island.
Location
Hackestown, Skerries, Co Dublin
Drive north on the N1 through Swords, taking the right fork of the R127 to Skerries.

Recommended hotels
Pier House B (01) 491708 Family-run hotel right on the harbour.

SLADE VALLEY
(01) 582207
An undulating 18 hole course (5337 metres, SSS 68). Visitors are welcome on weekdays but may be restricted on Wednesday and at weekends. Green fees are available on application. Bar snacks are available and dinner by arrangement.
Location
Lynch Park, Brittas, Co Dublin
Take the N81 south west for about 9 miles out of Dublin. The course is to the right of Brittas, on the hillside.

STACKSTOWN
An 18 hole course (5952 yards, SSS 72). Visitors are welcome on weekdays. Green fees are IR£8 on weekdays. Lunch, dinner and snacks are available. Within the southern suburbs of Dublin.
Location
Kellystown Road, Rathfarnham, Dublin 16
Drive south past St Patrick's cathedral and take the N81 through Terenure to Rathfarnham.

SUTTON
(01) 323013
A 9 hole seaside course (5522 yards, SSS 67). Visitors are welcome except on Tuesday and Saturday. Green fees are available on application. Catering by arrangement only. Places of local interest include St Mary's Abbey on the Howth peninsula; sailing is available in Dublin Bay.
Location
Cush Point, Barrow Road, Sutton, Dublin 13
Travel north east out of Dublin on the coast road towards Howth. The course is on the narrow isthmus leading to the peninsula.

Co GALWAY

ATHENRY
(091) 94466
A 9 hole parkland course (5448 yards, SSS 67). Visitors are welcome weekdays and Saturday. Green fees are IR£4 on weekdays, and IR£5 at weekends. Meals can be provided by arrangement. Situated 5 miles out of Athenry which retains some interesting medieval buildings.
Location
Derrydonnel, Dranmore, Co Galway
Travel east from Galway on the N6 branching on to the R348 along the railway towards Athenry.

BALLINASLOE
(0905) 42126
An 18 hole course of a park and meadowland mix (5800 yards, SSS 66). Visitors are welcome. Green fees are IR£5. Snacks and lunch are available. On the county borders, Ballinasloe is famous for its horse, cattle and sheep fair in October.
Location
Ballinasloe, Rosgloss, Co Galway
The course is about 2 miles south of the town on the east side of the R335 Portumna road.

Recommended hotels
Haydens A (0905) 42347 Family-owned and run hotel in landscaped gardens.

CONNEMARA
(095) 21153
An undulating championship links course (7107 yards, SSS 73). Visitors are welcome. Green fees are IR£12. Snacks are available and meals by arrangement. Situated on the tip of the Connemara peninsula with staggering views of the Atlantic and numerous inland lakes for good fishing.
Location
Ballyconneely, Co Galway
Drive west from Galway on the N59 to Clifden, then take the R341 to Ballyconneely. The course is out of town on the cliff-tops at Slyne Head.

Recommended hotels
Abbeyglen Castle A (095) 21201 Delightful mock castle, set in beautiful gardens with views of the village of Clifden and the bay.
Hotel Ardagh A (095) 21384 A family-run hotel beautifully located on the rocky edge of Ardbear Bay
Rock Glen Manor House A (095) 21035 A converted shooting lodge, built in 1815, now an owner-run hotel. Tennis, snooker.

GALWAY
(091) 22169
An 18 hole seaside course (6376 yards, SSS 70). Visitors welcome but play may be restricted on Tuesday and at weekends. Green fees are IR£12 and IR£15. Lunch and snacks available, and dinner by arrangement. Galway is full of historic buildings and churches and is a centre for salmon fishing and oysters.
Location
Blackrock, Salthill, Galway
Just 2 miles west of the centre of Galway at the coast resort of Salthill.

Recommended hotels
Great Southern A ★ (091) 64041 Large mid 19th-century hotel with a handsome facade in the heart of the city.
Ardilaum House A (091) 21433 Once a country mansion and situated in beautiful grounds.
Corrib Great Southern A (091) 55281 Modern hotel with spectacular views of Galway Bay.

GORT
(091) 31336
A 9 hole parkland course (4976 metres, SSS 66). Visitors are welcome at any time. Green fees are IR£5 per day. Snacks are available. Situated in a pleasant town with Yeats connections.
Location
Laughtry Shaughnessy, Gort, Co Galway
Travel south on the N18 from Galway to Gort. The course is on the right just before the town and past Kiltartan Church.

LOUGHREA
(091) 41049
A meadowland 9 hole course (5578 yards, SSS 67). Visitors are welcome at any time. Green fees are IR£4 on weekdays and IR£5 at weekends. Meals can be provided by arrangement. Situated on Lough Rea with many historic sites including the famous Turoe Stone reputed to be pre-Christian.
Location
Loughrea, Co Galway
Travel east on the N6 out of Galway to Lough Rea. The course is north of the town.

MOUNTBELLEW
(0905) 79259
A 9 hole meadowland course (5564 yards, SSS 67). Visitors are welcome. Green fees are IR£4 per day, IR£20 per week. Snacks are available and full meals by arrangement.
Location
Shankhill, Mountbellew, Co Galway
Travel north east on the N17 out of Galway. Take the N63 past Knockmoy Abbey on to Mount Bellew. The course is on the right before you reach the village.

OUGHTERARD
(091) 82131
An 18 hole course (6150 yards, SSS 69). Visitors are welcome. Green fees are IR£6 on weekdays and IR£8 at weekends. Snacks and meals are available. Scenic walks and fishing on the Connemara peninsula.
Location
Oughterard, Co Galway
On the N59 15 miles west of Galway.

Recommended hotels
Connemara Gateway A (091) 82328 Long, low modern hotel in well tended gardens.
Sweeney's Oughterard House A (091) 82207 Delightful creeper-clad hotel opposite the Owenriff River.
Corrib B ★ (091) 82329 Friendly, family-run hotel in the centre of village.
Currarevagh House A (091) 82313 A mid 19th-century mansion beside Lough Corrib.

TUAM
(093) 24354
An 18 hole parkland course (6321 yards, SSS 70). Visitors are welcome on weekdays. Green fees are IR£5 per person. Snacks and lunch are available. An interesting town with two fine cathedrals, the High Cross of Tuam and a 1000BC battle site with burial tumulus.
Location
Barnacurragh, Tuam, Co Galway
Tuam lies north of Galway on the N17. The course is half a mile out of town on the Athenry road.

Recommended hotels
Imperial B (093) 24188 Family-run Georgian hotel
Hermitage C (093) 24271

PORTUMNA
(0509) 41059
A 9 hole course of wooded parkland (5776 yards, SSS 68). Visitors are welcome and green fees on application. Situated on the shores at Lough Derg with fishing and sailing and several fine castles in the area.
Location
Portumna, Co Galway
From Galway, drive east on the N6 through Loughrea then fork to the right on the N65 which leads to Portumna. The course is half a mile to the west on the R352 Woodford road.

Co KILDARE

NAAS
(045) 97509
An 18 hole course (6233 yards, SSS 70). Visitors are welcome and green fees are IR£5 per day. Situated outside Naas near Dublin with Figginstowns House and Punchestown racecourse nearby.
Location
Kardiffstown, Salins, Naas, Co Kildare
Drive from Dublin on the N7, and take the link road at Johnstown round Naas then turn off on R407 at Salins.

Recommended hotel
Curryhills House B ★ (045) 68150

KNOCKANALLY
(045) 69322
An 18 hole inland course (6484 yards, SSS 72). Visitors are welcome at any time. Green fees are IR£8 weekdays, and IR£10 at weekends. Full meals can be provided by arrangement, otherwise bar snacks are available.
Location
Donadea, N Kildare
Drive west out of Dublin on the N4 following the Royal Canal. At Kilcock turn left on the R407; Donadea is on the right 3 miles further on.

FOUR LAKES
(045) 66003
An 18 hole course within a country club (yards, SSS 69). Visitors are welcome and green fees are IR£5 weekdays and IR£7 at weekends. Snacks are available and meals by arrangement. Situated outside Dublin towards Naas with other sports facilities on site.
Location
Kill, Co Kildare
Drive out of Dublin on the N7 for 17 miles.

CURRAGH
(045) 41238
A fine 18 hole parkland course (6565 yards, SSS 71). Visitors are welcome on most weekday mornings except Tuesday. Green fees are IR£6 weekdays, and IR£9 at weekends and Bank Holidays. Snacks and lunch are served and dinner by arrangement. Situated just outside Kildare on the plain of Curragh, the National Stud centre of horse breeding with the national stud museum is worth visiting.
Location
Curragh, Co Kildare
Drive from Dublin via Naas on the N7 on to Kildare. Turn left on the R413, towards Kilcullen to Curragh.

CILL DARA
(045) 21433
A 9 hole moorland course (6196 yards, SSS 68). Visitors are welcome. Green fees are IR£4 weekdays, and IR£6 weekends. Meals are available by arrangement. Situated in Kildare, with the National Stud and Museum, a round tower and an interesting cathedral.
Location
Kildare Town, Co Kildare
Drive south west from Dublin through Naas on the N7 in to Kildare. The course is north of the town on the R415.

BODENSTOWN
(045) 97096
Two 18 hole courses available here. The old course (7031 yards, SSS 72). The new with SSS 71. Visitors are welcome on weekdays, and by arrangement at weekends. Green fees are IR£6 weekdays and weekends, with a reduction for ladies on the old course. Snacks are available and dinner by arrangement. Naas, once the seat of ancient kings is now almost part of Dublin's sprawl. It has its own race course and the Punchestown course is nearby.
Location
Bodenstown, Sallins, Co Kildare
Drive from Dublin on the N7 to Naas. The course is north of the town on the R407.

Recommended hotels
Curryhills House B ★ (045) 68150

ATHY
(0507) 31729
A 9 hole undulating parkland course (6158 yards, SSS 69). Visitors are welcome on weekdays and Saturday. Green fees are available on application. Places of local interest include the White Castle ruins which stand on the famous Crom-A-Boo bridge.
Location
Geraldine, Athy, Co Kildare
Drive south west from Dublin, through Naas on the N7 and N9.
Just past Kilcullen, take the N78 to Athy. The course is 2 miles before the town just past the Mote of Ardscull.

Recommended hotel
Leinster Arms B (0507) 31269

Co KILKENNY

CALLAN
(052) 25136
A 9 hole meadowland (5844 yards, SSS 68). Visitors are welcome any time. Green fees are IR£4 weekdays, and IR£5 at weekends. Meals are available but only by appointment. Places of local interest include the ruins of Kell's Priory, Kilree Round tower and high cross. The delightful town of Kilkenny is only 8 miles away.
Location
Geraldine, Callan, Co Kilkenny
Drive south out of Kilkenny on the N76 straight to Callan. The course is 1 mile from town.

CASTLECOMER
(056) 41139
A 9 hole parkland course (6985 yards, SSS 71). Visitors are welcome any time and green fees are available on application. Snacks are served and lunch by arrangement. Situated 10 miles north of the county town of Kilkenny with its picturesque alleyways; cathedral and castle.
Location
Drumgoole, Castlecomer, Co Kilkenny
Drive south from Kilkenny on the N78 to Castlecomer. The course is to the right of the town.

KILKENNY
(056) 22125
An 18 hole parkland course, host to the Irish pro matchplay championship (6374 yards, SSS 70). Visitors are welcome. Green fees are IR£7 weekdays, and IR£8 at weekends. Full catering facilities are available except on Monday. The course is situated just outside Kilkenny with its Elizabethan architecture, castle, and fine cathedral.
Location
Glendine, Kilkenny
Drive 2 miles north of Kilkenny on the N77. The course is on the right.

Recommended hotels
Hotel Kilkenny A ( ) A modern hotel built around an attractive mansion.
Newpark A ( ) Modern hotel set in 30 acres of parkland
Club House B ( ) Originally the HQ of the Foxhunters Club with its traditional decor.
Lacken House B ( )

Co KERRY

BALLYBUNION
(068) 27146
Two superb 18-hole courses on the Atlantic Ocean. Old course (6542 yards, SSS72), runs amongst the sand dunes; new course (6477 yards, SSS 72). Visitors are welcome. Green fees are IR£20 per day which includes both courses. Snacks and full meals are available. Situated at the mouth of the River Shannon with long stretches of unspoilt Atlantic coast nearby. Some interesting caves in the cliffs.
Location
Sandhill Road, Ballybunion, Co Kerry
Driving south west from Limerick on the N69 coast road, turn inland at Tarbert to Listowel. Turn west on the R553 out to the coast and Ballybunion. The course is 1 mile out of town right on the dunes.

Recommended hotel
Marine B (068) 27139

CEANN SIBEAL
(066) 56255
A 9-hole course (6222 yards, SSS68). Visitors are welcome. Green fees are IR£6.
Location
Ballyferriter, Tralee, Co Kerry

DOOKS
(066) 67370
An 18-hole seaside course (5135 metres, SSS68). Visitors are welcome at weekends, but telephone in advance. Green fees are IR£8 on weekdays, IR£10 at weekends. Snacks are available. Situated at the end of the 'Ring of Kerry', the picturesque coast route round the peninsula, with noted salmon fishing in the River Laune.
Location
Dooks, Killorglin, Co Kerry
Drive out of Killarney on the R562, the course is 8 miles west of Killorglin at the bridge between Killorglin and Glenbeigh.

KENMARE
(064) 41291
A 9-hole parkland course (2410 yards, SSS64). Visitors are welcome. Green fees are IR£6. Situated at the head of Kenmare Bay near the Druid's Circle, Dunkerran Castle and in the centre of fine countryside.
Location
Kenmare, Killarney, Co Kerry

Drive south from Killarney on the N71 straight to Kenmare.

Recommended hotels
Park Hotel Kenmare A ★ (064) 41200 Luxurious hotel furnished with antiques and set in spacious gardens.
Lansdowne Arms B (064) 41368 An 18th century inn next to the golf course.

KILLARNEY
Two undulating parkland courses of championship standard; Kileen (7027 yards, SSS71) and Mahonys (6764 yards, SSS70). Visitors are welcome on weekdays. Green fees cover both courses and are IR£18. Meals and snacks are served. Situated in magnificent scenery amidst mountains and lakes, with famous fishing facilities. A cathedral, Ross Castle and Muckross House are also of local interest.
Location
Mahony's Point, Killarney, Co Kerry
Killarney is in the middle of Kerry at the junction of the N22 and N72. The course is 3 miles west of the town on the R562 overlooking Lough Leane.

Recommended hotels
Dunloe Castle A ★ (064) 44111
Europe A ★ (064) 31900 Elegant, modern hotel on the shores of Lough Leane.
Great Southern A ★ (064) 31262 A 19th century hotel set in beautiful grounds.
Dromhall B ★ (064) 31431 Low-built modern hotel.
International B ★ (064) 31816 A centrally situated hotel with live entertainment.

TRALEE
(066) 36379
An 18-hole link course (6047 yards, SSS72). Visitors are welcome on weekdays and after 12 noon at weekends. Green fees are IR£12 weekdays and £15 at weekends. Snacks and full catering facilities are available. Situated on the coast with good beaches. Inland, the mountains provide a fine climb and shooting is excellent at Derrymore Sloblands.
Location
West Barrow, Ardfort, Co Kerry
Drive north out of Killarney on the N22 joining the N21 just outside Tralee. The course is west of the town through the villages of Spa and Churchill to Barrow.

Recommended Hotels
Ballygarry House B ★ (066) 2123 Reburbished hotel just outside town on the Killarney Road.

WATERVILLE
(0667) 4102
An 18-hole seaside links course (7184 yards, SSS74). Visitors are welcome. Green fees are IR£18. Snacks are available and full meals at the Waterville hotel. Famed for its salmon fishing, the area has several interesting early Christian sites.
Location
Waterville, Co Kerry
Take the coastal road N70, The Ring of Kerry, round the south side of the peninsula. The links are 1 mile out of Waterville on the side of Ballinskellias Bay.

Recommended hotels
Butler Arms A (0667) 4144 White painted hotel overlooking the Atlantic.
Waterville Lake Hotel A (0667) 4133 Beautifully situated hotel.

Co LAOIS

ABBEYLEIX
(0502) 31450
A 9-hole parkland course (5680 yards, SSS 67). Visitors are welcome and green fees are IR£4 per day. Stradbally Steam Museum is a short journey east and is of interest.
Location
Abbeylieux, Co Laois
Drive south from Portlaoise on the N8. The course is off Main Street on the Stradbally Road.

HEATH
(0502) 26533
An 18-hole heathland course (6247 yards, SSS 70). Visitors are welcome on weekdays and by arrangement at weekends. Green fees are IR£6 on weekdays and IR£9 at weekends. There are reductions if playing with a member. Snacks are available and full meals if arranged with the Steward. Places of interest locally include Boolbanagher Church and the Stradbally Steam Museum.
Location
The Heath, Portlaoise, Co Laois
Take the N7 from Dublin through Naas, Kildare and onto Portlaoise. The course is opposite the R419 turn off before you reach the town.

Recommended hotels in Portlaoise
Montague A (0502) 26154
Killieshin B ★ (0502) 21663

Co LEITRIM

BALLINAMORE
(078) 44346
A 9-hole moorland course (5680 yards, SSS67). Visitors are welcome any time. Green fees are available on application. Snacks are available. Part of the Carrick on Shannon angling and boating area is nearby, also a megalithic tomb.
Location
Crevy, Ballinamore, Co Leitrim
Drive out of Carrick on Shannon eastwards on the R209 through Keshcarrigan to Fenagh, turn left towards Ballinamore

CARRICK ON SHANNON
(078) 67015
An undulating 9-hole parkland course (3922 yards, SSS68). Visitors are welcome any time. Green fees are available on application. The area is famous for its angling. The town has some interesting Georgian shop fronts.
Location
Woodbrook, Carrick on Shannon, Co Leitrim
South east from Sligo on the N4, through Boyle along the sides of the Loughs. The course is on the right before the town.

Recommended hotels
Bush B ★ (078) 20014 Six generations of one family have run this 200-year-old hotel which has an interesting collection of pictures.

Co LIMERICK

ADARE MANOR
(061) 86204
A 9-hole parkland course (5700 yards, SSS67). Visitors are welcome weekdays up to 4.30pm and by arrangement at other times. Green fees are £10 per day. Substantial snacks are available. A town of charming thatched cottages, salmon and trout stream, two abbeys, a castle and Adare Manor itself.
Location
Adare, Co Limerick
Drive north from Limerick on the N20 to Adare.

Recommended hotels
Dunraven Arms A (061) 86209 Attractive period building on the banks of the River Maigue.
Woodlands Hotel B (061) 86118 One storey modern hotel in 52 acres of ground.

CASTLE TROY
(061) 335261
An 18-hole parkland course (6340 yards, SSS71). Visitors are welcome on weekdays, weekends are restricted. Green fees are IR£10. Snacks and full meals are available. Located 3 miles from the city of Limerick. Fine cathedral, castle, abbey, museum and art galleries.
Location
Castletroy, Limerick
3 miles out of town on the Dublin road N7 signposted at Castletroy.

Recommended hotels in Limerick.

LIMERICK
(061) 44083
An 18-hole parkland course (5767 yards, SSS70). Visitors are welcome on weekdays except Tuesday and before 5pm. Green fees are IR£10 per day. Snacks and full meals are available. Situated on the outskirts of Eire's third largest city with its Georgian buildings, abbey, cathedral and castle.
Location
Ballyclough, Limerick
South out of Limerick on the Cork road. Turn left at Punches Cross.

Recommended hotels
Greenhills A (061) 53033. Modern Swiss-chalet style hotel.
Jurys A (061) 55266 Modern hotel in grounds overlooking River Shannon
Two Mile Inn A (061) 53122

NEWCASTLE WEST
(069) 62015
A 9-hole meadowland course (5482 yards, SSS66). Visitors are welcome. Green fees on application. Another course on the edge of Limerick with many places of interest.
Location
Newcastle West, Co Limerick
One mile from Limerick on the Cork road.
Recommended hotels in Limerick.

Co LONGFORD

COUNTY LONGFORD
(043) 46310
An undulating 18-hole course (5912 yards, SSS68). Visitors are welcome any time. Green fees are IR£6 weekdays and IR£7 weekends. Bar snacks are available and full meals by arrangement. Situated in Longford, which has a cathedral and church of interest.
Location
Dublin Road, Longford, Co Longford
Situated in the middle of the county of Longford. The course is on the N4 Dublin to Sligo road east of the town.

Recommended hotels
Longford Arms B ★ (043) 46296

Co LOUTH

ARDEE
(041) 53227
An 18-hole parkland course (5833 yards, SSS68). Visitors are welcome on weekdays and at weekends by arrangement. Green fees are IR£6 weekdays and IR£7 at weekends. Bar snacks and dinner are served. Places of interest include two 13th century castles and salmon and trout fishing on the River Dee.
Location
Town Parks, Ardee, Co Louth
South of the Irish border the N2 travels through Carrickmacross on to Ardee. The course is a quarter of a mile north of the town.

Recommended hotel
Gables House B ★ (041) 53789

COUNTY LOUGH
(041) 22329
A championship links course, 18 holes (6798 yards, SSS 72). Generally recognised as the 'best greens in Ireland'. Visitors are welcome but by prior arrangement. Green fees are IR£14 weekdays and IR£18 at weekends. Snacks and full catering facilities are available. Situated outside the historic city of Drogheda founded by the Vikings. Historic sites include a well preserved town gate with drum towers and the prehistoric site of Millmount with museum showing the town's history.
Location
Battray, Drogheda, Co Louth
On the N1 coastal road. Drive east out of Drogheda on the R167 to the mouth of the River Boyne.

Recommended hotels in Drogheda
Boyne Valley A (041) 37737 Country mansion in own grounds.
Glenside B ★ (041) 29185

DUNDALK
(042) 21731
An 18-hole parkland course (6115 metres, SSS72). Visitors are welcome except Tuesday and Sunday. Green fees are IR£8 weekdays and IR£10 weekends. Dinner and snacks available everyday. Places of interest include several fine churches and two breweries and seaside at Blackrock.
Location
Blackrock, Dundalk, Co Louth
Just over the border from Warrenpoint on the coast. Take the R172 through Dundalk to Blackrock.

Recommended hotels
Ballymascanlon A (042) 71124 Extended country mansion in extensive grounds
Carrickdale B ★ (042) 71397
Derryhale B ★ (042) 35471 Traditional family-run hotel in grounds
Imperial B ★ (042) 32241

GREENORE
(042) 73212
An 18-hole seaside course looking across to the Mourne Mountains (5614 metres, SSS69). Visitors are welcome weekdays and most weekends. Green fees are IR£7 weekdays and IR£8 at weekends. Snacks and meals are available except on Tuesday. Near the town of Dundalk with its fine buildings and a racecourse. There are sailing facilities in the beautiful Carlingford Lough.
Location
Greenore, Dundalk, Co Louth
Drive over the border at Warrenpoint along the side of the Lough on the R173 to the lighthouse at Greenore and the course or, up from Dundalk on the R73.

Recommended hotels see Dundalk.

Co MAYO

ACHILL ISLAND
(098) 45197
A 9-hole seaside course (5550 yards, SSS67). Visitors are welcome any time. Green fees are IR£2 per day. Located on a large island, noted for its peaceful, empty landscape with magnificent views.
Location
Keel, Achill, Co Mayo
Drive from Westport on the N59 coast road through Mallaranny onto the island on the R319. Follow this road over the Achill Sound to Keel.

BALLINA
(096) 21050
An undulating 9-hole course (5702 yards, SSS66). Visitors are welcome. Green fees are IR£5. Located near the estuary of the Moy; an excellent salmon and trout stream. Historic sites of interest include the Dolmen of the Four Maols.
Location
Mosgrove, Shanaghy, Ballina, Co Mayo
Travel from Sligo on the N59 coast road to Killala Bay and Ballina. The course is east of the town on the R294.

Recommended hotels
Downhill A (096) 21033. Situated on the River Moy in its own grounds.

BALLINROBE
(092) 41448
A 9-hole course (5790 yards, SSS68). Visitors welcome everyday except Sunday. Green fees very day except Sunday. Green fees are IR£4 per day.
Location
Coolnaha, Ballyhaunis, Co Mayo
Drive west from Roscommon on the N60 through Ballymoe, Castlerea to Ballyhaunis. The course is on the N83 Sligo road out of the town.

BELMULLET
(097) 81266
A 9-hole seaside links course (2829 yards, SSS67). Visitors are welcome any time. Green fees are IR£3 per day. Situated on Ireland's western coast with beautiful coastal walks and several prehistoric sites.
Location
Belmullet, Ballina, Co Mayo
Drive west from Ballina on the N59 towards the coast, taking the R313 out to Belmullet at the Bangor junction. The course is off to the right past Binghaustown church.

Recommended hotels
Western Strands C (097) 81096

CASTLEBAR
(094) 21649
An 18-hole parkland course (6109 yards, SSS69). Visitors are welcome on weekdays. Green fees are IR£6. Meals are available with three hours notice. Situated inland from beautiful Clew Bay and near to Westport with good angling and Westport House, one of Ireland's great mansions.
Location
Rocklands, Castlebar, Co Mayo
Drive east from Westport on the N60 to Castlebar. The course is south of town off the N84.

Recommended hotels
Breaffy House A (094) 22033 Stone-built mansion in 50 acres of parkland.

CLAREMORRIS
(094) 71527
A 9-hole parkland course (6454 yards, SSS69). Visitors are welcome. Green fees are IR£4 per day. Meals are available by arrangement. Situated 7 miles away from Knock Shrine with its pilgrimages.
Location
Rushbrook, Castlemaggaret, Claremorris, Co Mayo
Drive east from Westport on the N60 through Castlebar down to Claremorris. The course is south of town on the N17 to Tuam.

Recommended hotels
Knock International B (094) 88466 Single storey modern hotel set in its own gardens.

MULRANY OR MALLARANNY
(098) 36107
An undulating 9-hole seaside course (6380 yards, SSS70). Visitors are welcome any time. Green fees are IR£3 per day, IR£15 per week. Located on the isthmus leading to the Curraun peninsula, with beautiful scenery and fishing/boating facilities.
Location
Mulrany, Westport, Co Mayo
Drive northwards on the N50 from Westport round Clew Bay to Mulrany. The course is to the left on a small peninsula into the Bay.

SWINFORD
(094) 51378
A 9-hole parkland course (5230 yards, SSS65). Visitors are welcome any time. Green fees are IR£15. Meals are available by arrangement. A good fishing area towards Lough Conn and Aillin and Meelick round tower is nearby.
Location
Brabazon Park, Swinford, Co Mayo
Driving from Westport inland on the N60 to Castlebar on to the N5 through Belavery to Swinford, the course is out of town on the R320.

WESTPORT
(098) 25113
An 18-hole parkland course with views over Clew Bay (6950 yards, SSS73). Visitors are welcome except Sunday. Green fees are IR£9 weekdays and IR£10 weekends. Snacks and meals are available. A delightful town with many places of interest; Westport House, one of Ireland's great houses and Croagh Patrick the holy mountain nearby.
Location
Carroholly, Westport, Co Mayo
Situated on Clew Bay, the course is 2 miles out of town on the north side, past Westport Quay.

Recommended hotels
Westport Ryan A (098) 25811 Low modern hotel in quiet woodland setting.
Olde Railway B ★ (098) 25166 Family-run, 200-year-old inn overlooking the Carrowbeg river.

Co MEATH

HEADFORT
(046) 40146
An 18-hole parkland course (6372 yards, SSS70). Visitors are welcome on weekdays except Tuesday but limited at weekends. Green fees are IR£8 weekdays and IR£10 at weekends. Snacks are available at the bar and meals by arrangement. Situated close to Ceannus Mor (Kells). A historic town famous for the Book of Kells (now in Dublin), five high crosses and several early buildings.
Location
Ceanannus Mor (Kells), Co Meath
A quarter of a mile from Ceanannus Mor on the N3 Ceanannus Mor to Dublin road.

Recommended hotel
Headfort Arms B ★ (046) 40063

LAYTOWN AND BETTYSTOWN
(041) 27170
An 18-hole seaside links course (6254 yards, SSS69). Visitors are welcome on weekdays. Green fees are IR£9 weekdays and IR£14 at weekends. Snacks and meals are served. Situated on the coast outside Drogheda, a busy port with some interesting buildings and prehistoric sites.
Location
Bettystown, Drogheda, Co Meath
On the N1 coastal road drive out of Drogheda on the R150 following the River Boyne on the southside. The course is near the three lighthouses.

Recommended hotels in Drogheda see County Louth.

ROYAL TARA
(046) 25244
An 18-hole parkland course near the Hill of Tara (5757 metres, SSS70). Visitors are welcome on Monday, Thursday and Friday. Green fees are IR£8 weekdays and IR£10 at weekends. Full meals and snacks are available. Located beside the ancient seat of Irish Kings. Apart from the prehistoric earthworks, Tara has a donkey stud farm.

Location
Bellinter, Navan, Co Meath
Take the N3 north west from Dublin towards Navan. The course is on the left near Garlow Cross 6 miles outside Navan.

Recommended hotel
Ardboyne A (046) 23119. Modern hotel in own grounds.

TRIM
(046) 31463
A 9-hole course (6266 yards, SSS70). Visitors are welcome weekdays but restricted at weekends. Green fees are IR£5 weekdays and IR£6 at weekends. There are many historic buildings in Trim including Norman castles, the Duke of Wellington's School and Swifts church.
Location
Newtonmuynagh, Trim, Co Meath
Take the N3 north west from Dublin forking left onto the R154 at Black Bull through Batterstown to Trim. The course is south west of the town off the R160 Longwood Road.

Recommended hotel
Wellington Court B ★ (046) 31516

Co MONAGHAN

CASTLEBLAYNEY
(042) 40197
A 9-hole course (2678 yards, SSS66). Visitors are welcome. Green fees are IR£3 weekdays, IR£4 weekends.
Location
Castleblayney, Co Monaghan
Take N2 from Monaghan to Castleblayney.

CLONES
(049) 52354
A 9-hole parkland course (5570 yards, SSS67). Visitors are welcome any time. Green fees are IR£3 weekdays and IR£4 weekends. Meals are available except on Monday. The town has a high cross and round tower, and Monaghan is about 10 miles away.
Location
Hilton Park, Scotshouse, Clones, Co Monaghan
Drive across the border from Enniskillen on the A4/A34 or across from Monaghan on the N54. The course is to the south towards Scotshouse.

NUREMORE
(042) 61438
A 9-hole parkland course-part of a hotel complex (6032 yards, SSS69). Visitors are welcome any time. Green fees are IR£3 weekdays and IR£4 at weekends. Meals and snacks are available at the hotel. Carrickmacross is renowned for its lace; it has an interesting modern cathedral, Lough Fean House and caves at Tiragarvan.
Location
Carrickmacross, Co Monaghan
Take N2 from Monaghan through Castleblayney to Carrickmacross. The course is on the south side of town on the Dublin road.

Recommended hotel
Nuremore A (042) 61438. Family-owned hotel in extensive wooded grounds with fishing lakes.

ROSSMORE
(047) 81316
A 9-hole undulating parkland course (5859 yards, SSS68). Visitors are welcome on weekdays. Restrictions at weekends. Green fees are IR£4 weekdays and IR£5 weekends. Situated in Monaghan, with many fine Victorian buildings. There is an excellent museum and in July a festival of Irish music is held in the park.
Location
Rossmore Park, Monaghan
Across the border from Armagh on the A3/N12 or north from Castleblayney on the N2. The course is south of the city on the B189 in the Rossmore Forest Park.

Recommended hotel
Hillgrove B ★ (047) 81288

Co OFFALY

BIRR
(0509) 20082
An undulating parkland course of 18 holes (6216 yards, SSS70). Visitors are welcome most days but check on Sunday. Green fees are IR£6 weekdays and IR£7 weekends. Meals are available by arrangement. Places of interest include Birr Castle and its lovely gardens.
Location
Glenns, Birr, Co Offaly
In the centre of Ireland, south of Athlone on the N62. The course is north of Birr on the R439, Banagher Road.

Recommended hotel
County Arms B ★ (0509) 20791 Georgian mansion in delightful grounds
Dooly's B (0509) 20032

EDENBERRY
(0405) 31072
A mixed park and moorland course of 9 holes (5791 yards, SSS67). Visitors are welcome. Green fees are IR£4 and IR£5 respectively. A branch of the Grand Canal passes south of the town, and Carbury Castle is near.
Location
Boherberry, Edenberry, Co Offaly
Drive west from Dublin on the N4 taking the left turn at Innfield onto the R402 Carbury road. The course is just before the town.

GARRYHINCH
(0502) 23115
A 9-hole parkland course (5598 yards, SSS66). Visitors are welcome. Green fees are available on application. Meals are available by arrangement. Originally a 'French' town with a fine church, castle ruin and Emo Park and mansion.
Location
Portarlington, Co Offaly
Drive from Dublin on the N7 through Naas and Kildare to Monastereum, then take the R420 through Portarlington. The course is on the west side of town.

TULLAMORE
(0506) 21439
An 18-hole parkland course (6314 yards, SSS71). Visitors are welcome weekdays except Tuesday and are restricted at weekends. Green fees are IR£6 weekdays and IR£8 weekends. Snacks and full meals are served. The Grand Canal passes through the town, with its famous distillery.
Location
Brookfield, Tullamore, Co Offaly
Drive from Athlone east on the N6, then take the N80 to Tullamore. The course is outside of town on the R 421 Birr road.

Co ROSCOMMON

BALLAGHADERREEN
A 9-hole course (5686 yards, SSS65). Visitors are welcome. Green fees are IR£2 per day.
Location
Ballaghaderreen, Co Roscommon
Drive along the N5 from Langford to the western border of Roscommon. The course is on the R293, the left turn out of town.

BOYLE
(079) 62594
An undulating parkland course, 9 holes (4957 metres, SSS66). Visitors are welcome. Green fees are IR£4. Located on the Boyle river between Lough Key and Lough Gara with good fishing. An Abbey and Drumanore magalithic tombs are also of interest.
Location
Roscommon Road, Boyle, Co Roscommon
Drive west on the N4 north out of Longford through Carrick on Shannon to Boyle. The course is on the N61 road to Roscommon.

Recommended hotel
Royal B (079) 62016. Family run 18th century hotel beside the river.

CASTLEREA
(0907) 20068
A 9-hole parkland course (5466 yards, SSS66). Visitors are welcome weekdays except on Sunday. Green fees are IR£3 on weekdays and IR£5 at weekends. Located near Lough O'Plynnard. Lough Glinn with a high cross and Cloonshanville Abbey are in the area.
Location
Clonalis, Castlerea, Co Roscommon
Drive north out of Athlone on the N61 through Roscommon onto Castlerea. The course is just north of the town.

ROSCOMMON
(0903) 6382
A meadowland course (6215 yards, SSS68). Visitors are welcome. Green fees on application. Situated in the county town, with a friary, 18th century jail and castle ruins of interest.
Location
Mote Park, Roscommon, Co Roscommon
Drive north out of Athlone on the N61 to Roscommon. The course is south of town next to the railway.

Co SLIGO

BALLYMOTE
(071) 3460
A 9-hole course (5032 yards, SSS63). Visitors are welcome. Green fees are IR£2 per day. Places of interest include the fine castle in the town and the town of Boyle further south.
Location
Carrigans, Ballymote, Co Sligo
Drive south from Sligo on the N1 taking the R293 left fork to Ballymote. The course is on the hill to the left before reaching town.

COUNTY SLIGO
(071) 77186
An 18-hole seaside links course, venue of the Western Ireland Amateur Championships (6631 yards, SSS72). Visitors are welcome, except Tuesday but check before arriving. Green fees are IR£10 weekdays and IR£12 at weekends. Snacks available every day and an a la carte menu after 6pm though not on Thursday. The town of Sligo is full of interesting buildings, a ruined abbey, Venetian gothic courthouse and traditional Irish shop fronts. The course is part of Coney Island, a seaside resort with sandy beach.
Location
Rosses Point, Co Sligo
On the west coast south of Ballyshannan and Bundoran; take the N15 coast road. The course is north of town on the R291 spur out to Rosses Point and Coney Island.

Recommended hotels
Sligo Park A (071) 60291 Modern low rise hotel in rural surroundings.
Ballincar House A (071) 45361 Converted country house in 5 acres of mature gardens.
Yeats Country Ryan B ★ (071) 77211 Large modern holiday hotel near sandy beaches.

ENNISCRONE
(096) 36297
An 18-hole seaside course with magnificent views across Killala Bay (6610 yards, SSS72). Visitors are welcome anytime. Green fees are IR£8, ladies IR£4. Light snacks are available and meals by arrangement. A resort famous for sulphur baths, good sandy beach, a castle and large tumulus nearby.
Location
Enniscrone (Inniscrone), Co Sligo
Follow the N59 west round the coast from Sligo to Killala Bay. The course is on the R297 out on a peninsula near Bartragh Island.

Recommended hotels
Atlantic B (096) 36119
Castle Arms B (096) 36156

STRANDHILL
(071) 68188
An 18-hole seaside links course (5937 yards, SSS68). Visitors are welcome on weekdays and most weekends. Green fees are IR£6 weekdays and IR£7 weekends and Bank Holidays. Full catering is available. Located in a resort just outside Sligo city with its traditional shop fronts and various interesting buildings. Queen Maeve's Grave and Carrowmore megalithic remains are very close and worth visiting.
Location
Strandhill, Co Sligo
Travel west from Sligo to Strandhill, the course is signposted.

Recommended hotels
Sligo Park A (071) 60291 Modern, low-rise hotel in rural surroundings.
Silver Swan B ★ (071) 43231 Family-run hotel by Garavoque River.
Southern B ★ (071) 62101. Large wooden hotel in award-winning gardens.

Co TIPPERARY

CAHIR PARK
(052) 41474
A 9-hole parkland course (6262 yards, SSS69). Visitors are welcome. Green fees are IR£6. Situated on the River Suir with fine trout fishing, a large castle and the Mote of Knockgraffon, one of the coronation places of the Irish kings.
Location
Kilcommon, Cahir, Co Tipperary
Drive east out of Limerick on the N24 through Tipperary to Cahir or Caher. The course is on the R668 Clogheen Road south of the town.

CARRICK ON SUIR
(051) 40047
An undulating parkland course, 9 holes, (5948 yards, SSS68). Visitors are welcome except on Sunday. Green fees are IR£5. Meals can be supplied but by arrangement. Situated amidst good salmon and trout fishing country with rock climbing in the Comeraghs area. The town has a fortified Elizabethan manor of particular interest.
Location
Garravoone, Carrick on Suir, Co Tipperary
On the N24 road to Limerick from Waterford. The course is off the R676 south of the town.

CLONMEL
(052) 21138
An 18-hole parkland course at the foot of the Comeragh Mountains (6330 yards, SSS70). Visitors are welcome on weekdays but ring in advance. Green fees are IR£6 weekdays and IR£8 at weekends. Snacks and meals are available. Situated in a handsome town with many fine buildings, the area is famous for its trout fishing and greyhound racing.
Location
Lyteanearla, Mountain Road, Clonmel, Co Tipperary
On the N24 Waterford to Limerick Road, west of Carrick on Suir. The course is south of the town on the R678.

Recommended hotel
Hearn's B (052) 21611 Family run hotel in town centre, originally a 17th century coaching inn.

NENAGH
(067) 31476
An 18-hole course (5483 metres, SSS68). Visitors are welcome weekdays except Wednesday afternoon and Thursday. Bar snacks are available and meals by arrangement. Green fees are IR£6 weekdays and IR£7 weekends. Situated between the Silvermine mountains and the Arra mountains. The town has the ruins of a friary and Nenagh Castle.
Location
Beechwood, Nenagh, Co Tipperary
Take the N7 from Limerick to Nenagh; the course is 4 miles north of town off the R491.

ROSCREA
(0505) 21130
A 9-hole meadowland course (6059 yards, SSS69). Visitors are welcome. Green fees are IR£5. Meals can be provided but by arrangement. Situated in the picturesque town of Roscrea with a round tower, priory remains, castle, Georgian Damer house and the Timoney Standing Stones all of interest in the area.
Location
Derry Vale, Dublin Road, Roscrea, Co Tipperary.
Drive from Dublin on the N7 through Kildare, Portlaoise to Roscrea. The course is before the town, next to the main road by the railway bridge.

TEMPLEMORE
(0504) 31522
A 9-hole course (5442 yards, SSS67). Visitors are welcome. Green fees are IR£4 on weekdays and IR£5 at weekends. Meals can be arranged if required. Close to the town of Thurles which has an interesting cathedral and several castles.
Location
Manna, South Templemore, Co Tipperary.
Take N62 south from Roscrea to Templemore. The course is on the south side of town.

THURLES
(0504) 21983
An 18-hole parkland course (6300 yards, SSS70). Visitors are welcome weekdays except Tuesday and weekends are restricted. Green fees are IR£7 weekdays and IR£8 weekends. Snacks and full meals are available. Thurles has a fine cathedral, several castles, a racecourse and good brown trout fishing in the River Suir.
Location
Turtulla, Thurles, Co Tipperary
Take N62 south from Roscrea through Templemore on to Thurles. The course is just south of the town.

TIPPERARY
(062) 51119
A 9-hole parkland course (6074 yards, SSS69). Visitors are welcome. Green fees are IR£3 per day. Situated outside the town of Tipperary in the Golden Vale. Cashel, with its important historical Rock of Cashel, is well worth visiting.
Location
Rathanny, Tipperary
North east from Limerick on the N24, the course is on the south side of town off the R664.

Recommended hotel
The Glen B ★ (062) 56146.

Co WESTMEATH

ATHLONE
(0902) 92073
An undulating parkland course, 18 holes (6000 yards, SSS70). Visitors are welcome on weekdays and by arrangement at weekends. Green fees are available on application. Snacks and full meals are available all week except Monday. The town has interesting historical buildings and the Lough Ree good scenery and coarse fishing.
Location
Hodson Bay, Athlone, Co Westmeath
Situated in the centre of Ireland at the crossing of the River Shannon and the main Dublin-Galway road, N6. The course is north of the town along the shores of the Lough off the N61 towards Yan point.

Recommended hotels
Prince of Wales B ★ (0902) 72626 Modern hotel reconstructed from a Victorian one.
Royal B ★ (0902) 72924

MOATE
(0902) 81271
A 9-hole parkland course (5348 yards, SSS65). Visitors are welcome at all times. Green fees are available on application. Meals can be provided by arrangement.
Location
Moate, Co Westmeath
8 miles east of Athlone on the N6 Dublin road. The course is on the left behind the railway station.

MULLINGAR
(044) 48366
A rolling 18-hole parkland championship course (6370 yards, SSS72). Visitors are welcome on weekdays. Green fees are IR£10 weekdays and IR£15 weekends. Snacks and full meals are available. The town has a fine 20th century cathedral. Numerous lakes provide good fishing and Belvedere House is adjacent to the course.
Location
Belvedere, Mullingar, Co Westmeath
Take the N4 from Sligo and travel south east through Carrick on Shannon, Layford to Mullingar. The course is 3 miles south west of town off the N52 to Tullamore on the side of Lough Ennell.

Recommended hotel
Greville Arms B ★ (044) 48563 Traditional town hotel with nightclub.

Co WEXFORD

COURTOWN
(055) 25166
An 18-hole parkland course (6435 yards, SSS70). Visitors are welcome except on Wednesday and major competition days. Green fees are IR£6 weekdays and IR£9 at weekends. Snacks and full meals are available. A popular seaside resort, with Courtown House and an ancient cross of local interest.
Location
Kiltennel, Gorey, Co Wexford
Drive down from Dublin on the coast road N11 through Wicklow, Arklow and on to Gorey. The course is at Courtown on the R742 east of Gorey on the coast.

Recommended hotel
Courtown B ★ (055) 25108 Friendly hotel in town.

ENNISCORTHY
A 9-hole parkland course (6368 yards, SSS69). Visitors are welcome on weekdays. Green fees are IR£5 weekdays and IR£7 at weekends. Snacks and meals are available.

Location
Knockmarshal, Enniscorthy, Co Wexford
Take the N11 coast road down from Dublin through Arklow to Enniscorthy. The course is 1.5 miles from town on the New Ross Road.

Recommended hotel
Murphy-Floods B (054) 33413 Family-run hotel overlooking the market square.

NEW ROSS
(051) 21433
A 9-hole parkland course (6133 yards, SSS69). Visitors are welcome on weekdays and Saturday. Green fees are IR£5 weekdays and IR£7 at weekends. Snacks are always available and meals can be provided by arrangement.
Location
Tinneanny, New Ross, Co Wexford
Drive north from Waterford on the N25. The course is west of the town on the R704.

Recommended hotels
Five Counties A (051) 21703 Converted mansion in landscaped gardens overlooking the river.
Old Rectory B (051) 22053

ROSSLARE
(053) 32203
A famous 18-hole seaside links course. Visitors are welcome any time but with a handicap certificate. Green fees are available on application. Snacks and meals can be provided.
Location
Rosslaare, Co Wexford
The course is out of Wexford on the coast at Rosslare Point.

Recommended hotels
Casey's Cedars A (053) 32124
Great Southern A (053) 33233
Tuskar House B ★ (053) 33363

WEXFORD
(053) 42238
An 18-hole parkland course (6038 yards, SSS69). Visitors are welcome with a handicap certificate. Green fees are available on application.
Location
Mulganon, Wexford, Co Wexford
On the southernmost end of the N11 coast road. The course is half a mile on the south side of town.

Recommended hotels
Ferrycarrig A (053) 22999 Modern hotel beside the estuary.
Talbot A (053) 22566 Large town hotel with sea views.

Co WICKLOW

ARKLOW
(0402) 32492
A seaside course, 18 holes (5770 yards, SSS68). Visitors are welcome weekdays. Green fees are IR£7 weekdays and IR£8 weekends. Snacks and full meals are available.
Location
Abbeylands, Co Wicklow
Drive south from Dublin on the N11 coast road through Wicklow on to Arklow. The course is on the south side of the town.

BATTINGLASS
(0508) 81350
A 9-hole parkland course (6070 yards, SSS68). Visitors are always welcome. Green fees available on application. Meals can be provided by arrangement.
Location
Battinglass, Co Wicklow
Drive south west out of Dublin on the N81 Vale of Wicklow Road straight to Battinglass. The course is west of town off the R747.

BLAINROE
(0404) 68168
A fine 18-hole course (6681 yards, SSS72). Visitors are welcome weekdays but by arrangement. Green fees are IR£7 weekdays and IR£12 at weekends. Snacks and full meals are available.
Location
Blainroe, Co Wicklow
On the N11 south of Dublin, through Wicklow about 3 miles on the coast road.

Recommended hotel in Wicklow.

BRAY
(01) 862484
A 9-hole parkland course (5230 metres, SSS70). Visitors are welcome weekdays before 6pm. Green fees are IR£8 per day. Snacks are available.
Location
Ravenswell Road, Bray, Co Wicklow.
A short drive south of Dublin on the N11. The course is north of the town.

DELGANY
(404) 874536
An 18-hole parkland course (5249 yards, SSS69). Visitors are welcome weekdays preferably Monday, Thursday or Friday. Green fees are IR£8.50 weekdays and IR£11 at weekends. Snacks and full meals are available.
Location
Delgany, Co Wicklow
Drive out of Dublin on the N11 coast road through Bray turning inland to the R762. The course is just off the main road.

Recommended hotel
Glenview A (01) 862896 Family-run hotel in lovely gardens overlooking the Glen.

GREYSTONES
(01) 876624
An undulating parkland course (5227 yards, SSS68). Visitors are welcome Monday and Friday. Green fees are IR£8 weekdays. Bar snacks are available.
Location
Greystones, Co Wicklow
Drive out of Dublin on the N11, taking the coast road R761 out of Bray to Greystones. The course is on the left of the road.

WICKLOW
(0404) 67379
A 9-hole seaside course (5536 yards, SSS66). Visitors are welcome by introduction. Green fees are IR£6 weekdays and IR£10 at weekends. Snacks and meals are available except on Tuesday.
Location
Dunbar Road, Wicklow, Co Wicklow
Turn off the N11 coast road on to R750. The course is south of Wicklow on the way to Wicklow Head.

Recommended hotel
Old Rectory A (0404) 67048 Lovingly restored Georgian house in quiet garden.

WOODBROOK
(01) 824799
A championship parkland course with sea breezes and magnificent views, 18 holes (6541 yards, SSS71). Visitors are welcome on weekdays except Tuesday and Wednesday. Green fees are IR£13 weekdays and IR£16 at weekends.
Location
Bray, Co Wicklow
South out of Dublin on the N11. The course is before Bray on the coast side of the road.

Recommended hotel in Killiney
Fitzpatrick Castle A ★ (01) 851533 Luxury hotel in castle with modern extension.

WOODENBRIDGE
(0402) 5202
A 9-hole parkland course (6104 yards, SSS68). Visitors are welcome weekdays and Sunday. Green fees are IR£8 weekdays and IR£10 weekends. Meals are available except on Monday.
Location
Woodenbrige, Avoca, Co Wicklow
Drive to Wicklow on the N11 south from Dublin. Take the R752 west out of the town through Rathdrum and down the Vale of Avoca to Woodenbridge.

Co WATERFORD

DUNGARVAN
(058) 41605
A meadowland 9 hole course (5721 metres, SSS 69). Visitors are welcome on weekdays. Green fees are IR£5 per day.
Location
Ballinacourty, Dungarvan, Co Waterford
Drive south from Waterford on the N25. The course is out on the point off the R675 from town.

Recommended hotels
Lawlors B ★ (058) 41056 Bustling town centre hotel recently refurbished.

LISMORE
(058) 54026
A 9 hole parkland course (5127 metres, SSS 67). Visitors are welcome most days. Green fees are IR£5 per day. Meals are available if booked in advance.
Location
Lismore, Ballyin, Co Waterford
Driving south from Waterford on the N25 take the N72 outside Dungarvan along the River Blackwater valley to Lismore.

TRAMORE
(051) 81247
A championship parkland course of 18 holes (6660 yards, SSS 71). Visitors are welcome by arrangement. Green fees are IR£9 on weekdays and IR£10 at weekends. Snacks and full meals are available. The course offers additional facilities ot squash courts and snooker room.
Location
Newton Hill, Tramore, Co Waterford
Drive south from Waterford on the R675 to the coast and Tramore. The course is through the town.

Recommended hotels
Grand B ★ (051) 81414 Modern hotel overlooking Tramore Bay.

WATERFORD
(051) 76748
An 18 hole parkland course (6237 yards, SSS 70). Visitors are welcome but must be a member of a recognised club. Green fees are IR£8 on weekdays, and IR£12 at weekends and Bank Holidays. Snacks and full meals are available.
Location
New Rath, Waterford, Co Waterford
The town is south of Kilkenny on the N10/N9, east from Clonmel on the N24. The course is on the north side of the town over the river by the station.

Recommended hotels
Granville A (051) 55111 Town-centre hotel in restored period house.
Bridge B ★ (051) 77222 Large 'traditional' hotel.
Diamond Hill B ★ (051) 32855 Guest house
Dooley's B ★ (051) 73531 Old established hotel.

TOURNAMENT WINNERS

Tournaments have produced hundreds of champions, some of whom proved to be larger than life on and off the greens. There was Young Tom Morris, who won the Open in 1868 at the tender age of 17, went on to win over the next three consecutive years, but who then tragically died of a broken heart at 24, a few months after his young wife and baby died as she was giving birth.

A far less tragic champion was the flamboyant dresser and player, Walter Hagen. He dispensed with the formal tweed jacket and trousers worn by golfers, and opted for the Cowardesque playboy image, donning colourful clothes and black-and-white shoes. He amused hundreds, and no doubt shocked a few, when he arrived at Deal for the 1920 Open in a Rolls Royce complete with butler, who proceeded to serve champagne and caviar. His extraordinary skills on course won him the Open two years later. In typical Hagen fashion he dismissed the unimpressive prize money by passing the cheque to his caddie.

British pride in golf, after the domination of the Americans throughout the 'twenties, was restored by Henry Cotton, whose round of 65 at St. George's inspired the name for the famous Dunlop 65.

More recently selecting the golfer's golfer has proved more difficult. With so many young highly talented players around, the pressure to stay at the top is huge. Jack Nicklaus' phenomenal record of championship successes, along with his sportsman-like attitude must make the Big Bear a close contender for the title. Tom Watson and Lee Trevino are two other Americans whose service to the game has been invaluable, Trevino's as much for his witty one-liners as well as his wicked wedge. On the European side, Seve Ballesteros is still considered to be the best golfer today. His daring, courage and often unorthodox play make him an incredibly exciting player to watch. His film star looks ensure the ladies enjoy watching his swing more than the men do.

Our British players, particularly Nick Faldo, Sandy Lyle and Ian Woosnam have also given much to the game and provided millions of golfing fans with hours of great sporting entertainment.

The Open Golf Championship

Year	Winner	Venue	Score
1860	W. Park, Musselburgh	Prestwick	174
1861	T. Morris, Sen., Prestwick	Prestwick	163
1862	T. Morris, Sen., Prestwick	Prestwick	163
1863	W. Park, Musselburgh	Prestwick	168
1864	T. Morris, Sen., Prestwick	Prestwick	167
1865	A. Strath, St. Andrews	Prestwick	162
1866	W. Park, Musselburgh	Prestwick	169
1867	T. Morris, Sen., St. Andrews	Prestwick	170
1868	T. Morris, Jun., St. Andrews	Prestwick	157
1869	T. Morris, Jun., St. Andrews	Prestwick	154
1870	T. Morris, Jun., St. Andrews	Prestwick	149
1872	T. Morris, Jun., St. Andrews	Prestwick	166
1873	T. Kidd, St. Andrews	St. Andrews	179
1874	M. Park, Musselburgh	Musselburgh	159
1875	W. Park, Musselburgh	Prestwick	166
1876	B. Martin, St. Andrews	St. Andrews	176
1877	J. Anderson, St. Andrews	Musselburgh	160
1878	J. Anderson, St. Andrews	Prestwick	157
1879	J. Anderson, St. Andrews	St. Andrews	169
1880	B. Ferguson, Musselburgh	Musselburgh	162
1881	B. Ferguson, Musselburgh	Prestwick	170
1882	B. Ferguson, Musselburgh	St. Andrews	171
1883	W. Fernie, Dumfries*	Musselburgh	159
1884	J. Simpson, Carnoustie	Prestwick	160
1885	B. Martin, St. Andrews	St. Andrews	171
1886	D. Brown, Musselburgh	Musselburgh	157
1887	W. Park, Jun., Musselburgh	Prestwick	161
1888	J. Burns, Warwick	St. Andrews	171
1889	W. Park, Jun., Musselburgh*	Musselburgh	155
1890	J. Ball, Royal Liverpool (Am.)	Prestwick	164
1891	H. Kirkaldy, St. Andrews	St. Andrews	166
1892	H.H. Hilton, Royal Liverpool (Am.)	Muirfield	305
1893	W. Auchterlonie, St. Andrews	Prestwick	322
1894	J.H. Taylor, Winchester	Sandwich	326
1895	J.H. Taylor, Winchester	St. Andrews	322
1896	H. Vardon, Ganton*	Muirfield	316
1897	H.H. Hilton, Royal Liverpool (Am.)	Hoylake	314
1898	H. Vardon, Ganton	Prestwick	307
1899	H. Vardon, Ganton	Sandwich	310
1900	J.H. Taylor, Mid-Surrey	St. Andrews	309
1901	J. Braid, Romford	Muirfield	309
1902	A. Herd, Huddersfield	Hoylake	307
1903	H. Vardon, Totteridge	Prestwick	300
1904	J. White, Sunningdale	Sandwich	296
1905	J. Braid, Walton Heath	St. Andrews	318
1906	J. Braid, Walton Heath	Muirfield	300
1907	A. Massy, La Boulie	Hoylake	312
1908	J. Braid, Walton Heath	Prestwick	291
1909	J.H. Taylor, Mid-Surrey	Deal	295
1910	J. Braid, Walton Heath	St. Andrews	299
1911	H. Vardon, Totteridge*	Sandwich	303
1912	E. Ray, Oxhey	Muirfield	295
1913	J.H. Taylor, Mid-Surrey	Hoylake	304
1914	H. Vardon, Totteridge	Prestwick	306
1920	G. Duncan, Hanger Hill	Deal	303
1921	J. Hutchinson, Glenview, Chicago*	St. Andrews	296
1922	W. Hagen, Detroit, USA	Sandwich	300
1923	A.G. Havers, Coombe Hill	Troon	295
1924	W. Hagen, Detroit, USA	Hoylake	301
1925	J. Barnes, USA	Prestwick	300
1926	R.T. Jones, USA (Am.)	Royal Lytham & St. Annes	291
1927	R.T. Jones, USA (Am.)	St. Andrews	285
1928	W. Hagen, USA	Sandwich	292
1929	W. Hagen, USA	Muirfield	292
1930	R.T. Jones, USA (Am.)	Hoylake	291
1931	T.D. Armour, USA	Carnoustie	296
1932	G. Sarazen, USA	Prince's, Sandwich	283
1933	D. Shute, USA*	St. Andrews	292
1934	T.H. Cotton, Waterloo, Belgium	Sandwich	283
1935	A. Perry, Leatherhead	Muirfield	283
1936	A.H. Padgham, Sundridge Park	Hoylake	287
1937	T.H. Cotton, Ashridge	Carnoustie	290
1938	R.A. Whitcombe, Parkstone	Sandwich	295
1939	R. Burton, Sale	St. Andrews	290
1946	S. Snead, USA	St. Andrews	290
1947	F. Daly, Balmoral	Hoylake	293
1948	T.H. Cotton, Royal Mid-Surrey	Muirfield	284
1949	A.D. Locke, South Africa*	Sandwich	283
1950	A.D. Locke, South Africa	Troon	279
1951	M. Faulkner, Unattached	Royal Portrush	285

Year	Winner	Venue	Score
1952	A.D. Locke, South Africa	Royal Lytham & St. Annes	287
1953	B. Hogan, USA	Carnoustie	282
1954	P.W. Thompson, Australia	Royal Birkdale	283
1955	P.W. Thompson, Australia	St. Andrews	281
1956	P.W. Thompson, Australia	Hoylake	286
1957	A.D. Locke, South Africa	St. Andrews	279
1958	P.W. Thompson, Australia*	Royal Lytham & St. Annes	278
1959	G. Player, South Africa	Muirfield	284
1960	K.D.G. Nagle, Australia	St. Andrews	278
1961	A. Palmer, USA	Royal Birkdale	284
1962	A. Palmer, USA	Troon	276
1963	R.J. Charles, New Zealand*	Royal Lytham & St. Annes	277
1964	A. Lema, USA	St. Andrews	279
1965	P.W. Thompson, Australia	Royal Birkdale	285
1966	J. Nicklaus, USA	Muirfield	282
1967	R. de Vicenzo, Argentina	Hoylake	278
1968	G. Player, South Africa	Carnoustie	289
1969	A. Jacklin, Potters Bar	Royal Lytham & St. Annes	280
1970	J. Nicklaus, USA*	St. Andrews	283
1971	L. Trevino, USA	Royal Birkdale	278
1972	L. Trevino, USA	Muirfield	278
1973	T. Weiskopf, USA	Troon	276
1974	G. Player, South Africa	Royal Lytham & St. Annes	282
1975	T. Watson, USA*	Carnoustie	279
1976	J. Miller, USA	Royal Birkdale	279
1977	T. Watson, USA	Turnberry	268
1978	J. Nicklaus, USA	St. Andrews	281
1979	S. Ballesteros, Spain	Royal Lytham & St. Annes	283
1980	T. Watson, USA	Muirfield	271
1981	W. Rogers, USA	Royal St. George's	276
1982	T. Watson, USA	Royal Troon	284
1983	T. Watson, USA	Royal Birkdale	275
1984	S. Ballesteros, Spain	St. Andrews	276
1985	S. Lyle, Scotland	Royal St. George's	282
1986	G. Norman, Australia	Turnberry	280
1987	N. Faldo, England	Muirfield	280
1988	S. Ballesteros, Spain	Royal Lytham & St. Annes	273
1989	M. Calcavecchia, USA*	Royal Troon	275
1990	N. Faldo, England	St. Andrews	270

Won after play-off

US Masters

Augusta National Golf Club, Augusta, Georgia.

Year	Winner	Score
1934	Horton Smith	284
1935	Gene Sarazen*	282
1936	Horton Smith	285
1937	Byron Nelson	283
1938	Henry Picard	285
1939	Ralph Guldahl	279
1940	Jimmy Demaret	280
1941	Craig Wood	280
1942	Byron Nelson*	280
1946	Herman Keiser	282
1947	Jimmy Demaret	281
1948	Claude Harmon	279
1949	Sam Snead	282
1950	Jimmy Demaret	283
1951	Ben Hogan	280
1952	Sam Snead	286
1953	Ben Hogan	274
1954	Sam Snead*	289
1955	Cary Middlecoff	279
1956	Jack Burke, Jnr.	289
1957	Doug Ford	282
1958	Arnold Palmer	284
1959	Art Wall, Jnr.	284
1960	Arnold Palmer	282
1961	Gary Player	280
1962	Arnold Palmer*	280
1963	Jack Nicklaus	286
1964	Arnold Palmer	276
1965	Jack Nicklaus	271
1966	Jack Nicklaus*	288
1967	Gay Brewer, Jnr.	280
1968	Bob Goalby	277
1969	George Archer	281
1970	Billy Casper*	279
1971	Charles Coody	279
1972	Jack Nicklaus	286
1973	Tommy Aaron	283
1974	Gary Player	278
1975	Jack Nicklaus	276
1976	Ray Floyd	271
1977	Tom Watson	276
1978	Gary Player	277
1979	Fuzzy Zoeller*	280
1980	Seve Ballesteros	275
1981	Tom Watson	280
1982	Craig Stadler*	284
1983	Seve Ballesteros	280
1984	Ben Crenshaw	277
1985	Bernhard Langer	278
1986	Jack Nicklaus	279
1987	Larry Mize*	285
1988	Sandy Lyle	281
1989	Nick Faldo*	283
1990	Nick Faldo	278

Won after play-off

US Open Championship

Year	Winner	Venue	Score
1895	Horace Rawlins	Newport	173***
1896	James Foulis	Shinnecock Hills	153***
1897	Joe Floyd	Chicago	162***
1898	Fred Herd	Myopia Hunt Club	328**
1899	Willie Smith	Baltimore	315
1900	Harry Vardon	Chicago	313
1901	Willie Anderson*	Myopia Hunt Club	331
1902	Laurie Auchterlonie	Garden City	307
1903	Willie Anderson*	Baltusrol	307
1904	Willie Anderson	Glen View	303
1905	Willie Anderson	Myopia Hunt Club	314
1906	Alex Smith	Onwentsia Club	295
1907	Alex Ross	Phil. Cricket Club	302
1908	Fred McLeod*	Myopia Hunt Club	322
1909	George Sargent	Englewood	290
1910	Alex Smith*	Phil. Cricket Club	298
1911	John McDermott*	Chicago	307
1912	John McDermott	C.C. of Buffalo	294
1913	Francis Ouimet*	The C.C. Brookline	304
1914	Walter Hagen	Midlothian	290
1915	Jerome Travers	Baltusrol	297
1916	Charles Evans, Jnr.	Minikahada Club	286
1919	Walter Hagan	Brae Burn	301
1920	Edward Ray	Inverness	295
1921	James M. Barnes	Columbia	289
1922	Gene Sarazen	Skokie	288
1923	R.T. Jones, Jnr*	Inwood	296
1924	Cyril Walker	Oakland Hills	297
1925	W. MacFarlane*	Worcester	291
1926	R.T. Jones, Jnr.	Scioto	293
1927	Tommy Armour*	Oakmont	301
1928	Johnny Farrell*	Olympia Fields	294
1929	R.T. Jones, Jnr*	Winged Foot	294
1930	R.T. Jones, Jnr.	Interlachen	287
1931	Billy Burke*	Inverness	292
1932	Gene Sarazen	Fresh Meadows	286
1933	Johnny Goodman	North Shore	287
1934	Olin Dutra	Merion C.C.	293
1935	Sam Parks, Jnr.	Oakmont	299
1936	Tony Manero	Baltusrol	282
1937	Ralph Guldahl	Oakland Hills	281
1938	Ralph Guldahl	Cherry Hills	284
1939	Byron Nelson*	Philadelphia	284
1940	Lawson Little*	Canterbury	287
1941	Craig Wood	Colonial Club	284
1946	Lloyd Mangrum*	Canterbury	284
1947	Lew Worsham*	St. Louis	282
1948	Ben Hogan	Riviera	276
1949	Cary Middlecoff	Medinah	286
1950	Ben Hogan*	Merion	287
1951	Ben Hogan	Oakland Hills	287
1952	Julius Boros	Northwood	281
1953	Ben Hogan	Oakmont	283
1954	Ed Furgol	Baltusrol	284
1955	Jack Fleck*	Olympic Club	287
1956	Cary Middlecoff	Oak Hill	281
1957	Dick Mayer*	Inverness Club	282
1958	Tommy Bolt	Southern Hills	283
1959	Billy Casper	Winged Foot	282
1960	Arnold Palmer	Cherry Hills	280
1961	Gene Littler	Oakland Hills	281
1962	Jack Nicklaus*	Oakmont	283
1963	Julius Boros*	The C.C. Brookline	293
1964	Ken Venturi	Congressional	278
1965	Gary Player*	Bellerive	282
1966	Billy Casper*	Olympic Club	278
1967	Jack Nicklaus	Baltusrol	275
1968	Lee Trevino	Oak Hill	275
1969	Orville Moody	Champions G.C.	281
1970	Tony Jacklin	Hazeltine	281
1971	Lee Trevino*	Merion	280
1972	Jack Nicklaus	Pebble Beach	290
1973	Johnny Miller	Oakmont	279
1974	Hale Irwin	Winged Foot	287
1975	Lou Graham*	Medinah	287
1976	Jerry Pate	Atlantic Athletic C.	277
1977	Hubert Green	Southern Hills	278
1978	Andy North	Cherry Hills	285
1979	Hale Irwin	Inverness Club	284
1980	Jack Nicklaus	Baltusrol	272
1981	David Graham	Merion	273
1982	Tom Watson	Pebble Beach	282
1983	Larry Nelson	Oakmont	280
1984	Fuzzy Zoeller*	Winged Foot	276
1985	Andy North	Oakland Hills	279
1986	Ray Floyd	Shinnecock Hills	279
1987	Scott Simpson	Olympic Club	277
1988	Curtis Strange*	The C.C. Brookline	278
1989	Curtis Strange	Oak Hill	278
1990	Hale Irwin	Medinah	280

**Won after play-off   **72 Holes   ***36 Holes*

US PGA Championship

Year	Winner	Venue
1916	James M. Barnes	Siwanoy
1919	James M. Barnes	Engineers C.C.
1920	Jock Hutchinson	Flossmoor
1921	Walter Hagen	Inwood
1922	Gene Sarazen	Oakmont
1923	Gene Sarazen	Pelham
1924	Walter Hagen	French Lick C.C.
1925	Walter Hagen	Olympia Fields
1926	Walter Hagen	Salisbury
1927	Walter Hagen	Cedar Crest
1928	Leo Diegel	Five Farms
1929	Leo Diegel	Hillcrest
1930	Tommy Armour	Fresh Meadow
1931	Tom Creavy	Wannamoisett
1932	Olin Dutra	Keller
1933	Gene Sarazen	Blue Mound
1934	Paul Runyan	Park C.C.
1935	Johnny Revolta	Twin Hills
1936	Denny Shute	Pinehurst
1937	Denny Shute	Pittsburgh
1938	Paul Runyan	Shawnee
1939	Henry Picard	Pomonok
1940	Byron Nelson	Hershey
1941	Vic Ghezzi	Cherry Hills
1942	Sam Sneed	Seaview
1944	Bob Hamilton	Manito
1945	Byron Nelson	Morraine
1946	Ben Hogan	Portland
1947	Jim Ferrier	Plum Hollow
1948	Ben Hogan	Norwood Hills
1949	Sam Snead	Hermitage
1950	Chandler Harper	Scioto
1951	Sam Snead	Oakmont
1952	Jim Turnesa	Big Spring
1953	Walter Burkemo	Birmingham
1954	Chick Harbert	Keller
1955	Doug Ford	Meadowbrook
1956	Jack Burke	Blue Hill
1957	Lionel Herbert	Miami Valley

Until 1957 the championship was decided by match-play

Year	Winner	Venue	Score
1958	Dow Finsterwald	Llanerch	277
1959	Bob Rosburg	Minneapolis	277
1960	Jay Herbert	Firestone	281
1961	Jerry Barber*	Olympia Fields	277
1962	Gary Player	Aronomink	278
1963	Jack Nicklaus	Dalls Athletic C.	279
1964	Bobby Nichols	Columbus	271
1965	Dave Marr	Laurel Valley	280
1966	Al Geiberger	Firestone	280
1967	Don January*	Columbine	281
1968	Julius Boros	Pecan Valley	281
1969	Ray Floyd	NCR C.C.	276
1970	Dave Stockton	Southern Hills	279

Year	Winner	Venue	Score
1971	Jack Nicklaus	PGA National	281
1972	Gary Player	Oakland Hills	281
1973	Jack Nicklaus	Canterbury	277
1974	Lee Trevino	Tanglewood	276
1975	Jack Nicklaus	Firestone	276
1976	Dave Stockton	Congressional C.C.	281
1977	Lanny Wadkins*	Pebble Beach	282
1978	John Mahaffey*	Oakmont	276
1979	David Graham*	Oakland Hills	272
1980	Jack Nicklaus	Oak Hill	274
1981	Larry Nelson	Atlanta Athletic C.	273
1982	Ray Floyd	Southern Hills	272
1983	Hal Sutton	Riviera	274
1984	Lee Trevino	Shoal Creek	273
1985	Hubert Green	Cherry Hills	278
1986	Bob Tway	Inverness	276
1987	Larry Nelson*	PGA National Palm Beach	287
1988	Jeff Sluman	Oak Tree C.C.	272
1989	Payne Stewart	Kemper Lakes	276
1990	Wayne Grady	Shoal Creek	282

Stroke-play from 1958 **Won after play-off*

PGA European Tour Tenerife Open

Year	Winner	Venue	Score
1989	J.M. Olazabal	Golf del Sur	275
1990	V. Fernandez	Golf del Sur	282

Desert Classic

Year	Winner	Venue	Score
1989	M. James	Emirates	277
1990	E. Darcy	Emirates	276

Renault Open De Balearas Championship

Year	Winner	Venue	Score
1988	S. Ballesteros	Santa Ponsa	272
1989	O. Sellberg	Santa Ponsa	279
1990	S. Ballesteros	San Vida	269

Sanyo Open Championship

Year	Winner	Venue	Score
1982	N. Coles	Sant Cugat	266
1983	D. Smyth	El Prat	279
1984	S. Torrance	El Prat	281
1985	S. Ballesteros	El Prat	272
1986	J.M. Olazabal	El Prat	273

Not Contested since 1986

Catalan Open Championship

Year	Winner	Venue	Score
1988	D. Whelan	El Prat	276
1989	M. Roe	Pals	279
1990	Not played		

AGF Open Championship

Year	Winner	Venue	Score
1988	D. Llewellyn	Biarritz	258
1989	M. James	La Grande Motte	277
1990	B. Ogle	La Grande Motte	278

Volvo Open

Year	Winner	Venue	Score
1989	V. Singh	Is Molas	276
1990	E. Romero	Ugolino	265

Jersey Open Championship

Year	Winner	Venue	Score
1978	B.G.C. Huggett	La Moye	271
1979	S. Lyle	La Moye	271
1980	J.M. Canizares	La Moye	281
1981	A. Jacklin	La Moye	279
1982	B. Gallacher	La Moye	273
1983	J. Hall	La Moye	278
1984	B. Gallacher	La Moye	274
1985	H. Clark	La Moye	279
1986	J. Morgan	La Moye	275
1987	I. Woosnam	La Moye	279
1988	D. Smyth	La Moye	273
1989	C. O'Connor	La Moye	281
1990	Not played		

Cannes Open Championship

Year	Winner	Venue	Score
1984	D. Frost	Cannes Mougins	280
1985	R. Lee	Cannes Mougins	280
1986	J. Bland	Cannes Mougins	276
1987	S. Ballesteros	Cannes Mougins	275
1988	M. McNulty	Cannes Mougins	279
1989	P. Broadhurst	Cannes Mougins	207*
1990	M. McNulty	Cannes Mougins	280

**Rain shortened*

Cepsa Madrid Open Championship

Year	Winner	Venue	Score
1968	G. Garrido	R.A.C.E. Madrid	279
1969	R. Sota	R.A.C.E. Madrid	278
1970	M. Cabrera	R.A.C.E. Madrid	288
1971	V. Barrios	Puerta de Hierro	285
1972	J. Kinsella	Puerta de Hierro	283
1973	G. Garrido	R.A.C.E. Madrid	287
1974	M. Pinero	Puerta de Hierro	283
1975	R. Shearer	Lomas Bosque	135*
1976	F. Abreu	Puerta de Hierro	275
1977	A. Garrido	Hipica Espanola	278
1978	H. Clark	Puerta de Hierro	282
1979	S. Hobday	Puerta de Hierro	285
1980	S. Ballesteros	Puerta de Hierro	270
1981	M. Pinero	Puerta da Hierro	279
1982	S. Ballesteros	Puerta de Hierro	273
1983	S. Lyle	Puerta de Hierro	285
1984	H. Clark	Puerta de Hierro	274
1985	M. Pinero	Puerta de Hierro	278
1986	H. Clark	Puerta de Hierro	274
1987	I. Woosnam	Puerta de Hierro	269
1988	D. Cooper	Puerta de Hierro	275
1989	S. Ballesteros	Puerta de Hierro	272
1990	B. Langer	Puerta de Hierro	270

**2 rounds*

Peugeot Spanish Open Championship

Year	Winner	Venue	Score
1912	A. Massy	Polo GC, Madrid	
1916	A. de la Torre	Puerta de Hierro	
1917	A. de la Torre	Puerta de Hierro	
1919	A. de la Torre	Puerta de Hierro	
1921	E. Lafitte	Puerta de Hierro	
1923	A. de la Torre	Puerta de Hierro	
1925	A. de la Torre	Puerta de Hierro	
1926	J. Bernardino	Puerta de Hierro	
1927	A. Massy	Puerta de Hierro	
1928	A. Massy	Puerta de Hierro	
1929	E. Lafitte	Puerta de Hierro	
1930	J. Bernardino	Puerta de Hierro	
1932	G. Gonzalez	Puerta de Hierro	
1933	G. Gonzalez	Puerta de Hierro	
1934	J. Bernardino	Puerta de Hierro	
1935	A. de la Torre	Puerta de Hierro	
1941	M. Provencio	Puerta de Hierro	
1942	G. Gonzalez	Sant Cugat	
1943	M. Provencio	Puerta de Hierro	
1944	N. Sagardia	Pedrena	
1945	C. Celles	Puerta de Hierro	
1946	M. Morcillo	Pedrena	
1947	M. Gonzalez M. Morcillo	Puerta de Hierro	
1948	M. Morcillo	Negun	
1949	M. Morcillo	Puerta de Hierro	
1950	A. Cerda	Cedana	
1951	M. Provencio	Puerta de Hierro	
1952	M. Faulkner	Puerta de Hierro	
1953	M. Faulkner	Puerta de Hierro	
1954	S. Miguel	Puerta de Hierro	
1955	H. de Lamaze	Puerta de Hierro	
1956	P. Alliss	El Prat	
1957	M. Faulkner	Club de Campo	
1958	P. Alliss	Puerta de Hierro	

1959	P. Thompson	El Prat	
1960	S. Miguel	Club de Campo	
1961	A. Miguel	Puerta de Hierro	
1963	R. Sota	El Prat	
1964	A. Miguel	Tenerife	
1966	R. de Vincenzo	Sotogrande	
1967	S. Miguel	Sant Cugat	
1968	R. Shaw	La Galea	
1969	J. Garaialde	R.A.C.E. Madrid	
1970	A. Gallardo	Nueva Andalucia	
1971	D. Hayes	El Prat	275
1972	A. Garrido	Pals	293
1973	N. Coles	La Manga	282
1974	J. Heard	La Manga	279
1975	A. Palmer	La Manga	283
1976	E. Polland	La Manga	282
1977	B. Gallacher	La Manga	277
1978	B. Barnes	El Prat	276
1979	D. Hayes	Torrequebrada	278
1980	E. Polland	Escorpion	276
1981	S. Ballesteros	El Prat	273
1982	S. Torrance	Club de Campo	273
1983	E. Darcy	Las Brisas	277
1984	B. Langer	El Saler	275
1985	S. Ballesteros	Vallromanos	266
1986	H. Clark	La Moraleja	272
1987	N. Faldo	Las Brisas	286
1988	M. James	Pedrena	262
1989	B. Langer	El Saler	281
1990	R. Davis	Club de Campo	277

Epson Grand Prix of Europe Championship

Year	Winner	Venue	Score
1986	O. Sellberg	St. Pierre	3 & 2
1987	M. Lanner	St. Pierre	1 hole
1988	B. Langer	St. Pierre	4 & 3
1989	S. Ballesteros	St. Pierre	4 & 3
1990	I. Woosnam	St. Pierre	271

**From 1990 Stroke-play*

Belgian Open Championship

Year	Winner	Venue	Score
1987	E. Darcy	Royal Waterloo	200*
1988	J.M. Olazabal	Bercuit	269
1989	G.J. Brand	Royal Waterloo	273
1990	O. Sellberg	Royal Waterloo	272

**3 Rounds*

Italian Open Championship

Year	Winner	Venue	Score
1925	F. Pasquali	Stresa	154*
1926	A. Boyer	Stresa	147*
1927	P. Alliss	Stresa	145*
1928	A. Boyer	Villa d'Este	145*
1929	R. Golias	Villa d'Este	143*
1930	A. Boyer	Villa d'Este	140*
1931	A. Boyer	Villa d'Este	141*
1932	A. Boomer	Villa d'Este	143*
1934	N. Nutley	San Remo	132*
1935	P. Alliss	San Remo	262
1963	H. Cotton	Sestriere	268
1937	M. Dallemagne	San Remo	276
1938	F. van Donck	Villa d'Este	276
1947	F. van Donck	San Remo	263
1948	A. Casera	San Remo	267
1949	H. Hassanein	Villa d'Este	263
1950	U. Grappasonni	Rome	281
1951	J. Adams	Milan	289
1952	E. Brown	Milan	273
1953	F. van Donck	Villa d'Este	267
1954	U. Grappasonni	Villa d'Este	272
1955	F. van Donck	Venice	287
1956	A. Cerda	Milan	284
1957	H. Henning	Villa d'Este	273
1958	P. Alliss	Varese	282
1959	P. Thompson	Villa d'Este	269
1960	B. Wilkes	Venice	285
1971	R. Sota	Garlenda	282
1972	N. Wood	Villa d'Este	271
1973	A. Jacklin	Rome	284
1974	P. Oosterhuis	Venice	249**
1975	W. Casper	Monticello	286
1976	B. Dassu	Is Molas	280
1977	A. Gallardo	Monticello	286
1978	D. Hayes	Pevero	293
1979	B. Barnes	Monticello	281
1980	M. Mannelli	Rome	276
1981	J.M. Canizares	Milan	280
1982	M. James	Is Molas	280
1983	B. Langer	Ugolino	271
1984	S. Lyle	Milan	277
1985	M. Pinero	Milan	267
1986	D. Feherty	Albarella, Venice	270
1987	S. Torrance	Monticello	271
1988	G. Norman	Monticello	270
1989	R. Rafferty	Monticello	273
1990	R. Boxall	Milano	267

**2 Rounds   **63 holes   1933, 1961–70 Not played*

Volvo PGA Championship

Year	Winner	Venue	Score
1955	K. Bousfield	Pannal	277
1956	C.H. Ward	Maesdu	282
1957	P. Alliss	Maesdu	286
1958	H. Bradshaw	Llandudno	287
1959	D.J. Rees	Ashburnham	283
1960	A.F. Stickley	Coventry	247***
1961	B.J. Bamford	Royal Mid-Surrey	266
1962	P. Alliss	Little Ashton	287
1963	P.J. Butler	Royal Birkdale	306
1964	A.G. Grubb	Western Gailes	287
1965	P. Alliss	Prince's	286
1966	G. Wolstenholme	Saunton	278
1967	B.G.C. Huggett	Thorndon Park	271
1967	M.E. Gregson	Hunstanton	275*
1968	P.M. Townsend	Royal Mid-Surrey	275
1968	D. Talbot	Dunbar	276*
1969	B. Gallacher	Ashburnham	291
1972	A. Jacklin	Wentworth	279
1973	P. Oosterhuis	Wentworth	280
1974	M. Bembridge	Wentworth	278
1975	A. Palmer	Royal St. George's	285
1976	N.C. Coles	Royal St. George's	280
1977	M. Pinero	Royal St. George's	283
1978	N. Faldo	Royal Birkdale	278
1979	V. Fernandez	St. Andrews	288
1980	N. Faldo	Royal St. George's	283
1981	N. Faldo	Ganton	274
1982	A. Jacklin	Hillside	284
1983	S. Ballesteros	Royal St. George's	278
1984	H. Clark	Wentworth	204**
1985	P. Way	Wentworth	282
1986	R. Davis	Wentworth	281
1987	B. Langer	Wentworth	270
1988	I. Woosnam	Wentworth	274
1989	N. Faldo	Wentworth	272
1990	M. Harwood	Wentworth	271

*1970, 1971 Not Played   **3 Rounds   ***63 Holes*

Dunhill British Masters

Year	Winner	Venue	Score
1985	L. Trevino	Woburn	278
1986	S. Ballesteros	Woburn	275
1987	M. McNulty	Woburn	274
1988	S. Lyle	Woburn	273
1989	N. Faldo	Woburn	267
1990	M. James	Woburn	270

Wang Four Stars National Pro-Celebrity Tournament

Year	Winner	Venue	Score
1985	K. Brown	Moor Park	277
1986	A. Garrido	Moor Park	275
1987	M. McNulty	Moor Park	273
1988	R. Davis	Moor Park	275
1989	C. Parry	Moor Park	273
1990	R. Davis	Moor Park	271

NM English Open Championship

Year	Winner	Venue	Score
1988	H. Clark	Royal Birkdale	279
1989	M. James	The Belfry	279
1990	M. James	The Belfry	284

Carroll's Irish Open Championship

Year	Winner	Venue	Score
1975	C. O'Connor Jnr.	Woodbrook	275
1976	B. Crenshaw	Portmarnock	284
1977	H. Green	Portmarnock	283
1978	K. Brown	Portmarnock	281
1979	M. James	Portmarnock	282
1980	M. James	Portmarnock	284
1981	S. Torrance	Portmarnock	276
1982	J. O'Leary	Portmarnock	287
1983	S. Ballesteros	The Royal Dublin	271
1984	B. Langer	The Royal Dublin	267
1985	S. Ballesteros	The Royal Dublin	278
1986	S. Ballesteros	Portmarnock	285
1987	B. Langer	Portmarnock	269
1988	I. Woosnam	Portmarnock	278
1989	I. Woosnam	Portmarnock	278
1990	J. M. Olazabal	Portmarnock	282

Peugeot French Open Championship

Year	Winner	Venue	Score
1906	A. Massy	La Boulie	292
1907	A. Massy	La Boulie	298
1908	J.H. Taylor	La Boulie	300
1909	J.H. Taylor	La Boulie	293
1910	J. Braid	La Boulie	298
1911	A. Massy	La Boulie	284
1912	J. Gassiat	La Boulie	289
1913	G. Duncan	Chantilly	304
1914	J.D. Edgar	Le Touquet	288
1920	W. Hagen	La Boulie	298
1921	A. Boomer	Le Touquet	284
1922	A. Boomer	La Boulie	286
1923	J. Ockenden	Dieppe	288
1924	C.J.H. Tolley (Am)	La Boulie	290
1925	A. Massy	Chantilly	291
1926	A. Boomer	St. Cloud	280
1927	G. Duncan	St. Germain	299
1928	C.J.H. Tolley (Am)	La Boulie	283
1929	A. Boomer	Fourqueux	283
1930	E.R. Whitcombe	Dieppe	282
1931	A. Boomer	Deuville	291
1932	A.J. Lacey	St. Cloud	295
1933	B. Gadd	Chantilly	283
1934	S.F. Brews	Dieppe	284
1935	S.F. Brews	Le Touquet	293
1936	M. Dallemagne	St. Germain	277
1937	M. Dallemagne	St. Cloud	278
1938	M. Dallemagne	Fourqueux	282
1939	M. Pose	Le Touquet	285
1946	T.H. Cotton	St. Cloud	269
1947	T.H. Cotton	Chantilly	285
1948	F. Cavalo	St. Cloud	287
1949	U. Grappasonni	St. Germain	275
1950	R. de Vicenzo	Chantilly	279
1951	H. Hassanein	St. Cloud	278
1952	A.D. Locke	St. Germain	268
1953	A.D. Locke	La Boulie	276
1954	F. van Donck	St. Cloud	275
1955	B. Nelson	La Boulie	271
1956	A. Miguel	Deauville	277
1957	F. van Donck	St. Cloud	266
1958	F. van Donck	St. Germain	276
1959	D.C. Thomas	La Boulie	276
1960	R. de Vincenzo	St. Cloud	275
1961	K.D.G. Nagle	La Boulie	271
1962	A. Murray	St. Germain	274
1963	B. Devlin	St. Cloud	273
1964	R. de Vincenzo	Chantilly	272
1965	R. Sota	St. Nom-la-Breteche	268
1966	D.J. Hutchinson	La Boulie	274
1967	B.J. Hunt	St. Germain	271
1968	P.J. Butler	St. Cloud	272
1969	J. Garaialde	St. Nom-la-Breche	277
1970	D. Graham	Chantaco	268
1971	Lu Liang Huan	Biarritz	262
1972	B. Jaeckel	Biarritz & La Nivelle	265
1973	P. Oosterhuis	La Boulie	280
1974	P. Oosterhuis	Chantilly	284
1975	B. Barnes	La Boulie	281
1976	V. Tshabalala	Le Touquet	272
1977	S. Ballesteros	Le Touquet	282
1978	D. Hayes	La Baule	269
1979	B. Gallacher	Lyons	284
1980	G. Norman	St. Cloud	268
1981	S. Lyle	St. Germain	270
1982	S. Ballesteros	St. Nom-la-Breteche	278
1983	N. Faldo	La Boulie	277
1984	B. Langer	St. Cloud	270
1985	S. Ballesteros	St. Germain	263
1986	S. Ballesteros	La Boulie	269
1987	J. Rivero	St. Cloud	269
1988	N. Faldo	Chantilly	274
1989	N. Faldo	Chantilly	273
1990	P. Walton	Chantilly	275

Monte Carlo Championship

Year	Winner	Venue	Score
1984	I. Mosey	Mont Agel	131*
1985	S. Torrance	Mont Agel	264
1986	S. Ballesteros	Mont Agel	265
1987	P. Senior	Mont Agel	260
1988	J. Rivero	Mont Agel	261
1989	M. McNulty	Mont Agel	261
1990	I. Woosnam	Mont Agel	258

Bell's Scottish Open Championship

Year	Winner	Venue	Score
1986	D. Feherty	Haggs Castle	270
1987	I. Woosnam	Gleneagles Hotel	264
1988	B. Lane	Gleneagles Hotel	271
1989	M. Allen	Gleneagles Hotel	272
1990	I. Woosnam	Gleneagles Hotel	269

Volvo Seniors British Open

Year	Winner	Venue	Score
1977	N. Coles	Turnberry Hotel	279
1988	G. Player	Turnberry Hotel	272
1989	B. Charles	Turnberry Hotel	269
1990	G. Player	Turnberry Hotel	280

KLM Dutch Open Championship

Year	Winner	Venue	Score
1919	D. Oosterveer	The Hague	158*
1920	H. Burrows	Haarlem	155*
1921	H. Burrows	Domburg	151*
1922	G. Pannell	Noordwijk	160*
1923	H. Burrows	Hilversum	153*
1924	A. Boomer	The Hague	138*
1925	A. Boomer	The Hague	144*
1926	A. Boomer	The Hague	151*
1927	P. Boomer	The Hague	147*
1928	E.R. Whitcombe	The Hague	141*
1929	J.J. Taylor	Hilversum	153*
1930	J. Oosterveer	The Hague	152*
1931	F. Dyer	Haarlem	145*
1932	A. Boyer	The Hague	137*
1933	M. Dallemagne	Zandvoort	143*
1934	S.F. Brews	Utrecht	286
1935	S.F. Brews	Zandvoort	275
1936	F. van Donck	Hilversum	285
1937	F. van Donck	Utrecht	286
1938	A.H. Padgham	The Hague	281
1939	A.D. Locke	Zandvoort	281
1948	C. Denny	Hilversum	290
1949	J. Adams	The Hague	294
1950	R. de Vincenzo	Breda	269
1951	F. van Donck	Kennemer	281
1952	C. Denny	Hilversum	284
1953	F. van Donck	Eindhoven	286
1954	U. Grappasonni	The Hague	295
1955	A. Angelini	Zandvoort	280
1956	A. Cerda	Eindhoven	277
1957	J. Jacobs	Hilversum	284
1958	D. Thomas	Zandvoort	277
1959	S. Sewgolum	The Hague	283
1960	S. Sewgolum	Eindhoven	280
1961	B.B.S. Wilkes	Zandvoort	279
1962	B.G.C. Huggett	Hilversum	274
1963	R. Waltman	Wassenaar	279
1964	S. Sewgolum	Eindhoven	275
1965	A. Miguel	Breda	278
1966	R. Sota	Zandvoort	276
1967	P. Townsend	The Hague	282

1968	J. Cockin	Hilversum	292
1969	G. Wolstenholme	Utrecht	277
1970	V. Fernandez	Eindhoven	279
1971	R. Sota	Zandvoort	277
1972	J. Newton	The Hague	277
1973	D. McClelland	The Hague	279
1974	B. Barnes	Hilversum	211**
1975	H. Baiocchi	Hilversum	279
1976	S. Ballesteros	Kennemer	278
1977	R. Byman	Kennemer	214**
1978	R. Byman	Noordwijk	285
1979	G. Marsh	Noordwijk	285
1980	S. Ballesteros	Hilversum	280
1981	H. Henning	The Hague	280
1982	P. Way	Utrecht	276
1983	K. Brown	Kennemer	274
1984	B. Langer	Rosendaelsche	275
1985	G. Marsh	Noordwijk	282
1986	S. Ballesteros	Noordwijk	272
1987	G. Brand, Jnr.	Hilversum	272
1988	M. Mouland	Hilversum	274
1989	J.M. Olazabal	Kennemer	277
1990	S. McAllister	Kennemer	274

**2 Rounds* **54 Holes*

Scandinavian Enterprise Open Championship

Year	Winner	Venue	Score
1973	R. Charles	Drottningholm	278
1974	A. Jacklin	Bokskogen	279
1975	G. Burns	Bokskogen	279
1976	H. Baiocchi	Drottningholm	271
1977	R. Byman	Drottningholm	275
1978	S. Ballesteros	Vasatorp	279
1979	S. Lyle	Vasatorp	276
1980	G. Norman	Vasatorp	276
1981	S. Ballesteros	Linkoping	273
1982	R. Byman	Linkoping	275
1983	S. Torrance	Sven Tumba G&CC	280
1984	I. Woosnam	Sven Tumba G&CC	280
1985	I. Baker-Finch	Sven Tumba G&CC	274
1986	G. Turner	Sven Tumba G&CC	270
1987	G. Brand, Jnr.	Sven Tumba G&CC	277
1988	S. Ballesteros	Drottningholm	270
1989	R. Rafferty	Drottningholm	268
1990	C. Stadler	Drottningholm	268

Benson & Hedges International Open

Year	Winner	Venue	Score
1971	A. Jacklin	Fulford	279
1972	J. Newton	Fulford	281
1973	V. Baker	Fulford	276
1974	P. Toussaint	Fulford	276
1975	V. Fernandez	Fulford	266
1976	G. Marsh	Fulford	272
1977	A. Garrido	Fulford	280
1978	L. Trevino	Fulford	274
1979	M. Bembridge	St. Mellion	272
1980	G. Marsh	Fulford	272
1981	T. Weiskopf	Fulford	272
1982	G. Norman	Fulford	283
1983	J. Bland	Fulford	273
1984	S. Torrance	Fulford	270
1985	S. Lyle	Fulford	274
1986	M. James	Fulford	274
1987	N. Ratcliffe	Fulford	275
1988	P. Baker	Fulford	271
1989	G. Brand, Jnr.	Fulford	272
1990	J. M. Olazabal	St. Mellion	279

Murphy's Cup*

Year	Winner	Venue	Score
1989	H. Baiocchi	St. Pierre	156
1990	T. Johnston	Fulford	50

**Stableford competition*

PLM Open Championship

Year	Winner	Venue	Score
1986	P. Senior	Falsterbo	273
1987	H. Clark	Ljunghusens	271
1988	F. Nobilo	Flommen	270
1989	M. Harwood	Bokskogens	271
1990	R. Rafferty	Bokskogens	270

German Open Championship

Year	Winner	Venue	Score
1911	H. Vardon	Baden-Baden	279
1912	J.H. Taylor	Baden-Baden	279
1926	P. Alliss	Berlin	284
1927	P. Alliss	Berlin	288
1928	P. Alliss	Berlin	280
1929	P. Alliss	Berlin	285
1930	A. Boyer	Baden-Baden	266
1931	R. Golias	Berlin	298
1932	A. Boyer	Bad Ems	282
1933	P. Alliss	Bad Ems	284
1934	A.H. Padgham	Bad Ems	285
1935	A. Boyer	Bad Ems	280
1936	A. Boyer	Berlin	291
1937	T.H. Cotton	Bad Ems	274
1938	T.H. Cotton	Frankfurt	285
1939	T.H. Cotton	Bad Ems	280
1951	A. Cerda	Hamburg	286
1952	A. Cerda	Hamburg	283
1953	F. van Donck	Frankfurt	271
1954	A.D. Locke	Krefeld	277
1955	K. Bousfield	Hamburg	279
1956	F. van Donck	Frankfurt	271
1957	H. Weetman	Cologne	279
1958	F. de Luca	Krefeld	275
1959	K. Bousfield	Hamburg	271
1960	P.W. Thomson	Cologne	281
1961	B.J. Hunt	Krefeld	272
1962	R. Verwey	Hamburg	276
1963	B.G.C. Huggett	Cologne	278
1964	R. de Vincenzo	Krefeld	275
1965	H.R. Henning	Hamburg	274
1966	R. Stanton	Frankfurt	274
1967	D. Swaelens	Krefeld	273
1968	B. Franklin	Cologne	265
1969	J. Garaialde	Frankfurt	272
1970	J. Garaialde	Krefeld	276
1971	N.C. Coles	Bremen	279
1972	G. Marsh	Frankfurt	271
1973	F. Abreu	Hubbelrath	276
1974	S. Owen	Krefeld	276
1975	M. Bembridge	Bremen	285
1976	S. Hobday	Frankfurt	266
1977	T. Britz	Dusseldorf	275
1978	S. Ballesteros	Cologne	268
1979	A. Jacklin	Frankfurt	277
1980	M. McNulty	Berlin	280
1981	B. Langer	Hamburg	272
1982	B. Langer	Stuttgart	279
1983	C. Pavin	Cologne	275
1984	W. Grady	Frankfurt	268
1985	B. Langer	Garstedt	183*
1986	B. Langer	Hubbelrath	273
1987	M. McNulty	Frankfurt	259
1988	S. Ballesteros	Frankfurt	263
1989	C. Parry	Frankfurt	266
1990	M. McNulty	Hubbelrath	270

**3 rounds*

Ebel European Masters Swiss Open Championship

Year	Winner	Venue	Score
1923	A. Ross	Engen	149*
1924	P. Boomer	Engen	150*
1925	A. Ross	Engen	148*
1926	A. Ross	Lucerne	145*
1929	A. Wilson	Lucerne	142*
1930	A. Boyer	Samedan	150*
1931	M. Dallemagne	Lucerne	145*
1934	A. Boyer	Lausanne	133*
1935	A. Boyer	Lausanne	137*
1936	F. Francis (Am)	Lausanne	134*
1937	M. Dallemagne	Samedan	138*
1938	J. Saubaber	Zumikon	139*
1939	F. Cavalo	Crans s/Sierre	273
1948	U. Grappasonni	Crans s/Sierre	285
1949	M. Dallemagne	Crans s/Sierre	270
1950	A. Casera	Crans s/Sierre	276
1951	E.C. Brown	Crans s/Sierre	267
1952	U. Grappasonni	Crans s/Sierre	267
1953	F. van Donck	Crans s/Sierre	267
1954	A. D. Locke	Crans s/Sierre	276

1955	F. van Donck	Crans s/Sierre	277
1956	D.J. Rees	Crans s/Sierre	278
1957	A. Angelini	Crans s/Sierre	270
1958	K. Bousfield	Crans s/Sierre	272
1959	D.J. Rees	Crans s/Sierre	274
1960	H. Henning	Crans s/Sierre	270
1961	K.D.G. Nagle	Crans s/Sierre	268
1962	R.J. Charles	Crans s/Sierre	272
1963	D.J. Rees	Crans s/Sierre	278
1964	H.R. Henning	Crans s/Sierre	276
1965	H.R. Henning	Crans s/Sierre	208**
1966	A. Angelini	Crans s/Sierre	271
1967	R. Vines	Crans s/Sierre	272
1968	R. Bernardini	Crans s/Sierre	272
1969	R. Bernardini	Crans s/Sierre	277
1970	G. Marsh	Crans s/Sierre	274
1971	P.M. Townsend	Crans s/Sierre	270
1972	G. Marsh	Crans s/Sierre	270
1973	H. Baiocchi	Crans s/Sierre	278
1974	R.J. Charles	Crans s/Sierre	275
1975	D. Hayes	Crans s/Sierre	273
1976	M. Pinero	Crans s/Sierre	274
1977	S. Ballesteros	Crans s/Sierre	273
1978	S. Ballesteros	Crans s/Sierre	272
1979	H. Baiocchi	Crans s/Sierre	275
1980	N. Price	Crans s/Sierre	267
1981	M. Pinero	Crans s/Sierre	277
1982	I. Woosnam	Crans s/Sierre	272
1983	N. Faldo	Crans s/Sierre	268
1984	J. Anderson	Crans s/Sierre	261
1985	C. Stadler	Crans s/Sierre	267
1986	J.M. Olazabol	Crans s/Sierre	262
1987	A. Forsbrand	Crans s/Sierre	263
1988	C. Moody	Crans s/Sierre	268
1989	S. Ballesteros	Crans s/Sierre	266
1990	R. Raffertu	Crans s/Sierre	267

**2 rounds **3 rounds*

The Panasonic European Open Championship

Year	Winner	Venue	Score
1978	B. Wadkins	Walton Heath	283
1979	S. Lyle	Turnberry	275
1980	T. Kite	Walton Heath	284
1981	G. Marsh	Royal Liverpool	275
1982	M. Pinero	Sunningdale	266
1983	I. Aoki	Sunningdale	274
1984	G. Brand Jnr.	Sunningdale	270
1985	B. Langer	Sunningdale	269
1986	G. Norman	Sunningdale	269
1987	P. Way	Walton Heath	279
1988	I. Woosnam	Sunningdale	260
1989	A. Murray	Walton Heath	277
1990	P. Senior	Sunningdale	267

Lancome Trophy

Year	Winner	Venue	Score
1970	A. Jacklin	St. Nom-la Breteche	206
1971	A. Palmer	St. Nom-la Breteche	202
1972	T. Aaron	St. Nom-la Breteche	279
1973	J. Miller	St. Nom-la Breteche	277
1974	W. Casper	St. Nom-la Breteche	283
1975	G. Player	St. Nom-la Breteche	278
1976	S. Ballesteros	St. Nom-la Breteche	283
1977	G. Marsh	St. Nom-la Breteche	273
1978	L. Trevino	St. Nom-la Breteche	272
1979	J. Miller	St. Nom-la Breteche	281
1980	L. Trevino	St. Nom-la Breteche	280
1981	D. Graham	St. Nom-la Breteche	280
1982	D. Graham	St. Nom-la Breteche	276
1983	S. Ballesteros	St. Nom-la Breteche	269
1984	S. Lyle	St Nom-la Breteche	278
1985	N. Price	St. Nom-la Breteche	275
1986	S. Ballesteros and B. Langer**	St. Nom-la Breteche	274
1987	I. Woosnam	St. Nom-la Breteche	264
1988	S. Ballesteros	St. Nom-la Breteche	269
1989	E. Romero	St. Nom-la Breteche	266
1990	J. M. Olazabal	St. Nom-la Breteche	269

**3 Rounds **Tied*

Dunhill Cup

Year	Winner	Runner-up	Venue	By
1985	Australia	USA	St. Andrews	3-0
1986	Australia	Japan	St. Andrews	3-0
1987	England	Scotland	St. Andrews	2-1
1988	Ireland	Australia	St. Andrews	2-1
1989	USA	Japan	St. Andrews	3½-2½
1990	Ireland	England	St. Andrews	3½-2½

German Masters

Year	Winner	Venue	Score
1987	S. Lyle	Stuttgart	278
1988	J.M. Olazabal	Stuttgart	279
1989	B. Langer	Stuttgart	276
1990	S. Torrance	Stuttgart	272

BMW International Open

Year	Winner	Venue	Score
1989	D. Feherty	Munich	269
1990	P. Azinger	Munich	277

Portuguese Open Championship

Year	Winner	Venue	Score
1953	E.C. Brown	Estoril	260
1954	A. Miguel	Estoril	263
1955	F. van Donck	Estoril	267
1956	A. Miguel	Estoril	268
1958	P. Alliss	Estoril	264
1959	S. Miguel	Estoril	265
1960	K. Bousfield	Estoril	268
1961	K. Bousfield	Estoril	263
1962	A. Angelini	Estoril	269
1963	R. Sota	Estoril	204*
1964	A. Miguel	Estoril	279
1966	A. Angelini	Estoril	273
1967	A. Gallardo	Estoril	214*
1968	M. Faulkner	Estoril	273
1969	R. Sota	Estoril	270
1970	R. Sota	Estoril	274
1971	L. Platts	Estoril	277
1972	G. Garrido	Estoril	196*
1973	J. Benito	Penina	294
1974	B.G.C. Huggett	Estoril	272
1975	H. Underwood	Penina	292
1976	S. Balbuena	Quinta do Lago	283
1977	M. Ramos	Penina	287
1978	H. Clark	Penina	291
1979	B. Barnes	Vilamoura	287
1982	S. Torrance	Penina	207*
1983	S. Torrance	Troia	286
1984	A. Johnstone	Quinta do Lago	274
1985	W. Humphreys	Quinta do Lago	279
1986	M. McNulty	Quinta do Lago	270
1987	R. Lee	Estoril	195*
1988	M. Harwood	Quinta do Lago	280
1989	C. Montgomery	Quinta do Lago	264
1990	M. McLean	Quinta do Lago	274

**3 rounds*

Volvo Masters

Year	Winner	Venue	Score
1988	N. Faldo	Valderrama	284
1989	R. Rafferty	Valderrama	282
1990	???	Valderrama	???

Equity & Law Challenge

Year	Winner	Venue	Score
1987	B. Lane	Royal Mid-Surrey	15*
1988	R. Rafferty	Royal Mid-Surrey	21*
1989	B. Ogle	Royal Mid-Surrey	25*
1990	B. Marchbank	Royal Mid-Surrey	22*

**Points*

Benson and Hedges Trophy

Year	Winner	Venue	Score
1988	M. McNulty/ M.L. de Taya	La Moraleja	276
1989	M. Jimenez X. Hunsoh	Aloha	281
1990			

Mediterranean Open

Year	Winner	Runner-up	Score
1990	I. Woosnam	Las Brisas	210*

**Rain shortened*

Atlantic Open

Year	Winner	Runner-up	Score
1990	S. McAllister	Estela, Oporto	285

**Rain shortened*

Suntory World Match-play Championship
Venue: Wentworth

Year	Winner	Runner-up	Score
1964	A. Palmer	N.C. Coles	2 and 1
1965	G. Player	P.W. Thompson	3 and 2
1966	G. Player	J.W. Nicklaus	6 and 4
1967	A. Palmer	P.W. Thompson	1 hole
1968	G. Player	R. Charles	1 hole
1969	R. Charles	G. Littler	37th hole
1970	J.W. Nicklaus	L. Trevino	2 and 1
1971	G. Player	J.W. Nicklaus	5 and 4
1972	T. Weiskopf	L. Trevino	4 and 3
1973	G. Player	G. Marsh	40th hole
1974	H. Irwin	G. Player	3 and 1
1975	H. Irwin	A. Geiberger	4 and 2
1976	D. Graham	H. Irwin	38th hole
1977	G. Marsh	R. Floyd	5 and 3
1978	I. Aoki	S. Owen	3 and 2
1979	W. Rogers	I. Aoki	1 hole
1980	G. Norman	S. Lyle	1 hole
1981	S. Ballesteros	B. Crenshaw	1 hole
1982	S. Ballesteros	S. Lyle	37th hole
1983	G. Norman	N. Faldo	3 and 2
1984	S. Ballesteros	B. Langer	2 and 1
1985	S. Ballesteros	B. Langer	6 and 5
1986	G. Norman	S. Lyle	2 and 1
1987	I. Woosnam	S. Lyle	1 hole
1988	S. Lyle	N. Faldo	2 and 1
1989	N. Faldo	I. Woosnam	1 hole
1990	I. Woosnam	M. McNulty	4 and 2

World Cup
(Formerly Canada Cup, until 1966)

Year	Country	Venue	Score
1953	ARGENTINA A. Cerda, R. de Vincenzo (Ind: A. Cerda)	Montreal	287*
1954	AUSTRALIA P. Thompson, K. Nagle	Laval-sur-Lac	556
1955	UNITED STATES C. Herbert, E. Furgol (Ind: E. Furgol)	Washington	560
1956	UNITED STATES B. Hogan, S. Snead (Ind: B. Hogan)	Wentworth	567
1957	JAPAN T. Nakamura, K. Ono (Ind: T. Nakamura)	Tokyo	557
1958	IRELAND H. Bradshaw, C. O'Connor (Ind: A. Miguel, Sp.)	Mexico City	579
1959	AUSTRALIA P. Thompson, K. Nagle (Ind: S. Leonard, Can.)	Melbourne	563
1960	UNITED STATES S. Snead, A. Palmer (Ind: F. Von Donck, Bel.)	Portmarnock	565
1961	UNITED STATES S. Snead, J. Demaret (Ind: S. Snead)	Puerto Rico	560
1962	UNITED STATES S. Snead, A. Palmer (Ind: R. de Vincenzo, Arg.)	Buenos Aires	557
1963	UNITED STATES A. Palmer, J. Nicklaus (Ind: J. Nicklaus)	St. Nom-la-Breteche	482**
1964	UNITED STATES A. Palmer, J. Nicklaus (Ind: J. Nicklaus)	Maui, Hawaii	554
1965	SOUTH AFRICA G. Player, H. Henning (Ind: G. Player)	Madrid	571
1966	UNITED STATES J. Nicklaus, A. Palmer (Ind: G. Knudson, Can.)	Tokyo	548
1967	UNITED STATES J. Nicklaus, A. Palmer (Ind: A. Palmer)	Mexico City	557
1968	CANADA A. Balding, G. Knudson (Ind: A. Balding)	Olgiata, Rome	569
1969	UNITED STATES O. Moody, L. Trevino (Ind: L. Trevino)	Singapore	552
1970	AUSTRALIA B. Devlin, D. Graham (Ind: R. de Vicenzo, Arg.)	Buenos Aires	545
1971	UNITED STATES J. Nicklaus, L. Trevino (Ind: J. Nicklaus)	Palm Beach, Florida	555
1972	TAIWAN Hsieh Min Nan, Lu Liang Huan (Ind: Hsieh Min Nan)	Melbourne	438***
1973	UNITED STATES J. Nicklaus, J. Miller (Ind: J. Miller)	Marbella	558
1974	SOUTH AFRICA R. Cole, D. Hayes (Ind: R. Cole)	Caracas	554
1975	UNITED STATES J. Miller, L. Graham (Ind: J. Miller)	Bangkok	554
1976	SPAIN S. Ballesteros, M. Pinero (Ind: E. Acosta, Mex.)	Palm Springs	574
1977	SPAIN S. Ballesteros, A. Garrido (Ind: G. Player, SA)	Manila	591
1978	UNITED STATES J. Mahaffey, A. North (Ind: J. Mahaffey)	Hawaii	564
1979	UNITED STATES J. Mahaffey, H. Irwin (Ind: H. Irwin)	Glyfada	575
1980	CANADA D. Halldorson, J. Nelford (Ind: S. Lyle)	Bogota	572
1981	Not played		
1982	SPAIN M. Pinero, J.M. Canizares (Ind: M. Pinero)	Acapulco	563
1983	UNITED STATES R. Caldwell, J. Cook (Ind: D. Barr, Can.)	Jakarta	565
1984	SPAIN J.M. Canizares, J. Rivero (Ind: J.M. Canizares)	Olgiata, Rome	414***
1985	CANADA (D. Halldorson, D. Barr) (Ind: H. Clark, Eng.)	La Quinta	559
1986	Not played		
1987	WALES I. Woosnam, D. Llewellyn (Play-off against Scotland – S. Torrance, S. Lyle) (Ind: I. Woosnam)	Kapalua	574
1988	UNITED STATES B. Crenshaw, M. McCumber, (Ind: B. Crenshaw)	Melbourne	560
1989	AUSTRALIA P. Fowler, W. Grady (Ind: P. Fowler)	Las Brisas	278*
1990			

*36 holes   **63 holes   ***54 holes

Walker Cup

Year	Score	Venue
1922	US 8, GB & Ireland 4	National Links, Long Island
1923	US 6½, GB & Ireland 5½	St. Andrews, Scotland
1924	US 9, GB & Ireland 3	Garden City, NY
1926	US 6½, GB & Ireland 5½	St Andrews, Scotland
1928	US 11, GB & Ireland 1	Chicago GC, Ill
1930	US 10, GB & Ireland 2	Royal St. Georges, Sandwich
1932	US 9½, GB & Ireland 2½	Country Club, Brooklyn, Mass.
1934	US 9½, GB & Ireland 2½	St. Andrews, Scotland
1936	US 10½, GB & Ireland 1½	Pine Valley, NJ
1938	GB & Ireland 7½, US 4½	St. Andrews, Scotland
1940–1946 No competition		
1947	US 8, GB & Ireland 4	St. Andrews, Scotland
1949	US 10, GB & Ireland 2	Winged Foot, NY
1951	US 7½, GB & Ireland 4½	Royal Birkdale, Lancs
1953	US 9, GB & Ireland 3	Kittansett, Mass
1955	US 10, GB & Ireland 2	St. Andrews, Scotland
1957	US 8½, GB & Ireland 3½	Minikahda, Minn
1959	US 9, GB & Ireland 3	Muirfield, Scotland
1961	US 11, GB & Ireland 1	Seattle, Washington
1963	US 14, GB & Ireland 10	Turnberry, Scotland
1965	US 12, GB & Ireland 12	Baltimore, Md
1967	US 15, GB & Ireland 9	Royal St. Georges, Sandwich
1969	US 13, GB & Ireland 11	Milwaukee, Wis
1971	GB & Ireland 13, US 11	St. Andrews, Scotland
1973	US 14, GB & Ireland 10	Brooklyn, Mass
1975	US 15½, GB & Ireland 8½	St. Andrews, Scotland
1977	US 16, GB & Ireland 8	Shinnecock Hills, NY
1979	US 15½, GB & Ireland 8½	Muirfield, Scotland
1981	US 15, GB & Ireland 9	Cypress Point, Cal
1983	US 13½, GB & Ireland 10½	Royal Liverpool, England
1985	US 13, GB & Ireland 11	Pine Valley, New Jersey
1987	US 16½, GB & Ireland 7½	Sunningdale, Berkshire
1989	GB & Ireland 12½, US 11½	Peachtree, US

Eisenhower Trophy

(Men's world amateur team championship.)

Year	Winner	Venue
1958	Australia 918	St. Andrews, Scotland
1960	United States 834	Merion, US
1962	United States 854	Fuji, Japan
1964	Great Britain 895	Olgiata, Italy
1966	Australia 877	Mexico City
1968	United States 868	Royal Melbourne, Australia
1970	United States 857	Puerto de Hierro, Spain
1972	United States 865	Olivos, Argentina
1974	United States 888	Campo de Golf, Dominica
1976	Great Britain 892	Penina, Portugal
1978	United States 873	Pacific Harbour, Fiji
1980	United States 848	Pinehurst No 2, United States
1982	United States 859	Lausanne, Switzerland
1984	Japan 870	Royal Hong Kong
1986	Canada 860	Caracas, Venezuela
1988	GB & Ireland 882	Ullva, Sweden
1990		

British Women's Open

Year	Winner	Venue	Score
1976	Jenny Lee-Smith (GB)	Gosforth Park	299
1977	Vivien Saunders (GB)	Lindrick	306
1978	Janet Melville (GB)	Foxhills	310
1979	Alison Sherad (Sth Africa)	Southport & Ainsdale	301
1980	Debbie Massey (US)	Wentworth East	294
1981	Debbie Massey (US)	Northumberland	295
1982	Marta Figuearas-Dotti (Spain)	Royal Birkdale	296
1983		No competition	
1984	Ayako Okamoto (Japan)	Woburn	289
1985	Betsy King (US)	Moor Park	300
1986	Lawa Davis (GB)	Royal Birkdale	283
1987	Alison Nicholas (GB)	St. Mellion	296
1988	Corinne Dibnah (Australia)	Lindrick	295
1989	J. Geddes (USA)	Ferndown	274
1990	H. Alfredsson	Woburn	288

British Women's Amateur

(Players British unless otherwise stated.)

Year	Winner	Venue
1893	Lady Margaret Scott	St. Annes
1894	Lady Margaret Scott	Littlestone
1895	Lady Margaret Scott	Portrush
1896	Amy Pascoe	Hoylake
1897	Edith Orr	Gullane
1898	L. Thomson	Yarmouth
1899	May Hezlet	Newcastle, Co Down
1900	Rhona Adair	Westward Ho!
1901	Molly Graham	Aberdovey
1902	May Hezlet	Deal
1903	Rhona Adair	Portrush
1904	Lottie Dod	Troon
1905	B. Thompson	Cromer
1906	Mrs Kennion	Burnham
1907	May Hezlet	Newcastle, Co Down
1908	M. Titterton	St. Andrews
1909	Dorothy Campbell	Birkdale
1910	Mrs Grant Suttie	Westward Ho!
1911	Dorothy Campbell	Portrush
1912	Gladys Ravenscroft	Turnberry
1913	Muriel Dodd	St. Annes
1914	Cecil Leitch	Hunstanton
1915–1918 No competition		
1919		Cancelled
1920	Cecil Leitch	Newcastle, Co Down
1921	Cecil Leitch	Turnberry
1922	Joyce Wethered	Prince's, Sandwich
1923	Doris Chambers	Burnham
1924	Joyce Wethered	Portrush
1925	Joyce Wethered	Troon
1926	Cecil Leitch	Harlech
1927	T. de la Chaume (France)	Newcastle, Co Down
1928	Nanette Le Blan (France)	Hunstanton
1929	Joyce Wethered	St. Andrews
1930	Diana Fishwick	Formby
1931	Enid Wilson	Portmarnock
1932	Enid Wilson	Saunton
1933	Enid Wilson	Gleneagles
1934	Helen Holm	Royal Porthcrawl
1935	Wanda Morgan	Newcastle, Co Down
1936	Pam Barton	Southport & Ainsdale
1937	Jessie Anderson	Turnberry
1938	Helen Holm	Burnham
1939	Pam Barton	Portrush
1940–1945 No competition		
1946	Jean Hetherington	Hunstanton
1947	Babe Zaharias (US)	Gullane
1948	Louise Suggs (US)	Royal Lytham
1949	Frances Stephens	Harlech
1950	Vicoumtesse de St Sauveur (France)	Newcastle, Co Down
1951	P.G. MacCann	Broadstone
1952	Moira Paterson	Troon
1953	Marlene Stewart	Porthcawl
1954	Frances Stephens	Ganton
1955	Jessie Valentine	Portrush
1956	Margaret Smith	Sunningdale
1957	Philomena Garvey	Gleneagles
1958	Jessie Valentine	Hunstanton
1959	Elizabeth Price	Ascot
1960	Barbara McIntire (US)	Harlech
1961	Marley Spearman	Carnoustie
1962	Maryley Spearman	Royal Birkdale
1963	Brigitte Varangot (France)	Newcastle, Co Down
1964	Carol Sorenson (US)	Prince's, Sandwich
1965	Brigitte Varangot (France)	St. Andrews
1966	Elizabeth Chadwick	Ganton
1967	Elizabeth Chadwick	Harlech
1968	Brigitte Varangot (France)	Walton Heath
1969	Catherine Lacoste (France)	Portrush
1970	Dinah Oxley	Gullane
1971	Michelle Walker	Alwoodley
1972	Michelle Walker	Hunstanton
1973	Ann Irvin	Carnoustie
1974	Carol Semple (US)	Royal Porthcawl
1975	Nancy Syms (US)	St. Andrews
1976	Cathy Panton	Silloth
1977	Angela Uzielli	Hillside

1978	Edwina Kennedy (Australia)	Notts
1979	Maureen Madill	Nairn
1980	Ann Sander (US)	Woodhall Spa
1981	Belle Robertson	Caernarvonshire
1982	Kitrina Douglas	Walton Heath
1983	Jill Thornhill	Silloth
1984	Jody Rosenthal (US)	Royal Troon
1985	Lilian Beltan (Eire)	Ganton
1986	M. McGuire (NZ)	West Sussex
1987	Jane Conningham	Harlech
1988	Jane Furby	Deal
1989	Helen Dobson	Hoylake
1990	Julie Hall	Dunbar

Espirito Santo Trophy

(Women's world amateur team championship.)

Year	Winner	Venue
1964	France 588	St. Germain, France
1966	United States 580	Mexico City CC
1968	United States 616	Victoria GC, Australia
1970	United States 598	Club de Campo, Spain
1972	United States 583	Hindu CC, Argentina
1974	United States 620	Campo de Golf, Dominica
1976	United States 605	Vilamoura, Portugal
1978	Australia 596	Pacific Harbour, Fiji
1980	United States 588	Pinehurst No 2, USA
1982	United States 579	Geneva, Switzerland
1984	United States 585	Royal Hong Kong
1986	Spain 580	Caracas, Venezuala
1988	Sweden 587	Drottingham
1990		

Curtis Cup

Year	Result	Venue
1932	US 5½, GB & Ireland 3½	Wentworth, Surrey
1934	US 6½, GB & Ireland 2½	Chevy Chase, Md
1936	US 4½, GB & Ireland 4½	Gleneagles, Scotland
1938	US 5½, GB & Ireland 3½	Essex CC, Mass.
1948	US 6½, GB & Ireland 2½	Royal Birkdale, Lancs
1950	US 7½, GB & Ireland 1½	Buffalo, NY
1952	GB & Ireland 5, US 4	Muirfield, Scotland
1954	US 6, GB & Ireland 3	Merion, Pa
1956	GB & Ireland 5, US 4	Prince's, England
1958	GB & Ireland 4½, US 4½	Brae Burn, Mass
1960	US 6½, GB & Ireland 2½	Lindrick, Yorks
1962	US 8, GB & Ireland 1	Broadmoor, Colorado Springs
1964	US 10½, GB & Ireland 7½	Royal Porthcawl, Wales
1966	US 13, GB & Ireland 5	Cascades, Hot Springs, VA
1968	US 10½, GB & Ireland 7½	Royal County Down, Ireland
1970	US 11½, GB & Ireland 6½	Brae Burn, Mass
1972	US 10, GB & Ireland 8	Western Gailes, Scotland
1974	US 13, GB & Ireland 5	San Francisco, Calif
1976	US 11½, GB & Ireland 6½	Royal Lytham, Lancs
1978	US 12, GB & Ireland 6	Apawamis, NY
1980	US 13, GB & Ireland 5	St. Pierre, Chepstow, Wales
1982	US 14½, GB & Ireland 3½	Denver, Colo
1984	US 9½, GB & Ireland 8½	Muirfield, Scotland
1986	GB & Ireland 13, US 5	Prairie Dunes, Kansas
1988	GB & Ireland 11, US 7	Royal St. Georges
1990	US 14, GB & Ireland 4	Somerset Hills N.J.

Ryder Cup

Year	Result	Venue
1927	US 9½, GB 2½	Worcester, Mass
1929	GB 7, US 5	Moortown, Leeds
1931	US 9, GB 3	Scioto, Ohio
1933	GB 6½, US 5½	Southport & Ainsdale, Lancs
1935	US 9, GB 3	Ridgewood, NJ
1937	US 8, GB 4	Southport & Ainsdale, Lancs
1939–1945	Not played	
1947	US 11, GB 1	Portland, Ore
1949	US 7, GB 5	Ganton, Yorks
1951	US 9½, GB 2½	Pinehurst, NC
1953	US 6½, GB 5½	Wentworth, Surrey
1955	US 8, GB 4	Palm Springs, Calif.
1957	GB 7½, US 4½	Lindrick, Sheffield
1959	US 8½, GB 3½	Eldorado CC., Calif.
1961	US 14½, GB 9½	Royal Lytham, Lancs
1963	US 23, GB 9	Atlanta, Ga
1965	US 19½, GB 12½	Royal Birkdale, Lancs
1967	US 23½, GB 8½	Houston, Tex
1969	US 16, GB 16	Royal Birkdale, Lancs
1971	US 18½, GB 13½	St. Louis, Missouri
1973	US 19, GB 13	Muirfield, Scotland
1975	US 21, GB 11	Laurel Valley, Pa
1977	US 12½, GB 7½	Royal Lytham, Lancs
1979	US 17, Europe 11	Greenbrier, W. Virginia
1981	US 18½, Europe 9½	Walton Health, Surrey
1983	US 14½, Europe 13½	PGA National, Florida
1985	Europe 16½, US 11½	The Belfry, W. Midlands
1987	Europe 15, US 13	Muirfield Village, Ohio
1989	Europe 14, US 14	The Belfry, W. Midlands
1991		

INDEX